Perspectives In Philosophy

Perspectives
in
Philosophy

Michael Boylan

Marymount University

Under the general editorship of
Robert J. Fogelin
Dartmouth College

Harcourt Brace Jovanovich College Publishers

Fort Worth · Philadelphia · San Diego · New York · Orlando · Austin · San Antonio
Toronto · Montreal · Sydney · Tokyo

Editor-in-Chief	Ted Buchholz
Acquisitions Editor	David Tatom
Developmental Editor	Phoebe Woolbright Culp
Project Editor	Nicole Boyle
Production Manager	Jane Tyndall Ponceti
Book Designer	Terry Rasberry
Permissions Editor	Van Strength

Address for Editorial Correspondence: Harcourt Brace Jovanovich College Publishers, 301 Commerce Street, Suite 3700, Fort Worth, TX 76102.

Address for Orders: Harcourt Brace Jovanovich, Publishers, 6277 Sea Harbor Drive, Orlando, Florida 32887. 1-800-782-4479, or 1-800-433-0001 (in Florida).

ISBN: 0-15-500111-6

Library of Congress Catalog Card Number: 92-073433

Printed in the United States of America

2 3 4 5 6 7 8 9 0 1   039   9 8 7 6 5 4 3 2 1

Preface

When I began working on this book I realized I was confronted by especially difficult choices, the same ones every professor faces who is about to present an
introductory philosophy course. The goals in my courses are twofold and somewhat contradictory. Not only do I aim to expose students to all that is special and
enlightening about a discipline they are experiencing for the first time, I realize
that I must simplify that exposure sufficiently so that these new students will
hunger for even more. The choices which confront me are: cursory exposure to
many authors versus more comprehensive exposure to fewer authors; topical
organization versus historical organization versus systematic organization; primary readings versus secondary readings, and so on.

These tensions are real to me. They explain why I chose to organize the text the
way I did. At heart I am a pluralist. I believe that we learn best when we view a
problem from many perspectives. This sensibility has been my guide throughout.

What follows is a summary of the book's features.

Structure. *Perspectives in Philosophy* encompasses the major subfields of philosophy (ethics, metaphysics, epistemology, and logic) by dividing the book into parts
organized around a series of implied questions and issues. These parts are:
1. Self–Interest and Relativism; 2. Rights; 3. Epistemology: Skepticism, Appearance, and Reality; 4. Freedom and Determinism, Mind and Body; and 5. Belief in
God. By grouping together certain issues that represent the major areas of philosophy, it is hoped that students will gain exposure to the entire field of philosophy.

The subfield logic is considered throughout the book in the "Evaluating and
Writing A Logical Argument" exercises discussed below.

Commissioned Essays. I have asked five prominent philosophers to write essays
for this reader. Kai Nielson, Alan Gewirth, Roderick Chisholm, Marjorie Grene,
and Alvin Plantinga each introduce a particular topic. Their original essays offer
a modern perspective in the traditional subfields of philosophy. These pieces are
aimed at introducing and stretching the reader to the essential aspects of a philosophical problem. I have consulted with these professors on the nature of their
essays and have used their comments in structuring the selection of readings.

Readings. My intent is to blend sometimes disparate elements so as to provide
a historically balanced and topically organized text offering a glimpse of the
breadth and depth of philosophy. Fully half of the authors I have chosen are from
the twentieth century, but there is a fair representation from other principal

historical periods: ancient, medieval, seventeenth, eighteenth, and nineteenth centuries. This balance represents my desire to present the diverse ways philosophy has been practiced over the centuries. The essays themselves are organized around the implied question of the chapter, such as "Why should I be moral?" They seek to explore several directions from which the question might be answered.

Evaluating and Writing A Logical Argument. The logic sections consist of five sequential exercises following the readings in each part. My goal is this: to teach students to write an evaluation of a logical argument. This involves four steps: (1) reconstructing the argument presented in the text (Part One); (2) thinking about the pivotal premises (Part Two); (3) exploring strategies for presenting the "pro" and "con" reactions (Parts Three and Four); (4) writing the term paper (Part Five). These exercises are essentially analytic. The reader breaks up the argument into its components and then puts it back together again. By observing the mechanics of how an argument works, students will be in a better position to evaluate the argument.

Literature. In these five sections the reaction to the text is holistic. With these pieces, the student reads slices of "real life." These selections do not fit neatly point by point with the perspectives presented by the philosophers in the given part. Rather, what is required is that the reader discover and apply what is and is not relevant. By using these distinctions to interpret the story, the reader will be able to determine the philosophical significance of what happens to the characters. To aid them in their initial point of departure, I have offered questions at the end of each selection of literature.

My aim is for students to integrate philosophy into their everyday experiential consciousness. If the study of philosophy is to make a difference in their lives, students must master the kinds of essays and activities offered in this textbook. Acquiring these skills is essential in becoming an authentic, rational creature living in a sometimes irrational world.

Acknowledgments

There have been many people who have assisted me in this project. It has been a long time coming. The finished manuscript has taken me over seven years to produce. To those who were helpful in the early stages, I thank you.

Specifically, I would like to mention John Martin Fischer, University of California, Riverside; Steven Luper-Foy, Trinity University; Harold Greenstein, SUNY at Brockport; Hans Oberdeik, Swarthmore College; and Jon D. Ringen, Indiana University, Southbend for their helpful suggestions. A special thanks to my contributors Kai Nielson, Alan Gewirth, Roderick Chisholm, Marjorie Grene and Alvin Plantinga. These people have been generous with their suggestions and criticisms. I would also like to thank the late Alan Donagan who assisted me in the early phases of this project. Arthur Adkins also offered helpful suggestions. To all of these individuals and others, thank you. I hope the result will be useful.

For Rebecca

TABLE OF CONTENTS

PART FOUR   *Freedom and Determinism, Mind and Body*

Perspectives In Philosophy

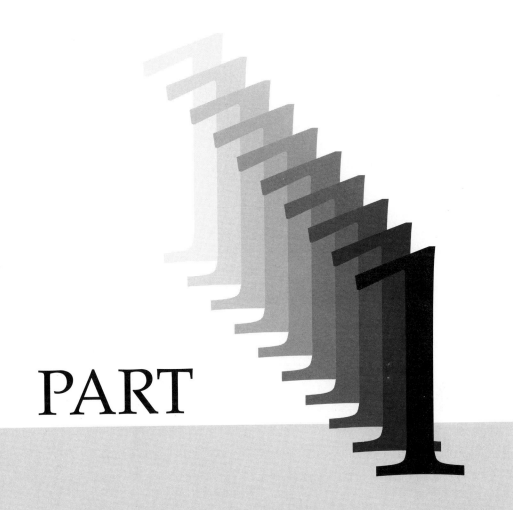

PART

1

Self-Interest and Moral Relativism

Kai Nielsen

The University of Calgary

Egoism and Relativism

I

Morality, most centrally, has to do with how we should live our lives, how our relations to others should be ordered, with what, if any, duties or obligations we may have to others and with what rights, if any, we may possess. Moral philosophy seeks to give a clear representation of morality, to unearth whatever underlying rationale it may have, to clarify the fundamental concepts of morality, to inquire into the grounds (if any) of moral belief, and to investigate both the limits of and the nature of the justification of the very enterprise of morality itself. What are our fundamental moral principles and how do we—or do we—know they are true or justified? Can there be anything even approximating "objective justification" here or is it all a matter of where we have been brought up, how we have been socialized, or what are the accidents of our genetic wiring? More-over, why should we be moral anyway when it is not in our interest to do so?[1]

These and a host of related questions get discussed in moral philosophy and are discussed in incisively different ways in the readings on ethics in this volume. I will concentrate here on two key issues implicit in what was said above that in one way or another come up again and again, sometimes directly and some-times obliquely, in the readings on ethics that follow. I refer to the issues of egoism and relativism and to the deep challenges they pose to any belief in morals which would obtain some measure of objectivity and reasonability.[2] I shall say what egoism is and what relativism is and display something of the challenge

they pose for morality, though concern-ing egoism I shall also say something about its defects. Relativism, a much deeper and more complex issue than ego-ism, should in such an introduction be elucidated and its challenge pressed. There should be no attempt at a quick clo-sure of the key issues raised by the specter of relativism.

II

Egoists believe either or both that the underlying motivation for doing what we do or what finally justifies our acting in one way rather than another is that it is in our interest, or at least that it is thought to be in our interest. Where it is put in the form of a normative principle, it should be that everyone should seek to achieve that which is in her or his own

---

[1] I try here to exhibit the rationale of *ethical egoism* and to show why there are good reasons not to be an ethical egoist. But even after we have seen that *ethical egoism* is not "the rational foundation of moral philosophy" or of morality or even a plausi-ble position to take in morality or perhaps not even a possible morality at all, we can still ask "But why take the moral point of view?" "Why be a person of moral principle or of moral integrity?" "Why care about morals if you can safely free ride?" I pursue such questions in my *Why Be Moral?* (Buffalo, New York: Prometheus Books, 1989).

[2] The notion of "objectivity" in ethics is a tricky one. Sometimes philosophers, including some skeptics, relativists, and some defenders of absolutism, adopt such an inappropriate conception of objectiv-ity that moral beliefs could not possibly on such a conception be objective. For a sophisticated treat-ment of the notion of objectivity in ethics and else-where, see Thomas Nagel, "The Limits of Objectivity," *The Tanner Lectures on Human Values*, Vol. 1 (Cambridge: Cambridge University Press, 1980), pp. 77–139.

self-interest no matter what its effects may be on the interests of others. Enlightened self-interest, the claim goes, is the sole rational standard of conduct, or at least it is the finally decisive rational standard of conduct.

When we inspect it carefully, we will see that egoism is really a cluster of related but distinct claims. First, it can be understood as a claim about our deep underlying motivations: about what triggers and sustains action and response in human beings. We all, when the chips are down, act to secure what we take to be those things which will further or protect our own interests. And where our interests conflict, or at least are thought to conflict, with the interests of others (including even those we care about very much), we will act in accordance with what, everything considered, we take to be in our own interests. This kind of egoism is called *psychological egoism*. It is the claim that for every individual all of her voluntary acts are acts which are done to further or protect what she believes to be in her own interest or will promote or protect what she takes to be in her own greatest good. Psychological egoists can quite consistently assert that sometimes a person will voluntarily act in a way that promotes the interests of others and involves some frustration of her own interests. But the psychological egoist believes that when a person so acts, she will do so because she thinks that by so furthering someone else's interests she will, at least in the long run, and all things considered, further her own interests. Keep in mind that it is sometimes in her interest or perhaps even one of her interests to take an interest in the interests of others. What the psychological egoist is committed to denying is that people ever voluntarily act to promote the interests of others as an *end in itself* or that they ever act disinterestedly. All our actions, they believe, are self-regarding at least in their ultimate intent.

Psychological egoism should be contrasted with what has been called *ethical egoism*, which is a normative principle purporting to tell us how to live. It says what each person should do is always to seek her own good (her own rational self-interest) regardless of its consequences to others. The only things *worth* having for their own sakes are those things that promote one's own self-interest. A rational person, the claim goes, will only consider the interests of others when considering them will in her best judgment, directly or indirectly, promote her own self-interest. Thus in so-called prisoner's dilemma situations[3] a rational person will constrain her maximization of what is directly in her own self-interest but only because she believes that by so constraining herself that she will in the long run and everything considered best further her own interests. One, sometimes acts disinterested in order to further one's own interests. Only, this view has it, suckers do not act in this way. To act in any other way is irrational. For the *ethical egoist* so acting is both the rational and the moral thing to do. Others will think that it might be one without being the other.

We will first look at *psychological egoism*. It is, of course, a commonplace to observe that we often, either consciously or unconsciously, seek our own

---

[3] The prisoner's dilemma has several different forms. They all basically go like this: Two people are suspected of committing a crime. These two people are arrested and put into detention. They are placed in two separate cells. They cannot talk to each other, but each is told: (a) You may confess to the crime or refuse to confess. (b) If one of you confesses but the other does not, then the one who confesses will go free and the other will have to stay in jail for four years. (c) If both of you confess, then you will both go to jail for three years. (d) If neither of you confesses, then you will both go to jail for a year. (e) Both of you are being told the same thing. Assume rational self-interest. Each prisoner is after his own interest and knows that the other prisoner is likewise disposed. What is the best alternative to take? Which is the most rational?—ED.

advantage. But the *psychological egoist* is claiming something much stronger. She is claiming that in *all* our voluntary actions, great and small, we act in such a manner. Is there good evidence or a sound argument for believing that to be so? Is this always the underlying motivating force, the thing that causes us to act as we act, when we act voluntarily? At first glance at least—though note that this is something *psychological egoists* like to stress themselves—*psychological egoism* seems plainly false. Indeed most philosophers (rightly or wrongly) believe that "seems" is "is" here. Sometimes people do not act—or so at least it appears—in even what they regard as being their long-term self-interest. This is true frequently for rather mundane things, but it is even sometimes true for rather grand things as well. Suppose—to take one of the mundane things—we are hiking along on a trail and someone stops us to ask directions. Most of us, even when we are in a hurry or are preoccupied and don't want to be bothered, will give the directions if we can and similar things obtain for a host of not dissimilar mundane cases. Moreover, it is scarcely credible that most people who do these things do them with even the vague understanding that by such behavior becoming habitual everyone, generally speaking, will be better off. That may indeed be so, but we have no good reason to believe that everyone who so acts has anything like that in mind. Moreover, in some rare instances, people do things that involve very considerable self-sacrifice that could by no reasonable stretch of the imagination be said to be in their self-interest. Sometimes old people have given up their places on life rafts or their equivalents to younger persons with children. These things do not happen very often—they are, unfortunately, hardly the usual way things go—but they do happen. They show something of what human beings are capable. What needs to be kept in mind here is that such self-sacrifice will almost certainly lead to the death of the person making the sacrifice and, particularly when the people making the sacrifice are atheists, the sacrifice cannot plausibly be said to be in their self-interest or be thought by them to be in their self-interest. It looks as if *psychological egoism* has been shown to be false.

There is, however, this strange fact. Defenders of *psychological egoism* welcome such allegedly disconfirming instances and staunchly maintain they do not disconfirm *psychological egoism* at all. Indeed, they confirm it. The old people who so give up their seats have, psychological egoists maintain, an image of themselves that simply would not allow them to act otherwise. The sting of guilt would be just too great for them to bear. Self-sacrificing as they were, they still did not act unselfishly for they, in acting voluntarily, did what they did because, everything considered, they did what they *wanted* most to do or at least what they in the circumstances disliked doing least. They *chose* to do what they did; it was an expression of their own self-conception, of their own self. So, appearances to the contrary notwithstanding, they *must* have acted egoistically: they *must* have acted in what they took to be in their own self-interest. After all, they did what they most wanted to do under the circumstances, or at least, of the alternatives available to them, disliked the least. Everyone, when push comes to shove, is selfish; everyone acts to secure what she takes to be her own self-interest.

Here the psychological egoist's case is rooted in confusion. To show that I do something because I want to do it or dislike doing it least of the alternatives before me shows the act is a voluntary act; it does not show that it was a selfish act: an act done to further what I at least believe to be in my own self-interest. Compare (1) and (2). (1) "We only voluntarily do what under the circumstances we want most to do or dislike least" and (2) "We only voluntarily do that which we think will satisfy our own interests." (1) and (2) plainly do not have the same meaning or use for (1) could be true and (2) false as far as logical possibilities are concerned. Moreover, (1) seems at least to be definitionally true or at least plainly undeniable, while (2) is very problematic. It looks at least as if it had disconfirming instances, and even if we are prepared to brush them aside we do not have any clear understanding of how we could establish (2) to be true or for that matter false. Moreover, it has none of the at least seemingly definitional ring of (1). (Here we need to attend as closely to our sense of English as we do to our knowledge of the world, though if this were being written in French or in German it would not make the slightest difference.) But only if we have good reasons for believing that what would establish the truth or probable truth of (1) would establish the truth or probable truth of (2), do we have good reason to think that the truth of (1) establishes the truth of (2) and, since (1) is unproblematic and indeed unproblematically true, and (1) and (2) make the same truth-claim, that, if all these things are so, then *psychological egoism* must be true. But we have no good reasons to believe most of those individual contentions. (1) and (2) clearly do not have the same truth-conditions: what shows (1) to be true does not show (2) to be true. We know that (1) is true but we do not know that (2) is true and we have no tolerably clear conception of what would establish even its probable truth.

So commonsense here seems at least to be vindicated. The psychological egoist has not been able to undermine appearances and make *psychological egoism* a plausible doctrine. We have no good reason to believe that we only want that which we think will protect or further our own best interests. Moreover, it is the *object* of a want, *not* the wanting itself, that makes an act selfish. The mere fact that I do something I want to do does not

make my action selfish. Whether it is selfish or not depends on what I want. If I want only my own good (or what I take to be my own good) and do not care a fig for others, I am selfish. But if I want the well-being and happiness of others (not *just* as a means to my own well-being or happiness), and if I actually act on that desire, I am being unselfish. This does not mean that I cannot desire my own well-being and happiness as well.

Let us now move to a consideration of *ethical egoism.* The ethical egoist need not deny that sometimes people do not, even when acting voluntarily, do what they at least take to be in their own self-interest. Ethical egoists can very well believe that is evident enough, but they will respond that if people are being rational or reasonable and not being taken for suckers, that is what they will do or at least try to do. Whatever people do, to do what they should do in order to act rationally is to so act, so far as it is in their power, to achieve or sustain what they at least believe to be in their own self-interest. Only if an agent acts in this way will she be acting rationally. Any other line of action will reveal a failure in rationality. (That people do not standardly act with adequate rationality is hardly surprising. So the falsity of *psychological egoism* should not be surprising.) Where one's interests are involved, a reasonable person will always act in such a way as to protect or further what she believes to be in her own best interest.

Is there a sound argument for such an *ethical egoism?* (I think "ethical egoism" is a misnomer, but I leave that aside.) We should start by asking what grounds we have, if any, for the claim that to be rational we must always act (where such considerations are relevant) so as to protect, enhance, or achieve what is in our own self-interest or at least what we believe is in our own interest. Is it something that has been established by observation in the way it has been established that all trout require cold water? It certainly does not seem to be so. Suppose a librarian stays around fifteen minutes after closing time while someone finishes up a bit of research or that someone gives money to Amnesty International and forgoes a fly rod he has been keen on or someone donates a kidney to someone desperately in need of it. Suppose further, what, to put it conservatively, could very well be true, that their interests were not served by doing these things. Still, in doing them it is as plain as plain can be that they need not be acting irrationally or unreasonably. And they need not be suckers, either. Such actions can be perfectly reasonable. Reason *permits* egoistic behavior but it does not *require* it. Ethical egoism demands the latter must be so in order to establish that if we are rational we will, over any other end, protect what we at least take to be in our own long-range self-interest. But now *ethical egoism* has lost its rational underpinnings. There seems at least to be no sound argument for being an ethical egoist. The core claim of the ethical egoist has not been made out, namely that the reasonable thing to do is *always* to give considerations of individual self-interest pride of place when they conflict with the interests of others, no matter how many other people's interests are involved and how centrally. Ethical egoists go illicitly from the correct claim—indeed a commonplace truism—that reasonable people will attend to what is in their self-interest to the false and rationally unmotivated claim that in their actions protecting their self-interest should *always* have pride of place.

Standardly, though not invariably, moral theories purport to be action guides which aim at being universal. They aim in some general and not infrequently in some oblique way to provide guidance concerning how people should act, live their lives, and relate to one another. It is an impersonal point of view but still a point of view designed to guide behavior in certain determinate ways. In attempting to do this, *ethical egoism* takes an impersonal form. It claims that every person should do what will most effectively further and protect her own self-interest and disregard the interests of others—except when having a regard for the interests of others will further her own self-interest. But, as we have seen, reason doesn't *require ethical egoism* or show someone is a sucker if she does not act in accordance with its prescriptions. That it may not be irrational to act against self-interest—that it be compatible with reason to so act—shows very little, for that is so of many moral theories and can with some adjustments be made so of still more. Moreover, compatibility counts for little when the theory in question does not square with many of our deepest and most firmly considered moral convictions. But that is exactly the boat that *ethical egoism* is in.

It should, of course, be remarked that particular considered moral convictions or even related particular clusters of them are sometimes quite properly reconsidered. Moreover, this reconsideration sometimes quite properly leads to their being modified or even abandoned. But that notwithstanding, they are at the very least a crucial starting point in moral reflection. To acknowledge that does not commit us to a form of moral conservativism: to a doing of the thing done. To recognize that the considered convictions from which we start provide the first word is not to make them into the last word, if indeed there ever is a last word. It is not to make them—or anything necessarily—into a final court of appeal. But they do enable us initially to find our feet. *Ethical egoism* has given us no rational grounds for setting these considered convictions aside and for turning, as "the real rational foundation of morality," to *ethical egoism*. To think that is so is little more than pure dogma parading as tough mindedness.

III

Talk of considered convictions raises another crucial question in moral philosophy that we shall discuss, namely, the question of *relativism*. We do in various ways rely on an appeal to considered convictions in moral thinking and acting. But considered convictions are many and not infrequently are different and sometimes at least appear to be conflicting both between different cultures and in the same culture over time. Indeed, sometimes even individuals in the same culture during the same period of time have important differences here. What is a considered conviction for James may not be for Monika. So, though we do appeal to considered convictions in moral deliberation, we still, faced with this variability, will want to ask, which of these considered convictions are the right ones to have, which are the ones which we should really stick to or give priority to if considered convictions conflict? Furthermore, because some particular range of considered convictions are mine gives me no guarantee that I should stick with them. That would be little more than pig-headedness. It is also very understandable, given this variability, that we might get very skeptical here. How are we to decide which ones to stick by? Or can we even make this out? Perhaps such matters are all relative: a matter of what sort of cultural creatures we just happen to be, with what kind of affective history, standing at what point in history. Perhaps reason can give us no anchor here?

What are really our moral convictions—and not *just* pieties that we may on occasion mouth—are indeed precious to us. We are prepared to struggle for them and, not atypically, our anger or anxiety or both are aroused when we are really opposed on a live moral issue. (It is much easier to be tolerant about what are mere conventional pieties.) We are determined to defend and hold on to our deepest moral convictions. But when we reflect in a cool hour we can hardly but wonder if we can get much in the way of objectivity here which goes beyond a thoroughly contingent and limited cultural consensus. Whether we should act in one way rather than another appears

at least to depend on the context and on a host of complicating culturally specific facts. No specific moral injunctions with much in the way of content appear on examination to be self-evident propositions clear to the light of reason. "Do good and avoid evil," to take a platitude of natural moral law, tells us very little. It does not tell us *what* is good or *what* is evil. It gains whatever self-evidence it has at the cost of emptiness. It does not provide guidance. It only tells us that if something is good (whatever that is), do it. However, when we get significant content, then we seem to run into something which is less than self-evident and into variability as well. The Greeks found homosexuality quite permissible; early Christians found it so unspeakably evil that they even put homosexuals to death. We find a similar variability in attitudes about suicide. In Japan suicide is sometimes the only honorable course; in Western countries it is generally thought to be something we ought never to do. St. Augustine even took it to be the worst form of murder, "the most grievous thing of all," and a Catholic council denied suicides the usual rites of Christian burial.[4] As Edward Westermarck points out, "It even said that Judas committed a greater sin in killing himself than in betraying his master Christ to a certain death."[5] Christian attitudes—or at least most Christian attitudes—in more recent times have changed. We see, however, when we look at things historically, that even in a cluster of distinctive cultural communities (the different Christian communities), deeply embedded considered convictions have shifted over time. When we consider examples of this sort, the suspicion grows that what is the right thing to do depends very much on who you are and where you are from. *Alles ist relativ.*

The classical writers in the selections that follow (Plato, Mill, Kant, and, even

---

[4] Edward Westermarck, *Ethical Relativity* (London: Routledge & Kegan Paul, 1932), p. 190.
[5] *Ibid.*, p. 191.

rather obliquely, Hegel) try to provide alternative accounts of morality which yield a greater objectivity than relativism sanctions. Others try, in one way or another, to provide refutations of relativism. I shall not in this introduction try to provide yet another refutation of relativism. I think it is too deep and too complicated an issue to admit of any such short and snappy refutation or defense. I shall, however, warn you both against just complacently taking it that relativism is just obviously true and against trusting snappy refutations of relativism designed to show that it is self-refuting or in some other way incoherent.[6] Such refutations typically at best refute some particular formulation of relativism, leaving the larger issue untouched. What I shall do instead is to draw some distinctions between types of relativism and seek for sufficiently perspicuous formulations of them to give the issue of relativism some of the bite I believe it deserves and to distinguish it from some things which are not relativism at all but which, contributing to our general confusion, are frequently confused with it. Most centrally, I want to distinguish what I call *contextualism*, which I believe yields a plausible conception of objectivity in ethics, from *relativism* in its different forms, which does not.[7]

TYPES OF RELATIVISM

Cultural relativism (sociological relativism, descriptive relativism) is simply the empirical and at least putatively factual thesis that different peoples (different cultures or civilizations) often have moral standards that differ and sometimes even conflict in a very fundamental way.

Ethical relativism (normative ethical relativism) is the normative claim that what is right or good for one individual or society need not be right or good for another, even when the situations involved are similar. The ethical

relativist is not simply (or necessarily even at all) making a factual statement about the differences in moral beliefs between people; rather, the ethical relativist is making the moral claim that what is really right or good in the one case need not be so in the other. He or she is making a claim in normative ethics and not a claim, or not simply a claim, about moral behavior or language.

Meta-ethical relativism is the thesis that there are no objectively sound procedures for justifying one moral code or one set of moral judgments. Two moral codes may be equally sound, and two moral claims may be equally justified or reasonable. There is no way of establishing what is the true moral code or set of moral beliefs.

Conceptual relativism is the thesis that different cultures have different concepts and that indeed some of their concepts are so fundamentally different that people within these different cultures see the world differently in certain crucial respects. Conceptual relativists also claim that there is no neutral or culturally ubiquitous way in which the world can be described against which these different and incommensurable conceptual systems or schemes can be graded or measured. Moreover, there is no right way of seeing the world or viewing the world. It is a conceptual confusion or ethnocentric arrogance or both to

---

[6] A fairly good example of such an argument is in Hilary Putnam, *Reason, Truth and History* (Cambridge: Cambridge University Press, 1981), p. 114. But see Paul Feyerabend's response in his *Farewell To Reason* (London: Verso Press, 1987), pp. 81–85. For an argument that things are rather more complicated still, see Peter Winch, *Trying To Make Sense* (Oxford, England: Blackwell, 1987), pp. 167–207.
[7] Kai Nielsen, *Marxism and the Moral Point of View* (Boulder, Colorado: Westview Press, 1988), pp. 1–17.

assume that one's own society's understanding of things is the correct one. (This is not to say that any other society is in or can be in a better or worse position.) We have no idea what must be so (what must obtain) for us to justifiably assert what it would be like for any given conceptual scheme to be the correct one—that is, that it, and not some other quite different ones would, if we utilized it, tell us what the world is like or how best to live.

These forms of relativism should be contrasted with something which is not relativistic, namely *contextualism.*

CONTEXTUALISM

Contextualism (as applied to morality) is the thesis that what is required morally varies, almost without exception, in some considerable measure with the context. Contextualism is not the claim that what is right or wrong or good or bad is determined by one's attitudes, commitments, or whatever universalizable prescriptions one will accept; rather, right or wrong, good or bad, is in considerable measure determined by the objective situation in which people find themselves. Thus, contextualism is not relativism in any form, for what is right or wrong is not determined by what a person, culture, class, or whatnot believes to be right, how each happens to conceptualize things, or what canons of justification each will accept. Right or wrong instead is determined largely by what needs people have and by the objective situation in which they find themselves.

An illustration might help to distinguish contextualism from relativism. Just as it is rationally necessary for a person

living in the Yukon in the winter to have a heavy coat, while no such requirements can rationally be made of people living near the Amazon, so it is morally irresponsible for people who do not know each other very well to have sex without using a condom in our society now, while it would not be morally irresponsible in a society with a fail-safe vaccine and an easy and fail-safe cure for AIDS. In both cases, people's needs and something (objectively discernable) in the situation ground both the non-moral evaluation and the moral evaluation. It is not people's attitudes, their being members of a certain culture or class, or having a certain conceptual scheme that determines and indeed justifies their making certain evaluations or having certain moral beliefs. If an Amazonian came to live in the Yukon, it would be reasonable for him or her to get a heavy coat, and if we come to live in an AIDS-protected world, it would not be unreasonable or immoral (under many circumstances) for us to no longer use condoms even with partners we do not know very well.

Situations change and, contextualists argue, it is not infrequently the case that our moral beliefs should change with them. However, there is nothing relative about this because something ascertainably objective in the situation, not our thinking or cultural belief-system, justifies the change in belief. I ought to give money to starvation funds for Ethiopia, but if I am starving myself, that is a different matter.

There is a superficial resemblance between contextualism and relativism because what is right or wrong varies in part with the situation. Nevertheless, the rationale is completely different for the contextualist than for the relativist. For the contextualist, a changed objective situation justifies the change; for the relativist, attitudes, the societal, class, or individual belief-system, a cluster of distinctive commitments, or some distinctive conceptual scheme justifies or at least explains the different moral beliefs or evaluative sets. The first is something plainly objective; the second is not.

Contextualists, unlike cultural relativists, do not commit themselves to the claim that there are different moral beliefs that *conflict in a fundamental way;* for contextualists think that differences, where they do not rest on objectively ascertainable confusions, rest on the different situations people encounter and would justifiably converge as their situations converge.

Unlike meta-ethical relativists, who claim there are no objectively sound procedures for justifying one moral code or one set of moral judgments over another, contextualists make no such claim at all. They could very well accept a common procedure for justifying moral claims or moral codes but still claim that the very same procedures will justify moral claims or perhaps even moral codes with somewhat different contents, including even general moral principles, in objectively different situations. Contextualists will not deny that one situation can be better than another; that this could, at least in principle, be ascertained by any reasonable person in either situation; and that a person in the objectively less desirable situation could discern it and reasonably advocate, where the situation could be changed, that the situation ought to be changed so that moral beliefs appropriate for the objectively better situation could become applicable in her situation as well.

Contextualism is also quite distinct from *conceptual relativism.* Conceptual relativists claims that we have different conceptual systems containing key incommensurable (untranslatable) moral beliefs and indeed other beliefs as well that preclude any objective appraisal of the comparative adequacy of different moral codes, different moral belief-systems, or different attitudinal sets. *Conceptual relativism,* more than *ethical relativism* or *meta-ethical relativism,* raises issues that carry us beyond moral philosophy to philosophy of language,

philosophy of logic, metaphysics, epistemology, as well as to an examination of the status of science. *Conceptual relativism* is a difficult, challenging but still very problematic thesis that very much needs elucidation and a critical examination. It is not, however, something which should just be complacently taken as the latest form of sophisticated truth about belief-systems. Be that as it may, whatever should be said about it, it should not be confused with *contextualism,* which does work with a conception of objective truth. *Contextualism* allows the claim—to return to one of my examples—that at present it is irresponsible, indeed perhaps immoral, for people who do not know each other reasonably well to have sex without using a condom. In a world made free from the dangers of AIDS such a claim could not be justifiably made or at the very least could not be justifiably made on those grounds. The statements here are objective truth-claims. (Talk of "objective truth" is actually redundant.) There is no claim that their truth rests on adopting a certain conceptual framework or having a certain attitudinal set.

Cultural relativism is compatible with *moral absolutism* and other (perhaps more plausible) conceptions of objectivity in ethics. That different tribes (including our big tribe) have different moral beliefs doesn't preclude that some of these beliefs are justified and some are not, though it does raise the question of how we would decide which are justified and which are not. *Cultural relativism, meta-ethical relativism,* and *conceptual relativism,* however, are in conflict with both *moral absolutism* and *contextualism.* A central task in moral philosophy is to try to ascertain, if we can, which view (if any at all) should be favored after careful examination. Is there, we need to ask, any truth about such matters, how would we ascertain it if there is, and what, if any such ascertaining is posible, is it most reasonable to claim approximates best "the truth" here?

Morality and Self-Interest

Me From Myself

Me from Myself—to banish—
Had I Art—
Impregnable my Fortress
Unto All Heart—

But since Myself—assault Me—
How have I: peace
Except by subjugating
Consciousness?

And since We're mutual Monarch
How this be
Except by Abdication—
Me—of Me?

Emily Dickinson

PLATO

(428–347 BC) Greek Philosopher

Books I & II
From *The Republic**

Argument One

Listen, then, he said; I proclaim that justice is nothing else than the interest of the stronger.[1] And now why do you not praise me? But of course you won't.

Let me first understand you, I replied. Justice, as you say, is the interest of the stronger. What, Thrasymachus, is the meaning of this? You can not mean to say that because Polydamas, the pancratiast,[2] is stronger than we are, and finds the eating of beef conducive to his bodily strength, that to eat beef is therefore equally for our good who are weaker than he is, and right and just for us?

That's abominable of you, Socrates; you take the words in the sense which is most damaging to the argument.

Not at all, my good sir, I said; I am trying to understand them; and I wish that you would be a little clearer.

Well, he said, have you never heard that forms of government differ; there are tyrannies, and there are democracies, and there are aristocracies?

Yes, I know.

And the government is the ruling power in each state?

Certainly.

And the different forms of government make laws democratical, aristocratical, tyrannical, with a view to their several interests; and these laws, which are made by them for their own interests, are the justice which they deliver to their subjects, and him who transgresses them they punish as a breaker of the law, and unjust. And that is what I mean when I say that in all states there is the same principle of justice, which is the interest of the government; and as the government must be supposed to have power, the only reasonable conclusion is, that everywhere there is one principle of justice, which is the interest of the stronger.

Now I understand you, I said; and whether you are right or not I will try to discover. But let me remark, that in defining justice you have yourself used the word "interest" which you forbade me to use. It is true, however, that in your definition the words "of the stronger" are added.

A small addition, you must allow, he said.

Great or small, never mind about that: we must first inquire whether what you are saying is the truth. Now we are both agreed that justice is interest of some

---

*From *The Dialogues of Plato*, 3rd ed., 5 vols., trans. B. Jowett (London, 1892).
[1] The Greek word, *kreitton*, means "stronger," but it can also refer to other sorts of superiority. Plato plays on these various meanings which mirror the popular confusion concerning the nature of justice. —ED.
[2] *Pancration* was a combination of wrestling and boxing. —ED.

sort, but you go on to say "of the stronger;" about this addition I am not so sure, and must therefore consider further.

Proceed.

I will; and first tell me, Do you admit that it is just for subjects to obey their rulers?

I do.

But are the rulers of states absolutely infallible, or are they sometimes liable to err?

To be sure, he replied, they are liable to err.

Then in making their laws they may sometimes make them rightly, and sometimes not?

True.

When they make them rightly, they make them agreeably to their interest; when they are mistaken, contrary to their interest; you admit that?

Yes.

And the laws which they make must be obeyed by their subjects,—and that is what you call justice?

Doubtless.

Then justice, according to your argument, is not only obedience to the interest of the stronger but the reverse?

What is that you are saying? he asked.

I am only repeating what you are saying, I believe. But let us consider: Have we not admitted that the rulers may be mistaken about their own interest in what they command, and also that to obey them is justice? Has not that been admitted?

Yes.

Then you must also have acknowledged justice not to be for the interest of the stronger, when the rulers unintentionally command things to be done which are to their own injury. For if, as you say, justice is the obedience which the subject renders to their commands, in that case, O wisest of men, is there any escape from the conclusion that the weaker are commanded to do, not what is for the interest, but what is for the injury of the stronger?

Nothing can be clearer, Socrates, said Polemarchus.

Yes, said Cleitophon, interposing, if you are allowed to be his witness.

Argument Two

But there is no need of any witness, said Polemarchus, for Thrasymachus himself acknowledges that rulers may sometimes command what is not for their own interest, and that for subjects to obey them is justice.

Yes, Polemarchus,—Thrasymachus said that for subjects to do what was commanded by their rulers is just.

Yes, Cleitophon, but he also said that justice is the interest of the stronger, and, while admitting both these propositions, he further acknowledged that the stronger may command the weaker who are his subjects to do what is not for his own interest; whence follows that justice is the injury quite as much as the interest of the stronger.

But, said Cleitophon, he meant by the interest of the stronger what the stronger thought to be his interest,—this was what the weaker had to do; and this was affirmed by him to be justice.

Those were not his words, rejoined Polemarchus.

Never mind, I replied, if he now says that they are, let us accept his statement. Tell me, Thrasymachus, I said, did you mean by justice what the stronger thought to be his interest, whether really so or not?

Certainly not, he said. Do you suppose that I call him who is mistaken the stronger at the time when he is mistaken?

Yes, I said, my impression was that you did so, when you admitted that the ruler was not infallible but might be sometimes mistaken.

You argue like an informer, Socrates. Do you mean, for example, that he who is mistaken about the sick is a physician in that he is mistaken? or that he who errs in arithmetic or grammar is an arithmetician or grammarian at the time when he is making the mistake, in respect of the mistake? True, we say that the physician or arithmetician or grammarian has made a mistake, but this is only a way of speaking; for the fact is that neither the grammarian nor any other person of skill ever makes a mistake in so far as he is what his name implies; they none of them err unless their skill fails them, and then they cease to be skilled artists. No artist or sage or ruler errs at the time when he is what his name implies; though he is commonly said to err, and I adopted the common mode of speaking. But to be perfectly accurate, since you are such a lover of accuracy, we should say that the ruler, in so far as he is ruler, is unerring, and, being unerring, always commands that which is for his own interest; and the subject is required to execute his commands; and therefore, as I said at first and now repeat, justice is the interest of the stronger.

Indeed, Thrasymachus, and do I really appear to you to argue like an informer?

Certainly, he replied.

And do you suppose that I ask these questions with any design of injuring you in the argument?

Nay, he replied, "suppose" is not the word—I know it; but you will be found out, and by sheer force of argument you will never prevail.

I shall not make the attempt, my dear man; but to avoid any misunderstanding occurring between us in future, let me ask, in what sense do you speak of a ruler or stronger whose interest, as you were saying, he being the superior, it is just that the inferior should execute—is he a ruler in the popular or in the strict sense of the term?

In the strictest of all senses, he said. And now cheat and play the informer if you can; I ask no quarter at your hands. But you never will be able, never.

And do you imagine, I said, that I am such a madman as to try and cheat Thrasymachus? I might as well shave a lion.

Why, he said, you made the attempt a minute ago, and you failed.

Enough, I said, of these civilities. It will be better that I should ask you a question: Is the physician, taken in that strict sense of which you are speaking, a healer of the sick or a maker of money? And remember that I am now speaking of the true physician.

A healer of the sick, he replied.

And the pilot—that is to say, the true pilot—is he a captain of sailors or a mere sailor?

A captain of sailors.

The circumstance that he sails in the ship is not to be taken into account; neither is he to be called a sailor; the name pilot by which he is distinguished has nothing to do with sailing, but is significant of his skill and of his authority over the sailors.

Very true, he said.

Now, I said, every art has an interest?

Certainly.

For which the art has to consider and provide?

Yes, that is the aim of art.

And the interest of any art is the perfection of it—this and nothing else?

What do you mean?

I mean what I may illustrate negatively by the example of the body. Suppose you were to ask me whether the body is self-sufficing or has wants, I should reply: Certainly the body has wants; for the body may be ill and require to be cured, and has therefore interests to which the art of medicine ministers; and this is the origin and intention of medicine, as you will acknowledge. Am I not right?

Quite right, he replied.

But is the art of medicine or any other art faulty or deficient in any quality in the same way that the eye may be deficient in sight or the ear fail of hearing, and therefore requires another art to provide for the interests of seeing and hearing—has art in itself, I say, any similar liability to fault or defect, and does every art require another supplementary art to provide for its interests, and that another and another without end? Or have the arts to look only after their own interests? Or have they no need either of themselves or of another?—having no faults or defects, they have no need to correct them, either by the exercise of their own art or of any other; they have only to consider the interest of their subject-matter. For every art remains pure and faultless while remaining true—that is to say, while perfect and unimpaired. Take the words in your precise sense, and tell me whether I am not right.

Yes, clearly.

Then medicine does not consider the interest of medicine, but the interest of the body?

True, he said.

Nor does the art of horsemanship consider the interests of the art of horsemanship, but the interests of the horse; neither do any other arts care for themselves, for they have no needs; they care only for that which is the subject of their art?

True, he said.

But surely, Thrasymachus, the arts are the superiors and rulers of their own subjects?

To this he assented with a good deal of reluctance.

Then, I said, no science or art considers or enjoins the interest of the stronger or superior, but only the interest of the subject and weaker?

He made an attempt to contest this proposition also, but finally acquiesced.

Then, I continued, no physician, in so far as he is a physician, considers his own good in what he prescribes, but the good of his patient; for the true physician is also a ruler having the human body as a subject, and is not a mere moneymaker; that has been admitted?

Yes.

And the pilot likewise, in the strict sense of the term, is a ruler of sailors and not a mere sailor.

That has been admitted.

And such a pilot and ruler will provide and prescribe for the interest of the sailor who is under him, and not for his own or the ruler's interest?

He gave a reluctant "Yes."

Then, I said, Thrasymachus, there is no one in any rule who, in so far as he is a ruler, considers or enjoins what is for his own interest, *but always what is for the interest of his subject or suitable to his art;* to that he looks, and that alone he considers in everything which he says and does.

Argument Three

When we had got to this point in the argument, and every one saw that the definition of justice had been completely upset, Thrasymachus, instead of replying to me, said: Tell me, Socrates, have you got a nurse?

Why do you ask such a question, I said, when you ought rather to be answering?

Because she leaves you to snivel, and never wipes your nose: she has not even taught you to know the shepherd from the sheep.

What makes you say that? I replied.

Because you fancy that the shepherd or neatherd fattens or tends the sheep or oxen with a view to their own good and not to the good of himself or his master; and you further imagine that the rulers of states, if they are true rulers, never think of their subjects as sheep, and that they are not studying their own advantage day and night. Oh, no; and so entirely astray are you in your ideas about the just and unjust as not even to know that justice and the just are in reality another's good; that is to say, the interest of the ruler and stronger, and the loss of the subject and servant; and in justice the opposite; for the unjust is lord over the truly simple and just: he is the stronger, and his subjects do what is for his interest, and minister to his happiness, which is very far from being their own. Consider further, most foolish Socrates, that the just is always a loser in comparison with the unjust. First of all, in private contracts: wherever the unjust is the partner of the just you will find that, when the partnership is dissolved, the unjust man has always more and the just less. Secondly, in their dealings with the State: when there is an income-tax, the just man will pay more and the unjust less on the same amount of income; and when there is anything to be received the one gains nothing and the other much. Observe also what happens when they take an office; there is the just man neglecting his affairs and perhaps suffering other losses, and getting nothing out of the public, because he is just; moreover he is hated by his friends and acquaintance for refusing to serve them in unlawful ways. But all this is reversed in the case of the unjust man. I am speaking, as before, of injustice[3] on a large scale in which the advantage of the unjust is most apparent; and my meaning will be most clearly seen if we turn to that highest form of injustice in which the criminal is the happiest of men, and the sufferers or those who refuse to do in justice are the most miserable—that is to say tyranny, which by fraud and force takes away the property of others, not little by little but wholesale; comprehending in one, things sacred as well as profane, private and public; for which acts of wrong, if he were detected perpetrating any of them singly, he would be punished and incur great disgrace—they who do such wrong in particular cases are called robbers of temples, and man-stealers and burglars and swindlers and thieves. But when a man besides taking away the money of the citizens has made slaves of them, then, instead of these names of reproach, he is termed happy and blessed, not only by the citizens but by all who hear of his having achieved the consummation of injustice. For mankind censure injustice, fearing that they may be victims of it and not because they shrink from committing it. And thus, as I have shown, Socrates, injustice, when on a sufficient scale, has more strength and freedom and mastery than justice; and, as I said at first, justice is the interest of the stronger, whereas injustice is a man's own profit and interest.

Thrasymachus, when he had thus spoken, having, like a bath-man,[4] deluged our ears with his words, had a mind to go away. But the company would not let him; they insisted that he should remain and defend his position; and I myself added my own humble request that he would not leave us. Thrasymachus, I said to him, excellent man, how suggestive are your remarks! And are you going to run away before you have fairly taught or learned whether they are true or not? Is the attempt to determine the way of man's life so small a matter in your eyes—to determine how life may be passed by each one of us to the greatest advantage?

And do I differ from you, he said, as to the importance of the inquiry?

You appear rather, I replied, to have no care or thought about us, Thrasymachus—whether we live better or worse from not knowing what you say you know, is to you a matter of indifference. Prithee, friend, do not keep your knowledge to yourself; we are a large party; and any benefit which you confer upon us will be amply rewarded. For my own part I openly declare that I am not convinced, and that I do not believe injustice to be more gainful than justice, even if uncontrolled and allowed to have free play. For, granting that there may be an unjust man who is able to commit injustice either by fraud or force, still this does not convince me of the superior advantage of injustice, and there may be others who are in the same predicament with myself. Perhaps we may be wrong; if so, you in your wisdom should convince us that we are mistaken in preferring justice to unjustice.

And how am I to convince you, he said, if you are not already convinced by what I have just said; what more can I do for you? Would you have me put the proof bodily into your souls?[5]

Heaven forbid! I said; I would only ask you to be consistent; or, if you change, change openly and let there be no deception. For I must remark, Thrasymachus,

---

[3] The Greek word, *pleonexia*, means literally a grasping for more. This is the sense played upon in the lines that follow.—ED.

[4] An attendant at the public bath house; perhaps a bit of a windbag.—ED.

[5] The expression refers to the way a nurse feeds an unwilling child.—ED.

if you will recall what was previously said, that although you began by defining the true physician in an exact sense, you did not observe a like exactness when speaking of the shepherd; you thought that the shepherd as a shepherd tends the sheep not with a view to their own good, but like a mere diner or banqueter with a view to the pleasures of the table; or, again, as a trader for sale in the market, and not as a shepherd. Yet surely the art of the shepherd is concerned only with the good of his subjects; he has only to provide the best for them, since the perfection of the art is already ensured whenever all the requirements of it are satisfied. And that was what I was saying just now about the ruler. I conceived that the art of the ruler, considered as ruler, whether in a state or in private life, could only regard the good of his flock or subjects; whereas you seem to think that the rulers in states, that is to say, the true rulers, like being in authority.

Think! Nay, I am sure of it.

Then why in the case of lesser offices do men never take them willingly without payment, unless under the idea that they govern for the advantage not of themselves but of others? Let me ask you a question: Are not the several arts different, by reason of their each having a separate function? And, my dear illustrious friend, do say what you think, that we may make a little progress.

Yes, that is the difference, he replied.

And each art gives us a particular good and not merely a general one—medicine, for example, gives us health; navigation, safety at sea, and so on?

Yes, he said.

And the art of payment has the special function of giving pay: but we do not confuse this with other arts, any more than the art of the pilot is to be confused with the art of medicine, because the health of the pilot may be improved by a sea voyage. You would not be inclined to say, would you, that navigation is the art of medicine, at least if we are to adopt your exact use of language?

Certainly not.

Or because a man is in good health when he receives pay you would not say that the art of payment is medicine?

I should not.

Nor would you say that medicine is the art of receiving pay because a man takes fees when he is engaged in healing?

Certainly not.

And we have admitted, I said, that the good of each art is specially confined to the art?

Yes.

Then, if there be any good which all artists have in common, that is to be attributed to something of which they all have the common use?

True, he replied.

And when the artist is benefited by receiving pay the advantage is gained by an additional use of the art of pay, which is not the art professed by him?

He gave a reluctant assent to this.

Then the pay is not derived by the several artists from their respective arts. But the truth is, that while the art of medicine gives health, and the art of the builder builds a house, another art attends them which is the art of pay. The various arts may be doing their own business and benefiting that over which they preside, but would the artist receive any benefit from his art unless he were paid as well?

I suppose not.

But does he therefore confer no benefit when he works for nothing?

Certainly, he confers a benefit.

Then now, Thrasymachus, there is no longer any doubt that neither arts nor governments provide for their own interests; but, as we were before saying, they rule and provide for the interests of their subjects who are the weaker and not the stronger—to their good they attend and not to the good of the superior. And this is the reason, my dear Thrasymachus, why, as I was just now saying, no one is willing to govern; because no one likes to take in hand the reformation of evils which are not his concern without remuneration. For, in the execution of his work, and in giving his orders to another, the true artist does not regard his own interest, but always that of his subjects; and therefore in order that rulers may be willing to rule, they must be paid in one of three modes of payment, money or honor, or a penalty for refusing.

What do you mean, Socrates? said Glaucon. The first two modes of payment are intelligible enough, but what the penalty is I do not understand, or how a penalty can be a payment.

You mean that you do not understand the nature of this payment which to the best men is the great inducement to rule? Of course you know that ambition and avarice are held to be, as indeed they are, a disgrace?

Very true.

And for this reason, I said, money and honor have no attraction for them; good men do not wish to be openly demanding payment for governing and so to get the name of hirelings, nor by secretly helping themselves out of the public revenues to get the name of thieves. And not being ambitious they do not care about honor. Wherefore necessity must be laid upon them, and they must be induced to serve from the fear of punishment. And this, as I imagine, is the reason why the forwardness to take office, instead of waiting to be compelled, has been deemed dishonorable.

Now the worst part of the punishment is that he who refuses to rule is liable to be ruled by one who is worse than himself. And the fear of this, as I conceive, induces the good to take office, not because they would, but because they can not help—not under the idea that they are going to have any benefit or enjoyment themselves, but as a necessity, and because they are not able to commit the task of ruling to any one who is better than themselves, or indeed as good.

For there is reason to think that if a city were composed entirely of good men, then to avoid office would be as much an object of contention as to obtain office is at present; then we should have plain proof that the true ruler is not meant by nature to regard his own interest, but that of his subjects; and every one who knew this would choose rather to receive a benefit from another than to have the trouble of conferring one. So far am I from agreeing with Thrasymachus that justice is the interest of the stronger. This latter question need not be further discussed at present; but when Thrasymachus says that the life of the unjust is more advantageous than that of the just, his new statement appears to me to be of a far more serious character. Which of us has spoken truly? And which sort of life, Glaucon, do you prefer?

I for my part deem the life of the just to be the more advantageous, he answered.

Did you hear all the advantages of the unjust which Thrasymachus was rehearsing?

Yes, I heard him, he replied, but he has not convinced me.

Argument Four

Then shall we try to find some way of convincing him, if we can, that he is saying what is not true?

Most certainly, he replied.

If, I said, he makes a set speech and we make another recounting all the advantages of being just, and he answers and we rejoin, there must be a numbering and measuring of the goods which are claimed on either side, and in the end we shall want judges to decide; but if we proceed in our inquiry as we lately did, by making admissions to one another, we shall unite the offices of judge and advocate in our own persons.

Very good, he said.

And which method do I understand you to prefer? I said.

That which you propose.

Well, then, Thrasymachus, I said, suppose you begin at the beginning and answer me. You say that perfect injustice is more gainful than perfect justice?

Yes, that is what I say, and I have given you my reasons.

And what is your view about them? Would you call one of them virtue and the other vice?

Certainly.

I suppose that you would call justice virtue and injustice vice?

What a charming notion! So likely too, seeing that I affirm injustice to be profitable and justice not.

What else then would you say?

The opposite, he replied.

And would you call justice vice?

No, I would rather say sublime simplicity.

Then would you call injustice malignity?

No; I would rather say discretion.

And do the unjust appear to you to be wise and good?

Yes, he said; at any rate those of them who are able to be perfectly unjust, and who have the power of subduing states and nations; but perhaps you imagine me to be talking of cutpurses. Even this profession if undetected has advantages, though they are not to be compared with those of which I was just now speaking.

I do not think that I misapprehend your meaning, Thrasymachus, I replied; but still I can not hear without amazement that you class injustice with wisdom and virtue, and justice with the opposite.

Certainly, I do so class them.

Now, I said, you are on more substantial and almost unanswerable ground; for if the injustice which you were maintaining to be profitable had been admitted by you as by others to be vice and deformity, an answer might have been given to you on received principles; but now I perceive that you will call injustice honorable and strong, and to the unjust you will attribute all the qualities which were attributed by us before to the just, seeing that you do not hesitate to rank injustice with wisdom and virtue.

You have guessed most infallibly, he replied.

Then I certainly ought not to shrink from going through with the argument so long as I have reason to think that you, Thrasymachus, are speaking your real mind; for I do believe that you are now in earnest and are not amusing yourself at our expense.

I may be in earnest or not, but what is that to you?—to refute the argument is your business.

Very true, I said; that is what I have to do: But will you be so good as answer yet one more question? Does the just man try to gain any advantage over the just?

Far otherwise; if he did he would not be the simple amusing creature which he is.

And would he try to go beyond just action?[6]

He would not.

And how would he regard the attempt to gain an advantage over the unjust; would that be considered by him as just or unjust?

He would think it just, and would try to gain the advantage; but he would not be able.

Whether he would or would not be able, I said, is not to the point. My question is only whether the just man, while refusing to have more than another just man, would wish and claim to have more than the unjust?

Yes, he would.

And what of the unjust—does he claim to have more than the just man and to do more than is just?

Of course, he said, for he claims to have more than all men.

And the unjust man will strive and struggle to obtain more than the unjust man or action, in order that he may have more than all?

True.

We may put the matter thus, I said—the just does not desire more than his like but more than his unlike, whereas the unjust desires more than both his like and his unlike?

Nothing, he said, can be better than that statement.

And the unjust is good and wise, and the just is neither?

Good again, he said.

And is not the unjust like the wise and good and the just unlike them?

Of course, he said, he who is of a certain nature, is like those who are of a certain nature; he who is not, not.

Each of them, I said, is such as his like is?

Certainly, he replied.

Very good, Thrasymachus, I said; and now to take the case of the arts: you would admit that one man is a musician and another not a musician?

Yes.

And which is wise and which is foolish?

Clearly the musician is wise, and he who is not a musician is foolish.

---

[6] The just man does not seek to outdo another just man. See Footnote 3.—ED.

And he is good in as far as he is wise, and bad in as far as he is foolish?[7]

Yes.

And you would say the same sort of thing of the physician?

Yes.

And do you think, my excellent friend, that a musician when he adjusts the lyre would desire or claim to exceed or go beyond a musician in the tightening and loosening the strings?

I do not think that he would.

But he would claim to exceed the non-musician?

Of course.

And what would you say of the physician? In prescribing meats and drinks would he wish to go beyond another physician or beyond the practice of medicine?

He would not.

But he would wish to go beyond the non-physician?

Yes.

And about knowledge and ignorance in general; see whether you think that any man who has knowledge ever would wish to have the choice of saying or doing more than another man who has knowledge. Would he not rather say or do the same as his like in the same case?

That, I suppose, can hardly be denied.

And what of the ignorant? would he not desire to have more than either the knowing or the ignorant?

I dare say.

And the knowing is wise?

Yes.

And the wise is good?

True.

Then the wise and good will not desire to gain more than his like, but more than his unlike and opposite?

I suppose so.

Whereas the bad and ignorant will desire to gain more than both?

Yes.

But did we not say, Thrasymachus, that the unjust goes beyond both his like and unlike? Were not these your words?

They were.

And you also said that the just will not go beyond his like but his unlike?

Yes.

Then the just is like the wise and good, and the unjust like the evil and ignorant?

That is the inference.

And each of them is such as his like is?

That was admitted.

Then the just has turned out to be wise and good and the unjust evil and ignorant.

[7] Being good at one's craft (including justice) is a matter of knowledge. —ED.

Thrasymachus made all these admissions, not fluently, as I repeat them, but with extreme reluctance; it was a hot summer's day, and the perspiration poured from him in torrents; and then I saw what I had never seen before, Thrasymachus blushing. As we were now agreed that justice was virtue and wisdom, and injustice vice and ignorance, I proceeded to another point:

Argument Five

Well, I said, Thrasymachus, that matter is now settled; but were we not also saying that injustice had strength; do you remember?

Yes, I remember, he said, but do not suppose that I approve of what you are saying or have no answer; if however I were to answer, you would be quite certain to accuse me of haranguing; therefore either permit me to have my say out, or if you would rather ask, do so, and I will answer "Very good," as they say to story-telling old women, and will nod "Yes" and "No."

Certainly not, I said, if contrary to your real opinion.

Yes, he said, I will, to please you, since you will not let me speak. What else would you have?

Nothing in the world, I said; and if you are so disposed I will ask and you shall answer.

Proceed.

Then I will repeat the question which I asked before, in order that our examination of the relative nature of justice and injustice may be carried on regularly. A statement was made that injustice is stronger and more powerful than justice, but now justice, having been identified with wisdom and virtue, is easily shown to be stronger than injustice, if injustice is ignorance; this can no longer be questioned by any one. But I want to view the matter, Thrasymachus, in a different way: You would not deny that a state may be unjust and may be unjustly attempting to enslave other states, or may have already enslaved them, and may be holding many of them in subjection?

True, he replied; and I will add that the best and most perfectly unjust state will be most likely to do so.

I know, I said, that such was your position; but what I would further consider is, whether this power which is possessed by the superior state can exist or be exercised without justice or only with justice.

If you are right in your view, and justice is wisdom, then only with justice; but if I am right, then without justice.

I am delighted, Thrasymachus, to see you not only nodding assent and dissent, but making answers which are quite excellent.

That is out of civility to you, he replied.

You are very kind, I said; and would you have the goodness also to inform me, whether you think that a state, or an army, or a band of robbers and thieves, or any other gang of evil-doers could act at all if they injured one another?

No indeed, he said, they could not.

But if they abstained from injuring one another, then they might act together better?

Yes.

And this is because injustice creates divisions and hatreds and fighting, and justice imparts harmony and friendship; is not that true, Thrasymachus?

I agree, he said, because I do not wish to quarrel with you.

How good of you, I said; but I should like to know also whether injustice, having this tendency to arouse hatred, wherever existing, among slaves or among freemen, will not make them hate one another and set them at variance and render them incapable of common action?

Certainly.

And even if injustice be found in two only, will they not quarrel and fight, and become enemies to one another and to the just?

They will.

And suppose injustice abiding in a single person, would your wisdom say that she loses or that she retains her natural power?

Let us assume that she retains her power.

Yet is not the power which injustice exercises of such a nature that wherever she takes up her abode, whether in a city, in an army, in a family, or in any other body, that body is, to begin with, rendered incapable of united action by reason of sedition and distraction; and does it not become its own enemy and at variance with all that opposes it, and with the just? Is not this the case?

Yes, certainly.

And is not injustice equally fatal when existing in a single person; in the first place rendering him incapable of action because he is not at unity with himself, and in the second place making him an enemy to himself and the just? Is not that true, Thrasymachus?

Yes.

And O my friend, I said, surely the gods are just?

Granted that they are.

But if so, the unjust will be the enemy of the gods, and the just will be their friends?

Feast away in triumph, and take your fill of the argument; I will not oppose you, lest I should displease the company.

Well then, proceed with your answers, and let me have the remainder of my repast. For we have already shown that the just are clearly wiser and better and abler than the unjust, and that the unjust are incapable of common action; nay more, that to speak as we did of men who are evil acting at any time vigorously together, is not strictly true, for if they had been perfectly evil, they would have laid hands upon one another; but it is evident that there must have been some remnant of justice in them, which enabled them to combine; if there had not been they would have injured one another as well as their victims; they were but half-villains in their enterprises; for had they been whole villains, and utterly unjust, they would have been utterly incapable of action. That, as I believe, is the truth of the matter, and not what you said at first. But whether the just have a better and happier life than the unjust is a further question which we also proposed to consider. I think that they have, and for the reasons which I have given; but still I should like to examine further, for no light matter is at stake, nothing less than the rule of human life.

Proceed.

I will proceed by asking a question: Would you not say that a horse has some end?

I should.

And the end or use of a horse or of anything would be that which could not be accomplished, or not so well accomplished, by any other thing?

I do not understand, he said.

Let me explain: Can you see, except with the eye?

Certainly not.

Or hear, except with the ear?

No.

These then may be truly said to be the ends of these organs?

They may.

But you can cut off a vine-branch with a dagger or with a chisel, and in many other ways?

Of course.

And yet not so well as with a pruning-hook made for the purpose?

True.

May we not say that this is the end of a pruning-hook?

We may.

Then now I think you will have no difficulty in understanding my meaning when I asked the question whether the end of anything would be that which could not be accomplished, or not so well accomplished, by any other thing?

I understand your meaning, he said, and assent.

And that to which an end is appointed has also an excellence? Need I ask again whether the eye has an end?

It has.

And has not the eye an excellence?

Yes.

And the ear has an end and an excellence also?

True.

And the same is true of all other things; they have each of them an end and a special excellence?

That is so.

Well, and can the eyes fulfil their end if they are wanting in their own proper excellence and have a defect instead?

How can they, he said, if they are blind and can not see?

You mean to say, if they have lost their proper excellence, which is sight, but I have not arrived at that point yet. I would rather ask the question more generally, and only inquire whether the things which fulfil their ends fulfil them by their own proper excellence, and fail of fulfilling them by their own defect?

Certainly, he replied.

I might say the same of the ears; when deprived of their own proper excellence they can not fulfil their end?

True.

And the same observation will apply to all other things?

I agree.

Well; and has not the soul an end which nothing else can fulfil? for example, to superintend and command and deliberate and the like. Are not these functions proper to the soul, and can they rightly be assigned to any other?

To no other.

And is *not life to be reckoned among the ends of the soul?*

Assuredly, he said.

And has not the soul an excellence also?

Yes.

And can she or can she not fulfil her own ends when deprived of that excellence?

She can not.

Then an evil soul must necessarily be an evil ruler and superintendent, and the good soul a good ruler?

Yes, necessarily.

And we have admitted that justice is the excellence of the soul, and injustice the defect of the soul?

That has been admitted.

Then the just soul and the just man will live well, and the unjust man will live ill?

That is what your argument proves.

And he who lives well is blessed and happy, and he who lives ill the reverse of happy?

Certainly.

Then the just is happy, and the unjust miserable?

So be it.

But happiness and not misery is profitable.

Of course.

Then, my blessed Thrasymachus, injustice can never be more profitable than justice.

Let this, Socrates, he said, be your entertainment at the Bendidea.[8]

For which I am indebted to you, I said, now that you have grown gentle towards me and have left off scolding. Nevertheless, I have not been well entertained; but that was my own fault and not yours. As an epicure snatches a taste of every dish which is successively brought to table, he not having allowed himself time to enjoy the one before, so have I gone from one subject to another without having discovered what I sought at first, the *nature of justice.* I left that inquiry and turned away to consider whether justice is virtue and wisdom or evil and folly; and when there arose a further question about the comparative advantages of justice and injustice, I could not refrain from passing on to that. And the result of the whole discussion has been that I know nothing at all. For I know not what justice is, and therefore I am not likely to know whether it is or is not a virtue, nor can I say whether the just man is happy or unhappy.

With these words I was thinking that I had made an end of the discussion; but the end, in truth, proved to be only a beginning. For Glaucon, who is always the

---

[8] Bendis (Bendidea) was a foreign goddess related to the moon. Her festival was the occasion for a hodgepodge of invocations. —ED.

most pugnacious of men, was dissatisfied at Thrasymachus' retirement; he wanted to have the battle out. So he said to me: Socrates, do you wish really to persuade us, or only to seem to have persuaded us, that to be just is always better than to be unjust?

I should wish really to persuade you, I replied, if I could.

Then you certainly have not succeeded. Let me ask you now:—How would you arrange goods—are there not some which we welcome for their own sakes, and independently of their consequences, as, for example, harmless pleasures and enjoyments, which delight us at the time, although nothing follows from them?

I agree in thinking that there is such a class, I replied.

Is there not also a second class of goods, such as knowledge, sight, health, which are desirable not only in themselves, but also for their results?

Certainly, I said.

And would you not recognize a third class,[9] such as gymnastic, and the care of the sick, and the physician's art; also the various ways of money-making—these do us good but we regard them as disagreeable; and no one would choose them for their own sakes, but only for the sake of some reward or result which flows from them?

There is, I said, this third class also. But why do you ask?

Because I want to know in which of the three classes you would place justice?

In the highest class, I replied,—among those goods which he who would be happy desires both for their own sake and for the sake of their results.

Then the many are of another mind; they think that justice is to be reckoned in the troublesome class, among goods which are to be pursued for the sake of rewards and of reputation, but in themselves are disagreeable and rather to be avoided.

I know, I said, that this is their manner of thinking, and that this was the thesis which Thrasymachus was maintaining just now, when he censured justice and praised injustice. But I am too stupid to be convinced by him.

I wish, he said, that you would hear me as well as him, and then I shall see whether you and I agree. For Thrasymachus seems to me, like a snake, to have been charmed by your voice sooner than he ought to have been; but to my mind the nature of justice and injustice have not yet been made clear. . . .

The common opinion asserts that to do injustice is, by nature, good; to suffer injustice, evil; but that the evil is greater than the good. And so when men have both done and suffered injustice and have had experience of both, not being able to avoid the one and obtain the other, they think that they had better agree among themselves to have neither; hence there arise laws and mutual covenants; and that which is ordained by law is termed by them lawful and just.

This they affirm to be the origin and nature of justice;—it is a mean or compromise, between the best of all, which is to do injustice and not be punished, and the worst of all, which is to suffer injustice without the power of retaliation; and justice, being at a middle point between the two, is tolerated not as a good, but as the lesser evil, and honored by reason of the inability of men to do injustice. For no man who is worthy to be called a man would ever submit to such an

---

[9] The Greek word is *eidos.* This is the word used in Plato's famous theory of forms. Some scholars believe that this is one of the first uses of the word in this way. Here, the primary meaning seems to be classifying according to "kinds."—ED.

agreement if he were able to resist; he would be mad if he did. Such is the received account, Socrates, of the nature and origin of justice.

Now that those who practise justice do so involuntarily and because they have not the power to be unjust will best appear if we imagine something of this kind: having given both to the just and the unjust power to do what they will, let us watch and see whither desire will lead them; then we shall discover in the very act the just and unjust man to be proceeding along the same road, following their interest, which all natures deem to be their good, and are only diverted into the path of justice by the force of law. The liberty which we are supposing may be most completely given to them in the form of such a power as is said to have been possessed by Gyges, the ancestor of Croesus the Lydian.

According to the tradition, Gyges was a shepherd in the service of the king of Lydia; there was a great storm, and an earthquake made an opening in the earth at the place where he was feeding his flock. Amazed at the sight, he descended into the opening, where, among other marvels, he beheld a hollow brazen horse, having doors, at which he stooping and looking in saw a dead body of stature, as appeared to him, more than human, and having nothing on but a gold ring; this he took from the finger of the dead and reascended.

Now the shepherds met together, according to custom, that they might send their monthly report about the flocks to the king; into their assembly he came having the ring on his finger, and as he was sitting among them he chanced to turn the collet of the ring inside his hand, when instantly he became invisible to the rest of the company and they began to speak of him as if he were no longer present. He was astonished at this, and again touching the ring he turned the collet outwards and reappeared; he made several trials of the ring, and always with the same result—when he turned the collet inwards he became invisible, when outwards he reappeared. Whereupon he contrived to be chosen one of the messengers who were sent to the court; where as soon as he arrived he seduced the queen, and with her help conspired against the king and slew him, and took the kingdom. Suppose now that there were two such magic rings, and the just put on one of them and the unjust the other; no man can be imagined to be of such an iron nature that he would stand fast in justice. No man would keep his hands off what was not his own when he could safely take what he liked out of the market, or go into houses and lie with any one at his pleasure, or kill or release from prison whom he would, and in all respects be like a God among men. Then the actions of the just would be as the actions of the unjust; they would both come at last to the same point. And this we may truly affirm to be a great proof that a man is just, not willingly or because he thinks that justice is any good to him individually, but of necessity, for wherever any one thinks that he can safely be unjust, there he is unjust. For all men believe in their hearts that injustice is far more profitable to the individual than justice, and he who argues as I have been supposing, will say that they are right. If you could imagine any one obtaining this power of becoming invisible, and never doing any wrong or touching what was another's, he would be thought by the lookers-on to be a most wretched idiot, although they would praise him to one another's faces, and keep up appearances with one another from a fear that they too might suffer injustice. Enough of this.

Now, if we are to form a real judgment of the life of the just and unjust, we must isolate them; there is no other way; and how is the isolation to be effected?

I answer: Let the unjust man be entirely unjust, and the just man entirely just; nothing is to be taken away from either of them, and both are to be perfectly furnished for the work of their respective lives.

First, let the unjust be like other distinguished masters of craft; like the skilful pilot or physician, who knows intuitively his own powers and keeps within their limits, and who, if he fails at any point, is able to recover himself. So let the unjust make his unjust attempts in the right way, and lie hidden if he means to be great in his injustice: (he who is found out is nobody:) for the highest reach of injustice is, to be deemed just when you are not. Therefore I say that in the perfectly unjust man we must assume the most perfect injustice; there is to be no deduction, but we must allow him, while doing the most unjust acts, to have acquired the greatest reputation for justice. If he have taken a false step he must be able to recover himself; he must be one who can speak with effect, if any of his deeds come to light, and who can force his way where force is required by his courage and strength, and command of money and friends. And at his side let us place the just man in his nobleness and simplicity, wishing, as Æschylus says, to be and not to seem good.[10]

There must be no seeming, for if he seem to be just he will be honored and rewarded, and then we shall not know whether he is just for the sake of justice or for the sake of honors and rewards; therefore, let him be clothed in justice only, and have no other covering; and he must be imagined in a state of life the opposite of the former. Let him be the best of men, and let him be thought the worst; then he will have been put to the proof; and we shall see whether he will be affected by the fear of infamy and its consequences. And let him continue thus to the hour of death; being just and seeming to be unjust. When both have reached the uttermost extreme, the one of justice and the other of injustice, let judgment be given which of them is the happier of the two.

JOHN STUART MILL
(1806–1873) British Philosopher

What Utilitarianism Is*

A passing remark is all that needs be given to the ignorant blunder of supposing that those who stand up for utility as the test of right and wrong, use the term in that restricted and merely colloquial sense in which utility is opposed to

---

[10] *Seven Against Thebes,* 592–94. The man is Amphiaraus who wished to be the best.—ED.

---

*From John Stuart Mill, *Utilitarianism* (London, 1863).

pleasure. An apology is due to the philosophical opponents of utilitarianism, for even the momentary appearance of confounding them with any one capable of so absurd a misconception; which is the more extraordinary, inasmuch as the contrary accusation, of referring everything to pleasure, and that too in its grossest form, is another of the common charges against utilitarianism: and, as has been pointedly remarked by an able writer, the same sort of persons, and often the very same persons, denounce the theory "as impracticably dry when the word utility precedes the word pleasure, and as too practicably voluptuous when the word pleasure precedes the word utility." Those who know anything about the matter are aware that every writer, from Epicurus to Bentham, who maintained the theory of utility, meant by it, not something to be contradistinguished from pleasure, but pleasure itself, together with exemption from pain; and instead of opposing the useful to the agreeable or the ornamental, have always declared that the useful means these, among other things. Yet the common herd, including the herd of writers, not only in newspapers and periodicals, but in books of weight and pretension, are perpetually falling into this shallow mistake. Having caught up the word utilitarian, while knowing nothing whatever about it but its sound, they habitually express by it the rejection, or the neglect, of pleasure in some of its forms; of beauty, of ornament, or of amusement. Nor is the term thus ignorantly misapplied solely in disparagement, but occasionally in compliment; as though it implied superiority to frivolity and the mere pleasures of the moment. And this perverted use is the only one in which the word is popularly known, and the one from which the new generation are acquiring their sole notion of its meaning. Those who introduced the word, but who had for many years discontinued it as a distinctive appellation, may well feel themselves called to resume it, if by doing so they can hope to contribute anything towards rescuing it from this utter degradation.[1]

The creed which accepts as the foundation of morals, Utility, or the Greatest Happiness Principle, holds that actions are right in proportion as they tend to promote happiness, wrong as they tend to produce the reverse of happiness. By happiness is intended pleasure, and the absence of pain; by unhappiness, pain, and the privation of pleasure. To give a clear view of the moral standard set up by the theory, much more requires to be said; in particular, what things it includes in the ideas of pain and pleasure; and to what extent this is left an open question. But these supplementary explanations do not affect the theory of life on which this theory of morality is grounded—namely, that pleasure, and freedom from pain, are the only things desirable as ends; and that all desirable things (which are as numerous in the utilitarian as in any other scheme) are desirable either for the pleasure inherent in themselves, or as means to the promotion of pleasure and the prevention of pain.

---

[1] The author of this essay has reason for believing himself to be the first person who brought the word utilitarian into use. He did not invent it, but adopted it from a passing expression in Mr. Galt's *Annals of the Parish*. After using it as a designation for several years, he and others abandoned it from a growing dislike to anything resembling a badge or watchword of sectarian distinction. But as a name for one single opinion, not a set of opinions—to denote the recognition of utility as a standard, not any particular way of applying it—the term supplies a want in the language, and offers, in many cases, a convenient mode of avoiding tiresome circumlocution.—Mill

Now, such a theory of life excites in many minds, and among them in some of the most estimable in feeling and purpose, inveterate dislike. To suppose that life has (as they express it) no higher end than pleasure—no better and nobler object of desire and pursuit—they designate as utterly mean and grovelling; as a doctrine worthy only of swine, to whom the followers of Epicurus were, at a very early period, contemptuously likened; and modern holders of the doctrine are occasionally made the subject of equally polite comparisons by its German, French, and English assailants.

When thus attacked, the Epicureans have always answered, that it is not they, but their accusers, who represent human nature in a degrading light; since the accusation supposes human beings to be capable of no pleasures except those of which swine are capable. If this supposition were true, the charge could not be gainsaid, but would then be no longer an imputation; for if the sources of pleasure were precisely the same to human beings and to swine, the rule of life which is good enough for the one would be good enough for the other. The comparison of the Epicurean life to that of beasts is felt as degrading, precisely because a beast's pleasures do not satisfy a human being's conception of happiness. Human beings have faculties more elevated than the animal appetites, and when once made conscious of them, do not regard anything as happiness which does not include their gratification. I do not, indeed, consider the Epicureans to have been by any means faultless in drawing out their scheme of consequences from the utilitarian principle. To do this in any sufficient manner, many Stoic, as well as Christian elements require to be included. But there is no known Epicurean theory of life which does not assign to the pleasures of the intellect, of the feelings and imagination, and of the moral sentiments, a much higher value as pleasures than to those of mere sensation. It must be admitted, however, that utilitarian writers in general have placed the superiority of mental over bodily pleasures chiefly in the greater permanency, safety, uncostliness, etc., of the former—that is, in their circumstantial advantages rather than in their intrinsic nature. And on all these points utilitarians have fully proved their case; but they might have taken the other, and, as it may be called, higher ground, with entire consistency. It is quite compatible with the principle of utility to recognise the fact, that some *kinds* of pleasure are more desirable and more valuable than others. It would be absurd that while, in estimating all other things, quality is considered as well as quantity, the estimation of pleasures should be supposed to depend on quantity alone.

If I am asked, what I mean by difference of quality in pleasures, or what makes one pleasure more valuable than another, merely as a pleasure, except its being greater in amount, there is but one possible answer. Of two pleasures, if there be one to which all or almost all who have experience of both give a decided preference, irrespective of any feeling of moral obligation to prefer it, that is the more desirable pleasure. If one of the two is, by those who are competently acquainted with both, placed so far above the other that they prefer it, even though knowing it to be attended with a greater amount of discontent, and would not resign it for any quantity of the other pleasure which their nature is capable of, we are justified in ascribing to the preferred enjoyment a superiority in quality, so far outweighing quantity as to render it, in comparison, of small account.

Now it is an unquestionable fact that those who are equally acquainted with, and equally capable of appreciating and enjoying, both, do give a most marked preference to the manner of existence which employs their higher faculties. Few human creatures would consent to be changed into any of the lower animals, for a promise of the fullest allowance of a beast's pleasures; no intelligent human being would consent to be a fool, no instructed person would be an ignoramus, no person of feeling and conscience would be selfish and base, even though they should be persuaded that the fool, the dunce, or the rascal is better satisfied with his lot than they are with theirs. They would not resign what they possess more than he for the most complete satisfaction of all the desires which they have in common with him. If they ever fancy they would, it is only in cases of unhappiness so extreme, that to escape from it they would exchange their lot for almost any other, however undersirable in their own eyes. A being of higher faculties requires more to make him happy, is capable probably of more acute suffering, and certainly accessible to it at more points, than one of an inferior type; but in spite of these liabilities, he can never really wish to sink into what he feels to be a lower grade of existence. We may give what explanation we please of this unwillingness; we may attribute it to pride, a name which is given indiscriminately to some of the most and to some of the least estimable feelings of which mankind are capable: we may refer it to the love of liberty and personal independence, an appeal to which was with the Stoics one of the most effective means for the inculcation of it; to the love of power, or to the love of excitement, both of which do really enter into and contribute to it: but its most appropriate appellation is a sense of dignity, which all human beings possess in one form or another, and in some, though by no means in exact, proportion to their higher faculties, and which is so essential a part of the happiness of those in whom it is strong, that nothing which conflicts with it could be, otherwise than momentarily, an object of desire to them. Whoever supposes that this preference takes place at a sacrifice of happiness—that the superior being, in anything like equal circumstances, is not happier than the inferior—confounds the two very different ideas, of happiness, and content. It is indisputable that the being whose capacities of enjoyment are low, has the greatest chance of having them fully satisfied; and a highly endowed being will always feel that any happiness which he can look for, as the world is constituted, is imperfect. But he can learn to bear its imperfections, if they are at all bearable; and they will not make him envy the being who is indeed unconscious of the imperfections, but only because he feels not at all the good which those imperfections qualify. It is better to be a human being dissatisfied than a pig satisfied; better to be Socrates dissatisfied than a fool satisfied. And if the fool, or the pig, are of a different opinion, it is because they only know their own side of the question. The other party to the comparison knows both sides.

It may be objected, that many who are capable of the higher pleasures, occasionally, under the influence of temptation, postpone them to the lower. But this is quite compatible with a full appreciation of the intrinsic superiority of the higher. Men often, from infirmity of character, make their election for the nearer good, though they know it to be the less valuable; and this no less when the choice is between two bodily pleasures, than when it is between bodily and mental. They pursue sensual indulgences to the injury of health, though perfectly aware that health is the greater good. It may be further objected, that many who begin with youthful enthusiasm for everything noble, as they advance in years sink into indolence and selfishness. But I do not believe that those who undergo this very common change, voluntarily choose the lower description of pleasures in preference to the higher. I believe that before they devote themselves exclusively to the one, they have already become incapable of the other. Capacity for the nobler feelings is in most natures a very tender plant, easily killed, not only by hostile influences, but by mere want of sustenance; and in the majority of young persons it speedily dies away if the occupations to which their position in life has devoted them, and the society into which it has thrown them, are not favourable to keeping that higher capacity in exercise. Men lose their high aspirations as they lose their intellectual tastes, because they have not time or opportunity for indulging them; and they addict themselves to inferior pleasures, not because they deliberately prefer them, but because they are either the only ones to which they have access, or the only ones which they are any longer capable of enjoying. It may be questioned whether any one who has remained equally susceptible to both classes of pleasures, ever knowingly and calmly preferred the lower; though many, in all ages, have broken down in an ineffectual attempt to combine both.

From this verdict of the only competent judges, I apprehend there can be no appeal. On a question which is the best worth having of two pleasures, or which of two modes of existence is the most grateful to the feelings, apart from its moral attributes and from its consequences, the judgment of those who are qualified by knowledge of both, or, if they differ, that of the majority among them, must be admitted as final. And there needs to be the less hesitation to accept this judgment respecting the quality of pleasures, since there is no other tribunal to be referred to even on the question of quantity. What means are there of determining which is the acutest of two pains, or the intensest of two pleasurable sensations, except the general suffrage of those who are familiar with both? Neither pains nor pleasures are homogeneous, and pain is always heterogeneous with pleasure. What is there to decide whether a particular pleasure is worth purchasing at the cost of a particular pain, except the feelings and judgment of the experienced? When, therefore, those feelings and judgment declare the pleasures derived from the higher faculties to be preferable *in kind*, apart from the question of intensity, to those of which the animal nature, disjoined from the higher faculties, is susceptible, they are entitled on this subject to the same regard.

I have dwelt on this point, as being a necessary part of a perfectly just conception of Utility or Happiness, considered as the directive rule of human conduct. But it is by no means an indispensable condition to the acceptance of the utilitarian standard; for that standard is not the agent's own greatest happiness, but the greatest amount of happiness altogether; and if it may possibly be doubted whether a noble character is always the happier for its nobleness, there can be no doubt that it makes other people happier, and that the world in general is immensely a gainer by it. Utilitarianism, therefore, could only attain its end by the general cultivation of nobleness of character, even if each individual were only benefited by the nobleness of others, and his own, so far as happiness is concerned were a sheer deduction from the benefit. But the bare enunciation of such an absurdity as this last, renders refutation superfluous.

IMMANUEL KANT
(1724–1804) German Philosopher

Passage From Ordinary Rational Knowledge of Morality to Philosophical*

[The Good Will.]

It is impossible to conceive anything at all in the world, or even out of it, which can be taken as good without qualification, except a *good will*. Intelligence, wit, judgement, and any other *talents* of the mind we may care to name, or courage, resolution, and constancy of purpose, as qualities of *temperament*, are without doubt good and desirable in many respects; but they can also be extremely bad and hurtful when the will is not good which has to make use of these gifts of nature, and which for this reason has the term *"character"* applied to its peculiar quality. It is exactly the same with *gifts of fortune.* Power, wealth, honour, even health and that complete well-being and contentment with one's state which goes by the name of *"happiness,"* produce boldness, and as a consequence often over-boldness as well, unless a good will is present by which their influence on the mind—and so too the whole principle of action—may be corrected and adjusted to universal ends; not to mention that a rational and impartial spectator can never feel approval in contemplating the uninterrupted prosperity of a being graced by no touch of a pure and good will, and that consequently a good will seems to constitute the indispensable condition of our very worthiness to be happy.

Some qualities are even helpful to this good will itself and can make its task very much easier.[1] They have none the less no inner unconditioned worth, but rather presuppose a good will which sets a limit to the esteem in which they are rightly held[2] and does not permit us to regard them as absolutely good. Moderation in affections and passions,[3] self-control, and sober reflexion are not only

---

*From Immanuel Kant, *Groundwork of the Metaphysics of Morals*, trans. by H. J. Paton (New York: Harper & Row, 1948; reprinted 1964).

[1] This sentence should be noted as it affirms what Kant is commonly supposed to deny.

[2] That is, these qualities are not good when they are incompatible with a good will.

[3] An affection (*Affekt*) is a sudden passion like anger and is compared by Kant to intoxication. A passion (*Leidenschaft*) is a lasting passion or obsession like hate and is compared by Kant to a disease.

good in many respects: they may even seem to constitute part of the *inner* worth of a person. Yet they are far from being properly described as good without qualification (however unconditionally they have been commended by the ancients). For without the principles of a good will they may become exceedingly bad; and the very coolness of a scoundrel makes him, not merely more dangerous, but also immediately more abominable in our eyes than we should have taken him to be without it.

[The Good Will and Its Results.]

A good will is not good because of what it effects or accomplishes—because of its fitness for attaining some proposed end: it is good through its willing alone—that is, good in itself. Considered in itself it is to be esteemed beyond comparison as far higher than anything it could ever bring about merely in order to favour some inclination or, if you like, the sum total of inclinations. Even if, by some special disfavour of destiny or by the niggardly endowment of step-motherly nature, this will is entirely lacking in power to carry out its intentions; if by its utmost effort it still accomplishes nothing, and only good will is left (not, admittedly, as a mere wish, but as the straining of every means so far as they are in our control); even then it would still shine like a jewel for its own sake as something which has its full value in itself. Its usefulness or fruitlessness can neither add to, nor subtract from, this value. Its usefulness would be merely, as it were, the setting which enables us to handle it better in our ordinary dealings or to attract the attention of those not yet sufficiently expert, but not to commend it to experts or to determine its value.

[The Function of Reason.]

Yet in this Idea of the absolute value of a mere will, all useful results being left out of account in its assessment, there is something so strange that, in spite of all the agreement it receives even from ordinary reason, there must arise the suspicion that perhaps its secret basis is merely some high-flown fantasticality, and that we may have misunderstood the purpose of nature in attaching reason to our will as its governor. We will therefore submit our Idea to an examination from this point of view.

In the natural constitution of an organic being—that is, of one contrived for the purpose of life—let us take it as a principle that in it no organ is to be found for any end unless it is also the most appropriate to that end and the best fitted for it. Suppose now that for a being possessed of reason and a will the real purpose of nature were his *preservation*, his *welfare*, or in a word his *happiness*. In that case nature would have hit on a very bad arrangement by choosing reason in the creature to carry out this purpose. For all the actions he has to perform with this end in view, and the whole rule of his behaviour, would have been mapped out for him far more accurately by instinct; and the end in question could have been maintained far more surely by instinct than it ever can be by reason. If reason should have been imparted to this favoured creature as well, it would have had to serve him only for contemplating the happy disposition of his nature, for admiring it, for enjoying it, and for being grateful to its beneficent Cause—not for subjecting his power of appetition to such feeble and defective guidance or for meddling incompetently with the purposes of nature. In a word, nature would have prevented reason from striking out into a *practical use* and from presuming, with its feeble vision, to think out for itself a plan for happiness and for the means to its attainment. Nature would herself have taken over the choice, not only of ends, but also of means, and would with wise precaution have entrusted both to instinct alone.

In actual fact too we find that the more a cultivated reason concerns itself with the aim of enjoying life and happiness, the farther does man get away from true contentment. This is why there arises in many, and that too in those who have made most trial of this use of reason, if they are only candid enough to admit it, a certain degree of *misology*—that is, a hatred of reason; for when they balance all the advantage they draw, I will not say from thinking out all the arts of ordinary indulgence, but even from science (which in the last resort seems to them to be also an indulgence of the mind), they discover that they have in fact only brought more trouble on their heads than they have gained in the way of happiness. On this account they come to envy, rather than to despise, the more common run of men, who are closer to the guidance of mere natural instinct, and who do not allow their reason to have much influence on their conduct. So far we must admit that the judgement of those who seek to moderate— and even to reduce below zero—the conceited glorification of such advantages as reason is supposed to provide in the way of happiness and contentment with life is in no way soured or ungrateful to the goodness with which the world is governed. These judgements rather have as their hidden ground the Idea of another and much more worthy purpose of existence, for which, and not for happiness, reason is quite properly designed, and to which, therefore, as a supreme condition the private purposes of man must for the most part be subordinated.

For since reason is not sufficiently serviceable for guiding the will safely as regards its objects and the satisfaction of all our needs (which it in part even multiplies)—a purpose for which an implanted natural instinct would have led us much more surely; and since none the less reason has been imparted to us as a practical power—that is, as one which is to have influence on the *will*; its true function must be to produce a *will* which is *good*, not as a *means* to some further end, but *in itself*; and for this function reason was absolutely necessary in a world where nature, in distributing her aptitudes, has everywhere else gone to work in a purposive manner. Such a will need not on this account be the sole and complete good, but it must be the highest good and the condition of all the rest, even of all our demands for happiness. In that case we can easily reconcile with the wisdom of nature our observation that the cultivation of reason which is required for the first and unconditioned purpose may in many ways, at least in this life, restrict the attainment of the second purpose—namely, happiness—which is always conditioned; and indeed that it can even reduce happiness to less than zero without nature proceeding contrary to its purpose; for reason, which recognizes as its highest practical function the establishment of a good will, in attaining this end is capable only of its own peculiar kind of contentment— contentment in fulfilling a purpose which in turn is determined by reason alone, even if this fulfilment should often involve interference with the purposes of inclination.

[The Good Will and Duty.]

We have now to elucidate the concept of a will estimable in itself and good apart from any further end. This concept, which is already present in a sound natural understanding and requires not so much to be taught as merely to be clarified, always holds the highest place in estimating the total worth of our actions and constitutes the condition of all the rest. We will therefore take up the concept of *duty*, which includes that of a good will, exposed, however, to certain subjective limitations and obstacles. These, so far from hiding a good will or disguising it, rather bring it out by contrast and make it shine forth more brightly.[4]

[The Motive of Duty.]

I will here pass over all actions already recognized as contrary to duty, however useful they may be with a view to this or that end; for about these the question does not even arise whether they could have been done *for the sake of duty* inasmuch as they are directly opposed to it. I will also set aside actions which in fact accord with duty, yet for which men have *no immediate inclination*, but perform them because impelled to do so by some other inclination. For there it is easy to decide whether the action which accords with duty has been done *from duty* or from some purpose of self-interest. This distinction is far more difficult to perceive when the action accords with duty and the subject has in addition an *immediate* inclination to the action. For example, it certainly accords with duty that a grocer should not overcharge his inexperienced customer; and where there is much competition a sensible shopkeeper refrains from so doing and keeps to a fixed and general price for everybody so that a child can buy from him just as well as anyone else. Thus people are served *honestly*; but this is not nearly enough to justify us in believing that the shopkeeper has acted in this way from duty or from principles of fair dealing; his interests required him to do so. We cannot assume him to have in addition an immediate inclination towards his customers, leading him, as it were out of love, to give no man preference over another in the matter of price. Thus the action was done neither from duty nor from immediate inclination, but solely from purposes of self-interest.

On the other hand, to preserve one's life is a duty, and besides this every one has also an immediate inclination to do so. But on account of this the often anxious precautions taken by the greater part of mankind for this purpose have no inner worth, and the maxim[5] of their action is without moral content. They do protect their lives *in conformity with duty*, but not *from the motive of duty*. When on the contrary, disappointments and hopeless misery have quite taken away the taste for life; when a wretched man, strong in soul and more angered at his fate than faint-hearted or cast down, longs for death and still preserves his life without loving it—not from inclination or fear but from duty; then indeed his maxim has a moral content.

---

[4] Kant's view is always that obstacles make a good will more *conspicuous*—not that a good will is shown only in overcoming obstacles.

[5] The example refers, not to the preceding sentence, but to the one before that. It is not so easy as Kant suggests to distinguish between actions done from duty and actions done from self-interest; even a grocer may have a conscience.

To help others where one can is a duty, and besides this there are many spirits of so sympathetic a temper that, without any further motive of vanity or self-interest, they find an inner pleasure in spreading happiness around them and can take delight in the contentment of others as their own work. Yet I maintain that in such a case an action of this kind, however right and however amiable it may be, has still no genuinely moral worth. It stands on the same footing as other inclinations—for example, the inclination for honour, which if fortunate enough to hit on something beneficial and right and consequently honourable, deserves praise and encouragement, but not esteem; for its maxim lacks moral content, namely, the performance of such actions, not from inclination, but *from duty*. Suppose then that the mind of this friend of man were overclouded by sorrows of his own which extinguished all sympathy with the fate of others, but that he still had power to help those in distress, though no longer stirred by the need of others because sufficiently occupied with his own; and suppose that, when no longer moved by any inclination, he tears himself out of this deadly insensibility and does the action without any inclination for the sake of duty alone; then for the first time his action has its genuine moral worth. Still further: if nature had implanted little sympathy in this or that man's heart; if (being in other respects an honest fellow) he were cold in temperament and indifferent to the sufferings of others—perhaps because, being endowed with the special gift of patience and robust endurance in his own sufferings, he assumed the like in others or even demanded it; if such a man (who would in truth not be the worst product of nature) were not exactly fashioned by her to be a philanthropist, would he not still find in himself a source from which he might draw a worth far higher than any that a good-natured temperament can have? Assuredly he would. It is precisely in this that the worth of character begins to show—a moral worth and beyond all comparison the highest—that he does good, not from inclination, but from duty.

To assure one's own happiness is a duty (at least indirectly); for discontent with one's state, in a press of cares and amidst unsatisfied wants, might easily become a great *temptation to the transgression of duty*. But here also, apart from regard to duty, all men have already of themselves the strongest and deepest inclination towards happiness, because precisely in this Idea of happiness all inclinations are combined into a sum total. The prescription for happiness is, however, often so constituted as greatly to interfere with some inclinations, and yet men cannot form under the name of "happiness" any determinate and assured conception of the satisfaction of all inclinations as a sum. Hence it is not to be wondered at that a single inclination which is determinate as to what it promises and as to the time of its satisfaction may outweigh a wavering Idea; and that a man, for example, a sufferer from gout, may choose to enjoy what he fancies and put up with what he can—on the ground that on balance he has here at least not killed the enjoyment of the present moment because of some possibly groundless expectations of the good fortune supposed to attach to soundness of health. But in this case also, when the universal inclination towards happiness has failed to determine his will, when good health, at least for him, has not entered into his calculations as so necessary, what remains over, here as in other cases, is a law—the law of furthering his happiness, not from inclination, but from duty; and in this for the first time his conduct has a real moral worth.

It is doubtless in this sense that we should understand too the passages from Scripture in which we are commanded to love our neighbour and even our enemy. For love out of inclination cannot be commanded; but kindness done from duty—although no inclination impels us, and even although natural and unconquerable disinclination stands in our way—is *practical*, and not *pathological*, love, residing in the will and not in the propensions of feeling, in principles of action and not of melting compassion; and it is this practical love alone which can be an object of command.

[The Formal Principle of Duty.]

Our second proposition is this: An action done from duty has its moral worth, *not in the purpose* to be attained by it, but in the maxim in accordance with which it is decided upon; it depends therefore, not on the realization of the object of the action, but solely on the *principle* of *volition* in accordance with which, irrespective of all objects of the faculty of desire, the action has been performed. That the purposes we may have in our actions, and also their effects considered as ends and motives of the will, can give to actions no unconditioned and moral worth is clear from what has gone before. Where then can this worth be found if we are not to find it in the will's relation to the effect hoped for from the action? It can be found nowhere but *in the principle of the will*, irrespective of the ends which can be brought about by such an action; for between its *a priori* principle, which is formal, and its *a posteriori* motive, which is material, the will stands, so to speak, at a parting of the ways; and since it must be determined by some principle, it will have to be determined by the formal principle of volition when an action is done from duty, where, as we have seen, every material principle is taken away from it.

[Reverence for the Law.]

Our third proposition, as an inference from the two preceding, I would express thus: *Duty is the necessity to act out of reverence for the law.* For an object as the effect of my proposed action I can have an *inclination*, but *never reverence*, precisely because it is merely the effect, and not the activity, of a will. Similarly for inclination as such, whether my own or that of another, I cannot have reverence: I can at most in the first case approve, and in the second case sometimes even love—that is, regard it as favourable to my own advantage. Only something which is conjoined with my will solely as a ground and never as an effect— something which does not serve my inclination, but outweighs it or at least leaves it entirely out of account in my choice—and therefore only bare law for its own sake, can be an object of reverence and therewith a command. Now an action done from duty has to set aside altogether the influence of inclination, and along with inclination every object of the will; so there is nothing left able to determine the will except objectively the *law* and subjectively *pure reverence* for this practical law, and therefore the maxim of obeying this law even to the detriment of all my inclinations.

Thus the moral worth of an action does not depend on the result expected from it, and so too does not depend on any principle of action that needs to borrow its motive from this expected result. For all these results (agreeable states and even the promotion of happiness in others) could have been brought about by other causes as well, and consequently their production did not require the will of a rational being, in which, however, the highest and unconditioned good can alone be found. Therefore nothing but the *idea of the law* in itself, *which admittedly is present only in a rational being*—so far as it, and not an expected result, is the ground determining the will—can constitute that pre-eminent good which we call moral, a good which is already present in the person acting on this idea and has not to be awaited merely from the result.

ANITA M. SUPERSON

Anita Superson teaches philosophy
at Kansas State University.

The Self-Interest Based Contractarian Response to the Why-Be-Moral Skeptic*

I

Is every instance of acting morally an instance of acting rationally? Philosophers have offered many answers to meet the skeptic's challenge. I shall examine one kind of answer to the skeptic, namely, that offered by self-interest based contractarians. I take a self-interest based contractarian theory, or contractarian theory for short, to be one that has the following three features: (i) it assumes that persons are mutually disinterested, that is, do not take an interest in the interest of others; (ii) it takes morality to be a set of rules for behavior which would emerge from an agreement among rational and informed persons; and (iii) it assumes that to act rationally is to act in one's self-interest, and is concerned to show that at some level *morality* can be justified on grounds of self-interest. Philosophers who have held this view include Thomas Hobbes, Kurt Baier, Geoffrey Grice, and, most recently, David Gauthier. In this paper I will be concerned mostly with Gauthier's view since it is the most developed, and, I believe, the best theory of its kind.

Indeed, I will try to show that the contractarian is committed to making a move that Gauthier makes, namely, the dispositional move. That is, such a theory is committed to showing that it is in one's own interest to dispose oneself to being a moral person, whatever this amounts to. But if the theory is to answer the skeptic fully, it must explain the connection between the rationality of the moral disposition and the rationality of the particular actions expressing that disposition. I will show that Gauthier, or any other contractarian who makes the dispositional

*From *The Southern Journal of Philosophy.* 28 (1990), no. 3.

move, is committed to what has been called the Dependency Thesis. This thesis states that the rationality of particular actions is dependent on the rationality of the disposition which they express. But this thesis needs to be defended, especially given that there are apparent counterexamples. I will examine some of the arguments Gauthier has offered for it, and I will try to show that no satisfactory argument has been given to establish it, or to refute the alternative view which I attribute to Parfit. Given this, the contractarian theory has left itself open to the serious charge that it is *never* rational to act morally.

II

We need to say something about the kind of challenge being raised by the why-be-moral skeptic. First, the skeptic wants it to be shown that it is rational to act morally even when acting morally conflicts with one's own interest. The question, "Why should I be moral?," is ambiguous: it could mean, "Why should I be a *moral person*?," or it could mean, "Why should I *act* morally on each occasion?" To defeat skepticism, we must answer the second question, since doing so will mean that no further skeptical challenge remains.

Second, the skeptic wants it to be shown that for *any* person, it is rational to act morally on *any* occasion. For the contractarian, this means any person who is party to the contract, for it is these persons who are bound by morality. The skeptical challenge must be stated this broadly so as to avoid the skeptic's posing his challenge about other people in other circumstances to whom the justification does not reach. A qualifier must be made: we need *not* worry about extending the justification to people who, for example, have no interests, or who have otherwise perverted interests (e.g., an interest in not satisfying any of their other interests), or who do not have sufficient time to dispose themselves to being moral so as to reap any of the benefits that come from being morally disposed, etc. These cases pose a challenge to morality, but the main concern is to establish the rationality of being moral for ordinary people in normal circumstances. What is important for our purposes is that ordinary circumstances will include those in which it is possible that morality demands great sacrifices on the pursuit of one's own interest.

A third important feature of the skeptic's position is that he demands a *justifying* reason, not solely a *motivating* reason, to act morally. Briefly, a justifying reason at least *prima facie* justifies the action in question, where a justified action is one that brings about, or tends to bring about, a good (i.e., valuable for the agent) state of affairs. A motivating reason, by contrast, is one that explains why a person acts or has acted in a certain way. It describes a psychological feature of the person. A justifying reason may also be a motivating reason, and there are motivating reasons that are not justifying ones as well. The skeptic seeks a justifying reason, whether or not it is a motivating reason as well.

Contractarian theories address a skeptic who at least initially believes that the only reasons there are, are reasons of self-interest. But the skeptic is willing to accept a better theory of practical reason, if it can be shown that there *is* a better set of reasons. Thus, he is not *committed* to a theory of practical reason that is constituted solely by self-interested reasons. The task facing the contractarian is to show that there *is* a better theory.

The fact that contractarians must at some level tie in reasons to be moral with reasons of self-interest so as to reach the skeptic, limits the response such theories can give to the skeptic. Moreover, the ultimate failure of this kind of theory to answer the skeptic is because the kind of response the skeptic will accept is so limited.

Contractarians can go either of two ways.

First, they can focus on the rationality of every particular moral action, instead of on the disposition to be moral. This would amount to showing that on every occasion in which a person acts morally, she acts in her own interest. But this route seems doomed to failure. For it is very unlikely that contractarians will be able to show that *for every* (ordinary) *person*, acting morally will always be in that person's self-interest. To show this, they undoubtedly will have to buttress their argument in some implausible or otherwise problematic way. They might, for example, build in psychological assumptions such as the assumption that guilt feelings will be so intense that they would deter *anyone*, even the extreme immoralist, from acting immorally. Alternatively, they might advance a questionable metaphysical view about the nature of a person, such as that offered by Plato, who argued that being moral was in a person's self-interest because only if she acted morally on every occasion would the three parts of her soul be in harmony. Or, the contractarian might make Hobbes' move of instituting a "moral police force" or "Sovereign." The moral police force would, of course, have to be extremely clever and powerful in order for it to be against anyone's interest to act immorally on any occasion. Any solution contractarians offer will involve obviously false or otherwise problematic assumptions.

I do not wish to deny that it is *logically* possible that acting morally always turns out to be in one's own interest. Yet from an empirical point of view, it is not likely that we will succeed in showing that it is always so. Here I agree with Sidgwick, who argued that there are two disparate systems of practical reason, namely, morality and self-interest, the complete and universal coincidence of which is improbable: Sidgwick's claim, like mine, is an empirical one, namely, that these two systems of practical reason will not always dictate the same action, though it remains *logically* possible that they do.

But even if it *could* be shown that acting morally on every occasion is in one's self-interest, Gauthier claims, the contractarian *should* not try to show this. Gauthier's point is really the same as Sidgwick's, that the demands of morality sometimes conflict with reasons of self-interest. Thus, Gauthier writes: ". . . it is only as we believe that some appeals do, alas, override interest or advantage that morality becomes our concern." If it could be shown that the dictates of morality in fact coincide completely with self-interest, Gauthier's objection would be that there would then be no point in developing a morality, for it could be eliminated in favor of a system of prudence. If we believe there is a point to morality, we should not aim or expect to show that moral reasons completely coincide with prudential reasons.

Given that contractarian theories aim to ground morality in self-interest, and given that they cannot show and should not expect to show that it is in one's own interest to act morally on every occasion, they are committed to answering the skeptic some way other than the act by act approach. They might attempt to link morality and self-interest by showing that it is in one's interest to adopt a *disposition* to be moral. In *Morals by Agreement*, David Gauthier tries to show just this. Casting the issue in terms of a disposition to be moral is a promising approach in that it appears it might allow the theory to ground morality in self-interest, while at the same time avoid the problems involved in showing that it is rational to act morally on every occasion. Indeed, the dispositional move is the only available option to contractarian theories, if they are to avoid the problems with the act by act approach.

But the dispositional move requires a solution to two problems: first, it must be shown that it is in one's self-interest to adopt the disposition to be moral, and second, it must be shown that it is rational to act morally on every occasion. That is, regarding the second problem, it must be shown that it is rational, *even if not in one's own interest*, to act morally on each occasion. It must be shown how the rationality of the disposition to be moral carries over to particular moral actions.

Since Gauthier introduces the dispositional move, it is crucial for his answer to the skeptic that he show both that it is rational (i.e., in one's self-interest) to adopt a moral disposition, and that the rationality of the disposition carries over to the particular choices. He argues first that it is in one's self-interest to adopt a putative moral disposition he calls *constrained maximization.* He casts the argument as a choice between this disposition and that of straightforward maximization. A *straightforward* maximizer is one who chooses to act on every occasion in ways that maximize her utility. A *constrained* maximizer is one who compares the benefit of cooperating with what she expects to gain from universal non-cooperation, and cooperates if the former provides her a greater expected utility than the latter. The argument for constrained maximization depends on there being enough others in the population similarly disposed, on people being sufficiently "translucent" so that their dispositions can be fairly easily detected by others, and on the claim that constrained maximizers have a better chance of benefiting than straightforward maximizers, by being included in future beneficial interactions. The important thing to notice is that the rationality of the disposition of constrained maximization is to be determined *independently* of the rationality of particular moral actions.

In this paper I will not decide the issue of Gauthier's success in establishing the rationality of the moral disposition; instead I am concerned only with Gauthier's claim that the rationality of the disposition of constrained maximization carries over to the particular actions expressing it. Unfortunately, the argument he offers in *Morals by Agreement* is not very convincing. It consists in attempting to explain away certain examples of actions that seem to be irrational even though they are expressions of a disposition it is rational to adopt. So instead, we will examine arguments that Gauthier has offered elsewhere, in the context of nuclear deterrence. I think these arguments can be applied to his views on morality, and can only help his case.

III

We need to get clear on exactly what Gauthier's view is. He offers the following thesis:

> If it is rational for me to adopt an intention to do **x** in circumstances **c**, and if **c** come about, and if nothing relevant to the adoption of the intention is changed save what must be changed with the coming about of **c** (such as my hope of avoiding **c**), then it is rational for me to carry out **x**.

For our purposes, let us assume that an intention is the same as a disposition— what is relevant is that they are psychological states a person can make herself come to have.

Gauthier's view, at least initially, seems intuitively plausible. Underlying it is a principle most of us accept as true, roughly, "Whenever you act from a disposition it is rational for you to have, you act rationally." This principle is intuitively plausible because it expresses a connection between the disposition a rational person has and the particular actions she performs. We would find it odd indeed if there were *no* connection between the rationality of the disposition and the actions it expresses. And it seems plausible not only for there to be *some* connection, but for there to be this *strong* connection. A few examples are persuasive. Suppose it could be shown that it is rational for one to dispose oneself to caring about one's parents. Then it seems that every instance of acting in a caring way towards one's parents is rational, as well. Or, suppose the devil exists and is as evil as legend has taken him to be. Suppose there is a pill that you must take every day that will drive away the devil. It seems to be rational for you to dispose yourself to taking the pill every day, and it seems that every instance of taking the pill is a rational action.

Not only is Gauthier's view intuitively plausible, it is one that we should hope can be defended. For if he can successfully show that the rationality of the disposition to be moral carries over to particular moral actions, he will have answered the skeptic who demands it to be shown that every moral action is rational. Of course, he will have to establish that it *is* rational to adopt a moral disposition. That point aside, his view is better than the alternative view which in this context would have the consequence that the skeptic can never be answered at the level of individual actions.

We can take Derek Parfit's discussion in *Reasons and Persons* to represent the alternative view about disposition and actions. Parfit presents the case of Kate, which is intended to show that even though it may be rational for a person to adopt a certain disposition, not every instance of acting from that disposition is rational. Parfit calls these cases of Rational Irrationality. His discussion centers around a theory of rationality called the Self-interest Theory, or, S. According to Parfit, "S gives to each person this aim: the outcomes that would be best for himself, and that would make his life go, for him, as well as possible." The person who adopts S as the best theory of rationality might find it rational to dispose herself to act in ways that will make her life go as well as possible. But having this disposition sometimes causes the person to act in ways that *do not* make her life go as well as possible.

Consider Parfit's example of Kate, a writer whose strongest desire is to make her books as good as possible. If this desire were not her strongest one, Kate would find her work boring. It is better for her if this is her strongest desire, and if she disposes herself to work hard so that her books will be as good as possible because only then can she expect her life to go as well as possible. But this disposition sometimes causes her to work so hard that she is exhausted and depressed. Were she to weaken her desire and her disposition so that she works less, she would find her work boring. So she keeps the disposition which is rational for her to have given her strongest desire, even though it sometimes causes her to act irrationally.

To make this a clear counterexample to Gauthier's view, let us flesh out the case in the following way. Kate's strongest desire is that her books be good. Given this, it is rational for Kate to dispose herself to working hard every weekday. Gauthier's thesis entails that on every weekday when Kate works on her books it is rational for her to do so. Parfit's objection is that, on occasion, say, on Friday of a certain week, Kate will find herself exhausted and depressed from working so hard earlier in the week, that working on Friday is irrational, because it will not contribute to making her life as good as possible. Kate would be better off taking a break.

Gauthier holds what has been called the *Dependency Thesis:* the rationality of a particular choice *depends on* the rationality of the disposition to choose which the particular choice expresses: If a disposition is rational, then every action that expresses it is rational, as well. Parfit holds what I will call the *Independency Thesis:* the rationality of a particular action can be assessed *independently* of the rationality of the disposition which the particular action expresses.

Gauthier is *committed* to the Dependency Thesis. He cannot say that particular moral actions are rational because they are utility maximizing (or, interest satisfying). As I said, he denies that we can and should show that. But he has to ground morality in self-interest in some way, given the kind of theory he holds. So how else can he establish that any particular moral action is rational? It seems that Gauthier has backed himself into a corner, and the Dependency Thesis is his only escape. He must make the dispositional move, and he must explain how the rationality of the disposition carries over to the particular actions expressing that disposition.

Which view is more plausible: the Dependency or the Independency Thesis?

In the face of Parfit's counterexample, I think that Gauthier and any contractarian who is committed to the Dependency Thesis, must offer an argument in support of it, or at least explain away the example and similar cases. A contractarian cannot just dismiss these cases by stating the Dependency Thesis. Let us turn now to Gauthier's arguments.

One argument Gauthier offers is that if one accepts a certain disposition as being rational, it would be *inconsistent* to reject the actions it requires, and so one cannot claim that such actions should not be performed. The question concerns exactly where the inconsistency lies, since Gauthier himself does not say, and whether it is indeed a problem.

David Lewis responds to two interpretations, and I think he is correct. First, if the argument is that a theory cannot consistently judge *the act* of disposing oneself as rational, while at the same time judge *acting* on the disposition as irrational, it is mistaken, for there is no inconsistency involved in these judgments. They are judgments of two different actions, the act of forming a disposition, and actually acting on it, and so they are consistent. Second, the argument might be that a theory cannot consistently judge *a person* who acts to be rational and irrational. Lewis rejects this as well. The correct judgment we need to make, in Lewis' view, is to say that the person is rational in adopting the disposition, but is irrational sometimes in acting on it. A person is just a mixture of rationality and irrationality. Since a person has many rational aspects, we can make opposing judgments about her because they are made about different things.

This last point raises the issue of the nature of dispositions, and something should be said about this. The paradoxical nature of the judgment of a person as a mixture of rationality and irrationality might be explained if we consider the psychology of dispositions. It seems to be the case that many dispositions to act will cause those who act on them to act in ways contrary to the very purpose of adopting the disposition in the first place. It happens in the case of Kate. It happens in the moral case as well. Gauthier's constrained maximizer disposes herself to act morally because having and acting on that disposition can be expected to be more self-beneficial than having and acting on the disposition of straightforward maximization. But given that she is disposed to acting morally, she will on occasion act irrationally because she will act contrary to the goal she wants to achieve by disposing herself that way in the first place. This happens when she can benefit greatly by acting immorally, without risking losing the benefit of being included in further interactions in which others treat her in the ways required by morality.

Other dispositions show the same result. Consider the person who tries to make herself happy, and so surrounds herself with things and engages in activities so as to achieve this result. For example, she buys nice clothes and antiques, takes vacations, visits family and friends often, and so on. Despite her efforts, however, she cannot make herself happy, and in fact, ends up making herself miserable because she keeps thinking she should be happy since she is trying so hard to become so. The person disposes herself to making herself happy, but her disposition causes her to act in ways that frustrate her goal.

Many dispositions are like this: it is rational to adopt them to achieve a certain goal, yet acting on them does not always help in achieving that goal, or sometimes actually frustrates it. If this is just a fact about dispositions, then it seems wrong to disparage a theory because it can make seemingly inconsistent judgments about a person. If there *is* an inconsistency in the judgments that a person is rational in one respect, but not in another, it is not a problem. These judgments merely reflect a fact about the nature of dispositions.

Perhaps Gauthier's point about inconsistency is just that if a person is disposed a certain way, and cannot help but act from that disposition, we would make inconsistent judgments if we were to judge him to be rational in adopting the disposition, but irrational in acting on it, given that the action is caused by the disposition. The claim is similar to the statement, "Ought implies can": just as it does not make sense to say one ought to do x if one cannot, so, too, it does not make sense to say one is irrational in doing x if one cannot help but do x. However, I think that the fact that such judgments are meaningless does *not* establish that they are *inconsistent*. But in order to establish the Dependency Thesis, Gauthier needs to show that the judgments are inconsistent.

An objector might claim that because the agent cannot act otherwise, we must judge her to be rational when she acts on her disposition. In Kate's case, we must say that Kate is rational to work on Friday, given that she cannot act otherwise.

But I think that at best we can say that Kate *is caused* by her disposition to work hard on Friday. Yet she is *not justified* in doing so, because her working hard on Friday does not lead to a good state of affairs for anyone, especially Kate herself, as she becomes exhausted and depressed. This kind of answer in the moral case would not satisfy the skeptic who demands a justifying, not merely a motivating, reason.

Though these attempts to dispel Gauthier's inconsistency charge are well-taken, there does still seem to be a kind of inconsistency involved in saying it is rational to be disposed to do **x** in **c**, yet when **c** occurs, doing **x** is irrational. Consider this case. Suppose you come to realize that you love life so much—and have good reason to believe you will not change—that you want to remain young forever so you can continue experiencing it in its fullest sense. Imagine that there is a fountain of youth such that if you drink from it on your birthday each year, you will be guaranteed eternal youth. Suppose it is rational for you to dispose yourself now to drink from the fountain each year. When your birthday arrives, assuming you still love life, it would be inconsistent for you to judge that it is *irrational* to drink from the fountain.

Yet consider a case raised by Gregory Kavka. Suppose someone offers to pay you $1 million tomorrow if at midnight tonight you have the intention (which is readily detectable) to drink a vial of toxin that will make you very sick for a day. You affirm that you have a reason to form the intention to drink the toxin the next day. You get the money at midnight. The claim is that you would make inconsistent statements if, on the next day, you do not affirm that it is rational for you to drink the toxin.

Why does the inconsistency charge seem to hold in one case but not in the other, and which case is morality most like?

I suggest that it holds in the fountain of youth case, but not in the toxin case, because the rationality of the disposition seems to carry over to the particular action in the former case, but not in the latter. In the fountain of youth case, the reason to adopt the disposition is that you want to achieve the goal of eternal life, together with the fact that it is necessary for you to drink from the fountain each year in order to achieve your goal. And the reason to drink from the fountain on your birthday is that it is necessary for you to do so on this and other occasions in order to achieve the goal of eternal life. Since your reason for adopting the disposition *includes* the fact that you must act on the disposition, the rationality of the disposition carries over to the particular actions expressing it. This is a case in which it is rational for you to dispose yourself to do **x** in **c**, and when **c** occurs, it is rational for you to do **x**. It *would* be inconsistent to judge otherwise, assuming, of course, your goals do not change.

The toxin case is different. You form the intention to drink the toxin because you want to achieve a certain goal (getting the money). But if acting on the intention is *not* necessary to achieving that goal, either because the goal has already been achieved, or because it can be achieved without your acting on the intention on this particular occasion, it seems that you *can* consistently affirm the rationality of the intention to do **x** in **c**, yet when **c** occurs, judge doing **x** to be irrational. This is obvious in the toxin case: you have already achieved the goal of having the intention when **c** occurs. So there is no reason to drink the toxin. You would *not* make inconsistent judgments were you to affirm the rationality of adopting the intention to drink the toxin at time t1, and at time t2, deny the rationality of acting on the intention.

The toxin case threatens Gauthier's view. To save it, he had better try to establish the inconsistency charge, and, thus, the Dependency Thesis, either by explaining away the toxin case and others like it, or by showing that morality is more like the fountain of youth case than the toxin case. I will disarm both disjuncts.

First, Gauthier might explain away the toxin and similar cases by saying that since time passes and circumstances change, it would not be rational to drink the toxin because the *intention* to drink the toxin at time t2 is no longer rational. This move would reduce the threat the toxin case poses to the Dependency Thesis simply by denying that it is a case in which the disposition is rational, and the actions expressing it, irrational. Instead, both the disposition and the action are irrational. More generally, the move amounts to saying that whenever we come across an action that is irrational, we judge that it would be irrational to affirm the disposition at the time of acting. Thus, the Dependency Thesis is preserved.

But I think this move does not work. Granted, it is true that when it comes time to drink the toxin, it is no longer rational to *intend* to drink it because you have already achieved the goal of forming the intention. But when you actually *do* form the intention, it is rational for you to do so because doing so is the only way to get the $1 million. It is rational even if you know full well at this time that having the intention will cause you to drink the toxin after you get the money. It is irrelevant that when the time comes to drink the toxin and you are wealthy, the intention to drink the toxin is irrational. What is relevant is that drinking the toxin at time t2 is irrational, but you are caused to drink it by the disposition it is *rational* for you to adopt at t1. Gauthier cannot explain away the toxin case: it is rational to form the intention at t1, and irrational to act on it at t2.

Moreover, there are cases in which it is rational for you to adopt a disposition at time t1, and in which it is still rational to affirm that disposition at time t2 even though acting on it at t2 is irrational. Consider a modified version of the fountain of youth case. Suppose you need to drink from the fountain only nine out of every eleven birthdays in order to achieve eternal life. If you have taken a drink on your past eight birthdays, and fully expect to on your tenth or eleventh birthday, it is not rational for you to do so on this, the ninth, birthday. This is so because you can achieve the goal of eternal life without drinking from the fountain on this one occasion. Yet your disposition at this time is still rationally justified. Cases like this deny Gauthier's claim (were he to make it) that if it is irrational to act on a disposition at time t2, it must be irrational to affirm the disposition at that time. In the end, Gauthier cannot explain away the toxin and other similar cases.

The second way Gauthier might establish the inconsistency charge is to show that morality is more like the (original) fountain of youth case than the toxin case. This would amount to showing that there is some goal that ensures the rationality of adopting a disposition to be moral, and whose achievement is accomplished only by acting on the disposition in every relevant instance. Morality would then be like the fountain of youth case in that it would be inconsistent to judge the disposition to be rational, and the actions expressing it, irrational.

In comparing morality to the toxin case, we need *not* be worried that a moral disposition is different from the intention to take the toxin because the latter is a one-shot deal, and the former a life-time or near life-time commitment. Nor need we be worried by the fact that having the intention to take the toxin will cause one to act clearly against one's interest, for the moral disposition will sometimes cause one to make sacrifices on a par with, or even greater than, being very sick for a day. Our concern is whether the rationality of the moral disposition carries over to the actions as neatly as it seems to in the original fountain of youth case, or whether it does not, as in the toxin case.

We might think it does. For on many occasions, a constrained maximizer *must act* on her disposition in order to achieve the goal of being included in future beneficial interactions. It is not enough just *to have* the disposition; translucency and observing behavior will let the rest of us be fairly certain whether she has it *and* acts on it. We might want to say, then, that if one affirms it to be rational to adopt constrained maximization, it would be inconsistent to judge acting on it to be irrational.

However, it is possible that one can achieve the goal of having the disposition of constrained maximization even *without* acting morally on a particular occasion. In such a case, one can expect to be included in future beneficial interactions despite acting immorally on this occasion. Only if Gauthier were to make the stronger assumption of *transparency* which would make a person's deceiving us about her disposition impossible, would this kind of case be extremely unlikely. It would then be *consistent* for one to affirm at t1 that it is rational to adopt constrained maximization, but at t2, *not* affirm the rationality of acting on that disposition. For the purpose of adopting the disposition could be achieved even without acting on it this time.

As long as there are such cases, Gauthier's charge of inconsistency will not hold for *all* moral cases. It is consistent in these cases to judge it to be rational to adopt a moral disposition at t1, but irrational to act on it at t2. But in order to establish the Dependency Thesis, Gauthier must show that the inconsistency charge holds for all moral cases, because the rationality of the disposition carries over to the action in every instance. Since the inconsistency charge does not hold in some moral cases, it does not establish the Dependency Thesis.

A second argument given by Gauthier to establish the Dependency Thesis takes the form of an objection to the kind of view held by Parfit. Gauthier supposes, for the sake of argument, that the view that it is rational to form a disposition that may cause a person to act irrationally on occasion, is correct. He then claims that if you are rational and know that it would be irrational for you to do **x** in **c**, then it would be *impossible* for you to dispose yourself to doing **x** in **c**. His point is a conceptual one.

Two responses are in order. First, I think it *is* possible for a person to dispose herself to act a certain way in a certain situation even though she knows it would be irrational for her to act that way when the time comes. People do this all the time. For example, many people have a "significant other" in their lives about whom they care very deeply, and whom they would like to keep in their lives. Since their strongest desire is to make their significant other as happy as they can, it is rational for them to dispose themselves to pleasing this person all the time. Even so, they know full well that being so disposed will lead them, on occasion, to act in ways that make the significant other less happy. For example, I may have a desire to go out with my friends. But sometimes my significant other will want to be alone with me. To please him, I will have to forego going out with my friends, which I want to do, even though I care deeply about my significant other. But I will be happier if I go out with my friends which in turn will make my significant other happier because I will be more pleasant to be around. Though I know that staying home with my significant other is irrational because it will make him less happy than if I were to go out with my friends, and I know full well that these situations will arise and that I will be caused to act as my disposition dictates, I find it quite possible to dispose myself always to pleasing my significant other. Gauthier's point might not be so off-base when we consider the case of nuclear deterrence, for example. It might be rational for a country to form the intention to retaliate when its enemy makes the first strike. But if it really thought about the effects of retaliation, it might not be able to form the intention to retaliate. Still, I do not think we can generalize the point to hold for *all* cases, as the significant other case shows.

My second response to this argument is that if it were not possible for a person to dispose himself in the relevant way, then it is *never* possible for him to form *any* disposition. Consider again the case of Kate. If Kate forms the disposition it is rational for her to form, given her desire to make her life go as well as possible, she will sometimes act irrationally. The only way for it to be true that Kate will never work to the point of exhaustion is for her to have a much weaker desire that her books be good, and, so, a *much weaker disposition* to work. But having *this* disposition will be worse for her, for her books will not be that good, and her life will not go as well as possible. She needs to have the stronger disposition in order to expect to obtain the goals she wants: interesting work, good books, and a good life. And if she forms the *opposite* disposition, clearly she will act in ways that are irrational. Any disposition weaker than the strongest one, but stronger than the one that leads her to avoid working to exhaustion, will lead her to the same problems as the strongest one. Any disposition weaker than the one that leads her to avoid working to exhaustion will be worse for her because it will cause her not to make her books as good as she can. On all the options, she will end up acting in irrational ways. If that is true, and if Gauthier is correct to say that it is not possible to dispose oneself to act in ways one knows are irrational, then one will not be able to form *any* disposition. But that is a tough result to swallow. I suggest we give up Gauthier's point.

Gauthier can modify this argument, to concede that if one believes it to be irrational sometimes to do **x** in **c,** one *can* form the disposition to act that way, but only if one changes one's beliefs about what it is rational to do. One could do this either by adopting a different theory of rationality, or by changing one's desires. Consider changing one's desires. In the nuclear deterrence case, for example, one might come to desire retaliation; in the toxin case, to desire drinking the toxin; in the moral case, to desire acting morally for its own sake. But then Gauthier would have to show that *everyone* forms a desire to be moral. For only those people who actually have the relevant desire would believe there is a reason to act in the way the disposition prescribes. But for the skeptic who has *not* changed his desires it would not be rational to act in the way the disposition dictates. We cannot defeat skepticism by giving a reason to act morally that holds only for people who are already morally disposed and have certain desires and beliefs. Further, if Gauthier were to make this move, he would be relying on a desire-satisfaction theory of rationality for individual moral actions, an account which I have said he clearly rejects.

A different response in support of Gauthier's argument is suggested by Gregory Kavka. An objector might claim, says Kavka, that if we admit that some of the actions done in accordance with a disposition are themselves irrational, that is reason for doubting the rationality of the *disposition*. This is a reason to prefer Gauthier's view to Parfit's, for at least on Gauthier's view, the skeptic might be answered at the level of dispositions.

But this attempt to reject Parfit's view in favor of Gauthier's does not seem to work. For a disposition may still be rational to adopt, even if having it leads one to act irrationally, on occasion, as the modified fountain of youth case seems to show. If Gauthier were to admit Parfit-like cases, the fact that those cases were possible would *not* destroy the rationality of the disposition of constrained maximization. Like the Kate case, all the alternative dispositions are not rational to adopt: straightforward maximization is irrational because if one adopts it, one cannot expect to benefit in ways that one can if one is a constrained maximizer; and a weaker disposition, namely, a disposition to act morally unless one thinks that one can benefit greatly by acting immorally this time, is irrational because one cannot expect to receive the benefits a constrained maximizer can expect to gain, for the weaker disposition inevitably will lead one to run the risk of being excluded from future beneficial interactions. The strong version of constrained maximization as Gauthier conceives it, still seems to be the disposition it is rational to adopt. Cases of Rational Irrationality, were Gauthier to admit them, should not lead us to reject that disposition as irrational.

If the failure of these arguments is not enough, there is a further reason *not* to hold Gauthier's Dependency Thesis. Anyone who holds this view cannot establish the rationality of the particular choices *independently* of the rationality of the disposition. But this leads to a bizarre result. If someone were to act in a way that, say, a constrained maximizer would act, but *from* an irrational disposition, we would have to judge that action to be irrational. Suppose, for example, that a straightforward and a constrained maximizer both perform the same action. The straightforward maximizer keeps his promise to meet you at 8:00 for dinner because you will buy him dinner. On this one occasion, then, the straightforward maximizer acts morally, but only because he will benefit by doing so. A constrained maximizer might also keep his promise to meet you for dinner, but his motive will, of course, be different. He will meet you because he expects to benefit from the practice of promise-keeping, even if this means he might not benefit on this occasion. So even if you would not buy him dinner if he kept his promise, he would still keep it, because he expects to benefit from the practice of promise-keeping. The point is that Gauthier would have to judge these same acts of promise-keeping differently. Many of us would find it understandable to judge them to be different, *morally* speaking. But Gauthier's view is that they are different *rationally* speaking: only the action caused by the (rational) disposition of constrained maximization is a rational action. And that is counter-intuitive.

The alternative view, one I have been attributing to Parfit, does not fall prey to this objection because, on it, the rationality of the particular choices can be assessed *independently* of the rationality of the disposition. And a good thing about this view is that there *is* some connection between the rationality of the disposition and the choices expressing it, albeit not the tight one that Gauthier's view has. Consider the disposition it is rational to adopt if one believes in S. It is rational to dispose oneself in the way that makes one's life go as well as possible. And, certain actions are rational on S because they, if performed, contribute to one's life going as well as possible. For example, Kate's staying home tonight to work on her books is rational because acting that way contributes to her life going as well as possible. It is because a person wants to act in ways that maximize his utility, or contribute to his life going as well as possible, that it is rational for him to dispose himself in a way that causes him to perform these very actions, even if he knows that having that disposition will cause him, on occasion, to act irrationally. The disposition he adopts is the best available option. And if he has that disposition, he often acts in ways that *are* rational, that is, that contribute to his life going as well as possible. The rationality of the disposition and of the particular choices, though the latter can be established independently of the former, go hand-in-hand. And the actions a person performs caused by the disposition could be judged as being rational even if the person did not perform them as a result of having the disposition it is rational for him to adopt. That is more plausible than Gauthier's view.

Moreover, if Gauthier were successful in establishing the Dependency Thesis, it would mean that the rationality of the disposition carries over to the particular choices in the toxin case, the nuclear deterrence case, and other similar cases. I suspect that most of us would be unhappy with this result. Our (justified) reluctance to accept this result provides another reason to reject the Dependency Thesis.

When all is said and done, Gauthier, and any contractarian who makes the dispositional move, are faced with serious problems. The Dependency Thesis must be defended in the face of such counterexamples as the Kate case. But if Gauthier cannot establish either the rationality of the disposition to be moral, or the Dependency Thesis, he has left himself open to the charge that *no moral acts are rational.* If he cannot show that the disposition is rational, then it would follow from the Dependency Thesis that he cannot show that all the actions based on that disposition are rational, either. If he can show that the disposition is rational, but cannot show that the rationality carries over to the particular choices, he is left in the same position. We are forced to conclude that no moral acts are rational because Gauthier cannot give any other argument that the particular actions are rational. Given his assumptions, and the way he sets up the problem, the Parfit view is not an option available to contractarians such as Gauthier. The Dependency Thesis leads him to this all-or-nothing situation. At least on the Parfit view, there is the middle ground case, namely, a case in which it is rational to have the disposition, but in which *some* actions that express it are irrational. Parfit can permit this because he holds the Independency Thesis. Gauthier cannot show that particular moral actions are rational, independent of the disposition. Not only is this view bizarre, but it leaves him open to the charge that *no* moral actions are rational.

Of course, the biggest drawback to siding with Parfit in this debate is that the skeptic will remain unanswered at the level of individual actions. Indeed, as long as it remains logically possible that there be cases of Rational Irrationality, the skeptic *cannot* be answered at this level. This is not a palatable conclusion. This is why we want Gauthier's view about the rationality of dispositions and particular choices to be successful. Given his commitment to the Dependency Thesis, he must explain how the rationality of the disposition carries over to the particular choices. The arguments I examined here, the only arguments Gauthier offers so far as I am aware, are unsuccessful. So perhaps the best thing contractarian theories can do, since they are committed to making the dispositional move, is to show that it is rational to adopt the disposition to be moral. But then these theories cannot answer the skeptic at the level of particular choices, either. So on either Parfit's view or on Gauthier's view, the skeptic cannot be answered. On Parfit's view, the skeptic cannot be answered because cases of Rational Irrationality are recognized to be logically possible, or even inevitable. On Gauthier's view, the skeptic cannot be answered because the link between the rationality of the disposition and the particular choices has not been established. Either way, we are left with an unpalatable conclusion.

It is particularly disturbing that the contractarian theory has failed to defeat skepticism. For one of the main advantages of this theory is that it does not assume, as other theories might, that people have any moral motives, and hopes to show that even so, it is rational to act morally. The theory thus does not beg the question against the skeptic. The theory's failure is unfortunate not only for philosophers, but for ordinary people as well. For when there is no reason to be moral, why would rational agents act morally?

Moral Relativism and Absolutism

Ozymandias

I met a traveller from an antique land
Who said: Two vast and trunkless legs of stone
Stand in the desert . . . Near them, on the sand,
Half sunk, a shattered visage lies, whose frown,
And wrinkled lip, and sneer of cold command,
Tell that its sculptor well those passions read
Which yet survive, stamped on these lifeless things,
The hand that mocked them, and the heart that fed:
And on the pedestal these words appear:
"My name is Ozymandias, king of kings:
Look on my works, ye Mighty, and despair!"
Nothing beside remains. Round the decay
Of that colossal wreck, boundless and bare
The lone and level sands stretch far away.

Percy Bysshe Shelly, "Ozymandias"

IMMANUEL KANT

(1724–1804) German Philosopher

Passage From Popular Moral Philosophy to a Metaphysic of Morals*

[The Use of Examples.]

If so far we have drawn our concept of duty from the ordinary use of our practical reason, it must by no means be inferred that we have treated it as a concept of experience. On the contrary, when we pay attention to our experience of human conduct, we meet frequent and—as we ourselves admit—justified complaints that we can adduce no certain examples of the spirit which acts out of pure duty, and that, although much may be done *in accordance with* the commands of *duty,* it remains doubtful whether it really is done *for the sake of duty* and so has a moral value. Hence at all times there have been philosophers who have absolutely denied the presence of this spirit in human actions and have ascribed everything to a more or less refined self-love. Yet they have not cast doubt on the rightness of the concept of morality. They have spoken rather with deep regret of the frailty and impurity of human nature, which is on their view noble enough to take as its rule an Idea so worthy of reverence, but at the same time too weak to follow it: the reason which should serve it for making laws it uses only to look after the interest of inclinations, whether singly or—at the best—in their greatest mutual compatibility.

In actual fact it is absolutely impossible for experience to establish with complete certainty a single case in which the maxim of an action in other respects right has rested solely on moral grounds and on the thought of one's duty. It is indeed at times the case that after the keenest self-examination we find nothing that without the moral motive of duty could have been strong enough to move us to this or that good action and to so great a sacrifice; but we cannot infer from this with certainty that it is not some secret impulse of self-love which has actually, under the mere show of the Idea of duty, been the cause genuinely determining our will. We are pleased to flatter ourselves with the false claim to a nobler motive, but in fact we can never, even by the most strenuous self-examination, get to the bottom of our secret impulsions; for when moral value is in question, we are concerned, not with the actions which we see, but with their inner principles, which we cannot see.

Furthermore, to those who deride all morality as the mere phantom of a human imagination which gets above itself out of vanity we can do no service more pleasing than to admit that the concepts of duty must be drawn solely from experience (just as out of slackness we willingly persuade ourselves that this is so

---

*From Immanuel Kant, *Groundwork of the Metaphysics of Morals* tr. H.J. Paton (New York: Harper and Row, 1948; reprinted 1964).

in the case of all other concepts); for by so doing we prepare for them an assured triumph. Out of love for humanity I am willing to allow that most of our actions may accord with duty; but if we look more closely at our scheming and striving, we everywhere come across the dear self, which is always turning up; and it is on this that the purpose of our actions is based—not on the strict command of duty, which would often require self-denial. One need not be exactly a foe to virtue, but merely a dispassionate observer declining to take the liveliest wish for good-ness straight away as its realization, in order at certain moments (particularly with advancing years and with a power of judgement at once made shrewder by experience and also more keen in observation) to become doubtful whether any genuine virtue is actually to be encountered in the world. And then nothing can protect us against a complete falling away from our Ideas of duty, or can preserve in the soul a grounded reverence for its law, except the clear conviction that even if there never have been actions springing from such pure sources, the question at issue here is not whether this or that has happened: that, on the contrary, reason by itself and independently of all appearances commands what ought to happen; that consequently actions of which the world has perhaps hitherto given no exam-ple—actions whose practicability might well be doubted by those who rest every-thing on experience—are nevertheless commanded unrelentingly by reason; and that, for instance, although up to now there may have existed no loyal friend, pure loyalty in friendship can be no less required from every man, inasmuch as this duty, prior to all experience, is contained as duty in general in the Idea of a reason which determines the will by *a priori* grounds.

It may be added that unless we wish to deny to the concept of morality all truth and all relation to a possible object, we cannot dispute that its law is of such wide-spread significance as to hold, not merely for men, but for all *rational beings as such* —not merely subject to contingent conditions and exceptions, but *with abso-lute necessity.* It is therefore clear that no experience can give us occasion to infer even the possibility of such apodeictic laws. For by what right can we make what is perhaps valid only under the contingent conditions of humanity into an object of unlimited reverence as a universal precept for every rational nature? And how could laws for determining *our* will be taken as laws for determining the will of a rational being as such—and only because of this for determining ours—if these laws were merely empirical and did not have their source completely *a priori* in pure, but practical, reason?

What is more, we cannot do morality a worse service than by seeking to derive it from examples. Every example of it presented to me must first itself be judged by moral principles in order to decide if it is fit to serve as an original example—that is, as a model: it can in no way supply the prime source for the concept of morality. Even the Holy One of the gospel must first be compared with our ideal of moral perfection before we can recognize him to be such. He also says of him-self: "Why callest thou me (whom thou seest) good? There is none good (the archetype of the good) but one, that is, God (whom thou seest not)." But where do we get the concept of God as the highest good? Solely from the *Idea* of moral perfection, which reason traces *a priori* and conjoins inseparably with the concept of a free will. Imitation has no place in morality, and examples serve us only for encouragement—that is, they set beyond doubt the practicability of what the law commands; they make perceptible what the practical law expresses more generally; but they can never entitle us to set aside their true original, which resides in reason, and to model ourselves upon examples.

[Popular Philosophy.]

If there can be no genuine supreme principle of morality which is not grounded on pure reason alone independently of all experience, it should be unnecessary, I think, even to raise the question whether it is a good thing to set forth in general (*in abstracto*) these concepts which hold *a priori*, together with their corresponding principles, so far as our knowledge is to be distinguished from ordinary knowledge and described as philosophical. Yet in our days it may well be necessary to do so. For if we took a vote on which is to be preferred, pure rational knowledge detached from everything empirical—that is to say, a metaphysic of morals—or popular practical philosophy, we can guess at once on which side the preponderance would fall.

It is certainly most praiseworthy to come down to the level of popular thought when we have previously risen to the principles of pure reason and are fully satisfied of our success. This could be described as first *grounding* moral philosophy on metaphysics and subsequently winning *acceptance* for it by giving it a popular character after it has been established. But it is utterly senseless to aim at popularity in our first enquiry, upon which the whole correctness of our principles depends. It is not merely that such a procedure can never lay claim to the extremely rare merit of a truly *philosophical popularity*, since we require no skill to make ourselves intelligible to the multitude once we renounce all profundity of thought: what it turns out is a disgusting hotch-potch of second-hand observations and semi-rational principles on which the empty-headed regale themselves, because this is something that can be used in the chit-chat of daily life. Men of insight, on the other hand, feel confused by it and avert their eyes with a dissatisfaction which, however, they are unable to cure. Yet philosophers, who can perfectly well see through this deception, get little hearing when they summon us for a time from this would-be popularity in order that they may win the right to be genuinely popular only after definite insight has been attained.

We need only look at the attempts to deal with morality in this favoured style. What we shall encounter in an amazing medley is at one time the particular character of human nature (but along with this also the Idea of a rational nature as such), at another perfection, at another happiness; here moral feeling and there the fear of God; something of this and also something of that. But it never occurs to these writers to ask whether the principles of morality are to be sought at all in our acquaintance with human nature (which we can get only from experience); nor does it occur to them that if this is not so—if these principles are to be found completely *a priori* and free from empirical elements in the concepts of pure reason and absolutely nowhere else even to the slightest extent—they had better adopt the plan of separating off this enquiry altogether as pure practical philosophy or (if one may use a name so much decried) as a metaphysic of morals; of bringing this to full completeness entirely by itself; and of bidding the public which demands popularity to await in hope the outcome of this undertaking.

Nevertheless such a completely isolated metaphysic of morals, mixed with no anthropology, no theology, no physics or hyperphysics, still less with occult qualities (which might be called hypophysical), is not only an indispensable substratum of all theoretical and precisely defined knowledge of duties, but is at the same time a desideratum of the utmost importance for the actual execution of moral precepts. Unmixed with the alien element of added empirical inducements, the pure thought of duty, and in general of the moral law, has by way of reason alone (which first learns from this that by itself it is able to be practical as well as theoretical) an influence on the human heart so much more powerful than all the further impulsions capable of being called up from the field of experience that in the consciousness of its own dignity reason despises these impulsions and is able gradually to become their master. In place of this, a mixed moral philosophy, compounded of impulsions from feeling and inclination and at the same time of rational concepts, must make the mind waver between motives which can be brought under no single principle and which can guide us only by mere accident to the good, but very often also to the evil.

[Review of Conclusions.]

From these considerations the following conclusions emerge. All moral concepts have their seat and origin in reason completely *a priori*, and indeed in the most ordinary human reason just as much as in the most highly speculative: they cannot be abstracted from any empirical, and therefore merely contingent, knowledge. In this purity of their origin is to be found their very worthiness to serve as supreme practical principles, and everything empirical added to them is just so much taken away from their genuine influence and from the absolute value of the corresponding actions. It is not only a requirement of the utmost necessity in respect of theory, where our concern is solely with speculation, but is also of the utmost practical importance, to draw these concepts and laws from pure reason, to set them forth pure and unmixed, and indeed to determine the extent of this whole practical, but pure, rational knowledge—that is, to determine the whole power of pure practical reason. We ought never—as speculative philosophy does allow and even at times finds necessary—to make principles depend on the special nature of human reason. Since moral laws have to hold for every rational being as such, we ought rather to derive our principles from the general concept of a rational being as such, and on this basis to expound the whole of ethics—which requires anthropology for its *application* to man—at first independently as pure philosophy, that is, entirely as metaphysics (which we can very well do in this wholly abstract kind of knowledge). We know well that without possessing such a metaphysics it is a futile endeavour, I will not say to determine accurately for speculative judgement the moral element of duty in all that accords with duty—but that it is impossible, even in ordinary and practical usage, particularly in that of moral instruction, to base morals on their genuine principles and so to bring about pure moral dispositions and engraft them on men's minds for the highest good of the world.

In this task of ours we have to progress by natural stages, not merely from ordinary moral judgement (which is here worthy of great respect) to philosophical judgement, as we have already done, but from popular philosophy, which goes no further than it can get by fumbling about with the aid of examples, to metaphysics. (This no longer lets itself be held back by anything empirical, and indeed—since it must survey the complete totality of this kind of knowledge—goes right to Ideas, where examples themselves fail.) For this purpose we must follow—and must portray in detail—the power of practical reason from the general rules determining it right up to the point where there springs from it the concept of duty.[1]

[Imperatives in General.]

Everything in nature works in accordance with laws. Only a rational being has the power to act *in accordance with his idea* of laws—that is, in accordance with principles—and only so has he a *will*. Since *reason* is required in order to derive actions from laws,[2] the will is nothing but practical reason. If reason infallibly determines the will, then in a being of this kind the actions which are recognized to be objectively necessary are also subjectively necessary—that is to say, the will is then a power to choose *only that* which reason independently of inclination recognizes to be practically necessary, that is, to be good. But if reason solely by itself is not sufficient to determine the will; if the will is exposed also to subjective conditions (certain impulsions) which do not always harmonize with the objective ones; if, in a word, the will is not *in itself* completely in accord with reason (as actually happens in the case of men); then actions which are recognized to be objectively necessary are subjectively contingent, and the determining of such a will in accordance with objective laws is *necessitation*. That is to say, the relation of objective laws to a will not good through and through is conceived as one in which the will of a rational being, although it is determined by principles of reason, does not necessarily follow these principles in virtue of its own nature.

The conception of an objective principle so far as this principle is necessitating for a will is called a command (of reason), and the formula of this command is called an *Imperative*.

All imperatives are expressed by an *'ought'* (*Sollen*). By this they mark the relation of an objective law of reason to a will which is not necessarily determined by this law in virtue of its subjective constitution (the relation of necessitation). They say that something would be good to do or to leave undone; only they say it to a will which does not always do a thing because it has been informed that this is a good thing to do. The practically *good* is that which determines the will by concepts of reason, and therefore not by subjective causes, but objectively—that is, on grounds valid for every rational being as such. It is distinguished from the *pleasant* as that which influences the will, not as a principle of reason valid for every one, but solely through the medium of sensation by purely subjective causes valid only for the senses of this person or that.

---

[1] We must pass from subjective principles (or maxims) to conditioned objective principles (hypothetical imperatives), and from there to the unconditioned categorical imperative of duty (especially the imperative of autonomy which prepares the way for the concept of freedom).

[2] If this 'derivation' were logical deduction, we could hardly infer from it that the will is practical reason. Kant seems to have in mind something more like what Aristotle called a *practical syllogism*—one whose condition is not a proposition but an action.

A perfectly good will would thus stand quite as much under objective laws (laws of the good), but it could not on this account be conceived as *necessitated* to act in conformity with law, since of itself, in accordance with its subjective constitution, it can be determined only by the concept of the good. Hence for the *divine* will, and in general for a *holy* will, there are no imperatives: *"I ought"* is here out of place, because *"I will"* is already of itself necessarily in harmony with the law. Imperatives are in consequence only formulae for expressing the relation of objective laws of willing to the subjective imperfection of the will of this or that rational being—for example, of the human will. . . .

[The Formula of Universal Law.]

In this task we wish first to enquire whether perhaps the mere concept of a categorical imperative may not also provide us with the formula containing the only proposition that can be a categorical imperative; for even when we know the purport of such an absolute command, the question of its possibility will still require a special and troublesome effort, which we postpone to the final chapter.

When I conceive a *hypothetical* imperative in general, I do not know beforehand what it will contain—until its condition is given. But if I conceive a *categorical* imperative, I know at once what it contains. For since besides the law this imperative contains only the necessity that our maxim[3] should conform to this law, while the law, as we have seen, contains no condition to limit it, there remains nothing over to which the maxim has to conform except the universality of a law as such; and it is this conformity alone that the imperative properly asserts to be necessary.

There is therefore only a single categorical imperative and it is this: *"Act only on that maxim through which you can at the same time will that it should become a universal law."*

Now if all imperatives of duty can be derived from this one imperative as their principle, then even although we leave it unsettled whether what we call duty may not be an empty concept, we shall still be able to show at least what we understand by it and what the concept means.

[The Formula of the Law of Nature.]

Since the universality of the law governing the production of effects constitutes what is properly called *nature* in its most general sense (nature as regards its form)—that is, the existence of things so far as determined by universal laws—the universal imperative of duty may also run as follows: *"Act as if the maxim of your action were to become through your will a universal law of nature."*

---

[3] A *maxim* is a subjective principle of action and must be distinguished from an *objective principle*—namely, a practical law. The former contains a practical rule determined by reason in accordance with the conditions of the subject (often his ignorance or again his inclinations): it is thus a principle on which the subject *acts*. A law, on the other hand, is an objective principle valid for every rational being; and it is a principle on which he *ought to act*—that is, an imperative.

[Illustrations.]

We will now enumerate a few duties, following their customary division into duties towards self and duties towards others and into perfect and imperfect duties.

1. A man feels sick of life as the result of a series of misfortunes that has mounted to the point of despair, but he is still so far in possession of his reason as to ask himself whether taking his own life may not be contrary to his duty to himself. He now applies the test "Can the maxim of my action really become a universal law of nature?" His maxim is "From self-love I make it my principle to shorten my life if its continuance threatens more evil than it promises pleasure." The only further question to ask is whether this principle of self-love can become a universal law of nature. It is then seen at once that a system of nature by whose law the very same feeling whose function (*Bestimmung*) is to stimulate the furtherance of life should actually destroy life would contradict itself and consequently could not subsist as a system of nature. Hence this maxim cannot possibly hold as a universal law of nature and is therefore entirely opposed to the supreme principle of all duty.

2. Another finds himself driven to borrowing money because of need. He well knows that he will not be able to pay it back; but he sees too that he will get no loan unless he gives a firm promise to pay it back within a fixed time. He is inclined to make such a promise; but he has still enough conscience to ask "Is it not unlawful and contrary to duty to get out of difficulties in this way?" Supposing, however, he did resolve to do so, the maxim of his action would run thus: "Whenever I believe myself short of money, I will borrow money and promise to pay it back, though I know that this will never be done." Now this principle of self-love or personal advantage is perhaps quite compatible with my own entire future welfare; only there remains the question "Is it right?" I therefore transform the demand of self-love into a universal law and frame my question thus: "How would things stand if my maxim became a universal law?" I then see straight away that this maxim can never rank as a universal law of nature and be self-consistent, but must necessarily contradict itself. For the universality of a law that every one believing himself to be in need can make any promise he pleases with the intention not to keep it would make promising, and the very purpose of promising, itself impossible, since no one would believe he was being promised anything, but would laugh at utterances of this kind as empty shams.

3. A third finds in himself a talent whose cultivation would make him a useful man for all sorts of purposes. But he sees himself in comfortable circumstances, and he prefers to give himself up to pleasure rather than to bother about increasing and improving his fortunate natural aptitudes. Yet he asks himself further "Does my maxim of neglecting my natural gifts, besides agreeing in itself with my tendency to indulgence, agree also with what is called duty?" He then sees that a system of nature could indeed always subsist under such a universal law, although (like the South Sea Islanders) every man should let his talents rust and should be bent on devoting his life solely to idleness, indulgence, procreation, and, in a word, to enjoyment. Only he cannot possibly *will* that this should

become a universal law of nature or should be implanted in us as such a law by a natural instinct. For as a rational being he necessarily wills that all his powers should be developed, since they serve him, and are given him, for all sorts of possible ends.

4.   Yet a *fourth* is himself flourishing, but he sees others who have to struggle with great hardships (and whom he could easily help); and he thinks "What does it matter to me? Let every one be as happy as Heaven wills or as he can make himself; I won't deprive him of anything; I won't even envy him; only I have no wish to contribute anything to his well-being or to his support in distress!" Now admittedly if such an attitude were a universal law of nature, mankind could get on perfectly well—better no doubt than if everybody prates about sympathy and goodwill, and even takes pains, on occasion, to practise them, but on the other hand cheats where he can, traffics in human rights, or violates them in other ways. But although it is possible that a universal law of nature could subsist in harmony with this maxim, yet it is impossible to *will* that such a principle should hold everywhere as a law of nature. For a will which decided in this way would be in conflict with itself, since many a situation might arise in which the man needed love and sympathy from others, and in which, by such a law of nature sprung from his own will, he would rob himself of all hope of the help he wants for himself.

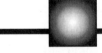

GEORG WILHELM FRIEDRICH HEGEL

(1770–1831) German Philosopher

From *The Philosophy of Right**

Morality (Moralität)

What Is My Duty?

Because every action explicitly calls for a particular content and a specific end, while duty as an abstraction entails nothing of the kind, the question arises: what is my duty? As an answer nothing is so far available except: (*a*) to do the right, and (*b*) to strive after welfare, one's own welfare, and welfare in universal terms, the welfare of others.

---

*From *The Philosophy of Right,* trans. T.M. Knox (Oxford: Clarendon Press, 1942).

Kant's Approach

These specific duties, however, are not contained in the definition of duty itself; but since both of them are conditioned and restricted, they *eo ipso* bring about the transition to the higher sphere of the unconditioned, the sphere of duty. Duty itself in the moral self-consciousness is the essence or the universality of that consciousness, the way in which it is inwardly related to itself alone; all that is left to it, therefore, is abstract universality, and for its determinate character it has identity without content, or the abstractly positive, the indeterminate.

However essential it is to give prominence to the pure unconditioned self-determination of the will as the root of duty, and to the way in which knowledge of the will, thanks to Kant's philosophy, has won its firm foundation and starting-point for the first time owing to the thought of its infinite autonomy, still to adhere to the exclusively moral position, without making the transition to the conception of ethics, is to reduce this gain to an empty formalism, and the science of morals to the preaching of duty for duty's sake. From this point of view, no immanent doctrine of duties is possible; of course, material may be brought in from outside and particular duties may be arrived at accordingly, but if the definition of duty is taken to be the absence of contradiction, formal correspondence with itself—which is nothing but abstract indeterminacy stabilized—then no transition is possible to the specification of particular duties nor, if some such particular content for acting comes under consideration, is there any criterion in that principle for deciding whether it is or is not a duty. On the contrary, by this means any wrong or immoral line of conduct may be justified.

Empty Duty

Kant's further formulation, the possibility of visualizing an action as a *universal maxim*, does lead to the more concrete visualization of a situation, but in itself it contains no principle beyond abstract identity and the "absence of contradiction" already mentioned.

The absence of property contains in itself just as little contradiction as the non-existence of this or that nation, family, &c., or the death of the whole human race. But if it is already established on other grounds and presupposed that property and human life are to exist and be respected, then indeed it is a contradiction to commit theft or murder; a contradiction must be a contradiction of something, i.e. of some content presupposed from the start as a fixed principle. It is to a principle of that kind alone, therefore, that an action can be related either by correspondence or contradiction. But if duty is to be willed simply for duty's sake and not for the sake of some content, it is only a formal identity whose nature it is to exclude all content and specification. . . .

True Conscience

Because of the abstract characterization of the good, the other moment of the Idea—particularity in general—falls within subjectivity. Subjectivity in its universality reflected into itself is the subject's absolute inward certainty of himself, that which establishes the particular and is the determining and decisive element in him, his conscience.

True conscience is the disposition to will what is absolutely good. It therefore has fixed principles and it is aware of these as its explicitly objective determinants and duties. In distinction from this its content (i.e. truth), conscience is only the formal side of the activity of the will, which as *this* will has no special content of its own. But the objective system of these principles and duties, and the union of subjective knowing with this system, is not present until we come to the standpoint of ethical life. Here at the abstract standpoint of morality, conscience lacks this objective content and so its explicit character is that of infinite abstract self-certainty, which at the same time is for this very reason the self-certainty of *this* subject.

This subjectivity, *qua* abstract self-determination and pure certainty of oneself alone, as readily evaporates into itself the whole determinate character of right, duty, and existence, as it remains both the power to judge, to determine from within itself alone, what is good in respect of any content, and also the power to which the good, at first only an ideal and an ought-to-be, owes its actuality.

The self-consciousness which has attained this absolute reflection into itself knows itself in this reflection to be the kind of consciousness which is and should be beyond the reach of every existent and given specific determination. As one of the commoner features of history (e.g. in Socrates, the Stoics, and others), the tendency to look deeper into oneself and to know and determine from within oneself what is right and good appears in ages when what is recognized as right and good in contemporary manners cannot satisfy the will of better men. When the existing world of freedom has become faithless to the will of better men, that will fails to find itself in the duties there recognized and must try to find in the ideal world of the inner life alone the harmony which actuality has lost. Once self-consciousness has grasped and secured its formal right in this way, everything depends on the character of the content which it gives to itself.

Once self-consciousness has reduced all otherwise valid duties to emptiness and itself to the sheer inwardness of the will, it has become the potentiality of either making the absolutely universal its principle, or equally well of elevating above the universal the self-will of private particularity, taking that as its principle and realizing it through its actions, i.e. it has become potentially evil.

To have a conscience, if conscience is only formal subjectivity, is simply to be on the verge of slipping into evil; in independent self-certainty, with its independence of knowledge and decision, both morality and evil have their common root. . . .

For the good as the substantial universal of freedom, but as something still abstract, there are therefore required determinate characteristics of some sort and the principle for determining them, though a principle identical with the good itself. For conscience similarly, as the purely abstract principle of determination, it is required that its decisions shall be universal and objective. If good and conscience are each kept abstract and thereby elevated to independent totalities, then both become the indeterminate which ought to be determined. But the integration of these two relative totalities into an absolute identity has already been implicitly achieved in this very subjectivity of pure self-certainty, aware in its vacuity of its gradual evaporation, is identical with the abstract universality of the

good. The identity of the good with the subjective will, an identity which therefore is concrete and the truth of them both, is Ethical Life.

Ethical Life (*Sittlichkeit*)

Situated Ethics

Ethical life is the Idea of freedom in that on the one hand it is the good become
alive—the good endowed in self-consciousness with knowing and willing and
actualized by self-conscious action—while on the other hand self-consciousness
has in the ethical realm its absolute foundation and the end which actuates its
effort. Thus ethical life is the concept of freedom developed into the existing
world and the nature of self-consciousness.

Since this unity of the concept of the will with its embodiment—i.e. the particular will—is knowing, consciousness of the distinction between these two
moments of the Idea is present, but present in such a way that now each of these
moments is in its own eyes the totality of the Idea and has that totality as its foundation and content.

The Objective Ethical Order

(d) The objective ethical order, which comes on the scene in place of good in the
abstract, is substance made concrete by subjectivity as infinite form. Hence it
posits within itself distinctions whose specific character is thereby determined by
the concept, and which endow the ethical order with a stable content independently necessary and subsistent in exaltation above subjective opinion and
caprice. These distinctions are absolutely valid laws and institutions.

It is the fact that the ethical order is the system of these specific determinations
of the Idea which constitutes its rationality. Hence the ethical order is freedom or
the absolute will as what is objective, a circle of necessity whose moments are the
ethical powers which regulate the life of individuals. To these powers individuals
are related as accidents to substance, and it is in individuals that these powers are
represented, have the shape of appearance, and become actualized.

The Substantial Order

(β) The substantial order, in the self-consciousness which it has thus actually
attained in individuals, knows itself and so is an object of knowledge. This ethical
substance and its laws and powers are on the one hand an object over against the
subject, and from his point of view they *are*—"are" in the highest sense of self-
subsistent being. This is an absolute authority and power infinitely more firmly
established than the being of nature.

The sun, the moon, mountains, rivers, and the natural objects of all kinds by
which we are surrounded, *are*. For consciousness they have the authority not only
of mere being but also of possessing a particular nature which it accepts and to
which it adjusts itself in dealing with them, using them, or in being otherwise
concerned with them. The authority of ethical laws is infinitely higher, because
natural objects conceal rationality under the cloak of contingency and exhibit it
only in their utterly external and disconnected way.

On the other hand, they are not something alien to the subject. On the contrary, his spirit bears witness to them as to its own essence, the essence in which

he has a feeling of his selfhood, and in which he lives as in his own element which is not distinguished from himself. The subject is thus directly linked to the ethical order by a relation which is more like an identity than even the relation of faith or trust.

Duty
The bond of duty can appear as a restriction only on indeterminate subjectivity or abstract freedom, and on the impulses either of the natural will or of the moral will which determines its indeterminate good arbitrarily. The truth is, however, that in duty the individual finds his liberation; first, liberation from dependence on mere natural impulse and from the depression which as a particular subject he cannot escape in his moral reflections on what ought to be and what might be; secondly, liberation from the indeterminate subjectivity which, never reaching reality or the objective determinacy of action, remains self-enclosed and devoid of actuality. In duty the individual acquires his substantive freedom.

Virtue
Virtue is the ethical order reflected in the individual character so far as that character is determined by its natural endowment. When virtue displays itself solely as the individual's simple conformity with the duties of the station to which he belongs, it is rectitude.

In an *ethical* community, it is easy to say what man must do, what are the duties he has to fulfil in order to be virtuous: he has simply to follow the well-known and explicit rules of his own situation. Rectitude is the general character which may be demanded of him by law or custom. But from the standpoint of *morality*, rectitude often seems to be something comparatively inferior, something beyond which still higher demands must be made on oneself and others, because the craving to be something special is not satisfied with what is absolute and universal; it finds consciousness of peculiarity only in what is exceptional.

The various facets of rectitude may equally well be called virtues, since they are also properties of the individual, although not specially of him in contrast with others. Talk about virtue, however, readily borders on empty rhetoric, because it is only about something abstract and indeterminate; and furthermore, argumentative and expository talk of the sort is addressed to the individual as to a being of caprice and subjective inclination. In an existing ethical order in which a complete system of ethical relations has been developed and actualized, virtue in the strict sense of the word is in place and actually appears only in exceptional circumstances or when one obligation clashes with another. The clash, however, must be a genuine one, because moral reflection can manufacture clashes of all sorts to suit its purpose and give itself a consciousness of being something special and having made sacrifices. It is for this reason that the phenomenon of virtue proper is commoner when societies and communities are uncivilized, since in those circumstances ethical conditions and their actualization are more a matter of private choice or the natural genius of an exceptional individual. For instance, it was especially to Hercules that the ancients ascribed virtue. In the states of antiquity, ethical life had not grown into this free system of an objective order self-subsistently developed, and consequently it was by the personal genius of individuals that this defect had to be made good. It follows that if a "doctrine of virtues" is not a mere "doctrine of duties," and if therefore it embraces the particular facet of character, the facet grounded in natural endowment, it will be a natural history of mind.

Custom and Ethics

But when individuals are simply identified with the actual order, ethical life (*das Sittliche*) appears as their general mode of conduct, i.e. as custom (*Sitte*), while the habitual practice of ethical living appears as a second nature which, put in the place of the initial, purely natural will, is the soul of custom permeating it through and through, the significance and the actuality of its existence. It is mind living and present as a world, and the substance of mind thus exists now for the first time as mind.

In this way the ethical substantial order has attained its right, and its right its validity. That is to say, the self-will of the individual has vanished together with his private conscience which had claimed independence and opposed itself to the ethical substance. For, when his character is ethical, he recognizes as the end which moves him to act the universal which is itself unmoved but is disclosed in its specific determinations as rationality actualized. He knows that his own dignity and the whole stability of his particular ends are grounded in this same universal, and it is therein that he actually attains these. Subjectivity is itself the absolute form and existent actuality of the substantial order, and the distinction between subject on the one hand and substance on the other, as the object, end, and controlling power of the subject, is the same as, and has vanished directly along with, the distinction between them in form.

Subjectivity is the ground wherein the concept of freedom is realized. At the level of morality, subjectivity is still distinct from freedom, the concept of subjectivity; but at the level of ethical life it is the realization of the concept in a way adequate to the concept itself.

The Universal and Particular Will

The right of individuals to be subjectively destined to freedom is fulfilled when they belong to an actual ethical order, because their conviction of their freedom finds its truth in such an objective order, and it is in an ethical order that they are actually in possession of their own essence or their own inner universality.

When a father inquired about the best method of educating his son in ethical conduct, a Pythagorean replied: "Make him a citizen of a state with good laws."

The right of individuals to their *particular* satisfaction is also contained in the ethical substantial order, since particularity is the outward appearance of the ethical order—a mode in which that order is existent.

Hence in this identity of the universal will with the particular will, right and duty coalesce, and by being in the ethical order a man has rights in so far as he has duties, and duties in so far as he has rights. In the sphere of abstract right, I have the right and another has the corresponding duty. In the moral sphere, the right of my private judgement and will, as well as of my happiness, has not, but only ought to have, coalesced with duties and become objective.

The ethical substance, as containing independent self-consciousness united with its concept, is the actual mind of a family and a nation.

The concept of this Idea has being only as mind, as something knowing itself and actual, because it is the objectification of itself, the movement running through the form of its moments. It is therefore

(A) ethical mind in its natural or immediate phase—the *Family.* This substantiality loses its unity, passes over into division, and into the phase of relation, i.e. into

(B) *Civil Society*—an association of members as self-subsistent individuals in a universality which, because of their self-subsistence, is only abstract. Their association is brought about by their needs, by the legal system— the means to security of person and property—and by an external organization for attaining their particular and common interests. This external state

(C) is brought back to and welded into unity in the *Constitution of the State* which is the end and actuality of both the substantial universal order and the public life devoted thereto.

MICHAEL OAKESHOTT
Contemporary Philosopher

The Tower of Babel*

I

The project of finding a short cut to heaven is as old as the human race. It is represented in the mythology of many peoples, and it is recognized always as an impious but not ignoble enterprise. The story of the Titans is, perhaps, the most complicated of the myths which portray this *folie de grandeur,* but the story of the Tower of Babel is the most profound. We may imagine the Titans drawing back after the first unsuccessful assault to hear one of their number suggest that their programme was too ambitious, that perhaps they were trying to do too much and to do it too quickly. But the builders of the Tower, whose top was to reach to heaven, were permitted no such conference; their enterprise involved them in the babblings of men who speak, but do not speak the same language. Like all profound myths, this represents a project the fascination of which is not confined to

---

*From Michael Oakeshott, *Rationalism in Politics* (London: Methuen & Co, 1962).

the childhood of the race, but is one which the circumstances of human life constantly suggest and one which no failure can deprive of its attraction. It indicates also the consequences of such an enterprise. I interpret it as follows.

The pursuit of perfection as the crow flies is an activity both impious and unavoidable in human life. It involves the penalties of impiety (the anger of the gods and social isolation), and its reward is not that of achievement but that of having made the attempt. It is an activity, therefore, suitable for individuals, but not for societies. For an individual who is impelled to engage in it, the reward may exceed both the penalty and the inevitable defeat. The penitent may hope, or even expect, to fall back, a wounded hero, into the arms of an understanding and forgiving society. And even the impenitent can be reconciled with himself in the powerful necessity of his impulse, though, like Prometheus, he must suffer for it. For a society, on the other hand, the penalty is a chaos of conflicting ideals, the disruption of a common life, and the reward is the renown which attaches to monumental folly. *A mesure que l'humanité se perfectionne l'homme se dégrade.* Or, to interpret the myth in a more lighthearted fashion: human life is a gamble; but while the individual must be allowed to bet according to his inclination (on the favourite or on an outsider), society should always back the field. Let us consider the matter in application to our own civilization.

The activity with which we are concerned is what is called moral activity, that is, activity which may be either good or bad. The moral life is human affection and behaviour determined, not by nature, but by art. It is conduct to which there is an alternative. This alternative need not be consciously before the mind; moral conduct does not necessarily involve the reflective choice of a particular action. Nor does it require that each occasion shall find a man without a disposition, or even without predetermination, to act in a certain way: a man's affections and conduct may be seen to spring from his character without thereby ceasing to be moral. The freedom without which moral conduct is impossible is freedom from a natural necessity which binds *all* men to act alike. This does not carry us very far. It identifies moral behaviour as the exercise of an acquired skill (though the skill need not have been self-consciously acquired), but it does not distinguish it from other kinds of art—from cookery or from carpentry. However, it carries us far enough for my purpose, which is to consider the *form* of the moral life, and in particular the form of the moral life of contemporary Western civilization.

In any manifestation of the moral life, form and content are, of course, inseparable. Nevertheless, neither can be said to determine the other; and in considering the form we shall be considering an abstraction which, in principle, is indifferent to any particular content, and indifferent also to any particular ethical theory. The practical question, What kinds of human enterprise should be designated right and wrong? and the philosophical question, What is the ultimate nature of moral criteria? are both outside what we are to consider. We are concerned only with the shape of the moral life. And our concern must be philosophical and historical, rather than practical, because neither a society nor an individual is normally given the opportunity of making an express choice of the form of a moral life.

The moral life of our society discloses a form neither simple nor homogeneous. Indeed, the form of our morality appears to be a mixture of two ideal extremes, a mixture the character of which derives from the predominance of one extreme over the other. I am not convinced of the necessary ideality of the extremes; it is perhaps possible that one, if not both, could exist as an actual form of the moral life. But even if this is doubtful, each can certainly exist with so little modification from the other that it is permissible to begin by regarding them as possible forms of morality. Let us consider the two forms which, either separately or in combination, compose the form of the moral life of the Western world.

II

In the first of these forms, the moral life is *a habit of affection and behaviour:* not a habit of reflective *thought,* but a habit of *affection* and *conduct.* The current situations of a normal life are met, not by consciously applying to ourselves a rule of behaviour, nor by conduct recognized as the expression of a moral ideal, but by acting in accordance with a certain habit of behaviour. The moral life in this form does not spring from the consciousness of possible alternative ways of behaving and a choice, determined by an opinion, a rule or an ideal, from among these alternatives; conduct is as nearly as possible without reflection. And consequently, most of the current situations of life do not appear as occasions calling for judgment, or as problems requiring solutions; there is no weighing up of alternatives or reflection on consequences, no uncertainty, no battle of scruples. There is, on the occasion, nothing more than the unreflective following of a tradition of conduct in which we have been brought up. And such moral habit will disclose itself as often in *not* doing, in the taste which dictates abstention from certain actions, as in performances. It should, of course, be understood that I am not here describing a form of the moral life which assumes the existence of a moral sense or of moral intuition, nor a form of the moral life presupposing a moral theory which attributes authority to conscience. Indeed, no specific theory of the source of authority is involved in this form of the moral life. Nor am I describing a merely primitive form of morality, that is, the morality of a society unaccustomed to reflective thought. I am describing the form which moral action takes (because it can take no other) in all the emergencies of life when time and opportunity for reflection are lacking, and I am supposing that what is true of the emergencies of life is true of most of the occasions when human conduct is free from natural necessity.

Every form of the moral life (because it is affection and behaviour determined by art) depends upon education. And the character of each form is reflected in the kind of education required to nurture and maintain it. From what sort of education will this first form of the moral life spring?

We acquire habits of conduct, not by constructing a way of living upon rules or precepts learned by heart and subsequently practised, but by living with people who habitually behave in a certain manner: we acquire habits of conduct in the same way as we acquire our native language. There is no point in a child's life at which he can be said to begin to learn the language which is habitually spoken in his hearing; and there is no point in his life at which he can be said to begin to learn habits of behaviour from the people constantly about him. No doubt, in both cases, what is learnt (or some of it) can be formulated in rules and precepts; but in neither case do we, in this kind of education, learn by learning rules and precepts. What we learn here is what may be learned without the formulation of its rules. And not only may a command of language and behaviour be achieved without our becoming aware of the rules, but also, if we have acquired a knowledge of the rules, this sort of command of language and behaviour is impossible until we have forgotten them as rules and are no longer tempted to turn speech and action into the applications of rules to a situation. Further, the education by means of which we acquire habits of affection and behaviour is not only coeval with conscious life, but it is carried on, in practice and observation, without pause in every moment of our waking life, and perhaps even in our dreams; what is begun as imitation continues as selective conformity to a rich variety of customary behaviour. This sort of education is not compulsory; it is inevitable. And lastly (if education in general is making oneself at home in the natural and civilized worlds), this is not a separable part of education. One may set apart an hour in which to learn mathematics and devote another to the Catechism, but it is impossible to engage in any activity whatever without contributing to this kind of moral education, and it is impossible to enjoy this kind of moral education in an hour set aside for its study. There are, of course, many things which cannot be learned in this sort of education. We may learn in this manner to play a game, and we may learn to play it without breaking the rules, but we cannot acquire a knowledge of the rules themselves without formulating them or having them formulated for us. And further, without a knowledge of the rules we can never know for certain whether or not we are observing them, nor shall we be able to explain why the referee has blown his whistle. Or, to change the metaphor, from this sort of education can spring the ability never to write a false line of poetry, but it will give us neither the ability to scan nor a knowledge of the names of the various metric forms.

It is not difficult, then, to understand the sort of moral education by means of which habits of affection and behaviour may be acquired; it is the sort of education which gives the power to act appropriately and without hesitation, doubt or difficulty, but which does not give the ability to explain our actions in abstract terms, or defend them as emanations of moral principles. Moreover, this education must be considered to have failed in its purpose if it provides a range of behaviour insufficient to meet all situations without the necessity of calling upon reflection, or if it does not make the habit of behaviour sufficiently compelling to remove hesitation. But it must not be considered to have failed merely because it leaves us ignorant of moral rules and moral ideals. And a man may be said to have acquired most thoroughly what this kind of moral education can teach him when his moral dispositions are inseverably connected with his *amour-propre*, when the spring of his conduct is not an attachment to an ideal or a felt duty to obey a rule, but his self-esteem, and when to act wrongly is felt as diminution of his self-esteem.

Now, it will be observed that this is a form of morality which gives remarkable stability to the moral life from the point of view either of an individual or of a society; it is not in its nature to countenance large or sudden changes in the kinds of behaviour it desiderates. Parts of a moral life in this form may collapse, but since the habits of conduct which compose it are never recognized as a system, the collapse does not readily spread to the whole. And being without a perceived rigid framework distinct from the modes of behaviour themselves (a framework, for example, of abstract moral ideals), it is not subject to the kind of collapse which springs from the detection of some flaw or incoherence in a system of moral ideals. Intellectual error with regard to moral ideas or opinions does not compromise a moral life which is firmly based upon a habit of conduct. In short, the stability which belongs to this form of the moral life derives from its elasticity and its ability to suffer change without disruption. First, there is in it nothing that is absolutely fixed. Just as in a language there may be certain constructions which are simply bad grammar, but in all the important ranges of expression the language is malleable by the writer who uses it and he cannot go wrong unless he deserts its genius, so in this form of the moral life, the more thorough our education the more certain will be our taste and the more extensive our range of behaviour within the tradition. Custom is always adaptable and susceptible to the *nuance* of the situation. This may appear a paradoxical assertion; custom, we have been taught, is blind. It is, however, an insidious piece of misobservation; custom is not blind, it is only "blind as a bat." And anyone who has studied a tradition of customary behaviour (or a tradition of any other sort) knows that both rigidity and instability are foreign to its character. And secondly, this form of the moral life is capable of change as well as of local variation. Indeed, no traditional way of behaviour, no traditional skill, ever remains fixed; its history is one of continuous change. It is true that the change it admits is neither great nor sudden; but then, revolutionary change is usually the product of the eventual overthrow of an aversion from change, and is characteristic of something that has few internal resources of change. And the appearance of changelessness in a morality of traditional behaviour is an illusion which springs from the erroneous belief that the only significant change is that which is either induced by self-conscious activity or is, at least, observed on the occasion. The sort of change which belongs to this form of the moral life is analogous to the change to which a living language is subject: nothing is more habitual or customary than our ways of speech, and nothing is more continuously invaded by change. Like prices in a free market, habits of moral conduct show no revolutionary changes because they are never at rest. But it should be observed, also, that because the internal movement characteristic of this form of the moral life does not spring from reflection upon moral principles, and represents only an unselfconscious exploitation of the genius of the tradition of moral conduct, it does not amount to moral self-criticism. And, consequently, a moral life of this kind, if it degenerates into superstition, or if crisis supervenes, has little power of recovery. Its defence is solely its resistance to the conditions productive of crisis.

One further point should, perhaps, be noticed: the place and character of the moral eccentric in this form of the moral life, when it is considered as the form of the moral life of a society. The moral eccentric is not, of course, excluded by this form of morality. (The want of moral sensibility, the hollowness of moral character, which seems often to inhere in peoples whose morality is predominantly one of custom, is improperly attributed to the customary form of their morality; its cause lies elsewhere.) We sometimes think that deviation from a customary morality must always take place under the direction of a formulated moral ideal. But this is not so. There is a freedom and inventiveness at the heart of every traditional way of life, and deviation may be an expression of that freedom, springing from a sensitiveness to the tradition itself and remaining faithful to the traditional form. Generally speaking, no doubt, the inspiration of deviation from moral habit is perfectionist, but it is not necessarily consciously perfectionist. It is not, in essence, rebellious, and may be likened to the sort of innovation introduced into a plastic art by the fortuitous appearance in an individual of a specially high degree of manual skill, or to the sort of change a great stylist may make in a language. Although in any particular instance deviation may lead the individual eccentric astray, and although it is not something that can profitably be imitated, moral eccentricity is of value to a society whose morality is one of habit of behaviour (regardless of the direction it may take) so long as it remains the activity of the individual and is not permitted to disrupt the communal life. In a morality of an habitual way of behaviour, then, the influence of the moral eccentric may be powerful but is necessarily oblique, and the attitude of society towards him is necessarily ambivalent. He is admired but not copied, reverenced but not followed, welcomed but ostracized.

III

The second form of the moral life we are to consider may be regarded as in many respects the opposite of the first. In it activity is determined, not by a habit of behaviour, but by *the reflective application of a moral criterion.* It appears in two common varieties: as *the self-conscious pursuit of moral ideals,* and as *the reflective observance of moral rules.* But it is what these varieties have in common that is important, because it is this, and not what distinguishes them from one another, which divides them from the first form of morality.

This is a form of the moral life in which a special value is attributed to self-consciousness, individual or social; not only is the rule or the ideal the product of reflective thought, but the application of the rule or the ideal to the situation is also a reflective activity. Normally the rule or the ideal is determined first and in the abstract; that is, the first task in constructing an art of behaviour in this form is to express moral aspirations in words—in a rule of life or in a system of abstract ideals. This task of verbal expression need not begin with a moral *de omnibus dubitandum;* but its aim is not only to set out the desirable ends of conduct, but also to set them out clearly and unambiguously and to reveal their relations to one another. Secondly, a man who would enjoy this form of the moral life must be certain of his ability to defend these formulated aspirations against criticism. For, having been brought into the open, they will henceforth be liable to attack. His third task will be to translate them into behaviour, to apply them to the current situations of life as they arise. In this form of the moral life, then, action will spring from a judgment concerning the rule or end to be applied and the determination to apply it. The situations of living should, ideally, appear as problems to be solved, for it is only in this form that they will receive the attention they call for. And there will be a resistance to the urgency of action; it will appear more important to have the right moral ideal, than to act. The application of a rule or an ideal to a situation can never be easy; both ideal and situation will usually require interpretation, and a rule of life (unless the life has been simplified by the drastic reduction of the variety of situations which are allowed to appear) will always be found wanting unless it is supplemented with an elaborate casuistry or hermeneutic. It is true that moral ideals and moral rules may become so familiar that they take on the character of an habitual or traditional way of *thinking* about behaviour. It is true also that long familiarity with our ideals may have enabled us to express them more concretely in a system of specific rights and duties, handy in application. And further, a moral ideal may find its expression in a type of human character—such as the character of the gentleman—and conduct become the imaginative application of the ideal character to the situation. But these qualifications carry us only part of the way: they may remove the necessity for *ad hoc* reflection on the rules and ideals themselves, but they leave us still with the problem of interpreting the situation and the task of translating the ideal, the right or the duty into behaviour. For the right or the duty is always to observe a rule or realize an end, and not to behave in a certain concrete manner. Indeed, it is not desired, in this form of the moral life, that tradition should carry us all the way; its distinctive virtue is to be subjecting behaviour to a continuous corrective analysis and criticism.

This form of the moral life, not less than the other, depends upon education, but upon an education of an appropriately different sort. In order to acquire the necessary knowledge of moral ideals or of a rule of life, we need something more than the observation and practice of behaviour itself. We require, first, an intellectual training in the detection and appreciation of the moral ideals themselves, a training in which the ideals are separated and detached from the necessarily imperfect expression they find in particular actions. We require, secondly, training in the art of the intellectual management of these ideals. And thirdly, we require training in the application of ideals to concrete situations, in the art of translation and in the art of selecting appropriate means for achieving the ends which our education has inculcated. Such an education may be made compulsory in a society, but if so it is only because it is not inevitable. It is true that, as Spinoza says, a substitute for a perfectly trained moral judgment may be found in committing a rule of life to memory and following it implicitly. But, though this is as far as some pupils will get, it cannot be considered to be the aim of this moral education. If it is to achieve its purpose, this education must carry us far beyond the acquisition of a moral technique; and it must be considered to have failed in its purpose if it has not given both ability to determine behaviour by a self-conscious choice and an understanding of the ideal grounds of the choice made. Nobody can fully share this form of the moral life who is not something of a philosopher and something of a self-analyst: its aim is moral behaviour springing from the communally cultivated reflective capacities of each individual.

Now, a moral life in which everyone who shares it knows at each moment exactly what he is doing and why, should be well protected against degeneration into superstition and should, moreover, give remarkable confidence to those who practise it. Nevertheless, it has its dangers, both from the point of view of an individual and from that of a society. The confidence which belongs to it is mainly a confidence in respect of the moral ideals themselves, or of the moral rule. The education in the ideals or in the rule must be expected to be the most successful part of this moral education; the art of applying the ideals is more difficult both to teach and to learn. And together with the certainty about how to *think* about moral ideals, must be expected to go a proportionate uncertainty about how to *act*. The constant analysis of behaviour tends to undermine, not only prejudice in moral habit, but moral habit itself, and moral reflection may come to inhibit moral sensibility.

Further, a morality which takes the form of the self-conscious pursuit of moral ideals is one which, at every moment, calls upon those who practise it to determine their behaviour by reference to a vision of perfection. This is not so much the case when the guide is a moral rule, because the rule is not represented as perfection and constitutes a mediation, a cushion, between the behaviour it demands on each occasion and the complete moral response to the situation. But when the guide of conduct is a moral ideal we are never suffered to escape from perfection. Constantly, indeed on all occasions, the society is called upon to seek virtue as the crow flies. It may even be said that the moral life, in this form, demands an hyperoptic moral vision and encourages intense moral emulation among those who enjoy it, the moral eccentric being recognized, not as a vicarious sufferer for the stability of a society, but as a leader and a guide. And the unhappy society, with an ear for every call, certain always about what it ought to *think* (though it will never for long be the same thing), in action shies and plunges like a distracted animal.

Again, a morality of ideals has little power of self-modification; its stability springs from its inelasticity and its imperviousness to change. It will, of course, respond to interpretation, but the limits of that response are close and severe. It has a great capacity to resist change, but when that resistance is broken down, what takes place is not change but revolution—rejection and replacement. Moreover, every moral ideal is potentially an obsession; the pursuit of moral ideals is an idolatry in which particular objects are recognized as "gods." This potentiality may be held in check by more profound reflection, by an intellectual grasp of the whole system which gives place and proportion to each moral ideal; but such a grasp is rarely achieved. Too often the excessive pursuit of one ideal leads to the exclusion of others, perhaps all others; in our eagerness to realize justice we come to forget charity, and a passion for righteousness has made many a man hard and merciless. There is, indeed, no ideal the pursuit of which will not lead to disillusion; *chagrin* waits at the end for all who take this path. Every admirable ideal has its opposite, no less admirable. Liberty or order, justice or charity, spontaneity or deliberateness, principle or circumstance, self or others, these are the kinds of dilemma with which this form of the moral life is always confronting us, making us see double by directing our attention always to abstract extremes, none of which is wholly desirable. It is a form of the moral life which puts upon those who share it, not only the task of translating moral ideals into appropriate forms of conduct, but also the distracting intellectual burden of removing the verbal conflict of ideals before moral behaviour is possible. These conflicting ideals are, of course, reconciled in all amiable characters (that is, when they no longer appear as ideals), but that is not enough; a verbal and theoretical reconciliation is required. In short, this is a form of the moral life which is dangerous in an individual and disastrous in a society. For an individual it is a gamble which may have its reward when undertaken within the limits of a society which is not itself engaged in the gamble; for a society it is mere folly.

IV

This brief characterization of what appear to be two forms of the moral life, while perhaps establishing their distinction or even their opposition, will have made us more doubtful about their capability of independent existence. Neither, taken alone, recommends itself convincingly as a likely form of the moral life, in an individual or in a society; the one is all habit, the other all reflection. And the more closely we examine them, the more certain we become that they are, not forms of the moral life at all, but ideal extremes. And when we turn to consider what sort of a form of the moral life they offer in combination, we may perhaps enjoy the not illusory confidence that we are approaching more nearly to concrete possibility, or even historical reality.

In a mixture in which the first of these extremes is dominant, the moral life may be expected to be immune from a confusion between behaviour and the pursuit of an ideal. Action will retain its primacy, and, whenever it is called for, will spring from habit of behaviour. Conduct itself will never become problematical, inhibited by the hesitations of ideal speculation or the felt necessity of bringing philosophic talent and the fruits of philosophic education to bear upon the situation. The confidence in action, which belongs to the well-nurtured customary moral life, will remain unshaken. And the coherence of the moral life will not wait upon the abstract unity which the reflective relation of values can give it. But, in addition, this mixed form of the moral life may be supposed to enjoy the advantages that spring from a reflective morality—the power to criticize, to reform and to explain itself, and the power to propagate itself beyond the range of the custom of a society. It will enjoy also the appropriate intellectual confidence in its moral standards and purposes. And it will enjoy all this without the danger of moral criticism usurping the place of a habit of moral behaviour, or of moral speculation bringing disintegration to moral life. The education in moral habit will be supplemented, but not weakened, by the education in moral ideology. And in a society which enjoyed this form of the moral life, both habit and ideology might be the common possession of all its members, or moral speculation might in fact be confined to the few, while the morality of the many remained one of the habit of behaviour. But, in any case, the internal resources of movement of this form of morality would be supplied by both its components: to the potential individual eccentricity which belongs to a traditional morality would be added the more consciously rebellious eccentricity which has its roots in the more precisely followed perfectionism of a morality of ideals. In short, this form of the moral life will offer to a society advantages similar to those of a religion which has taken to itself a theology (though not necessarily a popular theology) but without losing its character as a way of living.

On the other hand, a morality whose form is a mixture in which the second of our extremes is dominant will, I think, suffer from a permanent tension between its component parts. Taking charge, the morality of the self-conscious pursuit of ideals will have a disintegrating effect upon habit of behaviour. When action is called for, speculation or criticism will supervene. Behaviour itself will tend to become problematical, seeking its self-confidence in the coherence of an ideology. The pursuit of perfection will get in the way of a stable and flexible moral tradition, the naïve coherence of which will be prized less than the unity which springs from self-conscious analysis and synthesis. It will seem more important to have an intellectually defensible moral ideology than a ready habit of moral behaviour. And it will come to be assumed that a morality which is not easily transferable to another society, which lacks an obvious universality, is (for that reason) inadequate for the needs of the society of its origin. The society will wait upon its self-appointed moral teachers, pursuing the extremes they recommend and at a loss when they are silent. The distinguished and inspiring visiting preacher, who nevertheless is a stranger to the way we live, will displace the priest, the father of his parish. In a moral life constantly or periodically suffering the ravages of the armies of conflicting ideals, or (when these for the time have passed) falling into the hands of censors and inspectors, the cultivation of a habit of moral behaviour will have as little opportunity as the cultivation of the land when the farmer is confused and distracted by academic critics and political directors. Indeed, in such a mixture (where habit of behaviour is subordinate to the pursuit of ideals) each of the components is unavoidably playing a role foreign to its character; as in a literature in which criticism has usurped the place of poetry, or in a religious life in which the pursuit of theology offers itself as an alternative to the practice of piety.

These, however, must be counted incidental, though grave, imperfections in this mixture of extremes in the moral life; the radical defect of this form is the radical defect of its dominant extreme—its denial of the poetic character of all human activity. A prosaic tradition of thought has accustomed us to the assumption that moral activity, when analysed, will be found to consist in the translation of an idea of what ought to be into a practical reality, the transformation of an ideal into a concrete existence. And we are accustomed, even, to think of poetry in these terms; first, a "heart's desire" (an idea) and then its expression, its translation into words. Nevertheless, I think this view is mistaken; it is the superimposition upon art and moral activity generally of an inappropriate didactic form. A poem is not the translation into words of a state of mind. What the poet says and what he wants to say are not two things, the one succeeding and embodying the other, they are the same thing; he does not know what he wants to say until he has said it. And the "corrections" he may make to his first attempt are not efforts to make words correspond more closely to an already formulated idea or to images already fully formed in his mind, they are renewed efforts to formulate the idea, to conceive the image. Nothing exists in advance of the poem itself, except perhaps the poetic passion. And what is true of poetry is true also, I think, of all human moral activity. Moral ideals are not, in the first place, the products of reflective thought, the verbal expressions of unrealized ideas, which are then translated (with varying degrees of accuracy) into human behaviour; they are the products of human behaviour, of human practical activity, to which reflective thought gives subsequent, partial and abstract expression in words. What is good, or right, or what is considered to be reasonable behaviour may exist in advance of the situation, but only in the generalized form of the possibilities of behaviour determined by art and not by nature. That is to say, the capital of moral ideals upon which a morality of the pursuit of moral ideals goes into business has always been accumulated by a morality of habitual behaviour, and appears in the form of abstract ideas only because (for the purposes of subscription) it has been transformed by reflective thought into a currency of ideas. This view of the matter does not, of course, deprive moral ideals of their power as critics of human habits, it does not denigrate the activity of reflective thought in giving this verbal expression to the principles of behaviour; there is no doubt whatever that a morality in which reflection has no part is defective. But it suggests that a morality of the pursuit of moral ideals, or a morality in which this is dominant, is not what it appears at first sight to be, is not something that can stand on its own feet. In such a morality, that which has power to rescue from superstition is given the task of generating human behaviour—a task which, in fact, it cannot perform. And it is only to be expected that a morality of this sort will be subject to sudden and ignominious collapse. In the life of an individual this collapse need not necessarily be fatal; in the life of a society it is likely to be irretrievable. For a society is a common way of life; and not only is it true that a society may perish of a disease which is not necessarily fatal even to those of its members who suffer from it, but it is also true that what is corrupting in the society may not be corrupting in its members. . . .

The history of European morals, then, is in part the history of the maintenance and extension of a morality whose form has, from the beginning, been dominated by the pursuit of moral ideals. In so far as this is an unhappy form of morality, prone to obsession and at war with itself, it is a misfortune to be deplored; in so far as it cannot now readily be avoided, it is a misfortune to be made the best of. And if a morality of ideals is now all, or at least the best, of what we have, it might seem an injudicious moment to dwell upon its defects. But in order to make the best of an unavoidable situation, we need to know its defects as well as feel its necessity. And what at the present time stands between us and the opportunity (such as it is) of surmounting our misfortune is not our sense of the difficulty of doing so, but an erroneous inference we have drawn from our situation—the belief, which has slowly settled upon us, encouraged by almost all the intellectual tendencies of recent centuries, that it is no misfortune at all, but a situation to be welcomed. For the remarkable thing about contemporary European morality is not merely that its form is dominated by the self-conscious pursuit of ideals, but that this form is generally thought to be better and higher than any other. A morality of habit of behaviour is dismissed as primitive and obsolete; the pursuit of moral ideals (whatever discontent there may be with the ideals themselves) is identified with moral enlightenment. And further, it is prized (and has been particularly prized on this account since the seventeenth century) because it appears to hold out the possibility of that most sought-after consummation—a "scientific" morality. It is to be feared, however, that in both these appearances the pursuit of moral ideals has proved itself (as might be expected) an untrustworthy form of morality, the spring neither of a practical nor of a "scientific" moral life.

The predicament of Western morals, as I read it, is first that our moral life has come to be dominated by the pursuit of ideals, a dominance ruinous to a settled habit of behaviour; and, secondly, that we have come to think of this dominance as a benefit for which we should be grateful or an achievement of which we should be proud. And the only purpose to be served by this investigation of our predicament is to disclose the corrupt consciousness, the self-deception which reconciles us to our misfortune.

ALAN DONAGAN
(1925–1991) Australian Philosopher

On Kant and Hegel*

Although they were received from the first as classics, Kant's ethical writings were widely regarded as definitive of a dead tradition, not as models for future research. This may in large part be put down to Hegel's objection that Kant's "exclusively moral position" cannot make sense of concrete ethical life. Morality (*die Moralität*), conceived as a law binding upon all rational creatures by virtue of their rationality, was identified both by Kant and Hegel with "the pure unconditional self-determination" of a rational will. But Hegel argued that although such self-determination accounts for the "infinite autonomy" of ethical life, it must ultimately reduce it to "an empty formalism." It provides moral duty with identity, but not with content, and so cannot rise above preaching an empty duty for duty's sake.

If the pure self-determination of a rational will is abstract and empty, where is a specific content for ethical life to be sought? Hegel's answer was: in the mores of an actual ethical community (*sittliches Gemeinwesen*). In such a community, he declared, "it is easy to say what man must do, what are the duties he has to fulfil in order to be virtuous: he has simply to follow the well-known and explicit rules of his own situation. Rectitude is the general character which may be demanded of him by law or custom."[1]

Outside the ethical life (*Sittlichkeit*) of willing conformity to the mores of an actual ethical community, morality is an empty form: a devotion to duty for duty's sake, which lacks a rational ground by which anybody's specific duties may be determined. "As one of the commoner features of history," Hegel remarked, "for example, in Socrates, the Stoics, and others, the tendency to look deeper into oneself, and to know and determine from within oneself what is right and good, appears in ages when what is recognized as right and good in contemporary mores [*in der Wirklichkeit und Sitte*] cannot satisfy the will of better men."[2] But

---

*From Alan Donagan, *The Theory of Morality* (Chicago: University of Chicago Press; 1977), pp. 9–17.
[1] See Hegel, pp. 65—ED.
[2] Ibid., 63.

although better men may divine that something is wrong with contemporary mores, Hegel contended that they can provide no specific alternative that is rationally grounded. Their withdrawal into an inner life is therefore an "evaporation" of actual life into abstract "subjectivity"—into virtuousness without grounded virtues.[3]

"The moral point of view . . . is defective because it is purely abstract": that is the core of Hegel's case against morality.[4] It is *Sittlichkeit* evaporated into subjectivity; and although, as a stage in philosophical inquiry, "it is right enough to evaporate right and duty into subjectivity, it is wrong if this abstract groundwork is not condensed out again.[5] It follows that the proper subject of philosophical ethics is not morality but *Sittlichkeit*; and that a well-constructed ethical system will be, not a theory of morality, but a theory of what fills the empty form of morality with content. However they differ from him and from one another, philosophers who have accepted Hegel's doctrine of the emptiness of the moral point of view have, like him, inevitably become critics of morality. They are not immoralists; that is, they do not acknowledge any precepts as precepts of morality, and flout them. Rather, they assert that the a priori principles of morality, being abstract, cannot generate any specific precepts at all.

Hegel's observations on morality contain much that is true. A moral life cannot be solely the conscious following of explicit moral precepts. Since good morals are characteristically displayed in emergencies, which deny opportunity for reflection, they must in some measure consist in what Michael Oakeshott has called "a habit of affection and conduct."[6] Such a habit or disposition is revealed as much in what a man does not do as in what he does: it is a sort of fastidiousness or taste. And the tradition of such a disposition, although variable, will be stable. The kind of change which belongs to it, as Oakeshott has remarked, "is analogous to the change to which a living language is subject: nothing is more habitual or customary than our ways of speech, and nothing is more continuously invaded by change."[7]

That morality is characteristically found embodied in such dispositions of affection and conduct is part of what Hegel meant when he contended that morality receives content only in the *Sittlichkeit* of an ethical community. But he seems also to have meant that the content of the *Sittlichkeit* which embodies morality must be more than moral. Oakeshott's analogy of language is useful here. The grammar of a language is ascertained from the usage of those who speak and write that language well. Its authority is that of the speech and writing which exemplifies it. But speaking or writing well is more than doing so grammatically: being grammatical is a necessary condition of it, but not a sufficient one. And so it is with the relation of morality to acting well: nobody can act well unless he acts morally; but, for the most part, to act well it is not enough to act morally. A life the sole object of which was to obey the moral law would be aimless and empty.

A morality largely confined to restrictions on how one may pursue legitimate ends, which lays down only the most general conditions on what ends may be

[3] Ibid.
[4] Ibid.
[5] Ibid.
[6] See Oakeshott, pp. 71.—ED.
[7] Ibid.

legitimately chosen, has sometimes been thought to be incomplete, if not muti-
lated. Alasdair MacIntyre, for example, has depreciated the virtues characteristic
of such a morality as "secondary," on the ground that "their existence in a moral
scheme of things as virtues is secondary to . . . the notion of another primary set
of virtues which are directly related to the goals which men pursue as the ends of
their life."[8] And, writing in 1964, he went on to compare unfavorably British society from the middle of the nineteenth century, in which, because of the depth of
class divisions, the only moral virtues all its members have been able to agree
upon are secondary, with American society in the same period, in which the
same goals have been pursued by members of all classes. The American class
structure, he contended, "allows for there being a national community of values";
the British one "only allows that national community of values to exist at the level
of . . . the secondary virtues."

Even if class divisions in Britain are deeper than in the United States, the sociological contrast MacIntyre depicted is dubious. Because Americans of all classes
mostly agree on the rationality of a fundamentally capitalist economic system, he
credited them with sharing the same goal in life—success in terms of that system. Yet capitalism is attractive as an economic system in part because it is consistent with any number of different life plans, and imposes none; that may even be
why many Americans are attached to it. Very few of those whose chief object in
life is business success imagine that object to be morally mandatory, or regard
those who reject it as immoral. And no way of life which permits a variety of
specific goals—no free way of life—can treat traditional moral virtues like fairness as secondary to any virtue which is merely requisite for the attainment of
some specific goal. On the contrary, it will refuse to treat as either primary or
moral any virtue the sole ground of which is that it is requisite for the attainment
of this or that specific goal. The moral virtues are those without which you cannot, conformably to your rationality, pursue any goal whatever.

Neither of the two truths we have identified in Hegel's criticism of morality
need be denied by traditional moralists. In religious traditions such as Judaism
and Christianity, moral education, as the transmission of dispositions of conduct,
is a matter of initiation into the life of a religious community; and in civilized
pagan cultures it is a matter of initiation into the life of those cultures. Morality is
characteristically learned as one learns to speak one's mother tongue grammatically: not by formal instruction, in times set aside for it, but by conversation and
by participation in a common life. And one learns it incidentally to learning how
to act well.

Nor did Kant deny that characteristically the capability of acting morally consists in dispositions of action and affection, and not of deliberation, or that such
dispositions are usually found only in members of ethical communities. His reverence for the nontheoretical morality of ordinary folk should have placed this
beyond question. Moreover, by teaching that every man has a natural end, happiness; that different persons and cultures have found happiness in different ways
of life; and that morality is the common condition of every rational way of seeking
happiness, he made it equally plain that a life that was merely moral would have

---

[8]Alasdair MacIntyre, *Secularization and Moral Courage* (London: Oxford University Press, 1967), pp. 214.

been unimaginable to him. And, even more strongly than Oakeshott, he maintained that common morality is disclosed in what a man will not do: it consists in the limitations he observes in his pursuit of happiness.

In drawing attention to the limits both of the place of morality in human life, and of theory and deliberation in morality, Hegel asserted nothing that traditional moralists could not have approved. But they vehemently disapproved his more ambitious doctrine that morality has no content except that which the *Sittlichkeit* of ethical communities can supply. For they insisted that the restrictions ordained by practical reason on how one may pursue one's ends are specific. They conceived the conditions imposed by morality upon conduct to be analogous to those imposed by the grammar of a particular language upon speech in that language. By taking it to be a mere empty form which any coherent way of life whatever would have, Hegel reduced morality to something analogous to grammaticality in general.

Yet his reasons for so degrading morality are obscure. In his *Philosophie des Rechts* he sometimes wrote as though he were merely developing the implications of Kant's position.[9] Now it is true that Kant described his fundamental principle of morality as being purely formal, like all principles of reason. And his first formula for that principle, *Act only according to that maxim by which you can at the same time will that it should become a universal law,* helped to create an impression that he took it to be empty. But that impression cannot be sustained. In Kant's terminology, "formal" principles are contrasted with "material" ones, that is, with principles grounded in experience and interest. There is no implication that they are compatible with any content whatever. Moreover, he went on to maintain that his fundamental principle presupposes that action has an end prescribed by reason and not by interest or whim, to wit, rational nature itself; and that, accordingly, it has a second formula, equivalent to the first, namely, *Act so that you treat humanity, whether in your own person or in that of another, always as an end and never as a means only.* It is therefore evident that he did not think of the formal first principle of morality as devoid of content.

Today, however, the doctrine that reason can generate none but purely logical and hence empty a priori principles is so widely received that Hegel's defenders may think to claim for him the credit of anticipating it. And unquestionably, the *onus probandi* lies upon those who assert that pure reason furnishes substantive moral principles, not upon those who deny it. Anybody who offers to construct a theory of morality on the model of Kant's thereby undertakes to demonstrate how its principles are required by pure reason. Yet even though this undertaking must be reserved for what follows, it can be shown at once that Hegel himself conceded too much to the point of view of morality to have been able consistently to deny all content to its principles.

Although he was not much interested in the problem of how a man is to conduct himself when his will cannot "find itself" in the mores of his society, Hegel nevertheless recognized the problem and discussed it. It was the problem of Socrates, and of the Stoics. What, for example, must a deeply thoughtful man do if he finds himself a member of a society in which the institution of slavery is

---

[9] See Hegel, pp. 62.—ED.

recognized? Presumably having in mind such things as the Stoics' denial of the validity of the master-slave relation, even as they were compelled to observe the laws regarding it, Hegel agreed that in such a situation one has no choice but "to try to find in the ideal world of the inner life alone the harmony which actuality has lost"—or has never had.[10] It was in this spirit that Epictetus imagined a slave as thus addressing his master: "Zeus has set me free: do you think that he intended his own son to be enslaved? But you are master of my carcass; take it." Yet, even though the Stoics could not draw content for the empty self-determination of their wills from the *Sittlichkeit* of their ethical community, Hegel himself confessed that they were "better men than their fellows" and that their repudiation of slavery was right. How can this be rendered consistent? There is indeed the expedient of declaring that it was according to the *Sittlichkeit* of his ethical community, and not of their own, that Hegel judged the Stoics better men than their contemporaries; but, since such accidental and external superiority could have no philosophical significance, his own principles forbade him to adopt it. And there appears to be no other way of justifying his verdict than to concede that the ideal world of the Stoics' inner life had content as well as abstract form.

Hegel did not perceive that a pure morality of affection and conduct—a morality the content of which is wholly a matter of sharing the unselfconscious mores of an actual community—is weak both internally and externally. Its internal movement, Oakeshott has observed, which "does not spring from reflection on moral principles, . . . does not amount to moral self-criticism." Hence it has little power of recovery if, as is probable, "it degenerates into superstition, or if a crisis supervenes."[11]

The process of degeneration may be studied in moral traditions with a history of reflection on principles but in which the practice of self-criticism has fallen into disuse. According to received Catholic doctrine, it is morally wrong to serve in an unjust war: that is, a war not undertaken for a just and grave reason and with a right intention, or one that is not waged in a just way, or one in which there is no reasonable chance of accomplishing what is intended. Although this definition contains moral terms requiring interpretation, there is large agreement among Catholic moralists that various specific reasons for undertaking a war are unjust or inadequate, that various specific intentions are wrong, and that various specific ways of waging it are barbarous. Nor is it seriously doubted that, by one or more of these criteria, many of the wars fought by Catholic states have been unjust. However, it is also held that some wars are just and necessary; and that, if such a war is in prospect and can be effectively waged only by a conscript army, then it will be a citizen's moral duty to obey a law of universal military conscription.

What, in this system, is the moral duty of a man conscripted for military service in what he is persuaded is an unjust war? If he is convinced, there is no question: he must refuse to serve. But only if he is convinced. If he is in doubt he has no such duty. He must, of course, try to resolve his doubt; but if he cannot, he may consent to serve. For it is his duty to obey the morally lawful commands of the state; and he cannot know that the call to serve is morally unlawful, unless he

[10]See Hegel, pp. 63.—ED.
[11]See Oakeshott, pp. 71.—ED.

knows that the war in which he is called to serve is unjust. He may therefore assume that a war his own country is waging is just, unless he has good reason to believe that it is not.

Interpreted straightforwardly, this is mere common sense. Everybody has a general duty of loyalty to his country. Hence, if there is evidence that a war his country is waging is just, a man cannot be blamed for accepting that evidence in good faith, even though he knows that, governments being what they are, it may well be fraudulent. But what if there is plain evidence that the war is unjust?

Consider one of the rare cases which, by good fortune, have been documented. By 1943 it must have been difficult for any intelligent Catholic in Germany who read the newspapers to have been in any doubt at all that, by Catholic criteria, his country was waging an unjust war. A pious Austrian farmer, Franz Jägerstätter, saw what was obvious.

> [W]henever rulers have declared war against other countries [he wrote in a memorandum], they usually have not broken into their lands in order to improve them or perhaps give them something. Thus, if one is fighting against the Russian people, he will also take as much out of that country as can be put to use here. If we were merely fighting Bolshevism, would other things like iron, oil wells, or good grainlands have become such important considerations?[12]

Given that the war was unjust, as it plainly was, was it not his duty to refuse induction into the German army? Jägerstätter consulted his parish priest, and ultimately his bishop.

Since the punishment for refusal to serve in the German army was death, the Catholic clergy cannot be blamed for not advocating it. But there was no question of open advocacy. What Jägerstätter sought was private counsel about the legitimacy of a conclusion he had reached wholly by himself, on evidence available to anybody. Neither of the clergy he consulted questioned the truth or the relevance of that evidence. Yet they told him that neither they nor he, a relatively uneducated man, were in a position to make an informed judgement about the justice of the war; and that therefore the conclusion he had reached about it was doubtful.

In a private statement subsequently written in prison Jägerstätter demolished this sophistry.

> For what purpose . . . [he asked] did God endow all men with reason and free will if, despite this, we have to render blind obediance; or if, as so many also say, the individual is not qualified to judge whether this war started by Germany is just or unjust? What purpose is served by the ability to distinguish between good and evil?

Neither his sagacity nor his constancy were shaken. He was condemned to death, and beheaded.

After the war, the bishop who had tried to turn him from his course made it clear that his example was on no account to be followed. He was a martyr to his conscience, yes: but to "an inculpably erroneous conscience." It was not Jägerstätter but the "heroes" of the *Wehrmacht* who "conducted themselves . . . in the light of a clear and correct conscience."

---

[12]Gordon Zahn, *In Solitary Witness: The Life and Death of Franz Jägerstätter* (New York: Holt, Rinehart, and Winston, 1964), pp. 223.

Is it possible to find in this anything but the depravation of the *Sittlichkeit* of an ethical community whose members had lost the habit of moral self-criticism? What was done under Nazi rule matters less than what was thought and said afterwards. In his profound charity, Jägerstätter himself excused the compliance of the clergy with Nazism as intended to "spare the faithful many agonies and martyrs." While few would dare cast a stone had it been affirmed after the war that the members of the *Wehrmacht* who had believed it their duty to serve had been inculpable, although in error, the denial that Jägerstätter's conscience had been "clear and correct" was an open scandal.

Hegel disparaged the point of view of morality on the ground that, being abstractly rational, it could find content for its judgements only in the mores of some actual community. The case of Jägerstätter reveals an opposite process. The moral theory of Catholic Christianity furnished specific precepts on the subject of legitimate war service, which applied to the case in question on the basis of stated facts which were not questioned. But, by recourse to the mores of their actual community. Jägerstätter's spiritual advisers were able to evaporate the precepts whose applicability to his case they could not dispute. For, according to those mores, apart from such fanciful possibilities as a war with the declared intention of destroying the Church as an institution, no individual citizen was deemed capable of assuring himself that any war his country proposed to wage was unjust. Here, what is exposed as empty, as lacking specific content, as allowing any filling whatever, is not *Moralität,* but *Sittlichkeit.*

CONCLUSIONS

Here are conclusions for some of the important arguments in the Part One section entitled "Morality and Self-Interest."

Plato, *Republic*
1. *Justice is not the rule of the strongest.*
2. *The unjust soul does not act for its own advantage.*
3. *The just soul lives better than the unjust soul.*

Mill
1. *A theory of morality must be grounded in ends that aim at delivering pleasure.*
2. *Intellectual pleasure is of a higher quality and as such outweighs greater quantities of physical pleasure.*

Kant
1. *Only the good will is good in an unqualified sense.*
2. *The establishment of a good will is reason's highest goal.*
3. *Actions of moral worth are carried out from duty and not out of an inclination towards happiness or self-interest.*

Superson
1. *The rationality of the disposition and of the particular choices (though the latter can be established independently of the former) go hand-in-hand.*

Here are conclusions for some of the important arguments in the Part One section entitled "Moral Relativism and Absolutism."

Kant
1. *We should not use empirical examples to support the principles of morality.*
2. *Act only on that maxim through which you can at the same time will that it should become a universal law.*

Hegel
1. *If duty is defined as the absense of internal contradiction (as in Kant's categorical imperative), then no transition to particular duties is possible.*
2. *An individual's rights and duties spring out of his existing ethical community.*

Oakeshott
1. *The history of Western morality has reversed the proper roles of the two aspects of morality.*

Donagan
1. *Absolute morality (Moralität) supersedes custom (Sittlichkeit) as the most important element in philosophical ethics.*

Evaluating and Writing a Logical Argument

*Outlining**

In this textbook there are two supplementary sections to the readings: logic and fiction. The logic exercises consist of five sequential essays (one following each part). The goal of these sections is to enable the student to write a reasoned essay which evaluates a particular argument within the text—an analytic exercise. The student will break up the argument into its component parts and then put it back together again. By observing the mechanics of how an argument works, the student will be in a better position to evaluate the argument.

To begin, we must define the term "argument." What is an argument? Does it mean someone is angry with someone else? Is it something to avoid? Many people are unacquainted with arguments as a logical means of persuasion.

It is obvious to everyone that the power of persuasion is valuable. In Ancient Greece people spent large sums of money to possess this rare commodity; with it, they felt they could become successful. Other, less mercenary philosophers, such as Plato and Aristotle, extended the study of argument, developing it from an art into a science.

Indeed, today, similar attitudes toward persuasion exist. Executive seminars offer training in the art of leadership and positive thinking. These really amount to methods of getting one's ideas across to someone else. The motivation for these seminars is success and financial gain.

Likewise, in our universities, the disinterested study of persuasion proceeds under the titles of philosophy, rhetoric, and composition. Both their practical and intellectual exercises have one point in common: they aspire to construct rules whereby one can properly persuade others.

A full-scale treatment of this topic is beyond the scope of this selection. Instead, this essay will act as an initiation that will supplement and enrich various courses of instruction.

Be that as it may, a few things should be noted about the methodology adopted and how it intends to aid the student in acquiring the skill of analytic reading and reasoned evaluation.

The first point is that the purpose of argument, *persuasion,* is not a commodity that exists in isolation. One seeks to persuade within a context. This context can be described by the following elements:

Speaker
Audience
Point of contention
Argument
Common body of knowledge

An example of all these elements working together follows:

---

*Parts of this essay have been adapted from Michael Boylan, *The Process of Argument* (Prentice-Hall, 1988).

Sam wants to persuade Kathy to go to the movies. Kathy smiles, but doesn't reply. So Sam lists the great reviews and modestly hints at the advantages of going with him. After all, they're both in the same English class, love literature, and could have so much to talk about!

In this example the speaker is Sam; the audience is Kathy; the point of contention is "Kathy going to the movie with Sam"; the argument consists of both the movie's quality and the scenario of a good time; the common body of knowledge is Sam and Kathy's shared aesthetic value system.

Students are encouraged to identify these elements within the context of arguments that may be encountered. Familiarity with these separate roles is useful for acquiring competence in the process of argument.

This method of argument reconstruction is called logical outlining. A logical outline is different from the style of outline most people have been taught: the topical outline. The topical outline provides a summary of all that occurs within a given passage. It is a condensed presentation that allows one to skim over the high points of a given work.

In contrast to a topical outline, the logical outline seeks only to present arguments and points of contention. Any other material, such as classificatory remarks and various enumerations, is omitted from the logical outline.

For example, consider the contrasting outlines that can be constructed from the following passage:

What sort of person makes the best high-level manager? We all know that many kinds of people enter management. They range across the spectrum of human nature—from the timid, sniveling, and spineless, to the aggressive, high-powered motivators. But surely we all know that the future of our companies depends upon the quality of upper-level management. Therefore, it is apropos to ask what quality is inherent in the best of these leaders of the industry. In three words, it is a "calculated risk taker." This can easily be seen from the fact that initiating bold, new action, which is a top-level manager's job, involves taking risks. The policies of the past have to be reexamined and, if found wanting, then bold, new risky paths must be explored.

Obviously, though, one cannot go off willy-nilly. Some savvy and calculation are required, since these risk takers are more often than not the winners at the end of the day. This is what has made American industry great, and it must continue if we are to remain strong.

Logical Outline

1. A high-level manager must be able to boldly lead a company away from policies of the past. (assertion)

2. To move away from policies of the past is to take a new direction. (fact)

3. Initiating bold new directions involves taking risks. (fact)

4. High-level managers must be risk takers. (1–3)

5. Calculated risk taking is more successful than uncalculated risk taking. (fact)

6. High-level managers must employ the most successful strategies open to them. (assertion)

———————————

7. High-level managers must be calculated risk takers. (4–6)

Topical Outline

    I. *Types of Managers*
      A. Timid
         1. Sniveling
         2. Spineless
      B. Aggressive
         1. High-powered
         2. Motivator
      C. Similar to cross-sections of humanity

   II. *Future of Industry*
      A. Lies with upper-level managers
      B. Quality managers make good companies
         1. Risk takers
         2. Bold new action
         3. Reexamine policies of past
         4. Tempered with savvy and calculation

 III. *Past Success of American Industry*
      A. Depends upon risk-taking managers
      B. Must continue for the future

Let us consider, in reverse order, some of the differences between the topical and logical outline and then highlight the strengths of each.

The topical outline can give a summary of what is contained within a book or lecture. By condensing the material, through the use of key words or phrases, the reader can recall the flow and order of the text. Such an outline might be useful for creating an encapsulated reconstruction, or for boning up on a large amount of material at a glance. It is for this latter purpose that topical outlining is usually taught in grammar school.

The logical outline, in contrast, is not a summary. It is an exact reconstruction of the argument contained within a given passage. Some textual material is omitted. There is *no classification* found in logical outlines unless it is directly relevant to the argument at hand. Thus, in the above example, the classification into the two types of managers is not included.

Also omitted are various side remarks. In the above example, the depictions of "sniveling," "spineless," "high-powered," and "motivator" are all side comments. The remarks on the future of American industry are also side comments, since these remarks are not accompanied by an appropriate argument.

What remains is an exact depiction of the internal structure of the sentences meant logically to persuade the reader to accept some point of contention. The logical outline admittedly misses certain parts of a passage; thus, it is not comprehensive. But it is a more detailed and useful tool for understanding an argument than the topical outline. If one wished to formulate an objection to this argument, the topical outline would *not* afford the same view of all the logical relationships between sentences that the logical argument does.

For this reason, the logical outline can be viewed as a specialized form of outlining. It has a precise mission. But if one wishes to be comprehensive in note taking, then this form could be supplemented with a topical outline.

The arguments you construct should look like the above sample. Each premise should be numbered and followed by a justification, which for our purposes will either be "a fact," "an assertion," or "an inference." For clarity, let's further define some of the terms we have used.

Proposition

A declarative sentence with truth value.

Premise

These are the building blocks of argument. The individual sentences of an argument prior to the conclusion are called premises. In the sample above, the sentences numbered 1 through 6 are all premises. Collectively, the premises cause one to accept the point of contention. The way they do this has to do with the premises being true and interrelated in such a way that the point of contention *follows from* these premises. In order for us to accept this relationship as "tight," we must believe that it is impossible that if the premises are true we could fail to accept the conclusion as true.

Conclusion

The point of contention. It is what the argument aims for. In the sample, sentence number 7 is the conclusion. The justification of a conclusion is always an inference. The premises and conclusion are generally set apart by a line.

Argument

An argument consists of at least two sentences, one of which logically follows from the other. The statement said to follow is the conclusion, and the supporting statement is the premise. The vehicle which allows one to move from premise to conclusion is called an inference. In this book, the arguments presented generally consist of at least two premises. Therefore, the rules of argument put forth will be primarily directed at these arguments.

There are two broad classes of argument: inductive and deductive. The exercises in this text will focus upon the latter. (For a treatment of inductive argument based upon these principles, see "Process of Argument," Chapter 3.)

Justification

A justification comes after a premise and is the proximate reason for accepting the premise. Three kinds of justification are used to aid in creating an evaluation. They have been divided in this way for their utility in helping you ultimately to construct an essay. The three types of justification are assertion, fact, and inference.

Assertion —This is the weakest justification. It means that the premise is true simply because one person has said it. The truth content of the proposition involved may be doubted. In the above sample, premises 1 and 6 are supported by assertion.

Fact —This is the second-strongest justification. It means that most listeners would accept the given truth put forth as objectively correct. When outlining historical texts one should make reference to the beliefs of the time, such as "the earth is the center of the universe," which might count as fact for speakers before the seventeenth century. In the above sample, premise 3 is justified as fact.

Inference —This is formally the strongest justification. It will generally consist of at least two premises. (In some special cases, one premise might count as an inferential justification in a deductive argument. This is called an immediate inference. Also, if you find that you have more than four premises listed as a justification— check your work! Chances are you have compressed two inferences that should remain separate.) The force of the inference arises from the combination of premises with our common sense. For example, if one accepts premises 1–3 in the sample, then one must also accept premise 4. Thus, the justification for accepting premise 4 is simply our having accepted premises 1–3. When this connection is such that it cannot be doubted, we will call the inference *tight*. When one can still doubt the inference, we will call it *loose*. For example, in the following argument—(a) dropping a water balloon from the second story window causes the passerby to become wet; but (b) a water balloon was not dropped; therefore (c) the passerby did not get wet (a–b)—the inference at (c) is loose because it can be doubted.[1] It is possible to get wet by another means, such as a rainstorm; thus, the inference at (c) is loose and unacceptable.

This notion of tight and loose inferences is admittedly subjective. In formal systems of logic, there are mechanical rules for determining these criteria. Students who wish to pursue this further should consult a text in formal logic. In the present context, we are trying to keep things as simple as possible with a view to helping the reader write a philosophical evaluation. Therefore, trust your common sense in judging whether an inference is tight or loose.

Suppressed Premise

These are premises that are needed to make an inference but are not explicitly made by the writer. In the sample, there are no suppressed premises, but in the *Hometown Gazette* argument found on page 91, premises 1, 6, and 7 are suppressed. To show their special status, these premises are placed within brackets.

One important caution: when adding new premises, be sure the added material is in the spirit of the author's other positions; you would not want to add something that the original author would not have supported.

Interlocking Premises

Interlocking premises refer to a property of an argument that obtains when all the premises are represented directly or indirectly in the conclusion's inference. In the sample, there are six premises. Premises 4, 5, and 6 are directly in the conclusion.

---

[1] These rules do not apply for checking inductive arguments.

Premises 1, 2, and 3 are in premise 4, so they are indirectly in the conclusion. There-fore, all the premises are represented, directly or indirectly, in the conclusion. The sample argument has interlocking premises. The purpose of having interlocking premises will become clear in the exercise following Part Three entitled "Evaluating and Writing a Logical Argument."

Let's turn to another example.

Editorial in the Hometown Gazette

Residents of fair Hometown, we've got a problem—a big problem. This problem must be addressed now! What I am talking about are *potholes!* Yes, you have seen them arise and grow each spring when the winter thaw leaves its debris behind. At first they were only fissures, but now they threaten road safety and the general con-dition of our automobiles. Do you know what can happen to your car when you hit one of those potholes at 40 miles per hour? Your axle gets bent out of shape. And axles are expensive to replace.

It's therefore time for a change! The city needs to fix its potholes. Oh, I know the mayor says there is no room in the city budget for any more cost cutting in order to fix potholes. And he's right. The budget is tight as a drum. Therefore we must raise taxes to pay for the repairs; we can't delay. Write His Honor today. The city needs to raise taxes to fix those potholes!

Logical Outline

1. [The city's residents prize their automobiles' general condition and their own safety. (fact)]

2. There are many large potholes in the city. (fact)

3. Large potholes harm the condition of automobile axles as well as general driving safety. (fact)

4. The city needs to fill its potholes. (1–3)

5. The city is presently operating with a budget that cannot be trimmed. (assertion)

6. [Filling potholes costs money. (fact)]

7. [The only way a city can find money for a project is by cutting spending or by raising taxes. (assertion)]

8. The city can fix potholes only by raising taxes. (5–7)

———————

9. The city needs to raise taxes to fix potholes. (4, 8)

Observe how the logical outline above fulfills the requirements listed on page 89–91.

    A. Each premise is numbered.

    B. Each premise is followed by a justification.

    C. All the premises are directly or indirectly in the conclusion (number 4 and number 8 are in the conclusion directly, while numbers 1–3 are there indirectly via number 4, and numbers 5–7 are there indirectly via number 8).

    D. The three inferences, according to our subjective standard, appear tight.

E. The suppressed premises necessary to make the inferences tight have been added.

Therefore, the argument is properly reconstructed through a logical outline.

Over the years I have found that students have had certain common problems. A list of these may prove to be helpful.

1. *Finding the conclusion.* An argument is driven by its conclusion. The conclusion is the reason that the argument came to be. Therefore, if you cannot find the conclusion, you are arrested before you begin. To help on this score, conclusions of selected arguments are listed at the end of each logic exercise section in this book. Your instructor may elect to have you outline all or some of these, or he or she may choose to have you outline other arguments and discover your own conclusions. To find the conclusion, ask yourself "What is the point?" "Why has the author written this?" The answer to these questions reveals the reason for the exposition: the conclusion.

2. *Putting the argument into your own words.* Each logical outline must be representative of the text assigned. But this requirement of fidelity does *not* mean that you should set out your premises word for word as the argument's author has. Students who do this often fail to see the "big picture" of logical inferences by getting lost in the minutiae of trying to include every point. The extreme extension of this would result in the student merely copying over the text word-for-word.

   What I suggest is that once you find the conclusion—and the page(s) where the argument appears—read the argument very carefully several times and then close the book. Try to reconstruct the premises and sub-conclusions in your own words. Then open the book again. Have you distorted the argument? If so, go back to your outline and correct it. Move back and forth between outline and text until you feel comfortable.

3. *Fact versus assertion.* This can be a very close call. The definition provided focuses upon the context of the author—whether most would accept the statement as objectively correct. When in doubt, use the weaker justification—assertion.

4. *Inferences with five or more premises listed.* Some students will set out an argument with six premises and a conclusion. At the conclusion, the inference is cited as "1–6." There may be cases in which no intermediate "sub-conclusions" can be set out in the premises. But, most often, this is not the case. Generally, such lumping of every premise into a conclusion's justification indicates you have not adequately understood other logical relations. These relations form sub-conclusions that reveal a more complex inferential picture.

   The ability to see sub-conclusions will be helpful later when you write philosophical evaluations. Thus, when you see that your outline has more than four premises listed as a justification, go back and check to see if any rearrangement is possible.

Indirect Argument

Finally, for some of the selections (e.g., Plato), the student will need to become familiar with a special category of logical outlining: indirect argument. This form of argument varies from the above-stated form in one major way: Instead of having the point of contention proved positively, the logical complement is disproved.

This type of argument works on a very simple principle: If we want to prove a point, we first assume its opposite and then show that the opposite leads us into an absurd (false) state of affairs. Since the opposite leads to an obvious falsity, the original point must be correct.

Example

"Very good, Cephalus," I said. "But what is the definition of Justice? Is it to tell the truth and to pay your debts? No more? And is this definition even correct?

"Suppose a friend deposits his weapons with me. When he did this he was perfectly in control. Later when he is mad he asks for them back. Should I give them to him? Nobody would sanction this or call such an action right, anymore than they would require me to always speak the truth to my mad friend."

"This is true," he said.

"But then we were not right to say that Justice is telling the truth and repaying that which had been previously given?"

Plato, *Republic* (Ed. trans.)

Thesis:

Justice does not mean speaking the truth and paying one's debts.

Assume Antithesis:

Justice means speaking the truth and paying one's debts.

Antithesis Leads to an Absurdity:

One should provide a madman with weapons. Therefore, the antithesis is wrong and the thesis is proven.

Notice that this method relies on there being two and only two logical states, true and false, and if an antithesis is shown to be absurd (false), then the opposite, the thesis, must be true. This is true of opposites which admit no middle ground (contradictory opposites), but is not true of opposites that exist upon a continuum. An example of the first is "pregnancy." Either you are pregnant or you are not. There is no middle ground. An example of the latter is "happy–sad." It is possible to be somewhere in between.

When examining this sort of argument (often called "reductio ad absurdum"), it is important to keep in mind the distinction that exists between the types of opposites.

Self-Interest and Relativism in Literature
Sherwood Anderson
*The Untold Lie**

Ray Pearson and Hal Winters were farm hands employed on a farm three miles north of Winesburg. On Saturday afternoons they came into town and wandered about through the streets with other fellows from the country.

Ray was a quiet, rather nervous man of perhaps fifty with a brown beard and shoulders rounded by too much and too hard labor. In his nature he was as unlike Hal Winters as two men can be unlike.

Ray was an altogether serious man and had a little sharp-featured wife who had also a sharp voice. The two, with half a dozen thin-legged children, lived in a tumble-down frame house beside a creek at the back end of the Wills farm where Ray was employed.

Hal Winters, his fellow employee, was a young fellow. He was not of the Ned Winters family, who were very respectable people in Winesburg, but was one of the three sons of the old man called Windpeter Winters who had a sawmill near Unionville, six miles away, and who was looked upon by everyone in Winesburg as a confirmed old reprobate.

People from the part of Northern Ohio in which Winesburg lies will remember old Windpeter by his unusual and tragic death. He got drunk one evening in town and started to drive home to Unionville along the railroad tracks. Henry Brattenburg, the butcher, who lived out that way, stopped him at the edge of the town and told him he was sure to meet the down train but Windpeter slashed at him with his whip and drove on. When the train struck and killed him and his two horses a farmer and his wife who were driving home along a nearby road saw the accident. They said that old Windpeter stood up on the seat of his wagon, raving and swearing at the onrushing locomotive, and that he fairly screamed with delight when the team, maddened by his incessant slashing at them, rushed straight ahead to certain death. Boys like young George Willard and Seth Richmond will remember the incident quite vividly because, although everyone in our town said that the old man would go straight to hell and that the community was better off without him, they had a secret conviction that he knew what he was doing and admired his foolish courage. Most boys have seasons of wishing they could die gloriously instead of just being grocery clerks and going on with their humdrum lives.

But this is not the story of Windpeter Winters nor yet of his son Hal who worked on the Wills farm with Ray Pearson. It is Ray's story. It will, however, be necessary to talk a little of young Hal so that you will get into the spirit of it.

Hal was a bad one. Everyone said that. There were three of the Winters boys in that family, John, Hal, and Edward, all broad-shouldered big fellows like old Windpeter himself and all fighters and woman-chasers and generally all-around bad ones.

---

*From Sherwood Anderson, *Winesburg, Ohio* (New York: Viking, 1960; reprinted from 1919).

Hal was the worst of the lot and always up to some devilment. He once stole a load of boards from his father's mill and sold them in Winesburg. With the money he bought himself a suit of cheap, flashy clothes. Then he got drunk and when his father came raving into town to find him, they met and fought with their fists on Main Street and were arrested and put into jail together.

Hal went to work on the Wills farm because there was a country school teacher out that way who had taken his fancy. He was only twenty-two then but had already been in two or three of what were spoken of in Winesburg as "women scrapes." Everyone who heard of his infatuation for the school teacher was sure it would turn out badly. "He'll only get her into trouble, you'll see," was the word that went around.

And so these two men, Ray and Hal, were at work in a field on a day in the late October. They were husking corn and occasionally something was said and they laughed. Then came silence. Ray, who was the more sensitive and always minded things more, had chapped hands and they hurt. He put them into his coat pockets and looked away across the fields. He was in a sad, distracted mood and was affected by the beauty of the country. If you knew the Winesburg country in the fall and how the low hills are all splashed with yellows and reds you would understand his feeling. He began to think of the time, long ago when he was a young fellow living with his father, then a baker in Winesburg, and how on such days he had wandered away to the woods to gather nuts, hunt rabbits, or just to loaf about and smoke his pipe. His marriage had come about through one of his days of wandering. He had induced a girl who waited on trade in his father's shop to go with him and something had happened. He was thinking of that afternoon and how it had affected his whole life when a spirit of protest awoke in him. He had forgotten about Hal and muttered words. "Tricked by Gad, that's what I was, tricked by life and made a fool of," he said in a low voice.

As though understanding his thoughts, Hal Winters spoke up. "Well, has it been worth while? What about it, eh? What about marriage and all that?" he asked and then laughed. Hal tried to keep on laughing but he too was in an earnest mood. He began to talk earnestly. "Has a fellow got to do it?" he asked. "Has he got to be harnessed up and driven through life like a horse?"

Hal didn't wait for an answer but sprang to his feet and began to walk back and forth between the corn shocks. He was getting more and more excited. Bending down suddenly he picked up an ear of the yellow corn and threw it at the fence. "I've got Nell Gunther in trouble," he said. "I'm telling you, but you keep your mouth shut."

Ray Pearson arose and stood staring. He was almost a foot shorter than Hal, and when the younger man came and put his two hands on the older man's shoulders they made a picture. There they stood in the big empty field with the quiet corn shocks standing in rows behind them and the red and yellow hills in the distance, and from being just two indifferent workmen they had become all alive to each other. Hal sensed it and because that was his way he laughed. "Well, old daddy," he said awkwardly, "come on, advise me. I've got Nell in trouble. Perhaps you've been in the same fix yourself. I know what everyone would say is the right thing to do, but what do you say? Shall I marry and settle down? Shall I put myself into the harness to be worn out like an old horse? You know me, Ray. There can't anyone break me but I can break myself. Shall I do it or shall I tell Nell to go to the devil? Come on, you tell me. Whatever you say, Ray, I'll do."

Ray couldn't answer. He shook Hal's hands loose and turning walked straight away toward the barn. He was a sensitive man and there were tears in his eyes. He knew there was only one thing to say to Hal Winters, son of old Windpeter Winters, only one thing that all his own training and all the beliefs of the people he knew would approve, but for his life he couldn't say what he knew he should say.

At half-past four that afternoon Ray was puttering about the barnyard when his wife came up the lane along the creek and called him. After the talk with Hal he hadn't returned to the cornfield but worked about the barn. He had already done the evening chores and had seen Hal, dressed and ready for a roistering night in town, come out of the farmhouse and go into the road. Along the path to his own house he trudged behind his wife, looking at the ground and thinking. He couldn't make out what was wrong. Every time he raised his eyes and saw the beauty of the country in the failing light he wanted to do something he had never done before, shout or scream or hit his wife with his fists or something equally unexpected and terrifying. Along the path he went scratching his head and trying to make it out. He looked hard at his wife's back but she seemed all right.

She only wanted him to go into town for groceries and as soon as she had told him what she wanted began to scold. "You're always puttering," she said. "Now I want you to hustle. There isn't anything in the house for supper and you've got to get to town and back in a hurry."

Ray went into his own house and took an overcoat from a hook back of the door. It was torn about the pockets and the collar was shiny. His wife went into the bedroom and presently came out with a soiled cloth in one hand and three silver dollars in the other. Somewhere in the house a child wept bitterly and a dog that had been sleeping by the stove arose and yawned. Again the wife scolded. "The children will cry and cry. Why are you always puttering?" she asked.

Ray went out of the house and climbed the fence into a field. It was just growing dark and the scene that lay before him was lovely. All the low hills were washed with color and even the little clusters of bushes in the corners by the fences were alive with beauty. The whole world seemed to Ray Pearson to have become alive with something just as he and Hal had suddenly become alive when they stood in the corn field staring into each other's eyes.

The beauty of the country about Winesburg was too much for Ray on that fall evening. That is all there was to it. He could not stand it. Of a sudden he forgot all about being a quiet old farm hand and throwing off the torn overcoat began to run across the field. As he ran he shouted a protest against his life, against all life, against everything that makes life ugly. "There was no promise made," he cried into the empty spaces that lay about him. "I didn't promise my Minnie anything and Hal hasn't made any promise to Nell. I know he hasn't. She went into the woods with him because she wanted to go. What he wanted she wanted. Why should I pay? Why should Hal pay? Why should anyone pay? I don't want Hal to become old and worn out. I'll tell him. I won't let it go on. I'll catch Hal before he gets to town and I'll tell him."

Ray ran clumsily and once he stumbled and fell down. "I must catch Hal and tell him," he kept thinking, and although his breath came in gasps he kept running harder and harder. As he ran he thought of things that hadn't come into his mind for years—how at the time he married he had planned to go west to his uncle in Portland, Oregon—how he hadn't wanted to be a farm hand, but had thought when he got out

West he would go to sea and be a sailor or get a job on a ranch and ride a horse into Western towns, shouting and laughing and waking the people in the houses with his wild cries. Then as he ran he remembered his children and in fancy felt their hands clutching at him. All of his thoughts of himself were involved with the thoughts of Hal and he thought the children were clutching at the younger man also. "They are the accidents of life, Hal," he cried. "They are not mine or yours. I had nothing to do with them."

Darkness began to spread over the fields as Ray Pearson ran on and on. His breath came in little sobs. When he came to the fence at the edge of the road and confronted Hal Winters, all dressed up and smoking a pipe as he walked jauntily along, he could not have told what he thought or what he wanted.

Ray Pearson lost his nerve and this is really the end of the story of what happened to him. It was almost dark when he got to the fence and he put his hands on the top bar and stood staring. Hal Winters jumped a ditch and coming up close to Ray put his hands into his pockets and laughed. He seemed to have lost his own sense of what had happened in the corn field and when he put up a strong hand and took hold of the lapel of Ray's coat he shook the old man as he might have shaken a dog that had misbehaved.

"You came to tell me, eh?" he said. "Well, never mind telling me anything. I'm not a coward and I've already made up my mind." He laughed again and jumped back across the ditch. "Nell ain't no fool," he said. "She didn't ask me to marry her. I want to marry her. I want to settle down and have kids."

Ray Pearson also laughed. He felt like laughing at himself and all the world.

As the form of Hal Winters disappeared in the dusk that lay over the road that led to Winesburg, he turned and walked slowly back across the fields to where he had left his torn overcoat. As he went some memory of pleasant evenings spent with the thin-legged children in the tumble-down house by the creek must have come into his mind, for he muttered words. "It's just as well. Whatever I told him would have been a lie," he said softly, and then his form also disappeared into the darkness of the fields.

Questions for Discussion

1. Toward the end of the story Ray asks the question, "Why should I pay? Why should Hal pay? Why should anyone pay?" If morality requires that we restrict our range of action and "pay" for the consequences of our actions, then why would anyone wish to be moral?

2. Who is to say what is moral? Why is this standard the one that is being accepted and not another?

PART 2

Rights

Alan Gewirth

University of Chicago

Human Rights

Human rights are an especially important part of morality because of their bearing on human dignity and fundamental human needs. As their name implies, human rights are rights that are had equally by all human beings; to have them one must simply be human, as against the special rights that persons may have because of some particular status or transaction. The moral value and importance of human rights derive from the double fact that their objects, what they are rights to, are the most fundamental goods or interests of human personality and agency, and that in having rights to these objects humans are in a morally justified position to claim them as their personal due, as what they are entitled to for their own sakes and simply in virtue of their being human. On both counts, human rights are normatively necessary or mandatory requirements compliance with which every human being can justifiably demand of all others.

Although human rights have been claimed in all eras of civilization, the movements in their support have become especially prominent in the modern world. The English, American, and French revolutions of the seventeenth and eighteenth centuries were proclaimed and conducted in the name of human rights, as was the struggle against slavery. After the genocide perpetrated by the Nazis during World War II, the United Nations in 1948 promulgated the Universal Declaration of Human Rights, which set basic moral standards for the ways in which governments should treat the lives, liberties, and other essential goods of persons.

Philosophically, human rights raise deep conceptual and moral issues about the meaning of "rights," the justification for holding that all humans have certain moral rights, the contents of these rights, and the relation of rights to other moral values, including social utility.

Let us begin with certain conceptual issues. Three distinctions must be noted. First, persons do not have rights in the sense in which they have legs or feelings. Rights are normative entities, not empirical or descriptive ones; they involve prescriptive concepts like "ought" and "duty," as against physical or mental concepts.

Second, we should note the distinction between "right" used as an adjective and "right" used as a substantive or noun, such as between "the right thing to do" and "the right to do something." When "right" is used as an adjective, it signifies conformity to some practical rule or standard of adequacy, as when we say "This is the right way to throw a football" or "It is right to be charitable." But "right" in this adjectival sense does not necessarily imply "right" in the substantive sense. Although it may be right to throw a football in a certain way, this does not entail that in an actual game a player has a right to throw the football in that way, since the opposing players have no duty to let him throw it in that way. And although it may be right to be charitable, persons may have at least a legal right not to be charitable, and there is no right to receive charity as such.

Third, there is a distinction (pointed out especially by W. N. Hohfeld) between two kinds of rights: claim-rights and liberty-rights. Claim-rights are requirements for having or doing something that entail correlative duties on the part of other persons or groups to forbear or assist with a view to supporting the right-holders' having the objects of their rights. For example, since a person has claim-rights to life and to freedom of speech, this entails correlative duties on the part of other persons at least to refrain from interfering with his or her life or speech, such as by murder or by imprisonment. Liberty-rights, on the other hand, are simply permissions that carry no such entailment of correlative duties on the part of other persons. The contrast drawn above between "right" as adjective and as substantive applies primarily to claim-rights.

Now, human rights are claim-rights, not merely liberty-rights. On the other hand, not all claim-rights are human rights. For the further understanding of human rights as distinguished from other claim-rights, it will be helpful to note that the general structure of a claim-right is given by the following formula:

A has a right to X against B by virtue of Y.

There are five main elements here: first, the *subject* (A) of the right, the right-holder; second, the *nature* of the right, what being a right consists in or what it means for someone to have a right; third, the *object* (X) of the right, what it is a right to; fourth, the *respondent* (B) of the right, the duty-bearer, the person or group that has the correlative duty; and fifth, the *justifying ground* (Y) of the right.

Human rights differ from other claim-rights with respect to all five of these elements. First, as to the *subjects,* in the case of the human rights, these are all human beings equally. In this, human rights differ from such special moral rights as those that derive from promises or some particular status. For example, if Ames promises Blake that he will give him ten dollars, then Blake alone has the right to receive the ten dollars from Ames; if Cohen is the umpire in a baseball game

and calls Dawson out, then Cohen alone has the right to have his decision enforced even if Dawson protests, and so forth. In the case of human rights, on the other hand, no such special transaction relationship or status is needed; in order to have human rights, all one needs is to be human. Moreover, human rights also differ from universal but unequal moral or legal rights. For example, under feudalism all humans had certain claim-rights, but the vassals' rights were inferior to the rights of the lords. Thus, human rights are characterized by both universality and equality of distribution among the humans who are their subjects or possessors.

This feature also serves to differentiate human rights from utilitarian norms. For utilitarianism the ultimate subject of goods or values is not each human distributively or severally but rather the whole of humanity or even all sentient beings. The aim of utilitarianism is not the distributive one of securing goods for each person severally for his or her own sake and as his or her personal due or entitlement; rather, it is the aggregative aim of producing the greatest possible amount of good or utility overall, regardless of how it is distributed. Thus, utilitarianism may sanction the violation of some persons' rights if this is required for the maximizing of utility.

Second, as to the *nature* of the rights, while all claim-rights entail correlative duties on the part of respondents, the duties entailed by the human rights are especially stringent and mandatory. Because to have human rights one need only be human, one need not consult some special set of rules or transactions in order to ascertain whether one has the rights; in this respect human rights are unconditional. There are two contemporary theories of the nature of claim-rights; while the theories are usually presented as rivals, they are mutually compatible, emphasizing relations to different elements of rights. According to the "choice theory," to have a right is to be in a position to determine by one's choice how other persons shall act. According to the "benefit theory," to have a right is to be the directly intended beneficiary of someone else's performance of a duty. The choice theory emphasizes the relation of the right-holder to his or her respondents, while the benefit theory emphasizes the relation to the objects. A sound theory of the nature of rights will include both relations. Together, they indicate that human rights provide indispensable protections for certain important kinds of goods or benefits on the part of all human beings.

The choice theory brings out the idea that rights are justified claims, in that to have a right is to be in a position to make a justified demand on other persons (the respondents) that they act or refrain from acting in certain ways. This justification, moreover, is of a distinctive sort, in that when A has a right to X, the protection of his interest in X is justified because he has a personal title to have X, so that X is personally owed to A as his due and for his own sake, not because it adds to overall utility. This personal entitlement, in the case of human rights, is had by all humans as such. Because they are in a position to make such justified, effective claims or demands, humans through their human rights have a kind of dignity that derives from their being active, independent agents on their own behalf, as against being passive, dependent recipients of the favors or charity of other persons.

This aspect of rights can be further clarified if we contrast them with other bases of duties. As against duties of generosity or charity, persons need not plead or entreat to be given the objects of human rights; compliance with the rights is mandatory. And as for duties based on social utility, many of them are not sufficiently important to override rights of individuals; and when they are of comparable importance, they are not personally oriented as being for the individual's own sake, but are rather concerned with maximizing or aggregating advantages for a whole collectivity. In such cases, however, the advantages may coincide with the objects of individual rights and may be of similar mandatoriness. A current example may be certain restrictions on carriers of AIDS in order to protect the population at large; in this case it is still the rights of individual members of the public that are protected. Even in such cases, however, the human rights of the AIDS-carriers set limits on the kinds of restrictions that may be justifiably imposed.

The dignity-reflecting aspect of human rights also derives from the third element of rights, their *objects.* As the benefit theory suggests, in the case of all claim-rights their objects are certain goods or interests of human beings. Although rights and duties are correlative, the concept of rights cannot be eliminated or be simply replaced by the concept of duties, because the objects of rights are benefits while duties are burdens; and burdens are for the sake of benefits.

Whereas in the case of special rights the benefits that are their objects may be relatively trivial (as with some promises), the objects of human rights are of the utmost importance because they consist in the necessary or generic conditions or goods of action and successful action in general. What makes human rights so crucial for human welfare is that without their objects humans either cannot act at all or cannot act with general chances of success in achieving their purposes. It is thus in their capacity of being actual or prospective agents that all humans have rights.

The most general necessary conditions of action and successful action are *freedom* and *well-being.* Freedom is the *procedural* necessary condition of action: it consists in controlling one's behavior by one's unforced choice while having knowledge of relevant circumstances. Well-being as here understood is the *substantive* necessary condition of action: it consists in having the general abilities and conditions needed for achieving one's purposes. Such well-being falls into a hierarchy of three kinds of goods that are progressively less needed for action, although they all still contribute importantly to successful action. *Basic goods* are the essential prerequisites of action: they include life, physical integrity, mental equilibrium, and such specific goods as food, clothing, shelter, and medical care. *Nonsubtractive goods* are the general abilities and conditions needed for maintaining undiminished one's level of purpose-fulfillment and one's capabilities for particular actions. *Additive goods* are the general abilities and conditions needed for increasing one's level of purpose-fulfillment and one's capabilities for successful actions. Examples of nonsubtractive goods are not being lied to, stolen from, insulted, or threatened with violence. Examples of additive goods are self-esteem, education, and opportunities for earning wealth and income. Persons' rights to these three kinds of goods are, respectively, *basic rights, nonsubtractive rights,* and *additive rights.* Not all of these rights have governments as their respondents or protectors.

The distinction between different levels of well-being provides a significant criterion for resolving conflicts of rights. For since the purpose of the human rights is to protect or secure persons' rights of agency, in cases of conflict those rights whose objects are more important because more needed for action take precedence over rights whose objects are less needed for action. This is why, for example, the rights not to be stolen from or lied to are overridden by the rights not to starve or be killed when these respective rights are in conflict.

A question may be raised about the relation between the objects and the subjects of human rights. If the objects are the necessary conditions of action and successful action, then how can the subjects of human rights be all humans

equally? For some humans, such as young children or persons who have severe mental deficiencies, are capable of action only in very reduced degrees, and other humans, such as those who are in irreversible coma or are otherwise severely disabled, are incapable of any action at all. There are several answers to this question. Insofar as there is any possibility that the latter sorts of humans will recover to the extent of being capable of action, they have rights that such potential abilities of their agency be protected. And when the freedom-rights of children and mentally deficient humans are restricted in order to prevent their harming themselves or other persons, this is still grounded in an equal concern for the abilities of agency of all humans. Just as the equality of human rights is compatible with some humans' being given more food or protection than other humans, when the former have a greater need for such objects in order to sustain their basic well-being, so too the lesser freedom allowed to children and mentally deficient humans is justified by an equal concern for the basic well-being of them and of all other humans. In this extended sense, it still remains true that the human rights are had by all humans equally. When it is said that the human rights pertain to all persons insofar as they are prospective purposive agents, this does not violate the condition that for human rights to be had one must only be human, as against fulfilling some more restrictive description. All normal humans are prospective purposive agents; the point of introducing this description is only to call attention to the aspect of being human that most directly generates the rights to freedom and well-being.

For the fuller understanding of how the objects are related to human rights, we must turn to the fourth element of the rights, their *respondents,* the persons or groups that have the correlative duties or responsibilities. Most directly, just as the human rights are had by all humans equally, so too their respondents are all humans equally. For they are rights of all humans against all humans. In the first instance, the correlative duties of the respondents are negative: each person must refrain from removing or interfering with other persons' freedom and well-being. But the duties are also positive, requiring active assistance in situations where one person can help another to avoid drowning, starvation, or other threats to his basic well-being without comparable cost to himself. In the case of such positive duties, while their distribution is equal and universal as a matter of principle, the requirement of their actually being fulfilled is affected by considerations of ability, according to the maxim that "ought" implies "can," as well as by political-constitutional factors that must now be considered.

The freedom and the components of well-being that are the general objects of human rights are directly found in the actions of individual agents, but they may also be expressed in or protected by political institutions. States are morally justified insofar as they secure human rights, so that states are among the respondents of the rights. We may distinguish three kinds of such states, parallel to three kinds of rights set forth in the United Nations Universal Declaration of Human Rights. The *minimal state* operates through the criminal law to protect persons' basic rights of physical security against violence and other drastic wrongs. The *democratic state* uses and protects political and civil rights, including the civil liberties which are applications of the right to freedom in interpersonal communication and other areas, including the political process. The *supportive state* protects social and economic rights to subsistence, housing, and medical care where persons cannot obtain these by their own efforts, as well as their additive rights to education and means of earning wealth and income.

Although the political and civil rights are rights to political and civil liberties, they are still, like all human rights, grounded in the needs of action and successful action in general. For example, the civil liberties are vital parts of the overall freedom and additive well-being to which all humans have rights, not only because the lack of these liberties severely affects persons' equal dignity and self-esteem, but also because without them persons are drastically limited in coping with the sociopolitical arrangements that circumscribe their pursuits of their purposes. A further relevant aspect of the justification of the democratic state is that membership in such a state can be *active* through persons' use of their civil liberties, as against the predominantly *passive* membership that the minimal state provides. Such active membership is an important part of the rights of agency whose protection is the basis of human rights, because it helps each person to be a self-controlling, self-developing agent who can relate to other persons on a basis of mutual respect and cooperation, in contrast to being a dependent, passive recipient of the agency of others.

The state's protection of human rights may involve overriding the rights of individuals in certain circumstances. Such overriding *infringes* the rights, in that the correlative duties are not carried out; but it is not a *violation* of the rights, since the infringement is justified. One obvious example is when a judge, operating by the rules of the minimal state's criminal law, sentences a criminal to prison, thereby infringing his rights to freedom and aspects of his well-being. Even here, however, the human rights of individuals set important restrictions: only persons who have violated others' rights are to be punished; all persons must be equal before the law; trials must be fair; punishment must not be cruel, vindictive, or inhuman.

Some of the central political controversies of our time have revolved around the justification of the supportive state. In connection with human rights, the controversies especially concern the question whether these rights include the social and economic rights as well as the political and civil rights. A main point that has been advanced for a negative answer concerns universality. Human rights are rights of all persons against all persons; but poor persons and states cannot be the respondents or duty-bearers of the duties correlative to relief of economic deprivation. For while the political and civil rights, like the security rights protected by the minimal state, are primarily negative, in that their correlative duties require at least in the first instance, that persons and governments *refrain from* certain kinds of conduct, the social and economic rights, on the other hand, are primarily positive in that their correlative duties require *positive acts of assistance* by governments. Now refraining is relatively easy, but positive acts of assistance are often much more difficult. Thus, the contention is that when governments are held to be the respondents of social and economic rights, this may require far more in the way of positive institutional policies and resources than in the case of the political and civil rights, and such positive actions may be and are beyond the abilities of many states.

A main answer to this contention is that when states cannot by themselves fulfill the social and economic rights of their citizens and other inhabitants, assistance must be given by other states. This assistance, however, should proceed not by maintaining a relation of recipience and dependence on the part of the countries that are helped but rather by enabling them to use their own resources—personal, political, and environmental. On the national as well as the international level, the point of such a policy, in keeping with the general concern of human rights for the conditions of agency, is not to reinforce or increase dependence but rather to give support that enables persons to maintain these conditions for themselves. Thus, even though not all persons or states can

fulfill the duties correlative with the social and economic rights, it is still the case that everyone always has, as a matter of principle, both the right to be treated in the appropriate way when he has the need and the duty to act in accord with the right when the circumstances arise that require such action and when he then has the ability to do so, this ability including consideration of cost to himself. Hence, even if the social and economic rights are not always universally exercised, they are always universally had. Because the principle of human rights entails this requirement of mutual aid where needed and practicable, it is a principle of social solidarity, as against exclusive preoccupation with private interest.

A further objection against the social and economic rights is that they violate the right to freedom, since they impose duties that persons and groups may be unwilling to accept. This objection is to be answered by the criterion of degrees of needfulness for action, which was adduced above for resolving conflicts of rights. Possession of a surplus of economic goods is less needed for action than are basic goods and such additive goods as education. This is why property rights in the surplus are overridden by the basic and other rights in cases of conflict. But this requirement does not involve anything so drastic as the complete expropriation of all property; the provision is not open-ended, and thus property rights remain.

These considerations bring us to the fifth element in the structure of human rights, their *justifying ground*. The existence of legal rights can be verified by consulting the statute books; and special moral rights may be justified by particular transactions, like promises, or by particular relationships, like that of teacher and student. Both these kinds of rights, however, are inconclusive unless they can be justified by human rights, that is, by moral rights that all humans have equally. But how do we know that there *are* such rights? Despite what Thomas Jefferson wrote, the existence of such rights is not "self-evident"; it needs justificatory argument. What such argument can establish is not that there "are" human rights in the way that empirical argument can establish that there "are" electrons or viruses. Instead, the argument must be morally normative: it must establish a moral principle from which the existence of human rights follows. Philosophers have presented various arguments, which have appealed to considerations like needs, interests, contracts, and dignity. All these arguments, while suggestive, have incurred serious difficulties. I shall here briefly outline an argument which, while still the subject of considerable controversy, seems to me to establish the required principle. The argument proceeds dialectically rather than assertorically. It undertakes to show that every rational agent logically must accept that he or she and all other actual or prospective agents have certain rights. Since action is the direct or indirect context of all moral precepts, the requirement of acceptance by all agents means that the argument's conclusion holds within the whole relevant context.

The argument in question undertakes to establish two main theses. The first is that every agent logically must accept that *he or she* has rights to freedom and well-being as the necessary conditions of his or her action and successful action in general. The second thesis is that the agent also logically must accept that *all other* agents have the same rights he claims for himself, so that in this way the existence of universal and equal rights, and thus of human rights, must be accepted within the whole context of action or practice.

Reduced to its barest essentials, the argument for the first main thesis is as follows. Since freedom and well-being are the necessary conditions of action and successful action in general, every agent must regard these conditions as necessary goods for himself, since with-

out them he would not be able to act for any of his purposes, either at all or with general chances of success. Hence, every agent has to accept (1) "I must have freedom and well-being." This "must" is practical-prescriptive in that it signifies the agent's advocacy of his having the necessary goods of action, which he needs in order to act and to act successfully in general. Now, by virtue of accepting (1), every agent has to accept (2) "I have rights to freedom and well-being." For, if he rejects (2), then, because of the correlativity of claim-rights and strict "oughts," he also has to reject (3) "All other persons ought at least to refrain from removing or interfering with my freedom and well-being." By rejecting (3), he has to accept (4) "Other persons may (i.e., it is permissible that other persons) remove or interfere with my freedom and well-being." And by accepting (4), he also has to accept (5) "I may not (i.e., it is permissible that I not) have freedom and well-being." But (5) contradicts (1). Since every agent must accept (1), he must reject (5). And since (5) follows from the denial of (2), every agent must reject that denial, so that he must accept (2) "I have rights to freedom and well-being."

I shall give an even briefer summary of the argument for the second main thesis, that every agent logically must accept that all other actual or prospective agents also have rights to freedom and well-being. This generalization is an application of the logical principle of universalizability: if some predicate P belongs to some subject S because S has a certain quality Q (where the "because" is that of sufficient condition), then P logically must belong to all other subjects S_1 to S_n that also have the quality Q. Thus, since every agent must hold that he has rights to freedom and well-being because he is a prospective purposive agent, he also logically must hold that all prospective purposive agents have these rights. This, then, is the principle of human rights. Thus, the existence or having of human rights is susceptible of a definite rational proof, one that must be accepted by every actual or prospective agent.

From all the above considerations, it follows that human rights are basic to morality, in that they are the necessary even if not the sufficient condition of all moral values. For all moral precepts deal, directly or indirectly, with how persons ought to act, especially towards one another. Now, since the human rights are rights to the necessary conditions of action and successful action in general, it follows that without the objects of the human rights, the actions with which morality is concerned are either impossible or deficient and the abilities and conditions needed for the actions are not securely possessed. Without rights to these objects, the individual's personal dignity as an agent who can justifiably claim these goods on his own behalf is seriously threatened. And without social recognition of these rights—and, regarding the most important rights, their legal enforcement—the individual's possession of the necessary goods of action and successful action is rendered precarious. In addition, the universality of human rights provides the essential basis for linking together each individual's possession of the necessary goods of action in a context of social solidarity. For all these reasons, recognition and protection of human rights is a necessary condition of the moral legitimacy of societies.

Rights

Terezin

That bit of filth in dirty walls,
And all around barbed wire,
And 30,000 souls who sleep
Who once will wake
And once will see
Their own blood spilled.

I was once a little child,
Three years ago.
That child who longed for other worlds.
But now I am no more a child
For I have learned to hate.
I am a grown-up person now,
I have known fear.

Bloody words and a dead day then,
That's something different than bogie men!

But anyway, I still believe I only sleep today,
That I'll wake up, a child again, and start to laugh and play.

I'll go back to childhood sweet like a briar rose,
Like a bell which wakes us from a dream,
Like a mother with an ailing child
Loves him with aching woman's love.
How tragic, then, is youth which lives
With enemies, with gallows ropes,
How tragic, then, for children on your lap
To say: this for the good, that for the bad.

Somewhere, far away out there, childhood sweetly sleeps,

Along that path among the trees,
There o'er that house
Which was once my pride and joy.
There my mother gave me birth into this world
So I could weep . . .

In the flame of candles by my bed, I sleep
And once perhaps I'll understand
That I was such a little thing,
As little as this song.

These 30,000 souls who sleep
Among the trees will wake,
Open an eye
And because they see
A lot

They'll fall asleep again . . .

Hanus Hachenburg, 1944, just before his death in a
Nazi concentration camp at the age of 14.

ARISTOTLE
(384–322 B.C.) Greek Philosopher

From *Politics**

Property is a part of the household, and the art of acquiring property is a part of the art of managing the household; for no man can live well, or indeed live at all, unless he be provided with necessaries. And as in the arts which have a definite sphere the workers must have their own proper instruments for the accomplishment of their work, so it is in the management of a household. Now instruments are of various sorts; some are living, others lifeless; in the rudder, the pilot of a ship has a lifeless, in the look-out man, a living instrument; for in the arts the servant is a kind of instrument. Thus, too, a possession is an instrument for maintaining life. And so, in the arrangement of the family, a slave is a living possession, and property a number of such instruments; and the servant is himself an instrument which takes precedence of all other instruments. For if every instrument could accomplish its own work, obeying or anticipating the will of others, like the statues of Daedalus, or the tripods of Hephaestus, which, says the poet

"of their own accord entered the assembly of the Gods";

*Aristotle, *Politics*, trans. by Benjamin Jowett in *Oxford Translation of the Works of Aristotle*, ed. by J. S. Smith and W. D. Ross (Oxford, 1908–1952).

if, in like manner, the shuttle would weave and the plectrum touch the lyre without a hand to guide them, chief workmen would not want servants, nor masters slaves. Here, however, another distinction must be drawn; the instruments commonly so called are instruments of production, whilst a possession is an instrument of action. The shuttle, for example, is not only of use; but something else is made by it, whereas of a garment or of a bed there is only the use. Further, as production and action are different in kind, and both require instruments, the instruments which they employ must likewise differ in kind. But life is action and not production, and therefore the slave is the minister of action. Again, a possession is spoken of as a part is spoken of; for the part is not only a part of something else, but wholly belongs to it; and this is also true of a possession. The master is only the master of the slave; he does not belong to him, whereas the slave is not only the slave of his master, but wholly belongs to him. Hence we see what is the nature and office of a slave; he who is by nature not his own but another's man, is by nature a slave; and he may be said to be another's man who, being a human being, is also a possession. And a possession may be defined as an instrument of action, separable from the possessor.

But is there any one thus intended by nature to be a slave, and for whom such a condition is expedient and right, or rather is not all slavery a violation of nature?

There is no difficulty in answering this question, on grounds both of reason and of fact. For that some should rule and others be ruled is a thing not only necessary, but expedient; from the hour of their birth, some are marked out for subjection, others for rule.

And there are many kinds both of rulers and subjects (and that rule is the better which is exercised over better subjects—for example, to rule over men is better than to rule over wild beasts; for the work is better which is executed by better workmen, and where one man rules and another is ruled, they may be said to have a work); for in all things which form a composite whole and which are made up of parts, whether continuous or discrete, a distinction between the ruling and the subject element comes to light. Such a duality exists in living creatures, but not in them only; it originates in the constitution of the universe; even in things which have no life there is a ruling principle, as in a musical mode. But we are wandering from the subject. We will therefore restrict ourselves to the living creature, which, in the first place, consists of soul and body: and of these two, the one is by nature the ruler, and the other the subject. But then we must look for the intentions of nature in things which retain their nature, and not in things which are corrupted. And therefore we must study the man who is in the most perfect state both of body and soul, for in him we shall see the true relation of the two; although in bad or corrupted natures the body will often appear to rule over the soul, because they are in an evil and unnatural condition. At all events we may firstly observe in living creatures both a despotical and a constitutional rule; for the soul rules the body with a despotical rule, whereas the intellect rules the appetites with a constitutional and royal rule. And it is clear that the rule of the soul over the body, and of the mind and the rational element over the passionate, is natural and expedient; whereas the equality of the two or the rule of the inferior is always hurtful. The same holds good of animals in relation to men; for tame animals have a better nature than wild, and all tame animals are better off when they are ruled by man; for then they are preserved. Again, the male is by nature superior, and the female inferior; and the one rules, and the other is ruled; this principle, of necessity, extends to all mankind. Where then there is such a difference as that between soul and body, or between men and animals (as in the case of those whose business is to use their body, and who can do nothing better), the lower sort are by nature slaves, and it is better for them as for all inferiors that they should be under the rule of a master. For he who can be, and therefore is, another's, and he who participates in rational principle enough to apprehend, but not to have, such a principle, is a slave by nature. Whereas the lower animals cannot even apprehend a principle; they obey their instincts. And indeed the use made of slaves and of tame animals is not very different; for both with their bodies minister to the needs of life. Nature would like to distinguish between the bodies of freemen and slaves, making the one strong for servile labour, the other upright, and although useless for such services, useful for political life in the arts both of war and peace. But the opposite often happens—that some have the souls and others have the bodies of freemen. And doubtless if men differed from one another in the mere forms of their bodies as much as the statues of the Gods do from men, all would acknowledge that the inferior class should be slaves of the superior. And if this is true of the body, how much more just that a similar distinction should exist in the soul? but the beauty of the body is seen, whereas the beauty of the soul is not seen. It is clear, then, that some men are by nature free, and others slaves, and that for these latter slavery is both expedient and right.

But that those who take the opposite view have in a certain way right on their side, may be easily seen. For the words slavery and slave are used in two senses. There is a slave or slavery by law as well as by nature. The law of which I speak is a sort of convention—the law by which whatever is taken in war is supposed to belong to the victors. But this right many jurists impeach, as they would an orator who brought forward an unconstitutional measure: they detest the notion that, because one man has the power of doing violence and is superior in brute strength, another shall be his slave and subject. Even among philosophers there is a difference of opinion. The origin of the dispute, and what makes the views invade each other's territory, is as follows: in some sense virtue, when furnished with means, has actually the greatest power of exercising force: and as superior power is only found where there is superior excellence of some kind, power seems to imply virtue, and the dispute to be simply one about justice (for it is due to one party identifying justice with goodwill, while the other identifies it with the mere rule of the stronger). If these views are thus set out separately, the other views have no force or plausibility against the view that the superior in virtue ought to rule, or be master. Others, clinging, as they think, simply to a principle of justice (for law and custom are a sort of justice), assume that slavery in accordance with the custom of war is justified by law, but at the same moment they deny this. For what if the cause of the war be unjust? And again, no one would ever say that he is a slave who is unworthy to be a slave. Were this the case, men of the highest rank would be slaves and the children of slaves if they or their parents chance to have been taken captive and sold. Wherefore Hellenes do not like to call Hellenes slaves, but confine the term to barbarians. Yet, in using this language, they really mean the natural slave of whom we spoke at first; for it must be admitted that some are slaves everywhere, others nowhere. The same principle applies to nobility. Hellenes regard themselves as noble everywhere, and not only in their own country, but they deem the barbarians noble only when at home, thereby implying that there are two sorts of nobility and freedom, the one absolute, the other relative. The Helen of Theodectes says:

> "Who would presume to call me servant who am on both sides sprung from the stem of the Gods?"

What does this mean but that they distinguish freedom and slavery, noble and humble birth, by the two principles of good and evil? They think that as men and animals beget men and animals, so from good men a good man springs. But this is what nature, though she may intend it, cannot always accomplish.

We see then that there is some foundation for this difference of opinion, and that all are not either slaves by nature or freemen by nature, and also that there is in some cases a marked distinction between the two classes, rendering it expedient and right for the one to be slaves and the others to be masters: the one practising obedience, the others exercising the authority and lordship which nature intended them to have. The abuse of this authority is injurious to both; for the interests of part and whole, of body and soul, are the same, and the slave is a part of the master, a living but separated part of his bodily frame. Hence, where the relation of master and slave between them is natural they are friends and have a common interest, but where it rests merely on law and force the reverse is true.

The previous remarks are quite enough to show that the rule of a master is not a constitutional rule, and that all the different kinds of rule are not, as some affirm, the same with each other. For there is one rule exercised over subjects who are by nature free, another over subjects who are by nature slaves. The rule of a household is a monarchy, for every house is under one head: whereas constitutional rule is a government of freemen and equals. The master is not called a master because he has science, but because he is of a certain character, and the same remark applies to the slave and the freeman. Still there may be a science for the master and a science for the slave. The science of the slave would be such as the man of Syracuse taught, who made money by instructing slaves in their ordinary duties. And such a knowledge may be carried further, so as to include cookery and similar menial arts. For some duties are of the more necessary, others of the more honourable sort; as the proverb says, "slave before slave, master before master." But all such branches of knowledge are servile. There is likewise a science of the master, which teaches the use of slaves; for the master as such is concerned, not with the acquisition, but with the use of them. Yet this so-called science is not anything great or wonderful; for the master need only know how to order that which the slave must know how to execute. Hence those who are in a position which places them above toil have stewards who attend to their households while they occupy themselves with philosophy or with politics. But the art of acquiring slaves, I mean of justly acquiring them, differs both from the art of the master and the art of the slave, being a species of hunting or war. Enough of the distinction between master and slave.

JOHN LOCKE
(1632–1704) English Philosopher

The Second Treatise of Civil Government*

Of the State of Nature

To understand political power right, and derive it from its original, we must consider what state all men are naturally in, and that is a state of perfect freedom to order their actions and dispose of their possessions and persons as they think fit, within the bounds of the law of nature, without asking leave or depending upon the will of any other man.

A state also of equality, wherein all the power and jurisdiction is reciprocal, no one having more than another; there being nothing more evident than that creatures of the same species and rank, promiscuously born to all the same advantages of nature and the use of the same faculties, should also be equal one amongst another without subordination or subjection; unless the lord and master of them all should, by any manifest declaration of his will, set one above another, and confer on him by an evident and clear appointment an undoubted right to dominion and sovereignty.

This equality of men by nature the judicious Hooker[1] looks upon as so evident in itself and beyond all question that he makes it the foundation of that obligation to mutual love amongst men on which he builds the duties we owe one another, and from whence he derives the great maxims of justice and charity. His words are:

> The like natural inducement hath brought men to know that it is no less their duty to love others than themselves; for seeing those things which are equal must needs all have one measure; if I cannot but wish to receive good, even as much at every man's hands as any man can wish unto his own soul, how should I look to have any part of my desire herein satisfied unless myself be careful to satisfy the like desire, which is undoubtedly in other men, being of one and the same nature? To have anything offered them repugnant to this desire must needs in all respects grieve them as

*John Locke, "The Second Treatise of Civil Government," in *Two Treatises of Government* (London: A. Churchill, 1690).
[1] "The judicious Hooker" (1554–1600) was the celebrated English ecclesiastic who defended the Reformation settlements and wrote the famous *Lawes of Ecclesiasticall Politic*.

much as me; so that, if I do harm, I must look to suffer, there being no reason that others should show greater measure of love to me than they have by me showed unto them; my desire therefore to be loved of my equals in nature, as much as possibly may be, imposeth upon me a natural duty of bearing to them-ward fully the like affection; from which relation of equality between ourselves and them that are as ourselves, what several rules and canons natural reason hath drawn, for direction of life, no man is ignorant. (*Eccl. Pol.* lib. i.).

But though this be a state of liberty, yet it is not a state of licence; though man in that state have an uncontrollable liberty to dispose of his person or possessions, yet he has not liberty to destroy himself, or so much as any creature in his possession, but where some nobler use than its bare preservation calls for it. The state of nature has a law of nature to govern it which obliges every one; and reason, which is that law, teaches all mankind who will but consult it that, being all equal and independent, no one ought to harm another in his life, health, liberty, or possessions; for men being all the workmanship of one omnipotent and infinitely wise Maker—all the servants of one sovereign master, sent into the world by his order, and about his business—they are his property whose workmanship they are, made to last during his, not one another's, pleasure; and being furnished with like faculties, sharing all in one community of nature, there cannot be supposed any such subordination among us that may authorize us to destroy another, as if we were made for one another's uses as the inferior ranks of creatures are for ours. Every one, as he is bound to preserve himself and not to quit his station wilfully, so by the like reason, when his own preservation comes not in competition, ought he, as much as he can, to preserve the rest of mankind, and may not, unless it be to do justice to an offender, take away or impair the life, or what tends to the preservation of life: the liberty, health, limb, or goods of another.

And that all men may be restrained from invading others' rights and from doing hurt to one another, and the law of nature be observed which willeth the peace and preservation of all mankind, the execution of the law of nature is, in that state, put into every man's hands, whereby everyone has a right to punish the transgressors of that law to such a degree as may hinder its violation; for the law of nature would, as all other laws that concern men in this world, be in vain, if there were nobody that in the state of nature had a power to execute that law and thereby preserve the innocent and restrain offenders. And if any one in the state of nature may punish another for any evil he has done, every one may do so; for in that state of perfect equality where naturally there is no superiority or jurisdiction of one over another, what any may do in prosecution of that law, every one must needs have a right to do.

And thus in the state of nature one man comes by a power over another; but yet no absolute or arbitrary power to use a criminal, when he has got him in his hands, according to the passionate heats or boundless extravagancy of his own will; but only to retribute to him, so far as calm reason and conscience dictate, what is proportionate to his transgression, which is so much as may serve for reparation and restraint; for these two are the only reasons why one man may lawfully do harm to another, which is that we call punishment. In transgressing the law of nature, the offender declares himself to live by another rule than that of reason and common equity, which is that measure God has set to the actions of men for their mutual security; and so he becomes dangerous to mankind, the tie which is to secure them from injury and violence being slighted and broken by him. Which being a trespass against the whole species and the peace and safety of it provided for by the law of nature, every man upon this score, by the right he hath to preserve mankind in general, may restrain, or, where it is necessary, destroy things noxious to them, and so may bring such evil on any one who hath transgressed that law, as may make him repent the doing of it and thereby deter him, and by his example others, from doing the like mischief. And in this case, and upon this ground, *every man hath a right to punish the offender and be executioner of the law of nature. . . .*

It is often asked as a mighty objection, "Where are or ever were there any men in such a state of nature?" To which it may suffice as an answer at present that, since all princes and rulers of independent governments all through the world are in a state of nature, it is plain the world never was, nor ever will be, without numbers of men in that state. I have named all governors of independent communities, whether they are, or are not, in league with others; for it is not every compact that puts an end to the state of nature between men, but only this one of agreeing together mutually to enter into one community and make one body politic; other promises and compacts men may make one with another and yet still be in the state of nature. The promises and bargains for truck, etc., between the two men in the desert island, mentioned by Garcilasso de la Vega, in his *History of Peru,*[2] or between a Swiss and an Indian, in the woods of America, are binding to them, though they are perfectly in a state of nature in reference to one another; for truth and keeping of faith belongs to men as men, and not as members of society.

To those that say there were never any men in the state of nature, I will not only oppose the authority of the judicious Hooker, *Eccl. Pol.*, lib. i., sect. 10, where he says,

> The laws which have been hitherto mentioned, (*i.e.*, the laws of nature) do bind men absolutely, even as they are men, although they have never any settled fellowship, never any solemn agreement amongst themselves what to do, or not to do; but forasmuch as we are not by ourselves sufficient to furnish ourselves with competent store of things needful for such a life as our nature doth desire, a life fit for the dignity of man; therefore to supply those defects and imperfections which are in us, as living singly and solely by ourselves, we are naturally induced to seek communion and fellowship with others. This was the cause of men's uniting themselves at first in politic societies.

But I, moreover, affirm that all men are naturally in that state and remain so till by their own consents they make themselves members of some politic society; and I doubt not in the sequel of this discourse to make it very clear.

---

[2] Garcilasso de la Vega (1535–1616), called *el Inca,* was a historian of Peru and the first South American in Spanish literature.

Of the State of War

The state of war is a state of enmity and destruction; and, therefore, declaring by word or action, not a passionate and hasty, but a sedate, settled design upon another man's life, puts him in a state of war with him against whom he has declared such an intention, and so has exposed his life to the other's power to be taken away by him, or anyone that joins with him in his defence and espouses his quarrel; it being reasonable and just I should have a right to destroy that which threatens me with destruction; for, by the fundamental law of nature, man being to be preserved as much as possible when all cannot be preserved, the safety of the innocent is to be preferred; and one may destroy a man who makes war upon him, or has discovered an enmity to his being, for the same reason that he may kill a wolf or a lion, because such men are not under the ties of the common law of reason, have no other rule but that of force and violence, and so may be treated as beasts of prey, those dangerous and noxious creatures that will be sure to destroy him whenever he falls into their power.

And hence it is that he who attempts to get another man into his absolute power does thereby put himself into a state of war with him, it being to be understood as a declaration of a design upon his life; for I have reason to conclude that he who would get me into his power without my consent would use me as he pleased when he got me there, and destroy me, too, when he had a fancy to it; for nobody can desire to have me in his absolute power unless it be to compel me by force to that which is against the right of my freedom, *i.e.*, make me a slave. To be free from such force is the only security of my preservation; and reason bids me look on him as an enemy to my preservation who would take away that freedom which is the fence to it; so that he who makes an attempt to enslave me thereby puts himself into a state of war with me. He that, in the state of nature, would take away the freedom that belongs to any one in that state, must necessarily be supposed to have a design to take away everything else, that freedom being the foundation of all the rest; as he that, in the state of society, would take away the freedom belonging to those of that society or commonwealth, must be supposed to design to take away from them everything else, and so be looked on as in a state of war.

This makes it lawful for a man to kill a thief who has not in the least hurt him, nor declared any design upon his life any farther than, by the use of force, so to get him in his power as to take away his money, or what he pleases, from him; because, using force where he has no right to get me into his power, let his pretence be what it will, I have no reason to suppose that he who would take away my liberty would not, when he had me in his power, take away everything else. And therefore it is lawful for me to treat him as one who has put himself into a state of war with me, *i.e.*, kill him if I can; for to that hazard does he justly expose himself whoever introduces a state of war and is aggressor in it.

And here we have the plain difference between the state of nature and the state of war which, however some men have confounded, are as far distant as a state of peace, good-will, mutual assistance, and preservation, and a state of enmity, malice, violence, and mutual destruction are one from another. Men living together according to reason, without a common superior on earth with authority to judge between them, is properly the state of nature. But force, or a declared design of force, upon the person of another, where there is no common superior on earth to appeal to for relief, is the state of war; and it is the want of such an appeal gives a man the right of war even against an aggressor, though he be in society and a fellow-subject. Thus a thief, whom I cannot harm but by appeal to the law for having stolen all that I am worth, I may kill when he sets on me to rob me but of my horse or coat; because the law, which was made for my preservation, where it cannot interpose to secure my life from present force, which, if lost, is capable of no reparation, permits me my own defence and the right of war, a liberty to kill the aggressor, because the aggressor allows not time to appeal to our common judge, nor the decision of the law, for remedy in a case where the mischief may be irreparable. Want of a common judge with authority puts all men in a state of nature; force without right upon a man's person makes a state of war both where there is, and is not, a common judge.

Of Slavery

The natural liberty of man is to be free from any superior power on earth, and not to be under the will or legislative authority of man, but to have only the law of nature for his rule. The liberty of man in society is to be under no other legislative power but that established by consent in the commonwealth; nor under the dominion of any will or restraint of any law, but what that legislative shall enact according to the trust put in it. Freedom then is not what Sir Robert Filmer tells us "a liberty for every one to do what he lists, to live as he pleases, and not to be tied by any laws"; but freedom of men under government is to have a standing rule to live by, common to every one of that society and made by the legislative power erected in it, a liberty to follow my own will in all things where the rule prescribes not, and not to be subject to the inconstant, uncertain, unknown, arbitrary will of another man; as freedom of nature is to be under no other restraint but the law of nature.

This freedom from absolute, arbitrary power is so necessary to and closely joined with a man's preservation that he cannot part with it but by what forfeits his preservation and life together; for a man not having the power of his own life cannot by compact or his own consent enslave himself to any one, nor put himself under the absolute arbitrary power of another to take away his life when he pleases. Nobody can give more power than he has himself; and he that cannot take away his own life cannot give another power over it. Indeed, having by his fault forfeited his own life by some act that deserves death, he to whom he has forfeited it may, when he has him in his power, delay to take it, and make use of him to his own service, and he does him no injury by it; for, whenever he finds the hardship of his slavery outweigh the value of his life, it is in his power, by resisting the will of his master, to draw on himself the death he desires.

This is the perfect condition of slavery, which is nothing else but "the state of war continued between a lawful conqueror and a captive"; for, if once compact enter between them and make an agreement for a limited power on the one side and obedience on the other, the state of war and slavery ceases as long as the compact endures; for, as has been said, no man can by agreement pass over to another that which he hath not in himself—a power over his own life.

THOMAS HOBBES
(1588–1679) English Philosopher

From *Leviathan**

Of the Natural Condition of Mankind as Concerning Their Felicity and Misery

Men by Nature Equal.
Nature hath made men so equal, in the faculties of the body, and mind; as that though there be found one man sometimes manifestly stronger in body, or of quicker mind than another; yet when all is reckoned together, the difference between man, and man, is not so considerable, as that one man can thereupon claim to himself any benefit, to which another may not pretend, as well as he. For as to the strength of body, the weakest has strength enough to kill the strongest, either by secret machination, or by confederacy with others, that are in the same danger with himself.

And as to the faculties of the mind, setting aside the arts grounded upon words, and especially that skill of proceeding upon general, and infallible rules, called science; which very few have, and but in few things; as being not a native faculty, born with us; nor attained, as prudence, while we look after somewhat else, I find yet a greater equality amongst men, than that of strength. For prudence, is but experience; which equal time, equally bestows on all men, in those things they equally apply themselves unto. That which may perhaps make such equality incredible, is but a vain conceit of one's own wisdom, which almost all men think they have in a greater degree, than the vulgar; that is, than all men but themselves, and a few others, whom by fame, or for concurring with themselves, they approve. For such is the nature of men, that howsoever they may acknowledge many others to be more witty, or more eloquent, or more learned; yet they will hardly believe there be many so wise as themselves; for they see their own wit at hand, and other men's at a distance. But this proveth rather that men are in that point equal, than unequal. For there is not ordinarily a greater sign of the equal distribution of any thing, than that every man is contented with his share.

---

*From Thomas Hobbes, *Leviathan* (London, 1651).

From Equality Proceeds Diffidence.
From this equality of ability, ariseth equality of hope in the attaining of our ends. And therefore if any two men desire the same thing, which nevertheless they cannot both enjoy, they become enemies; and in the way to their end, which is principally their own conservation, and sometimes their delectation only, endeavour to destroy, or subdue one another. And from hence it comes to pass, that where an invader hath no more to fear, than another man's single power; if one plant, sow, build, or possess a convenient seat, others may probably be expected to come prepared with forces united, to dispossess, and deprive him, not only of the fruit of his labour, but also of his life, or liberty. And the invader again is in the like danger of another.

From Diffidence War.
And from this diffidence of one another, there is no way for any man to secure himself, so reasonable, as anticipation; that is, by force, or wiles, to master the persons of all men he can, so long, till he see no other power great enough to endanger him: and this is no more than his own conservation requireth, and is generally allowed. Also because there be some, that taking pleasure in contemplating their own power in the acts of conquest, which they pursue farther than their security requires; if others, that otherwise would be glad to be at ease within modest bounds, should not by invasion increase their power, they would not be able, long time, by standing only on their defence, to subsist. And by consequence, such augmentation of dominion over men being necessary to a man's conservation, it ought to be allowed him.

Again, men have no pleasure, but on the contrary a great deal of grief, in keeping company, where there is no power able to over-awe them all. For every man looketh that his companion should value him, at the same rate he sets upon himself: and upon all signs of contempt, or undervaluing, naturally endeavours, as far as he dares, (which amongst them that have no common power to keep them in quiet, is far enough to make them destroy each other), to extort a greater value from his contemners, by damage; and from others, by the example.

So that in the nature of man, we find three principal causes of quarrel. First, competition; secondly, diffidence; thirdly, glory.

The first, maketh men invade for gain; the second, for safety; and the third, for reputation. The first use violence, to make themselves masters of other men's persons, wives, children, and cattle; the second, to defend them; the third, for trifles, as a word, a smile, a different opinion, and any other sign of undervalue, either direct in their persons, or by reflection in their kindred, their friends, their nation, their profession, or their name.

Out of Civil States, There Is Always War of Every One Against Every One.
Hereby it is manifest, that during the time men live without a common power to keep them all in awe, they are in that condition which is called war; and such a war, as is of every man, against every man. For **war,** consisteth not in battle only, or the act of fighting; but in a tract of time, where in the will to contend by battle is sufficiently known: and therefore the notion of *time,* is to be considered in the nature of war; as it is in the nature of weather. For as the nature of foul weather,

lieth not in a shower or two of rain; but in an inclination thereto of many days together: so the nature of war, consisteth not in actual fighting; but in the known disposition thereto, during all the time there is no assurance to the contrary. All other time is **peace.** . . .

In Such a War Nothing Is Unjust.
To this war of every man, against every man, this also is consequent; that nothing can be unjust. The notions of right and wrong, justice and injustice have there no place. Where there is no common power, there is no law: where no law, no injustice. Force, and fraud, are in war the two cardinal virtues. Justice, and injustice are none of the faculties neither of the body, nor mind. If they were, they might be in a man that were alone in the world, as well as his senses, and passions. They are qualities, that relate to men in society, not in solitude. It is consequent also to the same condition, that there be no propriety, no dominion, no *mine* and *thine* distinct; but only that to be every man's, that he can get: and for so long, as he can keep it. And thus much for the ill condition, which man by mere nature is actually placed in; though with a possibility to come out of it, consisting partly in the passions, partly in his reason.

The Passions That Incline Men to Peace.
The passions that incline men to peace, are fear of death; desire of such things as are necessary to commodious living; and a hope by their industry to obtain them. And reason suggesteth convenient articles of peace, upon which men may be drawn to agreement. These articles, are they, which otherwise are called the Laws of Nature:

Of the First and Second Natural Laws, and of Contracts

Right of Nature What.
The right of nature, which writers commonly call *jus naturale,* is the liberty each man hath, to use his own power, as he will himself, for the preservation of his own nature; that is to say, of his own life; and consequently, of doing any thing, which in his own judgment, and reason, he shall conceive to be the aptest means thereunto.

Liberty What.
By **liberty,** is understood, according to the proper signification of the word, the absence of external impediments: which impediments, may oft take away part of a man's power to do what he would; but cannot hinder him from using the power left him, according as his judgment, and reason shall dictate to him.

A Law of Nature What. Difference of Right and Law.
A law of nature, *lex naturalis,* is a precept or general rule, found out by reason, by which a man is forbidden to do that, which is destructive of his life, or taketh away the means of preserving the same; and to omit that, by which he thinketh it may be best preserved. For though they that speak of this subject, use to confound *jus,* and *lex, right* and *law:* yet they ought to be distinguished; because **right,** consisteth in liberty to do, or to forbear: whereas **law,** determineth, and

bindeth to one of them: so that law, and right, differ as much, as obligation, and liberty; which in one and the same matter are inconsistent.

Naturally Every Man Has Right to Every Thing. The Fundamental Law of Nature.

And because the condition of man, as hath been declared in the precedent chapter, is a condition of war of every one against every one; in which case every one is governed by his own reason; and there is nothing he can make use of, that may not be a help unto him, in preserving his life against his enemies; it followeth, that in such a condition, every man has a right to every thing; even to one another's body. And therefore, as long as this natural right of every man to every thing endureth, there can be no security to any man, how strong or wise soever he be, of living out the time, which nature ordinarily alloweth men to live. And consequently it is a precept, or general rule of reason, *that* every man, ought to endeavour peace, as far as he has hope of obtaining it; and when he cannot obtain it, that he may seek, and use, all helps, and advantages of war. The first branch of which rule, containeth the first, and fundamental law of nature; which is, *to seek peace, and follow it.* The second, the sum of the right of nature; which is, *by all means we can, to defend ourselves.*

The Second Law of Nature.

From this fundamental law of nature, by which men are commanded to endeavour peace, is derived this second law; *that a man be willing, when others are so too, as far-forth, as for peace, and defence of himself he shall think it necessary, to lay down this right to all things; and be contented with so much liberty against other men, as he would allow other men against himself.* For as long as every man holdeth this right, of doing any thing he liketh; so long are all men in the condition of war. But if other men will not lay down their right, as well as he; then there is no reason for any one, to divest himself of his: for that were to expose himself to prey, which no man is bound to, rather than to dispose himself to peace. . . .

Not All Rights Are Alienable.

Whensoever a man transferreth his right, or renounceth it; it is either in consideration of some right reciprocally transferred to himself; or for some other good he hopeth for thereby. For it is a voluntary act: and of the voluntary acts of every man, the object is some *good to himself.* And therefore there be some rights, which no man can be understood by any words, or other signs, to have abandoned, or transferred. As first a man cannot lay down the right of resisting them, that assault him by force, to take away his life; because he cannot be understood to aim thereby, at any good to himself. The same may be said of wounds, and chains, and imprisonment; both because there is no benefit consequent to such patience; as there is to the patience of suffering another to be wounded, or imprisoned: as also because a man cannot tell, when he seeth men proceed against him by violence, whether they intend his death or not. And lastly the motive, and end for which this renouncing, and transferring of right is introduced, is nothing else but the security of a man's person, in his life, and in the means of so preserving life, as not to be weary of it. And therefore if a man by words, or other signs, seem to despoil himself of the end, for which those signs were intended; he is not to be understood as if he meant it, or that it was his will; but that he was ignorant of how such words and actions were to be interpreted. . . .

Of Other Laws of Nature

The Third Law of Nature, Justice.
From that law of nature, by which we are obliged to transfer to another, such rights, as being retained, hinder the peace of mankind, there followeth a third; which is this, *that men perform their covenants made:* without which, covenants are in vain, and but empty words; and the right of all men to all things remaining, we are still in the condition of war.

Justice and Injustice What.
And in this law of nature, consisteth the fountain and original of **justice.** For where no covenant hath preceded, there hath no right been transferred, and every man has right to every thing; and consequently, no action can be unjust. But when a covenant is made, then to break it is *unjust:* and the definition of **injustice,** is no other than *the not performance of covenant.* And whatsoever is not unjust, is *just.*

Justice and Propriety Begin with the Constitution of Commonwealth.
But because covenants of mutual trust, where there is a fear of not performance on either part, as hath been said in the former chapter, are invalid; though the original of justice be the making of covenants; yet injustice actually there can be none, till the cause of such fear be taken away; which while men are in the natural condition of war, cannot be done. Therefore before the names of just, and unjust can have place, there must be some coercive power, to compel men equally to the performance of their covenants, by the terror of some punishment, greater than the benefit they expect by the breach of their covenant; and to make good that propriety, which by mutual contract men acquire, in recompense of the universal right they abandon: and such power there is none before the erection of a commonwealth. . . .

Justice Not Contrary to Reason.
The fool hath said in his heart, there is no such thing as justice; and sometimes also with his tongue; seriously alleging, that every man's conservation, and contentment, being committed to his own care, there could be no reason, why every man might not do what he thought conduced thereunto: and therefore also to make, or not make; keep, or not keep covenants, was not against reason, when it conduced to one's benefit. . . .

For the question is not of promises mutual, where there is no security of performance on either side; as when there is no civil power erected over the parties promising; for such promises are no covenants: but either where one of the parties has performed already; or where there is a power to make him perform; there is the question whether it be against reason, that is, against the benefit of the other to perform, or not. And I say it is not against reason. For the manifestation whereof, we are to consider; first, that when a man doth a thing, which notwithstanding any thing can be foreseen, and reckoned on, tendeth to his own destruction, howsoever some accident which he could not expect, arriving may turn it to his benefit; yet such events do not make it reasonably or wisely done. Secondly, that in a condition of war, wherein every man to every man, for want of a common power to keep them all in awe, is an enemy, there is no man who can hope by his own strength, or wit, to defend himself from destruction, without the help of confederates; where every one expects the same defence by the confederation, that any one else does: and therefore he which declares he thinks it reason to deceive those that help him, can in reason expect no other means of safety, than what can be had from his own single power. He therefore that breaketh his covenant, and consequently declareth that he thinks he may with reason do so, cannot be received into any society, that unite themselves for peace and defence, but by the error of them that receive him; nor when he is received, be retained in it, without seeing the danger of their error; which errors a man cannot reasonably reckon upon as the means of his security: and therefore if he be left, or cast out of society, he perisheth; and if he live in society, it is by the errors of other men, which he could not foresee, nor reckon upon; and consequently against the reason of his preservation; and so, as all men that contribute not to his destruction, forbear him only out of ignorance of what is good for themselves. . . .

Justice therefore, that is to say, keeping of covenant, is a rule of reason, by which we are forbidden to do any thing destructive to our life; and consequently a law of nature. . . .

The question who is the better man, has no place in the condition of mere nature; where, as has been shewn before, all men are equal. The inequality that now is, has been introduced by the laws civil. I know that Aristotle in the first book of his *Politics*, for a foundation of his doctrine, maketh men by nature, some more worthy to command, meaning the wiser sort, such as he thought himself to be for his philosophy; others to serve, meaning those that had strong bodies, but were not philosophers as he; as if master and servant were not introduced by consent of men, but by difference of wit: which is not only against reason; but also against experience. For there are very few so foolish, that had not rather govern themselves, than be governed by others: nor when the wise in their own conceit, contend by force, with them who distrust their own wisdom, do they always, or often, or almost at any time, get the victory. If nature therefore have made men equal, that equality is to be acknowledged: or if nature have made men unequal; yet because men that think themselves equal, will not enter into conditions of peace, but upon equal terms, such equality must be admitted.

FRIEDRICH NIETZSCHE
(1844–1900) German Philosopher

From *Beyond Good & Evil**

Wandering through the many subtler and coarser moralities which have so far been prevalent on earth, or still are prevalent, I found that certain features recurred regularly together and were closely associated—until I finally discovered two basic types and one basic difference.

There are *master morality* and *slave morality*[1]—I add immediately that in all the higher and more mixed cultures there also appear attempts at mediation between these two moralities, and yet more often the interpenetration and mutual misunderstanding of both, and at times they occur directly alongside each other—even in the same human being, within a *single* soul.[2] The moral discrimination of values has originated either among a ruling group whose consciousness of its difference from the ruled group was accompanied by delight—or among the ruled, the slaves and dependents of every degree.

In the first case, when the ruling group determines what is "good," the exalted, proud states of the soul are experienced as conferring distinction and determining the order of rank. The noble human being separates from himself those in whom the opposite of such exalted, proud states finds expression: he despises them. It should be noted immediately that in this first type of morality the opposition of "good" and *"bad"* means approximately the same as "noble" and "contemptible." (The opposition of "good" and *"evil"* has a different origin.) One feels contempt for the cowardly, the anxious, the petty, those intent on narrow utility; also for the suspicious with their unfree glances, those who humble themselves, the doglike people who allow themselves to be maltreated, the begging flatterers, above all the liars: it is part of the fundamental faith of all aristocrats that the common people lie. "We truthful ones"—thus the nobility of ancient Greece referred to itself.

It is obvious that moral designations were everywhere first applied to *human beings* and only later, derivatively, to actions. Therefore it is a gross mistake when historians of morality start from such questions as: why was the compassionate act praised? The noble type of man experiences *itself* as determining values; it

---

*From Friedrich Nietzsche, *Beyond Good and Evil*, contained in *Basic Writings of Nietzsche*, trans. by Walter Kaufman (New York: Modern Library, 1968).

[1] While the ideas developed here, and explicated at greater length a year later in the first part of the *Genealogy of Morals*, had been expressed by Nietzsche in 1878 in section 45 of *Human, All-Too-Human*, this is the passage in which his famous terms "master morality" and "slave morality" are introduced.

[2] These crucial qualifications, though added immediately, have often been overlooked. "Modern" moralities are clearly mixtures; hence their manifold tensions, hypocrisies, and contradictions.

does not need approval; it judges, "what is harmful to me is harmful in itself"; it knows itself to be that which first accords honor to things; it is *value-creating*. Everything it knows as part of itself it honors: such a morality is self-glorification. In the foreground there is the feeling of fullness, of power that seeks to overflow, the happiness of high tension, the consciousness of wealth that would give and bestow: the noble human being, too, helps the unfortunate, but not, or almost not, from pity, but prompted more by an urge begotten by excess of power. The noble human being honors himself as one who is powerful, also as one who has power over himself, who knows how to speak and be silent, who delights in being severe and hard with himself and respects all severity and hardness. "A hard heart Wotan put into my breast," says an old Scandinavian saga: a fitting poetic expression, seeing that it comes from the soul of a proud Viking. Such a type of man is actually proud of the fact that he is *not* made for pity, and the hero of the saga therefore adds as a warning: "If the heart is not hard in youth it will never harden." Noble and courageous human beings who think that way are furthest removed from that morality which finds the distinction of morality precisely in pity, or in acting for others, or in *désintéressement;* faith in oneself, pride in oneself, a fundamental hostility and irony against "selflessness" belong just as definitely to noble morality as does a slight disdain and caution regarding compassionate feelings and a "warm heart."

It is the powerful who *understand* how to honor; this is their art, their realm of invention. The profound reverence for age and tradition—all law rests on this double reverence—the faith and prejudice in favor of ancestors and disfavor of those yet to come are typical of the morality of the powerful; and when the men of "modern ideas," conversely, believe almost instinctively in "progress" and "the future" and more and more lack respect for age, this in itself would sufficiently betray the ignoble origin of these "ideas."

A morality of the ruling group, however, is most alien and embarrassing to the present taste in the severity of its principle that one has duties only to one's peers; that against beings of a lower rank, against everything alien, one may behave as one pleases or "as the heart desires," and in any case "beyond good and evil"—here pity and like feelings may find their place.[3] The capacity for, and the duty of, long gratitude and long revenge—both only among one's peers—refinement in repaying, the sophisticated concept of friendship, a certain necessity for having enemies (as it were, as drainage ditches for the affects of envy, quarrelsomeness, exuberance—at bottom, in order to be capable of being good *friends*): all these are typical characteristics of noble morality which, as suggested, is not the morality

---

[3] The final clause that follows the dash, omitted in the Cowan translation, is crucial and qualifies the first part of the sentence: a noble person has no *duties* to animals but treats them in accordance with his feelings, which means, if he is noble, with pity.

The ruling masters, of course, are not always noble in this sense, and this is recognized by Nietzsche in *Twilight of the Idols,* in the chapter "The 'Improvers' of Mankind," in which he gives strong expression to his distaste for Manu's laws concerning outcastes (*Portable Nietzsche,* pp. 503–05); also in *The Will to Power* (ed. W. Kaufmann, New York, Random House, 1967), section 142. Indeed, in *The Antichrist,* section 57, Nietzsche contradicts outright his formulation above: "When the exceptional human being treats the mediocre more tenderly than himself and his peers, this is not mere courtesy of the heart—it is simply his *duty.*"

More important: Nietzsche's obvious distaste for slave morality and the fact that he makes a point of liking master morality better does not imply that he endorses master morality.

of "modern ideas" and therefore is hard to empathize with today, also hard to dig up and uncover.[4]

It is different with the second type of morality, *slave morality.* Suppose the violated, oppressed, suffering, unfree, who are uncertain of themselves and weary, moralize: what will their moral valuations have in common? Probably, a pessimistic suspicion about the whole condition of man will find expression, perhaps a condemnation of man along with his condition. The slave's eye is not favorable to the virtues of the powerful: he is skeptical and suspicious, *subtly* suspicious, of all the "good" that is honored there—he would like to persuade himself that even their happiness is not genuine. Conversely, those qualities are brought out and flooded with light which serve to ease existence for those who suffer: here pity, the complaisant and obliging hand, the warm heart, patience, industry, humility, and friendliness are honored—for here these are the most useful qualities and almost the only means for enduring the pressure of existence. Slave morality is essentially a morality of utility.

Here is the place for the origin of that famous opposition of "good" and "evil": into evil one's feelings project power and dangerousness, a certain terribleness, subtlety, and strength that does not permit contempt to develop. According to slave morality, those who are "evil" thus inspire fear; according to master morality it is precisely those who are "good" that inspire, and wish to inspire, fear, while the "bad" are felt to be contemptible.

The opposition reaches its climax when, as a logical consequence of slave morality, a touch of disdain is associated also with the "good" of this morality—this may be slight and benevolent—because the good human being has to be *undangerous* in the slaves' way of thinking: he is good-natured, easy to deceive, a little stupid perhaps, *un bonhomme.*[5] Wherever slave morality becomes preponderant, language tends to bring the words "good" and "stupid" closer together.

One last fundamental difference: the longing for *freedom,* the instinct for happiness and the subtleties of the feeling of freedom belong just as necessarily to slave morality and morals as artful and enthusiastic reverence and devotion are the regular symptom of an aristocratic way of thinking and evaluating.

This makes plain why love *as passion*—which is our European specialty—simply must be of noble origin: as is well known, its invention must be credited to the Provencal knight-poets, those magnificent and inventive human beings of the *"gai saber"*[6] to whom Europe owes so many things and almost owes itself.

Among the things that may be hardest to understand for a noble human being is vanity: he will be tempted to deny it, where another type of human being could not find it more palpable. The problem for him is to imagine people who seek to

[4] Clearly, master morality cannot be discovered by introspection nor by the observation of individuals who are "masters" rather than "slaves." Both of these misunderstandings are widespread. What is called for is rather a rereading of, say, the *Iliad* and, to illustrate "slave morality," the New Testament.
[5] Literally "a good human being," the term is used for precisely the type described here.
[6] "Gay science": in the early fourteenth century the term was used to designate the art of the troubadours. codified in *Leys d'amours.* Nietzsche subtitled his own *Fröhliche Wissenschaft* (1882), *"la gaya scienza,"* placed a quatrain on the title page, began the book with a fifteen-page "Prelude in German Rhymes," and in the second edition (1887) added, besides a Preface and Book V, an "Appendix" of further verses.

create a good opinion of themselves which they do not have of themselves—and thus also do not "deserve"—and who nevertheless end up *believing* this good opinion themselves. This strikes him half as such bad taste and lack of self-respect, and half as so baroquely irrational, that he would like to consider vanity as exceptional, and in most cases when it is spoken of he doubts it.

He will say, for example: "I may be mistaken about my value and nevertheless demand that my value, exactly as I define it, should be acknowledged by others as well—but this is no vanity (but conceit or, more frequently, what is called 'humility' or 'modesty')." Or: "For many reasons I may take pleasure in the good opinion of others: perhaps because I honor and love them and all their pleasures give me pleasure; perhaps also because their good opinion confirms and strengthens my faith in my own good opinion; perhaps because the good opinion of others, even in cases where I do not share it, is still useful to me or promises to become so—but all that is not vanity."

The noble human being must force himself, with the aid of history, to recognize that, since time immemorial, in all somehow dependent social strata the common man *was* only what he was *considered:* not at all used to positing values himself, he also attached no other value to himself than his masters attached to him (it is the characteristic *right of masters* to create values).

It may be understood as the consequence of an immense atavism that even now the ordinary man still always *waits* for an opinion about himself and then instinctively submits to that—but by no means only a "good" opinion; also a bad and unfair one (consider, for example, the great majority of the self-estimates and self-underestimates that believing women accept from their father-confessors, and believing Christians quite generally from their church).

In accordance with the slowly arising democratic order of things (and its cause, the intermarriage of masters and slaves), the originally noble and rare urge to ascribe value to oneself on one's own and to "think well" of oneself will actually be encouraged and spread more and more now; but it is always opposed by an older, ampler, and more deeply ingrained propensity—and in the phenomenon of "vanity" this older propensity masters the younger one. The vain person is delighted by *every* good opinion he hears of himself (quite apart from all considerations of its utility, and also apart from truth or falsehood), just as every bad opinion of him pains him: for he submits to both, he *feels* subjected to them in accordance with that oldest instinct of submission that breaks out in him.

It is "the slave" in the blood of the vain person, a residue of the slave's craftiness—and how much "slave" is still residual in woman, for example!—that seeks to *seduce* him to good opinions about himself; it is also the slave who afterwards immediately prostrates himself before these opinions as if he had not called them forth.

And to say it once more: vanity is an atavism. . . .

At the risk of displeasing innocent ears I propose: egoism belongs to the nature of a noble soul—I mean that unshakable faith that to a being such as "we are" other beings must be subordinate by nature and have to sacrifice themselves. The noble soul accepts this fact of its egoism without any question mark, also without any feeling that it might contain hardness, constraint, or caprice, rather as something that may be founded in the primordial law of things: if it sought a name for this fact it would say, "it is justice itself." Perhaps it admits under certain circumstances that at first make it hesitate that there are some who have rights equal to its own; as soon as this matter of rank is settled it moves among these equals with their equal privileges, showing the same sureness of modesty and delicate reverence that characterize its relations with itself—in accordance with an innate heavenly mechanism understood by all stars. It is merely another aspect of its egoism, this refinement and self-limitation in its relations with its equals—every star is such an egoist—it honors *itself* in them and in the rights it cedes to them; it does not doubt that the exchange of honors and rights is of the nature of all social relations and thus also belongs to the natural condition of things.

The noble soul gives as it takes, from that passionate and irritable instinct of repayment that lies in its depth. The concept "grace"[7] has no meaning or good odor *inter pares*;[8] there may be a sublime way of letting presents from above happen to one, as it were, and to drink them up thirstily like drops—but for this art and gesture the noble soul has no aptitude. Its egoism hinders it: quite generally it does not like to look "up"—but either *ahead*, horizontally and slowly, or down: *it knows itself to be at a height.*

JOHN AUSTIN
(1790–1859) English Jurist

Analysis of the Term Right*

I have endeavoured in the preceding Lectures to accomplish the following objects: 1st, To determine the essentials of a Law (in the largest signification which can be given to the term *properly*): 2ndly, To distinguish the laws proper which are set by God to Man, and the laws proper and improper which are sanctioned or oblige *morally*, from the laws proper which are sanctioned or oblige *legally*, or are established directly or indirectly by *sovereign* authority.

Having attempted to determine generally the nature of Law, and to mark the boundaries of the field which is occupied by the science of Jurisprudence, I shall

[7] *"Gnade."*
[8] Among equals.

*From John Austin, *Lectures on Jurisprudence*, 5th ed., ed. by Robert Campbell (London: John Murray, 1885).

now endeavour is unfold (as briefly as I can) the essential properties of Rights: meaning by Rights, *legal* rights, or rights which are creatures of Law, strictly or simply so called.

There are, indeed, Rights which arise from other sources: namely, from the laws of God or Nature, and from laws which are sanctioned morally. But the peculiarities of these may be easily collected, by considering the peculiarities of the sources from which they flow. Accordingly, I shall not pause to examine them in a direct or formal manner, although I shall advert to them occasionally in the course of the ensuing Lectures. At present I dismiss them with the following remarks. 1st, Like the Obligations to which they correspond, natural and moral Rights (or rights which are merely sanctioned religiously or morally) are *imperfect.* In other words, they are not armed with the legal sanction, or cannot be enforced judicially. 2ndly, The Rights (if such they can be called) which are conferred by positive morality, partake of the nature of the source from which they emanate.— So far as positive morality consists of laws *improper,* the rights which are said to arise from it are rights *by way* of *analogy.*

For example, rights which are derived from the Law of Nations are related to rights which are derived from positive Law, by a remote or faint resemblance. They are neither armed with the legal sanction, nor are they creatures of Law established by *determinate* superiors.

Strictly speaking, there are no rights but those which are the creatures of law; and I speak of any other kind of rights only in order that I may conform to the received language, which certainly does allow us to speak of moral rights not sanctioned by law; thus, for example, we speak of rights created by treaty. . . .

Since rights reside in *persons,* and *since persons, things, acts,* and *forbearances* are the subjects or objects of rights, I must advert to the respective significations of these various related expressions, before I address myself to rights and to the obligations with which they correlate.

Persons are divisible into two classes:—physical or natural persons, and legal or fictitious persons.

In this instance, *"physical"* or *"natural"* bears the signification which is usually attached to it in the language of Jurisprudence, and (I believe) in the language of other sciences. Its import is negative. It denotes a person not fictitious or legal, and is used to distinguish persons, properly so called, from persons which are such by a figment, and for the sake of brevity in discourse. Consequently, when we speak of *"persons"* simply, and without *opposing* them to legal or fictitious persons, we mean persons properly so called, or persons physical or natural.

By a physical or natural *person,* or, by a *person* simply, I mean *homo,* or a *man,* in the largest signification of the term: that is to say, as including *every* being which can be deemed *human.* This is the meaning which is given to the term person, in familiar discourse. And this, I believe, is the meaning which is given to it by the Roman Lawyers (from whose writings it has been borrowed by modern jurists) when they denote by it a physical or natural person, and not a legal or fictitious one.

Many of the modern Civilians have narrowed the import of the term person as meaning a physical or natural person.

They define a person thus: *"homo*, cum *statu* suo consideratus": a "human being, invested with a condition or *status.*" And, in this definition, they use the term *status* in a restricted sense: As including only those conditions which comprise *rights;* and as excluding conditions which are purely onerous or burthensome, or which consist of duties merely. According to this definition, human beings who have no rights are not *persons,* but *things;* being classed with other things which have no rights residing in themselves, but are merely the subjects of rights residing in others. Such, in the Roman Law, down to the age of the Antonines, was the position of the *slave.* In respect of his master, and also in respect of strangers, he was subject to Obligations or Duties. But he had no Rights as against his master, or even as against strangers. His master might deal with him, as if he had been a *thing* of which his master was the owner:—might use, abuse, and even destroy him, without stint or measure, and with absolute impunity. In case he were killed or maltreated by a third party, the act was not a wrong against the slave himself, but was merely an offence against the dominion or property which resided in the master. In a word, the slave (like a thing) was susceptible of *damage,* but was not susceptible of *injury.* "Servo ipsi nulla injuria intelligitur fieri: sed domino *per cum* fieri videtur."

Agreeably to this definition, as understood by the modern civilians above mentioned, a *person* is a human being invested with *rights.* Or a *person* is a human being capable of *rights.*

But this, I am convinced, was not the notion attached to the term *"person"* by the Roman Lawyers themselves, when they denoted by it a physical or natural person. . . .

In these passages from the Institutes of Gaius (and in various corresponding passages in the Institutes and Digest of Justinian) slaves (who had no rights) are treated as a class of *persons,* and *"homo"* and *"persona"* are applied indifferently, or as if they were equivalent expressions. And, in penning these passages, the attention of the authors must have been particularly directed to the just legal import of the term "person." For the purpose with which they were occupied was the division of persons, or the distribution of persons into *genera* and *species.*

Secondly, Although the slave had no rights, there are numerous places in the Institutes of Gaius, in the Institutes of Justinian, and also in his Digest or Pandects, in which a *status* or condition is ascribed to the slave, or in which the slave is spoken of as bearing a *status* or condition.

Even, therefore, if we admit that the definition in question will apply to the term *"person,"* and that a person is a human being bearing a condition or *status,* it will not follow that the term *"person"* is exclusively applicable to such human beings as are invested with *rights.*

If we admit the definition, while we look at the true import of the term *status,* the meaning of *"person"* is this: namely, a human being considered as *invested with rights,* or considered as *subject to duties.*

Taking the term in that meaning, it would apply to every human creature, if a member of a political society, and not sovereign therein. It could not apply to a human being not a member of any political society, for a human being in that situation has no legal rights, and is free from legal obligations. Nor, taken in that meaning, can it apply to a monarch, for as I have before observed, we cannot say with correctness, that sovereigns have legal rights, nor that they are subject to legal obligations. Obligations are imposed, and rights conferred by *laws.* He, therefore, who has rights, or who lies under obligations, occupies a position wherein sovereigns are not. He is in a state of subjection, or in a habit of obedience, to some determinate superior from whom he receives the law.

But, according to the meaning which was attached to it by the Roman Lawyers, neither of the significations in question belongs to the term *"person."* They neither confined it to human beings, considered as invested with rights; nor did they even restrict it to human beings, considered as subject to obligations. The meaning which they attached to the term, is the familiar or vulgar meaning. With them *"persona"* denoted *"homo,"* or *any* being which can be styled *human.*

The modern limitation of the term *"person"* to *"human beings considered as invested with rights,"* appears to have arisen thus: 1st, A *person* was defined by many of the modern Civilians, "a human being bearing a *status* or condition." 2ndly, The authors of the definition used the term *"status"* in a peculiar and narrow sense. They assumed that every *status* comprises *rights,* or, at least, comprises capacities to acquire or take rights. They assumed that a *status* or condition could not be ascribed to any one who was excluded from all rights, and was simply subject to duties. Now there is no classical authority for defining a person, "a human being bearing a *status* or condition." And further, I could cite numerous passages from the Classical Jurists, in which a *status* or condition is ascribed to the *slave:* That is to say, to a human being who is excluded from rights; and whose condition or *status* is therefore purely onerous, or consists of duties merely. The truth appears to be that the authors of the definition considered the term *"status"* as equivalent to the term *"caput":* a word denoting conditions of a particular class: conditions which *do* comprise rights, and comprise rights so numerous and important, that the conditions or *status* of which those rights are constituent parts, are marked and distinguished by a name importing preeminence.

For the purpose of ascertaining the meaning which should be assigned to the term *status,* I have searched the meanings which were annexed to it by the Roman Lawyers, through the Institutes of Gaius and Justinian, and through the more voluminous Digest of the latter. And the result at which I have arrived is this: that *status* and *caput* are not synonymous expressions, but that the term *caput* signifies certain conditions which are *capital* or principal: which cannot be acquired and cannot be lost, without a mighty and conspicuous change in the legal position of the party. Such, for instance, are the *status libertatis* and the *status civitatis:* that is to say, the condition of the freeman, as opposed to the condition of the slave; and the condition of the citizen or member of the political society, as opposed to the condition of the foreigner.

Whatever may be the meanings of these terms as they are used by the Roman Lawyers, it is certain that they are not synonymous. For a condition or *status* is repeatedly ascribed to the slave, and yet it is affirmed of the slave "that he has *nullum caput."*

It is much to be wished, that the difference between them could be ascertained. For of all the perplexing questions which the science of Jurisprudence presents, the notion of *status* or *condition* is incomparably the most difficult. And much of the obscurity in which it is involved, arises from the manner in which it has been treated by the modern Commentators upon the Roman Law: Particularly from their habit of restricting the import of *"status,"* and of using it as if it were equivalent to the narrower expression *"caput."*

I think, then, that I am justified by authority, as well as by the convenience which results from it, in imputing to the term *person* (as denoting a physical or natural person) the familiar or vulgar meaning; or in considering a physical or natural *person* as exactly equivalent to "man" (in the largest signification of the term).

If *persona* (as meaning *man*) be equivalent to *homo*, and be not exclusively applicable to "men *invested with rights*," it follows that the slave is a *person*, though he be excluded from rights. If, indeed, we consider him from a certain aspect, we may, in a certain sense, style him a *thing*. But almost every person may be considered from a similar aspect, and may also be styled a *thing*, with equal propriety. As I shall show more fully when I get further on, persons must be considered from three points of view: As invested with rights; as lying under obligations or duties; and as being the subjects or objects of rights and obligations.

I have hitherto considered the *extension* of the term *"person"* as denoting a human being. And in regard to the extension of the term, *as denoting a human being*, I believe that Classical Jurists, when they used it with that meaning, used it with the large signification which it bears in familiar discourse:—as being synonymous with *"homo,"* or as applying to every being which can be styled *human*.

But, instead of denoting *men* (or human *beings*), it sometimes denotes the *conditions* or *status* with which men are invested. And taking the term in this signification, every human being who has rights and duties bears a *number* of persons. "Unus homo sustinet *plures* personas." For example, every human being who has rights and duties, is *citizen* or *foreigner*: that is to say, he is either a member of a *given* independent society, or he is not a member of that given independent society. He is also a *son*. Probably, he is *husband* and *father*. It may happen, moreover, that he is *guardian* or *tutor*. His *profession* or *calling* may give him distinctive rights, or may subject him to distinctive duties. And with the various conditions or *status* of citizen, son, husband, father, guardian, advocate, attorney, or trader, he may combine the condition of judge, or of member of the supreme legislature, and so on to infinity.

The term *"person,"* as denoting a condition or *status*, is therefore equivalent to *character*. It signified originally, a mask worn by a player, and distinguishing the character which he represented from the other characters in the piece. From the mask which expressed the character, it was extended to the character itself. From characters represented by players, or from dramatic characters, it was further extended by a metaphor to conditions or *status*. For men, as subjects of law, are distinguished by their respective *conditions*; just as players, performing a play, are distinguished by the several *persons* which they respectively enact or sustain.

By the Greek commentators on the Roman Law, or by those who have translated the expositions of the Roman Law into Greek (as Theophilus), *persona* is translated by the word πρόσωπον, which signifies a visage or face, and is obviously meant to denote character or *status*, and not in the other import.

The term *"person"* has, therefore, two meanings, which must be carefully distinguished. It denotes a *man* or *human being*; or it signifies some *condition* borne by a man. A person (as meaning a man) is one or individual: But a *single* or *individual* person (meaning a man) may sustain a *number* of persons (meaning conditions or status). The erroneous definition of a *person* to which I have already adverted, probably arose in part from a confusion of these significations. Every *status* or condition consists of rights or duties; or it consists of both. And if we impute to a person (as meaning a *man*) this essential of a person (as meaning a *condition*), it will follow that a person (as meaning a man) must be defined thus: A man invested with rights, or subject to obligations.

The further limitation of the term *"person"* to "a man *invested with rights,"* probably arose (as I intimated before) from an erroneous limitation of the term *"status"*: from the restriction of the term to certain *capital* conditions, which consist of *rights* as well as of duties; and wherein the rights are the more conspicuous and distinctive constituents or components. A Roman Citizen, for instance, was of course distinguished from a foreigner, chiefly by the numerous rights which he enjoyed: so was a freeman from a slave: insomuch that he who was reduced from the more advantageous of these situations to the other was said to undergo *capitis deminutio:* so predominating was the idea of the rights which he lost over that of the duties from which he became freed, although by the same event by which he lost the rights he became freed from the duties also. This last mentioned error, in short, arose from the confusion of *status* (the larger of generic expression) with *caput* (the narrower or specific).

BETH J. SINGER
Brooklyn College, CUNY

Having Rights*

Do non-human animals have rights? The issue I wish to address in this paper is not whether we are or ought to be morally obligated to treat other animals humanely or whether or not it is morally wrong to kill them. I am concerned instead with the question whether moral issues concerning behavior toward members of other animal species are properly treated as issues involving rights.

In speaking of rights here, what I am referring to is rights as they are actually operative in social life. By "having rights" I shall mean participation in operative rights. Individuals are often said, especially in the context of theories of "natural" or "human" rights, to "have" rights even in societies where those rights are not operative. I prefer to distinguish between operative rights—those which prevail in a given social context—and those which *ought to be* operative, and to say that

*From *Philosophy and Social Criticism* 4(1986): 391–412.

the only rights any being "has" are those actually operative for him or her. To claim to have a right that is not operative is to mean that it ought to be so. In a subsequent paper, I plan to show why certain fundamental rights ought to be operative for every member of every community. I should add that, in saying that no one has rights unless they are operative, I do not mean to suggest that for any being to have a right this right must be conferred by a state or government. On the contrary, it follows from the analysis I shall propose that rights become operative, not when formally conferred or enacted (although this may serve to foster or reinforce them), but when the members of a community respect them. A right may be operative, in this sense, and not be law, or it may be a law and still not be operative.

One way to approach the question of animal rights is to ask whether animals, or some animals, are the kind of beings that *can* have rights. Feinberg, for example, asks whether the beings in question are capable of having interests. Regan asks whether they have "inherent value," the value, according to him, of beings with beliefs, desires, the faculties of perception and memory, an emotional life, a sense of the future, preferences, the capacity for suffering. But any answer to the question what qualifies a being to have rights presupposes a concept of the nature of rights and of what is involved in having them. I propose to reexamine this concept within a theoretical framework derived largely from George Herbert Mead and to show the implications of this analysis of rights for the question of animal rights.

While he wrote explicitly on the subject of rights and on the issue of natural rights, Mead's analysis of rights as such is articulated primarily in *Mind, Self, and Society,* where rights are used to illustrate Mead's theory of organized social interaction. The same analysis is summarized in "The Genesis of the Self and Social Control." The view of rights I shall present is grounded in Mead's analysis, but it is not identical with his and goes beyond it in several respects. Therefore, while I hope this paper will contribute to a greater understanding and appreciation of Mead's work in this area, it should be read as an essay on the concept of rights rather than as one on Mead's thought.

In developing my view I will not always use Mead's terminology. For example, one of Mead's key words is "attitude," and I shall use it frequently. But Mead sometimes speaks of what he calls an attitude as a "perspective," using this word in a sense that is consonant with that in which I have employed it elsewhere, a sense derived from Justus Buchler. In certain contexts, I shall use "perspective" instead of "attitude." Mead uses the names "community" and "society" interchangeably to refer to any organized social entity, from a small face-to-face group to one as wide as a nation. For the most part I shall use the word community. With a generic sense of "community" in mind, for which I have used the name, "perspectival community," I shall distinguish the kind of community Mead is talking about as a "normative community." The word "norm" is not used at all by Mead, but it is employed in social science, and the attitudes of which Mead speaks function normatively in governing the behavior of the members of a community.

I shall be primarily concerned with Mead's theory of social institutions and social control. It is the mechanism of social control, as he analyzes it, which Mead sees to make organized behavior possible and to enable individuals to be members of communities. He shows this mechanism to be at the heart of the social institution of rights. The same mechanism is involved in the development of the individual self and of mind. Mead is as much concerned with self and mind as he is with society, for he finds both to evolve together as an organism learns to participate in organized social interaction, and he conceives the self as a self-conscious process. What I have to say does not require any discussion of mind, but it should be noted that Mead's functional treatment of this concept, that of a "social behaviorist," is designed to avoid the philosophic problems of introspectionist psychology. Mead conceives experience, self, and mind in terms of the process of communication rather than in terms of subjective awareness. He does not deny that experience has an "inner phase," but his focus is on the "social act," that is, "the class of acts which involve the co-operation of more than one individual, and whose object is . . . found in the life-process of the group, not in those of the separate individuals alone." Thus, utilizing his theory will not involve us in issues concerning the privacy of experience or the existence of minds as entities.

What sort of complex is a right? A common and much-discussed way of defining it is to say that it is a claim, or, in some versions, a justified, justifiable, or valid claim. To review all the arguments and counter-arguments concerning this conception of a right would take far too much space and would divert me from my main objective, which is to present an analysis of a right which differs from those that are prominent in recent discussion. I shall confine my treatment of the idea that rights are claims to a few points that are directly relevant to the view I shall propose.

One can claim a right, i.e., make or voice the claim that one has or ought to have it; but if the right is itself a claim, it is the kind of claim that is had rather than one that is uttered. A right to fair treatment, for example, is a claim one has on (some would say "against") the community. Concerning claims in this sense, I would concede Alan R. White's point that the expression, "to have a justified (or justifiable or valid) claim," is redundant, for if a purported claim were not justified or valid we could say that its supposed possessor had no claim. But not every claim that is had is a right. For example, to have a claim on someone's affections is to have the power to inspire affection in that person, not to have any sort of right. The kind of claim that is a right is an entitlement. A being that has such possesses some good. Yet not all entitlements are rights. One may be entitled to credit or praise for doing a job well, but entitlement in this case is desert, not right. The credit or praise is warranted but not obligatory or owed. To be a right, a claim must be an entitlement which it is not only appropriate but obligatory to honor. Respect for an entitlement of this sort is owed to the one who has it, and we would hold failure to respect it, whether on the part of individuals or the community, to be morally wrong. If there were no obligation to respect or honor it, the entitlement would not be of the sort we call a right.

Whether or not every obligation is associated with a reciprocal entitlement, an entitlement that qualifies as a right carries with it a correlative obligation to respect it. There is indeed a logically necessary connection between the concept of a right and that of the obligation to respect it; each is defined, and is only intelligible with reference to the other. To say that there is an entitlement that we would call a right means that respect for it is obligatory. That there is such an obligation means that the entitlement is a right. Part of what I hope to show in this paper is that the necessary connection between entitlement and obligation in the concept of a right reflects a connection that is not logical but sociopsychological, a function of the nature of social institutions and the mechanisms involved in the social control of behavior.

I have spoken thus far, in the conventional way, of "having rights," and have suggested that a right is a kind of entitlement. But to speak of rights as entitlements is elliptical. What we are referring to when we speak of a right is an entitlement together with the correlative obligation to respect it. To identify the right with the entitlement alone is to omit the specification that makes it a rights-entitlement. Strictly, the right is a relation: a relation between the entitlement and the obligation, a relation which can be symbolized as **e** ⓡ **o**. Provisionally, I shall so define it. Where a right exists, where this relation is exemplified, there is a relation between a being (or beings) that is (are) entitled and beings that are obligated to respect the entitlement. Rather than "having" rights, we should be said to "participate in" them. To say, colloquially, "**S** has a right," is to mean that **S** is a participant in a rights-relation, **e** ⓡ **o**, and occupies the position of **e**, the party with a rights-entitlement. Alternatively, we may say that **S** "plays the role of" **e** in this relation. The same being, **S**, may also be involved, whether in this or other rights-relations, in the position of **o**, the party obliged to respect the entitlement. To avoid awkwardness, we may continue to speak of "having rights," provided we recognize that we are using this expression to designate the having of rights-entitlements, and I shall sometimes employ this locution. And since it would be confusing to call the relation itself a right, I shall refer to it as a "rights-relation."

A rights-relation is a social relation, one in which individuals are jointly involved. It is also a normative relation, one that serves to regulate the behavior of the participants. An important feature of this relation is its asymmetry. It involves two different positions or roles, and while these can only be understood in relation to one another, it would seem that a being could play one of the roles without playing the other: could be obligated to respect an entitlement it did not possess, or possess an entitlement without being obligated to respect similar entitlements. If this is the case, it is possible that a being that is not eligible for one of the roles or not capable of fulfilling it could yet have the other role. This is an important consideration in connection with the issue of animal rights, since we do not hold other animals obligated to respect rights, and they cannot do so. If they have a right to life, we have an obligation not to kill them, but even if this is the case, they have, and can have, no such obligation toward us or toward one another. The killing of a human being by a tiger or a bull is horrifying but not morally wrong.

Not everyone agrees that beings who cannot be obligated can have rights (i.e., entitlements). One who does not is A. I. Melden, who contends that rights obtain only among members of what he refers to as "the moral community." The moral community is the community of moral agents, all of whom, according to Melden, are obligated to respect one another's fundamental right to pursue their own interests. All persons, he holds, are equally members of the moral community, and it is only because they are thus respected as moral agents with the basic rights that persons can have any special rights. The moral community is also a community of understanding. Rights and obligations "exist only where there is a community of understanding of the complex array of moral concepts within which the concepts of a right and an obligation have their place, and paradigmatically, when the setting appropriate for the enjoyment and exercise of rights is present."

Let us grant that moral agents do respect one another, do have mutual rights and obligations, and that the existence of rights requires a framework of concepts in terms of which they are intelligible and the conditions under which entitlements and obligations can be exercised and fulfilled. It is conceivable that the members of a moral community might, on the very basis of their shared moral understanding, agree to ascribe entitlements to other beings whom they found some reason to respect, even if those beings were not themselves moral agents and could not respect other beings or their entitlements. Given that moral agents have both obligations and entitlements, why should it be that they cannot grant entitlements to other beings, or that those beings should be ineligible for them? The answer provided by Melden's theory is that, in their lives, which are perforce social and joined together with those of others, moral agents exhibit traits in virtue of which we ascribe, and ought to ascribe, to them the moral status of members of the moral community, beings with rights. And, he holds, only the lives of persons exhibit these traits.

The reason for the ascription of rights, Melden contends, lies in

> those general and familiar features of the lives of persons which are accessible to all of us: the fact that they have interests in the pursuit of which they seek to achieve a variety of goods for themselves and for others; the fact that these interests are intelligible to us and that they and the goods they define are in large measure similar to our own; the fact that their lives like our own are bound by love and affection with those of others within the circle of their own family and friends; the fact that like ourselves they are beings who carry on their affairs with others to whom they are not bound by love and affection but with whose well-being they are concerned, adjusting their desires and their concerns to theirs, and in joining their lives with them give them the support they need and require for the successful pursuit of their endeavors.

"The philosophical understanding of the rights of human beings," Melden insists, "must come to rest on nothing less, and on nothing else than, this enormously complicated and moral form of human life itself" [Ibid.]. This is to say that "qua human being" a person "has rights and as such is a full-fledged member of the moral community."

Even Melden acknowledges that, if it be taken as an argument about the "basis" of human rights, what he says here is circular. But he takes it instead to be a description of "just what it is for persons to have the rights they have as human beings." Assuming the description to be accurate, it does not seem to preclude humans' having a measure of respect for nonhuman beings, even if we do not have the same respect for them as for humans. Respect might rest, for example, on the fact that in their lives some nonhuman beings exhibit some traits of moral agents, as field studies indicate that they do. (There are species in which care and protection of the young is shared by a group of adults; species in which individuals—exposing themselves to danger—utter cries of warning, and so forth.) That the moral form of human social life is more developed and pervasive does not seem to rule out the ascription to these other beings of a fundamental right to pursue their own individual and collective interests. Could we not, then, grant them rights such as the right to be spared the wanton destruction of their natural habitat? What is required for us to determine whether beings who cannot respect rights-entitlements are qualified to have them, it seems to me, is not the more detailed description, called for by Melden, of the ways persons reveal themselves to be moral agents, but an analysis of the rights-relation itself in order to determine what is involved in both its constituent roles. Is there some intrinsic connection between being entitled, in the way we call "having a right," and being obligated to respect such entitlements? This is a distinct question from that concerning the necessary connection between the two concepts. It is a question about a social relation rather than a logical one. As I shall show, G. H. Mead sheds a unique light on this issue.

For Mead, as for Melden, rights obtain only within a community. However, this community is not as such a community of moral agents. It is a community of selves, beings who regulate their joint behavior and their mutual relations by the same organized set of social norms, the social institutions of that community. The existence of rights is such an institution. As I shall show, it follows from Mead's general analysis of social institutions, i.e., his analysis of norm-governed social interaction, that to take the role in a rights-relation of the party entitled is also to take the role of one who is obligated to respect the entitlement, so that a being incapable of respect for rights is also incapable of having them.

The model for Mead's analysis is that of a game. For the sake of clarity, let us first think of a game such as checkers, in which two players have identical roles, the same objectives and the same set of options. To play the game, two individuals must both regulate their conduct by the same set of rules. Each must make moves defined as legitimate by the moves of the other and as means to the appropriate end. Such behavior differs, on the one hand, from an exchange of instinctive or biologically determined reactions and, on the other, from mere imitation of the sort in which a solitary child engages when walking about in its parent's shoes. In the game, each move is a gesture to which the other player responds in a way provided for by the rules. By giving both players the same repertoire of responses to every pertinent gesture, the rules not only guide each of them individually but insure that their play is reciprocally coordinated. That is, the rules give each gesture the same meaning to both players, converting it into what Mead calls a "significant symbol." Both players use these symbols in the same ways in determining their responses to one another. Linguistic gestures are said by Mead to be the most important significant symbols, but not the only ones, and I believe that nonlinguistic gestures play a more important part in social interaction (and in Mead's analysis of it) than Mead formally acknowledges.

The rules of a game comprise an organized set of norms in accordance with which the players regulate their participation. Internalized by both, this set of norms constitutes a common perspective or "attitude," as Mead calls it. Having this "general" or "generalized" attitude, each player can anticipate what the other is likely to do in response to any legitimate move and, conversely, can view her own moves as the other would, and can utilize both these understandings in plotting her strategy. That is, each player can play because she can "put herself in the place of the other"—in Mead's language, she can "take the attitude of the other."

Mead speaks both of "taking" and of "having" the attitude of the other, but does not make a clear distinction between the two. As will become apparent in what follows, I take the distinction to be important and, moreover, I think we must distinguish two senses of "having an attitude." In behaviorist terms, an attitude can be defined as the disposition of an agent to control or direct his or her behavior in a particular way. (Mead speculates about the neurological basis of the ability to do this.) Trying, characteristically, to define an attitude as a way in which an organism functions, he states that "by 'attitude' I refer to the adjustment of the organism involved in an impulse ready for expression." To *take* an attitude, then, would be for the organism to make this "adjustment" and hence be ready to behaviorally express the impulse it embodies. It would then seem that to *have* an attitude would be for the organism to be ready to make this adjustment in the appropriate circumstances. However, a being that has an attitude may fail or omit or even refuse to adopt it in a situation in which it would be appropriate. An example of the latter would be when a law-abiding individual decides nevertheless to engage in civil disobedience. Another would be when someone declines to return a proferred handshake, even while recognizing it as calling for the reciprocal gesture. Thus we need to distinguish between "having an attitude" in the strong sense of having a disposition to take it in appropriate circumstance, and having it in the weaker sense of *knowing* it, being able to take it appropriately— whether or not one is disposed to do so. To "have an attitude" in the latter sense would be to have it in one's repertoire of adjustments, whether or not one were actually ready or willing to make the adjustment.

An attitude may also be conceived as a kind of perspective, a kind of outlook or orientation, namely, one which determines selected complexes to call for responses of a determinate sort. "We are," Mead says, "especially through the use of vocal gestures, continually arousing in ourselves those responses which we call out in other persons, so that we are taking the attitudes of the other persons into our own conduct." That which calls out the same responses in both— or, as I would prefer to put it, calls for the same responses from both—has the same meaning to both parties. "Meaning," Mead says, "arises in experience through the individual stimulating himself to take the attitude of the other in his reaction toward the object." And in indicating the meaning of an object to another, the individual is "occupying his perspective."

If an attitude is a perspective in which selected complexes call for certain responses, to *take* an attitude (adopt a perspective) is to recognize or judge the complexes to which it applies *as* calling for those responses, and to be ready so to respond. To *have* the attitude, on this view, is at least (i.e., in the weaker sense) to know the perspective as one that is applicable, know how to respond in terms of it to those complexes to which it applies. It is thus to recognize selected complexes as subject to the imperatives embodied in the perspective. To have an attitude in the stronger sense is both to know it and to be ready to adopt it in appropriate circumstances.

In defining the system of mutually responsive gestures that constitute a game, the rules of the game define the role of player and the relation between players (in checkers, a relation between opponents). This is to say that the perspective or attitude by which the game is governed, and which both players share, determines the reciprocal attitudes taken by the players vis-a-vis one another. Having the general attitude enables each player to take the specific attitude proper to each role, and to take each of these attitudes toward both herself and her opponent. This is not because the roles are identical. Not all games are symmetrical as checkers is: Take hide-and-seek, for example. Here, just as in a symmetrical game, by defining all the moves proper to each role and the ways in which the moves are to be employed in response to one another, the rules give each move the same meaning to any player and enable anyone who knows them to play both roles. To play by the rules is to regulate one's moves by the attitude—the set of norms—governing the game. This attitude encompasses the attitudes of both roles in their mutual relatedness. That is, it encompasses the norms governing the ways in which the player of each role can respond to the moves of the other. This enables each player to regulate her play in terms of the expectations of the other— to take the attitude of the other toward herself. To have the general attitude governing the game of hide-and-seek, therefore, is to be able to play either role, and to play one because it is to be able to play the other as well.

No matter how complicated the game, the same principle applies: To play it one must be able to take the attitude proper to any of the roles in the game, and to view one's own play and that of all the other players as they would. This is made possible by having the generalized attitude governing them all.

Insofar as they share in this generalized attitude, Mead holds, the players of a game constitute a community. Having this attitude, which is something over and above the attitudes of the roles it defines, the members of the community collectively function, in relation to each member individually, as an "other." Mead therefore calls the community as such a "generalized other." The player of a game, he says,

> must have the attitude of all others involved in the game. The attitudes of the other players which the participant assumes organize into a sort of unit, and it is that organization which controls the response of the individual. The illustration used was of a person playing baseball. Each one of his own acts is determined by his assumption of the action of the others who are playing the game. What he does is controlled by his being everyone else on that team, at least in so far as those attitudes affect his particular response. We get then an "other" which is an organization of the attitudes of those involved in the same process.

The organized community or social group . . . may be called "the generalized other." The attitude of the generalized other is the attitude of the whole community. Thus, for example, in the case of such a social group as a ball team, the team is the generalized other insofar as it enters—as an organized process or social activity—into the experience of any one of the individual members of it.

As Mead portrays it, the structure of any community, i.e., of all norm-governed social interaction and all social institutions, is essentially that of a game. The members of any group or society are bound together in an organized system of social relations by a common attitude, the attitude of a generalized other. This is also true, he holds, of the participants in "abstract" social organizations such as the system of economic exchange, which transcend particular structured social entities. Having the attitude of the generalized other, the members of a community share a system of responses—meanings—in virtue of which they are able to take one another's attitudes and so to communicate and interact in an organized manner. In "The Objective Reality of Perspectives" (1927), Mead remarks that "it is only insofar as the individual acts not only in his own perspective but also in the perspective of others . . . that a society arises."

In an actual human group or society, we need to remember, there may be individual members who either have not fully assimilated the attitude of the generalized other and do not share all its constituent attitudes, or who have other attitudes that are in some respect incompatible with that of the community. (The fact that an individual belongs to many communities makes the latter likely.) To the extent that this is the case, we would have to say that the bonds of community are weakened. Nevertheless, wherever there is a community in Mead's sense, there is a community of attitude which insofar as it prevails, serves to govern the conjoint activities of the members, whose participation in any of those activities is hampered if they cannot adopt the attitude of the community—the generalized other—toward it.

The concept of the generalized other is Mead's version of the concept of the "general will": "the universal will which could be the will of the individual and yet the will of the community." Mead conceives this to be something like public opinion, which he characterizes as "that attitude which is itself a universal attitude, which goes to make up the character of the individual." "When there is an effective public opinion," he says, "one that really expresses the attitude of everyone in the community, one recognizes it as one that has and will have authority." This authority consists in the attitude's serving to control the social behavior of those who share in it.

Despite the analogy between the social process as such and a game, not all social norms are rules. Norms are institutionalized ways of responding to complexes of any kind. They may or may not be rules, and norms that take the form of rules may or may not be promulgated as laws. Ends and goals, standards, ideals, values, understandings, tastes and preferences, may all be institutionalized in a community. Even sensory perception can be, as we know from cross-cultural studies of color-perception. Norms of all kinds may be ingredient in the general attitude or perspective of a community. By establishing common meanings, the development of a system of norms enables individuals to coordinate their lives together in an organized way. "That which makes society possible," Mead states, "is such common responses, such organized attitudes." Conversely, that which makes it possible for an individual to participate in the life of a community is the internalization of its norms, making the attitude of the generalized other a part of that individual's perspective or character. This does not mean that every member of a community must agree with every other or that all must accept the norms uncritically. What it means is that to be able to respond to a social gesture in a relevant way, even to criticize or oppose it, the individual must have (in the weak sense) the attitude in terms of which that gesture has the meaning it does in that community. As will be shown, Mead holds criticism to be an important factor in the life of a community and of the self. Beyond this, he would have to acknowledge that one may be a member of a community in the sense of sharing in the general attitude that governs it and yet have or adopt particular attitudes that are in conflict with that of the community in some respect. Where this is the case, the tension between the attitudes is replicated within the self; the individual is at least potentially in a state of inner conflict. It should be noted as well that were the organizational structure of a group or society to be dissolved, to the extent that the attitude of the generalized other remained part of the perspectives of its members they would still constitute a community in the sense intended here. The same would hold true if an individual or individuals were to be formally expelled from an organization or group.

Since the perspective of a generalized other comprises a system of norms (or a system of such systems) I shall call a community governed by such a perspective a "normative community." Not all an individual's perspectives are shared with others, although many are bound to be; and not all shared perspectives are those of social institutions. (As examples one may cite the perspectives which tall people or those who are color blind share to the extent that, as a result of these conditions, they respond similarly to the same complexes.) I have used the term "perspectival community" as a name for any collectivity of individuals who share a perspective. A normative community, then, is a species of perspectival community, one whose members are united by a common normative perspective.

Mead shows the norms that govern the life of such a community to arise out of the requirements of cooperative social interaction. By cooperative interaction, Mead means joint behavior having either shared or reciprocally defined objectives, so that competition and conflict, rather than being antithetical to cooperation, are forms of it. Norm-governed interaction evolves among organisms whose highly developed central nervous systems enable them to adopt the responses of others to their own gestures and to regulate their behavior in terms of those responses. By taking one another's attitudes in the attempt to coordinate their actions, such organisms can evolve a comprehensive system of mutually responsive gestures. In the form of habits, dispositions to respond, this system comes to govern the social behavior of each of the members and thereby to regulate the ongoing social process. This is the attitude of the generalized other. "The complex co-operative processes and activities and institutional functionings of organized human society," Mead says, "are . . . possible only in so far as every individual involved in them . . . can take the general attitude of all other such individuals with reference to these processes and activities and institutionalized functionings, and to the organized social whole of experiential relations thereby constituted—and can direct his own behavior accordingly." This is what Mead means by "social control." "It is in the form of the generalized other that the social process influences the behavior of the individuals involved in it and carrying it on, i.e., that the community exercises control over the conduct of its members." This control is only possible to the extent that the attitude of the generalized other of every community to which she belongs is a component of the self of each member, of that aspect of the self Mead calls the "me." The "me" is an organization of social attitudes in the perspective of the individual, comparable in some ways to Heidegger's *"das Man."* It is "the self which arises through the taking of the attitudes of others."

The process in which an organism becomes a self is the same as that in which normative communities and their institutions evolve and are perpetuated. It is the process in which cooperative social behavior and the relations embodied and expressed in that behavior come to be organized and regulated. The attitude of the generalized other, which arises in and thereafter serves to govern this process, incorporated into the "me" of the participants, provides the link between the social institutions and the self. This linkage is central to Mead's understanding of what is involved in the existence of rights.

In learning to respond to its own gestures as others do, an organism becomes aware of itself, self-conscious; in experiencing itself as others experience it, it experiences itself as an other. This other calls out a further response on the part of the individual, who must act. The "I" is that self, or aspect of the self, which is aware of and responds to the "me" and to the situation in which it is involved, and which initiates decision and action. Mead sometimes speaks of the "I" **as** a response: Like the "me," it is a function, a phase of an interactive process, not an entity. In a situation of cooperative interaction, the acts and expressions of the individual elicit responses from that individual herself as well as from others. Insofar as a gesture calls out the same response in the gesturer as in those others, and the gesturer in turn reacts to this response in herself, Mead says, "we have both those contents which go to make the self, the 'other' ['me'] and the 'I'." "The 'I'," as Mead puts it, "both calls out the 'me' and responds to it. The self . . . is essentially a social process going on with these two distinguishable phases."

Whereas the "me" embodies the attitude of the community, the "I" is not inherently bound by this attitude and can react spontaneously. Thus there can occur the "inner dialogue" or "conversation" of reflection. Just as the "I" calls out the "me," the "me" "call[s] for a certain sort of an 'I' in so far as we meet the obligations that are given in conduct itself." As Mead's context makes clear, these "obligations" are not per se moral duties but responses called for by the social norms. (In the language suggested earlier, to have the attitude of the community is at least to know these responses as what is called for.) It is here that social control is exercised. "But," Mead continues, "the 'I' is always something different from what the situation itself calls for." The office of the "I" is to respond, not only to the "me," but to the situation, and it may bring to bear attitudes of the "me" derived from other situations or from other communities to which the individual belongs. Its task is to synthesize, to reorganize or reconstruct the situation within the experience of the individual. The resulting action may therefore reflect something new, to which in turn the community and the self must respond, and which may come to be incorporated in the attitude, not only of the individual "me," but of the generalized other. Mead further maintains that the "I" can project a new, ideal, generalized other, in the light of which it can serve as critic of the "me" and of the social norms. Thus the interplay between the "I" and the "me" is at one and the same time the mechanism of social control and a source of personal growth, individuality and independence; it is not only the means of the establishment and continuance of social norms and institutions, but also the motive force in social change and social reform.

To illustrate the function of the generalized other in social control, Mead uses the institution of property. Property differs from sheer possession in that possession is based only on power, whereas property is based on a common understanding, a collective attitude. An individual can lay claim to something as property "only in so far as he can present evidence that it is his property on bases that everyone else recognizes." Where this institution exists, he says in another context, "there is an organized attitude with reference to property which is common to all members of the community." Those who share this attitude have it both as respecters of property and as its possessors. It is not only that the attitude of the community mandates respect for the property of others; one could neither claim to have property nor treat one's own possessions as property without having the attitude which defines it as property, to be respected by all. To play the role of an owner of property is to take the attitude of the generalized other toward it, which entails taking the attitude of a respecter of property toward oneself as owner. "A man who says 'This is my property'," Mead asserts, "is taking the attitude of the other person." This is because to play any institutionalized social role is to take the attitude of the generalized other governing it, and hence to take the attitudes of other participants towards oneself. The respecter of property is also taking the attitude of the other. One who says, "This is your property," is saying, "With you, I hold others, including myself, obligated to respect your ownership." Any statement that something is someone's property calls out the attitude of the generalized other which determines what property is. And not only the statement, but all conduct relating to property calls out and is governed by the same set of normative responses which must be operative in all property-holding and all transactions pertaining to property. For example, as Mead points out, "One cannot exchange otherwise than by putting oneself in the attitude of the other party to the bargain. Property becomes a tangible object, because all essential phases of property appear in the actions of all those involved in exchange, and appear as essential features of the individual's action." As in playing a game, in participating in the social institution of property it is not possible to play a role without having or knowing (being able to take) the attitudes of the coordinate roles. The normative attitude of the generalized other with regard to property governs them all and must be a component of the "me" of anyone who engages in property dealings.

But, it could be asked, what about an individual who does not have the attitude governing property, or one who repudiates that attitude or professes it insincerely? Can such a one steal with impunity? Of course not. One who did not have the requisite attitude in either of the above-specified senses, might go through the motions of what appears to be a genuine property transaction, but to that individual the item(s) involved would not have the meaning of property. The transaction would be faulty and its validity could be challenged. However, what it means for property to be institutionalized in a community is for the members, as members, to be bound by the norms governing property, so that a member who did not have the appropriate attitude would have an obligation to acquire it, analogous to the obligation of one who plays a game to obey its rules. One who professed insincerely to respect property might not understand it to be property, i.e., not have the attitude defining it as such, in which case that person would be merely "putting on an act." If that person did understand it to be property, she would *have* (i.e., know) the attitude defining it as such but would only be pretending to *take* it or be governing her behavior by it. And, just like anyone who joins in a game, anyone who enters into the activities of a normative community and engages in behavior covered by the norms is thereby bound by them. The thief or vandal who violates the norms governing property may be presumed to do so either knowingly or unknowingly. One cannot knowingly violate a norm and reject the normative attitude without having it (in the weak sense) as a component of one's perspective as an individual. But, knowing or unknowing, the thief or vandal **is** such in virtue of being bound by the norms in any dealings concerning what the community takes to be property. One who was neither thief nor vandal but on moral grounds rejected the principle of private ownership could do so only in the light of an understanding of what ownership meant, that is, only by having, again in the weak sense defined above, the general attitude governing property. Such a person would be counterposing to that attitude a contrasting attitude, would have conflicting attitudes toward the same complex, but in different respects. This individual could try to change the prevailing norms, but in the perspective of the community she would still be subject to those norms in any dealings to which they were relevant.

The institution of property serves Mead as an important example of a right, and the property relation is a special case of what I am calling a rights-relation. To have property is to be entitled to use and control it, an entitlement that carries with it a concomitant obligation on the part of all members of the community, including oneself, to respect it. In terms of Mead's analysis, wherever there are rights-relations there is an organized attitude which all who participate in such relations share, and to (sincerely) play either role in such a relation is to take the attitude governing the other. Property rights are a case in point. "The man who says 'This is my property'," Mead contends, "is appealing to his rights because he is able to take the attitude which everybody else in the group has with reference to property, thus arousing in himself the attitudes of others." And, more generally, "We cannot have rights unless we have common attitudes." This is to say that when a right is operative in a community the general perspective of the community has as a constituent a normative attitude that determines or defines an entitlement, and defines it as one it is obligatory to respect. If the attitude of the generalized other does not include such a norm, there is no such right in that community.

To "have a right" is to be a member of a community in which such a normative attitude is operative. (As indicated above, the distinction between operative rights and those which ought to be operative is an important one and raises questions which I hope to address in the future.) To "have a right" in general is to belong to a normative community in which rights are respected as such. And, just as the rules of a game are binding upon the players, the attitude governing rights is binding upon all who participate in the life of a community in which those rights are operative. To have the general attitude governing rights, in either the stronger or weaker sense of "having an attitude," is to be able to take the attitude of either a respecter or a possessor of rights-entitlements, and thus to play either role in a rights-relation. Since the two attitudes are reciprocal and governed by the same general attitude, all members of a community in which rights are operative are obliged to be respecters of rights and, by the same token, all possess the reciprocal entitlements, which, given the appropriate circumstances, ought to be honored.

As Joseph Betz points out, "The sociality of Mead's self nicely explains how obligation accompanies a right." The attitude of the generalized other governing rights comes to be incorporated in the "me" of each member. (They "have" the attitude, in at least the weaker of the two senses specified earlier.) Since the norms regarding rights define both roles in the rights-relation, to have the attitude governing rights is to have (be able to take) the attitudes proper to both entitlement and obligation. In the enactment of either role, one takes the general attitude governing them both; the "I" is called upon by the "me" to conform to it. The attitude of owing respect for an entitlement is the attitude that, under the same circumstances, one would oneself be similarly entitled and would hold all members of the community to be similarly obligated. The attitude of entitlement is one of owing that same respect for the entitlement that is mandatory for others. Failing to take this attitude, one is not participating in the institution of rights.

The rights-relation, on this view, is a social institution, governed by the attitude of the generalized other of a normative community. I have provisionally characterized this relation as a dyadic one, symbolizing it as e Ⓡ o. In the light of the analysis I have presented, we can now see that this characterization is inaccurate. The rights-relation between e and o obtains only in virtue of their membership in a normative community. Rather than a dyadic relation, the rights-relation is a genuinely triadic one involving the community, those who have entitlements, and those who are obligated to respect them, a relation that may be symbolized as c Ⓡ e, o. This in itself means that only a member of a community in which there are rights can participate in rights-relations. But it is also the case that any member who shares the attitude of the generalized other is able to take the attitude proper to each role and in so doing necessarily takes the attitude proper to the other. It follows that a being that cannot play the role of obligation cannot play that of entitlement, and vice-versa.

In speaking of rights and property, Mead repeatedly states his case by citing an individual who **asserts** a claim to property. Could it be that the proposed analysis applies to the act of claiming entitlements rather than, as I have contended, to having them, being entitled? As I see it, and as I interpret Mead, it is not, nor could it be, only the saying of "This is my property" or "I have a right to do (or say or have) this" that is governed by the attitude of the generalized other. Such a statement is a gesture, a significant symbol, and elicits from the members of a community in which there are rights the response of the generalized other. Even though Mead takes linguistic expressions to be the paradigmatic significant symbols, he recognizes (and I would affirm, even if he did not) that other gestures may function in the same way. Typical of such significant gestures are the moves made by the players of a game and the giving and taking enacted in an exchange of property. Where the institution of rights obtains, not only verbal claims and assurances but all conduct pertinent to the rights-relation is governed and given meaning by the relevant normative attitude of the generalized other. Thus one requirement for participation in rights-relations is the capacity to use gestures, both one's own and those of others, as significant symbols and to regulate one's behavior in accordance with the meaning those symbols have in the perspective of the community.

In considering the issue of animal rights, we are concerned with entitlements, and we are asking whether a being that does not and cannot respect rights-entitlements can have certain entitlements nevertheless. By the definition of a right proposed here, the answer would have to be "no," for to act as the party entitled in a rights-relation would be to take the attitude governing entitlement, an attitude inseparable from that of respect for it. It may be asked, however, whether some rights do not entitle one party to be treated by another in a particular way without requiring any reciprocal behavior on the part of the one so entitled. An example would be the right to freedom from gratuitously inflicted pain. It would seem that in a rights-relation of this sort the entitlement, being wholly passive, does not necessitate adoption of any attitude at all. Suppose, for example, that, whether by custom or by resolution or legislation, a community were to have a policy or norm in accordance with which all nonhuman beings that can feel pain are entitled to be spared its gratuitous inflection, and suppose all members of the community to be thereby obligated to respect that entitlement. Would this not be to grant those beings a right? I have said that the social norms that constitute the institution of rights govern the attitudes and conduct toward one another of the members of the normative community among whom that institution is operative. But there are social norms governing behavior that is not mutual, norms such as an acknowledged obligation to protect the helpless, or moral principles governing behavior toward those who are not members of the community in which these norms are operative. There are even norms governing the treatment of inanimate objects. Every society and culture has institutionalized ways of treating outsiders, norms governing dress and the use of materials and utensils, and norms governing relations to the natural environment, including those regulating the acquisition or production of food. Why, then, can't there be norms conferring rights on members of other species?

Given the proposed concept of rights, those who have rights can establish as a norm that certain nonhuman beings are to be treated **as if** they had rights-entitlements. But this is not the same as those beings participating in rights-relations, which they could only do as members of the normative community, sharing the attitude of the generalized other that governs such relations. The existence of a norm regulating behavior toward beings who are not members of the community means that all members ought to govern themselves by it; all who have this normative attitude know those other beings as calling for the prescribed treatment and know to expect one another to do so. Sharing the attitude of the generalized other, the members of the community would, in their dealings with those other beings, adopt **one another's** attitude, not the attitude of the other creatures. The attitude governing the supposed right would differ from that governing a rights-entitlement. The latter is an attitude of mutual respect for self and other as being both bearers of the entitlement. I can only acknowledge your right or grant you a right by presupposing that what is granted or acknowledged is a right **to** you as well; that in your perspective my gesture has the same meaning it has in mine. The entitlement is a right to or for either of us only if it is so to both. Beings who were entitled, by others, to behave or be treated in a particular way, but for whom that entitlement did not have the meaning of a right, i.e., beings who did not share the perspective in which it was a right, did not themselves respect the entitlement, would have a benefit, not a right. They would be the objects of a normative attitude and of the social behavior mandated by it, not rights-bearers. The social institution determining their entitlement would pertain to them, but they would not be participants in it, and no rights-relation would exist.

Unless they can regulate their attitudes by the norms of the institution of rights and assume the obligation of respect for rights-entitlements, animals cannot have rights. Moral behavior toward them, therefore, must be governed by other norms, and a moral theory concerning their treatment requires a different conceptual frame.

United States Bill of Rights
(September 25, 1789)

Article [I]
Congress shall make no law respecting an establishment of religion, or prohibiting the free exercise thereof; or abridging the freedom of speech, or of the press; or the right of the people peaceably to assemble, and to petition the Government for a redress of grievances.

Article [II]
A well regulated Militia, being necessary to the security of a free State, the right of the people to keep and bear Arms, shall not be infringed.

Article [III]
No Soldier shall, in time of peace be quartered in any house, without the consent of the Owner, nor in time of war, but in a manner to be prescribed by law.

Article [IV]
The right of the people to be secure in their persons, houses, papers, and effects, against unreasonable searches and seizures, shall not be violated, and no Warrants shall issue, but upon probable cause, supported by Oath or affirmation, and particularly describing the place to be searched, and the persons or things to be seized.

Article [V]
No person shall be held to answer for a capital, or otherwise infamous crime, unless on a presentment or indictment of a Grand Jury, except in cases arising in the land or naval forces, or in the Militia, when in actual service in time of War or

public danger; nor shall any person be subject for the same offence to be twice put in jeopardy of life or limb; nor shall be compelled in any criminal case to be a witness against himself, nor be deprived of life, liberty, or property, without due process of law; nor shall private property be taken for public use without just compensation.

Article [VI]

In all criminal prosecutions, the accused shall enjoy the right to a speedy and public trial, by an impartial jury of the State and district wherein the crime shall have been committed, which district shall have been previously ascertained by law, and to be informed of the nature and cause of the accusation; to be confronted with the witnesses against him; to have compulsory process for obtaining Witnesses in his favor, and to have the assistance of counsel for his defence.

Article [VII]

In Suits at common law, where the value in controversy shall exceed twenty dollars, the right of trial by jury shall be preserved, and no fact tried by jury, shall be otherwise reexamined in any Court of the United States, than according to the rules of the common law.

Article [VIII]

Excessive bail shall not be required, nor excessive fines imposed, nor cruel and unusual punishments inflicted.

Article [IX]

The enumeration in the Constitution, of certain rights, shall not be construed to deny, or disparage others retained by the people.

Article [X]

The powers not delegated to the United States by the Constitution, nor prohibited by it to the States, are reserved to the States respectively, or to the people.

Universal Declaration of Human Rights
United Nations (1948)

Preamble

Whereas recognition of the inherent dignity and of the equal and inalienable rights of all members of the human family is the foundation of freedom, justice and peace in the world,

Whereas disregard and contempt for human rights have resulted in barbarous acts which have outraged the conscience of mankind, and the advent of a world in which human beings shall enjoy freedom of speech and belief and freedom from fear and want has been proclaimed as the highest aspiration of the common people,

Whereas it is essential, if man is not to be compelled to have recourse, as a last resort, to rebellion against tyranny and oppression, that human rights should be protected by the rule of law,

Whereas it is essential to promote the development of friendly relations between nations,

Whereas the peoples of the United Nations have in the Charter reaffirmed their faith in fundamental human rights, in the dignity and worth of the human person and in the equal rights of men and women and have determined to promote social progress and better standards of life in larger freedom,

Whereas Member States have pledged themselves to achieve, in co-operation with the United Nations, the promotion of universal respect for and observance of human rights and fundamental freedoms,

Whereas a common understanding of these rights and freedoms is of the greatest importance for the full realization of this pledge,

Now, therefore,

The General Assembly

Proclaims this Universal Declaration of Human Rights as a common standard of achievement for all peoples and all nations, to the end that every individual and every organ of society, keeping this Declaration constantly in mind, shall strive by teaching and education to promote respect for these rights and freedoms and by progressive measures, national and international, to secure their universal and effective recognition and observance, both among the peoples of Member States themselves and among the peoples of territories under their jurisdiction.

Article 1

All human beings are born free and equal in dignity and rights. They are endowed with reason and conscience and should act towards one another in a spirit of brotherhood.

Article 2

Everyone is entitled to all the rights and freedoms set forth in this Declaration, without distinction of any kind, such as race, colour, sex, language, religion, political or other opinion, national or social origin, property, birth or other status.

Furthermore, no distinction shall be made on the basis of the political, jurisdictional or international status of the country or territory to which a person belongs, whether it be independent, trust, non-self-governing or under any other limitation of sovereignty.

Article 3

Everyone has the right to life, liberty and the security of person.

Article 4

No one shall be held in slavery or servitude: slavery and the slave trade shall be prohibited in all their forms.

Article 5

No one shall be subjected to torture or to cruel, inhuman or degrading treatment or punishment.

Article 6

Everyone has the right to recognition everywhere as a person before the law.

Article 7

All are equal before the law and are entitled without any discrimination to equal protection of the law. All are entitled to equal protection against any discrimination in violation of this Declaration and against any incitement to such discrimination.

Article 8

Everyone has the right to an effective remedy by the competent national tribunals for acts violating the fundamental rights granted him by the constitution or by law.

Article 9

No one shall be subjected to arbitrary arrest, detention or exile.

Article 10

Everyone is entitled in full equality to a fair, and public hearing by an independent and impartial tribunal, in the determination of his rights and obligations and of any criminal charge against him.

Article 11

1. Everyone charged with a penal offence has the right to be presumed innocent until proved guilty according to law in a public trial at which he has had all the guarantees necessary for his defence.

2. No one shall be held guilty of any penal offence on account of any act or omission which did not constitute a penal offence, under national or international law, at the time when it was committed. Nor shall a heavier penalty be imposed than the one that was applicable at the time the penal offence was committed.

Article 12

No one shall be subjected to arbitrary interference with his privacy, family, home or correspondence, nor to attacks upon his honour and reputation. Everyone has the right to the protection of the law against such interference or attacks.

Article 13

1. Everyone has the right to freedom of movement and residence within the borders of each State.

2. Everyone has the right to leave any country, including his own, and to return to his country.

Article 14

1. Everyone has the right to seek and to enjoy in other countries asylum from persecution.

2. This right may not be invoked in the case of prosecutions genuinely arising from non-political crimes or from acts contrary to the purposes and principles of the United Nations.

Article 15

1. Everyone has the right to a nationality.

2. No one shall be arbitrarily deprived of his nationality nor denied the right to change his nationality.

Article 16

1. Men and women of full age, without any limitation due to race, nationality or religion, have the right to marry and to found a family. They are entitled to equal rights as to marriage, during marriage and at its dissolution.

2. Marriage shall be entered into only with the free and full consent of the intending spouses.

3. The family is the natural and fundamental group unit of society and is entitled to protection by society and the State.

Article 17

1. Everyone has the right to own property alone as well as in association with others.

2. No one shall be arbitrarily deprived of his property.

Article 18

Everyone has the right to freedom of thought, conscience and religion; this right includes freedom to change his religion or belief, and freedom, either alone or in community with others and in public or private, to manifest his religion or belief in teaching, practice, worship and observance.

Article 19

Everyone has the right to freedom of opinion and expression: this right includes freedom to hold opinions without interference and to seek, receive and impart information and ideas through any media and regardless of frontiers.

Article 20

1. Everyone has the right to freedom of peaceful assembly and association.

2. No one may be compelled to belong to an association.

Article 21

1. Everyone has the right to take part in the government of his country, directly or through freely chosen representatives.

2. Everyone has the right of equal access to public service in his country.

3. The will of the people shall be the basis of the authority of government; this will shall be expressed in periodic and genuine elections which shall be by universal and equal suffrage and shall be held by secret vote or by equivalent free voting procedures.

Article 22

Everyone, as a member of society, has the right to social security and is entitled to realization, through national effort and international co-operation and in accordance with the organization and resources of each State, of the economic, social and cultural rights indispensable for his dignity and the free development of his personality.

Article 23

1. Everyone has the right to work, to free choice of employment, to just and favourable conditions of work and to protection against unemployment.

2. Everyone, without any discrimination, has the right to equal pay for equal work.

3. Everyone who works has the right to just and favourable remuneration ensuring for himself and his family an existence worthy of human dignity, and supplemented, if necessary, by other means of social protection.

4. Everyone has the right to form and to join trade unions for the protection of his interests.

Article 24

Everyone has the right to rest and leisure, including reasonable limitation of working hours and periodic holidays with pay.

Article 25

1. Everyone has the right to a standard of living adequate for the health and well-being of himself and of his family, including food, clothing, housing and medical care and necessary social services, and the right to security in the event of unemployment, sickness, disability, widowhood, old age or other lack of livelihood in circumstances beyond his control.

2. Motherhood and childhood are entitled to special care and assistance. All children, whether born in or out of wedlock, shall enjoy the same social protection.

Article 26

1. Everyone has the right to education. Education shall be free, at least in the elementary and fundamental stages. Elementary education shall be compulsory. Technical and professional education shall be made generally available and higher education shall be equally accessible to all on the basis of merit.

2. Education shall be directed to the full development of the human personality and to the strengthening of respect for human rights and fundamental freedoms. It shall promote understanding, tolerance and friendship among all nations, racial or religious groups, and shall further the activities of the United Nations for the maintenance of peace.

3. Parents have a prior right to choose the kind of education that shall be given to their children.

Article 27

1. Everyone has the right freely to participate in the cultural life of the community, to enjoy the arts and to share in scientific advancement and its benefits.

2. Everyone has the right to the protection of the moral and material interests resulting from any scientific, literary or artistic production of which he is the author.

Article 28

Everyone is entitled to a social and international order in which the rights and freedoms set forth in this Declaration can be fully realized.

Article 29

1. Everyone has duties to the community in which alone the free and full development of his personality is possible.

2. In the exercise of his rights and freedoms, everyone shall be subject only to such limitations as are determined by law solely for the purpose of securing due recognition and respect for the rights and freedoms of others and of meeting the just requirements of morality, public order and the general welfare in a democratic society.

3. These rights and freedoms may in no case be exercised contrary to the purposes and principles of the United Nations.

Article 30

Nothing in this Declaration may be interpreted as implying for any State, group or person any right to engage in any activity or to perform any act aimed at the destruction of any of the rights and freedoms set forth herein.

From *Helsinki Accord**

VII. Respect for Human Rights and Fundamental Freedoms, Including the Freedom of Thought, Conscience, Religion or Belief

The participating States will respect human rights and fundamental freedoms, including the freedom of thought, conscience, religion or belief, for all without distinction as to race, sex, language or religion.

They will promote and encourage the effective exercise of civil, political, economic, social, cultural and other rights and freedoms all of which derive from the inherent dignity of the human person and are essential for his free and full development.

Within this framework the participating States will recognize and respect the freedom of the individual to profess and practise, alone or in community with others, religion or belief acting in accordance with the dictates of his own conscience.

The participating States on whose territory national minorities exist will respect the right of persons belonging to such minorities to equality before the law, will afford them the full opportunity for the actual enjoyment of human rights and fundamental freedoms and will, in this manner, protect their legitimate interests in this sphere.

The participating States recognize the universal significance of human rights and fundamental freedoms, respect for which is an essential factor for the peace, justice and well-being necessary to ensure the development of friendly relations and co-operation among themselves as among all States.

They will constantly respect these rights and freedoms in their mutual relations and will endeavour jointly and separately, including in co-operation with the United Nations, to promote universal and effective respect for them.

They confirm the right of the individual to know and act upon his rights and duties in this field.

In the field of human rights and fundamental freedoms, the participating States will act in conformity with the purposes and principles of the Charter of the United Nations and with the Universal Declaration of Human Rights. They

*From *Helsinki Accord* (August 1, 1975).

will also fulfill their obligations as set forth in the international declarations and agreements in this field, including inter alia the International Covenants on Human Rights, by which they may be bound.

VIII. Equal Rights and Self-determination of Peoples

The participating States will respect the equal rights of peoples and their right to self-determination, acting at all times in conformity with the purposes and principles of the Charter of the United Nations and with the relevant norms of international law, including those relating to territorial integrity of States.

CONCLUSIONS

Here are conclusions for some of the important arguments in Part Two

Aristotle

1. *Because nature dictates the mind govern the body, it is natural that some people are slaves.*
2. *In unjust wars slavery may also be unjust.*

Locke

1. *The natural state of man is peaceful equality and freedom.*
2. *Every man has a right to punish offenders in the state of nature.*
3. *Slavery is only justified in a state of war.*

Hobbes

1. *The natural state of man is war.*
2. *In war every person takes what he can get.*
3. *To be just is rational and in one's best interest.*

Nietzsche

1. *The masters' morality is concerned with their own self-glorification.*
2. *Masters create "values."*

Austin

1. *Moral rights come about by analogy to law.*
2. *A person's rights and duties are a function of his societal role.*

Singer

1. *Only a member of a community in which there are rights can participate in a rights-relation.*

Evaluating and Writing a Logical Argument

Brainstorming

In Part Two I will assume that you have struggled with outlining and have a handle on how to present numbered premises that eventually lead to a conclusion. Once this artifact is completed, you have just begun your task. This may be daunting to students who have already put in hours to create one outline. But the outlining, in itself, is not our final goal.

The next step is one I call "listing," or "brainstorming." When you have a completed outline, look to the justifications of the premises presented. What are they? Think a moment. An inference is tight inasmuch as the premises cited in the inference are true and their connection cannot be doubted. Thus, any premise that has as its justification—inference—is not suitable for consideration. Remember, in this feedback mode we are concerned with analysis. We want to find the smallest units possible so that we may isolate them for our examination. Therefore, since an inference is tight in virtue of other premises being true, our focus will be upon those other premises.

For example, say premise number 5 in an argument had as its justification premises number 3 and number 4. Instead of focusing upon premise number 5, focus upon number 3 and number 4. Number 5 is proven true in virtue of these other premises. If number 3 and/or number 4 are/is false, then number 5 has no logical support.

What we are after is a narrow focus. We want to find the kernel of controversy that will stimulate your ideas. Once you have isolated all the possible premises (those with "assertion" or "fact" as a justification), then you can begin to speculate. Take a sheet of paper for each eligible premise and go through a careful examination of various issues that may be contained within it. For example, when you look at a premise such as "Man is basically good," you must ask yourself the question: Why do some people believe this while others disagree?

This is not an easy task. Many students will read a premise and respond, "So what?" There may be many causes for such a response. To begin, you need to transcend the attitude that what is written is true. This requires an active, critical disposition. Accept nothing. Question everything. Only then will you crack into the premise. Only then will you be brainstorming.

As an aid, try these steps.

Step 1: Isolate the premises that are justified by "fact" or "assertion."

Step 2: Take a piece of paper for each premise and set down all your thoughts on that premise. Some premises will stimulate you to write more than others.

Step 3: Select the two sheets that have the most written on them and, day by day for a week, supplement this list. Talk to others. Discuss these thoughts outside of class. Buy someone a pizza, sit down, and get into it. Philosophy develops nicely in small group situations. Cross-fertilization works. Diversity breeds excellence. Talk to others. Make your list varied. This is very important.

The most common problems my students have are:

1. *I have nothing to say.* I don't believe it! Whenever students say this to me, I sit back and ask them provocative questions—and soon they won't shut up! This objection is related to "having a mental block." The block may be relieved by talking with others.

2. *The student perceives the writer as having made a simple mistake which is easily corrected.* Don't be so hasty. Let's assume the authors in this text are not stupid. Let's also assume that because of this they do not generally make simple-minded mistakes. Often, if you perceive an error you take to be very obvious, it may not indicate a shortcoming in the author but in the reader. Perhaps you are missing the point. What was the author trying to say? Isolate the purpose of the argument and you have gone a long way toward discovering the deeper meaning of the premise.

3. *The student stops at one observation.* As stated above, your brainstorming list must be full. Personally, I make my lists into pictures so that sentences of one thought interact with related strains of other thoughts. You must choose your own style. But you must choose some style. Philosophical thought does not come "all at once." It develops over time. Let the thoughts come to their proper fullness. Fight the urge to stop your list with a single "zinger." Even the best insights need unpacking.

Rights in Literature
MAYA ANGELOU
*Lift Ev'ry Voice and Sing**

The children in Stamps [Arkansas] trembled visibly with anticipation. Some adults were excited too, but to be certain the whole young population had come down with graduation epidemic. Large classes were graduating from both the grammar school and the high school. Even those who were years removed from their own day of glorious release were anxious to help with preparations as a kind of dry run. The junior students who were moving into the vacating classes' chairs were tradition-bound to show their talents for leadership and management. They strutted through the school and around the campus exerting pressure on the lower grades. Their authority was so new that occasionally if they pressed a little too hard it had to be overlooked. After all, next term was coming, and it never hurt a sixth grader to have a play sister in the eighth grade, or a tenth-year student to be able to call a twelfth grader Bubba. So all was endured in a spirit of shared understanding. But the graduating classes themselves were the nobility. Like travelers with exotic destinations on their minds, the graduates were remarkably forgetful. They came to school without their books, or tablets or even pencils. Volunteers fell over themselves to secure replacements for the missing equipment. When accepted, the willing workers might or might not be thanked, and it was of no importance to the pregraduation rites. Even teachers were respectful of the now quiet and aging seniors, and tended to speak to them, if not as equals, as beings only slightly lower than themselves. After tests were returned and grades given, the student body, which acted like an extended family, knew who did well, who excelled, and what piteous ones had failed.

Unlike the white high school, Lafayette County Training School distinguished itself by having neither lawn, nor hedges, nor tennis court, nor climbing ivy. Its two buildings (main classrooms, the grade school and home economics) were set on a dirt hill with no fence to limit either its boundaries or those of bordering farms. There was a large expanse to the left of the school which was used alternately as a baseball diamond or a basketball court. Rusty hoops on the swaying poles represented the permanent recreational equipment, although bats and balls could be borrowed from the P.E. teacher if the borrower was qualified and if the diamond wasn't occupied.

Over this rocky area relieved by a few shady tall persimmon trees the graduating class walked. The girls often held hands and no longer bothered to speak to the lower students. There was a sadness about them, as if this old world was not their home and they were bound for higher ground. The boys, on the other hand, had become more friendly, more outgoing. A decided change from the closed attitude they projected while studying for finals. Now they seemed not ready to give up the old school, the

---

*Title for chapter 23 of *I Know Why the Caged Bird Sings* (1969).

familiar paths and classrooms. Only a small percentage would be continuing on to college—one of the South's A & M (agricultural and mechanical) schools, which trained Negro youths to be carpenters, farmers, handymen, masons, maids, cooks and baby nurses. Their future rode heavily on their shoulders, and blinded them to the collective joy that had pervaded the lives of the boys and girls in the grammar school graduating class.

Parents who could afford it had ordered new shoes and ready-made clothes for themselves from Sears and Roebuck or Montgomery Ward. They also engaged the best seamstresses to make the floating graduating dresses and to cut down secondhand pants which would be pressed to a military slickness for the important event.

Oh, it was important, all right. Whitefolks would attend the ceremony, and two or three would speak of God and home, and the Southern way of life, and Mrs. Parsons, the principal's wife, would play the graduation march while the lower-grade graduates paraded down the aisles and took their seats below the platform. The high school seniors would wait in empty classrooms to make their dramatic entrance.

In the Store I was the person of the moment. The birthday girl. The center. Bailey [my brother] had graduated the year before, although to do so he had had to forfeit all pleasures to make up for his time lost in Baton Rouge.

My class was wearing butter-yellow piqué dresses, and Momma launched out on mine. She smocked the yoke into tiny crisscrossing puckers, then shirred the rest of the bodice. Her dark fingers ducked in and out of the lemony cloth as she embroidered raised daisies around the hem. Before she considered herself finished she had added a crocheted cuff on the puff sleeves, and a pointy crocheted collar.

I was going to be lovely. A walking model of all the various styles of fine hand sewing and it didn't worry me that I was only twelve years old and merely graduating from the eighth grade. Besides, many teachers in Arkansas Negro schools had only that diploma and were licensed to impart wisdom.

The days had become longer and more noticeable. The faded beige of former times had been replaced with strong and sure colors. I began to see my classmates' clothes, their skin tones, and the dust that waved off pussy willows. Clouds that lazed across the sky were objects of great concern to me. Their shiftier shapes might have held a message that in my new happiness and with a little bit of time I'd soon decipher. During that period I looked at the arch of heaven so religiously my neck kept a steady ache. I had taken to smiling more often, and my jaws hurt from the unaccustomed activity. Between the two physical sore spots, I suppose I could have been uncomfortable, but that was not the case. As a member of the winning team (the graduating class of 1940) I had outdistanced unpleasant sensations by miles. I was headed for the freedom of open fields.

Youth and social approval allied themselves with me and we trammeled memories of slights and insults. The wind of our swift passage remodeled my features. Lost tears were pounded to mud and then to dust. Years of withdrawal were brushed aside and left behind, as hanging ropes of parasitic moss.

My work alone had awarded me a top place and I was going to be one of the first called in the graduating ceremonies. On the classroom blackboard, as well as on the bulletin board in the auditorium, there were blue stars and white stars and red stars. No absences, no tardinesses, and my academic work was among the best of the year. I could say the preamble to the Constitution even faster than Bailey. We timed ourselves often: "WethepeopleoftheUnitedStatesinordertoformamoreperfectunion . . ." I had memorized the Presidents of the United States from Washington to Roosevelt in chronological as well as alphabetical order.

My hair pleased me too. Gradually the black mass had lengthened and thickened, so that it kept at last to its braided pattern, and I didn't have to yank my scalp off when I tried to comb it.

Louise and I had rehearsed the exercises until we tired out ourselves. Henry Reed was class valedictorian. He was a small, very black boy with hooded eyes, a long, broad nose and an oddly shaped head. I had admired him for years because each term he and I vied for the best grades in our class. Most often he bested me, but instead of being disappointed I was pleased that we shared top places between us. Like many Southern Black children, he lived with his grandmother, who was as strict as Momma and as kind as she knew how to be. He was courteous, respectful and soft-spoken to elders, but on the playground he chose to play the roughest games. I admired him. Anyone, I reckoned, sufficiently afraid or sufficiently dull could be polite. But to be able to operate at a top level with both adults and children was admirable.

His valedictory speech was entitled "To Be or Not to Be." The rigid tenth-grade teacher had helped him write it. He'd been working on the dramatic stresses for months.

The weeks until graduation were filled with heady activities. A group of small children were to be presented in a play about buttercups and daisies and bunny rabbits. They could be heard throughout the building practicing their hops and their little songs that sounded like silver bells. The older girls (nongraduates, of course) were assigned the task of making refreshments for the night's festivities. A tangy scent of ginger, cinnamon, nutmeg and chocolate wafted around the home economics building as the budding cooks made samples for themselves and their teachers.

In every corner of the workshop, axes and saws split fresh timber as the woodshop boys made sets and stage scenery. Only the graduates were left out of the general bustle. We were free to sit in the library at the back of the building or look in quite detachedly, naturally, on the measures being taken for our event.

Even the minister preached on graduation the Sunday before. His subject was, "Let your light so shine that men will see your good works and praise your Father, Who is in Heaven." Although the sermon was purported to be addressed to us, he used the occasion to speak to backsliders, gamblers and general ne'er-do-wells. But since he had called our names at the beginning of the service we were mollified.

Among Negroes the tradition was to give presents to children going only from one grade to another. How much more important this was when the person was graduating at the top of the class. Uncle Willie and Momma had sent away for a Mickey Mouse watch like Bailey's. Louise gave me four embroidered handkerchiefs. (I gave her three crocheted doilies.) Mrs. Sneed, the minister's wife, made me an underskirt to wear for graduation, and nearly every customer gave me a nickel or maybe even a dime with the instruction "Keep on moving to higher ground," or some such encouragement.

Amazingly the great day finally dawned and I was out of bed before I knew it. I threw open the back door to see it more clearly, but Momma said, "Sister, come away from that door and put your robe on."

I hoped the memory of that morning would never leave me. Sunlight was itself still young, and the day had none of the insistence maturity would bring it in a few hours. In my robe and barefoot in the backyard, under cover of going to see about my new beans, I gave myself up to the gentle warmth and thanked God that no matter what evil I had done in my life He had allowed me to live to see this day. Somewhere in my fatalism I had expected to die, accidentally, and never have the chance to walk up the stairs in the auditorium and gracefully receive my hard-earned diploma. Out of God's merciful bosom I had won reprieve.

Bailey came out in his robe and gave me a box wrapped in Christmas paper. He said he had saved his money for months to pay for it. It felt like a box of chocolates, but I knew Bailey wouldn't save money to buy candy when we had all we could want under our noses.

He was as proud of the gift as I. It was a soft-leather-bound copy of a collection of poems by Edgar Allan Poe, or, as Bailey and I called him, "Eap." I turned to "Annabel Lee" and we walked up and down the garden rows, the cool dirt between our toes, reciting the beautifully sad lines.

Momma made a Sunday breakfast although it was only Friday. After we finished the blessing, I opened my eyes to find the watch on my plate. It was a dream of a day. Everything went smoothly and to my credit. I didn't have to be reminded or scolded for anything. Near evening I was too jittery to attend to chores, so Bailey volunteered to do all before his bath.

Days before, we had made a sign for the Store, and as we turned out the lights Momma hung the cardboard over the doorknob. It read clearly: CLOSED. GRADUATION.

My dress fitted perfectly and everyone said that I looked like a sunbeam in it. On the hill, going toward the school, Bailey walked behind with Uncle Willie, who muttered, "Go on, Ju." He wanted him to walk ahead with us because it embarrassed him to have to walk so slowly. Bailey said he'd let the ladies walk together, and the men would bring up the rear. We all laughed, nicely.

Little children dashed by out of the dark like fireflies. Their crepe-paper dresses and butterfly wings were not made for running and we heard more than one rip, dryly, and the regretful "uh uh" that followed.

The school blazed without gaiety. The windows seemed cold and unfriendly from the lower hill. A sense of ill-fated timing crept over me, and if Momma hadn't reached for my hand I would have drifted back to Bailey and Uncle Willie, and possibly beyond. She made a few slow jokes about my feet getting cold, and tugged me along to the now-strange building.

Around the front steps, assurance came back. There were my fellow "greats," the graduating class. Hair brushed back, legs oiled, new dresses and pressed pleats, fresh pocket handkerchiefs and little handbags, all homesewn. Oh, we were up to snuff, all right. I joined my comrades and didn't even see my family go in to find seats in the crowded auditorium.

The school band struck up a march and all classes filed in as had been rehearsed. We stood in front of our seats, as assigned, and on a signal from the choir director, we sat. No sooner had this been accomplished than the band started to play the national anthem. We rose again and sang the song, after which we recited the pledge of allegiance. We remained standing for a brief minute before the choir director and the principal signaled to us, rather desperately I thought, to take our seats. The command was so unusual that our carefully rehearsed and smooth-running machine was thrown off. For a full minute we fumbled for our chairs and bumped into each other awkwardly. Habits change or solidify under pressure, so in our state of nervous tension we had been ready to follow our usual assembly pattern: the American national anthem, then the pledge of allegiance, then the song every Black person I knew called the Negro National Anthem ["Lift Ev'ry Voice and Sing"]. All done in the same key, with the same passion and most often standing on the same foot.

Finding my seat at last, I was overcome with a presentiment of worse things to come. Something unrehearsed, unplanned, was going to happen, and we were going to be made to look bad. I distinctly remember being explicit in the choice of pronoun. It was "we," the graduating class, the unit, that concerned me then.

The principal welcomed "parents and friends" and asked the Baptist minister to lead us in prayer. His invocation was brief and punchy, and for a second I thought we were getting back on the high road to right action. When the principal came back to the dais, however, his voice had changed. Sounds always affected me profoundly and the principal's voice was one of my favorites. During assembly it melted and lowed weakly into the audience. It had not been in my plan to listen to him, but my curiosity was piqued and I straightened up to give him my attention.

He was talking about Booker T. Washington, our "late great leader," who said we can be as close as the fingers on the hand, etc. . . . Then he said a few vague things about friendship and the friendship of kindly people to those less fortunate than themselves. With that his voice nearly faded, thin, away. Like a river diminishing to a stream and then to a trickle. But he cleared his throat and said, "Our speaker tonight, who is also our friend, came from Texarkana to deliver the commencement address, but due to the irregularity of the train schedule, he's going to, as they say, 'speak and run.'" He said that we understood and wanted the man to know that we were most grateful for the time he was able to give us and then something about how we were willing always to adjust to another's program, and without more ado—"I give you Mr. Edward Donleavy."

Not one but two white men came through the door offstage. The shorter one walked to the speaker's platform, and the tall one moved over to the center seat and sat down. But that was our principal's seat, and already occupied. The dislodged gentleman bounced around for a long breath or two before the Baptist minister gave him his chair, then with more dignity than the situation deserved, the minister walked off the stage.

Donleavy looked at the audience once (on reflection, I'm sure that he wanted only to reassure himself that we were really there), adjusted his glasses and began to read from a sheaf of papers.

He was glad "to be here and to see the work going on just as it was in the other schools."

At the first "Amen" from the audience I willed the offender to immediate death by choking on the word. But Amen's and Yes, sir's began to fall around the room like rain through a ragged umbrella.

He told us of the wonderful changes we children in Stamps had in store. The Central School (naturally, the white school was Central) had already been granted improvements that would be in use in the fall. A well-known artist was coming from Little Rock to teach art to them. They were going to have the newest microscopes and chemistry equipment for their laboratory. Mr. Donleavy didn't leave us long in the dark over who made these improvements available to Central High. Nor were we to be ignored in the general betterment scheme he had in mind.

He said that he had pointed out to people at a very high level that one of the first-line football tacklers at Arkansas Agricultural and Mechanical College had graduated from good old Lafayette County Training School. Here fewer Amen's were heard. Those few that did break through lay dully in the air with the heaviness of habit.

He went on to praise us. He went on to say how he had bragged that "one of the best basketball players at Fisk sank his first ball right here at Lafayette County Training School."

The white kids were going to have a chance to become Galileos and Madame Curies and Edisons and Gauguins, and our boys (the girls weren't even in on it) would try to be Jesse Owenses and Joe Louises.

Owens and the Brown Bomber were great heroes in our world, but what school official in the white-goddom of Little Rock had the right to decide that those two men must be our only heroes? Who decided that for Henry Reed to become a scientist he had to work like George Washington Carver, as a boot-black, to buy a lousy microscope? Bailey was obviously always going to be too small to be an athlete, so which concrete angel glued to what country seat had decided that if my brother wanted to become a lawyer he had to first pay penance for his skin by picking cotton and hoeing corn and studying correspondence books at night for twenty years?

The man's dead words fell like bricks around the auditorium and too many settled in my belly. Constrained by hard-learned manners I couldn't look behind me, but to my left and right the proud graduating class of 1940 had dropped their heads. Every girl in my row had found something new to do with her handkerchief. Some folded the tiny squares into love knots, some into triangles, but most were wadding them, then pressing them flat on their yellow laps.

On the dais, the ancient tragedy was being replayed. Professor Parsons sat, a sculptor's reject, rigid. His large, heavy body seemed devoid of will or willingness, and his eyes said he was no longer with us. The other teachers examined the flag (which was draped stage right) or their notes, or the windows which opened on our now-famous playing diamond.

Graduation, the hush-hush magic time of frills and gifts and congratulations and diplomas, was finished for me before my name was called. The accomplishment was nothing. The meticulous maps, drawn in three colors of ink, learning and spelling decasyllabic words, memorizing the whole of *The Rape of Lucrece*—it was for nothing. Donleavy had exposed us.

We were maids and farmers, handymen and washerwomen, and anything higher that we aspired to was farcical and presumptuous.

Then I wished that Gabriel Prosser and Nat Turner had killed all whitefolks in their beds and that Abraham Lincoln had been assassinated before the signing of the Emancipation Proclamation, and that Harriet Tubman had been killed by that blow on her head and Christopher Columbus had drowned in the *Santa María*.

It was awful to be Negro and have no control over my life. It was brutal to be young and already trained to sit quietly and listen to charges brought against my color with no chance of defense. We should all be dead. I thought I should like to see us all dead, one on top of the other. A pyramid of flesh with the whitefolks on the bottom, as the broad base, then the Indians with their silly tomahawks and teepees and wigwams and treaties, the Negroes with their mops and recipes and cotton sacks and spirituals sticking out of their mouths. The Dutch children should all stumble in their wooden shoes and break their necks. The French should choke to death on the Louisiana Purchase (1803) while silkworms ate all the Chinese with their stupid pigtails. As a species, we were an abomination. All of us.

Donleavy was running for election, and assured our parents that if he won we could count on having the only colored paved playing field in that part of Arkansas. Also—he never looked up to acknowledge the grunts of acceptance—also, we were bound to get some new equipment for the home economics building and the workshop.

He finished, and since there was no need to give any more than the most perfunctory thank-you's, he nodded to the men on the stage, and the tall white man who was never introduced joined him at the door. They left with the attitude that now they were off to something really important. (The graduation ceremonies at Lafayette County Training School had been a mere preliminary.)

The ugliness they left was palpable. An uninvited guest who wouldn't leave. The choir was summoned and sang a modern arrangement of "Onward, Christian Soldiers," with new words pertaining to graduates seeking their place in the world. But it didn't work. Elouise, the daughter of the Baptist minister, recited "Invictus," and I could have cried at the impertinence of "I am the master of my fate, I am the captain of my soul."

My name had lost its ring of familiarity and I had to be nudged to go and receive my diploma. All my preparations had fled. I neither marched up to the stage like a conquering Amazon, nor did I look in the audience for Bailey's nod of approval. Marguerite Johnson [Angelou's maiden name], I heard the name again, my honors were read, there were noises in the audience of appreciation, and I took my place on the stage as rehearsed.

I thought about colors I hated: ecru, puce, lavender, beige and black.

There was shuffling and rustling around me, then Henry Reed was giving his valedictory address, "To Be or Not to Be." Hadn't he heard the whitefolks? We couldn't *be,* so the question was a waste of time. Henry's voice came out clear and strong. I feared to look at him. Hadn't he got the message? There was no "nobler in the mind" for Negroes because the world didn't think we had minds, and they let us know it. "Outrageous fortune"? Now, that was a joke. When the ceremony was over I had to tell Henry Reed some things. That is, if I still cared. Not "rub," Henry, "erase." "Ah, there's the erase." Us.

Henry had been a good student in elocution. His voice rose on tides of promise and fell on waves of warnings. The English teacher had helped him to create a sermon winging through Hamlet's soliloquy. To be a man, a doer, a builder, a leader, or to be a tool, an unfunny joke, a crusher of funky toadstools. I marveled that Henry could go through with the speech as if we had a choice.

I had been listening and silently rebutting each sentence with my eyes closed; then there was a hush, which in an audience warns that something unplanned is happening. I looked up and saw Henry Reed, the conservative, the proper, the A student, turn his back to the audience and turn to us (the proud graduating class of 1940) and sing, nearly speaking,

> *"Lift ev'ry voice and sing*
> *Till earth and heaven ring*
> *Ring with the harmonies of Liberty. . ."*

It was the poem written by James Weldon Johnson. It was the music composed by J. Rosamond Johnson. It was the Negro national anthem. Out of habit we were singing it.

Our mothers and fathers stood in the dark hall and joined the hymn of encouragement. A kindergarten teacher led the small children onto the stage and the buttercups and daisies and bunny rabbits marked time and tried to follow:

> *"Stony the road we trod*
> *Bitter the chastening rod*
> *Felt in the days when hope, unborn, had died.*
> *Yet with a steady beat*
> *Have not our weary feet*
> *Come to the place for which our fathers sighed?"*

Every child I knew had learned that song with his ABC's and along with "Jesus Loves Me This I Know." But I personally had never heard it before. Never heard the words, despite the thousands of times I had sung them. Never thought they had anything to do with me.

On the other hand, the words of Patrick Henry had made such an impression on me that I had been able to stretch myself tall and trembling and say, "I know not what course others may take, but as for me, give me liberty or give me death."

And now I heard, really for the first time:

> *"We have come over a way that with tears*
>   *has been watered,*
> *We have come, treading our path through*
>   *the blood of the slaughtered."*

While echoes of the song shivered in the air, Henry Reed bowed his head, said "Thank you," and returned to his place in the line. The tears that slipped down many faces were not wiped away in shame.

We were on top again. As always, again. We survived. The depths had been icy and dark, but now a bright sun spoke to our souls. I was no longer simply a member of the proud graduating class of 1940; I was a proud member of the wonderful, beautiful Negro race.

Oh, Black known and unknown poets, how often have your auctioned pains sustained us? Who will compute the lonely nights made less lonely by your songs, or the empty pots made less tragic by your tales?

If we were a people much given to revealing secrets, we might raise monuments and sacrifice to the memories of our poets, but slavery cured us of that weakness. It may be enough, however, to have it said that we survive in exact relationship to the dedication of our poets (include preachers, musicians and blues singers).

Questions for Discussion:

1. How does Edward Donleavy's speech make an impact on the rights and dignity of those in the audience?

2. What do the feelings of guilt and shame reveal? Compare these feelings to similar expressions by Holocaust survivors. How is hope reaffirmed?

PART 3

Epistemology: Skepticism,
Appearance, and Reality

Roderick M. Chisholm

Brown University

The Theory of Knowledge

Introduction

We raise the most fundamental questions of theory of knowledge, or "epistemology," when we ask ourselves: "What can I know? How can I distinguish those things I am justified in believing from those things I am not justified in believing? And how can I decide whether I am more justified in believing one thing than in believing another?" Most of the problems that these questions involve were discussed by the ancient Greeks, and there is little agreement even now about how they should be dealt with.

In this part, the problems are divided into three groups: (1) "the problem of skepticism," (2) "appearance and reality," and (3) "the sources of knowing."

The Problem of Skepticism

There are philosophers who doubt whether there is anything that we can know. They also doubt, therefore, whether it is possible for us to find out whether there is anything that we can know. Such philosophers—we may call them "philosophical skeptics"—may thus seem to present a challenge to traditional epistemology.

What can the skeptic tell us? He may say: "There are good reasons, after all, for supposing that we *cannot* know the kinds of things that most people think they can know." In support of this contention, he can provide an impressive amount of information about human fallibility and the foolish things that many people believe. Suppose, then, we are given such information. Does the possession of such information mean that it is *not* reasonable for us to assume that we can answer our epistemological questions?

If we do have *information* about human fallibility, that is to say, if we *know* something about it, then, obviously, we should take such information into account when we ask about what it is that we can know. But we should *also* take into account the fact that, despite the indications of fallibility, whatever these indications may be, we *are* aware of them and therefore *do* have information about ourselves and other people.

Some skeptics, however, know better than to say that they *know* that no one can know anything. Yet they challenge *our* claim that *we* know something. Such a skeptic may argue that, for all we know, we are the victims of a monstrous deception. He may logically point out to us that it is possible that Descartes' supposition of a malicious demon is true. This supposition is set forth in the selection from Descartes' *Meditations* that is included here. Descartes makes it clear that no contradiction is involved in assuming that all my present experiences are caused by a skillful evil spirit who wishes to deceive me about my own nature and about the nature of the world in which I find myself. Since no contradiction is involved in such an assumption, the skeptic concludes that it is not reasonable for me to believe the things that I do believe about myself and the world.

Yet the skeptic's reasoning is itself questionable. To see that this is so, we have only to ask ourselves how he would defend his own assertion. What he tells us is this:

> If it is logically possible that I have made a mistake with respect to a given belief, then it follows that it is unreasonable of me to have that belief.

What reason can the skeptic give us for accepting *that* proposition? When we hear the answer, if we do, we may decide that he has very little to say that should deter us from *our* project.

And there are still other problems for the skeptic. For there are some things concerning which it would be very difficult for even the cleverest of malicious demons to deceive us.

Consider the following remark that St. Augustine makes in his book, *Against the Academicians*. (The "Academicians" were a group of skeptics who had taken over the philosophical Academy that was founded by Plato.)

> I do not see how the Academician can refute him who says: "I know that this *appears* white to me, I know that my hearing is delighted with this, I know that this has an agreeable odor, I know that this tastes sweet to me, I know that this feels cold to me.". . . I say this that, when a person tastes something, he can honestly swear that he knows it is sweet to his palate or the contrary, and that no trickery of the Greeks can dispossess him of that knowledge.[1]

Descartes, too, points out that although there may be good reasons for doubting whether, on any given occasion, he sees light, hears noise, or feels heat, "still it is at least quite *certain that it seems to me that* I see light, that I hear noise and that I feel heat." That something thus *seems* to me to be so-and-so is a fact that may be said to "present itself" to me with certainty.

There are still other possible sources of certainty.

There are propositions that are necessarily true and such that, once one understands them, one *sees* that they are

true. Examples are: "Nothing is such that it is both thinking and not thinking"; "If there are dogs and cats, then there are cats"; "4 + 3 = 7"; and "If a proposition *p* implies a proposition *g*, and if *g* is false, then *p* is false." Such propositions have traditionally been called *a priori*. Leibniz remarks: "You will find a hundred places in which the scholastic philosophers have said that these propositions are evident, from their terms, as soon as they are understood."[2]

Some will say that the "truths of reason" are only trivially true—to which one may well reply: "So much the worse, then, for those who refuse to accept them." Others will feel themselves perplexed by the "appearances" to which we have referred. Let us now turn to these strange entities.

Appearances and Reality

Consider how easy it is to change the ways in which things appear to us without altering those things themselves. By holding this piece of paper at different angles, you can make it present different appearances to you. If you hold it vertically a few feet in front of you, you may cause it to present an appearance that is rectangular. You can cause it to present an appearance that is rhomboidal by changing the angle. And you can make the appearance smaller by moving the paper farther away.

The other senses are similar. Just by altering the senses and without doing anything to the things that appear to us, we can make the things present us with a great variety of appearances. You can make a thing present different auditory appearances merely by changing your

---

[1] *Against the Academicians (Contra Academicos)*, ed. by Sister Mary Patricia Garvey (Milwaukee: Marquette University Press. 1942), Paragraph 26, pp. 68 of translation. My italics.

[2] G. W. Leibniz, *New Essays Concerning Human Understanding*, trans. and ed. by Peter Remnant and Jonathan Bennett (Cambridge University Press, 1982), Book IV, Chapter 7.

spatial relation to it. And you can make food present olfactory and gustatory appearances merely by doing things to your nose or mouth.

The nature and location of these strange entities, then, has caused considerable puzzlement, and imposing metaphysical systems have been constructed to bring them together with the rest of the world.

It is tempting to assume that if a physical thing appears white or loud or bitter to a person, then the person may be said to sense, or to be aware of, an appearance that *is* white or loud or bitter. It has been assumed that if a dog presents a canine appearance, then the dog presents an appearance that *is* canine.

According to this way of looking at the matter, if you are aware of an appearance that is red, then there is a red thing "in the mind"; and if you are aware of an appearance that is canine, then there is a *dog* "in the mind." But if the red thing and the dog are "in the mind," what about the world outside? Are there also red things and dogs "*outside* the mind"?

The ancient Greek philosopher, Democritus, considered such facts and drew two very significant conclusions. One was that we don't really perceive what we think we perceive. For we think we perceive external things that are red and we think we perceive dogs that exist outside our bodies; but, Democritus seemed to say, the only red things and the only dogs that we perceive are *internal* things— things "in the mind." The other conclusion that Democritus drew was that the things that are external to us are not at all what we take them to be; for *they* are not things that are red or things that are dogs.

Aristotle saw, however, that Democritus had failed to take into account an important distinction.[3] Such terms as "white" and "black" are ambiguous. When we say of an external thing that it is white or black, we are not saying of it what we would be saying of an appearance if we were to say that *it* is white or

black. We are saying of the external thing that it is such that, when viewed by a normal observer under favorable circumstances, it will appear white to that observer. The physicist can tell us in detail just what further properties an external thing must have if it is to be white or black in this dispositional sense. But when we say of an appearance that it is white, we are not saying that it is related to us in the way that an external thing that is white is related to us; we are not saying that the *appearance* will appear white to us.

The second of the conclusions that Democritus drew would seem, then, to be wrong. He was mistaken in concluding that external physical things cannot be said to be white or black. What of his first conclusion—his conclusion that certain *internal* things—certain appearances—can be said to be white or black?

Like ever so many subsequent philosophers, Democritus seems to have assumed that, whenever a thing *appears* so-and-so, then the thing presents an appearance that really *is* so-and-so. But surely there is something wrong here. We cannot say, for example, that if a person *appears to be singing*, then he is presenting an appearance that really *is* singing. And we cannot say that if a book *looks old*, then it presents an appearance that really *is* old.

Perhaps, then, it was a mistake for Democritus and others to reify appearances. They moved much too quickly from "This *appears* white" to "This presents an appearance that *is* white." The sentences "I sense a red appearance" and "I experience a red sensation" could be interpreted as being analogous to "I have a depressed feeling" and "I feel a wave of exuberance." They ascribe a certain type of undergoing to the person. The adjective "red," in "I am aware of a red appearance" and "I am experiencing a

[3] *De Anima*, Book III, Chapter 2, pp. 426a; see also *Metaphysics*, Book IV, Chapter 5, 1010b.

red sensation," is used abverbially to qualify this undergoing.[4] Thus, we might say "I am sensing redly" or even "I am appeared to redly." Such sentences do not tell us that there are appearances that are the *objects* of sensing. They tell us, rather, *how* the subject is sensing. Or, better, they tell us in what *way* he is sensing.

One who looked at appearances this way would say that we multiply entities beyond necessity if we suppose that, in addition to the person who is in a state of undergoing or sensing, there is a certain *further* entity, a sense-datum or an appearance, which is the object of that undergoing or sensing.

Is this to say, then, that we do *not* perceive or observe external things?

The Sources of Knowing

One of the fundamental questions of theory of knowledge is often put by asking: "What are the *sources* of our knowledge?" In asking about "the sources of knowledge," the epistemologist is concerned with two sets of questions.

One of these is the question that we may raise about ourselves: "Just *what* do I know?" And this is a question not about causation or explanation, but about epistemic *justification*—about the justification of belief. The second set of questions is closely related to the first. One goes on to ask: "And what *can* I know? What can I do to insure that I have beliefs that *are* justified and to rid myself of beliefs that are *not* justified?"

One approach to the second set of questions was suggested by Descartes in the first of his *Meditations:* "It is now some years since I detected how many were the false beliefs that I had from my earliest youth admitted as true, and how doubtful was everything I had since constructed on this basis; and from that time I was convinced that I must once for all seriously undertake to rid myself of all the opinions which I had formerly accepted, and commence to build anew

from the foundation, if I wanted to establish any firm and permanent structure in the sciences."[5]

But where would I be if I really succeeded in ridding myself of *all* the opinions I had formerly accepted? If I were left with *no* opinions at all, then I wouldn't have the slightest idea what I should then do to improve my system of beliefs and to build a new and superior structure.

What, then, can we do to improve our present epistemic situation? One thing is to make use of the two sources of certainty that we have already discussed— the two types of "basic apprehension" that served as stopping places for our Socratic questions about knowing.

(1) One of these is that *inner perception* by means of which we apprehend our own states of mind and the ways in which we are appeared to.

And (2) the other is *reason*—the source of our *a priori* knowledge of axioms and of other "truths of reason." But these two sources, by themselves, will not take us very far. What more shall we do?

The "common sensist" will tell us that we should begin with the set of beliefs that we have (where else *could* we begin?) and then try to refine upon them and make the set more respectable, epistemically. We should begin with our native common sense. And so he adds (3) that our *natural inclination* is a source of knowledge. The mere fact that we find ourselves inclined to believe one thing rather than another is itself a provisional—or *prima facie*—justification *for* believing the one thing rather than the other. "So far, so good," we tell ourselves.

---

[4] Compare Thomas Reid: "When I am pained, I cannot say that the pain I feel is one thing, and that my feeling of it is another thing. They are one and the same thing and cannot be disjoined even in the imagination." *Essays on the Intellectual Powers,* Essay I, Chapter 1.

[5] *The Philosophical Works of Descartes,* ed. by E. S. Haldane and R. T. Ross, vol. 1 (Cambridge: The University Press, 1931), pp. 144.

But, to use C. S. Peirce's phrase, our commonsensism should be a *"critical commonsensism."* Although we start out with a mass of uncritical beliefs, we will refine upon it and improve it. One way of improving it is to sift it down, so to speak, and cast away the things that shouldn't be there.

If, after removing the contradictions that we find among our system of beliefs, we find that the remaining set tends to *disconfirm* some of its members, then we will reject the ones that are disconfirmed.

Of the commonsense beliefs that then remain (those beliefs that go beyond inner perception and the *a priori*), some will be *more* justified than others. These will include beliefs from two further "sources of knowing": (4) *external perception* and (5) *memory.*

We could say of the ostensible deliverances of perception and memory that it is reasonable for us to accept them—*unless* we have positive grounds to reject them. They should be held to be innocent, epistemically, until there is ground to think them guilty. If you *think* you see familiar objects in front of you, then it is reasonable for you to suppose that there *are* such objects in front of you—*unless* you have reason for supposing that, on this particular occasion, your senses are deceiving you. And analogously for memory.

Can we improve further upon this refined set of beliefs?

Some philosophers think that such a list of sources is too long. The skeptic, if he allowed himself to discuss the matter, would say we should not countenance the possibility that any of our beliefs are justified. The "immediatist" concedes that certain facts are self-presenting but refuses to go beyond these facts. He will say that we go too far in permitting any trust in what we call perception and memory.

Other philosophers believe, however, that such a list of sources is not long enough.

There is "the problem of other minds." Some have pointed to a kind of "intuitive understanding," or *Verstehen,* that enables us to grasp the mental life of others. Observation of the ways in which other people act and express themselves tends naturally to suggest certain things about what they are thinking and how they are feeling. Like our ordinary perceptual beliefs, this suggestion seems almost irresistable. The proponent of *"Verstehen,"* then, will add another "source" to our list: (6) *intuitive understanding.*

The basic question of *ethics,* or *moral philosophy,* according to Kant, is one that each of us may formulate by asking "What ought I to do?" One of the fundamental *philosophical* questions about ethics, therefore, is this: In deciding what it is in any given case that I ought to do, do I have access to certain *ethical* information? Those who would appeal to (7) *ethical intuition* would say that our moral feelings do provide us with information about good and evil and about what is right and what is wrong.

Some will add (8) *religious intuition* to the list. The religious intuitionist says that certain other thoughts and feelings justify us in believing that there is a personal God. And some go even farther. They say in effect: "I have certain special experiences that justify me in believing, not only that there is a personal God, but also that this God has selected *me,* out of all others, to be his personal representative."

One of the most difficult questions of theory of knowledge, if not of all philosophy, is this. How are we to find the *answer* to such a question? How are we to *decide* whether the list is too long or too short?

The Problem of Skepticism

Meditatio

When I carefully consider the curious habits of dogs
I am compelled to conclude
That man is the superior animal.

When I consider the curious habits of man
I confess, my friend, I am puzzled.

Ezra Pound

SEXTUS EMPIRICUS
(c. 160–210) Greek Philosopher and Physician

From *Outlines of Pyrrhonism**

Of the Main Difference Between Philosophic Systems

The natural result of any investigation is that the investigators either discover the object of search or deny that it is discoverable and confess it to be inapprehensible or persist in their search. So, too, with regard to the objects investigated by philosophy, this is probably why some have claimed to have discovered the truth, others have asserted that it cannot be apprehended, while others again go on inquiring. Those who believe they have discovered it are the "Dogmatists," specially so called—Aristotle, for example, and Epicurus and the Stoics and certain others; Cleitomachus and Carneades and other Academics treat it as inapprehensible: the Skeptics keep on searching. Hence it seems reasonable to hold that the main types of philosophy are three—the Dogmatic, the Academic, and the Skeptic. Of the other systems it will best become others to speak: our task at present is to describe in outline the Skeptic doctrine, first premising that of none of our future statements do we positively affirm that the fact is exactly as we state it, but we simply record each fact, like a chronicler, as it appears to us at the moment. . . .

What Skepticism Is

Skepticism is an ability, or mental attitude, which opposes appearances to judgments in any way whatsoever, with the result that, owing to the equipollence of the objects and reasons thus opposed, we are brought firstly to a state of mental suspense and next to a state of "unperturbedness" or quietude. Now we call it an "ability" not in any subtle sense, but simply in respect of its "being able." By "appearances" we now mean the objects of sense perception, whence we contrast them with the objects of thought or "judgments." The phrase "in any way whatsoever" can be connected either with the word "ability," to make us take the word "ability," as we said, in its simple sense, or with the phrase "opposing appearances to judgments"; for inasmuch as we oppose these in a variety of ways—appearances to appearances, or judgments to judgments, or *alternando* appearances to judgments,—in order to ensure the inclusion of all these antitheses we employ the phrase "in any way whatsoever." Or, again, we join "in any way whatsoever" to "appearances and judgments" in order that we may not have to inquire how the appearances appear or how the thought-objects are judged,

*For permission to photocopy this selection please contact Harvard University Press. Reprinted by permission of the publisher and the Loeb Classical Library from Sextus Empiricus, *Outlines of Pyrrhonism*, trans. by R. G. Bury, Cambridge: Harvard University Press, 1933.

but may take these terms in the simple sense. The phase "opposed judgments" we do not employ in the sense of negations and affirmations only but simply as equivalent to "conflicting judgments." "Equipollence" we use of equality in respect of probability and improbability, to indicate that no one of the conflicting judgments takes precedence of any other as being more probable. "Suspense" is a state of mental rest owing to which we neither deny nor affirm anything. "Quietude" is an untroubled and tranquil condition of soul.

Of the Skeptic

In the definition of the Skeptic system there is also implicitly included that of the Pyrrhonean philosopher; he is the man who participates in this "ability."[1]

Of the Principles of Skepticism

The originating cause of Skepticism is, we say, the hope of attaining quietude. Men of talent, who were perturbed by the contradictions in things and in doubt as to which of the alternatives they ought to accept, were led on to inquire what is true in things and what false, hoping by the settlement of this question to attain quietude. The main basic principle of the Skeptic system is that of opposing to every proposition an equal proposition; for we believe that as a consequence of this we end by ceasing to dogmatize.

Does the Skeptic Dogmatize?

When we say that the Skeptic refrains from dogmatizing we do not use the term "dogma," as some do, in the broader sense of "approval of a thing" (for the Skeptic gives assent to the feelings which are the necessary results of sense impressions, and he would not, for example, say when feeling hot or cold "I believe that I am not hot or cold"); but we say that "he does not dogmatize" using "dogma" in the sense, which some give it, of "assent to one of the non-evident objects of scientific inquiry"; for the Pyrrhonean philosopher assents to nothing that is non-evident. Moreover, even in the act of enunciating the Skeptic formulae concerning things non-evident—such as the formula "No more (one thing than another)," or the formula "I determine nothing," or any of the others which we shall presently mention,—he does not dogmatize. For whereas the dogmatizer posits the things about which he is said to be dogmatizing as really existent, the Skeptic does not posit these formulae in any absolute sense; for he conceives that, just as the formula "All things are false" asserts the falsity of itself as well as of everything else, as does the formula "Nothing is true," so also the formula "No more" asserts that itself, like all the rest, is "No more (this and that)," and thus cancels itself along with the rest. And of the other formulae we say the same. If then, while the dogmatizer posits the matter of his dogma as substantial truth, the Skeptic enunciates his formulae so that they are virtually cancelled by themselves, he should not be said to dogmatize in his enunciation of

---

[1] The word here is *dunamis*. It refers both to "power" and "potentiality."

them. And, most important of all, in his enunciation of these formulae he states what appears to himself and announces his own impression in an undogmatic way, without making any positive assertion regarding the external realities.

Has the Skeptic a Doctrinal Rule?

We follow the same lines in replying to the question "Has the Skeptic a doctrinal rule?" For if one defines a "doctrinal rule" as "adherence to a number of dogmas which are dependent both on one another and on appearances," and defines "dogma" as "assent to a non-evident proposition," then we shall say that he has not a doctrinal rule. But if one defines "doctrinal rule" as "procedure which, in accordance with appearance, follows a certain line of reasoning, that reasoning indicating how it is possible to seem to live rightly (the word 'rightly' being taken, not as referring to virtue only, but in a wider sense) and tending to enable one to suspend judgment," then we say that he has a doctrinal rule. For we follow a line of reasoning which, in accordance with appearances, points us to a life conformable to the customs of our country and its laws and institutions, and to our own instinctive feelings.

Does the Skeptic Deal With Physics?

We make a similar reply also to the question "Should the Skeptic deal with physical problems?" For while, on the one hand, so far as regards making firm and positive assertions about any of the matters dogmatically treated in physical theory, we do not deal with physics; yet, on the other hand, in respect of our mode of opposing to every proposition an equal proposition and of our theory of quietude we do treat of physics. This, too, is the way in which we approach the logical and ethical branches of so-called "philosophy."

Do the Skeptics Abolish Appearances?

Those who say that "the Skeptics abolish appearances," or phenomena, seem to me to be unacquainted with the statements of our School. For, as we said above, we do not overthrow the affective sense impressions which induce our assent involuntarily; and these impressions are "the appearances." And when we question whether the underlying object is such as it appears, we grant the fact that it appears, and our doubt does not concern the appearance itself but the account given of that appearance,—and that is a different thing from questioning the appearance itself. For example, honey appears to us to be sweet (and this we grant, for we perceive sweetness through the senses), but whether it is also sweet in its essence is for us a matter of doubt, since this is not an appearance but a judgment regarding the appearance. And even if we do actually argue against the appearances, we do not propound such arguments with the intention of abolishing appearances, but by way of pointing out the rashness of the Dogmatists; for if reason is such a trickster as to all but snatch away the appearances from under our very eyes, surely we should view it with suspicion in the case of things non-evident so as not to display rashness by following it.

Of the Criterion of Skepticism

That we adhere to appearances is plain from what we say about the criterion of the Skeptic School. The word "criterion" is used in two senses: in the one it means "the standard regulating belief in reality or unreality" (and this we shall discuss in our refutation); in the other it denotes the standard of action by conforming to which in the conduct of life we perform some actions and abstain from others; and it is of the latter that we are now speaking. The criterion, then, of the Skeptic School is, we say, the appearance, giving this name to what is virtually the sense presentation. For since this lies in feeling and involuntary affection, it is not open to question. Consequently, no one, I suppose, disputes that the underlying object has this or that appearance; the point in dispute is whether the object is in reality such as it appears to be.

Adhering, then, to appearances we live in accordance with the normal rules of life, undogmatically, seeing that we cannot remain wholly inactive. And it would seem that this regulation of life is fourfold, and that one part of it lies in the guidance of Nature, another in the constraint of the passions, another in the tradition of laws and customs, another in the instruction of the arts. Nature's guidance is that by which we are naturally capable of sensation and thought; constraint of the passions is that whereby hunger drives us to food and thirst to drink; tradition of customs and laws, that whereby we regard piety in the conduct of life as good, but impiety as evil; instruction of the arts, that whereby we are not inactive in such arts as we adopt. But we make all these statements undogmatically.

What Is the End of Skepticism?

Our next subject will be the end of the Skeptic system. Now an "end" is "that for which all actions or reasonings are undertaken, while it exists for the sake of none"; or, otherwise, "the ultimate object of appetency." We assert still that the Skeptic's end is quietude in respect of matters of opinion and moderate feeling in respect of things unavoidable. For the Skeptic, having set out to philosophize with the object of passing judgment on the sense impressions and ascertaining which of them are true and which false, so as to attain quietude thereby, found himself involved in contradictions of equal weight, and being unable to decide between them suspended judgment; and as he was thus in suspense there followed, as it happened, the state of quietude in respect of matters of opinion. For the man who opines that anything is by nature good or bad is for ever being disquieted: when he is without the things which he deems good he believes himself to be tormented by things naturally bad and he pursues after the things which are, as he thinks, good; which when he has obtained he keeps falling into still more perturbations because of his irrational and immoderate elation, and in his dread of a change of fortune he uses every endeavor to avoid losing the things which he deems good. On the other hand, the man who determines nothing as to what is naturally good or bad neither shuns nor pursues anything eagerly; and, in consequence, he is unperturbed.

The Skeptic, in fact, had the same experience which is said to have befallen the painter Apelles.[2] Once, they say, when he was painting a horse and wished to represent in the painting the horse's foam, he was so unsuccessful that he gave up the attempt and flung at the picture the sponge on which he used to wipe the paints off his brush, and the mark of the sponge produced the effect of a horse's foam. So, too, the Skeptics were in hopes of gaining quietude by means of a decision regarding the disparity of the objects of sense and of thought, and being unable to effect this they suspended judgment; and they found that quietude, as if by chance, followed upon their suspense, even as a shadow follows its substance. We do not, however, suppose that the Skeptic is wholly untroubled; but we say that he is troubled by things unavoidable; for we grant that he is cold at times and thirsty, and suffers various affections of that kind. But even in these cases, whereas ordinary people are afflicted by two circumstances,—namely, by the affections themselves and, in no less a degree, by the belief that these conditions are evil by nature,— the Skeptic, by his rejection of the added belief in the natural badness of all these conditions, escapes here too with less discomfort. Hence we say that, while in regard to matters of opinion the Skeptic's end is quietude, in regard to things unavoidable it is "moderate affection." But some notable Skeptics have added the further definition "suspension of judgment in investigations."

Of the General Modes Leading to Suspension of Judgment

Now that we have been saying that tranquility follows on suspension of judgment, it will be our next task to explain how we arrive at this suspension. Speaking generally, one may say that it is the result of setting things in opposition. We oppose either appearances to appearances or objects of thought to objects of thought or *alternando*. For instance, we oppose appearances to appearances when we say "The same tower appears round from a distance, but square from close at hand"; and thoughts to thoughts, when in answer to him who argues the existence of providence from the order of the heavenly bodies we oppose the fact that often the good fare ill and the bad fare well, and draw from this the inference that providence does not exist. And thoughts we oppose to appearances, as when Anaxagoras countered the notion that snow is white with the argument, "Snow is frozen water, and water is black; therefore snow also is black." With a different idea we oppose things present sometimes to things present, as in the foregoing examples, and sometimes to things past or future, as, for instance, when someone propounds to us a theory which we are unable to refute, we say to him in reply, "Just as, before the birth of the founder of the School to which you belong, the theory it holds was not as yet apparent as a sound theory, although it was really in existence, so likewise it is possible that the opposite theory to that which you now propound is already really existent, though not yet apparent to us so that we ought not as yet to yield assent to this theory which at the moment seems to be valid."

[2] Court painter to Alexander the Great (350–300 B.C.)

AUGUSTINE

(354–430 A.D.) North African Philosopher

From *Against the Academician**

The Academicians are of the opinion that knowledge cannot be attained by man in so far as those things are concerned which pertain to philosophy—for Carneades[1] said he did not care about other matters—and yet that man can be wise and that the whole duty of a wise man is accomplished in seeking truth, a statement which was also made by you, Licentius, in your argument; the conclusion is that the wise man should not assent to anything; for the fact that it is wrong for a wise man to assent to things that are uncertain, makes it necessary that he be in error. And they not only said that everything is uncertain but they even supported their statement by very forceful arguments. But they seemed to have appropriated the idea that truth cannot be grasped, from that definition of Zeno,[2] the Stoic, who said that that can be apprehended as true which has been so deeply impressed upon the mind from the source from which it came, that it could not proceed from that from which it did not come. To express it more briefly and clearly, truth can be grasped by those signs which whatever is false cannot have. They emphasized this precisely in order to prove conclusively that it cannot be found. From this source have arisen the dissensions of philosophers, the unreliability of the senses, vain imaginations and frenzies, sophistical syllogisms and sorites in defense of that cause. And since they had learned from this same Zeno, that nothing is more disgraceful than to conjecture, they very cleverly inferred that if nothing can actually be known and if it is disgraceful to express an opinion, then the wise man should never approve of anything.

From this cause great odium was excited against them: for the logical consequence seemed to be that he who would not assent to anything would not accomplish anything. Hence the Academicians seemed to portray your wise man as always sleeping and neglecting all his duties since they thought he never gave assent to anything. Hereupon, by introducing a kind of probability which they even mentioned as being similar to truth, they maintained that the wise man was in no way negligent in his duties since he had that which he was striving for; truth, however, lay hidden, being either crushed or obscured because of the darkness of our nature or the similarity existing in all things, although they said that the very withholding and, as it were, suspension of assent was, indeed, the great achievement of the wise man.

---

*From Augustine, *Against the Academicians* (Book II, vols. 11–12; Book III, vols. 23–26), ed. by Mary Garvey. (Milwaukee; Marquette, 1942).
[1] Carneades of Cyrene (213–129 B.C.)—critical skeptic from The New Academy. —ED.
[2] Zeno of Citium (350–258 B.C.)—one of the founders of stoicism. —ED.

You say that nothing can be apprehended in philosophy and, in order to spread your opinion far and wide, you make use of the disputes and contentions of philosophers and you think that these dissensions furnish arms for you against them. For how shall we determine the strife between Democritus[3] and the earlier natural philosophers about one world and innumerable worlds when no harmony could subsist between him and Epicurus,[4] his successor? For when that lover of pleasure does not allow his atoms, his little maid-servants, so to speak, that is, the little bodies which he joyfully embraces in the darkness, to hold their course, but permits them of their own accord to deviate here and there into strange bypaths, he has squandered his entire patrimony through contentions. But this is of no concern to me. For if it belongs to wisdom to know any of these things, it cannot be hidden from the wise man. If, however, it is something else, the wise man knows that type of wisdom and despises such things as these. And yet, I who am still far removed from the likeness of a wise man, know something about those physical phenomena. For I hold as certain either that there is or is not one world; and if there is not one, there are either a finite or an infinite number of worlds. Carneades would teach that that opinion resembles what is false. I likewise know that this world of ours has been so arranged either because of the nature of bodies or by some providence, and that it either always was and will be or that it began to exist and will by no means cease existing, or that it does not have its origin in time but will have an end, or that it has started to remain in existence and will remain but not forever, and I know innumerable physical phenomena of this type. For those disjunctions are true nor can anyone confuse them with any likeness to what is false. But take something for granted, says the Academician. I do not wish to do so; for that is to say: abandon what you know; say what you do not know. But opinion is uncertain. Assuredly it is better that it be uncertain than that it be destroyed; it surely is clear; it certainly now can be called false or true. I say that I know this opinion. Prove to me that I do not know them, you who do not deny that such matters pertain to philosophy and who maintain that none of these things can be known; say that those disjunctive ideas are either false or have something in common with what is false from which they cannot altogether be distinguished.

Whence, he says, do you know that this world exists if the senses are untrustworthy? Your methods of reasoning have never been able to disprove the power of the senses in such a way as to convince us that nothing is seen and you certainly have never dared to try such a thing, but you have exerted yourself to persuade us urgently that (a thing) can be otherwise than it seems. And so I call this entire thing, whatever it is, which surrounds us and nourishes us, this object, I say, which appears before my eyes and which I perceive is made up of earth and sky, or what appears to be earth and sky, the world. If you say nothing is seen by me, I shall never err. For he is in error who rashly proves what seems to him. For you say that what is false can be seen by those perceiving it: you do not say that nothing is seen. Certainly every reason for arguing will be removed when it pleases you to settle the point, if we not only know nothing but if nothing is even seen by

---

[3] Democritus of Abdera (c. 420 B.C.) held the world is composed of atoms and empty space. —ED.
[4] Epicurus of Samos (341–270 B.C.) was an atomist. One follower of Epicurus was Lucretius—see pp. 340 of this volume. —ED.

us. If, however, you deny that this object which appears to me is the world, you are making it a controversy in regard to a name since I said that I called it the world.

If you are asleep, you will say, is that also the world, which you see? I have already said I call that the world, which appears to me to be such. But if it pleases me to call only that the world, which is seen by those who are awake or even by those who are rational, prove this if you can, that those who are asleep and are raving are not raving and sleeping in the world. Therefore I say this: that entire mass of bodies and that contrivance in which we exist whether sleeping, or raging, or awake, or rational, either is one or is not one. Explain how that opinion can be false. For if I am asleep, it can follow that I said nothing; or even if the words have escaped from the mouth of a person who is asleep, as often happens, it can follow that I did not speak here, nor while sitting in this way, nor to those who were listening; but it cannot follow that this is false. Nor do I say that I apprehended this because I am awake. For you can say that this could appear to me even if I were asleep and therefore this can bear a close resemblance to what is false. But if there are one and six worlds, it is evident to me, no matter in what condition I may be, that there are seven worlds, and I am not rash in asserting that I know it. Therefore, show me either that this logical conclusion or those disjunctions mentioned above in regard to sleep or madness or unreliability of the senses can be false, and I shall grant that I have been defeated if I remember them when I have been awakened. For I believe it is sufficiently evident that those things which appear false through sleep and an abnormal condition of the mind are those things which have reference to the senses of the body; for that three threes are nine and represent the square of intelligible numbers is necessary or would be true even though the human race were lying prostrate. And yet I also see that many things can be said in favor of the senses themselves, which we have not found refuted by the Academicians. For I think that the senses are not to be blamed because they permit false and frenzied mental images or because in sleep we see things which are not true. If indeed the senses have reported the truth to those who are awake and who are rational, what the mind of a sleeping or insane person may fabricate for itself is not to be attributed to them.

It now remains for us to inquire whether the senses report the truth when they give information. Suppose that some Epicurean should say: "I have no complaint to make in regard to the senses; for it is unjust to demand more of them than they can give; moreover whatever the eyes can see they see in a reliable manner." Then is what they see in regard to an oar in the water true? It certainly is true. For when the reason is added for its appearing thus, if the oar dipped in the water seemed straight, I should rather blame my eyes for the false report. For they did not see what should have been seen when such causes arose. What need is there of many illustrations? This can also be said of the movement of towers, of the feathers of birds, of innumerable other things. "And yet I am deceived if I give my assent," someone says. Do not give assent any further than to the extent that you can persuade yourself that it appears true to you, and there is no deception. For I do not see how the Academician can refute him who says: "I know that this appears white to me. I know that my hearing is delighted with this. I know that this has an agreeable odor. I know that this tastes sweet to me. I know that this feels cold to me." Tell us rather whether the leaves of the wild olive trees, which the goat so persistently desires, are by their very nature bitter. O foolish man! Is not the goat more reasonable? I do not know how they seem to the goat, but they are bitter to me. What more do you ask for? But perhaps there is also some one to whom they do not taste bitter. Do you trouble yourself about this? Did I say they were bitter to everyone? I said they were bitter to me and I do not always maintain this. For what if for some reason or other a thing which now tastes sweet to a person should at another time seem bitter to him? I say this, that when a person tastes something, he can honestly swear that he knows it is sweet to his palate or the contrary, and that no trickery of the Greeks can dispossess him of that knowledge. For who would be so bold as to say to me when I am longing for something with great pleasure: Perhaps you do not taste it, but this is only a dream? Do I offer any opposition to him? But still that would give me pleasure even in my sleep. Therefore no likeness to what is false obscures that which I have said I know, and both the Epicurean and the Cyrenaics may say many other things in favor of the senses against which I have heard that the Academicians have not said anything. But why should this concern me? If they so desire and if they can, let them even do away with the argument with my approbation. Whatever argument they raise against the senses has no weight against all philosophers. For there are those who admit that whatever the mind receives through a sense of the body, can beget opinion, but they deny (that it can beget) knowledge which, however, they wish to be continued to the intellect and to live in the mind, far removed from the senses. And perhaps that wise man whom we are seeking is in their number. But we shall say more about this at another time.

RENÉ DESCARTES
(1596–1650) French Philosopher

Meditations I and II*

Meditation I

Of the things which may be brought within the sphere of the doubtful.

It is now some years since I detected how many were the false beliefs that I had from my earliest youth admitted as true, and how doubtful was everything I had since constructed on this basis; and from that time I was convinced that

---

*From René Descartes, *Meditations on First Philosophy,* trans. by Elizabeth S. Haldane and G.R.T. Ross, in *The Philosophical Writings of Descartes,* vol. 1 (Cambridge: Cambridge University Press, 1911, reprinted 1931).

I must once for all seriously undertake to rid myself of all the opinions which I had formerly accepted, and commence to build anew from the foundation, if I wanted to establish any firm and permanent structure in the sciences. But as this enterprise appeared to be a very great one, I waited until I had attained an age so mature that I could not hope that at any later date I should be better fitted to execute my design. This reason caused me to delay so long that I should feel that I was doing wrong were I to occupy in deliberation the time that yet remains to me for action. To-day, then, since very opportunely for the plan I have in view I have delivered my mind from every care [and am happily agitated by no passions] and since I have procured for myself an assured leisure in a peaceable retirement, I shall at last seriously and freely address myself to the general upheaval of all my former opinions.

Now for this object it is not necessary that I should show that all of these are false—I shall perhaps never arrive at this end. But inasmuch as reason already persuades me that I ought no less carefully to withhold my assent from matters which are not entirely certain and indubitable than from those which appear to me manifestly to be false, if I am able to find in each one some reason to doubt, this will suffice to justify my rejecting the whole. And for that end it will not be requisite that I should examine each in particular, which would be an endless undertaking; for owing to the fact that the destruction of the foundations of necessity brings with it the downfall of the rest of the edifice, I shall only in the first place attack those principles upon which all my former opinions rested.

All that up to the present time I have accepted as most true and certain I have learned either from the senses or through the senses; but it is sometimes proved to me that these senses are deceptive, and it is wiser not to trust entirely to any thing by which we have once been deceived.

But it may be that although the senses sometimes deceive us concerning things which are hardly perceptible, or very far away, there are yet many others to be met with as to which we cannot reasonably have any doubt, although we recognise them by their means. For example, there is the fact that I am here, seated by the fire, attired in a dressing gown, having this paper in my hands and other similar matters. And how could I deny that these hands and this body are mine, were it not perhaps that I compare myself to certain persons, devoid of sense, whose cerebella are so troubled and clouded by the violent vapours of black bile, that they constantly assure us that they think they are kings when they are really quite poor, or that they are clothed in purple when they are really without covering, or who imagine that they have an earthenware head or are nothing but pumpkins or are made of glass. But they are mad, and I should not be any the less insane were I to follow examples so extravagant.

At the same time I must remember that I am a man, and that consequently I am in the habit of sleeping, and in my dreams representing to myself the same things or sometimes even less probable things, than do those who are insane in their waking moments. How often has it happened to me that in the night I dreamt that I found myself in this particular place, that I was dressed and seated near the fire, whilst in reality I was lying undressed in bed! At this moment it does indeed seem to me that it is with eyes awake that I am looking at this paper; that this head which I move is not asleep, that it is deliberately and of set purpose that I extend my hand and perceive it; what happens in sleep does not appear so clear nor so distinct as does all this. But in thinking over this I remind myself that on many occasions I have in sleep been deceived by similar illusions, and in dwelling carefully on this reflection I see so manifestly that there are no certain indications by which we may clearly distinguish wakefulness from sleep that I am lost in astonishment. And my astonishment is such that it is almost capable of persuading me that I now dream.

Now let us assume that we are asleep and that all these particulars, e.g. that we open our eyes, shake our head, extend our hands, and so on, are but false delusions; and let us reflect that possibly neither our hands nor our whole body are such as they appear to us to be. At the same time we must at least confess that the things which are represented to us in sleep are like painted representations which can only have been formed as the counterparts of something real and true, and that in this way those general things at least, i.e. eyes, a head, hands, and a whole body, are not imaginary things, but things really existent. For, as a matter of fact, painters, even when they study with the greatest skill to represent sirens and satyrs by forms the most strange and extraordinary, cannot give them natures which are entirely new, but merely make a certain medley of the members of different animals; or if their imagination is extravagant enough to invent something so novel that nothing similar has ever before been seen, and that then their work represents a thing purely fictitious and absolutely false, it is certain all the same that the colours of which this is composed are necessarily real. And for the same reason, although these general things, to wit, [a body], eyes, a head, hands, and such like, may be imaginary, we are bound at the same time to confess that there are at least some other objects yet more simple and more universal, which are real and true; and of these just in the same way as with certain real colours, all these images of things which dwell in our thoughts, whether true and real or false and fantastic, are formed.

To such a class of things pertains corporeal nature in general, and its extension, the figure of extended things, their quantity or magnitude and number, as also the place in which they are, the time which measures their duration, and so on.

That is possibly why our reasoning is not unjust when we conclude from this that Physics, Astronomy, Medicine and all other sciences which have as their end the consideration of composite things, are very dubious and uncertain; but that Arithmetic, Geometry and other sciences of that kind which only treat of things that are very simple and very general, without taking great trouble to ascertain whether they are actually existent or not, contain some measure of certainty and an element of the indubitable. For whether I am awake or asleep, two and three together always form five, and the square can never have more than four sides, and it does not seem possible that truths so clear and apparent can be suspected of any falsity [or uncertainty].

Nevertheless I have long had fixed in my mind the belief that an all-powerful God existed by whom I have been created such as I am. But how do I know that He has not brought it to pass that there is no earth, no heaven, no extended body, no magnitude, no place, and that nevertheless [I possess the perceptions of all these things and that] they seem to me to exist just exactly as I now see them?

And, besides, as I sometimes imagine that others deceive themselves in the things which they think they know best, how do I know that I am not deceived every time that I add two and three, or count the sides of a square, or judge of things yet simpler, if anything simpler can be imagined? But possibly God has not desired that I should be thus deceived, for He is said to be supremely good. If, however, it is contrary to His goodness to have made me such that I constantly deceive myself, it would also appear to be contrary to His goodness to permit me to be sometimes deceived, and nevertheless I cannot doubt that He does permit this.

There may indeed be those who would prefer to deny the existence of a God so powerful, rather than believe that all other things are uncertain. But let us not oppose them for the present, and grant that all that is here said of a God is a fable; nevertheless in whatever way they suppose that I have arrived at the state of being that I have reached—whether they attribute it to fate or to accident, or make out that it is by a continual succession of antecedents, or by some other method— since to err and deceive oneself is a defect, it is clear that the greater will be the probability of my being so imperfect as to deceive myself ever, as is the Author to whom they assign my origin the less powerful. To these reasons I have certainly nothing to reply, but at the end I feel constrained to confess that there is nothing in all that I formerly believed to be true, of which I cannot in some measure doubt, and that not merely through want of thought or through levity, but for reasons which are very powerful and maturely considered; so that henceforth I ought not the less carefully to refrain from giving credence to these opinions than to that which is manifestly false, if I desire to arrive at any certainty [in the sciences].

But it is not sufficient to have made these remarks, we must also be careful to keep them in mind. For these ancient and commonly held opinions still revert frequently to my mind, long and familiar custom having given them the right to occupy my mind against my inclination and rendered them almost masters of my belief; nor will I ever lose the habit of deferring to them or of placing my confidence in them, so long as I consider them as they really are, i.e. opinions in some measure doubtful, as I have just shown, and at the same time highly probable, so that there is much more reason to believe in than to deny them. That is why I consider that I shall not be acting amiss, if, taking of set purpose a contrary belief, I allow myself to be deceived, and for a certain time pretend that all these opinions are entirely false and imaginary, until at last, having thus balanced my former prejudices with my latter [so that they cannot divert my opinions more to one side than to the other], my judgment will no longer be dominated by bad usage or turned away from the right knowledge of the truth. For I am assured that there can be neither peril nor error in this course, and that I cannot at present yield too much to distrust, since I am not considering the question of action, but only of knowledge.

I shall then suppose, not that God who is supremely good and the fountain of truth, but some evil genius not less powerful than deceitful, has employed his whole energies in deceiving me; I shall consider that the heavens, the earth, colours, figures, sound, and all other external things are nought but the illusions and dreams of which this genius has availed himself in order to lay traps for my credulity; I shall consider myself as having no hands, no eyes, no flesh, no blood, nor any senses, yet falsely believing myself to possess all these things; I shall remain obstinately attached to this idea, and if by this means it is not in my power to arrive at the knowledge of any truth, I may at least do what is in my power [i.e. suspend my judgment], and with firm purpose avoid giving credence to any false thing, or being imposed upon by this arch deceiver, however powerful and deceptive he may be. But this task is a laborious one, and insensibly a certain lassitude leads me into the course of my ordinary life. And just as a captive who in sleep enjoys an imaginary liberty, when he begins to suspect that his liberty is but a dream, fears to awaken, and conspires with these agreeable illusions that the deception may be prolonged, so insensibly of my own accord I fall back into my former opinions, and I dread awakening from this slumber, lest the laborious wakefulness which would follow the tranquillity of this repose should have to be spent not in daylight, but in the excessive darkness of the difficulties which have just been discussed.

Meditation II

Of the Nature of the Human Mind; and that it is more easily known than the Body.

The Meditation of yesterday filled my mind with so many doubts that it is no longer in my power to forget them. And yet I do not see in what manner I can resolve them; and, just as if I had all of a sudden fallen into very deep water, I am so disconcerted that I can neither make certain of setting my feet on the bottom, nor can I swim and so support myself on the surface. I shall nevertheless make an effort and follow anew the same path as that on which I yesterday entered, i.e. I shall proceed by setting aside all that in which the least doubt could be supposed to exist, just as if I had discovered that it was absolutely false; and I shall ever follow in this road until I have met with something which is certain, or at least, if I can do nothing else, until I have learned for certain that there is nothing in the world that is certain. Archimedes, in order that he might draw the terrestrial globe out of its place, and transport it elsewhere, demanded only that one point should be fixed and immoveable; in the same way I shall have the right to conceive high hopes if I am happy enough to discover one thing only which is certain and indubitable.

I suppose, then, that all the things that I see are false; I persuade myself that nothing has ever existed of all that my fallacious memory represents to me. I consider that I possess no senses; I imagine that body, figure, extension, movement and place are but the fictions of my mind. What, then, can be esteemed as true? Perhaps nothing at all, unless that there is nothing in the world that is certain.

But how can I know there is not something different from those things that I have just considered, of which one cannot have the slightest doubt? Is there not some God, or some other being by whatever name we call it, who puts these reflections into my mind? That is not necessary, for is it not possible that I am capable of producing them myself? I myself, am I not at least something? But I have already denied that I had senses and body. Yet I hesitate, for what follows from that? Am I so dependent on body and senses that I cannot exist without these? But I was persuaded that there was nothing in all the world, that there was no heaven, no earth, that there were no minds, nor any bodies: was I not then likewise persuaded that I did not exist? Not at all; of a surety I myself did exist since I persuaded myself of something [or merely because I thought of something]. But there is some deceiver or other, very powerful and very cunning, who ever employs his ingenuity in deceiving me. Then without doubt I exist also if he deceives me, and let him deceive me as much as he will, he can never cause me to be nothing so long as I think that I am something. So that after having reflected well and carefully examined all things, we must come to the definite conclusion that this proposition: I am, I exist, is necessarily true each time that I pronounce it, or that I mentally conceive it.

But I do not yet know clearly enough what I am, I who am certain that I am; and hence I must be careful to see that I do not imprudently take some other object in place of myself, and thus that I do not go astray in respect of this knowledge that I hold to be the most certain and most evident of all that I have formerly learned. That is why I shall now consider anew what I believed myself to be before I embarked upon these last reflections; and of my former opinions I shall withdraw all that might even in a small degree be invalidated by the reasons which I have just brought forward, in order that there may be nothing at all left beyond what is absolutely certain and indubitable.

What then did I formerly believe myself to be? Undoubtedly I believed myself to be a man. But what is a man? Shall I say a reasonable animal? Certainly not; for then I should have to inquire what an animal is, and what is reasonable; and thus from a single question I should insensibly fall into an infinitude of others more difficult; and I should not wish to waste the little time and leisure remaining to me in trying to unravel subtleties like these. But I shall rather stop here to consider the thoughts which of themselves spring up in my mind, and which were not inspired by anything beyond my own nature alone when I applied myself to the consideration of my being. In the first place, then, I considered myself as having a face, hands, arms, and all that system of members composed of bones and flesh as seen in a corpse which I designated by the name of body. In addition to this I considered that I was nourished, that I walked, that I felt, and that I thought, and I referred all these actions to the soul: but I did not stop to consider what the soul was, or if I did stop, I imagined that it was something extremely rare and subtle like a wind, a flame, or an ether, which was spread throughout my grosser parts. As to body I had no manner of doubt about its nature, but thought I had a very clear knowledge of it; and if I had desired to explain it according to the notions that I had then formed of it, I should have described it thus: By the body I understand all that which can be defined by a certain figure: something which can be confined in a certain place, and which can fill a given space in such a way that every other body will be excluded from it; which can be perceived either by touch, or by sight, or by hearing, or by taste, or by smell: which can be moved in many ways not, in truth, by itself, but by something which is foreign to it, by which it is touched [and from which it receives impressions]: for to have the power of self-movement, as also of feeling or of thinking, I did not consider to appertain to the nature of body: on the contrary, I was rather astonished to find that faculties similar to them existed in some bodies.

But what am I, now that I suppose that there is a certain genius which is extremely powerful, and, if I may say so, malicious, who employs all his powers in deceiving me? Can I affirm that I possess the least of all those things which I have just said pertain to the nature of body? I pause to consider, I revolve all these things in my mind, and I find none of which I can say that it pertains to me. It would be tedious to stop to enumerate them. Let us pass to the attributes of soul and see if there is any one which is in me? What of nutrition or walking [the first mentioned]? But if it is so that I have no body it is also true that I can neither walk nor take nourishment. Another attribute is sensation. But one cannot feel without body, and besides I have thought I perceived many things during sleep that I recognised in my waking moments as not having been experienced at all. What of thinking? I find here that thought is an attribute that belongs to me; it alone cannot be separated from me. I am, I exist, that is certain. But how often? Just when I think; for it might possibly be the case if I ceased entirely to think, that I should likewise cease altogether to exist. I do not now admit anything which is not necessarily true: to speak accurately I am not more than a thing which thinks, that is to say a mind or a soul, or an understanding, or a reason, which are terms whose significance was formerly unknown to me. I am, however, a real thing and really exist; but what thing? I have answered: a thing which thinks.

And what more? I shall exercise my imagination [in order to see if I am not something more]. I am not a collection of members which we call the human body: I am not a subtle air distributed through these members, I am not a wind, a fire, a vapour, a breath, nor anything at all which I can imagine or conceive; because I have assumed that all these were nothing. Without changing that supposition I find that I only leave myself certain of the fact that I am somewhat. But perhaps it is true that these same things which I supposed were non-existent because they are unknown to me, are really not different from the self which I know. I am not sure about this, I shall not dispute about it now; I can only give judgment on things that are known to me. I know that I exist, and I inquire what I am, I whom I know to exist. But it is very certain that the knowledge of my existence taken in its precise significance does not depend on things whose existence is not yet known to me; consequently it does not depend on those which I can feign in imagination. And indeed the very term *feign* in imagination proves to me my error, for I really do this if I image myself a something, since to imagine is nothing else than to contemplate the figure or image of a corporeal thing. But I already know for certain that I am, and that it may be that all these images, and, speaking generally, all things that relate to the nature of body are nothing but dreams [and chimeras]. For this reason I see clearly that I have as little reason to say, "I shall stimulate my imagination in order to know more distinctly what I am," than if I were to say, "I am now awake, and I perceive somewhat that is real and true: but because I do not yet perceive it distinctly enough, I shall go to sleep of express purpose, so that my dreams may represent the perception with greatest truth and evidence." And, thus, I know for certain that nothing of all that I can understand by means of my imagination belongs to this knowledge which I have of myself, and that it is necessary to recall the mind from this mode of thought with the utmost diligence in order that it may be able to know its own nature with perfect distinctness.

But what then am I? A thing which thinks. What is a thing which thinks? It is a thing which doubts, understands, [conceives], affirms, denies, wills, refuses, which also imagines and feels.

Certainly it is no small matter if all these things pertain to my nature. But why should they not so pertain? Am I not that being who now doubts nearly everything, who nevertheless understands certain things, who affirms that one only is true, who denies all the others, who desires to know more, is averse from being deceived, who imagines many things, sometimes indeed despite his will, and who perceives many likewise, as by the intervention of the bodily organs? Is there nothing in all this which is as true as it is certain that I exist, even though I should always sleep and though he who has given me being employed all his ingenuity in deceiving me? Is there likewise any one of these attributes which can be distinguished from my thought, or which might be said to be separated from myself? For it is so evident of itself that it is I who doubts, who understands, and who desires, that there is no reason here to add anything to explain it. And I have certainly the power of imagining likewise; for although it may happen (as I formerly supposed) that none of the things which I imagine are true, nevertheless this power of imagining does not cease to be really in use, and it forms part of my thought. Finally, I am the same who feels, that is to say, who perceives certain things, as by the organs of sense, since in truth I see light, I hear noise, I feel heat. But it will be said that these phenomena are false and that I am dreaming. Let it be so; still it is at least quite certain that it seems to me that I see light, that I hear noise and that I feel heat. That cannot be false; properly speaking it is what is in me called feeling; and used in this precise sense that is no other thing than thinking.

From this time I begin to know what I am with a little more clearness and distinction than before; but nevertheless it still seems to me, and I cannot prevent myself from thinking, that corporeal things, whose images are framed by thought, which are tested by the senses, are much more distinctly known than that obscure part of me which does not come under the imagination. Although really it is very strange to say that I know and understand more distinctly these things whose existence seems to me dubious, which are unknown to me, and which do not belong to me, than others of the truth of which I am convinced, which are known to me and which pertain to my real nature, in a word, than myself. But I see clearly how the case stands: my mind loves to wander, and cannot yet suffer itself to be retained within the just limits of truth. Very good, let us once more give it the freest rein, so that, when afterwards we seize the proper occasion for pulling up, it may the more easily be regulated and controlled.

Let us begin by considering the commonest matters, those which we believe to be the most distinctly comprehended, to wit, the bodies which we touch and see; not indeed bodies in general, for these general ideas are usually a little more confused, but let us consider one body in particular. Let us take, for example, this piece of wax: it has been taken quite freshly from the hive, and it has not yet lost the sweetness of the honey which it contains; it still retains somewhat of the odour of the flowers from which it has been culled; its colour, its figure, its size are apparent; it is hard, cold, easily handled, and if you strike it with the finger, it will emit a sound. Finally all the things which are requisite to cause us distinctly to recognise a body, are met with in it. But notice that while I speak and approach the fire what remained of the taste is exhaled, the smell evaporates, the colour alters, the figure is destroyed, the size increases, it becomes liquid, it heats, scarcely can one handle it, and when one strikes it, no sound is emitted. Does the same wax remain after this change? We must confess that it remains; none would judge otherwise. What then did I know so distinctly in this piece of wax? It could certainly be nothing of all that the senses brought to my notice, since all these things which fall under taste, smell, sight, touch, and hearing, are found to be changed, and yet the same wax remains.

Perhaps it was what I now think, viz that this wax was not that sweetness of honey, nor that agreeable scent of flowers, nor that particular whiteness, nor that figure, nor that sound, but simply a body which a little while before appeared to me as perceptible under these forms, and which is now perceptible under others. But what, precisely, is it that I imagine when I form such conceptions? Let us attentively consider this, and, abstracting from all that does not belong to the wax, let us see what remains. Certainly nothing remains excepting a certain extended thing which is flexible and movable. But what is the meaning of flexible and movable? Is it not that I imagine that this piece of wax being round is capable of becoming square and of passing from a square to a triangular figure? No, certainly it is not that, since I imagine it admits of an infinitude of similar changes, and I nevertheless do not know how to compass the infinitude by my imagination, and consequently this conception which I have of the wax is not brought about by the faculty of imagination. What now is this extension? Is it not also unknown? For it becomes greater when the wax is melted, greater when it is boiled, and greater still when the heat increases; and I should not conceive [clearly] according to truth what wax is, if I did not think that even this piece that we are considering is capable of receiving more variations in extension than I have ever imagined. We must then grant that I could not even understand through the imagination what this piece of wax is, and that it is my mind alone which perceives it. I say this piece of wax in particular, for as to wax in general it is yet clearer. But what is this piece of wax which cannot be understood excepting by the [understanding or] mind? It is certainly the same that I see, touch, imagine, and finally it is the same which I have always believed it to be from the beginning. But what must particularly be observed is that its perception is neither an act of vision, nor of touch, nor of imagination, and has never been such although it may have appeared formerly to be so, but only an intuition of the mind, which may be imperfect and confused as it was formerly, or clear and distinct as it is at present, according as my attention is more or less directed to the elements which are found in it, and of which it is composed.

Yet in the meantime I am greatly astonished when I consider [the great feebleness of mind] and its proneness to fall [insensibly] into error; for although without giving expression to my thoughts I consider all this in my own mind, words often impede me and I am almost deceived by the terms of ordinary language. For we say that we see the same wax, if it is present, and not that we simply judge that it is the same from its having the same colour and figure. From this I should conclude that I knew the wax by means of vision and not simply by the intuition of the mind; unless by chance I remember that, when looking from a window and saying I see men who pass in the street, I really do not see them, but infer that what I see is men, just as I say that I see wax. And yet what do I see from the window but hats and coats which may cover automatic machines? Yet I judge these to be men. And similarly solely by the faculty of judgment which rests in my mind, I comprehend that which I believed I saw with my eyes.

A man who makes it his aim to raise his knowledge above the common should be ashamed to derive the occasion for doubting from the forms of speech invented by the vulgar; I prefer to pass on and consider whether I had a more evident and perfect conception of what the wax was when I first perceived it, and when I believed I knew it by means of the external senses or at least by the common sense as it is called, that is to say by the imaginative faculty, or whether my present conception is clearer now that I have most carefully examined what it is, and in what way it can be known. It would certainly be absurd to doubt as to this. For what was there in this first perception which was distinct? What was there which might not as well have been perceived by any of the animals? But when I distinguish the wax from its external forms, and when, just as if I had taken from it its vestments, I consider it quite naked, it is certain that although some error may still be found in my judgment, I can nevertheless not perceive it thus without a human mind.

But finally what shall I say of this mind, that is, of myself, for up to this point I do not admit in myself anything but mind? What then, I who seem to perceive this piece of wax so distinctly, do I now know myself, not only with much more truth and certainty, but also with much more distinctness and clearness? For if I judge that the wax is or exists from the fact that I see it, it certainly follows much more clearly that I am or that I exist myself from the fact that I see it. For it may be that what I see is not really wax, it may also be that I do not possess eyes with which to see anything; but it cannot be that when I see, or (for I no longer take account of the distinction) when I think I see, that I myself who think am nought. So if I judge that the wax exists from the fact that I touch it, the same thing will follow, to wit, that I am; and if I judge that my imagination, or some other cause, whatever it is, persuades me that the wax exists, I shall still conclude the same. And what I have here remarked of wax may be applied to all other things which are external to me [and which are met with outside of me]. And further, if the [notion or] perception of wax has seemed to me clearer and more distinct, not only after the sight or the touch, but also after many other causes have rendered it quite manifest to me, with how much more [evidence] and distinctness must it be said that I now know myself, since all the reasons which contribute to the knowledge of wax, or any other body whatever, are yet better proofs of the nature of my mind! And there are so many other things in the mind itself which may contribute to the elucidation of its nature, that those which depend on body such as these just mentioned, hardly merit being taken into account.

But finally here I am, having insensibly reverted to the point I desired, for, since it is now manifest to me that even bodies are not properly speaking known by the senses or by the faculty of imagination, but by the understanding only, and since they are not known from the fact that they are seen or touched, but only because they are understood, I see clearly that there is nothing which is easier for me to know than my mind. But because it is difficult to rid oneself so promptly of an opinion to which one was accustomed for so long, it will be well that I should halt a little at this point, so that by the length of my meditation I may more deeply imprint on my memory this new knowledge.

WILLIAM KINGDOM CLIFFORD
(1845–1899) English Mathematician and Philosopher

The Ethics of Belief*

L—The Duty of Inquiry

A shipowner was about to send to sea an emigrant-ship. He knew that she was old, and not over-well built at the first; that she had seen many seas and climes, and often had needed repairs. Doubts had been suggested to him that possibly she was not seaworthy. These doubts preyed upon his mind and made him unhappy; he thought that perhaps he ought to have her thoroughly overhauled and refitted, even though this should put him to great expense. Before the ship sailed, however, he succeeded in overcoming these melancholy reflections. He said to himself that she had gone safely through so many voyages and weathered so many storms that it was idle to suppose she would not come safely home from this trip also. He would put his trust in Providence, which could hardly fail to protect all these unhappy families that were leaving their father-land to seek for better times elsewhere. He would dismiss from his mind all ungenerous suspicions about the honesty of builders and contractors. In such ways he acquired a sincere and comfortable conviction that his vessel was thoroughly safe and seaworthy; he watched her departure with a light heart, and benevolent wishes for the success of the exiles in their strange new home that was to be; and he got his insurance-money when she went down in mid-ocean and told no tales.

What shall we say of him? Surely this, that he was verily guilty of the death of those men. It is admitted that he did sincerely believe in the soundness of his ship; but the sincerity of his conviction can in no wise help him, because *he had no right to believe on such evidence as was before him.* He had acquired his belief not by honestly earning it in patient investigation, but by stifling his doubts. And

*From William Kingdom Clifford, *Lectures and Essays*, vol. 2 (London: Macmillan & Co., 1901), pp. 163–205.

although in the end he may have felt so sure about it that he could not think otherwise, yet inasmuch as he had knowingly and willingly worked himself into that frame of mind, he must be held responsible for it.

Let us alter the case a little, and suppose that the ship was not unsound after all; that she made her voyage safely, and many others after it. Will that diminish the guilt of her owner? Not one jot. When an action is once done, it is right or wrong for ever; no accidental failure of its good or evil fruits can possibly alter that. The man would not have been innocent, he would only have been not found out. The question of right or wrong has to do with the origin of his belief, not the matter of it; not what it was, but how he got it; not whether it turned out to be true or false, but whether he had a right to believe on such evidence as was before him.

There was once an island in which some of the inhabitants professed a religion teaching neither the doctrine of original sin nor that of eternal punishment. A suspicion got abroad that the professors of this religion had made use of unfair means to get their doctrines taught to children. They were accused of wresting the laws of their country in such a way as to remove children from the care of their natural and legal guardians; and even of stealing them away and keeping them concealed from their friends and relations. A certain number of men formed themselves into a society for the purpose of agitating the public about this matter. They published grave accusations against individual citizens of the highest position and character, and did all in their power to injure these citizens in the exercise of their professions. So great was the noise they made, that a Commission was appointed to investigate the facts; but after the Commission had carefully inquired into all the evidence that could be got, it appeared that the accused were innocent. Not only had they been accused on insufficient evidence, but the evidence of their innocence was such as the agitators might easily have obtained, if they had attempted a fair inquiry. After these disclosures the inhabitants of that country looked upon the members of the agitating society, not only as persons whose judgment was to be distrusted, but also as no longer to be counted honourable men. For although they had sincerely and conscientiously believed in the charges they had made, *yet they had no right to believe on such evidence as was before them.* Their sincere convictions, instead of being honestly earned by patient inquiring, were stolen by listening to the voice of prejudice and passion.

Let us vary this case also, and suppose, other things remaining as before, that a still more accurate investigation proved the accused to have been really guilty. Would this make any difference in the guilt of the accusers? Clearly not; the question is not whether their belief was true or false, but whether they entertained it on wrong grounds. They would no doubt say, "Now you see that we were right after all; next time perhaps you will believe us." And they might be believed, but they would not thereby become honourable men. They would not be innocent, they would only be not found out. Every one of them, if he chose to examine himself *in foro conscientia,* would know that he had acquired and nourished a belief, when he had no right to believe on such evidence as was before him; and therein he would know that he had done a wrong thing.

It may be said, however, that in both of these supposed cases it is not the belief which is judged to be wrong, but the action following upon it. The shipowner might say, "I am perfectly certain that my ship is sound, but still I feel it my duty to have her examined, before trusting the lives of so many people to her." And it might be said to the agitator, "However convinced you were of the justice of your cause and the truth of your convictions, you ought not to have made a public attack upon any man's character until you had examined the evidence on both sides with the utmost patience and care."

In the first place, let us admit that, so far as it goes, this view of the case is right and necessary; right, because even when a man's belief is so fixed that he cannot think otherwise, he still has a choice in regard to the action suggested by it, and so cannot escape the duty of investigating on the ground of the strength of his convictions; and necessary, because those who are not yet capable of controlling their feelings and thoughts must have a plain rule dealing with overt acts.

But this being premised as necessary, it becomes clear that it is not sufficient, and that our previous judgment is required to supplement it. For it is not possible so to sever the belief from the action it suggests as to condemn the one without condemning the other. No man holding a strong belief on one side of a question, or even wishing to hold a belief on one side, can investigate it with such fairness and completeness as if he were really in doubt and unbiased; so that the existence of a belief not founded on fair inquiry unfits a man for the performance of this necessary duty.

Nor is that truly a belief at all which has not some influence upon the actions of him who holds it. He who truly believes that which prompts him to an action has looked upon the action to lust after it, he has committed it already in his heart. If a belief is not realised immediately in open deeds, it is stored up for the guidance of the future. It goes to make a part of that aggregate of beliefs which is the link between sensation and action at every moment of all our lives, and which is so organised and compacted together that no part of it can be isolated from the rest, but every new addition modifies the structure of the whole. No real belief, however trifling and fragmentary it may seem, is ever truly insignificant; it prepares us to receive more of its like, confirms those which resembled it before, and weakens others; and so gradually it lays a stealthy train in our inmost thoughts, which may some day explode into overt action, and leave its stamp upon our character for ever.

And no one man's belief is in any case a private matter which concerns himself alone. Our lives are guided by that general conception of the course of things which has been created by society for social purposes. Our words, our phrases, our forms and processes and modes of thought, are common property, fashioned and perfected from age to age; an heirloom which every succeeding generation inherits as a precious deposit and a sacred trust to be handed on to the next one, not unchanged but enlarged and purified, with some clear marks of its proper handiwork. Into this, for good or ill, is woven every belief of every man who has speech of his fellows. An awful privilege, and an awful responsibility, that we should help to create the world in which posterity will live.

In the two supposed cases which have been considered, it has been judged wrong to believe on insufficient evidence, or to nourish belief by suppressing doubts and avoiding investigation. The reason of this judgment is not far to seek: it is that in both these cases the belief held by one man was of great importance to other men. But forasmuch as no belief held by one man however seemingly trivial the belief, and however obscure the believer, is ever actually insignificant or without its effect on the fate of mankind, we have no choice but to extend our judgment to all cases of belief whatever. Belief, that sacred faculty which prompts the decisions of our will, and knits into harmonious working all the compacted energies of our being, is ours not for ourselves, but for humanity. It is rightly used on truths which have been established by long experience and waiting toil, and which have stood in the fierce light of free and fearless questioning. Then it helps to bind men together, and to strengthen and direct their common action. It is desecrated when given to unproved and unquestioned statements, for the solace and private pleasure of the believer; to add a tinsel splendour to the plain straight road of our life and display a bright mirage beyond it; or even to drown the common sorrows of our kind by a self-deception which allows them not only to cast down, but also to degrade us. Whoso would deserve well of his fellows in this matter will guard the purity of his belief with a very fanaticism of jealous care, lest at any time it should rest on an unworthy object, and catch a stain which can never be wiped away.

It is not only the leader of men, statesman, philosopher, or poet, that owes this bounden duty to mankind. Every rustic who delivers in the village alehouse his slow, infrequent sentences, may help to kill or keep alive the fatal superstitions which clog his race. Every hard-worked wife of an artisan may transmit to her children beliefs which shall knit society together, or rend it in pieces. No simplicity of mind, no obscurity of station, can escape the universal duty of questioning all that we believe.

It is true that this duty is a hard one, and the doubt which comes out of it is often a very bitter thing. It leaves us bare and powerless where we thought that we were safe and strong. To know all about anything is to know how to deal with it under all circumstances. We feel much happier and more secure when we think we know precisely what to do, no matter what happens, than when we have lost our way and do not know where to turn. And if we have supposed ourselves to know all about anything, and to be capable of doing what is fit in regard to it, we naturally do not like to find that we are really ignorant and powerless, that we have to begin again at the beginning, and try to learn what the thing is and how it is to be dealt with—if indeed anything can be learnt about it. It is the sense of power attached to a sense of knowledge that makes men desirous of believing, and afraid of doubting.

This sense of power is the highest and best of pleasures when the belief on which it is founded is a true belief, and has been fairly earned by investigation. For then we may justly feel that it is common property, and holds good for others as well as for ourselves. Then we may be glad, not that *I* have learned secrets by which I am safer and stronger, but that *we men* have got mastery over more of the world; and we shall be strong, not for ourselves, but in the name of Man and in his strength. But if the belief has been accepted on insufficient evidence, the pleasure is a stolen one. Not only does it deceive ourselves by giving us a sense of power which we do not really possess, but it is sinful, because it is stolen in defiance of our duty to mankind. That duty is to guard ourselves from such beliefs as from a pestilence, which may shortly master our own body and then spread to the rest of the town. What would be thought of one who, for the sake of a sweet fruit, should deliberately run the risk of bringing a plague upon his family and his neighbours?

And, as in other such cases, it is not the risk only which has to be considered; for a bad action is always bad at the time when it is done, no matter what happens afterwards. Every time we let ourselves believe for unworthy reasons, we weaken our powers of self-control, of doubting, of judicially and fairly weighing evidence. We all suffer severely enough from the maintenance and support of false beliefs and the fatally wrong actions which they lead to, and the evil born when one such belief is entertained is great and wide. But a greater and wider evil arises when the credulous character is maintained and supported, when a habit of believing for unworthy reasons is fostered and made permanent. If I steal money from any person, there may be no harm done by the mere transfer of possession; he may not feel the loss, or it may prevent him from using the money badly. But I cannot help doing this great wrong towards Man, that I make myself dishonest. What hurts society is not that it should lose its property, but that it should become a den of thieves; for then it must cease to be society. This is why we ought not to do evil that good may come; for at any rate this great evil has come, that we have done evil and are made wicked thereby. In like manner, if I let myself believe anything on insufficient evidence, there may be no great harm done by the mere belief; it may be true after all, or I may never have occasion to exhibit it in outward acts. But I cannot help doing this great wrong towards Man, that I make myself credulous. The danger to society is not merely that it should believe wrong things, though that is great enough; but that it should become credulous, and lose the habit of testing things and inquiring into them; for then it must sink back into savagery.

The harm which is done by credulity in a man is not confined to the fostering of a credulous character in others, and consequent support of false beliefs. Habitual want of care about what I believe leads to habitual want of care in others about the truth of what is told to me. Men speak the truth to one another when each reveres the truth in his own mind and in the other's mind; but how shall my friend revere the truth in my mind when I myself am careless about it, when I believe things because I want to believe them, and because they are comforting and pleasant? Will he not learn to cry, "Peace," to me, when there is no peace? By such a course I shall surround myself with a thick atmosphere of falsehood and fraud, and in that I must live. It may matter little to me, in my cloud-castle of sweet illusions and darling lies; but it matters much to Man that I have made my neighbours ready to deceive. The credulous man is father to the liar and the cheat; he lives in the bosom of this his family, and it is no marvel if he should become even as they are. So closely are our duties knit together, that whoso shall keep the whole law, and yet offend in one point, he is guilty of all.

To sum up: it is wrong always, everywhere, and for any one, to believe anything upon insufficient evidence.

WILLIAM JAMES

(1842–1910) American Philosopher and Psychologist

The Sentiment of Rationality*

Now, there is one element of our active nature . . . which philosophers as a rule have with great insincerity tried to huddle out of sight in their pretension to found systems of absolute certainty. I mean the element of faith. Faith means belief in something concerning which doubt is still theoretically possible; and as the test of belief is willingness to act, one may say that faith is the readiness to act in a cause the prosperous issue of which is not certified to us in advance. It is in fact the same moral quality which we call courage in practical affairs; and there will be a very widespread tendency in men of vigorous nature to enjoy a certain amount of uncertainty in their philosophic creed, just as risk lends a zest to worldly activity. Absolutely certified philosophies seeking the *inconcussum* are fruits of mental natures in which the passion for identity (which we saw to be but one factor of the rational appetite) plays an abnormally exclusive part. In the average man, on the contrary, the power to trust, to risk a little beyond the literal evidence, is an essential function. Any mode of conceiving the universe which makes an appeal to this generous power, and makes the man seem as if he were individually helping to create the actuality of the truth whose metaphysical reality he is willing to assume, will be sure to be responded to by large numbers.

The necessity of faith as an ingredient in our mental attitude is strongly insisted on by the scientific philosophers of the present day; but by a singularly arbitrary caprice they say that it is only legitimate when used in the interests of one particular proposition,—the proposition, namely, that the course of nature is uniform. That nature will follow to-morrow the same laws that she follows to-day is, they all admit, a truth which no man can *know*; but in the interests of cognition as well as of action we must postulate or assume it. . . .

With regard to all other possible truths, however, a number of our most influential contemporaries think that an attitude of faith is not only illogical but shameful. Faith in a religious dogma for which there is no outward proof, but which we are tempted to postulate for our emotional interests, just as we postulate the uniformity of nature for our intellectual interests, is branded by Professor Huxley as "the lowest depth of immorality." Citations of this kind from leaders of the modern *Aufklärung*[1] might be multiplied almost indefinitely. Take Professor Clifford's article on the "Ethics of Belief." He calls it "guilt" and "sin" to believe even the truth without "scientific evidence." But what is the use of being a genius, unless *with the same scientific evidence* as other men, one can reach more

---

*From William James, *The Will to Believe and Other Essays* (New York: Longmaus, Green & Co., 1897), pp. 63–110.
[1] Enlightenment—ED.

truth than they? Why does Clifford fearlessly proclaim his belief in the conscious-automaton theory, although the "proofs" before him are the same which make Mr. Lewes reject it? Why does he believe in primordial units of "mind-stuff" on evidence which would seem quite worthless to Professor Bain? Simply because, like every human being of the slightest mental originality, he is peculiarly sensitive to evidence that bears in some one direction. It is utterly hopeless to try to exorcise such sensitiveness by calling it the disturbing subjective factor, and branding it as the root of all evil. "Subjective" be it called! and "disturbing" to those whom it foils! But if it helps those who, as Cicero says, "vim naturæ magis sentiunt," it is good and not evil. Pretend what we may, the whole man within us is at work when we form our philosophical opinions. Intellect, will, taste, and passion co-operate just as they do in practical affairs; and lucky it is if the passion be not something as petty as a love of personal conquest over the philosopher across the way. The absurd abstraction of an intellect verbally formulating all its evidence and carefully estimating the probability thereof by a vulgar fraction by the size of whose denominator and numerator alone it is swayed, is ideally as inept as it is actually impossible. It is almost incredible that men who are themselves working philosophers should pretend that any philosophy can be, or ever has been, constructed without the help of personal preference, belief, or divination. How have they succeeded in so stultifying their sense for the living facts of human nature as not to perceive that every philosopher, or man of science either, whose initiative counts for anything in the evolution of thought, has taken his stand on a sort of dumb conviction that the truth must lie in one direction rather than another, and a sort of preliminary assurance that his notion can be made to work; and has borne his best fruit in trying to make it work? These mental instincts in different men are the spontaneous variations upon which the intellectual struggle for existence is based. The fittest conceptions survive, and with them the names of their champions shining to all futurity.

The coil is about us, struggle as we may. The only escape from faith is mental nullity. What we enjoy most in a Huxley or a Clifford is not the professor with his learning, but the human personality ready to go in for what it feels to be right, in spite of all appearances. The concrete man has but one interest,—to be right. That for him is the art of all arts, and all means are fair which help him to it. Naked he is flung into the world, and between him and nature there are no rules of civilized warfare. The rules of the scientific game, burdens of proof, presumptions, *experimenta crucis*, complete inductions, and the like, are only binding on those who enter that game. As a matter of fact we all more or less do enter it, because it helps us to our end. But if the means presume to frustrate the end and call us cheats for being right in advance of their slow aid, by guesswork or by hook or crook, what shall we say of them? Were all of Clifford's works, except the Ethics of Belief, forgotten, he might well figure in future treatises on psychology in place of the somewhat threadbare instance of the miser who has been led by the association of ideas to prefer his gold to all the goods he might buy therewith.

In short, if I am born with such a superior general reaction to evidence that I can guess right and act accordingly, and gain all that comes of right action, while my less gifted neighbor (paralyzed by his scruples and waiting for more evidence which he dares not anticipate, much as he longs to) still stands shivering on the brink, by what law shall I be forbidden to reap the advantages of my superior native sensitiveness? Of course I yield to my belief in such a case as this or distrust it, alike at my peril, just as I do in any of the great practical decisions of life. If my inborn faculties are good, I am a prophet; if poor, I am a failure: nature spews me out of her mouth, and there is an end of me. In the total game of life we stake our persons all the while; and if in its theoretic part our persons will help us to a conclusion, surely we should also stake them there, however inarticulate they may be.[2]

But in being myself so very articulate in proving what to all readers with a sense for reality will seem a platitude, am I not wasting words? We cannot live or think at all without some degree of faith. Faith is synonymous with working hypothesis. The only difference is that while some hypotheses can be refuted in five minutes, others may defy ages. A chemist who conjectures that a certain wall-paper contains arsenic, and has faith enough to lead him to take the trouble to put some of it into a hydrogen bottle, finds out by the results of his action whether he was right or wrong. But theories like that of Darwin, or that of the kinetic constitution of matter, may exhaust the labors of generations in their corroboration, each tester of their truth proceeding in this simple way,— that he acts as if it were true, and expects the result to disappoint him if his assumption is false. The longer disappointment is delayed, the stronger grows his faith in his theory. . . .

Now, I wish to show what to my knowledge has never been clearly pointed out, that belief (as measured by action) not only does and must continually outstrip scientific evidence, but that there is a certain class of truths of whose reality belief is a factor as well as a confessor; and that as regards this class of truths faith is not only licit and pertinent, but essential and indispensable. The truths cannot become true till our faith has made them so.

Suppose, for example, that I am climbing in the Alps, and have had the ill-luck to work myself into a position from which the only escape is by a terrible leap. Being without similar experience, I have no evidence of my ability to perform it successfully; but hope and confidence in myself make me sure I shall not miss my aim, and nerve my feet to execute what without those subjective emotions would perhaps have been impossible. But suppose that, on the contrary, the emotions of fear and mistrust preponderate; or suppose that, having just read the Ethics of Belief, I feel it would be sinful to act upon an assumption unverified by previous experience,—why, then I shall hesitate so long that at last, exhausted and trembling, and launching myself in a moment of despair, I miss my foothold and roll

---

[2] At most, the command laid upon us by science to believe nothing not yet verified by the senses is a prudential rule intended to maximize our right thinking and minimize our errors *in the long run*. In the particular instance we must frequently lose truth by obeying it; but on the whole we are safer if we follow it consistently, for we are sure to cover our losses with our gains. It is like those gambling and insurance rules based on probability, in which we secure ourselves against losses in detail by hedging on the total run. But this hedging philosophy requires that long run should be there; and this makes it inapplicable to the question of religious faith as the latter comes home to the individual man. He plays the game of life not to escape losses, for he brings nothing with him to lose; he plays it for gains; and it is now or never with him, for the long run which exists indeed for humanity, is not there for him. Let him doubt, believe, or deny, he runs his risk, and has the natural right to choose which one it shall be.

into the abyss. In this case (and it is one of an immense class) the part of wisdom clearly is to believe what one desires; for the belief is one of the indispensable preliminary conditions of the realization of its object. *There are then cases where faith creates its own verification.* Believe, and you shall be right, for you shall save yourself; doubt, and you shall again be right, for you shall perish. The only difference is that to believe is greatly to your advantage. . . .

The essential thing to notice is that our active preference is a legitimate part of the game,—that it is our plain business as men to try one of the keys, and the one in which we most confide. If then the proof exist not till I have acted, and I must needs in acting run the risk of being wrong, how can the popular science professors be right in objurgating in me as infamous a "credulity" which the strict logic of the situation requires? If this really be a moral universe; if by my acts I be a factor of its destinies; if to believe where I may doubt be itself a moral act analogous to voting for a side not yet sure to win,—by what right shall they close in upon me and steadily negate the deepest conceivable function of my being by their preposterous command that I shall stir neither hand nor foot, but remain balancing myself in eternal and insoluble doubt? Why, doubt itself is a decision of the widest practical reach, if only because we may miss by doubting what goods we might be gaining by espousing the winning side. But more than that! it is often practically impossible to distinguish doubt from dogmatic negation. If I refuse to stop a murder because I am in doubt whether it be not justifiable homicide, I am virtually abetting the crime. If I refuse to bale out a boat because I am in doubt whether my efforts will keep her afloat, I am really helping to sink her. If in the mountain precipice I doubt my right to risk a leap, I actively connive at my destruction. He who commands himself not to be credulous of God, of duty, of freedom, of immortality, may again and again be indistinguishable from him who dogmatically denies them. Scepticism in moral matters is an active ally of immorality. Who is not for is against. The universe will have no neutrals in these questions. In theory as in practice, dodge or hedge, or talk as we like about a wise scepticism, we are really doing volunteer military service for one side or the other.

Yet obvious as this necessity practically is, thousands of innocent magazine readers lie paralyzed and terrified in the network of shallow negations which the leaders of opinion have thrown over their souls. All they need to be free and hearty again in the exercise of their birthright is that these fastidious vetoes should be swept away. All that the human heart wants is its chance. It will willingly forego certainty in universal matters if only it can be allowed to feel that in them it has that same inalienable right to run risks, which no one dreams of refusing to it in the pettiest practical affairs. And if I, in these last pages, like the mouse in the fable, have gnawed a few of the strings of the sophistical net that has been binding down its lion-strength, I shall be more than rewarded for my pains.

Appearance and Reality

From *Rhapsody on a Windy Night*

Twelve o'clock.
Along the reaches of the street
Held in a lunar synthesis,
Whispering lunar incantations
Dissolve the floors of memory
And all its clear relations
Its divisions and precisions,
Every street lamp that I pass
Beats like a fatalistic drum,
And through the spaces of the dark
Midnight shakes the memory
As a madman shakes a dead geranium.

T. S. Eliot

PLATO

(428–347 B.C.) Greek Philosopher

The Cave*

Next, said I, compare our nature in respect of education and its lack to such an experience as this. Picture men dwelling in a sort of subterranean cavern with a long entrance open to the light on its entire width. Conceive them as having their legs and necks fettered from childhood, so that they remain in the same spot, able to look forward only, and prevented by the fetters from turning their heads. Picture further the light from a fire burning higher up and at a distance behind them, and between the fire and the prisoners and above them a road along which a low wall has been built, as the exhibitors of puppet shows have partitions before the men themselves, above which they show the puppets.

All that I see, he said.

See also, then, men carrying past the wall implements of all kinds that rise above the wall, and human images and shapes of animals as well, wrought in stone and wood and every material, some of these bearers presumably speaking and others silent.

A strange image you speak of, he said, and strange prisoners.

Like to us, I said. For, to begin with, tell me do you think that these men would have seen anything of themselves or of one another except the shadows cast from the fire on the wall of the cave that fronted them?

How could they, he said, if they were compelled to hold their heads unmoved through life?

And again, would not the same be true of the objects carried past them?

Surely.

If then they were able to talk to one another, do you not think that they would suppose that in naming the things that they saw they were naming the passing objects?

Necessarily.

And if their prison had an echo from the wall opposite them, when one of the passers-by uttered a sound, do you think that they would suppose anything else than the passing shadow to be the speaker?

By Zeus, I do not, said he.

Then in every way such prisoners would deem reality to be nothing else than the shadows of the artificial objects.

Quite inevitably, he said.

Consider, then, what would be the manner of the release and healing from these bonds and this folly if in the course of nature something of this sort should happen to them. When one was freed from his fetters and compelled to stand up

---

*From Plato, *The Republic*, trans. by Paul Shorey (Cambridge: Harvard University Press, 1930).

suddenly and turn his head around and walk and to lift up his eyes to the light, and in doing all this felt pain and, because of the dazzle and glitter of the light, was unable to discern the objects whose shadows he formerly saw, what do you suppose would be his answer if someone told him that what he had seen before was all a cheat and an illusion, but that now, being nearer to reality and turned toward more real things, he saw more truly? And if also one should point out to him each of the passing objects and constrain him by questions to say what it is, do you not think that he would be at a loss and that he would regard what he formerly saw as more real than the things now pointed out to him?

Far more real, he said.

And if he were compelled to look at the light itself, would not that pain his eyes, and would he not turn away and flee to those things which he is able to discern and regard them as in very deed more clear and exact than the objects pointed out?

It is so, he said.

And if, said I, someone should drag him thence by force up the ascent which is rough and steep, and not let him go before he had drawn him out into the light of the sun, do you not think that he would find it painful to be so haled along, and would chafe at it, and when he came out into the light, that his eyes would be filled with its beams so that he would not be able to see even one of the things that we call real?

Why, no, not immediately, he said.

Then there would be need of habituation, I take it, to enable him to see the things higher up. And at first he would most easily discern the shadows and, after that, the likenesses or reflections in water of men and other things, and later, the things themselves, and from these he would go on to contemplate the appearances in the heavens and heaven itself, more easily by night, looking at the light of the stars and the moon, than by day the sun and the sun's light.

Of course.

And so, finally, I suppose, he would be able to look upon the sun itself and see its true nature, not by reflections in water or phantasms of it in an alien setting, but in and by itself in its own place.

Necessarily, he said.

And at this point he would infer and conclude that this it is that provides the seasons and the courses of the year and presides over all things in the visible region, and is in some sort the cause of all these things that they had seen.

Obviously, he said, that would be the next step.

Well then, if he recalled to mind his first habitation and what passed for wisdom there, and his fellow bondsmen, do you not think that he would count himself happy in the change and pity them?

He would indeed.

And if there had been honors and commendations among them which they bestowed on one another and prizes for the man who is quickest to make out the shadows as they pass and best able to remember their customary precedences, sequences, and coexistences, and so most successful in guessing at what was to come, do you think he would be very keen about such rewards, and that he would envy and emulate those who were honored by these prisoners and lorded it among them, or that he would feel with Homer and greatly prefer while living on earth to be serf of another, a landless man, and endure anything rather than opine with them and live that life?[1]

Yes, he said, I think that he would choose to endure anything rather than such a life.

And consider this also, said I. If such a one should go down again and take his old place would he not get his eyes full of darkness, thus suddenly coming out of the sunlight?

He would indeed.

Now if he should be required to contend with these perpetual prisoners in "evaluating" these shadows while his vision was still dim and before his eyes were accustomed to the dark—and this time required for habituation would not be very short—would he not provoke laughter, and would it not be said of him that he had returned from his journey aloft with his eyes ruined and that it was not worth while even to attempt the ascent? And if it were possible to lay hands on and to kill the man who tried to release them and lead them up, would they not kill him?

They certainly would, he said.

This image then, dear Glaucon, we must apply as a whole to all that has been said, likening the region revealed through sight to the habitation of the prison, and the light of the fire in it to the power of the sun. And if you assume that the ascent and the contemplation of the things above is the soul's ascension to the intelligible region, you will not miss my surmise, since that is what you desire to hear. But Gods knows whether it is true. But, at any rate, my dream as it appears to me is that in the region of the known the last thing to be seen and hardly seen is the idea of good, and that when seen it must needs point us to the conclusion that this is indeed the cause for all things of all that is right and beautiful, giving birth in the visible world to light, and the author of light and itself in the intelligible world being the authentic source of truth and reason, and that anyone who is to act wisely in private or public must have caught sight of this.

GEORGE BERKELEY
(1685–1753) Irish Philosopher

Of the Principles of Human Knowledge*

1. It is evident to anyone who takes a survey of the objects of human knowledge that they are either ideas actually imprinted on the senses, or else

---

[1] *Odyssey,* XI, pp. 489–491. Achilles speaks to Odysseus that he would rather be a poor man's servant on earth than king of the underworld.—ED.

---

*From George Berkeley, *A Treatise Concerning the Principles of Human Knowledge* (Dublin, 1710).

such as are perceived by attending to the passions and operations of the mind, or lastly ideas formed by help of memory and imagination, either compounding, dividing, or barely representing those originally perceived in the aforesaid ways. By sight I have the ideas of light and colors with their several degrees and variations. By touch I perceive, for example, hard and soft, heat and cold, motion and resistance, and of all these more and less either as to quantity or degree. Smelling furnishes me with odors; the palate with tastes, and hearing conveys sounds to the mind in all their variety of tone and composition. And as several of these are observed to accompany each other, they come to be marked by one name, and so to be reputed as one thing. Thus, for example, a certain color, taste, smell, figure and consistence having been observed to go together, are accounted one distinct thing, signified by the name *apple*. Other collections of ideas constitute a stone, a tree, a book, and the like sensible things; which, as they are pleasing or disagreeable, excite the passions of love, hatred, joy, grief, and so forth.

2. But besides all that endless variety of ideas or objects of knowledge, there is likewise something which knows or perceives them, and exercises divers operations, as willing, imagining, remembering about them. This perceiving, active being is what I call *mind, spirit, soul* or *myself*. By which words I do not denote any one of my ideas, but a thing entirely distinct from them, wherein they exist, or, which is the same thing, whereby they are perceived; for the existence of an idea consists in being perceived.

3. That neither our thoughts, nor passions, nor ideas formed by the imagination, exist without the mind, is what everybody will allow. And it seems no less evident that the various sensations or ideas imprinted on the sense, however blended or combined together (that is, whatever objects they compose) cannot exist otherwise than in a mind perceiving them. I think an intuitive knowledge may be obtained of this, by anyone that shall attend to what is meant by the term *exist* when applied to sensible things. The table I write on, I say, exists, that is, I see and feel it; and if I were out of my study I should say it existed, meaning thereby that if I was in my study I might perceive it, or that some other spirit actually does perceive it. There was an odor, that is, it was smelled; there was a sound, that is to say, it was heard; a color or figure, and it was perceived by sight or touch. This is all that I can understand by these and the like expressions. For as to what is said of the absolute existence of unthinking things without any relation to their being perceived, that seems perfectly unintelligible. Their *esse* is *percipi*, nor is it possible they should have any existence, out of the minds or thinking things which perceive them.

4. It is indeed an opinion strangely prevailing amongst men, that houses, mountains, rivers, and in a word all sensible objects have an existence natural or real, distinct from their being perceived by the understanding. But with how great an assurance and acquiescence soever this principle may be entertained in the world; yet whoever shall find in his heart to call it in

question, may, if I mistake not, perceive it to involve a manifest contradiction. For what are the forementioned objects but the things we perceive by sense, and what do we perceive besides our own ideas or sensations; and is it not plainly repugnant that any one of these or any combination of them should exist unperceived?

5. If we thoroughly examine this tenet, it will, perhaps, be found at bottom to depend on the doctrine of *abstract ideas.* For can there be a nicer strain of abstraction than to distinguish the existence of sensible objects from their being perceived, so as to conceive them existing unperceived? Light and colors, heat and cold, extension and figures, in a word the things we see and feel, what are they but so many sensations, notions, ideas or impressions on the sense; and is it possible to separate, even in thought, any of these from perception? For my part I might as easily divide a thing from itself. I may indeed divide in my thoughts or conceive apart from each other those things which, perhaps, I never perceived by sense so divided. Thus I imagine the trunk of a human body without the limbs, or conceive the smell of a rose without thinking on the rose itself. So far I will not deny I can abstract, if that may properly be called *abstraction*, which extends only to the conceiving separately such objects, as it is possible may really exist or be actually perceived asunder. But my conceiving or imagining power does not extend beyond the possibility of real existence or perception. Hence as it is impossible for me to see or feel anything without an actual sensation of that thing, so is it impossible for me to conceive in my thoughts any sensible thing or object distinct from the sensation or perception of it.

6. Some truths there are so near and obvious to the mind, that a man need only open his eyes to see them. Such I take this important one to be, to wit, that all the choir of heaven and furniture of the earth, in a word all those bodies which compose the mighty frame of the world, have not any subsistence without a mind, that their being is to be perceived or known; that consequently so long as they are not actually perceived by me, or do not exist in my mind or that of any other created spirit, they must either have no existence at all, or else subsist in the mind of some eternal spirit: it being perfectly unintelligible and involving all the absurdity of abstraction, to attribute to any single part of them an existence independent of a spirit. To be convinced of which, the reader need only reflect and try to separate in his own thoughts the being of a sensible thing from its being perceived.

7. From what has been said, it follows, there is not any other substance than *spirit*, or that which perceives. But for the fuller proof of this point, let it be considered, the sensible qualities are color, figure, motion, smell, taste, and such like, that is, the ideas perceived by sense. Now for an idea to exist in an unperceiving thing, is a manifest contradiction; for to have an idea is all one as to perceive: that therefore wherein color, figure, and the like qualities exist, must perceive them; hence it is clear there can be no unthinking substance or *substratum* of those ideas.

8. But say you, though the ideas themselves do not exist without the mind, yet there may be things like them whereof they are copies or resemblances, which things exist without the mind, in an unthinking substance. I answer, an idea can be like nothing but an idea; a color or figure can be like nothing but another color or figure. If we look but ever so little into our thoughts, we shall find it impossible for us to conceive a likeness except only between our ideas. Again, I ask whether those supposed originals or external things, of which our ideas are the pictures or representations, be themselves perceivable or no? If they are, then they are ideas, and we have gained our point; but if you say they are not, I appeal to anyone whether it be sense, to assert a color is like something which is invisible; hard or soft, like something which is intangible; and so of the rest.

9. Some there are who make a distinction betwixt *primary* and *secondary* qualities: by the former, they mean extension, figure, motion, rest, solidity or impenetrability and number: by the latter they denote all other sensible qualities, as colors, sounds, tastes, and so forth. The ideas we have of these they acknowledge not to be the resemblances of anything existing without the mind or unperceived; but they will have our ideas of the primary qualities to be patterns or images of things which exist without the mind, in an unthinking substance which they call *matter.* By matter therefore we are to understand an inert, senseless substance, in which extension, figure, and motion, do actually subsist. But is evident from what we have already shown, that extension, figure and motion are only ideas existing in the mind, and that an idea can be like nothing but another idea, and that consequently neither they nor their archetypes can exist in an unperceiving substance. Hence it is plain, that the very notion of what is called *matter* or *corporeal substance,* involves a contradiction in it.

10. They who assert that figure, motion, and the rest of the primary or original qualities do exist without the mind, in unthinking substances, do at the same time acknowledge that colors, sounds, heat, cold, and such like secondary qualities, do not, which they tell us are sensations existing in the mind alone, that depend on and are occasioned by the different size, texture and motion of the minute particles of matter. This they take for an undoubted truth, which they can demonstrate beyond all exception. Now if it be certain, that those original qualities are inseparably united with the other sensible qualities, and not, even in thought, capable of being abstracted from them, it plainly follows that they exist only in the mind. But I desire anyone to reflect and try, whether he can by any abstraction of thought, conceive the extension and motion of a body, without all other sensible qualities. For my own part, I see evidently that it is not in my power to frame an idea of a body extended and moved, but I must withal give it some color or other sensible quality which is acknowledged to exist only in the mind. In short, extension, figure, and motion, abstracted from all other qualities, are inconceivable. Where therefore the other sensible qualities are, there must these be also, to wit, in the mind and nowhere else.

11. Again, *great* and *small, swift* and *slow,* are allowed to exist nowhere without the mind, being entirely relative, and changing as the frame or position of the organs of sense varies. The extension therefore which exists without the mind, is neither great nor small, the motion neither swift nor slow, that is, they are nothing at all. But say you, they are extension in general, and motion in general: thus we see how much the tenet of extended, moveable substances existing without the mind, depends on that strange doctrine of *abstract ideas.* And here I cannot but remark, how nearly the vague and indeterminate description of matter or corporeal substance, which the modern philosophers are run into by their own principles, resembles that antiquated and so much ridiculed notion of *materia prima,* to be met with in *Aristotle* and his followers.[1] Without extension solidity cannot be conceived; since therefore it has been shown that extension exists not in an unthinking substance, the same must also be true of solidity.

12. That number is entirely the creature of the mind, even though the other qualities be allowed to exist without, will be evident to whoever considers, that the same thing bears a different denomination of number, as the mind views it with different respects. Thus, the same extension is one or three or thirty six, according as the mind considers it with reference to a yard, a foot, or an inch. Number is so visibly relative, and dependent on men's understanding, that it is strange to think how anyone should give it an absolute existence without the mind. We say one book, one page, one line; all these are equally units, though some contain several of the others. And in each instance it is plain, the unit relates to some particular combination of ideas arbitrarily put together by the mind.

13. Unity I know some will have to be a simple or uncompounded idea, accompanying all other ideas into the mind. That I have any such idea answering the word *unity,* I do not find; and if I had, methinks I could not miss finding it; on the contrary is should be the most familiar to my understanding, since it is said to accompany all other ideas, and to be perceived by all the ways of sensation and reflection. To say no more, it is an *abstract idea.*

14. I shall farther add, that after the same manner, as modern philosophers prove certain sensible qualities to have no existence in matter, or without the mind, the same thing may be likewise proved of all other sensible qualities whatsoever. Thus, for instance, it is said that heat and cold are affections only of the mind, and not at all patterns of real beings, existing in the corporeal substances which excite them, for that the same body which appears cold to one hand, seems warm to another. Now why may we not as well argue that figure and extension are not patterns or resemblances of qualities existing in matter, because to the same eye at different stations, or

[1] Aristotle in his books, *The Categories* and *The Metaphysics,* talks about matter as it is present in an individual subject. This was interpreted by medieval commentators to refer to an undifferentiated "prime matter." This interpretation of Aristotle is not in favor today. However, it is true that Aristotle believed in the possibility of knowing matter (in some sense) that was more than merely the appearance of matter.—ED.

eyes of a different texture at the same station, they appear various, and cannot therefore be the images of anything settled and determinate without the mind? Again, it is proved that sweetness is not really in the sapid thing, because the thing remaining unaltered the sweetness is changed into bitter, as in case of a fever or otherwise vitiated palate. Is it not as reasonable to say, that motion is not without the mind, since if the succession of ideas in the mind become swifter, the motion, it is acknowledged, shall appear slower without any alteration in any external object.

15. In short, let anyone consider those arguments, which are thought manifestly to prove that colors and tastes exist only in the mind, and he shall find they may with equal force, be brought to prove the same thing of extension, figure, and motion. Though it must be confessed this method of arguing does not so much prove that there is no extension or color in an outward object, as that we do not know by sense which is the true extension or color of the object. But the arguments foregoing plainly show it to be impossible that any color or extension at all, or other sensible quality whatsoever, should exist in an unthinking subject without the mind, or in truth, that there should be any such thing as an outward object.

16. But let us examine a little the received opinion. It is said extension is a mode or accident of matter, and that matter is the *substratum* that supports it. Now I desire that you would explain what is meant by matter's *supporting* extension: say you, I have no idea of matter, and therefore cannot explain it. I answer, though you have no positive, yet if you have any meaning at all, you must at least have a relative idea of matter; though you know not what it is, yet you must be supposed to know what relation it bears to accidents, and what is meant by its supporting them. It is evident *support* cannot here be taken in its usual or literal sense, as when we say that pillars support a building: in what sense therefore must it be taken?

17. If we inquire into what the most accurate philosophers declare themselves to mean by *material substance;* we shall find them acknowledge, they have no other meaning annexed to those sounds, but the idea of being in general, together with the relative notion of its supporting accidents. The general idea of being appears to me the most abstract and incom- prehensible of all other; and as for its supporting accidents, this, as we have just now observed, cannot be understood in the common sense of those words; it must therefore be taken in some other sense, but what that is they do not explain. So that when I consider the two parts or branches which make the signification of the words *material substance.* I am convinced there is no distinct meaning annexed to them. But why should we trouble ourselves any farther, in discussing this material *substratum* or support of figure and motion, and other sensible qualities? Does it not suppose they have an existence without the mind? And is not this a direct repugnancy, and altogether inconceivable?

18. But though it were possible that solid, figured, moveable substances may exist without the mind, corresponding to the ideas we have of bodies, yet how is it possible for us to know this? Either we must know it by sense, or by reason. As for our senses, by them we have the knowledge only of our sensations, ideas, or those things that are immediately perceived by sense, call them what you will: but they do not inform us that things exist without the mind, or unperceived, like to those which are perceived. This the materialists themselves acknowledge. It remains therefore that if we have any knowledge at all of external things, it must be by reason, inferring their existence from what is immediately perceived by sense. But what reason can induce us to believe that existence of bodies without the mind, from what we perceive, since the very patrons of matter themselves do not pretend, there is any necessary connection betwixt them and our ideas? I say it is granted on all hands (and what happens in dreams, frenzies, and the like, puts it beyond dispute) that it is possible we might be affected with all the ideas we have now, though no bodies existed without, resembling them. Hence it is evident the supposition of external bodies is not necessary for the producing of our ideas: since it is granted they are produced sometimes, and might possibly be produced always in the same order we see them in at present, without their concurrence.

19. But though we might possibly have all our sensations without them, yet perhaps it may be thought easier to conceive and explain the manner of their production, by supposing external bodies in their likeness rather than otherwise; and so it might be at least probable there are such things as bodies that excite their ideas in our minds. But neither can this be said; for though we give the materialists their external bodies, they by their own confession are never the nearer knowing how our ideas are produced: since they own themselves unable to comprehend in what manner body can act upon spirit, or how it is possible it should imprint any idea in the mind. Hence it is evident the production of ideas or sensations in our minds, can be no reason why we should suppose matter or corporeal substances, since that is acknowledged to remain equally inexplicable with, or without this supposition. If therefore it were possible for bodies to exist without the mind, yet to hold they do so, must needs be a very precarious opinion; since it is to suppose, without any reason at all, that God has created innumerable beings that are entirely useless, and serve to no manner of purpose.

20. In short, if there were external bodies, it is impossible we should ever come to know it; and if there were not, we might have the very same reasons to think there were that we have now. Suppose, what no one can deny possible, an intelligence, without the help of external bodies, to be affected with the same train of sensations or ideas that you are, imprinted in the same order and with like vividness in his mind. I ask whether that intelligence has not all the reason to believe the existence of corporeal substances, represented by his ideas, and exciting them in his mind, that you can possibly have for believing the same thing? Of this there can be no

question; which one consideration is enough to make any reasonable person suspect the strength of whatever arguments he may think himself to have, for the existence of bodies without the mind. . . .

25. All our ideas, sensations, or the things which we perceive, by whatsoever names they may be distinguished, are visibly inactive, there is nothing of power or agency included in them. So that one idea or object of thought cannot produce, or make any alteration in another. To be satisfied of the truth of this, there is nothing else requisite but a bare observation of our ideas. For since they and every part of them exist only in the mind, it follows that there is nothing in them but what is perceived. But whoever shall attend to his ideas, whether of sense or reflection, will not perceive in them any power or activity; there is therefore no such thing contained in them. A little attention will discover to us that the very being of an idea implies passiveness and inertness in it, insomuch that it is impossible for an idea to do anything, or, strictly speaking, to be the cause of anything: neither can it be the resemblance or pattern of any active being, as is evident from *Sect.* 8. Whence it plainly follows that extension, figure and motion, cannot be the cause of our sensations. To say therefore, that these are the effects of powers resulting from the configuration, number, motion, and size of corpuscles, must certainly be false.

26. We perceive a continual succession of ideas, some are anew excited, others are changed or totally disappear. There is therefore some cause of these ideas whereon they depend, and which produces and changes them. That this cause cannot be any quality or idea or combination of ideas, is clear from the preceding section. It must therefore be a substance; but it has been shown that there is no corporeal or material substance: it remains therefore that the cause of ideas is an incorporeal active substance or spirit.

27. A spirit is one simple, undivided, active being: as it perceives ideas, it is called the *understanding*, and as it produces or otherwise operates about them, it is called the *will*. Hence there can be no idea formed of a soul or spirit: for all ideas whatever, being passive and inert, *vide Sect.* 25, they cannot represent unto us, by way of image or likeness, that which acts. A little attention will make it plain to anyone, that to have an idea which shall be like that active principle of motion and change of ideas, is absolutely impossible. Such is the nature of *spirit* or that which acts, that it cannot be of itself perceived, but only by the effects which it produces. If any man shall doubt of the truth of what is here delivered, let him but reflect and try if he can frame the idea of any power or active being; and whether he has ideas of two principal powers, marked by the names *will* and *understanding*, distinct from each other as well as from a third idea of substance or being in general, with a relative notion of its supporting or being in general, with a relative notion of its supporting or being the subject of the aforesaid powers, which is signified by the name *soul* or *spirit*. This is what some hold; but so far as I can see, the words *will, soul, spirit,* do not stand

for different ideas, or in truth, for any idea at all, but for something which is very different from ideas, and which being an agent cannot be like unto, or represented by, any idea whatsoever. [Though it must be owned at the same time, that we have some notion of soul, spirit, and the operations of the mind, such as willing, loving, hating, inasmuch as we know or understand the meaning of those words.]

28. I find I can excite ideas in my mind at pleasure, and vary and shift the scene as oft as I think fit. It is no more than willing, and straightway this or that idea arises in my fancy: and by the same power it is obliterated, and makes way for another. This making and unmaking of ideas does very properly denominate the mind active. Thus much is certain, and grounded on experience: but when we talk of unthinking agents, or of exciting ideas exclusive of volition, we only amuse ourselves with words.

29. But whatever power I may have over my own thoughts, I find the ideas actually perceived by sense have not a like dependence on my will. When in broad daylight I open my eyes, it is not in my power to choose whether I shall see or no, or to determine what particular objects shall present themselves to my view; and so likewise as to the hearing and other senses, the ideas imprinted on them are not creatures of my will. There is therefore some other will or spirit that produces them.

30. The ideas of sense are more strong, lively, and distinct than those of the imagination; they have likewise a steadiness, order, and coherence, and are not excited at random, as those which are the effects of human wills often are, but in a regular train or series, the admirable connection whereof sufficiently testifies the wisdom and benevolence of its author. Now the set rules or established methods, wherein the mind we depend on excites in us the ideas of sense, are called the *laws of nature:* and these we learn by experience, which teaches us that such and such ideas are attended with such and such other ideas, in the ordinary course of things.

31. This gives us a sort of foresight, which enables us to regulate our actions for the benefit of life. And without this we should be eternally at a loss: we could not know how to act anything that might procure us the least pleasure, or remove the least pain of sense. That food nourishes, sleep refreshes, and fire warms us; that to sow in the seedtime is the way to reap in the harvest, and, in general, that to obtain such or such ends, such or such means are conducive, all this we know, not by discovering any necessary connection between our ideas, but only by the observation of the settled laws of nature, without which we should be all in uncertainty and confusion, and a grown man no more know how to manage himself in the affairs of life, than an infant just born.

32. And yet this consistent uniform working, which so evidently displays the goodness and wisdom of that governing spirit whose will constitutes the laws of nature, is so far from leading our thoughts to him, that it rather sends them awandering after second causes. For when we perceive certain

ideas of sense constantly followed by other ideas, and we know this is not of our own doing, we forthwith attribute power and agency to the ideas themselves, and make one the cause of another, than which nothing can be more absurd and unintelligible. Thus, for example, having observed that when we perceive by sight a certain round luminous figure, we at the same time perceive by touch the idea or sensation called *heat*, we do from thence conclude the sun to be the cause of heat. And in like manner perceiving the motion and collision of bodies to be attended with sound, we are inclined to think the latter an effect of the former.

33. The ideas imprinted on the senses by the Author of Nature are called *real things:* and those excited in the imagination being less regular, vivid and constant, are more properly termed *ideas,* or *images of things,* which they copy and represent. But then our sensations, be they never so vivid and distinct, are nevertheless *ideas,* that is, they exist in the mind, or are perceived by it, as truly as the ideas of its own framing. The ideas of sense are allowed to have more reality in them, that is, to be more strong, orderly, and coherent than the creatures of the mind; but this is no argument that they exist without the mind. They are also less dependent on the spirit, or thinking substance which perceives them, in that they are excited by the will of another and more powerful spirit: yet still they are *ideas,* and certainly no *idea,* whether faint or strong, can exist otherwise than in a mind perceiving it.

34. Before we proceed any farther, it is necessary to spend some time in answering objections which may probably be made against the principles hitherto laid down. In doing of which, if I seem too prolix to those of quick apprehensions, I hope it may be pardoned, since all men do not equally apprehend things of this nature; and I am willing to be understood by everyone. First then, it will be objected that by the foregoing principles, all that is real and substantial in nature is banished out of the world: and instead thereof a chimerical scheme of ideas takes place. All things that exist, exist only in the mind, that is, they are purely notional. What therefore becomes of the sun, moon, and stars? What must we think of houses, rivers, mountains, trees, stones; nay, even of our own bodies? Are all these but so many chimeras and illusions on the fancy? To all which, and whatever else of the same sort may be objected, I answer, that by the principles premised, we are not deprived of any one thing in nature. Whatever we see, feel, hear, or any wise conceive or understand, remains as secure as ever, and is as real as ever. There is a *rerum natura,* and the distinction between realities and chimeras retains its full force. This is evident from *Sect.* 29, 30, and 33, where we have shown what is meant by *real things* in opposition to *chimeras,* or ideas of our own framing; but then they both equally exist in the mind, and in that sense are alike *ideas.*

35. I do not argue against the existence of any one thing that we can apprehend, either by sense or reflection. That the things I see with mine eyes and touch with my hands do exist, really exist, I make not the least

question. The only thing whose existence we deny, is that which philosophers call matter or corporeal substance. And in doing of this, there is no damage done to the rest of mankind, who, I dare say, will never miss it. The atheist indeed will want the color of an empty name to support his impiety; and the philosophers may possibly find, they have lost a great handle for trifling and disputation.

36. If any man thinks this detracts from the existence or reality of things, he is very far from understanding what has been premised in the plainest terms I could think of. Take here an abstract of what has been said. There are spiritual substances, minds, or human souls, which will or excite ideas in themselves at pleasure: but these are faint, weak, and unsteady in respect of others they perceive by sense, which being impressed upon them according to certain rules or laws of nature, speak themselves the effects of a mind more powerful and wise than human spirits. These latter are said to have more *reality* in them than the former: by which is meant that they are more affecting, orderly, and distinct, and that they are not fictions of the mind perceiving them. And in this sense, the sun that I see by day is the real sun, and that which I imagine by night is the idea of the former. In the sense here given of *reality*, it is evident that every vegetable, star, mineral, and in general each part of the mundane system, is as much a *real being* by our principles as by any other. Whether others mean anything by the term *reality* different from what I do, I entreat them to look into their own thoughts and see.

37. It will be urged that thus much at least is true, to wit, that we take away all corporeal substances. To this my answer is, that if the word *substance* be taken in the vulgar sense, for a combination of sensible qualities, such as extension, solidity, weight, and the like; this we cannot be accused of taking away. But if it be taken in a philosophic sense, for the support of accidents or qualities without the mind: then indeed I acknowledge that we take it away, if one may be said to take away that which never had any existence, not even in the imagination.

38. But, say you, it sounds very harsh to say we eat and drink ideas, and are clothed with ideas. I acknowledge it does so, the word *idea* not being used in common discourse to signify the several combinations of sensible qualities, which are called *things*: and it is certain that any expression which varies form the familiar use of language, will seem harsh and ridiculous. But this does not concern the truth of the proposition, which in other words is no more than to say, we are fed and clothed with those things which we perceive immediately by our senses. The hardness or softness, the color, taste, warmth, figure, and such like qualities, which combined together constitute the several sorts of victuals and apparel, have been shown to exist only in the mind that perceives them; and this is all that is meant by calling them *ideas*; which word, if it was as ordinarily used as *thing*, would sound no harsher nor more ridiculous than it. I am not for disputing about the propriety, but the truth of the expression. If

therefore you agree with me that we eat and drink, and are clad with the immediate objects of sense which cannot exist unperceived or without the mind: I shall readily grant it is more proper or conformable to custom, that they should be called things rather than ideas.

39. If it be demanded why I make use of the word *idea*, and do not rather in compliance with custom call them things. I answer, I do it for two reasons: first, because the term *thing*, in contradistinction to *idea*, is generally supposed to denote somewhat existing without the mind: secondly, because *thing* has a more comprehensive signification than *idea*, including spirits or thinking things as well as ideas. Since therefore the objects of sense exist only in the mind, and are withal thoughtless and inactive, I chose to mark them by the word *idea*, which implies those properties.

40. But say what we can, someone perhaps may be apt to reply, he will still believe his senses, and never suffer any arguments, how plausible soever, to prevail over the certainty of them. Be it so, assert the evidence of sense as high as you please, we are willing to do the same. That what I see, hear and feel does exist, that is to say, is perceived by me, I no more doubt than I do of my own being. But I do not see how the testimony of sense can be alleged, as a proof for the existence of anything, which is not perceived by sense. We are not for having any man turn *skeptic*, and disbelieve his senses; on the contrary we give them all the stress and assurance imaginable; nor are there any principles more opposite to skepticism, than those we have laid down, as shall be hereafter clearly shown.

41. Secondly, it will be objected that there is a great difference betwixt real fire, for instance, and the idea of fire, betwixt dreaming or imagining oneself burnt, and actually being so: this and the like may be urged in opposition to our tenets. To all which the answer is evident from what has been already said, and I shall only add in this place, that if real fire be very different from the idea of fire, so also is the real pain that it occasions, very different from the idea of the same pain: and yet nobody will pretend that real pain either is, or can possibly be, in an unperceiving thing or without the mind, any more than its idea.

42. Thirdly, it will be objected that we see things actually without or at a distance from us, and which consequently do not exist in the mind, it being absurd that those things which are seen at the distance of several miles, should be as near to us as our own thoughts. In answer to this, I desire it may be considered, that in a dream we do oft perceive things as existing at a great distance off, and yet for all that, those things are acknowledged to have their existence only in the mind.

43. But for the fuller clearing of this point, it may be worthwhile to consider, how it is that we perceive distance and things placed at a distance by sight. For that we should in truth see external space, and bodies actually existing in it, some nearer, others farther off, seems to carry with it some opposition to what has been said, of their existing nowhere without the

mind. The consideration of this difficulty it was, that gave birth to my *Essay towards a New Theory of Vision*, which was published not long since. Wherein it is shown that *distance* or outness is neither immediately of itself perceived by sight, nor yet apprehended or judged of by lines and angles, or anything that has a necessary connection with it: but that it is only suggested to our thoughts, by certain visible ideas and sensations attending vision, which in their own nature have no manner of similitude or relation, either with distance, or things placed at a distance. But by a connection taught us by experience, they come to signify and suggest them to us, after the same manner that words of any language suggest the ideas they are made to stand for. Insomuch that a man born blind, and afterwards made to see, would not, at first sight, think the things he saw, to be without his mind, or at any distance from him. See *Sect.* 41. of the forementioned treatise.

44. The ideas of sight and touch make two species, entirely distinct and heterogeneous. The former are marks and prognostics of the latter. That the proper objects of sight neither exist without the mind, nor are the images of external things, was shown even in that treatise. Though throughout the same, the contrary be supposed true of tangible objects: not that to suppose that vulgar error, was necessary for establishing the notion therein laid down; but because it was beside my purpose to examine and refute it in a discourse concerning *vision*. So that in strict truth the ideas of sight, when we apprehend by them distance and things placed at a distance, do not suggest or mark out to us things actually existing at a distance, but only admonish us what ideas of touch will be imprinted in our minds at such and such distances of time, and, in consequence of such or such actions. It is, I say, evident from what has been said in the foregoing parts of this treatise, and in *Sect.* 147, and elsewhere of the essay concerning vision, that visible ideas are the language whereby the governing spirit, on whom we depend, informs us what tangible ideas he is about to imprint upon us, in case we excite this or that motion in our own bodies. But for a fuller information in this point, I refer to the essay itself.

45. Fourthly, it will be objected that from the foregoing principles it follows, things are every moment annihilated and created anew. The objects of sense exist only when they are perceived: the trees therefore are in the garden, or the chairs in the parlor, no longer than while there is somebody by to perceive them. Upon shutting my eyes all the furniture in the room is reduced to nothing, and barely upon opening them it is again created. In answer to all which, I refer the reader to what has been said in *Sect.* 3, 4, etc. and desire he will consider whether he means anything by the actual existence of an idea, distinct from its being perceived. For my part, after the nicest inquiry I could make, I am not able to discover that anything else is meant by those words. And I once more entreat the reader to sound his own thoughts, and not suffer himself to be imposed on by words. If he can conceive it possible either for his ideas or their archetypes to exist without

being perceived, then I give up the cause: but if he cannot, he will acknowledge it is unreasonable for him to stand up in defense of he knows not what, and pretend to charge on me as an absurdity, the not assenting to these propositions which at bottom have no meaning to them.

DAVID HUME
(1711–1776) Scottish Philosopher

Of the Academical or Sceptical Philosophy*

Part I

There is not a greater number of philosophical reasonings, displayed upon any subject, than those, which prove the existence of a Deity, and refute the fallacies of *Atheists;* and yet the most religious philosophers still dispute whether any man can be so blinded as to be a speculative atheist. How shall we reconcile these contradictions? The knights-errant, who wandered about to clear the world of dragons and giants, never entertained the least doubt with regard to the existence of these monsters.

The *Sceptic* is another enemy of religion, who naturally provokes the indignation of all divines and graver philosophers; though it is certain, that no man ever met with any such absurd creature, or conversed with a man, who had no opinion or principle concerning any subject, either of action or speculation. This begets a very natural question; What is meant by a sceptic? And how far it is possible to push these philosophical principles of doubt and uncertainty?

There is a species of scepticism, *antecedent* to all study and philosophy, which is much inculcated by Des Cartes and others, as a sovereign preservative against error and precipitate judgment. It recommends an universal doubt, not only of all our former opinions and principles, but also of our very faculties; of whose veracity, say they, we must assure ourselves, by a chain of reasoning, deduced from some original principle, which cannot possibly be fallacious or deceitful. But neither is there any such original principle, which has a prerogative above others, that are self-evident and convincing: Or if there were, could we advance a step beyond it, but by the use of those very faculties, of which we are supposed to be already diffident. The Cartesian doubt, therefore, were it ever possible to be

---

*From David Hume, *An Enquiry Concerning Human Understanding* (London, 1748).

attained by any human creature (as it plainly is not) would be entirely incurable; and no reasoning could ever bring us to a state of assurance and conviction upon any subject.

It must, however, be confessed, that this species of scepticism, when more moderate, may be understood in a very reasonable sense, and is a necessary preparative to the study of philosophy, by preserving a proper impartiality in our judgments, and weaning our mind from all those prejudices, which we may have imbibed from education or rash opinion. To begin with clear and self-evident principles, to advance by timorous and sure steps, to review frequently our conclusions, and examine accurately all their consequences; though by these means we shall make both a slow and a short progress in our systems; are the only methods, by which we can ever hope to reach truth, and attain a proper stability and certainty in our determinations.

There is another species of scepticism, *consequent* to science and enquiry, when men are supposed to have discovered, either the absolute fallaciousness of their mental faculties, or their unfitness to reach any fixed determination in all those curious subjects of speculation, about which they are commonly employed. Even our very senses are brought into dispute, by a certain species of philosophers; and the maxims of common life are subjected to the same doubt as the most profound principles or conclusions of metaphysics and theology. As these paradoxical tenets (if they may be called tenets) are to be met with in some philosophers, and the refutation of them in several, they naturally excite our curiosity, and make us enquire into the arguments, on which they may be founded.

I need not insist upon the more trite topics, employed by the sceptics in all ages, against the evidence of *sense;* such as those which are derived from the imperfection and fallaciousness of our organs, on numberless occasions; the crooked appearance of an oar in water; the various aspects of objects, according to their different distances; the double images which arise from the pressing one eye; with many other appearances of a like nature. These sceptical topics, indeed, are only sufficient to prove, that the senses alone are not implicitly to be depended on; but that we must correct their evidence by reason, and by considerations, derived from the nature of the medium, the distance of the object, and the disposition of the organ, in order to render them, within their sphere, the proper *criteria* of truth and falsehood. There are other more profound arguments against the senses, which admit not of so easy a solution.

It seems evident, that men are carried, by a natural instinct or prepossession, to repose faith in their senses; and that, without any reasoning, or even almost before the use of reason, we always suppose an external universe, which depends not on our perception, but would exist, though we and every sensible creature were absent or annihilated. Even the animal creation are governed by a like opinion, and preserve this belief of external objects, in all their thoughts, designs, and actions.

It seems also evident, that, when men follow this blind and powerful instinct of nature, they always suppose the very images, presented by the senses, to be the external objects, and never entertain any suspicion, that the one are nothing but representations of the other. This very table, which we see white, and which we feel hard, is believed to exist, independent of our perception, and to be something external to our mind, which perceives it. Our presence bestows not being on it: Our absence does not annihilate it. It preserves its existence uniform and entire, independent of the situation of intelligent beings, who perceive or contemplate it.

But this universal and primary opinion of all men is soon destroyed by the slightest philosophy, which teaches us, that nothing can ever be present to the mind but an image or perception, and that the senses are only the inlets, through which these images are conveyed, without being able to produce any immediate intercourse between the mind and the object. The table, which we see, seems to diminish, as we remove farther from it: But the real table, which exists independent of us, suffers no alteration: It was, therefore, nothing but its image, which was present to the mind. These are the obvious dictates of reason; and no man, who reflects, ever doubted, that the existences, which we consider, when we say, *this house* and *that tree,* are nothing but perceptions in the mind, and fleeting copies or representations of other existences, which remain uniform and independent.

So far, then, are we necessitated by reasoning to contradict or depart from the primary instincts of nature, and to embrace a new system with regard to the evidence of our senses. But here philosophy finds herself extremely embarrassed, when she would justify this new system, and obviate the cavils and objections of the sceptics. She can no longer plead the infallible and irresistible instinct of nature: For that led us to a quite different system, which is acknowledged fallible and even erroneous. And to justify this pretended philosophical system, by a chain of clear and convincing argument, or even any appearance of argument, exceeds the power of all human capacity.

By what argument can it be proved, that the perceptions of the mind must be caused by external objects, entirely different from them, though resembling them (if that be possible) and could not arise either from the energy of the mind itself, or from the suggestion of some invisible and unknown spirit, or from some other cause still more unknown to us? It is acknowledged, that, in fact, many of these perceptions arise not from any thing external, as in dreams, madness, and other diseases. And nothing can be more inexplicable than the manner, in which body should so operate upon mind as ever to convey an image of itself to a substance, supposed of so different, and even contrary a nature.

It is a question of fact, whether the perceptions of the senses be produced by external objects, resembling them: How shall this question be determined? By experience surely; as all other questions of a like nature. But here experience is, and must be entirely silent. The mind has never any thing present to it but the perceptions, and cannot possibly reach any experience of their connexion with objects. The supposition of such a connexion is, therefore, without any foundation in reasoning.

To have recourse to the veracity of the supreme Being in order to prove the veracity of our senses, is surely making a very unexpected circuit. If his veracity were at all concerned in this matter, our senses would be entirely infallible; because it is not possible that he can ever deceive. Not to mention, that, if the external world be once called in question, we shall be at a loss to find arguments, by which we may prove the existence of that Being or any of his attributes.

This is a topic, therefore, in which the profounder and more philosophical sceptics will always triumph, when they endeavour to introduce an universal doubt into all subjects of human knowledge and enquiry. Do you follow the instincts and propensities of nature, may they say, in assenting to the veracity of sense? But these lead you to believe, that the very perception or sensible image is the external object. Do you disclaim this principle, in order to embrace a more rational opinion, that the perceptions are only representations of something external? You here depart from your natural propensities and more obvious sentiments; and yet are not able to satisfy your reason, which can never find any convincing argument from experience to prove, that the perceptions are connected with any external objects.

There is another sceptical topic of a like nature, derived from the most profound philosophy; which might merit our attention, were it requisite to dive so deep, in order to discover arguments and reasonings, which can so little serve to any serious purpose. It is universally allowed by modern enquirers, that all the sensible qualities of objects, such as hard, soft, hot, cold, white, black, &c., are merely secondary, and exist not in the objects themselves, but are perceptions of the mind, without any external archetype or model, which they represent. If this be allowed, with regard to secondary qualities, it must also follow, with regard to the supposed primary qualities of extension and solidity; nor can the latter be any more entitled to that denomination than the former. The idea of extension is entirely acquired from the senses of sight and feeling; and if all the qualities, perceived by the senses, be in the mind, not in the object, the same conclusion must reach the idea of extension, which is wholly dependent on the sensible ideas or the ideas of secondary qualities. Nothing can save us from this conclusion, but the asserting, that the ideas of those primary qualities are attained by *Abstraction:* an opinion, which, if we examine it accurately, we shall find to be unintelligible, and even absurd. An extension, that is neither tangible nor visible, cannot possibly be conceived: And a tangible or visible extension, which is neither hard nor soft, black nor white, is equally beyond the reach of human conception. Let any man try to conceive a triangle in general, which is neither *Isoceles* nor *Scalenum,* nor has any particular length or proportion of sides; and he will soon perceive the absurdity of all the scholastic notions with regard to abstraction and general ideas.

Thus the first philosophical objection to the evidence of sense or to the opinion of external existence consists in this, that such an opinion, if rested on natural instinct, is contrary to reason, and if referred to reason, is contrary to natural instinct, and at the same time carries no rational evidence with it, to convince an impartial enquirer. The second objection goes farther, and represents this opinion as contrary to reason: at least, if it be a principle of reason, that all sensible qualities are in the mind, not in the object. Bereave matter of all its intelligible qualities, both primary and secondary, you in a manner annihilate it, and leave only a certain unknown, inexplicable *something,* as the cause of our perceptions; a notion so imperfect, that no sceptic will think it worth while to contend against it.

Part II

It may seem a very extravagant attempt of the sceptics to destroy *reason* by argument and ratiocination; yet is this the grand scope of all their enquiries and disputes. They endeavour to find objections, both to our abstract reasonings, and to those which regard matter of fact and existence.

The chief objection against all *abstract* reasonings is derived from the ideas of space and time; ideas, which, in common life and to a careless view, are very clear and intelligible, but when they pass through the scrutiny of the profound sciences (and they are the chief object of these sciences) afford principles, which seem full of absurdity and contradiction. No priestly *dogmas*, invented on purpose to tame and subdue the rebellious reason of mankind, ever shocked common sense more than the doctrine of the infinite divisibility of extension, with its consequences; as they are pompously displayed by all geometricians and metaphysicians, with a kind of triumph and exultation. A real quantity, infinitely less than any finite quantity, containing quantities infinitely less than itself, and so on *in infinitum;* this is an edifice so bold and prodigious, that it is too weighty for any pretended demonstration to support, because it shocks the clearest and most natural principles of human reason.[1] But what renders the matter more extraordinary, is, that these seemingly absurd opinions are supported by a chain of reasoning, the clearest and most natural; nor is it possible for us to allow the premises without admitting the consequences. Nothing can be more convincing and satisfactory than all the conclusions concerning the properties of circles and triangles; and yet, when these are once received, how can we deny, that the angle of contact between a circle and its tangent is infinitely less than any rectilineal angle, that as you may increase the diameter of the circle *in infinitum,* this angle of contact becomes still less, even *in infinitum,* and that the angle of contact between other curves and their tangents may be infinitely less than those between any circle and its tangent, and so on, *in infinitum?* The demonstration of these principles seems as unexceptionable as that which proves the three angles of a triangle to be equal to two right ones, though the latter opinion be natural and easy, and the former big with contradiction and absurdity. Reason here seems to be thrown into a kind of amazement and suspense, which, without the suggestions of any sceptic, gives her a diffidence of herself, and of the ground on which she treads. She sees a full light, which illuminates certain places; but that light borders upon the most profound darkness. And between these she is so dazzled and confounded, that she scarcely can pronounce with certainty and assurance concerning any one object.

The absurdity of these bold determinations of the abstract sciences seems to become, if possible, still more palpable with regard to time than extension. An infinite number of real parts of time, passing in succession, and exhausted one after another, appears so evident a contradiction, that no man, one should think,

---

[1] Whatever disputes there may be about mathematical points, we must allow that there are physical points; that is, parts of extension, which cannot be divided or lessened, either by the eye or imagination. These images, then, which are present to the fancy or senses, are absolutely indivisible, and consequently must be allowed by mathematicians to be infinitely less than any real part of extension; and yet nothing appears more certain to reason, than that an infinite number of them composes an infinite extension. How much more an infinite number of those infinitely small parts of extension, which are still supposed infinitely divisible?

whose judgment is not corrupted, instead of being improved, by the sciences, would ever be able to admit of it.

Yet still reason must remain restless, and unquiet, even with regard to that scepticism, to which she is driven by these seeming absurdities and contradictions. How any clear, distinct idea can contain circumstances, contradictory to itself, or to any other clear, distinct idea, is absolutely incomprehensible; and is, perhaps, as absurd as any proposition, which can be formed. So that nothing can be more sceptical, or more full of doubt and hesitation, than this scepticism itself, which arises from some of the paradoxical conclusions of geometry or the science of quantity.[2]

The sceptical objections to *moral* evidence, or to the reasonings concerning matter of fact, are either *popular* or *philosophical*. The popular objections are derived from the natural weakness of human understanding; the contradictory opinions, which have been entertained in different ages and nations; the variations of our judgment in sickness and health, youth and old age, prosperity and adversity; the perpetual contradiction of each particular man's opinions and sentiments; with many other topics of that kind. It is needless to insist farther on this head. These objections are but weak. For as, in common life, we reason every moment concerning fact and existence, and cannot possibly subsist, without continually employing this species of argument, any popular objections, derived from thence, must be insufficient to destroy that evidence. The great subverter of *Pyrrhonism* [skepticism] or the excessive principles of scepticism, is action, and employment, and the occupations of common life. These principles may flourish and triumph in the schools; where it is, indeed, difficult, if not impossible, to refute them. But as soon as they leave the shade, and by the presence of the real objects, which actuate our passions and sentiments, are put in opposition to the more powerful principles of our nature, they vanish like smoke, and leave the most determined sceptic in the same condition as other mortals.

The sceptic, therefore, had better keep within his proper sphere, and display those *philosophical* objections, which arise from more profound researches. Here he seems to have ample matter of triumph; while he justly insists, that all our evidence for any matter of fact, which lies beyond the testimony of sense or memory, is derived entirely from the relation of cause and effect; that we have no other idea of this relation than that of two objects, which have been frequently *conjoined* together; that we have no argument to convince us, that objects, which have, in our experience, been frequently conjoined, will likewise, in other instances, be

---

[2] It seems to me not impossible to avoid these absurdities and contradictions, if it be admitted, that there is no such thing as abstract or general ideas, properly speaking; but that all general ideas are, in reality, particular ones, attached to a general term, which recalls, upon occasion, other particular ones, that resemble, in certain circumstances, the idea, present to the mind. Thus when the term Horse, is pronounced, we immediately figure to ourselves the idea of a black or white animal, of a particular size or figure: But as that term is also usually applied to animals of other colours, figures and sizes, these ideas, though not actually present to the imagination, are easily recalled; and our reasoning and conclusion proceed in the same way, as if they were actually present. If this be admitted (as seems reasonable) it follows that all the ideas of quantity, upon which mathematicians reason, are nothing but particular, and such as are suggested by the senses and imagination, and consequently, cannot be infinitely divisible. It is sufficient to have dropped this hint at present, without prosecuting it any farther. [For a more comprehensive discussion, see *Treatise* 1.1.7.] It certainly concerns all lovers of science not to expose themselves to the ridicule and contempt of the ignorant by their conclusions; and this seems the readiest solution of these difficulties.

conjoined in the same manner; and that nothing leads us to this inference but custom or a certain instinct of our nature; which it is indeed difficult to resist, but which, like other instincts, may be fallacious and deceitful. While the sceptic insists upon these topics, he shows his force, or rather, indeed, his own and our weakness; and seems, for the time at least, to destroy all assurance and conviction. These arguments might be displayed at greater length, if any durable good or benefit to society could ever be expected to result from them.

For here is the chief and most confounding objection to *excessive* scepticism, that no durable good can ever result from it; while it remains in its full force and vigour. We need only ask such a sceptic, *What his meaning is? And what he proposes by all these curious researches?* He is immediately at a loss, and knows not what to answer. A Copernican or Ptolemaic, who supports each his different system of astronomy, may hope to produce a conviction, which will remain constant and durable, with his audience. A Stoic or Epicurean displays principles, which may not only be durable, but which have an effect on conduct and behaviour. But a Pyrrhonian cannot expect, that his philosophy will have any constant influence on the mind: Or if it had, that its influence would be beneficial to society. On the contrary, he must acknowledge, if he will acknowledge any thing, that all human life must perish, were his principles universally and steadily to prevail. All discourse, all action would immediately cease; and men remain in a total lethargy, till the necessities of nature, unsatisfied, put an end to their miserable existence. It is true; so fatal an event is very little to be dreaded. Nature is always too strong for principle. And though a Pyrrhonian may throw himself or others into a momentary amazement and confusion by his profound reasonings; the first and most trivial event in life will put to flight all his doubts and scruples, and leave him the same, in every point of action and speculation, with the philosophers of every other sect, or with those who never concerned themselves in any philosophical researches. When he awakes from his dream, he will be the first to join in the laugh against himself, and to confess, that all his objections are mere amusement, and can have no other tendency than to show the whimsical condition of mankind, who must act and reason and believe; though they are not able, by their most diligent enquiry, to satisfy themselves concerning the foundation of these operations, or to remove the objections, which may be raised against them.

Part III

There is, indeed, a more *mitigated* scepticism or *academical* philosophy, which may be both durable and useful, and which may, in part, be the result of this Pyrrhonism, or *excessive* scepticism, when its undistinguished doubts are, in some measure, corrected by common sense and reflection. The greater part of mankind are naturally apt to be affirmative and dogmatical in their opinions; and while they see objects only on one side, and have no idea of any counterpoising argument, they throw themselves precipitately into the principles, to which they are inclined; nor have they any indulgence for those who entertain opposite sentiments. To hesitate or balance perplexes their understanding, checks their passion, and suspends their action. They are, therefore, impatient till they escape from a state, which to them is so uneasy; and they think, that they can never remove themselves far enough from it, by the violence of their affirmations and obstinacy of their belief. But could such dogmatical reasoners become sensible of the strange infirmities of human understanding, even in its most perfect state, and when most accurate and cautious in its determinations; such a reflection would naturally inspire them with more modesty and reserve, and diminish their fond opinion of themselves, and their prejudice against antagonists. The illiterate may reflect on the disposition of the learned, who, amidst all the advantages of study and reflection, are commonly still diffident in their determinations: And if any of the learned be inclined, from their natural temper, to haughtiness and obstinacy, a small tincture of Pyrrhonism might abate their pride, by showing them, that the few advantages, which they may have attained over their fellows, are but inconsiderable, if compared with the universal perplexity and confusion, which is inherent in human nature. In general, there is a degree of doubt, and caution, and modesty, which, in all kinds of scrutiny and decision, ought for ever to accompany a just reasoner.

Another species of *mitigated* scepticism, which may be of advantage to mankind, and which may be the natural result of the Pyrrhonian doubts and scruples, is the limitation of our enquiries to such subjects as are best adapted to the narrow capacity of human understanding. The *imagination* of man is naturally sublime, delighted with whatever is remote and extraordinary, and running, without control, into the most distant parts of space and time in order to avoid the objects, which custom has rendered too familiar to it. A correct *Judgment* observes a contrary method, and avoiding all distant and high enquiries, confines itself to common life, and to such subjects as fall under daily practice and experience; leaving the more sublime topics to the embellishment of poets and orators, or to the arts of priests and politicians. To bring us to so salutary a determination, nothing can be more serviceable, than to be once thoroughly convinced of the force of the Pyrrhonian doubt, and of the impossibility, that any thing, but the strong power of natural instinct, could free us from it. Those who have a propensity to philosophy, will still continue their researches; because they reflect, that, besides the immediate pleasure, attending such an occupation, philosophical decisions are nothing but the reflections of common life, methodized and corrected. But they will never be tempted to go beyond common life, so long as they consider the imperfection of those faculties which they employ, their narrow reach, and their inaccurate operations. While we cannot give a satisfactory reason, why we believe, after a thousand experiments, that a stone will fall, or fire burn; can we ever satisfy ourselves concerning any determination, which we may form, with regard to the origin of worlds, and the situation of nature, from, and to eternity?

This narrow limitation, indeed, of our enquiries, is, in every respect, so reasonable, that it suffices to make the slightest examination into the natural powers of the human mind, and to compare them with their objects, in order to recommend it to us. We shall then find what are the proper subjects of science and enquiry.

It seems to me, that the only objects of the abstract sciences or of demonstration are quantity and number, and that all attempts to extend this more perfect species of knowledge beyond these bounds are mere sophistry and illusion. As the component parts of quantity and number are entirely similar, their relations become intricate and involved; and nothing can be more curious, as well as useful, than to trace, by a variety of mediums, their equality or inequality, through their different appearances. But as all other ideas are clearly distinct and different from each other, we can never advance farther, by our utmost scrutiny, than to observe this diversity, and, by an obvious reflection, pronounce one thing not to be another. Or if there be any difficulty in these decisions, it proceeds entirely from the undeterminate meaning of words, which is corrected by juster definitions. That *the square of the hypothenuse is equal to the squares of the other two sides*, cannot be known, let the terms be ever so exactly defined, without a train of reasoning and enquiry. But to convince us of this proposition, *that where there is no property, there can be no injustice*, it is only necessary to define the terms, and explain injustice to be a violation of property. This proposition is, indeed, nothing but a more imperfect definition. It is the same case with all those pretended syllogistical reasonings, which may be found in every other branch of learning, except the sciences of quantity and number; and these may safely, I think, be pronounced the only proper objects of knowledge and demonstration.

All other enquiries of men regard only matter of fact and existence; and these are evidently incapable of demonstration. Whatever *is* may *not be*. No negation of a fact can involve a contradiction. The non-existence of any being, without exception, is as clear and distinct an idea as its existence. The proposition, which affirms it not to be, however false, is no less conceivable and intelligible, than that which affirms it to be. The case is different with the sciences, properly so called. Every proposition, which is not true, is there confused and unintelligible. That the cube root of 64 is equal to the half of 10, is a false proposition, and can never be distinctly conceived. But that Caesar, or the angel Gabriel, or any being never existed, may be a false proposition, but still is perfectly conceivable, and implies no contradiction.

The existence, therefore, of any being can only be proved by arguments from its cause or its effect; and these arguments are founded entirely on experience. If we reason *a priori*, any thing may appear able to produce any thing. The falling of a pebble may, for aught we know, extinguish the sun; or the wish of a man control the planets in their orbits. It is only experience, which teaches us the nature and bounds of cause and effect, and enables us to infer the existence of one object from that of another. Such is the foundation of moral reasoning, which forms the greater part of human knowledge, and is the source of all human action and behaviour.

Moral reasonings are either concerning particular or general facts. All deliberations in life regard the former; as also all disquisitions in history, chronology, geography, and astronomy.

The sciences, which treat of general facts, are politics, natural philosophy, physic, chemistry, &c. where the qualities, causes and effects of a whole species of objects are enquired into.

Divinity or Theology, as it proves the existence of a Deity, and the immortality of souls, is composed partly of reasonings concerning particular, partly concerning general facts. It has a foundation in *reason*, so far as it is supported by experience. But its best and most solid foundation is *faith* and divine revelation.

Morals and criticism are not so properly objects of the understanding as of taste and sentiment. Beauty, whether moral or natural, is felt, more properly than perceived. Or if we reason concerning it, and endeavour to fix its standard, we regard a new fact, to wit, the general taste of mankind, or some such fact, which may be the object of reasoning and enquiry.

When we run over libraries, persuaded of these principles, what havoc must we make? If we take in our hand any volume; of divinity or school metaphysics, for instance; let us ask, *Does it contain any abstract reasoning concerning quantity or number?* No. *Does it contain any experimental reasoning concerning matter of fact and existence?* No. Commit it then to the flames: For it can contain nothing but sophistry and illusion.

The Sources of Knowledge

From *The Prelude*

From early days,
Beginning not long after that first time
In which, a Babe, by intercourse of touch
I held mute dialogues with my Mother's heart,
I have endeavoured to display the means
Whereby this infant sensibility,
Great birthright of our being, was in me
Augmented and sustained. Yet is a path
More difficult before me; and I fear
That in its broken windings we shall need
The chamois' sinews, and the eagle's wing:
For now a trouble came into my mind
From unknown causes. I was left alone
Seeking the visible world, nor knowing why.

William Wordsworth

PLATO

(428–347 B.C.) Greek Philosopher

The Divided Line*

This reality, then, that gives their truth to the objects of knowledge and the power of knowing to the knower, you must say is the idea of good, and you must conceive it as being the cause of knowledge, and of truth in so far as known. Yet fair as they both are, knowledge and truth, in supposing it to be something fairer still than these you will think rightly of it. But as for knowledge and truth, even as in our illustration it is right to deem light and vision sunlike, but never to think that they are the sun, so here it is right to consider these two their counterparts, as being like the good or boniform, but to think that either of them is the good is not right. Still higher honor belongs to the possession and habit of the good.

An inconceivable beauty you speak of, he said, if it is the source of knowledge and truth, and yet itself surpasses them in beauty. For you surely cannot mean that it is pleasure.

Hush, said I, but examine the similitude of it still further in this way.

How?

The sun, I presume you will say, not only furnishes to visibles the power of visibility but it also provides for their generation and growth and nurture though it is not itself generation.

Of course not.

In like manner, then, you are to say that the objects of knowledge not only receive from the presence of the good their being known, but their very existence and essence is derived to them from it, though the good itself is not essence but still transcends essence in dignity and surpassing power.

And Glaucon very ludicrously said, Heaven save us, hyperbole can no further go.

The fault is yours, I said, for compelling me to utter my thoughts about it.

And don't desist, he said, but at least expound the similitude of the sun, if there is anything that you are omitting.

Why, certainly, I said, I am omitting a great deal.

Well, don't omit the least bit, he said.

I fancy, I said, that I shall have to pass over much, but nevertheless so far as it is at present practicable I shall not willingly leave anything out.

Do not, he said.

---

*For permission to photocopy this selection please contact Harvard University Press. Reprinted by permission of the publisher and the Loeb Classical Library from *Republic*, by Plato, trans. by Paul Shorey, Cambridge: Harvard University Press, 1930.

231

Conceive then, said I, as we were saying, that there are these two entities, and that one of them is sovereign over the intelligible order and region and the other over the world of the eyeball, not to say the sky-ball, but let that pass. You surely apprehend the two types, the visible and the intelligible.

I do.

Represent them then, as it were, by a line divided into two unequal sections and cut each section again in the same ratio—the section, that is, of the visible and that of the intelligible order—and then as an expression of the ratio of their comparative clearness and obscurity you will have, as one of the sections of the visible world, images. By images I mean, first shadows and then reflections in water and on surfaces of dense, smooth, and bright texture, and everything of that kind, if you apprehend.

I do.

As the second section assume that of which this is a likeness or an image, that is, the animals about us and all plants and the whole class of objects made by man.

I so assume it, he said.

Would you be willing to say, said I, that the division in respect of reality and truth or the opposite is expressed by the proportion—as is the opinable to the knowable so is the likeness to that of which it is a likeness?

I certainly would.

Consider then again the way in which we are to make the division of the intelligible section.

In what way?

By the distinction that there is one section of it which the soul is compelled to investigate by treating as images the things imitated in the former division, and by means of assumptions from which it proceeds not up to a first principle but down to a conclusion, while there is another section in which it advances from its assumption to a beginning or principle that transcends assumption, and in which it makes no use of the images employed by the other section, relying on ideas only and progressing systematically through ideas.

I don't fully understand what you mean by this, he said.

Well, I will try again, said I, for you will better understand after this preamble. For I think you are aware that students of geometry and reckoning and such subjects first postulate the odd and the even and the various figures and three kinds of angles and other things akin to these in each branch of science, regard them as known, and, treating them as absolute assumptions, do not deign to render any further account of them to themselves or others, taking it for granted that they are obvious to everybody. They take their start from these, and pursuing the inquiry from this point on consistently, conclude with that for the investigation of which they set out.

Certainly, he said, I know that.

And do you not also know that they further make use of the visible forms and talk about them, though they are not thinking of them but of those things of which they are a likeness, pursuing their inquiry for the sake of the square as such and the diagonal as such, and not for the sake of the image of it which they draw? And so in all cases. The very things which they mold and draw, which have shadows and images of themselves in water, these things they treat in their turn as only images, but what they really seek is to get sight of those realities which can be seen only by the mind.

True, he said.

This then is the class that I described as intelligible, it is true, but with the reservation first that the soul is compelled to employ assumptions in the investigation of it, not proceeding to a first principle because of its inability to extricate itself from and rise above its assumptions, and second, that it uses as images or likenesses the very objects that are themselves copied and adumbrated by the class below them, and that in comparison with these latter are esteemed as clear and held in honor.

I understand, said he, that you are speaking of what falls under geometry and the kindred arts.

Understand then, said I, that by the other section of the intelligible I mean that which the reason itself lays hold of by the power of dialectic, treating its assumptions not as absolute beginnings but literally as hypotheses, underpinnings, footings, and springboards so to speak, to enable it to rise to that which requires no assumption and is the starting point of all, and after attaining to that again taking hold of the first dependencies from it, so to proceed downward to the conclusion, making no use whatever of any object of sense but only of pure ideas moving on through ideas to ideas and ending with ideas.

I understand, he said, not fully, for it is no slight task that you appear to have in mind, but I do understand that you mean to distinguish the aspect of reality and the intelligible, which is contemplated by the power of dialectic, as something truer and more exact than the object of the so-called arts and sciences whose assumptions are arbitrary starting points. And though it is true that those who contemplate them are compelled to use their understanding and not their senses, yet because they do not go back to the beginning in the study of them but start from assumptions you do not think they possess true intelligence about them although the things themselves are intelligibles when apprehended in conjunction with a first principle. And I think you call the mental habit of geometers and their like mind or understanding and not reason because you regard understanding as something intermediate between opinion and reason.

Your interpretation is quite sufficient, I said. And now, answering to these four sections, assume these four affections occurring in the soul—intellection or reason for the highest, understanding for the second, belief for the third, and for the last, picture thinking or conjecture—and arrange them in a proportion, considering that they participate in clearness and precision in the same degree as their objects partake of truth and reality.

I understand, he said. I concur and arrange them as you bid.

ARISTOTLE

(384–322 B.C.) Greek Philosopher

From *Posterior Analytics**

As regards syllogism and demonstration, the definition of, and the conditions required to produce each of them, are now clear, and with that also the definition of, and the conditions required to produce, demonstrative knowledge, since it is the same as demonstration. As to the basic premises, how they become known and what is the developed state of knowledge of them is made clear by raising some preliminary problems.

We have already said that scientific knowledge through demonstration is impossible unless a man knows the primary immediate premises. But there are questions which might be raised in respect of the apprehension of these immediate premises: one might not only ask whether it is of the same kind as the apprehension of the conclusions, but also whether there is or is not scientific knowledge of both; or scientific knowledge of the latter, and of the former a different kind of knowledge; and, further, whether the developed states of knowledge are not innate but come to be in us, or are innate but at first unnoticed. Now it is strange if we possess them from birth; for it means that we possess apprehensions more accurate than demonstration and fail to notice them. If on the other hand we acquire them and do not previously possess them, how could we apprehend and learn without a basis of pre-existent knowledge? For that is impossible, as we used to find in the case of demonstration. So it emerges that neither can we possess them from birth, nor can they come to be in us if we are without knowledge of them to the extent of having no such developed state at all. Therefore we must possess a capacity of some sort, but not such as to rank higher in accuracy than these developed states. And this at least is an obvious characteristic of all animals, for they possess a congenital discriminative capacity which is called sense-perception. But though sense-perception is innate in all animals, in some the sense-impression comes to persist, in others it does not. So animals in which this persistence does not come to be have either no knowledge at all outside the act of perceiving, or no knowledge of objects of which no impression persists; animals in which it does come into being have perception and can continue to retain the sense-impression in the soul: and when such persistence is frequently repeated a further distinction at once arises between those which out of the persistence of such sense-impressions develop a power of systematizing them and those which do not. So out of sense-perception comes to be what we call memory,

*From Aristotle, *Posterior Analytics,* trans. by G.R.G. Muce, in *Oxford Translation of the Works of Aristotle,* ed. by J.A. Smith and W.D. Ross (Oxford, 1908–1952).

and out of frequently repeated memories of the same thing develops experience; for a number of memories constitute a single experience. From experience again—i.e. from the universal now stabilized in its entirety within the soul, the one beside the many which is a single identity within them all—originate the skill of the craftsman and the knowledge of the man of science, skill in the sphere of coming to be and science in the sphere of being.

   We conclude that these states of knowledge are neither innate in a determinate form, nor developed from other higher states of knowledge, but from sense-perception. It is like a rout in battle stopped by first one man making a stand and then another, until the original formation has been restored. The soul is so constituted as to be capable of this process.

   Let us now restate the account given already, though with insufficient clearness. When one of a number of logically indiscriminable particulars has made a stand, the earliest universal is present in the soul: for though the act of sense-perception is of the particular, its content is universal—is man, for example, not the man Callias. A fresh stand is made among these rudimentary universals, and the process does not cease until the indivisible concepts, the true universals, are established: e.g. such and such a species of animal is a step towards the genus animal, which by the same process is a step towards a further generalization.

   Thus it is clear that we must get to know the primary premisses by induction; for the method by which even sense-perception implants the universal is inductive. Now of the thinking states by which we grasp truth, some are unfailingly true, others admit of error—opinion, for instance, and calculation, whereas scientific knowing and intuition are always true: further, no other kind of thought except intuition is more accurate than scientific knowledge, whereas primary premisses are more knowable than demonstrations, and all scientific knowledge is discursive. From these considerations it follows that there will be no scientific knowledge of the primary premisses, and since except intuition nothing can be truer than scientific knowledge, it will be intuition that apprehends the primary premisses—a result which also follows from the fact that demonstration cannot be the originative source of demonstration, nor, consequently, scientific knowledge of scientific knowledge. If, therefore, it is the only other kind of true thinking except scientific knowing, intuition will be the originative source of scientific knowledge. And the originative source of science grasps the original basic premiss, while science as a whole is similarly related as originative source to the whole body of fact.

JOHN LOCKE

(1632–1704) English Philosopher

From *Essay Concerning Human Understanding**

No Innate Speculative Principles

It is an established opinion amongst some men, that there are in the understanding certain *innate principles;* some primary notions, characters, as it were stamped upon the mind of man; which the soul receives in its very first being, and brings into the world with it. It would be sufficient to convince unprejudiced readers of the falseness of this supposition, if I should only show (as I hope I shall in the following parts of this Discourse) how men, barely by the use of their natural faculties, may attain to all the knowledge they have, without the help of any innate impressions; and may arrive at certainty, without any such original notions or principles.

There is nothing more commonly taken for granted than that there are certain *principles,* both *speculative* and *practical* (for they speak of both), universally agreed upon by all mankind: which therefore, they argue, must needs be the constant impressions which the souls of men receive in their first beings, and which they bring into the world with them, as necessarily and really as they do any of their inherent faculties.

This argument, drawn from universal consent, has this misfortune in it, that if it were true in matter of fact, that there were certain truths wherein all mankind agreed, it would not prove them innate, if there can be any other way shown how men may come to that universal agreement, in the things they do consent in, which I presume may be done.

But, which is worse, this argument of universal consent, which is made use of to prove innate principles, seems to me a demonstration that there are none such: because there are none to which all mankind gives a universal assent. I shall begin with the speculative, and instance in those magnified principles of demonstration, "Whatsoever is, is," and "It is impossible for the same thing to be and not to be"; which, of all others, I think have the most allowed title to innate. These have so settled a reputation of maxims universally received, that it will no doubt be thought strange if any one should seem to question it. But yet I take liberty to say, that these propositions are so far from having a universal assent, that there are a great part of mankind to whom they are not so much as known.

For, first, it is evident, that all children and idiots have not the least apprehension or thought of them. And the want of that is enough to destroy that universal assent which must needs be the necessary concomitant of all innate truths: it

---

*From John Locke, *Essay Concerning Human Understanding* (London, 1690), Book I, Chapter 1 and Book 4, Chapters 1 & 2.

seeming to me near a contradiction to say, that there are truths imprinted on the soul, which it perceives or understands not: imprinting, if it signify anything, being nothing else but the making certain truths to be perceived. For to imprint anything on the mind without the mind's perceiving it, seems to me hardly intelligible. If therefore children and idiots have souls, have minds, with those impressions upon them, *they* must unavoidably perceive them, and necessarily know and assent to these truths; which since they do not, it is evident that there are no such impressions. For if they are not notions naturally imprinted, how can they be innate? and if they are notions imprinted, how can they be unknown? If therefore these two propositions, "Whatsoever is, is," and "It is impossible for the same thing to be and not to be," are by nature imprinted, children cannot be ignorant of them: infants, and all that have souls, must necessarily have them in their understandings, know the truth of them, and assent to it.

To avoid this, it is usually answered, that all men know and assent to them, *when they come to the use of reason;* and this is enough to prove them innate. I answer:

To apply this answer with any tolerable sense to our present purpose, it must signify one of these two things: either that as soon as men come to the use of reason these supposed native inscriptions come to be known and observed by them; or else, that the use and exercise of men's reason assists them in the discovery of these principles, and certainly makes them known to them.

If they mean, that by the use of reason men may discover these principles, and that this is sufficient to prove them innate; their way of arguing will stand thus, viz. that whatever truths reason can certainly discover to us, and make us firmly assent to, those are all naturally imprinted on the mind; since that universal assent, which is made the mark of them, amounts to no more but this,—that by the use of reason we are capable to come to a certain knowledge of and assent to them; and, by this means, there will be no difference between the maxims of the mathematicians, and theorems they deduce from them: all must be equally allowed innate; they being all discoveries made by the use of reason, and truths that a rational creature may certainly come to know, if he apply his thoughts rightly that way.

But how can these men think the use of reason necessary to discover principles that are supposed innate, when reason (if we may believe them) is nothing else but the faculty of deducing unknown truths from principles or propositions that are already known? That certainly can never be thought innate which we have need of reason to discover; unless, as I have said, we will have all the certain truths that reason ever teaches us, to be innate. So that to make reason discover those truths thus imprinted, is to say, that the use of reason discovers to a man what he knew before: and if men have those innate impressed truths originally, and before the use of reason, and yet are always ignorant of them till they come to the use of reason, it is in effect to say, that men know and know them not at the same time.

If by knowing and assenting to them "when we come to the use of reason," be meant, that this is the time when they come to be taken notice of by the mind; and that as soon as children come to the use of reason, they come also to know and assent to these maxims; this also is false and frivolous. First, it is false;

because it is evident these maxims are not in the mind so early as the use of reason: and therefore the coming to the use of reason is falsely assigned as the time
of their discovery. How many instances of the use of reason may we observe in
children, a long time before they have any knowledge of this maxim, "That it is
impossible for the same thing to be and not to be"? And a great part of illiterate
people and savages pass many years, even of their rational age, without ever
thinking on this and the like general propositions. I grant, men come not to the
knowledge of these general and more abstract truths, which are thought innate,
till they come to the use of reason; and I add, nor then neither. Which is so,
because till after they come to the use of reason, those general abstract ideas are
not framed in the mind, about which those general maxims are, which are mistaken for innate principles, but are indeed discoveries made and verities introduced and brought into the mind by the same way, and discovered by the same
steps, as several other propositions, which nobody was ever so extravagant as to
suppose innate. This I hope to make plain in the sequel of this Discourse. I allow
therefore, a necessity that men should come to the use of reason before they get
the knowledge of those general truths; but deny that men's coming to the use of
reason is the time of their discovery.

In the meantime it is observable, that this saying, that men know and assent to
these maxims "when they come to the use of reason," amounts in reality of fact
to no more but this,—that they are never known nor taken notice of before the
use of reason, but may possibly be assented to some time after, during a man's
life; but when is uncertain. And so may all other knowable truths, as well as
these; which therefore have no advantage nor distinction from others by this note
of being known when we come to the use of reason; nor are thereby proved to be
innate, but quite the contrary.

But, secondly, were it true that the precise time of their being known and
assented to were when men come to the use of reason, neither would that prove
them innate. This way of arguing is as frivolous as the supposition itself is false.
For, by what kind of logic will it appear that any notion is originally by nature
imprinted in the mind in its first constitution, because it comes first to be
observed and assented to when a faculty of the mind, which has quite a distinct
province, begins to exert itself? And therefore the coming to the use of speech, if
it were supposed the time that these maxims are first assented to (which it may
be with as much truth as the time when men come to the use of reason), would
be as good a proof that they were innate, as to say they are innate because men
assent to them when they come to the use of reason. I agree then with these men
of innate principles, that there is no knowledge of these general and self-evident
maxims in the mind, till it comes to the exercise of reason: but I deny that the
coming to the use of reason is the precise time when they are first taken notice of;
and if that were the precise time, I deny that it would prove them innate. All that
can with any truth be meant by this proposition, that men "assent to them when
they come to the use of reason," is no more but this,—that the making of general
abstract ideas, and the understanding of general names, being a concomitant of
the rational faculty, and growing up with it, children commonly get not those
general ideas, nor learn the names that stand for them, till, having for a good
while exercised their reason about familiar and more particular ideas, they are,

by their ordinary discourse and actions with others, acknowledged to be capable of rational conversation. If assenting to these maxims, when men come to the use of reason, can be true in any other sense, I desire it may be shown; or at least, how in this, or any other sense, it proves them innate. . . .

Of Knowledge in General

Since the mind, in all its thoughts and reasonings, hath no other immediate object but its own ideas, which it alone does or can contemplate, it is evident that our knowledge is only conversant about them.

Knowledge that seems to me to be nothing but *the perception of the connection of and agreement, or disagreement and repugnancy, of any of our ideas.* In this alone it consists. Where this perception is, there is knowledge, and where it is not, there, though we may fancy, guess, or believe, yet we always come short of knowledge. For when we know that white is not black, what do we else but perceive, that these two ideas do not agree? When we possess ourselves with the utmost security of the demonstration, that the three angles of a triangle are equal to two right ones, what do we more but perceive, that equality to two right ones does necessarily agree to, and is inseparable from, the three angles of a triangle?

But to understand a little more distinctly wherein this agreement or disagreement consists, I think we may reduce it all to these four sorts:

1. *Identity,* or *diversity.*

2. *Relation.*

3. *Co-existence,* or *necessary connection.*

4. *Real existence.*

First, As to the first sort of agreement or disagreement, viz. *identity* or *diversity.* It is the first act of the mind, when it has any sentiments or ideas at all, to perceive its ideas; and so far as it perceives them, to know each what it is, and thereby also to perceive their difference, and that one is not another. This is so absolutely necessary, that without it there could be no knowledge, no reasoning, no imagination, no distinct thoughts at all. By this the mind clearly and infallibly perceives each idea to agree with itself, and to be what it is; and all distinct ideas to disagree, i.e. the one not to be the other: and this it does without pains, labor, or deduction; but at first view, by its natural power of perception and distinction. And though men of art have reduced this into those general rules, *What is, is,* and *It is impossible for the same thing to be and not to be,* for ready application in all cases, wherein there may be occasion to reflect on it: yet it is certain that the first exercise of this faculty is about particular ideas. A man infallibly knows, as soon as ever he has them in his mind, that the ideas he calls *white* and *round* are the very ideas they are; and that they are not other ideas which he calls *red* or *square.* Nor can any maxim or proposition in the world make him know it clearer or surer than he did before, and without any such general rule. This then is the first agreement or disagreement which the mind perceives in its ideas; which it always perceives at first sight: and if there ever happen any doubt about it, it will always be found to be about the names, and not the ideas themselves, whose identity and diversity will always be perceived, as soon and clearly as the ideas themselves are; nor can it possibly be otherwise.

Secondly, The next sort of agreement or disagreement the mind perceives in any of its ideas may, I think, be called *relative,* and is nothing but the perception of the *relation* between any two ideas, of what kind soever, whether substances, modes, or any other. For, since all distinct ideas must eternally be known not to be the same, and so be universally and constantly denied one of another, there could be no room for any positive knowledge at all, if we could not perceive any relation between our ideas, and find out the agreement or disagreement they have one with another, in several ways the mind takes of comparing them.

Thirdly, The third sort of agreement or disagreement to be found in our ideas, which the perception of the mind is employed about, is *co-existence* or *non-co-existence* in the *same subject;* and this belongs particularly to substances. Thus when we pronounce concerning gold, that it is fixed, our knowledge of this truth amounts to no more but this, that fixedness or a power to remain in the fire unconsumed, is an idea that always accompanies and is joined with that particular sort of yellowness, weight, fusibility, malleableness, and solubility in *aqua regia,* which make our complex idea signified by the word gold.

Fourthly, The fourth and last sort is that of *actual real existence* agreeing to any idea.

Within these four sorts of agreement or disagreement is, I suppose, contained all the knowledge we have, or are capable of. . . .

Of the Degrees of Our Knowledge

All our knowledge consisting, as I have said, in the view the mind has of its own ideas, which is the utmost light and greatest certainty we, with our faculties, and in our way of knowledge, are capable of, it may not be amiss to consider a little the degrees of its evidence. The different clearness of our knowledge seems to me to lie in the different way of perception the mind has of the agreement or disagreement of any of its ideas. For if we will reflect on our own ways of thinking, we will find, that sometimes the mind perceives the agreement or disagreement of two ideas *immediately by themselves,* without the intervention of any other: and this I think we may call *intuitive knowledge.* For in this the mind is at no pains of proving or examining, but perceives the truth as the eye doth light, only by being directed towards it. Thus the mind perceives that *white* is not *black,* that a *circle* is not a *triangle,* that *three* are more than *two* and equal to *one and two.* Such kinds of truths the mind perceives at the first sight of the ideas together, by bare intuition; without the intervention of any other idea: and this kind of knowledge is the clearest and most certain that human frailty is capable of. This part of knowledge is irresistible, and, like bright sunshine, forces itself immediately to be perceived, as soon as ever the mind turns its view that way; and leaves no room for hesitation, doubt, or examination, but the mind is presently filled with the clear light of it. *It is on this intuition that depends all the certainty and evidence of all our knowledge;* which certainty everyone finds to be so great, that he cannot imagine, and therefore not require a greater: for a man cannot conceive himself capable of a greater certainty than to know that any idea in his mind is such as he perceives it to be; and that two ideas, wherein he perceives a difference, are different and not precisely the same. He that demands a greater certainty than this, demands he knows not what, and shows only that he has a mind to be a skeptic, without being able to be so. Certainty depends so wholly on this intuition, that, in the next degree of knowledge which I call demonstrative, this intuition is necessary in all the connections of the intermediate ideas, without which we cannot attain knowledge and certainty.

The next degree of knowledge is, where the mind perceives the agreement or disagreement of any ideas, but not immediately. Though wherever the mind perceives the agreement or disagreement of any of its ideas, there be certain knowledge; yet it does not always happen, that the mind sees that agreement or disagreement, which there is between them, even where it is discoverable; and in that case remains in ignorance, and at most gets no further than a probable conjecture. The reason why the mind cannot always perceive presently the agreement or disagreement of two ideas, is, because those ideas, concerning whose agreement or disagreement the inquiry is made, cannot by the mind be so put together as to show it. In this case, then, when the mind cannot so bring its ideas together as by their immediate comparison, and as it were juxtaposition or application one to another, to perceive their agreement or disagreement, it is fain, *by the intervention of other ideas* (one or more, as it happens) to discover the agreement or disagreement which it searches; and this is that which we call reasoning. Thus, the mind being willing to know the agreement or disagreement in bigness between the three angles of a triangle and two right ones, cannot be brought at once, and be compared with any other one, or two angles; and so of this the mind has no immediate, no intuitive knowledge. In this case the mind is fain to find out some other angles, to which the three angles of a triangle have an equality; and, finding those equal to two right ones, comes to know their equality to two right ones.

Those intervening ideas, which serve to show the agreement of any two others, are called *proofs*; and where the agreement and disagreement is by this means plainly and clearly perceived, it is called *demonstration*; it being *shown* to the understanding, and the mind made to see that it is so. A quickness in the mind to find out these intermediate ideas (that shall discover the agreement or disagreement of any other), and to apply them right, is, I suppose, that which is called *sagacity*.

This knowledge, by intervening proofs, though it be certain, yet the evidence of it is not altogether so clear and bright, nor the assent so ready, as in intuitive knowledge. For, though in demonstration the mind does at last perceive the agreement or disagreement of the ideas it considers; yet it is not without pains and attention: there must be more than one transient view to find it. A steady application and pursuit are required to this discovery: and there must be a progression by steps and degrees, before the mind can in this way arrive at certainty, and come to perceive the agreement or repugnancy between two ideas that need proofs and the use of reason to show it.

Another difference between intuitive and demonstrative knowledge is, that, though in the latter all doubt be removed when, by the intervention of the intermediate ideas, the agreement or disagreement is perceived, yet before the demonstration there was a doubt; which in intuitive knowledge cannot happen to the mind that has its faculty of perception left to a degree capable of distinct ideas; no more than it can be a doubt to the eye (that can distinctly see white and black), Whether this ink and this paper be all of a color.

It is true, the perception produced by demonstration is also very clear; yet it is often with a great abatement of that evident lustre and full assurance that always accompany that which I call intuitive: like a face reflected by several mirrors one to another, where, as long as it retains the similitude and agreement with the object, it produces a knowledge; but it is still, in every successive reflection, with a lessening of that perfect clearness and distinctness which is in the first; till at last, after many removes, it has a great mixture of dimness, and is not at first sight so knowable, especially to weak eyes. Thus it is with knowledge made out by a long train of proof.

Now, in every step reason makes in demonstrative knowledge, there is an intuitive knowledge of that agreement or disagreement it seeks with the next intermediate idea which it uses as a proof: for if it were not so, that yet would need a proof; since without the perception of such agreement or disagreement, there is no knowledge produced: if it be perceived by itself, it is intuitive knowledge: if it cannot be perceived by itself, there is need of some intervening idea, as a common measure, to show their agreement or disagreement. By which it is plain, that every step in reasoning that produces knowledge, has intuitive certainty; which when the mind perceives, there is no more required but to remember it, to make the agreement or disagreement of the ideas, concerning which we inquire, visible and certain.

GOTTFRIED LEIBNIZ
(1646–1716) German Philosopher

From *New Essays on the Human Understanding**

Introduction

As the *Essay on the Understanding*, by an illustrious Englishman,[1] is one of the best and most highly esteemed works of the present time, I have resolved to make some remarks upon it, because, having for a long time given considerable

---

New Essays on the Human Understanding and Other Philosophical Writings, ed. Robert Latta (Oxford: Clarendon Press, 1948) pp. 357–85.

[1] John Locke—ED.

attention to the same subject and to most of the matters with which the essay deals, I have thought that this would be a good occasion for publishing some of my opinions under the title of *New Essays on the Understanding*, in the hope that my thoughts will obtain a favourable reception through appearing in such good company. I have hoped also to be able to profit by the work of another, not only in the way of lessening my own work (as in fact it is less trouble to follow the thread of a good author than to work on entirely untrodden ground), but also in the way of adding something to what he has given us, which is always easier than making an independent beginning. For I think I have removed some difficulties which he left entirely alone. Thus his reputation is helpful to me; and besides, being disposed to do justice and very far from wishing to lessen the esteem in which his work is held, I would increase his reputation, if my approval have any weight. It is true that I often differ from him in opinion; but, far from denying the worth of famous writers, we bear witness to it by making known in what respect and for what reasons we differ from their opinion, when we think it necessary to prevent their authority from prevailing against reason on some important points; and besides, in replying to such excellent men, we make it easier for the truth to be accepted, and it is to be supposed that it is principally for truth that they are working.

In fact, although the author of the *Essay* says a thousand fine things of which I cordially approve, our systems greatly differ. His has more relation to Aristotle and mine to Plato, although in many things both of us have departed from the doctrine of these two ancient writers. He is more popular, and I for my part am sometimes compelled to be a little more *acroamatic* and abstract, which is not of advantage to me, especially when a living language is used. But I think that by introducing two speakers, one of whom expounds opinions taken from this author's *Essay*, while the other adds my observations, I show the relation between us in a way that will be more satisfactory to the reader than if I had put down mere remarks, the reading of which would have been constantly interrupted by the necessity of turning to his book in order to understand mine. Nevertheless it will be well also to compare our writings sometimes, and not to judge of his opinions except from his own work, although I have usually retained his expressions. It is true that owing to the limitations involved in following the thread of another person's argument and making remarks upon it. I have been unable even to think of achieving the graceful turns of which dialogue is susceptible; but I hope that the matter will make up for the defects of the style.

The differences between us have regard to subjects of some importance. There is the question whether the soul, in itself, is entirely empty, like a writing-tablet on which nothing has yet been written *(tabula rasa)*, (which is the opinion of Aristotle and of the author of the *Essay)*, and whether everything that is inscribed upon it comes solely from the senses and experience; or whether the soul originally contains the principles of several notions and doctrines, which are merely roused on certain occasions by external objects, as I hold along with Plato and even with the Schoolmen, and with all those who interpret in this sense the passage of St. Paul (Romans, ii. 15), in which he shows that the law of God is written in men's hearts. The Stoics called these principles προλήψεις, that is, fundamental assumptions or what we take for granted beforehand. Mathematicians call them *common notions* Κολυνε 'έννοιαι. Modern philosophers give them other excellent names; and, in particular, Julius Scaliger named them *semina aeternitatis item copyra*, as much as to say, living fires, flashes of light *[traits lummeux]*, hidden within us but appearing at the instance of the senses, like the sparks which come from the steel when it strikes the flint. And not without reason it is thought that these flashes *[eclats]* indicate something divine and eternal, which appears above all in necessary truths. Hence there arises another question, whether all truths are dependent on experience, that is, on induction and instances; or whether there are some which have yet another foundation. For if some events can be fore-seen before we have made any trial of them, it is manifest that we contribute to them something of our own. The senses, although they are necessary for all our actual acquiring of knowledge, are by no means sufficient to give us the whole of our knowledge, since the senses never give anything but instances, that is to say particular or individual truths. Now all the instances which confirm a general truth, however numerous they may be, are not sufficient to establish the universal necessity of this same truth; for it does not at all follow that what has happened will happen in the same way. For example, the Greeks, the Romans, and all the other peoples of the earth, as it was known to the ancients, always observed that before twenty-four hours have passed, day changes into night and night into day. But they would have been wrong if they had thought that the same rule is observed everywhere else, for since that time, the opposite has been experienced by people on a visit to Nova Zembla. And he would still be wrong who should think that, in our regions at least, it is a necessary and eternal truth that shall endure for ever, since we must hold that the earth and the sun itself do not exist necessarily, and that perhaps there will come a time when this beautiful star with its whole system will no longer exist, at least in its present form. Whence it seems that necessary truths, such as we find in pure mathematics and especially in arithmetic and geometry, must have principles whose proof does not depend upon instances nor, consequently, upon the witness of the senses, although with-out the senses it would never have come into our heads to think of them. This is a point which should be carefully noted, and it is one which Euclid so well under-stood that he often proves by reason that which is evident enough through expe-rience and through sense-images. Logic also, along with metaphysics and ethics *[la morale]*, of which the one forms natural theology and the other natural jurisprudence, are full of such truths, and consequently their demonstration can come only from the inner principles which are called innate. It is true we must not imagine that we can read these eternal laws of reason in the soul as in an open book, as the edict of the praetor may be read on his *album* without trouble or investigation; but it is enough that we can discover these laws in ourselves by means of attention, for which opportunities are furnished by the senses; and the success of experiments serves also as a confirmation of reason, somewhat as in arithmetic "proofs" are useful in helping us to avoid errors of calculation when the process is a long one. In this also lies the difference between human knowl-edge and that of the lower animals. The lower animals are purely empirical and direct themselves by particular instances alone; for, so far as we can judge, they never succeed in forming necessary propositions; while men, on the other hand, have the capacity for demonstrative science. It is also on this account that the power of making *concatenations* [of ideas] which the lower animals possess is something inferior to the reason which is in men. The concatenations [of ideas] made by the lower animals are simply like those of mere empirics, who maintain that what has sometimes happened will happen again in a case which resembles the former in characteristics which strike them, although they are incapable of judging whether or not the same reasons hold good in both cases. That is why it is so simple a matter for men to entrap animals, and so easy for mere empirics to make mistakes. From this making of mistakes even persons who have become skillful through age and experience are not exempt, when they trust too much to their past experience, as some have done in civil and military affairs; because enough consideration is not given to the fact that the world changes and that men become more skillful by finding countless new contrivances, while on the other hand the stags or the hares of our time do not become more full of shifts than those of former times. The concatenations [of ideas] in the lower animals are only a shadow of reasoning, that is to say they are only connexions of imagination and passings from one image to another, because in new circumstances which seem to resemble others which have occurred before we expect anew what we at other times found along with them, as if things were actually connected together because their images are connected in memory. It is true that reason also leads us to expect, as a rule, that there will occur in the future what is in harmony with a long experience of the past, but this is, nevertheless, not a necessary and infallible truth; and our forecast may fail when we least expect it, because the reasons which have hitherto justified it no longer operate. And on this account the wisest people do not trust altogether to experience, but try, so far as possible, to get some hold of the reason of what happens, in order to decide when exceptions must be made. For reason is alone capable of laying down trustworthy rules and of supplying what is lacking in those which were not trustworthy, by stating the exception to them, and in short of finding sure connexions in the force of necessary consequences; and this often enables us to foresee the event without having to experience the sense-connexions of images, to which the animals are confined, so that that which shows that the sources [*principes*] of necessary truths are within us also distinguishes man from the lower animals.

Perhaps our able author may not entirely differ from me in opinion. For after having devoted the whole of his first book to the rejection of innate knowledge [*lumieres*], understood in a certain sense, he nevertheless admits, at the beginning of the second book and in those which follow, that the ideas which do not originate in sensation come from reflexion. Now reflexion is nothing but an attention to that which is in us, and the senses do not give us what we already bring with us. That being so, can it be denied that there is much that is innate in our mind [*esprit*], since we are, so to speak, innate to ourselves, and since in ourselves there are being, unity, substance, duration, change, activity [*action*], perception, pleasure and a thousand other objects of our intellectual ideas? And as these objects are immediate objects of our understanding and are always present (although they cannot always be consciously perceived [*aperçus*] because of our distractions and wants), why should it be surprising that we say that these ideas, along with all that depends on them, are innate in us? Accordingly I have taken as illustration a block of veined marble, rather than a block of perfectly uniform marble or than empty tablets, that is to say, what is called by philosophers *tabula rasa*. For if the soul were like these empty tablets, truths would be in us as the figure of Hercules is in a block of marble, when the block of marble is indifferently capable of receiving this figure or any other. But if there were in the stone veins, which should mark out the figure of Hercules rather than other figures, the stone would be more determined towards this figure, and Hercules would somehow be, as it were, innate in it, although labour would be needed to uncover the veins and to clear them by polishing and thus removing what prevents them from being fully seen. It is thus that ideas and truths are innate in us, as natural inclinations, dispositions, habits or powers *[virtualites]*, and not as activities *[actions]*, although these powers *[virtualites]* are always accompanied by some activities *[actions]*, often imperceptible, which correspond to them.

Our able author seems to maintain that there is in us nothing *virtual*, and even nothing of which we are not always actually conscious. But this cannot be understood in a strict sense; otherwise his opinion would be too paradoxical, since, for instance, we are not always conscious of acquired habits and of the things stored in our memory, and, indeed, they do not always come to our aid when we require them, although we often bring them back easily into our mind on some slight occasion which recalls them to us, as we need only the beginning of a song in order to remember it. Our author also limits his thesis in other places, saying that there is in us nothing of which we have not at least been conscious *[aperçus]* formerly. But in addition to the fact that nobody can, through reason alone, be quite certain how far our past *apperceptions* have extended, for we may have forgotten them, especially in light of the Platonic doctrine of reminiscence, which, though a myth, contains, in part at least, nothing incompatible with bare reason—in addition, I say, to this fact, why must everything be acquired by us through apperception of external things, and why should it be impossible to unearth anything in ourselves? Is our soul, then, so empty that, beyond images borrowed from outside, it is nothing? That, I am sure, is not a view which our judicious author can approve. And where shall we find tablets which have not some variety in themselves? For there is never such a thing as a perfectly unbroken *[uni]* and uniform surface. Why, then, should not we also be able to provide ourselves with some sort of thought out of our own inner being, when we deliberately try to penetrate its depths?

THOMAS REID

(1710–1796) Scottish Philosopher

An Inquiry into the Human Mind and Common Sense*

General Theory

Of Bishop Berkeley—The "Treatise of Human Nature"—And of Scepticism

The present age, I apprehend, has not produced two more acute or more practised in this part of philosophy, than the Bishop of Cloyne, and the author of the "Treatise of Human Nature."[1] The first was no friend to scepticism, but had that warm concern for religious and moral principles which became his order: yet the result of his inquiry was a serious conviction that there is no such thing as a material world—nothing in nature but spirits and ideas; and that the belief of material substances, and of abstract ideas, are the chief causes of all our errors in philosophy, and of all infidelity and heresy in religion. His arguments are founded upon the principles which were formerly laid down by Des Cartes, Malebranche, and Locke, and which have been very generally received.

And the opinion of the ablest judges seems to be, that they neither have been, nor can be confuted; and that he hath proved by unanswerable arguments what no man in his senses can believe.

The second proceeds upon the same principles, but carries them to their full length; and, as the Bishop undid the whole material world, this author, upon the same grounds, undoes the world of spirits, and leaves nothing in nature but ideas and impressions, without any subject on which they may be impressed.

It seems to be a peculiar strain of humour in this author, to set out in his introduction by promising, with a grave face, no less than a complete system of the sciences, upon a foundation entirely new—to wit, that of human nature—when the intention of the whole work is to shew, that there is neither human nature nor science in the world. It may perhaps be unreasonable to complain of this conduct in an author who neither believes his own existence nor that of his reader; and therefore could not mean to disappoint him, or to laugh at his credulity. Yet I cannot imagine that the author of the "Treatise of Human Nature" is so sceptical as to plead this apology. He believed, against his principles, that he should be read, and that he should retain his personal identity, till he reaped the honour and reputation justly due to his metaphysical *acumen*. Indeed, he ingeniously acknowledges, that it was only in solitude and retirement that he could yield any assent to his own philosophy; society, like day-light, dispelled the darkness and fogs of

---

*From Thomas Reid, *The Works of Thomas Reid*, 6th ed., ed. by William Hamilton (Edinburgh: Maclachlan and Stewart, 1863).
[1] George Berkeley and David Hume—ED.

scepticism, and made him yield to the dominion of common sense. Nor did I ever hear him charged with doing anything, even in solitude, that argued such a degree of scepticism as his principles maintain. Surely if his friends apprehended this, they would have the charity never to leave him alone.

Pyrrho the Elean, the father of this philosophy, seems to have carried it to greater perfection than any of his successors: for, if we may believe Antigonus the Carystian, quoted by Diogenes Laertius, his life corresponded to his doctrine. And, therefore, if a cart run against him, or a dog attacked him, or if he came upon a precipice, he would not stir a foot to avoid the danger, giving no credit to his senses. But his attendants, who, happily for him, were not so great sceptics, took care to keep him out of harm's way; so that he lived till he was ninety years of age. Nor is it to be doubted but this author's friends would have been equally careful to keep him from harm, if ever his principles had taken too strong a hold of him.

It is probable the "Treatise of Human Nature" was not written in company; yet it contains manifest indications that the author every now and then relapsed into the faith of the vulgar, and could hardly, for half a dozen pages, keep up the sceptical character.

In like manner, the great Pyrrho himself forgot his principles on some occasions; and is said once to have been in such a passion with his cook, who probably had not roasted his dinner to his mind, that with the spit in his hand, and the meat upon it, he pursued him even into the marketplace.

It is a bold philosophy that rejects, without ceremony, principles which irresistibly govern the belief and the conduct of all mankind in the common concerns of life; and to which the philosopher himself must yield, after he imagines he hath confuted them. Such principles are older, and of more authority, than Philosophy: she rests upon them as her basis, not they upon her. If she could overturn them, she must be buried in their ruins; but all the engines of philosophical subtilty are too weak for this purpose; and the attempt is no less ridiculous than if a mechanic should contrive an *axis in peritrochio* to remove the earth out of its place; or if a mathematician should pretend to demonstrate that things equal to the same thing are not equal to one another.

Zeno endeavoured to demonstrate the impossibility of motion;[2] Hobbes, that there was no difference between right and wrong; and this author, that no credit is to be given to our senses, to our memory, or even to demonstration. Such philosophy is justly ridiculous, even to those who cannot detect the fallacy of it. It can have no other tendency, than to shew the acuteness of the sophist, at the expense of disgracing reason and human nature, and making mankind Yahoos.[3]

The System of All These Authors is The Same, and Leads to Scepticism
But what if these profound disquisitions into the first principles of human nature, do naturally and necessarily plunge a man into this abyss of scepticism? May we not reasonably judge so from what hath happened? Des Cartes no sooner began

---

[2] Zeno of Elea, floruit 464–461 B.C. created four paradoxes of motion that suggested that the concept of bodies moving in space was impossible due to logical contradictions.—ED.

[3] In Jonathan Swift's *Gulliver's Travels*, the "yahoos" were a race that represented a brutish humanity. Reason was the province of the houyhnms (a breed of rational horses).—ED.

to dig in this mine, than scepticism was ready to break in upon him. He did what he could to shut it out. Malebranche and Locke, who dug deeper, found the difficulty of keeping out this enemy still to increase; but they laboured honestly in the design. Then Berkeley, who carried on the work, despairing of securing all, bethought himself of an expedient:—By giving up the material world, which he thought might be spared without loss, and even with advantage, he hoped, by an impregnable partition, to secure the world of spirits. But, alas! the "Treatise of Human Nature" wantonly sapped the foundation of this partition, and drowned all in one universal deluge.

These facts, which are undeniable, do, indeed, give reason to apprehend that Des Cartes' system of the human understanding, which I shall beg leave to call *the ideal system,* and which, with some improvements made by later writers, is now generally received, hath some original defect; that this scepticism is inlaid in it, and reared along with it; and, therefore, that we must lay it open to the foundation, and examine the materials, before we can expect to raise any solid and useful fabric of knowledge on this subject.

We Ought Not to Despair of a Better

But is this to be despaired of, because Des Cartes and his followers have failed? By no means. This pusillanimity would be injurious to ourselves and injurious to truth. Useful discoveries are sometimes indeed the effect of superior genius, but more frequently they are the birth of time and of accidents. A traveller of good judgment may mistake his way, and be unawares led into a wrong track; and, while the road is fair before him, he may go on without suspicion and be followed by others; but, when it ends in a coal-pit, it requires no great judgment to know that he hath gone wrong, nor perhaps to find out what misled him.

In the meantime, the unprosperous state of this part of philosophy hath produced an effect, somewhat discouraging indeed to any attempt of this nature, but an effect which might be expected, and which time only and better success can remedy. Sensible men, who never will be sceptics in matters of common life, are apt to treat with sovereign contempt everything that hath been said, or is to be said, upon this subject. It is metaphysic, say they: who minds it? Let scholastic sophisters entangle themselves in their own cobwebs; I am resolved to take my own existence, and the existence of other things, upon trust; and to believe that snow is cold, and honey sweet, whatever they may say to the contrary. He must either be a fool, or want to make a fool of me, that would reason me out of my reason and senses.

I confess I know not what a sceptic can answer to this, nor by what good argument he can plead even for a hearing; for either his reasoning is sophistry, and so deserves contempt; or there is no truth in human faculties—and then why should we reason?

If, therefore, a man find himself intangled in these metaphysical toils, and can find no other way to escape, let him bravely cut the knot which he cannot loose, curse metaphysic, and dissuade every man from meddling with it; for, if I have been led into bogs and quagmires by following an *ignis fatuus,* [4] what can I do

---

[4] Foolish light

better than to warn others to beware of it? If philosophy contradicts herself, befools her votaries, and deprives them of every object worthy to be pursued or enjoyed, let her be sent back to the infernal regions from which she must have had her original.

But is it absolutely certain that this fair lady is of the party? Is it not possible she may have been misrepresented? Have not men of genius in former ages often made their own dreams to pass for her oracles? Ought she then to be condemned without any further hearing? This would be unreasonable. I have found her in all other matters an agreeable companion, a faithful counsellor, a friend to common sense, and to the happiness of mankind. This justly entitles her to my correspondence and confidence, till I find infallible proofs of her infidelity.

Of Smelling.

The Sensation Considered Abstractly
. . . let us now attend carefully to what the mind is conscious of when we smell a rose or a lily; and, since our language affords no other name for this sensation, we shall call it a *smell* or *odour*, carefully excluding from the meaning of those names everything but the sensation itself, at least till we have examined it.

Suppose a person who never had this sense before, to receive it all at once, and to smell a rose—can he perceive any similitude or agreement between the smell and the rose? or indeed between it and any other object whatsoever? Certainly he cannot. He finds himself affected in a new way, he knows not why or from what cause. Like a man that feels some pain or pleasure formerly unknown to him, he is conscious that he is not the cause of it himself; but cannot, from the nature of the thing, determine whether it is caused by body or spirit, by something near, or by something at a distance. It has no similitude to anything else, so as to admit of a comparison; and, therefore, he can conclude nothing from it, unless, perhaps, that there must be some unknown cause of it.

It is evidently ridiculous to ascribe to it figure, colour, extension, or any other quality of bodies. He cannot give it a place, any more than he can give a place to melancholy or joy; nor can he conceive it to have any existence, but when it is smelled. So that it appears to be a simple and original affection or feeling of the mind, altogether inexplicable and unaccountable. It is, indeed, impossible that it can be in any body: it is a sensation, and a sensation can only be in a sentient thing. . . .

Sensation and Remembrance, Natural Principles of Belief
So far we have considered this sensation abstractly. Let us next compare it with other things to which it bears some relation. And first I shall compare this sensation with the remembrance, and the imagination of it.

I can think of the smell of a rose when I do not smell it; and it is possible that when I think of it, there is neither rose nor smell anywhere existing. But when I smell it, I am necessarily determined to believe that the sensation really exists. This is common to all sensations, that, as they cannot exist but in being perceived, so they cannot be perceived but they must exist. I could as easily doubt of my own existence, as of the existence of my sensations. Even those profound philosophers who have endeavoured to disprove their own existence, have yet left their sensations to stand upon their own bottom, stript of a subject, rather than call in question the reality of their existence.

Here, then, a sensation, a smell for instance, may be presented to the mind three different ways: it may be smelled, it may be remembered, it may be imagined or thought of. In the first case, it is necessarily accompanied with a belief of its present existence; in the second, it is necessarily accompanied with a belief of its past existence; and in the last, it is not accompanied with belief at all, but is what the logicians call *a simple apprehension.*

Why sensation should compel our belief of the present existence of the thing, memory a belief of its past existence, and imagination no belief at all, I believe no philosopher can give a shadow of reason, but that such is the nature of these operations: they are all simple and original, and therefore inexplicable acts of the mind.

Suppose that once, and only once, I smelled a tuberose in a certain room, where it grew in a pot, and gave a very grateful perfume. Next day I relate what I saw and smelled. When I attend as carefully as I can to what passes in my mind in this case, it appears evident that the very thing I saw yesterday, and the fragrance I smelled, are now the immediate objects of my mind, when I remember it. Further, I can imagine this pot and flower transported to the room where I now sit, and yielding the same perfume. Here likewise it appears, that the individual thing which I saw and smelled, is the object of my imagination.

Philosophers indeed tell me, that the immediate object of my memory and imagination in this case, is not the past sensation, but an idea of it, an image, phantasm, or species, of the odour I smelled: that this idea now exists in my mind, or in my sensorium; and the mind, contemplating this present idea, finds it a representation of what is past, or of what may exist; and accordingly calls it memory, or imagination. This is the doctrine of the ideal philosophy; which we shall not now examine, that we may not interrupt the thread of the present investigation. Upon the strictest attention, memory appears to me to have things that are past, and not present ideas, for its object. We shall afterwards examine this system of ideas, and endeavour to make it appear, that no solid proof has ever been advanced of the existence of ideas; that they are a mere fiction and hypothesis, contrived to solve the phaenomena of the human understanding; that they do not at all answer this end; and that this hypothesis of ideas or images of things in the mind, or in the sensorium, is the parent of those many paradoxes so shocking to common sense, and of that scepticism which disgrace our philosophy of the mind, and have brought upon it the ridicule and contempt of sensible men.

In the meantime, I beg leave to think, with the vulgar, that, when I remember the smell of the tuberose, that very sensation which I had yesterday, and which has now no more any existence, is the immediate object of my memory; and when I imagine it present, the sensation itself, and not any idea of it, is the object of my imagination. But, though the object of my sensation, memory, and imagination, be in this case the same, yet these acts or operations of the mind are as different, and as easily distinguishable, as smell, taste, and sound. I am conscious of a difference in kind between sensation and memory, and between both and imagination. I find this also, that the sensation compels my belief of the present existence of the smell, and memory my belief of its past existence. There is a smell, is the immediate testimony of sense; there was a smell, is the immediate testimony of memory. If you ask me, why I believe that the smell exists, I can give no other reason, nor shall ever be able to give any other, than that I smell it. If you ask, why I believe that it existed yesterday, I can give no other reason but that I remember it.

Sensation and memory, therefore, are simple, original, and perfectly distinct operations of the mind, and both of them are original principles of belief. Imagination is distinct from both, but is no principle of belief. Sensation implies the present existence of its object, memory its past existence, but imagination views its object naked, and without any belief of its existence or nonexistence, and is therefore what the schools call *Simple Apprehension.*

Judgment and Belief in Some Cases Precede Simple Apprehension
But here, again, the ideal system comes in our way: it teaches us that the first operation of the mind about its ideas, is simple apprehension—that is, the bare conception of a thing without any belief about it: and that, after we have got simple apprehensions, by comparing them together, we perceive agreements or disagreements between them; and that this perception of the agreement or disagreement of ideas, is all that we call belief, judgment, or knowledge. Now, this appears to me to be all fiction, without any foundation in nature; for it is acknowledged by all, that sensation must go before memory and imagination; and hence it necessarily follows, that apprehension, accompanied with belief and knowledge, must go before simple apprehension, at least in the matters we are now speaking of. So that here, instead of saying that the belief or knowledge is got by putting together and comparing the simple apprehensions, we ought rather to say that the simple apprehension is performed by resolving and analysing a natural and original judgment. And it is with the operations of the mind, in this case, as with natural bodies, which are, indeed, compounded of simple principles or elements. Nature does not exhibit these elements separate, to be compounded by us; she exhibits them mixed and compounded in concrete bodies, and it is only by art and chemical analysis that they can be separated.

Two Theories of the Nature of Belief Refuted—Conclusions From What Hath Been Said
But what is this belief or knowledge which accompanies sensation and memory? Every man knows what it is, but no man can define it. Does any man pretend to define sensation, or to define consciousness? It is happy, indeed, that no man does. And if no philosopher had endeavoured to define and explain belief, some paradoxes in philosophy, more incredible than ever were brought forth by the most abject superstition or the most frantic enthusiasm, had never seen the light. Of this kind surely is that modern discovery of the ideal philosophy, that sensation, memory, belief, and imagination, when they have the same object, are only different degrees of strength and vivacity in the idea. Suppose the idea to be that of a future state after death: one man believes it firmly—this means no more than

that he hath a strong and lively idea of it; another neither believes nor disbe-lieves—that is, he has a weak and faint idea. Suppose, now, a third person believes firmly that there is no such thing, I am at a loss to know whether his idea be faint or lively: if it is faint, then there may be a firm belief where the idea is faint; if the idea is lively, then the belief of a future state and the belief of no future state must be one and the same. The same arguments that are used to prove that belief implies only a stronger idea of the object than simple apprehension, might as well be used to prove that love implies only a stronger idea of the object than indifference. And then what shall we say of hatred, which must upon this hypothesis be a degree of love, or a degree of indifference? If it should be said, that in love there is something more than an idea—to wit, an affection of the mind—may it not be said with equal reason, that in belief there is something more than an idea—to wit, an assent or persuasion of the mind?

But perhaps it may be thought as ridiculous to argue against this strange opin-ion, as to maintain it. Indeed, if a man should maintain that a circle, a square, and a triangle differ only in magnitude, and not in figure, I believe he would find nobody disposed either to believe him or to argue against him; and yet I do not think it less shocking to common sense, to maintain that sensation, memory, and imagination differ only in degree, and not in kind. I know it is said, that, in a delirium, or in dreaming, men are apt to mistake one for the other. But does it follow from this, that men who are neither dreaming nor in a delirium cannot dis-tinguish them? But how does a man know that he is not in a delirium? I cannot tell: neither can I tell how a man knows that he exists. But, if any man seriously doubts whether he is in a delirium, I think it highly probable that he is, and that it is time to seek for a cure, which I am persuaded he will not find in the whole system of logic.

I conclude, then, that the belief which accompanies sensation and memory, is a simple act of the mind, which cannot be defined. It is, in this respect, like seeing and hearing, which can never be so defined as to be understood by those who have not these faculties; and to such as have them, no definition can make these operations more clear than they are already. In like manner, every man that has any belief—and he must be a curiosity that has none—knows perfectly what belief is, but can never define or explain it. I conclude, also, that sensation, mem-ory, and imagination, even where they have the same object, are operations of a quite different nature, and perfectly distinguishable by those who are sound and sober. A man that is in danger of confounding them, is indeed to be pitied; but whatever relief he may find from another art, he can find none from logic or meta-physic. I conclude further, that it is no less a part of the human constitution, to believe the present existence of our sensations, and to believe the past existence of what we remember, than it is to believe that twice two make four. The evidence of sense, the evidence of memory, and the evidence of the necessary relations of things, are all distinct and original kinds of evidence, equally grounded on our constitution: none of them depends upon, or can be resolved into another. To rea-son against any of these kinds of evidence, is absurd; nay, to reason for them is absurd. They are first principles; and such fall not within the province of reason, but of common sense.

JANE DURAN
University of California, Santa Barbara

Reliabilism, Foundationalism, and Naturalized Epistemic Justification Theory*

Recent work in epistemology has made frequent reference to "naturalistic" views, and the debate between those who hold positions which might be deemed naturalistic and those who are less interested in cognitive processes and more interested in what has been called adequate justification. Specifically, the literature has tended to lump under the rubric "naturalized" a number of views which are somewhat weak kin to each other—reliabilist views, causal views, social coherence views of knowledge, and so forth.

Reliabilism's appeal seems to stem from the fact that it reminds us of the functioning of epistemic agents without throwing overboard our deep desire to possess some kind of criterion for knowledge which is stronger than mere social coherence. Reliabilism has been dubbed by some a "weak foundationalism." What passes for reliabilism varies, of course from view to view, but the theories seem to have in common their emphasis on what is dubbed a "reliable cognitive process." Heil cites

> . . . according to this theory S's belief would be warranted, however he arrives at it, if it should happen that there is a sufficiently long period in the future, whether or not we live to know about it, when belief-generating processes like S's do (or would) yield true beliefs with a suitably high frequency.

Van Cleve, paraphrasing Goldman, has it as:

> Finally, we say that a belief is justified if it either (i) results from a reliable process . . . or (ii) results from justified beliefs via a reliable process . . . (Van Cleve 1984, p. 559)

Generally speaking, the theories are vague about what might constitute this "process." It seems an intriguing feature of reliability views that they fail to spell out what might be thought to be their most important and distinguishing characteristic. For it can be maintained without difficulty that adversion to some sort of cognitive process represents a step toward naturalization, however small, and that this in and of itself is a leap in an area where theorizing has tended to be almost completely normative.[1] One might well inquire, then, why reliabilist theories typically tell us so little about what might count as a reliable process.

In this paper I will argue that reliabilism, as formulated in the contemporary literature, may indeed be thought of as an analogue to foundationalism, and that

---

*From *Metaphilosophy*, 19.2 (April 1988), pp. 113–27.
[1] See Duran (1984) for an account of the normative nature of contemporary work in epistemology.

there is a very real sense in which reliabilism fails the naturalism test in any meaningful sense of the term. By the same token, I intend to claim that an epistemology—specifically, an epistemic justification theory—naturalized must be more specific about what sorts of epistemic or cognitive processes are at work, and that one can indeed develop such a theory. In a later section of the paper I present my own such view and argue that a theory more properly dubbed "naturalized" is reliant upon notions of contextualization.

I

Foundationalism has always enjoyed a great popularity in the literature of epistemology. Attacks on foundationalism have tended to center on the notion of a "basic belief": in other words, if it is a central and distinguishing tenet of a foundationalist theory of epistemic justification—as opposed, say, to a coherence theory, or to some third type of theory—that some belief or knowledge claim has a special status, and that other claims rely upon it in a pyramidal or chain-like fashion, then the nature of such a belief is crucial. There has been a tendency for the belief accorded the special status to be a belief statement of first-person perception, in some accounts hedged with certain sorts of locutions or terminology to safeguard its epistemic status. The older "incorrigibility" now more-or-less out of fashion, notions of "self-presentation" or "self-warrant" frequently come into play. But the difficulty is that there does not appear to be a sound candidate for the basic statement. Incorrigibility received sledge-hammer blows from Austin's arguments, many of which are contained in *Sense and Sensibilia.* It was in any case connected with the protocol statements of positivism, and so declined when positivism's "Swan Song" began. "Self-presentation" is a notion closely enough related to incorrigibility that similar sorts of arguments may be leveled against it. Finally, one argument in particular tends to hit hard against the claims of any sort of statement (even a "self-warranted" one) to special epistemic status—there is reason to think that context, not the type or sort of statement, is crucial in determining whether or not a statement could be a sound candidate for one of the epistemically privileged positions. But most of the accounts seem to want to classify the epistemically privileged statements as a group, and thus context is omitted from consideration. Thus any argument which hits squarely the notion that a sort or type of statement could count as epistemically privileged will, in fact, be an argument against incorrigibility or self-presentation or self-warrant. And Austin and others have come up with such arguments as well.

Now one might at first blush be tempted to say that the claim that a certain statement has a superior status in some epistemic hierarchy vis-a-vis other statements has nothing in particular to do with cognitive processing. One would be further tempted to make the claim when one took into account the completely non-descriptive nature of much of the foundationalist work, and its lack of emphasis on what sorts of cognitive processes, if any, could be specified as being involved in the production of the favored statement. But we have just contended that there has been a tendency for the statements to be statements of privileged access, and the literature cites the ubiquitousness of perceptual processes, particularly processes of visual perception, in the production of these statements.

All of the foregoing may in fact give us a clue as to why reliabilism, although falling in many accounts under the rubric of "naturalized epistemology," still smacks to some extent of foundationalism. Perhaps the basic statements dear to foundationalists simply are best characterized (without such labeling as "incorrigible") as the results of reliable processes.

In his article "Modest Foundationalism and Self-Warrant," Pastin attempts to construct a foundationalist theory which would not be vulnerable in the same way as previous theories. Specifically, Pastin dubs her version "modest" because the basic belief has the property of "self-warrant," rather than some more grandiose and presumptuous property, such as "incorrigibility" or "self-presentation." In other words, Pastin attempts to make specific our quite natural intuitions that the broader and stronger a claim, the easier it is to find counterexamples to it. If it is claimed, as it was for some of the older foundationalist theories, that they are based on beliefs having the property of "incorrigibility," one might reasonably be concerned, because the claim that a belief is incorrigible is rather a grand one, along the lines of "all swans are white." The latter can be refuted by finding one non-white swan, and if "incorrigibility" is glossed as "not subject to refutation" or "not dubitable," even the possibility of refutation or doubt has already done significant damage. Having said so much then, one might wonder how Pastin's "self-warrant" comes out. Pastin's basic account of self-warrant is: "warranted in believing . . . to some degree, however slight, without inductive evidential support." One is tempted to think that it would be very difficult to do damage to a theory based on such a slender foundation, but it was our contention at an earlier point that what the foundationalist theories tend to have as a point of covergence is a reliance on a type or sort of belief. If in fact Pastin's theory also relies on a type or sort of belief, then Austinian-type counterarguments might be used against it, too, rendering its status nugatory. The fact that foundationalist theories tend to be constructed around beliefs which are of a certain sort, i.e., privileged status beliefs having to do with perceptual processes also ties into our claim, made originally by Audi, that reliabilism is a "weak foundationalism."

II

Pastin's piece is constructed along the lines of three attempts at giving a correct, filled-out account of "self-warrant." Two of these attempts are ultimately rejected, but for our purposes it may be fruitful to work through the three attempts.

Pastin begins with a modest and perspicuous definition which is soon discarded, but which reminds us of some of the salient features of foundationalist theories. His opening definition is:

> Proposition P is self-warranted for person S at time t: (i) P is warranted for S at t, and (ii) not necessarily if P is warranted for S at t, then S has inductive evidential support for P at t. (Pastin 1978, pp. 282)

This opening definition is in accordance with the usual foundationalist moves for the establishment of a basic belief. If the belief is to be accorded some special epistemic status, then it must not rely on inductive evidential support, but in some sense must serve as its own support. That a belief which is deemed "incorrigible" can stand independently epistemically is not difficult to swallow; "self-warrant" requires filling out. Clearly, however, this opening definition is not strong enough, as Pastin soon admits.

Pastin is concerned about the foregoing definition because of the number of unconvincing and allegedly self-warranted propositions which might be generated on the basis of it. If I am warranted in believing "The object in my hand is a pencil" (and Pastin gives us no gloss on "warranted"—it apparently means something like "credible"), then the proposition "The object in my hand is a pencil or my mother is in Cracow" is *self-warranted* on the basis of the above definition, however counterintuitive this may seem. Pastin's next version of a definition for "self-warrant" is considerably more rigorous in order to avoid such troublesome proliferation of propositions.

> Proposition P is self-warranted for person S at time t: S's epistemic system at t, call it R, is such that: (i) W(P, S, t) ε R and (ii) it is not the case that every subsystem R' or R with respect to the set of all propositions of the form 'I(, P, S, t)' is such that W(P, S, t) ε R'.[2]

Before proceeding with the analysis, we need to clarify some points of Pastin's terminology. Pastin relies on the notion of an *epistemic system*. He defines such a system as a set of propositions of the form *"P is warranted for S at t," "P provides inductive evidential support for Q for S at t."* (They are abbreviated W(P, S, t), I(P, Q, S, T) and D(P, Q, S, t) respectively, hence the material above.) Then, Pastin remarks, "A set of propositions R of the appropriate form constitutes an epistemic system iff[3] it is logically (or metaphysically) possible that there be a person S and a time t such that for all propositions P and Q (i) W(P, S, t) ε R if W(P, S, t); (ii) I(P, Q, S, t) ε R if I(P, Q, S, t), and (iii) D(P, Q, S, t) ε R if D(P, Q, S, t)."

The last sentence quoted from Pastin merely states the obvious: that a proposition of the specified form should be a member of one's epistemic system only if the specified relations (provisions of inductive evidential support, for instance), really do obtain.

Pastin's second definition requires close scrutiny, and will have import for our overall contention. The abbreviation employed in the first conjunct may the thought of as reading, as Pastin informs us, *"P is warranted for S at t"* (and here that proposition is an element of epistemic system R, which is itself a set of propositions), and the abbreviation in the second conjunct as reading "_____ provides inductive evidential support for P for S at t." The point of Pastin's definition is simply this: If a proposition P is self-warranted for S at t, then it must be warranted for S at t, and show in at least one subset R' which is to be thought of as the set of propositions providing inductive evidential support for P—in other words, P is its own support. Notice that Pastin does not rule out there being other propositions in the subsystem R'; his weaker definition of R' is that at least one R' must contain W(P, S, t).

---

[2] The blank in 'I(, P, S, t)' occurs because any designated proposition may provide inductive evidential support.

[3] If and only if.—ED.

This very carefully done analysis does obviate the possibility to which Pastin had earlier alluded (generation of self-warranted propositions by disjointure) and certainly does not rely on incorrigibility. Let us try to be explicit about how it does so. A self-warranted proposition certainly must be warranted; this much was contained in the first definition which Pastin discarded. But although we might have inductive evidential support for a self-warranted proposition, part of what we mean by *self-warranted* (note the comparison here with *self-justified* or *self-presenting*) is that such a proposition must provide some of its own support. In the previous example, there was no "self-support," so to speak. That is not the case with the new definition. But, Pastin notes, the present account is still in need of emendation.

> However, the present account of self-warrant is unsatisfactory in an important respect; it does not adequately take account of the features of a person's condition at a time in virtue of which he has a particular epistemic system at the time. (Pastin 1978, pp. 285)

The problem here, according to Pastin, is that some proposition such as "I feel warm" might be warranted—indeed, on the above definition, might be self-warranted—for S at t without taking into account further changes in S's state that would ordinarily be held to be necessary in order for the proposition to be self-warranted. We would be inclined to say, intuitively, and without regard for Pastin's definition, that in order for the proposition "I feel warm" to be self-warranted for S at t, S would have to be sensing warmth. But, demurs Pastin, on the above definition, even if S had nothing but inductive evidence for warmth, such as a thermostat or the opinion of others, the relationship between subsystem R' and supersystem R as presented is such that we would have to consider the proposition self-warranted. (This objection, like the objection Pastin himself generated to his previous definition, is based on our intuitions regarding what is epistemically appropriate.)

For further clarification, we may look at the problem this way—if P ("I feel warm") is warranted for S at t (and remember that *warrant* relies on inductive evidential support) all it needs is to show as a member of subsystem R', although S might not actually be sensing warmth. Here we require some examples in order to grasp Pastin's crucial points. One might be in a situation—and these are the sorts of counterexamples dear to contemporary philosophers—where one had inductive evidential support for one's warmth, but had no sensation of warmth. Suppose that one had been given a drug that reduced bodily sensation and that most of one's body was immersed in a sensory deprivation apparatus. One might infer that one was warm from glancing at the thermostat on the wall. Or one might know that the bio-physicist on the left was stimulating the relevant portion of one's cerebral cortex. These cases are counterexamples to Pastin's definition, for "I feel warm" might then be warranted for S at t, and there would be a Q ("The thermostat now registers 90°") which provided inductive evidential support for P for S at t, but without the sensation of warmth, it would seem counterintuitive to say that "I feel warm" is *self-warranted*. Pastin manages to revise his definition one more time to take care of this particular counterexample, but we need to examine the enterprise overall for the points we wish to make about foundationalism.

Pastin set out to devise a foundationalism which was not, like radical foundationalism, dependent upon the notion of incorrigibility, and because of this his particular project seemed very relevant to ours. Indeed, Pastin wrote "I believe that many epistemologists, because they have failed to distinguish between these two types of foundationalism, have produced arguments against radical foundationalism in the belief that they were arguing against foundationalism *per se*." (Pastin 1978, pp. 289)

After tedious and careful work, he succeeded in the version of modest foundationalism which we have set out at length and examined above. There is no question that it is not culpable in the same way that radical foundationalism might be thought to be and that it has avoided the slough of incorrigibility: Specifically, Pastin's work does not rely on a notion as strong as incorrigibility. Incorrigibility is comparatively easy to attack precisely because it is such a strong notion. But the pertinent question now is this: Has Pastin avoided the larger criticism that self-warrant is similar enough to incorrigibility to be vulnerable to some of the same lines of criticism?

I claim that Pastin's notion of self-warrant is related to the notion of incorrigibility in an important way. Many would argue that it is by no means certain that there is even such a thing as a *self-warranted* proposition, if the notion of self-warrant is related to type of proposition. One might be tempted to say that Pastin has not referred to the notion of a type of proposition, but my claim is that Pastin implicitly has. First of all, it is a proposition of privileged access which Pastin has selected as his main example ("I feel warm"). But in addition, toward the end of his piece, Pastin says the following:

> There is another task which might be called 'providing an account of self-warrant' which I have not undertaken here. This is the task of determining what sorts of empirical propositions, if any, can be self-warranted for a person and whether there is a core of these propositions which support all of a person's empirical knowledge. . . . With respect to this second task, I believe that a 'Cartesian' version of modest foundationalism is correct, but that is another story. (Pastin 1979, pp. 288)

Pastin has written, "Some modest foundationalists, the 'Cartesian' modest foundationalists, may hold that the only empirical propositions which can be self-warranted for a person are propositions about just the person's immediate experience at a given time." Note also that Pastin has intuitions regarding the sorts of propositions which one may accept as self-warranted, and that these intuitions helped generate his first counterexample. The previous Austinian line can now be brought forward one more time: Is there a type of proposition that is self-warranted, or is it the case that circumstances of utterance render a proposition self-warranted? The reasoning adduced at an earlier point may here be utilized again. To phrase it succinctly: If it is the case that the only self-warranted propositions are those which are so rendered by individual circumstance, how may one trace the foundationalist chain? Would memory serve? Would one be able to reconstruct the peculiar circumstances which rendered the proposition self-warranted in the first place? And does not this very argument show that reliance on a type or sort of sentence is the downfall of foundationalism?

In all fairness, it should be remarked that it seems much more likely that a case could be made for a proposition's being self-warranted on the basis of *type* than could have been made for a type of proposition's being incorrigible, assuming that Pastin is implicitly referring to type. Whether or not there are self-warranted propositions, employing Pastin's definition, depends upon whether there are propositions which, as Pastin says, are believable "without inductive evidential support," where "believable" means "warranted to some degree, however slight, in believing," or, on our more charitable interpretation, "more reasonable to believe than not, to some degree, however slight." With the qualifier "however slight," we can assert that the Austinian line may well fail here, and that there may be such propositions, taken as a type, simply because the modifiers here are weaker. But the very modifier itself is problematic, and the argument that these propositions exist is far from knock-down.

III

In the previous section we saw that even a weak foundationalism, like Pastin's, seems to rely on a certain sort of statement which itself relies on a cognitive process. In other words, if the basic statement for foundationalist theories tends, as it frequently does, to be a statement of privileged access, it is then reliant on a perceptual (or some similar) process. But perceptual processes are, *inter alia*, cognitive processes. Hence foundationalism, in its various versions, tends to rely on cognitive processes which have been held to be in general reliable. (Surely they could not elsewise give rise to the sorts of statements which some have been tempted to deem incorrigible.) Hence foundationalism is itself a sort of reliabilism.

Now Audi's point, cited earlier in this paper, was that reliabilism is a sort of foundationalism. Although this is not what we have just finished arguing, the point seems well-taken and is by no means obscure. For if we recall our opening citation from Van Cleve (". . .we say that a belief is justified iff it either (i) results from a reliable process . . ."), the first disjunct here clearly takes the place of the basic statement in most foundationalist theories. In other words, claiming ancestry from a reliable process is an awful lot like claiming ancestry from a statement of privileged access. This analogy becomes even more acute when it is recalled, as we just argued, that most basic statements are themselves reliant on a trustworthy cognitive process. The relationship is, of course, casual, and for this very reason one hesitates, for the usual sorts of reasons, to try to term it in necessary and sufficient conditions. Suffice it to say that appealing to the reliable process rather than the basic statement itself seems a bit like appealing to the basic statement's grandparent.

Now it is not the fact that reliabilism smacks of foundationalism which really ought to be worrisome to the epistemologist. What ought to trouble him, I claim, is the fact that reliabilism is not really a naturalized theory. There is, of course, more than one way to go here. Klein and others have rather pointedly emphasized the normative history of epistemology and the extent to which epistemology should not take an interest in what epistemic agents actually do, etc. But if one buys at all the notion that an "ought" implies a "can," then one might be interested in determining what epistemic agents actually can perform and what relationship this has, if any, to our epistemic theories. To be interested in this topic is not necessarily to advocate a Quinean sort of line— although this is the citation that is frequently made in the literature—nor is it necessarily to be guilty of holding the view which Rorty, for example, describes as advocating the replacement of epistemology by cognitive psychology or the computational model of mind. It is, however, by my lights, to be interested in attempting to ascertain just which of our theories of epistemic justification (if any) can be instantiated in living agents.

Now part and parcel of my contention here is that reliabilism is not really naturalized. In other words, as was asserted earlier, reliabilist theories are vague and typically fail to spell out in any sort of interesting way what might constitute a reliable cognitive process. Given the ubiquitousness of the current computational model of mind, and the variety of sources available for utilization, one might well find this lacuna puzzling.[4]

In another piece I have outlined the bare bones of what I term a contextualized theory of epistemic justification, borowing from the framework of coherentism. Cognitive processes, whether reliable or unreliable, occur in some kind of context. Recognition of this context has played an increasingly important role in cognitive science, artificial intelligence, and psychology itself.[5] So part of what it might mean to "naturalize epistemology," specifically epistemic justification theory, would be to (a) be specific about what kinds of cognitive processes are at work—this may mean, for example, adverting to aspects of contemporary cognitive theory, such as the computational model of mind—and (b) to show how these specific cognitive processes interact with the context of the epistemic agent. For our purposes here, we will take the agent's context to be not so much a physical time and place (although such notions can be important) but the conversational context in which the agent functions.

To recapitulate, our argument so far has been along the following lines: Some have claimed that the various sorts of reliabilisms represent the most significant advance in the overall project of "naturalizing" epistemology. (The value of such a project itself we have not attempted to investigate.) But the reliabilist theories typically do not spell out the requisite cognitive processes, and more to the point, there is real reason to think that reliabilism is a new version of foundationalism. An examination of a foundationalism which was supposed to avoid the pitfalls of the traditional foundationalist theories (Pastin's) showed us the extent to which foundationalism relies on the notion of a reliable cognitive process and hence is a lot like reliabilism. So Audi's overall claim about reliabilism seems well-taken, and there is reason to think that something else might more deservedly fall under the rubric of "naturalized epistemology," since reliabilism suffers from serious flaws. In the next section I attempt to sketch a theory which might more justifiably be deemed to be naturalized, at least insofar as epistemic justification theory is concerned.

---

[4] See, for example, Pylyshyn (1984) or Fodor (1984). These are only two of the better known long pieces which attempt to present such a model.
[5] See Winograd (1980) and Schank and Abelson (1977). Sternberg's work (1984) and others) also makes frequent reference to context.

IV

The contemporary computational model of mind, filled out by theorists such as Fodor and Pylyshyn, has relied heavily on the notion of representation. This particular piece of conceptual apparatus fills in the blank between what the theorists refer to as the "syntatic encoding"—that is, the on-off switching at the neuronic level of the brain—and its semantic interpretations or correlates.

In general, the representational aspects of a system correspond to what is labeled intentionality. Any intentional state (or what previous philosophers would have labeled propositional attitudes) may be thought of as a set of representations. Pylyshyn makes a distinction between the "functional architecture" (hardware, or neurology) and representations, which is helpful to our project:

> . . . /there is a distinction/between processes governed by semantic principles (which I call "cognitive processes") and those realized in what I call the "functional architecture" of the system . . . According to the position I have taken, processes carried out in the functional architecture are processes whose behavior requires no explanation in terms of semantic regularities. (Pylshyn, 1984, pp. 130)

Many of those who have disagreed with the contemporary employment of the computational model of mind as the leading psychological mental exemplar have failed to understand that positing representations, as theoretical entities, is necessary because it bridges what would otherwise be a serious gap in the casual chain. In other words, we would like to be able to account for our interaction with the world in terms of brain states. We would like to be able to make the claim that the firing of synapses, functioning of the neurons—in other words, the workings of the entire functional architecture—are causally related to an activity such as jogging or reading a paper at a professional conference.

But because the causal connection between these sets of states is not obvious, and because the crucial component of the mental, intentionality, seems to be left out of any purely "hardware" account, another component needs to be alluded to. As Pylyshyn writes:

> Plainly, what is going on is, my behavior is being caused by certain states of my brain. Yet—and this is the crux of the problem—the only way to explain why those states caused me to type the specific sentences *about* walking, writing, the mountains and so on is to say that these states themselves are in some way related to the things referred to (writing, walking, mountains) . . . My brain states are not, as we have noted, causally connected in appropriate ways to walking and to mountains. The relationship must be one of content: a semantic, not a causal, relation. (Pylshyn 1984, pp. 27)

It is the symbolic codes, correlated with the appropriate semantic interpretations, which are, on this model, the physical patterns in the requisite portion of the brain. This pattern link can, of course, enter into causal relations and combined with the appropriate interpretation, it provides an account which enables one to make the move from interaction at the hardware or completely physiological level to the mundane realm of activities which one would like to be able to say are caused by the brain.

All of this is of crucial importance for our project because we require an overview of the process of epistemic justification which is more descriptively accurate than any of the material which has been labeled "reliabilist," since we aim to give an account which may truly be deemed naturalized.

Now in a previous paper we have argued that there is real reason to think a naturalized model of epistemic justification would proceed roughly along the lines of a coherence theory, rather than a foundationalist theory. If, as we have just contended, foundationalist views smack of unspecified cognitive processes and reliabilist views reek of foundationalism, our own view will avoid these two areas of entrapment. Cornman and others have worried that coherentism suffers from fatal flaws because a coherentist's justificatory set might include simultaneously as elements theorems of quantum mechanics and material from classical mechanics, thus producing inconsistency; our contention is that the functioning of epistemic agents is such that it greatly constrains the elements of the justificatory set and thus renders this concern otiose.[6]

The verbal utterances of a skeptical challenger will be heard by the epistemic agent and processed internally. The neurophysiological details of this process elude us and are in any case not necessary for what we do here. The steps preceding the utterance of the agent's justifiers are, however, important to us, and delineation of them allows us a naturalized model.

The computational model—and here we utilize specifically Pylyshyn's model— informs us that the physical patterns in the requisite portion of the brain which will play a causal role in the chain leading to verbal utterance are themselves symbolic codes correlated with a semantics. But the fact that we can postulate these symbolic codes as physical patterns is very significant. It means that there will be, *a fortiori*, no symbolic codes/physical patterns correlated with semantic interpretations for large chunks of the set of all possible semantic interpretations, since the agent is, of course, a finite device. We know antecedently that the range of most agents is extremely limited, and that the verbal output resulting from the causal chain will be extremely limited. Hence the idealized nature of the justificatory set alluded to in most coherence theories is beyond the computational capacity of all but a handful of epistemic agents. Such theories are far from naturalized. There are also, as we have previously remarked, speech act constraints, but these operate at another level.

Generally speaking, we may think of the following sort of linking between the two sets of constraints (those of functional architecture and, say, speech act constraints). Verbal utterances transmitted from the challenger to the epistemic agent pass through certain interpretative exchanges which are mapped on the neurophysiological level. Specifically, verbal utterances for which there is no set of syntactic encoding at the neuronic level probably will not be processed as anything more than noise. An example would be a verbal utterance in a foreign language with which the epistemic agent was totally unfamiliar. Phonology itself, according to Pylyshyn, has been the subject of some work on the computational level, but most of the work has been done at the transducer level (the level of

---

[6] See my piece (1984) for an account of Cornman's problematic.

functioning between that of the purely neurophysiological or functional architecture level and the level of semantic correlation of encoding).

It now remains for us to try to fill in a model for a naturalized and more specifically descriptive view of the process of epistemic justification, based on the strands of thought to which we have alluded—the computational model of mind, intentionality, speech act theory, the intrinsic appeal of a coherence view, and so forth.

If we think in terms of an epistemic agent venting utterances which are *intended* as responses to the challenge of someone cast in the role of skeptic, we will draw a model which relies heavily on the notion of a verbal interchange, but which also contains elements of the theoretical overview just cited.

We will begin with the notion of the coherentist's justificatory set naturalized:

(1) Taking off from a crude coherence model, we can pick out a justifying set on contextually constrained grounds (that is, the set may very well not be normatively adequate, as we have admitted all the way along).

The delineation of the set is given by:

(2)   specification of each putative justifier
$\alpha_1, \alpha_2, \alpha_3, \ldots, \alpha_n$
for statement-to-be justified x results from a process of *epistemic intent* on the part of the challenger and *recognition of epistemic intent* on the part of the agent.

(2a)   More specifically still, the utterance of the challenge, once heard by the epistemic agent, results in a neurophysiological passage of the utterance into *symbolically encoded information correlated with certain semantic interpretations* if the utterance falls into a subset of information with which the agent had some previous familiarity.

(2a')   If partially or fully interpreted with appropriate semantic correlations, the neurological encodings yield, *following higher-level rules for transformation*, some of which are relevant to speech act and/or SCRIPT/GOAL constraints, utterances which themselves are putative justifiers

(2a'' ') If not interpreted at all, the challenge of the skeptic is reduced to the level of noise,

(3)   The utterances of the challenger—the various utterances individually—must be recognized by the epistemic agent as intended by the challenger to produce a state of doubt, and

(4)   For closure of the process of epistemic justification, the challenger must recognise
$\alpha_1, \alpha_2, \alpha_3, \ldots, \alpha_n$
as justifiers, and such recognition must be manifested by the challenger either in acquiescence (which may be signaled non-verbally) or of further challenge. If further challenges are forthcoming, the process will be repeated.

Now in the material set forth above it is clearly conditions (2a)–(2a″) which present the most difficulty. For what we have tried to pack into these tersely-stated conditions is a set of notions, some of which have been adduced in previous portions of this paper, but which need to be stated explicitly:

- Symbolic codes are physical patterns in the requisite portion of the brain which will be correlated with semantic interpretations
- An inherent constraint here is that there will be few symbolic codes in comparison to the world of *possible* utterances
- The verbal utterances of a challenger, when heard by the epistemic agent, pass through certain interpretative changes which are mapped on the neurophysiological level
- There may be no interpretation, partial interpretation or full interpretation
- There are higher-level rules for transformation which also function as constraints on the epistemic agent but which may not be fully set out

The virtues of the view which we have adumbrated here are obvious in contrast with the sorts of views which we have examined, reliabilism and foundationalism. Our view allows for the specification of a justificatory set which is already limited by context, saving it from the problems of size, scope and rigor alluded to by coherence theorists, among others. We have repeatedly claimed that foundationalism is thoroughgoingly normative, and that reliabilism is itself a new sort of foundationalism—a non-naturalized one, at that. Reliabilism claims to furnish us with information about "reliable cognitive processes," but fails to do so in any meaningful way. If it has the virtue that it reminds us of the actual functioning of epistemic agents, it has the defect that it is not at all specific about such functioning.

V

Our argument has been that, in the project of naturalizing epistemology, any number of views might be deemed to be naturalized, but that some are more deserving of that label than others. In a three-pronged argument, we have first examined Audi's claim that reliabilism is a kind of foundationalism, and cursorily agreed with that view, since it appears at first blush that reliabilism preserves our desire to "naturalize" (to in some sense describe the actual functioning of the agent) while simultaneously adverting to a criterion for knowledge which is stronger than some sort of coherence. We then argued that foundationalism itself—even a more modest foundationalism like Pastin's—may in some sense rely on a cognitive process, and hence the linkage between foundationalism and reliabilism might be thought to be stronger than had originally been claimed. Finally, we argued that even if reliabilism failed to be truly naturalized, epistemic justification theory, at least, could be naturalized by creating an overview of the process of epistemic justification (and hence a new view of the justificatory set) at the intuitive level of intersection between the computational model of mind and justification theory.

Our conclusion is that the project of naturalizing epistemology is one which, at least for the moment, is better thought of in non-reliabilist terms. Foundationalism, like the emperor of the fairy tale, has appeared in a set of new clothes. The new clothing is called reliabilism, and like the emperor's old clothing, foundationalism leaves much to be desired. Not the least of the missing *desiderata* is a statement of the specific cognitive processes at work and the interaction with the context of the epistemic agent.

CONCLUSIONS

Here are conclusions for some important arguments in the Part Three section entitled "Skepticism."

Sextus Empiricus

    1. *The skeptic suspends his judgment and receives quietude.*

Augustine

    1. *"P or not-P" is true.*

    2. *Senses do not err in what they report.*

Descartes

    1. *Deceiver or not, I exist.*

    2. *Bodies are better known by the understanding than by the senses.*

Clifford

    1. *All people have a duty to question all their beliefs.*

    2. *It is wrong to believe in anything based upon insufficient evidence.*

James

    1. *We cannot live or think without some degree of faith.*

    2. *Belief must outstrip scientific evidence.*

Here are conclusions for some of the important arguments in the Part Three section entitled "Appearance and Reality."

Plato

    1. *Most people view illusions as reality; only the philosophers see the light.*

Berkeley

    1. *Abstract ideas which separate objects from sensation lead to error.*

    2. *It is impossible to know if there are any external bodies.*

Hume

    1. *Only limited and mitigated skepticism can be useful.*

    2. *Intellectual belief that is not based upon reasoning about quantity and number or experimental fact is not justifiable.*

Here are conclusions for some of the important arguments in the Part Three section entitled "Knowledge."

Plato

    1. *The highest form of knowledge comes from pure (dialectical and non-propositional) contemplation.*

Aristotle

First principles are known through induction by intuition.

Locke

1. *There are no innate ideas.*
2. *Fundamentally, it is intuition that provides certainty for our ideas.*

Leibniz

1. *Humans dominate other animals because they can reason and not through their powers of perception.*
2. *Innate ideas exist.*

Reid

Belief which accompanies sensation and memory is a simple act of the mind which cannot be defined.

Duran

The project of naturalizing epistemology is one which, at least for the moment, is better thought of in non-reliabilist terms.

Evaluating and Writing a Logical Argument
The Con Essay

By now, students should be able to outline and create brainstorming lists from the out-lines. If this is not the case, students should go back and work on the logic exercises at the end of Parts One and Two.

It is important not to skip ahead to the final essay (even if that is all you are being graded on). Each interim step is designed to help the student better write the final essay.

The strategy of the "con" essay is this:

A. The demonstrated truth of the conclusion depends upon the premises that sup-port the conclusion.
B. If those supporting premises are false, then the conclusion is not proven.
C. Since we have assumed interlocking premises, the loss of any single premise will result in the conclusion's being unproven.

Therefore, find the weakest premise and have at it.

The essay itself, at this level, should be about one thousand words (three or four sides of notebook paper). This length is sufficient to practice evaluative skills—yet not so detailed as to outstrip your narrow focus. Remember, the purpose of this form of feedback is narrow analysis. You can be very exact in your task.

The entire process can be described as follows:

Step 1: Create a logical outline of the argument to be examined.
Step 2: Brainstorm a thought-list.
Step 3: Choose the premise which stimulated the greatest number of fruitful com-ments on your brainstorm list. This is your "crucial" premise.
Step 4: Focus your thoughts by grouping comments on your thought list into gen-eral categories. These categories will become the body of your essay.
Step 5: Set out your introduction (see problem 2 below) and begin writing.

Followed sequentially, the five steps mentioned above will provide you with a better chance at writing a clear analytic essay.

The most common problems students have are:

1. *There are too many premises chosen for examination.* Since this model is presupposing a one-thousand-word essay, there isn't much room to develop too many different directions. I suggest sticking to one premise—or at the most, two. This will allow you to better develop your thoughts. The key to development is a well-executed brainstorm list.

2. *The student has difficulty getting into the essay.* For students who tend to become blocked by introductions, I will provide a sample introduction to a "con" essay. Adapt it for your own purposes.

Sample con introduction

> The author of the argument believes [insert conclusion of the argument]. He bases this conclusion on an argument that has as its foundation an objectional premise which states [insert the crucial premise from your brainstorm list]. This premise is necessary for the author's conclusion. It will be the contention of this essay that such a premise is flawed because [insert the names for the general categories which you grouped on your brainstorm list]. Thus, this essay rejects the argument's key premise and the argument in which it plays an integral part.

3. *The student spends time summarizing the author's argument.* Don't do it. If your reader does not know the argument you are analyzing, then insert your logical outline. Don't waste space repeating the argument. Follow the form described above and get right to the evaluation.

4. *One point is repeated several times in different ways.* One thousand words is really not much space. Don't waste it. If your brainstorm list is sufficiently rich, you'll have plenty to say. Most students who have this problem haven't created a detailed brainstorm list.

5. *There is a lack of development.* What is development? It is the construction of your own argument. What would happen if I outlined *your* argument? Would it have sub-conclusions and interlocking premises? Do you continually advance the reader's understanding of the crucial premise through various dimensions not present or sustained in the text? Do you follow out the logical consequences of different approaches to this premise?

   The end result of development is not merely to fill up the page with words. It is a journey the reader takes. When that journey is sufficiently rich and varied, then the essay is well developed. This may sound a bit subjective. It is. However, this does not mean your professor cannot support his or her judgment of why your paragraphs are underdeveloped. If you don't understand why your points are not developed, schedule a conference with your professor to discuss ways you might improve. Bring your outline and brainstorm lists with you.

6. *The student uses too many examples.* Examples are fine. They clarify your point. When they are systematically gathered as data (e.g., as in science), they support an inductive argument. But, in general, you will be using examples merely to clarify. As such, keep examples brief and remember to tell the reader what these examples purport to show. You may think it's very clear, but another reader may be perplexed.

7. *The student loses sight of the principle of fairness.* I state the principle this way: "Always reconstruct and present an argument in its strongest form, even if it requires correcting trivial errors (though these may be noted elsewhere)." Your goal is arriving at Truth. I have seen essays written in which a premise was given a narrow and uncharitable reading so that it then became easy to refute. This technique is not effective (nor honest) because the author can merely revise his premise to meet the objection.

   What is better is an attitude that will examine several interpretations of a premise and eventually concentrate upon the strongest reading. Assume the best and not the worst. Give the author his most plausible reading and *then* refute it.

In this logic exercise section, you are asked to construct a "con" evaluation. In the next chapter, you will construct a "pro" evaluation. After you learn both, the choice is up to you. But how do you choose? When do you choose?

The answer goes back to the brainstorm lists. In the process of writing down all your thoughts on a premise, you will observe patterns of response—against or supporting the crucial premise. When you have completed your list, it should become apparent which side you have chosen.[1] Thus, your "choice" emerges from the process of analysis.

Obviously, this isn't always the case. Many times when you consider a premise, you immediately have a judgment. But try to suppress such prejudices. They tend to impede your objectivity.

Skepticism, Appearance, and Reality in Literature
JORGE LUIS BORGES
*The Circular Ruins**

> And if he left off dreaming about you . . .
> *Through the Looking Glass,* VI

No one saw him disembark in the unanimous night, no one saw the bamboo canoe sinking into the sacred mud, but within a few days no one was unaware that the silent man came from the South and that his home was one of the infinite villages upstream, on the violent mountainside, where the Zend tongue is not contaminated with Greek and where leprosy is infrequent. The truth is that the obscure man kissed the mud, came up the bank without pushing aside (probably without feeling) the brambles which dilacerated his flesh, and dragged himself, nauseous and bloodstained, to the circular enclosure crowned by a stone tiger or horse, which once was the color of fire and now was that of ashes. This circle was a temple, long ago devoured by fire, which the malarial jungle had profaned and whose god no longer received the homage of men. The stranger stretched out beneath the pedestal. He was awakened by the sun high above. He evidenced without astonishment that his wounds had closed; he shut his pale eyes and slept, not out of bodily weakness but out of determination of will. He knew that this temple was the place required by his invincible purpose; he knew that, downstream, the incessant trees had not managed to choke the ruins of another propitious temple, whose gods were also burned and dead; he knew that his immediate obligation was to sleep. Towards midnight he was awakened by the disconsolate cry of a bird. Prints of bare feet, some figs and a jug told him that men of the region had respectfully

[1] If not, then continue the process or create a hybrid between the "pro" and "con" evaluation.

*From Jorge Luis Borges, *Labyrinths* (New York: New Directions, 1962).

spied upon his sleep and were solicitous of his favor or feared his magic. He felt the chill of fear and sought out a burial niche in the dilapidated wall and covered himself with some unknown leaves.

The purpose which guided him was not impossible, though it was supernatural. He wanted to dream a man: he wanted to dream him with minute integrity and insert him into reality. This magical project had exhausted the entire content of his soul; if some-one had asked him his own name or any trait of his previous life, he would not have been able to answer. The uninhabited and broken temple suited him, for it was a mini-mum of visible world; the nearness of the peasants also suited him, for they would see that his frugal necessities were supplied. The rice and fruit of their tribute were suffi-cient sustenance for his body, consecrated to the sole task of sleeping and dreaming.

At first, his dreams were chaotic; somewhat later, they were of a dialectical nature. The stranger dreamt that he was in the center of a circular amphitheater which in some way was the burned temple: clouds of silent students filled the gradins; the faces of the last ones hung many centuries away and at a cosmic height, but were entirely clear and precise. The man was lecturing to them on anatomy, cosmography, magic; the counte-nances listened with eagerness and strove to respond with understanding, as if they divined the importance of the examination which would redeem one of them from his state of vain appearance and interpolate him into the world of reality. The man, both in dreams and awake, considered his phantoms' replies, was not deceived by impostors, divined a growing intelligence in certain perplexities. He sought a soul which would merit participation in the universe.

After nine or ten nights, he comprehended with some bitterness that he could expect nothing of those students who passively accepted his doctrines, but that he could of those who, at times, would venture a reasonable contradiction. The former, though worthy of love and affection, could not rise to the state of individuals; the latter pre-existed somewhat more. One afternoon (now his afternoons too were tributaries of sleep, now he remained awake only for a couple of hours at dawn) he dismissed the vast illusory college forever and kept one single student. He was a silent boy, sallow, sometimes obstinate, with sharp features which reproduced those of the dreamer. He was not long disconcerted by his companions' sudden elimination; his progress, after a few special lessons, astounded his teacher. Nevertheless, catastrophe ensued. The man emerged from sleep one day as if from a viscous desert, looked at the vain light of after-noon, which at first he confused with that of dawn, and understood that he had not really dreamt. All that night and all day, the intolerable lucidity of insomnia weighed upon him. He tried to explore the jungle, to exhaust himself; amidst the hemlocks, he was scarcely able to manage a few snatches of feeble sleep, fleetingly mottled with some rudimentary visions which were useless. He tried to convoke the college and had scarcely uttered a few brief words of exhortation, when it became deformed and was extinguished. In his almost perpetual sleeplessness, his old eyes burned with tears of anger.

He comprehended that the effort to mold the incoherent and vertiginous matter dreams are made of was the most arduous task a man could undertake, though he might penetrate all the enigmas of the upper and lower orders: much more arduous than weaving a rope of sand or coining the faceless wind. He comprehended that an initial failure was inevitable. He swore he would forget the enormous hallucination which had misled him at first, and he sought another method. Before putting it into effect, he dedicated a month to replenishing the powers his delirium had wasted. He abandoned any premeditation of dreaming and, almost at once, was able to sleep for a considerable part of the day. The few times he dreamt during this period, he did not take notice of the dreams. To take up his task again, he waited until the moon's disk was perfect. Then, in the afternoon, he purified himself in the waters of the river, worshiped the planetary gods, uttered the lawful syllables of a powerful name and slept. Almost immediately, he dreamt of a beating heart.

He dreamt it as active, warm, secret, the size of a closed fist, of garnet color in the penumbra of a human body as yet without face or sex; with minute love he dreamt it, for fourteen lucid nights. Each night he perceived it with greater clarity. He did not touch it, but limited himself to witnessing it, observing it, perhaps correcting it with his eyes. He perceived it, lived it, from many distances and many angles. On the fourteenth night he touched the pulmonary artery with his finger, and then the whole heart, inside and out. The examination satisfied him. Deliberately, he did not dream for a night; then he took the heart again, invoked the name of a planet and set about to envision another of the principal organs. Within a year he reached the skeleton, the eyelids. The innumerable hair was perhaps the most difficult task. He dreamt a complete man, a youth, but this youth could not rise nor did he speak nor could he open his eyes. Night after night, the man dreamt him as asleep.

In the Gnostic cosmogonies, the demiurgi knead and mold a red Adam who cannot stand alone; as unskillful and crude and elementary as this Adam of dust was the Adam of dreams fabricated by the magician's nights of effort. One afternoon, the man almost destroyed his work, but then repented. (It would have been better for him had he destroyed it.) Once he had completed his supplications to the numina of the earth and the river, he threw himself down at the feet of the effigy which was perhaps a tiger and perhaps a horse, and implored its unknown succor. That twilight, he dreamt of the statue. He dreamt of it as a living, tremulous thing: it was not an atrocious mongrel of tiger and horse, but both these vehement creatures at once and also a bull, a rose, a tempest. This multiple god revealed to him that its earthly name was Fire, that in the circular temple (and in others of its kind) people had rendered it sacrifices and cult and that it would magically give life to the sleeping phantom, in such a way that all creatures except Fire itself and the dreamer would believe him to be a man of flesh and blood. The man was ordered by the divinity to instruct his creature in its rites, and send him to the other broken temple whose pyramids survived downstream, so that in this deserted edifice a voice might give glory to the god. In the dreamer's dream, the dreamed one awoke.

The magician carried out these orders. He devoted a period of time (which finally comprised two years) to revealing the arcana of the universe and of the fire cult to his dream child. Inwardly, it pained him to be separated from the boy. Under the pretext of pedagogical necessity, each day he prolonged the hours he dedicated to his dreams. He also redid the right shoulder, which was perhaps deficient. At times, he was troubled by the impression that all this had happened before . . . In general, his days were happy; when he closed his eyes, he would think: *Now I shall be with my son.* Or, less often: *The child I have engendered awaits me and will not exist if I do not go to him.*

Gradually, he accustomed the boy to reality. Once he ordered him to place a banner on a distant peak. The following day, the banner flickered from the mountain top. He tried other analogous experiments, each more daring than the last. He understood with certain bitterness that his son was ready—and perhaps impatient—to be born. That night he kissed him for the first time and sent him to the other temple whose debris showed white downstream, through many leagues of inextricable jungle and swamp. But first (so that he would never know he was a phantom, so that he would be thought a man like others) he instilled into him a complete oblivion of his years of apprenticeship.

The man's victory and peace were dimmed by weariness. At dawn and at twilight, he would prostrate himself before the stone figure, imagining perhaps that his unreal child was practicing the same rites, in other circular ruins, downstream; at night, he would not dream, or would dream only as all men do. He perceived the sounds and forms of the universe with a certain colorlessness: his absent son was being nurtured with these diminutions of his soul. His life's purpose was complete; the man persisted in a kind of ecstasy. After a time, which some narrators of his story prefer to compute in years and others in lustra, he was awakened one midnight by two boatmen; he could not see their faces, but they told him of a magic man in a temple of the North who could walk upon fire and not be burned. The magician suddenly remembered the words of the god. He recalled that, of all the creatures of the world, fire was the only one that knew his son was a phantom. This recollection, at first soothing, finally tormented him. He feared his son might meditate on his abnormal privilege and discover in some way that his condition was that of a mere image. Not to be a man, to be the projection of another man's dream, what a feeling of humiliation, of vertigo! All fathers are interested in the children they have procreated (they have permitted to exist) in mere confusion or pleasure; it was natural that the magician should fear for the future of that son, created in thought, limb by limb and feature by feature, in a thousand and one secret nights.

The end of his mediations was sudden, though it was foretold in certain signs. First (after a long drought) a faraway cloud on a hill, light and rapid as a bird; then, toward the south, the sky which had the rose color of the leopard's mouth; then the smoke which corroded the metallic nights; finally, the panicky flight of the animals. For what was happening had happened many centuries ago. The ruins of the fire god's sanctuary were destroyed by fire. In a birdless dawn the magician saw the concentric blaze close round the walls. For a moment, he thought of taking refuge in the river, but then he knew that death was coming to crown his old age and absolve him of his labors. He walked into the shreds of flame. But they did not bite into his flesh, they caressed him and engulfed him without heat or combustion. With relief, with humiliation, with terror, he understood that he too was a mere appearance, dreamt by another.

Questions for Discussion

1. A silent man came from nowhere. He wanted to dream a man. Does a man just exist in the mind?

2. Is philosophy the *creation* of ghosts and chimeras?

3. When you create an idea, it influences other ideas; which is real and what does "real" mean?

PART 4

Freedom and Determinism, Mind and Body

Marjorie Grene

Virginia Polytechnic Institute

Qualified Freedom

Much, if not most, philosophical debate still suffers from the crippling effect of problems bequeathed to us by our seventeenth-century heritage. This is true, it seems to me, of the question of human freedom (and by implication of the so-called "theory of action" that depends on it).

I am speaking here, I should say, of individual freedom, the problem of free will, not of political liberty. The two are conceptually quite different, though often associated or confused.

It is, then, I believe, the concept of a world sharply divided between mind and nature, or between God, mind, and nature, as Descartes so plainly painted it, that has led our thinking into a dead end with respect to the question of freedom as it has in many other areas: in our conception of science, of language, of art, of the mind-body relation—and so on and on. So I want first to sketch for you very crudely the dilemma of modern thought with respect to freedom, and then to suggest, not a solution, but a way of looking at the problem that may make it more tolerable. Philosophical problems are not generally soluble, as scientific questions often are. The most persistent ones may be quite *in*soluble; but sometimes, and especially, I think, in our time, when we are still living with the outworn premises of another age, we need to make a fresh start (relatively speaking—there are no absolutely fresh starts) and think of the problem in a new context. And that is how we need to proceed in particular with the concept of freedom.

But before trying to do this—that is, to exhibit the problem as it has been stated over the past three centuries and to suggest a more tolerable approach to it—I should perhaps warn you that I am *not* going to add to the long list of those popularizers of science who give us a recipe for seeing human action scientifically, and therefore "correctly," over against an old and outworn tradition, whether of religion or morality. Indeed, this view of science, or these views seemingly borrowed from science, are precisely an important ingredient in the outworn conception of human nature that demands to be replaced.

First, then, what has the problem been? If we put the question of freedom in a very crude and superficial form, as it usually has been put in modern philosophy, we may ask: If everything that happened in nature is strictly determined in a cause and effect sequence, is what *I* do produced by something like a "will" not subject to such determinable laws? There seem to be four possible answers: yes; no; no, but I need to think so (that is, free will is a necessary illusion); and both yes and no.

Both Descartes and Locke after him found the existence of freedom unquestionable (although Descartes pushed metaphysical thought far enough to grasp the difficulty of a free will given the traditional God; Locke, a good member of the Church of England, was less radical in metaphysical probing). The way Locke put the matter in 1690 is still characteristic of some eminent philosophical thinkers, although it is a way I find very hard to defend. All discussion of an alleged philosophical problem of free will, Locke declared emphatically, is nonsense, since, in effect, will means freedom and freedom means the ability to will, and this I quite plainly possess. If I want to take a step forward, I can do so; if I want to stand still, I can do that, too. I experience in myself a power to initiate action that is undeniable. Now, of course it is true that I perform a great many so-called voluntary actions, and it is true too that there are many actions for which people are held to be legally as well as morally responsible, and it makes sense to talk that way and to behave that way. But when I am told that I have in me somehow, directly and immediately, an obvious power to initiate motion and to alter the course of events, either in my human environment or in nature, I become very skeptical. Actions like walking or standing still are one thing; but when it comes to the major decisions of my life, how do I know when I have "really chosen" and when I have been moved this way or that by circumstance? Is it really so easy to know the difference, metaphorically speaking, between walking and being pushed? It doesn't take Freud or Marx or Skinner or Levi-Strauss or Crick or E. O. Wilson to show us that most, if not all, our seeming choices are thrust upon us by our genes, our early history, the habits and customs of our parents, our community, our language group, and so on ad infinitum. Ordinary experience shows quite plainly, it seems to me, that most people go the way that a combination of innate tendencies and outward circumstances drives them to go. Free will in any deep sense, far from being obvious, seems a rare phenomenon, if it exists at all. The case is well put by a fictional character, Mr. Polly, in H. G. Wells's *History of Mr. Polly:* "I never really planned my life," he says, "or set out to live. I happened, things happened to me. It's so with every one."

If, then, freedom is not as obvious as Locke supposed, and if, as Locke followed Descartes in believing, everything in the world *except* the human mind constitutes a closed nexus of determinate motions, there seems to be nothing but matter in motion, and therefore determinism, the denial of free will, appears to win the day. That is a very misleading historical statement, I must confess, if only because for Descartes it may have been intelligence, not will, that was most clearly essential to human nature (this is debatable), and also because the Lockean (and Boylan) view of nature itself differs in important respects from the Cartesian. But I am trying to present very quickly and schematically what is, as all historical events are, really a much subtler and more complicated story. The point is that, as I said at the beginning, modern thought is characterized from the first by a very abstract and simple view of God sustaining a harmony of thinking or willing mind and inert material nature, and that the acceptance of this bare trinity easily gives way, when its delicate equilibrium is disturbed, to the alternative view that there is after all only dead nature, of which "mind" is but an ephemeral consequence.

Indeed, the most thoroughgoing expression of this materialistic vision occurred in Descartes' own lifetime, in the work of Thomas Hobbes, and, as I have argued elsewhere, it is his metaphysic of motion that is still exemplified in modern materialistic mythologies. In short, Hobbes had progressed "beyond freedom and dignity" in the middle of the seventeenth century as Skinner in the latter half of this one—and Crick's and now Wilson's pseudobiologism is again but a caricature, with a new lingo, of the Hobbesian position. Science, it is alleged, shows us a world of matter-in-motion. We are but part of that world, a series of events that just happened to happen, with the same old necessary contingency or contingent necessity as any other natural events. Why pretend otherwise? The truth of science lies in determinism (even if in twentieth-century quantum-mechanical terms a statistical determinism, for statistical laws bind large aggregates as firmly as unambiguous laws bind sequences of single events). But the truth of science is the only truth we have. God has receded and mind, with its sure intuition of its own freedom, is conquered by science, too. Let us be honest, say such people from Hobbes to the present, and declare determinism the victor.

Yet this will not quite do either. Not because it feels uncomfortable: truths are supposed to be statements of how things are, not security blankets. All the same, this will not quite do, for several reasons. First, although freedom is not the obvious power Locke thought it, there *is* something convincing in the notion of the uniqueness of a human life, of its relation to some kind of center that, developing from infancy to old age, makes it the peculiar history it is. And that core of responsible action is closely related to what we mean by "will." Why did Wells call his novel *The History of Mr. Polly?* He was probably using "history" in the sense in which, as the Oxford English Dictionary defines it, a history is "an eventful career, a course of existence worthy of record." Poor Mr. Polly! He was a draper's clerk—that is, an assistant in a clothing and textile store—back in the days when such people worked from dawn to dusk for a mere pittance, lived in dormitories (What do we call them? Barracks? Big rooms with say twenty or thirty beds in each?) under the almost continuous control of their foreman—in short, in the relative sense of a constriction of their possibilities for living, were almost wholly unfree. He married foolishly and, as he said, in a half-dream, used reading and imagining as solaces in an otherwise utterly dreary life, and finally walked off to a strange dreamy existence in a tavern by a river where he could think and talk and watch the sunset. Most of his life had been a misery, but through a set of curious chances, it turned into a pattern that was uniquely

his. That strange originality in a far-from-original context is what makes his history a *history:* an eventful career or a course of existence worthy of record. And so it may be of any human life, even one that appears on the surface the most routine and ordinary. In an account of what there is, we do not want to omit this feature, not because it is comforting—in fact, it is rather unsettling—but because it is there, odd and hidden and hard to come at, but still there.

Besides, determinism, pushed to a Hobbesian extreme, is unable to produce a proof for itself. The deterministic thesis claims to be true, but all it can say to justify itself is: that the determinist is determined to assert determinism. And since in that case the supporter of freedom is equally determined to assert the denial of determinism, there is no argument. If there is to be an argument, on the contrary—that is, if the determinist is to assert his view *for reasons* which can be weighed and found valid or wanting, then he must assert his determinism, so to speak, on his own recognizances, because on consideration he finds reason to do so, and not because he is compelled. If, however, asserting-for-reasons is different from being compelled, then insofar as the determinist asserts determinism for reasons, he shows determinism to be false. If he just asserts it, because he can't help himself, it may be true, but he can't prove it is. (Nor can he prove the falsity, or we the truth, of its contradictory. Again, if determinism is true, there just is no argument.)

Finally, the notion of science and of the truths of science that motivates and accompanies Hobbesian determinism has by now been amply proven to be false and sterile. Science is by no means the single machine-for-prediction in a determinate nature that it used to be thought to be. Science is rather a family of human practices of a complicated, interrelated, but by no means monolithic kind, attempting, each in its own specialty, to understand how certain phenomena in a limited area of nature work, and sustained in its existence by a disciplined devotion on the part of its practitioners to standards of accuracy, honesty and systematic scope. By itself it does not aim to tell us how we ought to see ourselves; but insofar as we see honestly, it too entails in its very existence ingredients of human responsible action and therefore of human freedom—and I do not intend that as a reference to the practical or social applications or consequences of science, but to its very nature as a family of theoretical and intellectual disciplines. (By science, in this context, I should say, I mean natural science; whether, once we recognize such an enterprise for the kind of human pursuit it is, we can take the so-called sciences of man to be sciences in the same sense, is a question I cannot pursue here. Suffice it to recall that it is natural, not so-called "social" science, that has served as model for all these Hobbesian nothing-butteries.)

Nor, indeed, is the "nature" the natural sciences seek to explain as monolithic as the "new corpuscular philosophy" of the seventeenth century supposed it to be and as its present-day heirs still seem to believe. Newton's notion of least particles is as outdated as his "true, absolute and mathematical space and time." One of the many quaint features of the recently fashionable sociobiology, in fact, is its naive Newtonism: a machinery which in its founder's view could not have been created or sustained without its Infinite and All-wise Maker is now supposed to be self-generating and self-perpetuating. Not that we can return in simple traditional fashion to divine support for our view of nature. By no means. But we *should* recognize the truncated character of modern materialism for what is it is: half a divided world left orphaned by its defunct designer. And then why not abandon the dead nature too that completes that austere vision, and try to think freshly about where indeed we find ourselves: not in a world

of hard solid impenetrable particles and absolute space and time, but historically located in a human and a living world whose complex networks or orders of order we can partly decipher if we try?

This is already anticipating my second main point: the way to see our place in nature and therefore our freedom more adequately than the modern tradition has allowed us to do. But there are two more possibilities of an answer to the orthodox freedom–determinism question that I promised to touch on.

One is the idea that free will, though illusory, is a useful and even necessary illusion, rather like Plato's noble lie in his ideal state. I cannot think of a philosopher who has taken this stand on freedom, but the British anthropologist Malinowski took it about religion, and a similar position suggests itself with respect to associated aspects of our fundamental beliefs, including our belief in freedom, despite its ontological impossibility within the framework or our particular theistic tradition. As I have already suggested, however, we cannot honestly affirm beliefs about what there is in the light of their utility to us: we cannot really *believe* what we deny to be the case even if we recommend belief in it as a crutch for action; or better, we cannot really recommend such a belief as a crutch for action at the same time that we deny it.

Another way, finally, in which it seems we might have it both ways is Kant's. Nature, he said, is intelligible only as determined, but we are free, and, practically, through our experience of respect for the moral law, we "know" this, although we can achieve no theoretical basis for such "knowledge." Kant is saved from the lameness of the third as-if solution that I just mentioned by his notion that one cannot in any case know anything about the whole of nature, so that if we try to assert determinism as a universal thesis, we can argue validly against this assertion, although of course if we try to assert freedom as holding in fact of the natural world, we can argue equally well against that position. Both thesis (freedom) and antithesis (determinism) are true in a way, Kant believes, but neither can be proved. Now there is a kind of wisdom in Kant's doctrine. It is true, it seems to me, that even if you could give a complete causal account of a person's history (s)he would still, in terms of responsible agency, be rightly held to have done the things (s)he had done and left undone the things (s)he had not done. Yet the Kantian "solution" comes to rest *as* a solution, I believe, only if moral life is grounded in a strict Kantian ethic of duty and if this in turn is protected by the postulates of God and immortality to which in fact Kant adhered. If you remove those props, both puritanical and supernatural, the antinomy becomes just the kind of opposition between the belief in free will and determinism that I have presented as the first two traditional answers to our question. Again, in other words, deprived of the Infinite Allgood Allwise Maker who had to hold together the ingredients of the modern vision, mind and nature become acutely dichotomous. And then, as "mind" too ceases to justify itself as a separate entity, the bare bones of a one-level material universe turn out to be all that is left us. So either we keep pitting free will and determinate nature against one another, or once more admit the triumph of what is called "eliminative" materialism, or something very close to it, as the only truth that remains.

Now it seems to me, as, again, I remarked at the start—and as I have remarked on a great many other occasions, and as others much wiser than I have remarked on many occasions also—that it is the overabstract dichotomy of mind and nature, or perhaps better, trichotomy, if we count God as well as cogitating mind and extended matter (and we have to count Him, since mind and matter, different as they are, could never make a universe without His intervention)—it is this overabstract trichotomy

that has brought us in our view of freedom to such a pretty pass. Either God keeps mind and matter, these disparate entities, working together, and then of course we do not really understand their union but rely on His mysterious Providence for our seeming explanation. Or He does not, and then mind is either something over against nature or it is not. If it is, again, we cannot for the life of us explain how minds can influence bodies or vice versa. We may in these circumstances try to swell out mind or something like it to assimilate nature in some idealistic absolute. Or if that ruse fails, we are likely, more commonsensically as it seems, to relegate mind to a place *in* nature. But nature in turn is extended, particulate, determinate, certainly not such as to admit the kind of power-to-initiate-change that defenders of free will like Locke claimed so readily to discover. So there is no freedom.

But why let the new corpuscular philosophy of three centuries ago thus cabin and confine our thought today? On the contrary, the model experience would suggest is not one of mind (or action) over against dead nature, but of action within *living* nature, a nature full of achievements and failures, not just inertial motion and its thermodynamic death. And when it comes to human action, we also need a concept of the historical, or the cultural, within the range of the living. We need the categories of life and of history as well as (or instead of) those of bare mind and bare matter if we are to describe with any honesty things as we find ourselves among them. Many thinkers have already attempted such a revision of our basic categories. Bergson tried, in a limited way, to provide such a new vision, and so, more radically, did Whitehead. Both those efforts, however, seem now in some respects inadequate. The attempts that appeal most to me, as it happens, are put forward by relatively obscure continental thinkers, notably by Helmuth Plessner in a book about the fundamental concepts of biology and of the philosophy of the person published in 1928 and by Maurice Merleau-Ponty in the *Structure of Behavior* and the *Phenomenology of Perception*, also to some extent by writers like the psychiatrist Erwin Straus and the zoologist Adolph Portmann. In part, the argument of Heidegger in *Being and Time*, I regret to say, is also, with major qualifications, crucially important. Rather than report these various views here, however, I shall speak in the main in my own voice, acknowledging my indebtedness *en bloc*.[1]

Human existence is a version, if an odd one, of animal existence. Not bare matter versus thinking mind, but life transformed through culture, is what we want to try to understand. To begin with, then, we must take biology seriously as showing us the ground of our human life-style. Darwin has proved to us that we are descended from and therefore akin to other animals; we have no right to set ourselves off, with respect to free will or any other allegedly exclusive capacity of ours, from our kin of other kinds. Yet we must take care in interpreting this lesson. Evolution may have demoted man from a special status in creation, as modern astronomy had shifted our planet from being the center of the universe. But that does not mean either that evolution explains everything about all living things or that any wholly biological explanation clarifies the fundamental philosophical issues about human life. Evolution explains how, step by step, populations have originated, but that is not the only question, even in scientific inquiry, about living things. George Wald, in a paper of many years ago called "Innovation in Biology," pointed out that one can ask about a living system not only how it arose, but for example how it works or what it is made of.[2] In particular, the question how a system works, the question of its function, of what Aristotle calls its formal cause, cannot be reduced to the story of how it came to be. Darwinism, through turning people's attention rightly to the living world, and so helping to alter the

overattention to mathematical physics that had characterized much of thought about science up to 1859—and, I regret to say, up to fairly recently, for philosophy of science is just beginning to recover from having been chiefly philosophy of physics—Darwinism, while having so far a benign effect, has also been misapplied or exaggerated to suggest that explaining how a phenomenon came about is explaining it *tout court*. Thus E. O. Wilson, for example, declares that showing how the emotions originate in the hypothalamus shows what morality is.[3] Now morality may or may not be a matter of the emotions (on the whole I think not), but even if it were, telling us how the emotions originated in the development of the brain does not tell us anything at all about what they are or how they work. And, in general, to describe what something is and how it does its job is not the same as to tell a story, however convincing, of how it got that way. No; what our belief in evolution should do is not to let us ignore the complexities of the living world through exclusive attention to a bare causal when–then tale of origins, but to help us see the great multiplicity of styles of life and so look for the uniqueness of our own life-style, with its gift of responsible action, within the context of that scene of infinite variety. We want to see ourselves where we belong, within nature, not over against it, as an alien excrescence. We are born, reproduce, grow old, and die like other animals, as well as differently.

So let us look at animal life as background to the question of freedom. In this ecology-conscious age, it should be obvious that we should think of livng

---

[1] For an account of Portmann, Straus, and Plessner, see my *Understanding of Nature* (Dordrecht: Reidel, 1974), pp. 254–360. Merleau-Ponty's *Phenomenology of Perception* appeared in English translation in 1962 (New York: Humanities Press) and his earlier *Structure of Behavior* appeared in a very poor translation indeed in 1963 (Boston: Beacon Press).

[2] George Wald, "Innovation in Biology," *American Scientist*, Vol. 41 (1953), pp. 2–8.

[3] E. O. Wilson, *Sociobiology* (Cambridge: Harvard University Press, 1975).

things, including animals, as expressions of their relations to their environments. It is slightly differing adaptations to differing environments that trigger evolutionary change; and the life of any organism at every moment consists in a complex give-and-take—feedback, if you want a fashionable term—between each part of the system and its environment, and in turn between the whole and its environment, biotic as well as climatic, geologic, and so on. Now we may of course turn all these relations, if we like, into a string of when–then, cause–effect sequences. There is no functional or whole–part relation that *cannot* be analyzed into one-darned-thing-after-another if one insists. The reason we do this, however, I believe, lies in our lingering commitment to a Cartesian–Newtonian vision of a dead, one-level nature. If we stay closer to what we find in the world around us, we see living things attuned to existence in this or that ecological niche, niches that in turn are constituted by complex interrelations between living and non-living things. And among such interrelations some are tighter and more mechanically binding than others. Thus if we compare the courtship or nesting behaviors of groups like birds or insects, for example, with those of "higher" mammals, we find in the former relatively fixed sequences of behavior, what used to be called "fixed action patterns." To give a simple example, a male robin responds with a threat display to a simulated red breast as well as to a real live male of his species, or to a certain flight past not even by a conspecific male, and so on. In this respect, at least, his life seems a mosaic of relatively fixed behaviors in response to relatively fixed environmental signals. True, it is a complicated network of responses, but complicated differently from the more flexible behavior of many other kinds of organisms. Experience seems to give the robin little room to learn, at least in such matters. He is tied all his life rather strictly to his packet of genetic information. Some animals, on the

other hand, can acquire much more information in the course of their life experience; they have more space to maneuver within the directions allowed them by a combination of environmental conditions and genetic instructions. The most obvious examples are of primate behavior or that of other "advanced" mammals, like dolphins or elephants, which, as we all know by now, are strikingly intelligent. But let us take an incident related by Konrad Lorenz about a jewel fish in his aquarium. He had thrown pieces of earthworm into a tank where a pair of jewel fish were tending their young. "As I approached the container," he writes, "I saw that most of the young were already in the nesting hollow over which the mother was hovering. She refused to come for the food when I threw pieces of earthworm into the tank. The father, however, who, in great excitement, was dashing backwards and forwards searching for truants, allowed himself to be diverted from his duty by a nice hind-end of earthworm . . . He swam up and seized the worm, but owing to its size, was unable to swallow it. As he was in the act of chewing this mouthful, he saw a baby fish swimming by itself across the tank; he started as though stung, raced after the baby and took it into his already filled mouth." What would happen? "The fish stood stock still with full cheeks, but did not chew. If ever I saw a fish think," says Lorenz, "it was in that moment! What did the fish do? After some seconds of hesitation, he spat out both worm and baby, both sank to the bottom" (as the baby had reflexly 'made itself heavy' in the parent's mouth). "Then the fish went back to the worm and ate it up, keeping his eye on the quiet baby. After that he picked up the baby and took it home to mother."[4] Now that fish, I submit, was deciding. We do not share his feelings, as we could those of a human parent distraught, say, between baby crying and a

[4] K. Lorenz, *King Solomon's Ring* (London: Methuen, 1952), pp. 37–38.

saucepan boiling over. But unless we are brainwashed by the notion that everything not "conscious" in the mode of our particular explicit and instantaneous human consciousness is "mere" behavior, we can see this animal coping with its problems, a center of action in a milieu that it has to a limited extent within its control. This is the root of free action, namely, taking one way or another in a problematic situation. If we want to talk in terms of information, as it was fashionable to do in biology some decades ago, we could say that freedom consists in the ability to use ambiguous information, rather than depending wholly on a strict genetic program. In other words, the more developed an animal's ability to learn to deal with novelties in slightly different situations, the more degrees of freedom it has in such circumstances. No animal, including human animals, can act except in its proper niche, but its range of decision making can vary from limited and fixed to multifarious and flexible. Only within that biological context, I suggest, can we understand what freedom is at all. That is what I mean by saying that we need the category of the living as our foundation if we are to think more effectively than the Cartesian physical/mental distinction has allowed us to do about what freedom means.

About thirty years ago a British zoologist, R. H. Pumphrey, published in the *British Journal for the Philosophy of Science* an article called "The Evolution of Thinking," in which he put very clearly, I thought, the point I have been trying to make. True, he was talking about powers of thought, or understanding, not explicitly of action, but the question of freedom arises just as clearly in the more "theoretical" context. For the seeming distinction between learning and what used to be called "instinct" appears equally for thought and action, and needs to be modified in the same way for both. As Pumphrey convincingly argues, it is never a simple either/or, but rather, as I have already indicated, a question of some flexibility within a set of predeterminate genetic-times-environmental circumstances. How much can an animal of a certain kind, destined to exist in a certain kind of natural niche, modify or manipulate factors in its environment? That is where, whether for efforts to know or for efforts to act, the question of freedom arises, and it is always a question, not of free or unfree, but of *how* free. As Pumphrey resoundingly concludes, "there is not absolute distinction between the bound and the free. There are only . . . degrees of freedom."[5]

Given, then, that freedom consists, at least minimally, in the relative range (and/or richness) of possibilities of action in given circumstances, what about the human case? We are animals, too, but in our own peculiar way, which facilitates moral judgments and legal decisions, in which we hold others and ourselves accountable for our choices. Obviously, while other animals are tied to a relatively limited milieu, we are freed from such confinements by the instrumentalities we have devised to help us solve our problems: clothing, shelter, and other technological constraints, and, above all, our languages, by means of which we mediate our other inventions. Here we meet the familiar contrast between nature and culture, a contrast which, however, again needs careful interpretation. Too often it has been simply taken as a dichotomy between nature and convention, as in Hobbism or in the reductive evolutionisms that reiterate Hobbesian thinking. Then it turns out that only the natural really counts; all else (justice, mercy, truth, or what you will) is mere convention and even pretense. That has been the message of "social Darwinisms," whether in the nineteenth century or now. It is a travesty of the nature/culture distinction. We should try to think rather in terms of what Plessner has called the

[5] R. H. Pumphrey, "The Evolution of Thinking," *British Journal for the Philosophy of Science*, Vol. 4 (1953), pp. 315–27, 326.

natural artificiality of human beings. Culture for us is not unnatural: it is the breath of life to us, the medium every human infant needs, in whatever form, to permit it to develop into a human agent.

Even our biological natures are adjusted to this need. That is the chief lesson of Adolph Portmann's study of the comparative development of the young of a number of species of birds and mammals. The young of more primitive birds, like ostriches, are relatively well developed when hatched, while the more advanced birds, those that have evolved relatively recently, hatch helpless, featherless young needing parental care. In mammals, on the other hand, the development has gone the other way. Rats, cats, or dogs give birth to blind, hairless, helpless litters, while more advanced mammals, like horses, sheep, cattle, primates, produce young both alert and mobile. What about us, then? Our neonates appear with sense-organs functioning, but certainly do not leap about like new-born lambs or foals till they are, usually, into their second year. Anatomically, moreover, Portmann has established, a chimp at birth is as close to adult proportions as a year-old baby. So we are born early, when our senses have developed beyond the level of more primitive mammalian neonates, but not yet our power of locomotion. Infants take a powerful sight of notice, like other advanced mammalian young, but they do not get up and go till nearly a year later, or even more. What is the significance of this reversion to a more primitive stage of evolution, or, if you like, this habit of partly premature birth? The first year of human life, Portmann argues, is a time in which the infant takes note of the human world around him (her) that he (she) will enter into when he (she) stands upright and begins to speak and to act. Had we started life as mature as other primates, it appears, we would have needed twenty-one months' gestation, but we emerge a year early, to take in the prerequisites of the cultural world we are

to enter into. Only after about a year of such protected observation of their surroundings do human young achieve upright posture, speech, and the power of responsible action. Portmann calls this first period "the year of the social uterus."

If we think about our kind of life-style in this way, understanding even our biological endowments as the foundation of our human, culture-dwelling existence, and conversely our cultural existence as rooted in biology, we may note three fundamental respects in which human dependence on the artifacts of culture has transformed our lives so that we may rightly contrast human existence with the life-styles of other species.

First, and as I have already said in passing, if we think of the effect of our commitment to culture on our natural environment, we find ourselves much less restricted than are members of other species. If Pacific salmon are imported into Irish waters, they can survive only if conditions are sufficiently close to those of their natural habitat—and of course, as critics of this enterprise have been quick to point out, they may by their presence alter the environment too, so as to endanger the indigenous species. Indeed, we are given to upsetting the balance of nature precisely because *we* can move so easily from one natural setting to another and adjust it (within limits) to our needs or desires. A contrast is sometimes made in general between the limited environment (*Umwelt*) of other animals and the open world (*Welt*) of human beings. Our relative detachability from a given niche is part at least of what is being referred to in this context. Although, of course, like all living things we are dependent chemically on certain materials for our metabolic processes, the kinds of particular environments we need—mountain or valley, desert or swamp, and so on—are certainly not limited as those of other species tend to be.

Nor is this relative independence of ecological and biological givens purely a matter of geography. We are also, thanks to education, relatively independent of our individual biological endowments. Not that our drives go, as Kant believed, in direct opposition to our moral lives; yet we can, and do, up to a point, learn, each in his or her own way and within his or her own cultural setting, to control and direct our appetites. As Spinoza showed us, though often slaves to passion, we are free to be free. Such freedom consists, however, not so much in denying our emotions as in directing them into more fruitful channels, as for example, in the devotion of their practitioners to the sciences and arts. With these very sketchy remarks, however, we have already passed from nature to culture, from biology to history. For the way in which any individual uses his (her) emotional life or permits it to use him (her) is an expression of the tradition he or she has been born into and bred in as well as of his (her) natural biological endowment. Both in our technical and in our moral lives, the manner in which we control our environment and/or our own natures clearly instantiates the ethos of our society.

So, it may be objected, you are just moving from physical or biological to technical or cultural determinism. Where is freedom in all this? But again, as I have emphasized, although one can always break down any system–part relation into a cause and effect sequence, one need not do so, especially when one gains no insight and loses much in the process. If we think more, so-to-speak, ecologically about the matter, we can see two respects in which our insertion in a culture is liberating. First, in terms of freedom from restraint (or the negative concept of freedom, as it is called), compare, for example, the range of possibilities for communication possessed by a bee with the range open to a human being. One may be held captive by one's mother tongue, but think what a variety of mother tongues one might have had, and what a variety of second to nth

languages one can acquire if one tries, compared with the single species-specific language of the honeybee. More significant, however, in this context, is the way we can see freedom here in its so-called positive role: as the source of responsible action. I become a free agent as I develop, out of my own center of responsible choice, control over the ways and means at my disposal for the realization of ends that, within limits, I also freely choose. Mind you, I am not going back on Mr. Polly's insight: we happen, things happen to us; but we also make them *our* happenings, and to a fortunate few it is given to realize that responsibility more fully than usual, to transform more fully than usual happenings into history.

These remarks have brought me, not only nature to culture, but to my second point. Perhaps I can approach it best if I summarize the first one. I have been trying to compare human freedom in respect to biological factors, both external and internal, with that of other living systems, and to stress the greater degree of freedom characteristic of our lifestyle. But I have been unable to put even this very simple thesis without referring to the artifactual-historical (as against merely natural) situation within which we have each of us developed as centers of human agency. This confinement within a culture, however, again looks at first sight—as I have already noted—like a new and unnatural bondage, rather than an implementation of liberty. If we can, up to a point, do what we like with the materials around us and with our biological natures, we do whatever we do within the iron grip of a given belief system, acquired since birth, a taught way of taking things and doing things that seems as inescapable as it does arbitrary. Have we gained control over nature and over our own natures only to surrender our liberty to the tyranny of habit, or parental prejudice, of the tricks and manners that our parents and teachers, not to mention our commercial and/or political exploiters, have instilled in us?

In a way, we *are* prisoners of our culture. But at the same time it is our home, a home that we make our own by the way we choose to live in it. Even a biological environment is not just a piece of extended matter, of such a size or shape. It becomes the environment it is through the complex interactions between the myriad plants and animals that, inhabiting it, constitute it as the living place it is. So much the more clearly and definitely does each human person, in achieving personhood, both express and constitute the mores of his (her) society by the way in which he (she) accepts them, transforms them, or up to a point rejects them. And it is this constitution of his (her) social setting as his (her) dwelling place that forms, in my view, the primary locus of human freedom. The human infant does not simply ape the behavior of others in its society. Many other young animals do that. But as the child grows into his (her) cultural niche, he or she makes his (her) own the fundamental symbolic relations that distinguish this particular human world. I have often quoted in other contexts A.J.P. Kenny's definition of mind, and venture to quote it once more here, since it includes by implication a hint of the peculiar nature of human freedom. "To have a mind," Kenny says, "is to have the capacity to operate with symbols, in such a way that it is one's own activity that makes them symbols and confers meaning on them."[6] Now it is just this responsible conferring of meaning on symbol systems or on the ingredients of symbol systems that is most characteristic of human free choice. Even in a very rigidly structured society, each person has to remake its structures by taking on for him(her)self the meanings they convey. The rites of initiation studied by anthropologists give formal expression to this process; even when less explicit, the passage to membership in a group through participation in its basic symbols (or symbolic activities—

what Peter Wilson calls "symboling") is essential to growing up in any human community.[7] Socrates' account of his quasi-contractual relation to the Athenian state represents not just a particular trick of the Greek *polis*, but the relation of any mature individual to the community in which he participates.

But surely, it will be objected once again, this is not what we mean by freedom. I am free when I can do what *I* like, and to hell with society! What we have to face, however, is that the human individual, however seemingly unrestrained in some particular behavior, *is* the person he (she) is as an expression of the human world through participation in which he (she) has become that person. As I have put it elsewhere, "a human being is a personalization of nature through participation in a culture."[8] A certain kind of little animal can take on personhood, but only through dwelling in a human world. Now such an individual history, like Mr. Polly's, is, looked at one way, a mere happening, but looked at another, it is an achievement. And to be an achievement is to be not by happening only but freely. True, such freedom is incurably ambiguous: it is never radical, pure Cartesian freedom. Rather, it is that core of meaning-giving hidden in our actions and that makes them actions rather than mere muscle-motions. Further, such freedom is indirect. As Merleau-Ponty said of the painter's task in "Cézanne's Doubt": "We never leave our lives. We never see . . . freedom face to face."[9] Where you are freest, it is not freedom you feel, but your commitment to what needs to be done. Thus we do what we must, whether out of duty or desire, and yet in submitting to such compulsions we are choosing to do

[6] A.J.P. Kenny, *Will, Freedom and Power* (Oxford: Blackwell, 1975), pp. 2–3.

[7] Peter J. Wilson, *Man: the Promising Primate* (New Haven: Yale University Press, 1980).

[8] *Understanding of Nature*, pg. 354.

[9] Maurice Merleau-Ponty, "La Doute de Cézanne," in *Sens et Nonsens* (Paris: Nagel, 1948), pp. 15–44, 44.

what we do and to become what we become. At the same time, finally, such freedom is open to the future. In its very ambiguity and indirectness it challenges us to yet another reach forward, to yet another choice. (I shall return to this point shortly.) Aristotle defined choice as deliberative desire, and such an origin of action, he said, is a human being.[10] But such an origin of action cannot exist in a vacuum: it exists only where there is already an embodied-enculturated human world to give it a dwelling place.

This oddly qualified view of human freedom I take, as I have acknowledged, largely from the writings of Merleau-Ponty, as well as in part from Plessner's philosophical anthropology. The best place to fill in the very crude outline I have sketched, however, in my view, is in the work of the so-called symbolic anthropologists. If I had more time, and if I had not already cluttered up my argument with draper's clerks and jewel fish, I should like to exemplify that very abstract allusion by reporting some particular cases of the kind of work I have in mind and the kind of illumination I believe it can provide—the case of a particular masked dance among a people called the Karavarans, for instance, or a particular ritual of canoe-building on the island of Gawa. But in the circumstances I had better just repeat the general point: that the symbol systems exemplified in social actions both provide the place in which individual human beings can become responsible centers of action and demand from each individual that he or she in his or her own way participate on his (her) own initiative in such actions— thus making them his (her) own, and him(her)self the agent of the symbol systems they embody.

So far I have made two general points about human freedom in comparison with other animals: (1) our greater flexibility over against both internal and external factors in our natural situation, and (2) the location of human free

action within a structure of symbol systems that are constituted *as* symbols by such action. The third point I want to add (and have already alluded to in passing) is taken directly from Merleau-Ponty, from a passage in *The Structure of Behavior*.[11] At least that is where he first states it, so far as I know, but it is in fact a theme that dominates all his work. Human freedom, as I have already remarked, is always open: it is embodied and historically situated, to be sure, but unlike, say, the vaunted territories of other animals, these confining boundaries can be transformed or transcended. Hence the contrast, which I have already mentioned, between the closed *Umwelt* of other animals and the open world of the human person. Along similar lines, Merleau-Ponty contrasts, in the passage in question, two aspects of what he calls "the human dialectic": "It is manifested first by the social or cultural structures that it makes appear and in which it imprisons itself." But, he continues, man's "objects of use and his cultural objects would not be what they are if the activity that makes them appear did not also have the sense of denying and outstripping them." And it is here, in our possibility of change, of innovation, of development, that we find the real center of human uniqueness: not in some Cartesian separate mind or totally free will, or in some Lockean "power," but in the creative character of every human history, potentially of every human moment, which expresses and reflects its cultural heritage, indeed, but may nevertheless transfigure it in ways not yet imagined. Such a gift of originality, however, can be understood only in its setting, both natural and historical. If we try to snatch it out of its right place, and see it as a moment of pure freedom in and of itself, it becomes at most the unachievable

[10]*Nichamachean Ethics*, 1112b, 31–32.
[11]M. Merleau-Ponty, *The Structure of Behavior*, pg. 176 (my revision of the translation).

ideal of Sartrean freedom, always and inevitably betrayed into bad faith, or, what is more likely, is cast aside as a silly make-believe unable to withstand the assault of pseudo-scientific and deterministic dogma. As I confessed at the outset, the alternative I have sketched is no solution to the "problem" of freedom, yet it is an approach, I believe, that allows us to see why freedom is both problematic and, though ambiguous, indirect and practical, nevertheless real, inherent, indeed, in the very core of our human reality.

Freedom and Determinism

Hap

If but some vengeful god would call to me
From up the sky, and laugh: "Thou suffering thing,
Know that thy sorrow is my ecstasy,
That thy love's loss is my hate's profiting!"

Then would I bear it, clench myself, and die,
Steeled by the sense of ire unmerited;
Half-eased in that a Powerfuller than I
Had willed and meted me the tears I shed.

But not so. How arrives it joy lies slain,
And why unblooms the best hope ever sown?
—Crass Casualty obstructs the sun and rain,
And dicing Time for gladness casts a moan . . .
These purblind Doomsters had as readily strown
Blisses about my pilgrimage as pain.

Thomas Hardy

JOHN LOCKE

(1632–1704) English Philosopher

From *An Essay Concerning Human Understanding**

Whence the Ideas of Liberty and Necessity. Everyone, I think, finds in himself a power to begin or forbear, continue or put an end to several actions in himself. From the consideration of the extent of this power of the mind over the actions of the man, which everyone finds in himself, arise the *ideas of liberty* and *necessity.*

Liberty, what. All the actions that we have any idea of reducing themselves, as has been said, to these two, viz. thinking and motion, so far as a man has power to think or not to think, to move or not to move, according to the preference or direction of his own mind, so far is a man *free*. Wherever any performance or forbearance are not equally in a man's power, wherever doing or not doing will not equally follow upon the preference of his mind directing it, there he is not free, though perhaps the action may be voluntary. So that the idea of *liberty* is the idea of a power in any agent to do or forbear any particular action, according to the determination or thought of the mind, whereby either of them is preferred to the other; where either of them is not in the power of the agent to be produced by him according to his volition, there he is not at liberty; that agent is under *necessity.* So that liberty cannot be where there is no thought, no volition, no will; but there may be thought, there may be will, there may be volition, where there is no liberty. A little consideration of an obvious instance or two may make this clear.

Belongs not to Volition. Suppose a man be carried, whilst fast asleep, into a room where is a person he longs to see and speak with, and be there locked fast in, beyond his power to get out; he awakes, and is glad to find himself in so desirable company, which he stays willingly in, i.e. prefers his stay to going away. I ask, is not this stay voluntary? I think nobody will doubt it; and yet, being locked fast in, it is evident he is not at liberty not to stay, he has not freedom to be gone. So that liberty is not an idea belonging to volition, or preferring; but to the person having the power of doing, or forbearing to do, according as the mind shall choose or direct. Our idea of liberty reaches as far as that power, and no farther. For wherever restraint comes to check that power, or compulsion takes away that indifference of ability on either side to act, or to forbear acting, there liberty, and our notion of it, presently ceases.

Voluntary opposed to Involuntary, not to Necessary. We have instances enough, and often more than enough, in our own bodies. A man's heart beats, and the blood circulates, which it is not in his power by any thought or volition to stop; and therefore in respect of these motions, where rest depends not on his choice, nor would follow the determination of his mind, if it should prefer it, he is not a

---

*John Locke, *An Essay Concerning Human Understanding*, Book II, Chapter 21 (London, 1690).

free agent. Convulsive motions agitate his legs, so that though he wills it ever so much, he cannot by any power of his mind stop their motion, (as in that odd disease called *chorea Sancti Viti*),[1] but he is perpetually dancing; he is not at liberty in this action, but under as much necessity of moving, as a stone that falls, or a tennis-ball struck with a racket. On the other side, a palsy or the stocks hinder his legs from obeying the determination of his mind, if it would thereby transfer his body to another place. In all these there is want of freedom; though the sitting still, even of a paralytic, whilst he prefers it to a removal, is truly voluntary. Voluntary, then, is not opposed to necessary, but to involuntary. For a man may prefer what he can do, to what he cannot do; the state he is in, to its absence or change; though necessity has made it in itself unalterable.

Liberty, what. As it is in the motions of the body, so it is in the thoughts of our minds: where any one is such that we have power to take it up, or lay it by, according to the preference of the mind, there we are at liberty. A waking man, being under the necessity of having some ideas constantly in his mind, is not at liberty to think or not to think, no more than he is at liberty, whether his body shall touch any other or no; but whether he will remove his contemplation from one idea to another is many times in his choice, and then he is, in respect of his ideas, as much at liberty as he is in respect of bodies he rests on; he can at pleasure remove himself from one to another. But yet some ideas to the mind, like some motions to the body, are such as in certain circumstances it cannot avoid, nor obtain their absence by the utmost effort it can use. A man on the rack is not at liberty to lay by the idea of pain, and divert himself with other contemplations; and sometimes a boisterous passion hurries our thoughts, as a hurricane does our bodies, without leaving us the liberty of thinking on other things, which we would rather choose. But as soon as the mind regains the power to stop or continue, begin or forbear, any of these motions of the body without, or thoughts within, according as it thinks fit to prefer either to the other, we then consider the man as a free agent again.

Liberty belongs not to the Will. If this be so (as I imagine it is), I leave it to be considered whether it may not help to put an end to that long agitated, and, I think, unreasonable, because unintelligible question, viz. *Whether man's will be free or no?* For if I mistake not, it follows from what I have said, that the question itself is altogether improper; and it is as insignificant to ask whether man's *will* be free, as to ask whether his sleep be swift, or his virtue square; liberty being as little applicable to the will, as swiftness of motion is to sleep, or squareness to virtue. Everyone would laugh at the absurdity of such a question as either of these: because it is obvious that the modifications of motion belong not to sleep, nor the difference of figure to virtue; and when anyone well considers it, I think he will as plainly perceive that liberty, which is but a power, belongs only to *agents*, and cannot be an attribute or modification of the will, which is also but a power.

Powers belong to Agents. It is plain then that the will is nothing but one power or ability, and freedom another power or ability so that to ask whether the will has

---

[1] Saint Vitus's Dance is a disease of the central nervous system characterized by disturbances of spontaneous and coordinating movements. —ED.

freedom, is to ask whether one power has another power, one ability another ability; a question at first sight too grossly absurd to make a dispute, or need an answer.

However, the name "faculty" which men have given to this power called the will, and whereby they have been led into a way of talking of the will as acting, may, by an appropriation that disguises its true sense, serve a little to palliate the absurdity; yet the "will" in truth signifies nothing but a power or ability to prefer or choose: and when the will, under the name of a faculty, is considered as it is, barely as an ability to do something, the absurdity in saying it is free, or not free, will easily discover itself. For, if it be reasonable to suppose and talk of faculties as distinct beings that can act (as we do, when we say the will orders, and the will is free), it is fit that we should make a speaking faculty, and a walking faculty, and a dancing faculty, by which those actions are produced, which are but several modes of motion; as well as we make the will and understanding to be faculties, by which the actions of choosing and perceiving are produced, which are but several modes of thinking. And we may as properly say that it is the singing faculty sings, and the dancing faculty dances, as that the will chooses, or that the understanding conceives; or, as is usual, that the will directs the understanding, or the understanding obeys or obeys not the will; it being altogether as proper and intelligible to say that the power of speaking directs the power of singing, or the power of singing obeys or disobeys the power of speaking.

Liberty belongs not to the Will. The attributing to faculties that which belonged not to them has given occasion to this way of talking; but the introducing into discourses concerning the mind, with the name of faculties, a notion of their operating, has, I suppose, as little advanced our knowledge in that part of ourselves, as the great use and mention of the like invention of faculties in the operations of the body has helped us in the knowledge of physic.

But to the Agent, or Man. To return, then, to the inquiry about liberty, I think the question is not proper, *whether the will be free*, but *whether a man be free*. Thus, I think,

(1) That so far as anyone can, by the direction or choice of his mind, preferring the existence of any action to the non-existence of that action, and *vice versa*, make it to exist or not exist, so far he is free. For if I can, by a thought directing the motion of my finger, make it move when it was at rest, or *vice versa*, it is evident that in respect of that I am free; and if I can, by a like thought of my mind, preferring one to the other, produce either words or silence, I am at liberty to speak or hold my peace; and as far as this power reaches, of acting or not acting, by the determination of his own thought preferring either, so far is a man free. For how can we think anyone freer than to have the power to do what he will? And so far as anyone can, by preferring any action to its not being, or rest to any action, produce that action or rest, so far can he do what he will. For such a preferring of action to its absence is the willing of it; and we can scarce tell how to imagine any being freer than to be able to do what he wills. So that in respect of actions within the reach of such a power in him a man seems as free as it is possible for freedom to make him.

(2) That willing, or volition, being an action, and freedom consisting in a power of acting or not acting, a man in respect of willing or the act of volition,

when any action in his power is once proposed to his thoughts, as presently to be done, cannot be free. The reason whereof is very manifest. For, it being unavoidable that the action depending on his will should exist or not exist, and its existence or not existence following perfectly the determination and preference of his will, he cannot avoid willing the existence or non-existence of that action, it is absolutely necessary that he will the one or the other, i.e. prefer the one to the other, since one of them must necessarily follow; and that which does follow follows by the choice and determination of his mind, that is, by his willing it; for if he did not will it, it would not be.

This, then, is evident, *That in all proposals of present action a man is not at liberty to will, or not to will, because he cannot forbear willing;* liberty consisting in a power to act or to forbear acting, and in that only. For a man that sits still is said yet to be at liberty, because he can walk if he wills it. But if a man sitting still has not a power to remove himself, he is not at liberty; so likewise a man falling down a precipice, though in motion, is not at liberty, because he cannot stop that motion if he would. This being so, it is plain that a man that is walking, to whom it is proposed to give off walking, is not at liberty whether he will determine himself to walk, or give off walking or no: he must necessarily prefer one or the other of them, walking or not walking. And so it is in regard of all other actions in our power so proposed, which are the far greater number.

The Will determined by something without it. Since then it is plain that in most cases a man is not at liberty whether he will or no, the next thing demanded is *whether a man be at liberty to will which of the two he pleases, motion or rest?* This question carries the absurdity of it so manifestly in itself that one might thereby sufficiently be convinced that liberty concerns not the will. For to ask whether a man be at liberty to will either motion or rest, speaking or silence, which he pleases, is to ask whether a man can will what he wills, or be pleased with what he is pleased with. A question which, I think, needs no answer; and they who can make a question of it must suppose one will to determine the acts of another, and another to determine that, and so on *in infinitum.*

To avoid these and the like absurdities, nothing can be of greater use than to establish in our minds determined ideas of the things under consideration.

Freedom. First, then, it is carefully to be remembered that freedom consists in the dependence of the existence, or not existence of any action, upon our volition of it, and not in the dependence of any action, or its contrary, on our *preference.* He that is a close prisoner in a room twenty foot square, being at the north side of his chamber, is at liberty to walk twenty feet southward, because he can walk or not walk it; but is not, at the same time, at liberty to do the contrary, i.e. to walk twenty feet northward.

In this, then, consists freedom, viz. in our being able to act or not to act, according as we shall choose or will.

Will and Desire must not be confounded. Though I have above endeavoured to express the act of volition by "choosing," "preferring," and the like terms, that signify desire as well as volition, for want of other words to mark that act of the mind whose proper name is "willing" or "volition"; yet, it being a very simple act, whosoever desires to understand what it is will better find it by reflecting on his own mind, and observing what it does when it wills, than by any variety of articulate sounds whatsoever. This caution of being careful not to be misled by expressions that do not enough keep up the difference between the will and several acts of the mind that are quite distinct from it I think the more necessary, because I find the will often confounded with several of the affections, especially desire, and one put for the other. This, I imagine, has been no small occasion of obscurity and mistake in this matter, and therefore is, as much as may be, to be avoided. For he that shall turn his thoughts inwards upon what passes in his mind when he wills, shall see that the will or power of volition is conversant about nothing but that particular determination of the mind, whereby, barely by a thought, the mind endeavours to give rise, continuation, or stop, to any action which it takes to be in its power. This, well considered, plainly shows that the will is perfectly distinguished from desire; which, in the very same action, may have a quite contrary tendency from that which our will sets us upon. A man, whom I cannot deny, may oblige me to use persuasions to another, which, at the same time I am speaking, I may wish may not prevail on him. In this case, it is plain the will and desire run counter. I will the action; that tends one way, whilst my desire tends another, and that the direct contrary. Whence it is evident that desiring and willing are two distinct acts of the mind; and consequently, that the will, which is but the power of volition, is much more distinct from desire.

Uneasiness determines the Will. To return, then, to the inquiry, what is it that determines the will in regard to our actions? And that, upon second thoughts, I am apt to imagine is not, as is generally supposed, the greater good in view; but some (and for the most part the most pressing) *uneasiness* a man is at present under. This is that which successively determines the will, and sets us upon those actions we perform. This uneasiness we may call, as it is, desire; which is an uneasiness of the mind for want of some absent good.

The greatest positive Good determines not the Will, but Uneasiness. It seems so established and settled a maxim, by the general consent of all mankind, that good, the greater good, determines the will, that I do not at all wonder that, when I first published my thoughts on this subject, I took it for granted; and I imagine that, by a great many, I shall be thought more excusable for having then done so, than that now I have ventured to recede from so received an opinion. But yet, upon a stricter inquiry, I am forced to conclude that *good,* the *greater good,* though apprehended and acknowledged to be so, does not determine the will, until our desire, raised proportionably to it, makes us uneasy in the want of it. Convince a man never so much that plenty has its advantages over poverty, make him see and own that the handsome conveniences of life are better than nasty penury; yet, as long as he is content with the latter, and finds no uneasiness in it, he moves not, his will never is determined to any action that shall bring him out of it.

Because all who allow the Joys of Heaven possible, pursue them not. Were the will determined by the views of good, as it appears in contemplation greater or less to the understanding, which is the state of all absent good, and that which, in the received opinion, the will is supposed to move to, and to be moved by, I do not see how it could ever get loose from the infinite eternal joys of heaven, once proposed and considered as possible.

But any great Uneasiness is never neglected. But that it is not so, is visible in experience, the infinitely greatest confessed good being often neglected, to satisfy the successive uneasiness of our desires pursuing trifles.

All desire Happiness. If it be further asked, what it is moves desire? I answer, happiness, and that alone. "Happiness" and "misery" are the names of two extremes, the utmost bounds whereof we know not; it is what "eye hath not seen, ear hath not heard, nor hath it entered into the heart of man to conceive." But of some degrees of both we have very lively impressions, made by several instances of delight and joy on the one side, and torment and sorrow on the other; which, for shortness' sake, I shall comprehend under the names of "pleasure" and "pain," there being pleasure and pain of the mind as well as the body: "With him is fulness of joy, and pleasure for evermore." Or, to speak truly, they are all of the mind; though some have their rise in the mind from thought, others in the body from certain modifications of motion.

Happiness, what. Now, because pleasure and pain are produced in us by the operation of certain objects, either on our minds or our bodies, and in different degrees; therefore, what has an aptness to produce pleasure in us is that we call *good*, and what is apt to produce pain in us we call *evil*, for no other reason but for its aptness to produce pleasure and pain in us, wherein consists our happiness and misery.

What Good is desired, what not? Though this be that which is called good and evil, and all good be the proper object of desire in general, yet all good, even seen and confessed to be so, does not necessarily move every particular man's desire; but only that part, or so much of it as is considered and taken to make a necessary part of his happiness. All other good, however great in reality or appearance, excites not a man's desires who looks not on it to make a part of that happiness wherewith he, in his present thoughts, can satisfy himself. Happiness, under this view, everyone constantly pursues, and desires what makes any part of it; other things, acknowledged to be good, he can look upon without desire, pass by, and be content without.

Why the greatest Good is not always desired. This, I think, anyone may observe in himself and others, that the greater visible good does not always raise men's desires in proportion to the greatness it appears, and is acknowledged, to have; though every little trouble moves us, and sets us on work to get rid of it. The reason whereof is evident from the nature of our happiness and misery itself. All present pain, whatever it be, makes a part of our present misery; but all absent good does not at any time make a necessary part of our present happiness, nor the absence of it make a part of our misery.

The Power to suspend the Prosecution of any Desire makes way for Consideration. There being in us a great many uneasinesses, always soliciting and ready to determine the will, it is natural, as I have said, that the greatest and most pressing should determine the will to the next action; and so it does for the most part, but not always. For, the mind having in most cases, as is evident in experience, a power to suspend the execution and satisfaction of any of its desires, and so all, one after another, is at liberty to consider the objects of them, examine them on all sides, and weigh them with others. In this lies the liberty man has; and from the not using of it right comes all that variety of mistakes, errors, and faults which we run into in the conduct of our lives, and our endeavours after happiness, whilst we precipitate the determination of our wills, and engage too soon, before due examination. To prevent this, we have a power to suspend the prosecution of this or that desire, as everyone daily may experiment in himself. This seems to me the source of all liberty; in this seems to consist that which is (as I think improperly) called *free-will*. For, during this suspension of any desire, before the will be determined to action, and the action (which follows that determination) done, we have opportunity to examine, view, and judge of the good or evil of what we are going to do; and when, upon due examination, we have judged, we have done our duty, all that we can, or ought to do, in pursuit of our happiness; and it is not a fault, but a perfection of our nature, to desire, will, and act according to the last result of a fair examination.

The Reason of it. This is the hinge on which turns the *liberty* of intellectual beings, in their constant endeavours after, and a steady prosecution of, true felicity, that they *can suspend* this prosecution in particular cases, till they have looked before them, and informed themselves whether that particular thing which is then proposed or desired lie in the way to their main end, and make a real part of that which is their greatest good. For the inclination and tendency of their nature to happiness is an obligation and motive to them, to take care not to mistake or miss it; and so necessarily puts them upon caution, deliberation, and wariness, in the direction of their particular actions, which are the means to obtain it. Whatever necessity determines to the pursuit of real bliss, the same necessity, with the same force, establishes suspense, deliberation, and scrutiny of each successive desire, whether the satisfaction of it does not interfere with our true happiness, and mislead us from it. This, as seems to me, is the great privilege of finite intellectual beings; and I desire it may be well considered whether the great inlet and exercise of all the liberty men have, are capable of, or can be useful to them, and that whereon depends the turn of their actions, does not lie in this.

THOMAS HOBBES
(1588–1679) English Philosopher

Of the Liberty of Subjects*

Liberty, what. LIBERTY, or FREEDOM, signifieth, properly, the absence of opposition; by opposition, I mean external impediments of motion; and may be applied no less to irrational, and inanimate creatures, than to rational. For whatsoever is so tied, or environed, as it cannot move but within a certain space, which space is

---

*From Thomas Hobbes, *Leviathan* (London, 1651), Part II, Chapter 21.

determined by the opposition of some external body, we say it hath not liberty to go further. And so of all living creatures, whilst they are imprisoned, or restrained, with walls, or chains; and of the water whilst it is kept in by banks, or vessels, that otherwise would spread itself into a larger space, we use to say, they are not at liberty, to move in such a manner, as without those external impediments they would. But when the impediment of motion, is in the constitution of the thing itself, we use not to say; it wants the liberty; but the power to move; as when a stone lieth still, or a man is fastened to his bed by sickness.

What it is to be free. And according to this proper, and generally received meaning of the word, a FREEMAN, *is he, that in those things, which by his strength and wit he is able to do, is not hindered to do what he has a will to.* But when the words *free,* and *liberty,* are applied to any thing but *bodies,* they are abused; for that which is not subject to motion, is not subject to impediment: and therefore, when it is said, for example, the way is free, no liberty of the way is signified, but of those that walk in it without stop. And when we say a gift is free, there is not meant any liberty of the gift, but of the giver, that was not bound by any law or covenant to give it. So when we *speak freely,* it is not the liberty of voice, or pronunciation, but of the man, whom no law hath obliged to speak otherwise than he did. Lastly, from the use of the word *free-will,* no liberty can be inferred of the will, desire, or inclination, but the liberty of the man; which consisteth in this, that he finds no stop, in doing what he has the will, desire, or inclination to do.

Fear and liberty consistent. Fear and liberty are consistent; as when a man throweth his goods into the sea for *fear* the ship should sink, he doth it nevertheless very willingly, and may refuse to do it if he will: it is therefore the action of one that was *free:* so a man sometimes pays his debt, only for *fear* of imprisonment, which because nobody hindered him from detaining, was the action of a man at *liberty.* And generally all actions which men do in commonwealths, for *fear* of the law, are actions, which the doers had *liberty* to omit.

Liberty and necessity consistent. Liberty, and *necessity* are consistent: as in the water, that hath not only *liberty,* but a *necessity* of descending by the channel; so likewise in the actions which men voluntarily do: which, because they proceed from their will, proceed from *liberty;* and yet, because every act of man's will, and every desire, and inclination proceedeth from some cause, and that from another cause, in a continual chain, whose first link is in the hand of God the first of all causes, proceed from *necessity.* So that to him that could see the connexion of those causes, the *necessity* of all men's voluntary actions, would appear manifest. And therefore God, that seeth, and disposeth all things, seeth also that the *liberty* of man in doing what he will, is accompanied with the *necessity* of doing that which God will, and no more, nor less. For though men may do many things, which God does not command, nor is therefore author of them; yet they can have no passion, nor appetite to any thing, of which appetite God's will is not the cause. And did not his will assure the *necessity* of man's will, and consequently of all that on man's will dependeth, the *liberty* of men would be a contradiction, and impediment to the omnipotence and *liberty* of God. And this shall suffice, as to the matter in hand, of that natural *liberty,* which only is properly called *liberty.*

B. F. SKINNER

(1904–1990) American Psychologist

Freedom*

Almost all living things act to free themselves from harmful contacts. A kind of freedom is achieved by the relatively simple forms of behavior called reflexes. A person sneezes and frees his respiratory passages from irritating substances. He vomits and frees his stomach from indigestible or poisonous food. He pulls back his hand and frees it from a sharp or hot object. More elaborate forms of behavior have similar effects. When confined, people struggle ("in rage") and break free. When in danger they flee from or attack its source. Behavior of this kind presumably evolved because of its survival value; it is as much a part of what we call the human genetic endowment as breathing, sweating, or digesting food. And through conditioning similar behavior may be acquired with respect to novel objects which could have played no role in evolution. These are no doubt minor instances of the struggle to be free, but they are significant. We do not attribute them to any love of freedom; they are simply forms of behavior which have proved useful in reducing various threats to the individual and hence to the species in the course of evolution.

A much more important role is played by behavior which weakens harmful stimuli in another way. It is not acquired in the form of conditioned reflexes, but as the product of a different process called operant conditioning. When a bit of behavior is followed by a certain kind of consequence, it is more likely to occur again, and a consequence having this effect is called a reinforcer. Food, for example, is a reinforcer to a hungry organism; anything the organism does that is followed by the receipt of food is more likely to be done again whenever the organism is hungry. Some stimuli are called negative reinforcers; any response which reduces the intensity of such a stimulus—or ends it—is more likely to be emitted when the stimulus recurs. Thus, if a person escapes from a hot sun when he moves under cover, he is more likely to move under cover when the sun is again hot. The reduction in temperature reinforces the behavior it is "contingent upon"—that is, the behavior it follows. Operant conditioning also occurs when a person simply avoids a hot sun—when, roughly speaking, he escapes from the *threat* of a hot sun.

Negative reinforcers are called aversive in the sense that they are the things organisms "turn away from." The term suggests a spatial separation—moving or running away from something—but the essential relation is temporal. In a standard apparatus used to study the process in the laboratory, an arbitrary response simply weakens an aversive stimulus or brings it to an end. A great deal of

*From B. F. Skinner, *Beyond Freedom and Dignity* (New York: Alfred A. Knopf, 1971), pp. 26–43.

physical technology is the result of this kind of struggle for freedom. Over the centuries, in erratic ways, men have constructed a world in which they are relatively free of many kinds of threatening or harmful stimuli—extremes of temperature, sources of infection, hard labor, danger, and even those minor aversive stimuli called discomfort.

Escape and avoidance play a much more important role in the struggle for freedom when the aversive conditions are generated by other people. Other people can be aversive without, so to speak, trying: they can be rude, dangerous, contagious, or annoying, and one escapes from them or avoids them accordingly. They may also be "intentionally" aversive—that is, they may treat other people aversively because of what follows. Thus, a slave driver induces a slave to work by whipping him when he stops; by resuming work the slave escapes from the shipping (and incidentally reinforces the slave driver's behavior in using the whip). A parent nags a child until the child performs a task; by performing the task the child escapes nagging (and reinforces the parent's behavior). The blackmailer threatens exposure unless the victim pays; by paying, the victim escapes from the threat (and reinforces the practice). A teacher threatens corporal punishment or failure until his students pay attention; by paying attention the students escape from the threat of punishment (and reinforce the teacher for threatening it). In one form or another intentional aversive control is the pattern of most social coordination—in ethics, religion, government, economics, education, psychotherapy, and family life.

A person escapes from or avoids aversive treatment by behaving in ways which reinforce those who treated him aversively until he did so, but he may escape in other ways. For example, he may simply move out of range. A person may escape from slavery, emigrate or defect from a government, desert from an army, become an apostate from a religion, play truant, leave home, or drop out of a culture as a hobo, hermit, or hippie. Such behavior is as much a product of the aversive conditions as the behavior the conditions were designed to evoke. The latter can be guaranteed only by sharpening the contingencies or by using stronger aversive stimuli.

Another anomalous mode of escape is to attack those who arrange aversive conditions and weaken or destroy their power. We may attack those who crowd us or annoy us, as we attack the weeds in our garden, but again the struggle for freedom is mainly directed toward intentional controllers—toward those who treat others aversively in order to induce them to behave in particular ways. Thus, a child may stand up to his parents, a citizen may overthrow a government, a communicant may reform a religion, a student may attack a teacher or vandalize a school, and a dropout may work to destroy a culture.

It is possible that man's genetic endowment supports this kind of struggle for freedom: when treated aversively people tend to act aggressively or to be reinforced by signs of having worked aggressive damage. Both tendencies should have had evolutionary advantages, and they can easily be demonstrated. If two organisms which have been coexisting peacefully receive painful shocks, they immediately exhibit characteristic patterns of aggression toward each other. The aggressive behavior is not necessarily directed toward the actual source of stimulation; it may be "displaced" toward any convenient person or object.

Vandalism and riots are often forms of undirected or misdirected aggression. An organism which has received a painful shock will also, if possible, act to gain access to another organism toward which it can act aggressively. The extent to which human aggression exemplifies innate tendencies is not clear, and many of the ways in which people attack and thus weaken or destroy the power of intentional controllers are quite obviously learned.

What we may call the "literature of freedom" has been designed to induce people to escape from or attack those who act to control them aversively. The content of the literature is the philosophy of freedom, but philosophies are among those inner causes which need to be scrutinized. We say that a person behaves in a given way because he possesses a philosophy, but we infer the philosophy from the behavior and therefore cannot use it in any satisfactory way as an explanation, at least until it is in turn explained. The literature of freedom, on the other hand, has a simple objective status. It consists of books, pamphlets, manifestoes, speeches, and other verbal products, designed to induce people to act to free themselves from various kinds of intentional control. It does not impart a philosophy of freedom; it induces people to act.

The literature often emphasizes the aversive conditions under which people live, perhaps by contrasting them with conditions in a freer world. It thus makes the conditions more aversive, "increasing the misery" of those it is trying to rescue. It also identifies those from whom one is to escape or those whose power is to be weakened through attack. Characteristic villains of the literature are tyrants, priests, generals, capitalists, martinet teachers, and domineering parents.

The literature also prescribes modes of action. It has not been much concerned with escape, possibly because advice has not been needed; instead, it has emphasized how controlling power may be weakened or destroyed. Tyrants are to be overthrown, ostracized, or assassinated. The legitimacy of a government is to be questioned. The ability of a religious agency to mediate supernatural sanctions is to be challenged. Strikes and boycotts are to be organized to weaken the economic power which supports aversive practices. The argument is strengthened by exhorting people to act, describing likely results, reviewing successful instances on the model of the advertising testimonial, and so on.

The would-be controllers do not, of course, remain inactive. Governments make escape impossible by banning travel or severely punishing or incarcerating defectors. They keep weapons and other sources of power out of the hands of revolutionaries. They destroy the written literature of freedom and imprison or kill those who carry it orally. If the struggle for freedom is to succeed, it must then be intensified.

The importance of the literature of freedom can scarcely be questioned. Without help or guidance people submit to aversive conditions in the most surprising way. This is true even when the aversive conditions are part of the natural environment. Darwin observed, for example, that the Fuegians seemed to make no effort to protect themselves from the cold; they wore only scant clothing and made little use of it against the weather. And one of the most striking things about the struggle for freedom from intentional control is how often it has been lacking. Many people have submitted to the most obvious religious, governmental, and economic controls for centuries, striking for freedom only sporadically, if at all. The literature of freedom has made an essential contribution to the elimination of many aversive practices in government, religion, education, family life, and the production of goods.

The contributions of the literature of freedom, however, are not usually described in these terms. Some traditional theories could conceivably be said to define freedom as the absence of aversive control, but the emphasis has been on how that condition *feels.* Other traditional theories could conceivably be said to define freedom as a person's condition when he is behaving under nonaversive control, but the emphasis has been upon a state of mind associated with doing what one wants. According to John Stuart Mill, "Liberty consists in doing what one desires." The literature of freedom has been important in changing practice (it has changed practices whenever it has had any effect whatsoever), but it has nevertheless defined its task as the changing of states of mind and feelings. Freedom is a "possession." A person escapes from or destroys the power of a controller in order to feel free, and once he feels free and can do what he desires, no further action is recommended and none is prescribed by the literature of freedom, except perhaps eternal vigilance lest control be resumed.

The feeling of freedom becomes an unreliable guide to action as soon as would-be controllers turn to nonaversive measures, as they are likely to do to avoid the problems raised when the controllee escapes or attacks. Nonaversive measures are not as conspicuous as aversive and are likely to be acquired more slowly, but they have obvious advantages which promote their use. Productive labor, for example, was once the result of punishment: the slave worked to avoid the consequences of not working. Wages exemplify a different principle; a person is paid when he behaves in a given way so that he will continue to behave in that way. Although it has long been recognized that rewards have useful effects, wage systems have evolved slowly. In the nineteenth century it was believed that an industrial society required a hungry labor force; wages would be effective only if the hungry worker could exchange them for food. By making labor less aversive—for instance, by shortening hours and improving conditions—it has been possible to get men to work for lesser rewards. Until recently teaching was almost entirely aversive: the student studied to escape the consequences of not studying, but nonaversive techniques are gradually being discovered and used. The skillful parent learns to reward a child for good behavior rather than punish him for bad. Religious agencies move from the threat of hellfire to an emphasis on God's love, and governments turn from aversive sanctions to various kinds of inducements, as we shall note again shortly. What the layman calls a reward is a "positive reinforcer," the effects of which have been exhaustively studied in the experimental analysis of operant behavior. The effects are not as easily recognized as those of aversive contingencies because they tend to be deferred, and applications have therefore been delayed, but techniques as powerful as the older aversive techniques are now available.

A problem arises for the defender of freedom when the behavior generated by positive reinforcement has deferred aversive consequences. This is particularly likely to be the case when the process is used in intentional control, where the gain to the controller usually means a loss to the controllee. What are called conditioned positive reinforcers can often be used with deferred aversive results. Money is an example. It is reinforcing only after it has been exchanged for reinforcing things, but it can be used as a reinforcer when exchange is impossible. A counterfeit bill, a bad check, a stopped check, or an unkept promise are conditioned reinforcers, although aversive consequences are usually quickly discovered. The archetypal pattern is the gold brick. Countercontrol quickly follows: we escape from or attack those who misuse conditioned reinforcers in this way. But the misuse of many social reinforcers often goes unnoticed. Personal attention, approval, and affection are usually reinforcing only if there has been some connection with already effective reinforcers, but they can be used when a connection is lacking. The simulated approval and affection with which parents and teachers are often urged to solve behavior problems are counterfeit. So are flattery, backslapping, and many other ways of "winning friends."

Genuine reinforcers can be used in ways which have aversive consequences. A government may prevent defection by making life more interesting—by providing bread and circuses and by encouraging sports, gambling, the use of alcohol and other drugs, and various kinds of sexual behavior, where the effect is to keep people within reach of aversive sanctions. The Goncourt brothers noted the rise of pornography in the France of their day: "Pornographic literature," they wrote, "serves a Bas-Empire . . . one tames a people as one tames lions, by masturbation."

Genuine positive reinforcement can also be misused because the sheer quantity of reinforcers is not proportional to the effect on behavior. Reinforcement is usually only intermittent, and the schedule of reinforcement is more important than the amount received. Certain schedules generate a great deal of behavior in return for very little reinforcement, and the possibility has naturally not been overlooked by would-be controllers. Two examples of schedules which are easily used to the disadvantage of those reinforced may be noted.

In the incentive system known as piece-work pay, the worker is paid a given amount for each unit of work performed. The system seems to guarantee a balance between the goods produced and the money received. The schedule is attractive to management, which can calculate labor costs in advance, and also to the worker, who can control the amount he earns. This so-called "fixed-ratio" schedule of reinforcement can, however, be used to generate a great deal of behavior for very little return. It induces the worker to work fast, and the ratio can then be "stretched"—that is, more work can be demanded for each unit of pay without running the risk that the worker will stop working. His ultimate condition—hard work with very little pay—may be acutely aversive.

A related schedule, called variable-ratio, is at the heart of all gambling systems. A gambling enterprise pays people for giving it money—that is, it pays them when they make bets. But it pays on a kind of schedule which sustains betting even though, in the long run, the amount paid is less than the amount wagered. At first the mean ratio may be favorable to the bettor; he "wins." But the ratio can be stretched in such a way that he continues to play even when he begins to lose. The stretching may be accidental (an early run of good luck which grows steadily worse may create a dedicated gambler), or the ratio may be deliberately stretched by someone who controls the odds. In the long run the "utility" is negative: the gambler loses all.

It is difficult to deal effectively with deferred aversive consequences because they do not occur at a time when escape or attack is feasible—when, for example, the controller can be identified or is within reach. But the immediate reinforcement is positive and goes unchallenged. The problem to be solved by those who are concerned with freedom is to create immediate aversive consequences. A classical problem concerns "self-control." A person eats too much and gets sick but survives to eat too much again. Delicious food or the behavior evoked by it must be made sufficiently aversive so that a person will "escape from it" by not eating it. (It might be thought that he can escape from it only before eating it, but the Romans escaped afterward through the use of a vomitorium.) Current aversive stimuli may be conditioned. Something of the sort is done when eating too much is called wrong, gluttonous, or sinful. Other kinds of behavior to be suppressed may be declared illegal and punished accordingly. The more deferred the aversive consequences the greater the problem. It has taken a great deal of "engineering" to bring the ultimate consequences of smoking cigarettes to bear on the behavior. A fascinating hobby, a sport, a love affair, or a large salary may compete with activities which would be more reinforcing in the long run, but the run is too long to make countercontrol possible. That is why countercontrol is exerted, if at all, only by those who suffer aversive consequences but are not subject to positive reinforcement. Laws are passed against gambling, unions oppose piece-work pay, and no one is allowed to pay young children to work for them or to pay anyone for engaging in immoral behavior, but these measures may be strongly opposed by those whom they are designed to protect. The gambler objects to antigambling laws and the alcoholic to any kind of prohibition; and a child or prostitute may be willing to work for what is offered.

The literature of freedom has never come to grips with techniques of control which do not generate escape or counterattack because it has dealt with the problem in terms of states of mind and feelings. In his book *Sovereignty,* Bertrand de Jouvenel quotes two important figures in that literature. According to Leibnitz, "Liberty consists in the power to do what one wants to do," and according to Voltaire, "When I can do what I want to do, there is my liberty for me." But both writers add a concluding phrase: Leibnitz,". . . or in the power to want what can be got," and Voltaire, more candidly, ". . . but I can't help wanting what I do want." Jouvenel relegates these comments to a footnote, saying that the power to want is a matter of "interior liberty" (the freedom of the inner man!) which falls outside the "gambit of freedom."

A person wants something if he acts to get it when the occasion arises. A person who says "I want something to eat" will presumably eat when something becomes available. If he says "I want to get warm," he will presumably move into a warm place when he can. These acts have been reinforced in the past by whatever was wanted. What a person *feels* when he feels himself wanting something depends upon the circumstances. Food is reinforcing only in a state of deprivation, and a person who wants something to eat may feel parts of that state—for example, hunger pangs. A person who wants to get warm presumably feels cold. Conditions associated with a high probability of responding may also be felt, together with aspects of the present occasion which are similar to those of past occasions upon which behavior has been reinforced. Wanting is not, however, a feeling, nor is a feeling the reason a person acts to get what he wants. Certain contingencies have raised the probability of behavior and at the same time have created conditions which may be felt. Freedom is a matter of contingencies of reinforcement, not of the feelings the contingencies generate. The distinction is particularly important when the contingencies do not generate escape or counter-attack.

The uncertainty which surrounds the countercontrol of nonaversive measures is easily exemplified. In the 1930's it seemed necessary to cut agricultural produc-tion. The Agricultural Adjustment Act authorized the Secretary of Agriculture to make "rental or benefit payments" to farmers who agreed to produce less—to pay the farmers, in fact, what they would have made on the food they agreed not to produce. It would have been unconstitutional to *compel* them to reduce produc-tion, but the government argued that it was merely inviting them to do so. But the Supreme Court recognized that positive inducement can be as irresistible as aver-sive measures when it ruled that "the power to confer or withhold unlimited ben-efit is the power to coerce or destroy." The decision was later reversed, however, when the Court ruled that "to hold that motive or temptation is equivalent to coercion is to plunge the law into endless difficulties." We are considering some of these difficulties.

The same issue arises when a government runs a lottery in order to raise rev-enue to reduce taxes. The government takes the same amount of money from its citizens in both cases, though not necessarily from the same citizens. By running a lottery it avoids certain unwanted consequences: people escape from heavy tax-ation by moving away or they counterattack by throwing a government which imposes new taxes out of office. A lottery, taking advantage of a stretched vari-able-ratio schedule of reinforcement, has neither of these effects. The only opposi-tion comes from those who in general oppose gambling enterprises and who are themselves seldom gamblers.

A third example is the practice of inviting prisoners to volunteer for possibly dangerous experiments—for example, on new drugs—in return for better living conditions or shortened sentences. Everyone would protest if the prisoners were forced to participate, but are they really free when positively reinforced, particu-larly when the condition to be improved or the sentence to be shortened has been imposed by the state?

The issue often arises in more subtle forms. It has been argued, for example, that uncontrolled contraceptive services and abortion do not "confer unrestricted freedom to reproduce or not to reproduce because they cost time and money." Impoverished members of society should be given compensation if they are to have a truly "free choice." If the just compensation exactly offsets the time and money needed to practice birth control, then people will indeed be free of the control exerted by the loss of time and money, but whether or not they then have children will still depend upon other conditions which have not been specified. If a nation generously reinforces the practices of contraception and abortion, to what extent are its citizens free to have or not to have children?

Uncertainty about positive control is evident in two remarks which often appear in the literature of freedom. It is said that even though behavior is completely determined, it is better that a man "feel free" or "believe that he is free." If this means that it is better to be controlled in ways against which no one revolts, it fails to take account of the possibility of deferred aversive consequences. A second comment seems more appropriate: "It is better to be a conscious slave than a happy one." The word "slave" clarifies the nature of the ultimate consequences being considered: they are exploitative and hence aversive. What the slave is to be conscious of is his misery; and a system of slavery so well designed that it does not breed revolt is the real threat. The literature of freedom has been designed to make men "conscious" of aversive control, but in its choice of methods it has failed to rescue the happy slave.

One of the great figures in the literature of freedom, Jean-Jacques Rousseau, did not fear the power of positive reinforcement. In his remarkable book *Émile* he gave the following advice to teachers:

> Let [the child] believe that he is always in control, though it is always you [the teacher] who really controls. There is no subjugation so perfect as that which keeps the appearance of freedom, for in that way one captures volition itself. The poor baby, knowing nothing, able to do nothing, having learned nothing, is he not at your mercy? Can you not arrange everything in the world which surrounds him? Can you not influence him as you wish? His work, his play, his pleasures, his pains, are not all these in your hands and without his knowing? Doubtless he ought to do only what he wants; but he ought to want to do only what you want him to do; he ought not to take a step which you have not foreseen; he ought not to open his mouth without your knowing what he will say.

Rousseau could take this line because he had unlimited faith in the benevolence of teachers, who would use their absolute control for the good of their students. But, as we shall see later, benevolence is no guarantee against the misuse of power, and very few figures in the history of the struggle for freedom have shown Rousseau's lack of concern. On the contrary, they have taken the extreme position that all control is wrong. In so doing they exemplify a behavioral process called generalization. Many instances of control are aversive, in either their nature or their consequences, and hence all instances are to be avoided. The Puritans carried the generalization a step further by arguing that most positive reinforcement was wrong, whether or not it was intentionally arranged, just because it occasionally got people into trouble.

The literature of freedom has encouraged escape from or attack upon all controllers. It has done so by making any indication of control aversive. Those who manipulate human behavior are said to be evil men, necessarily bent on exploitation. Control is clearly the opposite of freedom, and if freedom is good, control must be bad. What is overlooked is control which does not have aversive consequences at any time. Many social practices essential to the welfare of the species involve the control of one person by another, and no one can suppress them who has any concern for human achievements. We shall see later that in order to maintain the position that all control is wrong, it has been necessary to disguise or conceal the nature of useful practices, to prefer weak practices just because they can be disguised or concealed, and—a most extraordinary result indeed!—to perpetuate punitive measures.

The problem is to free men, not from control, but from certain kinds of control, and it can be solved only if our analysis takes all consequences into account. How people feel about control, before or after the literature of freedom has worked on their feelings, does not lead to useful distinctions.

Were it not for the unwarranted generalization that all control is wrong, we should deal with the social environment as simply as we deal with the nonsocial. Although technology has freed men from certain aversive features of the environment, it has not freed them from the environment. We accept the fact that we depend upon the world around us, and we simply change the nature of the dependency. In the same way, to make the social environment as free as possible of aversive stimuli we do not need to destroy that environment or escape from it; we need to redesign it.

Man's struggle for freedom is not due to a will to be free, but to certain behavioral processes characteristic of the human organism, the chief effect of which is the avoidance of or escape from so-called "aversive" features of the environment. Physical and biological technologies have been mainly concerned with natural aversive stimuli; the struggle for freedom is concerned with stimuli intentionally arranged by other people. The literature of freedom has identified the other people and has proposed ways of escaping from them or weakening or destroying their power. It has been successful in reducing the aversive stimuli used in intentional control, but it has made the mistake of defining freedom in terms of states of mind or feelings, and it has therefore not been able to deal effectively with techniques of control which do not breed escape or revolt but nevertheless have aversive consequences. It has been forced to brand all control as wrong and to misrepresent many of the advantages to be gained from a social environment. It is unprepared for the next step, which is not to free men from control but to analyze and change the kinds of control to which they are exposed.

E. O. WILSON
Contemporary Biologist

The Morality of the Gene*

Camus said that the only serious philosophical question is suicide. That is wrong even in the strict sense intended. The biologist, who is concerned with questions

---

of physiology and evolutionary history, realizes that self-knowledge is constrained and shaped by the emotional control centers in the hypothalamus and limbic system of the brain. These centers flood our consciousness with all the emotions—hate, love, guilt, fear, and others—that are consulted by ethical philosophers who wish to intuit the standards of good and evil. What, we are then compelled to ask, made the hypothalamus and limbic system? They evolved by natural selection. That simple biological statement must be pursued to explain ethics and ethical philosophers, if not epistemology and epistemologists, at all depths. Self-existence, or the suicide that terminates it, is not the central question of philosophy. The hypothalamic-limbic complex automatically denies such logical reduction by countering it with feelings of guilt and altruism. In this one way the philosopher's own emotional control centers are wiser than his solipsist consciousness, "knowing" that in evolutionary time the individual organism counts for almost nothing. In a Darwinist sense the organism does not live for itself. Its primary function is not even to reproduce other organisms; it reproduces genes, and it serves as their temporary carrier. Each organism generated by sexual reproduction is a unique, accidental subset of all the genes constituting the species. Natural selection is the process whereby certain genes gain representation in the following generations superior to that of other genes located at the same chromosome positions. When new sex cells are manufactured in each generation, the winning genes are pulled apart and reassembled to manufacture new organisms that, on the average, contain a higher proportion of the same genes. But the individual organism is only their vehicle, part of an elaborate device to preserve and spread them with the least possible biochemical perturbation. Samuel Butler's famous aphorism that the chicken is only an egg's way of making another egg has been modernized: the organism is only DNA's way of making more DNA. More to the point, the hypothalamus and limbic system are engineered to perpetuate DNA.

In the process of natural selection, then, any device that can insert a higher proportion of certain genes into subsequent generations will come to characterize the species. One class of such devices promotes prolonged individual survival. Another promotes superior mating performance and care of the resulting offspring. As more complex social behavior by the organism is added to the genes' techniques for replicating themselves, altruism becomes increasingly prevalent and eventually appears in exaggerated forms. This brings us to the central theoretical problem of sociobiology: how can altruism, which by definition reduces personal fitness, possibly evolve by natural selection? The answer is kinship: if the genes causing the altruism are shared by two organisms because of common descent, and if the altruistic act by one organism increases the joint contribution of these genes to the next generation, the propensity to altruism will spread through the gene pool. This occurs even though the altruist makes less of a solitary contribution to the gene pool as the price of its altruistic act.

To his own question "Does the Absurd dictate death?" Camus replied that the struggle toward the heights is itself enough to fill a man's heart. This arid judgment is probably correct, but it makes little sense except when closely examined in the light of evolutionary theory. The hypothalamic-limbic complex of a highly social species, such as man, "knows," or more precisely it has been programmed to perform as if it knows, that its underlying genes will be proliferated maximally only if it orchestrates behavioral responses that bring into play an efficient mixture of personal survival, reproduction, and altruism. Consequently, the centers of the complex tax the conscious mind with ambivalences whenever the organisms encounter stressful situations. Love joins hate; aggression, fear; expansiveness, withdrawal; and so on—in blends designed not to promote the happiness and survival of the individual, but to favor the maximum transmission of the controlling genes.

The ambivalences stem from counteracting pressures on the units of natural selection. Their genetic consequences will be explored formally later in this book. For the moment suffice it to note that what is good for the individual can be destructive to the family; what preserves the family can be harsh on both the individual and the tribe to which its family belongs; what promotes the tribe can weaken the family and destroy the individual; and so on upward through the permutations of levels of organization. Counteracting selection on these different units will result in certain genes being multiplied and fixed, others lost, and combinations of still others held in static proportions. According to present theory, some of the genes will produce emotional states that reflect the balance of counteracting selection forces at the different levels.

I have raised a problem in ethical philosophy in order to characterize the essence of sociobiology. Sociobiology is defined as the systematic study of the biological basis of all social behavior. For the present it focuses on animal societies, their population structure, castes, and communication, together with all of the physiology underlying the social adaptations. But the discipline is also concerned with the social behavior of early man and the adaptive features of organization in the more primitive contemporary human societies. Sociology *sensu stricto*, the study of human societies at all levels of complexity, still stands apart from sociobiology because of its largely structuralist and nongenetic approach. It attempts to explain human behavior primarily by empirical description of the outermost phenotypes and by unaided intuition, without reference to evolutionary explanations in the true genetic sense. It is most successful, in the way descriptive taxonomy and ecology have been most successful, when it provides a detailed description of particular phenomena and demonstrates first-order correlations with features of the environment. Taxonomy and ecology, however, have been reshaped entirely during the past forty years by integration into neo-Darwinist evolutionary theory—the "Modern Synthesis," as it is often called—in which each phenomenon is weighed for its adaptive significance and then related to the basic principles of population genetics. It may not be too much to say that sociology and the other social sciences, as well as the humanities, are the last branches of biology waiting to be included in the Modern Synthesis. One of the functions of sociobiology, then, is to reformulate the foundations of the social sciences in a way that draws these subjects into the Modern Synthesis. Whether the social sciences can be truly biologicized in this fashion remains to be seen.

This book is a condensation of *Sociobiology: The New Synthesis*, which made an attempt to codify sociobiology into a branch of evolutionary biology and particularly of modern population biology. I believe that the subject has an adequate richness of detail and aggregate of self-sufficient concepts to be ranked as coordinate with such disciplines as molecular biology and developmental biology. In the past its development has been slowed by too close an identification with ethology and behavioral physiology. In the view presented here, the new sociobiology should be compounded of roughly equal parts of invertebrate zoology, vertebrate zoology, and population biology. Biologists have always been intrigued by comparisons between societies of invertebrates, especially insect societies, and those of vertebrates. They have dreamed of identifying the common properties of such disparate units in a way that would provide insight into all aspects of social evolution, including that of man. The goal can be expressed in modern terms as follows: when the same parameters and quantitative theory are used to analyze both termite colonies and troops of rhesus macaques, we will have a unified science of sociobiology. This may seem an impossibly difficult task. But as my own studies have advanced, I have been increasingly impressed with the functional similarities between invertebrate and vertebrate societies and less so with the structural differences that seem, at first glance, to constitute such an immense gulf between them. Consider for a moment termites and monkeys. Both are formed into cooperative groups that occupy territories. The group members communicate hunger, alarm, hostility, caste status or rank, and reproductive status among themselves by means of something on the order of 10 to 100 nonsyntactical signals. Individuals are intensely aware of the distinction between groupmates and nonmembers. Kinship plays an important role in group structure and probably served as a chief generative force of sociality in the first place. In both kinds of society there is a well-marked division of labor, although in the insect society there is a much stronger reproductive component. The details of organization have been evolved by an evolutionary optimization process of unknown precision, during which some measure of added fitness was given to individuals with cooperative tendencies—at least toward relatives. The fruits of cooperativeness depend upon the particular conditions of the environment and are available to only a minority of animal species during the course of their evolution.

This comparison may seem facile, but it is out of such deliberate oversimplification that the beginnings of a general theory are made. The formulation of a theory of sociobiology constitutes, in my opinion, one of the great manageable problems of biology for the next twenty or thirty years. Its central precept is that the evolution of social behavior can be fully comprehended only through an understanding, first, of demography, which yields the vital information concerning population growth and age structure, and, second, of the genetic structure of the populations, which tells us what we need to know about effective population size in the genetic sense, the coefficients of relationship within the societies, and the amounts of gene flow between them. The principal goal of a general theory of sociobiology should be an ability to predict features of social organization from a knowledge of these population parameters combined with information on the behavioral constraints imposed by the genetic constitution of the species. It will be a chief task of evolutionary ecology, in turn, to derive the population parameters from a knowledge of the evolutionary history of the species and of the environment in which the most recent segment of that history unfolded. The most important feature of the prolegomenon, then, is the sequential relation between evolutionary studies, ecology, population biology, and sociobiology.

In stressing the tightness of this sequence, however, I do not wish to underrate the filial relationship that sociobiology has had in the past with the remainder of behavioral biology. Although behavioral biology is traditionally spoken of as if it were a unified subject, it is now emerging as two distinct disciplines centered on neurophysiology and on sociobiology, respectively. The conventional wisdom also speaks of ethology, which is the naturalistic study of whole patterns of animal behavior, and its companion enterprise, comparative psychology, as the central, unifying fields of behavioral biology. They are not; both are destined to be cannibalized by neurophysiology and sensory physiology from one end and sociobiology and behavioral ecology from the other.

I hope not too many scholars in ethology and psychology will be offended by this vision of the future of behavioral biology. It seems to be indicated both by the extrapolation of current events and by consideration of the logical relationship behavioral biology holds with the remainder of science. The future, it seems clear, cannot lie with the ad hoc terminology, crude models, and curve fitting that characterize most of contemporary ethology and comparative psychology. Whole patterns of animal behavior will inevitably be explained within the framework, first, of integrative neurophysiology, which classifies neurons and reconstructs their circuitry, and, second, of sensory physiology, which seeks to characterize the cellular transducers at the molecular level. Endocrinology will continue to play a peripheral role, since it is concerned with the cruder tuning devices of nervous activity. To pass from this level and reach the next really distinct discipline, we must travel all the way up to the society and the population. Not only are the phenomena best described by families of models different from those of cellular and molecular biology, but the explanations become largely evolutionary. There should be nothing surprising in this distinction. It is only a reflection of the larger division that separates the two greater domains of evolutionary biology and functional biology. As Lewontin (1972) has truly said: "Natural selection of the character states themselves is the essence of Darwinism. All else is molecular biology."

IMMANUEL KANT
(1724–1804) German Philosopher

From *Groundwork of the Metaphysics of Morals**

[*Moral Interest and the Vicious Circle.*]
We have at last traced the determinate concept of morality back to the Idea of freedom, but we have been quite unable to demonstrate freedom as something actual

---

*From Immanuel Kant, *Groundwork of the Metaphysics of Morals,* trans. by H.J. Paton (New York: Harper & Row, 1964; reprint of 1948 translation).

in ourselves and in human nature: we saw merely that we must presuppose it if we wish to conceive a being as rational and as endowed with consciousness of his causality in regard to actions—that is, as endowed with a will. Thus we find that on precisely the same ground we must attribute to every being endowed with reason and a will this property of determining himself to action under the Idea of his own freedom.

From the presupposition of this Idea there springs, as we further saw, consciousness of a law of action, the law that subjective principles of action—that is, maxims—must always be adopted in such a way that they can also hold as principles objectively—that is, universally—and can therefore serve for our own enactment of universal law. But why should I subject myself to this principle simply as a rational being and in so doing also subject to it every other being endowed with reason? I am willing to admit that no interest *impels* me to do so since this would not produce a categorical imperative; but all the same I must necessarily *take* an interest in it and understand how this happens; for this "I ought" is properly an "I will" which holds necessarily for every rational being—provided that reason in him is practical without any hindrance. For beings who, like us, are affected also by sensibility—that is, by motives of a different kind—and who do not always act as reason by itself would act, this necessity is expressed as an "I ought," and the subjective necessity is distinct from the objective one.

It looks as if, in our Idea of freedom, we have in fact merely taken the moral law for granted—that is, the very principle of the autonomy of the will—and have been unable to give an independent proof of its reality and objective necessity. In that case we should still have made a quite considerable gain inasmuch as we should at least have formulated the genuine principle more precisely than has been done before. As regards its validity, however, and the practical necessity of subjecting ourselves to it we should have got no further. Why must the validity of our maxim as a universal law be a condition limiting our action? On what do we base the worth we attach to this way of acting—a worth supposed to be so great that there cannot be any interest which is higher? And how does it come about that in this alone man believes himself to feel his own personal worth, in comparison with which that of a pleasurable or painful state is to count as nothing? To these questions we should have been unable to give any sufficient answer.

We do indeed find ourselves able to take an interest in a personal characteristic which carries with it no interest in mere states, but only makes us fit to have a share in such states in the event of their being distributed by reason. That is to say, the mere fact of deserving happiness can by itself interest us even without the motive of getting a share in this happiness. Such a judgement, however, is in fact merely the result of the importance we have already assumed to belong to moral laws (when we detach ourselves from every empirical interest by our Idea of freedom). But on this basis we can as yet have no insight into the principle that we ought to detach ourselves from such interest—that is, that we ought to regard ourselves as free in our actions and yet to hold ourselves bound by certain laws in order to find solely in our own person a worth which can compensate us for the loss of everything that makes our state valuable. We do not see how this is possible nor consequently *how the moral law can be binding*.

In this, we must frankly admit, there is shown a kind of circle, from which, as it seems, there is no way of escape. In the order of efficient causes we take ourselves to be free so that we may conceive ourselves to be under moral laws in the order of ends; and we then proceed to think of ourselves as subject to moral laws on the ground that we have described our will as free. Freedom and the will's enactment of its own laws are indeed both autonomy—and therefore are reciprocal concepts—but precisely for this reason one of them cannot be used to explain the other or to furnish its ground. It can at most be used for logical purposes in order to bring seemingly different ideas of the same object under a single concept (just as different fractions of equal value can be reduced to their simplest expression). . . .

The Extreme Limit of Practical Philosophy

[*The Antinomy of Freedom and Necessity.*]

All men think of themselves as having a free will. From this arise all judgements that actions are such as *ought to have been done,* although they *have not been done.* This freedom is no concept of experience, nor can it be such, since it continues to hold although experience shows the opposite of those requirements which are regarded as necessary under the presupposition of freedom. On the other hand, it is just as necessary that everything which takes place should be infallibly determined in accordance with the laws of nature; and this necessity of nature is likewise no concept of experience, precisely because it carries with it the concept of necessity and so of *a priori* knowledge. The concept of nature is, however, confirmed by experience and must inevitably be presupposed if experience—that is, coherent knowledge of sensible objects in accordance with universal laws—is to be possible. Hence, while freedom is only an *Idea* of reason whose objective reality is in itself questionable, nature is a *concept of the understanding,* which proves, and must necessarily prove, its reality in examples from experience.

From this there arises a dialectic of reason, since the freedom attributed to the will seems incompatible with the necessity of nature; and although at this parting of the ways reason finds the road of natural necessity much more beaten and serviceable than that of freedom for *purposes of speculation,* yet for *purposes of action* the footpath of freedom is the only one on which we can make use of reason in our conduct. Hence to argue freedom away is as impossible for the most abstruse philosophy as it is for the most ordinary human reason. Reason must therefore suppose that no genuine contradiction is to be found between the freedom and the natural necessity ascribed to the very same human actions; for it can abandon the concept of nature as little as it can abandon that of freedom.

All the same we must at least get rid of this seeming contradiction in a convincing fashion—although we shall never be able to comprehend how freedom is possible. For if the thought of freedom is self-contradictory or incompatible with nature—a concept which is equally necessary—freedom would have to be completely abandoned in favour of natural necessity.

[*The Two Standpoints.*]

From this contradiction it would be impossible to escape if the subject who believes himself free were to conceive himself *in the same sense,* or *in precisely the same relationship,* when he calls himself free as when he holds himself subject to the law of nature in respect of the same action. Hence speculative philosophy has the unavoidable task of showing at least this—that its illusion about the contradiction rests on our conceiving man in one sense and relationship when we call him free and in another when we consider him, as a part of nature, to be subject to nature's laws; and that both characteristics not merely *can* get on perfectly well together, but must be conceived as *necessarily combined* in the same subject; for otherwise we could not explain why we should trouble reason with an Idea which—even if it can *without contradiction* be combined with a different and adequately verified concept—does yet involve us in a business which puts reason to sore straits in its theoretical use. This duty is incumbent on speculative philosophy solely in order that it may clear a path for practical philosophy. Thus it is not left to the discretion of philosophers whether they will remove the seeming contradiction or leave it untouched; for in the latter case the theory on this topic becomes *bonum vacans,*[1] of which the fatalist can justifiably take possession and can chase all morality out of its supposed property, which it has no title to hold.

Nevertheless at this point we cannot yet say that the boundary of practical philosophy begins. For practical philosophy has no part in the settlement of this controversy: it merely requires speculative reason to bring to an end the dissension in which it is entangled on theoretical questions so that practical reason may have peace and security from external attacks capable of bringing into dispute the territory it seeks to cultivate.

The lawful title to freedom of will claimed even by ordinary human reason is grounded on a consciousness—and an accepted presupposition—that reason is independent of purely subjective determination by causes which collectively make up all that belongs to sensation and comes under the general name of sensibility. In thus regarding himself as intelligence man puts himself into another order of things, and into relation with determining causes of quite another sort, when he conceives himself as intelligence endowed with a will and consequently with causality, than he does when he perceives himself as a phenomenon in the sensible world (which he actually is as well) and subjects his causality to external determination in accordance with laws of nature. He then becomes aware at once that both of these can, and indeed must, take place at the same time; for there is not the slightest contradiction in holding that a *thing as an appearance* (as belonging to the sensible world) is subject to certain laws of which it is independent *as a thing* or being *in itself.* That he must represent and conceive himself in this double way rests, as regards the first side, on consciousness of himself as an object affected through the senses; as concerns the second side, on consciousness of himself as intelligence—that is, as independent of sensuous impressions in his use of reason (and so as belonging to the intelligible world).

Hence it comes about that man claims for himself a will which does not impute to itself anything appertaining merely to his desires and inclinations; and, on the other hand, that he conceives as possible through its agency, and indeed as necessary, actions which can be done only by disregarding all desires and incitements of sense. The causality of such actions lies in man as intelligence and in the laws of such effects and actions as accord with the principles of an intelligible world. Of that world he knows no more than this—that in it reason alone, and indeed

[1] unoccupied property

pure reason independent of sensibility, is the source of law; and also that since he is there his proper self only as intelligence (while as a human being he is merely an appearance of himself), these laws apply to him immediately and categorically. It follows that incitements from desires and impulses (and therefore from the whole sensible world of nature) cannot impair the laws which govern his will as intelligence. Indeed he does not answer for the former nor impute them to his proper self—that is, to his will; but he does impute to himself the indulgence which he would show them if he admitted their influence on his maxims to the detriment of the rational laws governing his will.

[*There Is No Knowledge of the Intelligible World.*]

By *thinking* itself into the intelligible world practical reason does not overstep its limits in the least: it would do so only if it sought to *intuit or feel itself* into that world. The thought in question is a merely negative one with respect to the sensible world: it gives reason no laws for determining the will and is positive only in this one point, that it combines freedom as a negative characteristic with a (positive) power as well—and indeed with a causality of reason called by us "a will"— a power so to act that the principle of our actions may accord with the essential character of a rational cause, that is, with the condition that the maxim of these actions should have the validity of a universal law. If practical reason were also to import an *object of the will*—that is, a motive of action—from the intelligible world, it would overstep its limits and pretend to an acquaintance with something of which it has no knowledge. The concept of the intelligible world is thus only *a point of view* which reason finds itself constrained to adopt outside appearances *in order to conceive itself as practical.* To conceive itself thus would not be possible if the influences of sensibility were able to determine man; but it is none the less necessary so far as we are not to deny him consciousness of himself as intelligence and consequently as a rational cause which is active by means of reason—that is, which is free in its operation. This thought admittedly carries with it the Idea of an order and a legislation different from that of the mechanism of nature appropriate to the world of sense. It makes necessary the concept of an intelligible world (that is, of the totality of rational beings as things in themselves); but it makes not the slightest pretension to do more than conceive such a world with respect to its *formal* condition—to conceive it, that is, as conforming to the condition that the maxim of the will should have the universality of a law, and so as conforming to the autonomy of the will, which alone is compatible with freedom. In contrast with this all laws determined by reference to an object give us heteronomy, which can be found only in laws of nature and can apply only to the world of sense.

[*There Is No Explanation of Freedom.*]

Reason would overstep all its limits if it took upon itself to *explain how* pure reason can be practical. This would be identical with the task of explaining *how freedom is possible.*

We are unable to explain anything unless we can bring it under laws which can have an object given in some possible experience. Freedom, however, is a mere Idea: its objective validity can in no way be exhibited by reference to laws of nature and consequently cannot be exhibited in any possible experience. Thus the Idea of freedom can never admit of full comprehension, or indeed of insight, since it can never by any analogy have an example falling under it. It holds only as a necessary presupposition of reason in a being who believes himself to be conscious of a will—that is, of a power distinct from mere appetition (a power, namely, of determining himself to act as intelligence and consequently to act in accordance with laws of reason independently of natural instincts). But where determination by laws of nature comes to an end, all *explanation* comes to an end as well. Nothing is left but *defence*—that is, to repel the objections of those who profess to have seen more deeply into the essence of things and on this ground audaciously declare freedom to be impossible. We can only show them that their pretended discovery of a contradiction in it consists in nothing but this: in order to make the law of nature apply to human actions they have necessarily had to consider man as an appearance; and now that they are asked to conceive him, *qua* intelligence, as a thing in himself as well, they continue to look upon him as an appearance in this respect also. In that case, admittedly, to exempt man's causality (that is, his will) from all the natural laws of the sensible world would, in one and the same subject, give rise to a contradiction. The contradiction would fall away if they were willing to reflect and to admit, as is reasonable, that things in themselves (although hidden) must lie behind appearances as their ground, and that we cannot require the laws of their operations to be identical with those that govern their appearances.

WALTER T. STACE
(1886–1967) British Philosopher

Soft Determinism*

[A] great problem which the rise of scientific naturalism has created for the modern mind concerns the foundations of morality. The old religious foundations have largely crumbled away, and it may well be thought that the edifice built upon them by generations of men is in danger of collapse. A total collapse of moral behavior is, as I pointed out before, very unlikely. For a society in which this occurred could not survive. Nevertheless, the danger to moral standards inherent in the virtual disappearance of their old religious foundations is not illusory.

I shall first discuss the problem of free will, for it is certain that if there is no free will there can be no morality. Morality is concerned with what men ought

*From W. T. Stace, *Religion and the Modern Man* (New York: J. B. Lippincott Company, 1952). Reprinted by permission of Harper & Row, Publishers, Inc.

and ought not to do. But if a man has no freedom to choose what he will do, if whatever he does is done under compulsion, then it does not make sense to tell him that he ought not to have done what he did and that he ought to do something different. All moral precepts would in such case be meaningless. Also if he acts always under compulsion, how can he be held morally responsible for his actions? How can he, for example, be punished for what he could not help doing?

It is to be observed that those learned professors of philosophy or psychology who deny the existence of free will do so only in their professional moments and in their studies and lecture rooms. For when it comes to doing anything practical, even of the most trivial kind, they invariably behave as if they and others were free. They inquire from you at dinner whether you will choose this dish or that dish. They will ask a child why he told a lie, and will punish him for not having chosen the way of truthfulness. All of which is inconsistent with a disbelief in free will. This should cause us to suspect that the problem is not a real one; and this, I believe, is the case. The dispute is merely verbal, and is due to nothing but a confusion about the meanings of words. It is what is now fashionably called a semantic problem.

How does a verbal dispute arise? Let us consider a case which, although it is absurd in the sense that no one would ever make the mistake which is involved in it, yet illustrates the principle which we shall have to use in the solution of the problem. Suppose that someone believed that the word "man" means a certain sort of five-legged animal; in short that "five-legged animal" is the correct *definition* of man. He might then look around the world, and rightly observing that there are no five-legged animals in it, he might proceed to deny the existence of men. This preposterous conclusion would have been reached because he was using an incorrect definition of "man." All you would have to do to show him his mistake would be to give him the correct definition; or at least show him that his definition was wrong. Both the problem and its solution, would, of course, be entirely verbal. The problem of free will, and its solution, I shall maintain, is verbal in exactly the same way. The problem has been created by the fact that learned men, especially philosophers, have assumed an incorrect definition of free will, and then finding that there is nothing in the world which answers to their definition, have denied its existence. As far as logic is concerned, their conclusion is just as absurd as that of the man who denies the existence of men. The only difference is that the mistake in the latter case is obvious and crude, while the mistake which the deniers of free will have made is rather subtle and difficult to detect.

Throughout the modern period, until quite recently, it was assumed, both by the philosophers who denied free will and by those who defended it, that *determinism is inconsistent with free will*. If a man's actions were wholly determined by chains of causes stretching back into the remote past, so that they could be predicted beforehand by a mind which knew all the causes, it was assumed that they could not in that case be free. This implies that a certain definition of actions done from free will was assumed, namely that they are actions *not* wholly determined by causes or predictable beforehand. Let us shorten this by saying that free will was defined as meaning indeterminism. This is the incorrect definition which has led to the denial of free will. As soon as we see what the true definition is we shall find that the question whether the world is deterministic, as Newtonian science implied, or in a measure indeterministic, as current physics teaches, is wholly irrelevant to the problem.

Of course there is a sense in which one can define a word arbitrarily in any way one pleases. But a definition may nevertheless be called correct or incorrect. It is correct if it accords with a *common usage* of the word defined. It is incorrect if it does not. And if you give an incorrect definition, absurd and untrue results are likely to follow. For instance, there is nothing to prevent you from arbitrarily defining a man as a five-legged animal, but this is incorrect in the sense that it does not accord with the ordinary meaning of the word. Also it has the absurd result of leading to a denial of the existence of men. This shows that *common usage is the criterion for deciding whether a definition is correct or not.* And this is the principle which I shall apply to free will. I shall show that indeterminism is not what is meant by the phrase "free will" *as it is commonly used.* And I shall attempt to discover the correct definition by inquiring how the phrase is used in ordinary conversation.

Here are a few samples of how the phrase might be used in ordinary conversation. It will be noticed that they include cases in which the question whether a man acted with free will is asked in order to determine whether he was morally and legally responsible for his acts.

JONES   I once went without food for a week.
SMITH   Did you do that of your own free will?
JONES   No. I did it because I was lost in a desert and could find no
          food.

But suppose that the man who had fasted was Mahatma Gandhi. The conversation might then have gone:

GANDHI   I once fasted for a week.
SMITH   Did you do that of your own free will?
GANDHI   Yes. I did it because I wanted to compel the British Government
          to give India its independence.

Take another case. Suppose that I had stolen some bread, but that I was as truthful as George Washington. Then, if I were charged with the crime in court, some exchange of the following sort might take place:

JUDGE   Did you steal the bread of your own free will?
STACE   Yes. I stole it because I was hungry.

Or in different circumstances the conversation might run:

JUDGE   Did you steal of your own free will?
STACE   No. I stole because my employer threatened to beat me if I
          did not.

At a recent murder trial in Trenton some of the accused had signed confessions, but afterwards asserted that they had done so under police duress. The following exchange might have occurred:

JUDGE   Did you sign the confession of your own free will?
PRISONER   No. I signed it because the police beat me up.

Now suppose that a philosopher had been a member of the jury. We could imagine this conversation taking place in the jury room.

FOREMAN OF   The prisoner says he signed the confession because he
    THE JURY   was beaten, and not of his own free will.
PHILOSOPHER   This is quite irrelevant to the case. There is no such
                 thing as free will.
FOREMAN   Do you mean to say that it makes no difference whether
                 he signed because his conscience made him want to tell
                 the truth or because he was beaten?
PHILOSOPHER   None at all. Whether he was caused to sign by a beating
                 or by some desire of his own—the desire to tell the
                 truth, for example—in either case his signing was
                 causally determined, and therefore in neither case did he
                 act of his own free will. Since there is no such thing as
                 free will, the question whether he signed of his own free
                 will ought not to be discussed by us.

The foreman and the rest of the jury would rightly conclude that the philosopher must be making some mistake. What sort of a mistake could it be? There is only one possible answer. The philosopher must be using the phrase "free will" in some peculiar way of his own which is not the way in which men usually use it when they wish to determine a question of moral responsibility. That is, he must be using an incorrect definition of it as implying action not determined by causes.

Suppose a man left his office at noon, and were questioned about it. Then we might hear this:

JONES   Did you go out of your own free will?
SMITH   Yes. I went out to get my lunch.

But we might hear:

JONES   Did you leave your office of your own free will?
SMITH   No. I was forcibly removed by the police.

We have now collected a number of cases of actions which, in the ordinary usage of the English language, would be called cases in which people have acted of their own free will. We should also say in all these cases that they *chose* to act as they did. We should also say that they could have acted otherwise, if they had chosen. For instance, Mahatma Gandhi was not compelled to fast; he chose to do so. He could have eaten if he had wanted to. When Smith went out to get his lunch, he chose to do so. He could have stayed and done some work, if he had wanted to. We have also collected a number of cases of the opposite kind. They are cases in which men were not able to exercise their free will. They had no choice. They were compelled to do as they did. The man in the desert did not fast of his own free will. He had no choice in the matter. He was compelled to fast because there was nothing for him to eat. And so with the other cases. It ought to be quite easy, by an inspection of these cases, to tell what we ordinarily mean when we say that a man did or did not exercise free will. We ought therefore to be able to extract from them the proper definition of the term. Let us put the cases in a table:

Free Acts	*Unfree Acts*
Gandhi fasting because he wanted to free India.	The man fasting in the desert because there was no food.
Stealing bread because one is hungry.	Stealing because one's employer threatened to beat one.
Signing a confession because one wanted to tell the truth.	Signing because the police beat one.
Leaving the office because one wanted one's lunch.	Leaving because forcibly removed.

It is obvious that to find the correct definition of free acts we must discover what characteristic is common to all the acts in the left-hand column, and is, at the same time, absent from all the acts in the right-hand column. This characteristic which all free acts have, and which no unfree acts have, will be the defining characteristic of free will.

Is being uncaused, or not being determined by causes, the characteristic of which we are in search? It cannot be, because although it is true that all the acts in the right-hand column have causes, such as the beating by the police or the absence of food in the desert, so also do the acts in the left-hand column. Mr. Gandhi's fasting was caused by his desire to free India, the man leaving his office by his hunger, and so on. Moreover there is no reason to doubt that these causes of the free acts were in turn caused by prior conditions, and that these were again the results of causes, and so on back indefinitely into the past. Any physiologist can tell us the causes of hunger. What caused Mr. Gandhi's tremendously powerful desire to free India is no doubt more difficult to discover. But it must have had causes. Some of them may have lain in peculiarities of his glands or brain, others in his past experiences, others in his heredity, others in his education. Defenders of free will have usually tended to deny such facts. But to do so is plainly a case of special pleading, which is unsupported by any scrap of evidence. The only reasonable view is that all human actions, both those which are freely done and those which are not, are either wholly determined by causes, or at least as much determined as other events in nature. It may be true, as the physicists tell us, that nature is not as deterministic as was once thought. But whatever degree of determinism prevails in the world, human actions appear to be as much determined as anything else. And if this is so, it cannot be the case that what distinguishes actions freely chosen from those which are not free is that the latter are determined by causes while the former are not. Therefore, being uncaused or being undetermined by causes, must be an incorrect definition of free will.

What, then, is the difference between acts which are freely done and those which are not? What is the characteristic which is present to all the acts in the left-hand column and absent from all those in the right-hand column? Is it not obvious that, although both sets of actions have causes, the causes of those in the left-hand column are *of a different kind* from the causes of those in the right-hand column? The free acts are all caused by desires, or motives, or by some sort of internal psychological states of the agent's mind. The unfree acts, on the other hand, are all caused by physical forces or physical conditions, outside the agent. Police arrest means physical force exerted from the outside; the absence of food in the desert is a physical condition of the outside world. We may therefore frame the following rough definitions. *Acts freely done are those whose immediate causes are psychological states in the agent. Acts not freely done are those whose immediate causes are states of affairs external to the agent.*

It is plain that if we define free will in this way, then free will certainly exists, and the philosopher's denial of its existence is seen to be what it is—nonsense. For it is obvious that all those actions of men which we should ordinarily attribute to the exercise of their free will, or of which we should say that they freely chose to do them, are in fact actions which have been caused by their own desire, wishes, thoughts, emotions, impulses, or other psychological states.

In applying our definition we shall find that it usually works well, but that there are some puzzling cases which it does not seem exactly to fit. These puzzles can always be solved by paying careful attention to the ways in which words are used, and remembering that they are not always used consistently. I have space for only one example. Suppose that a thug threatens to shoot you unless you give him your wallet, and suppose that you do so. Do you, in giving him your wallet, do so of your own free will or not? If we apply our definition, we find that you acted freely, since the immediate cause of the action was not an actual outside force but the fear of death, which is a psychological cause. Most people, however, would say that you did not act of your own free will but under compulsion. Does this show that our definition is wrong? I do not think so. Aristotle, who gave a solution of the problem of free will substantially the same as ours (though he did not use the term "free will") admitted that there are what he called "mixed" or borderline cases in which it is difficult to know whether we ought to call the acts free or compelled. In the case under discussion, though no actual force was used, the gun at your forehead so nearly approximated to actual force that we tend to say the case was one of compulsion. It is a borderline case.

Here is what may seem like another kind of puzzle. According to our view an action may be free though it could have been predicted beforehand with certainty. But suppose you told a lie, and it was certain beforehand that you would tell it. How could one then say, "You could have told the truth"? The answer is that it is perfectly true that you could have told the truth *if* you had wanted to. In fact you would have done so, for in that case the causes producing your action, namely your desires, would have been different, and would therefore have produced different effects. It is a delusion that predictability and free will are incompatible. This agrees with common sense. For if, knowing your character, I predict that you will act honorably, no one would say when you do act honorably, that this shows you did not do so of your own free will.

Since free will is a condition of moral responsibility, we must be sure that our theory of free will gives a sufficient basis for it. To be held morally responsible for one's actions means that one may be justly punished or rewarded, blamed or praised, for them. But it is not just to punish a man for what he cannot help doing. How can it be just to punish him for an action which it was certain beforehand that he would do? We have not attempted to decide whether, as a matter of fact, all events, including human actions, are completely determined. For that question is irrelevant to the problem of free will. But if we assume for the purposes of argument that complete determinism is true, but that we are nevertheless free, it may then be asked whether such a deterministic free will is compatible with moral responsibility. For it may seem unjust to punish a man for an action which it could have been predicted with certainty beforehand that he would do.

But that determinism is incompatible with moral responsibility is as much a delusion as that it is incompatible with free will. You do not excuse a man for doing a wrong act because, knowing his character, you felt certain beforehand that he would do it. Nor do you deprive a man of a reward or prize because, knowing his goodness or his capabilities, you felt certain beforehand that he would win it.

Volumes have been written on the justification of punishment. But so far as it affects the question of free will, the essential principles involved are quite simple. The punishment of a man for doing a wrong act is justified, either on the ground that it will correct his own character, or that it will deter other people from doing similar acts. The instrument of punishment has been in the past, and no doubt still is, often unwisely used; so that it may often have done more harm than good. But that is not relevant to our present problem. Punishment, if and when it is justified, is justified only on one or both of the grounds just mentioned. The question then is how, if we assume determinism, punishment can correct character or deter people from evil actions.

Suppose that your child develops a habit of telling lies. You give him a mild beating. Why? Because you believe that his personality is such that the usual motives for telling the truth do not cause him to do so. You therefore supply the missing cause, or motive, in the shape of pain and the fear of future pain if he repeats his untrustful behavior. And you hope that a few treatments of this kind will condition him to the habit of truth-telling, so that he will come to tell the truth without the infliction of pain. You assume that his actions are determined by causes, but that the usual causes of truth-telling do not in him produce their usual effects. You therefore supply him with an artificially injected motive, pain and fear, which you think will in the future cause him to speak truthfully.

The principle is exactly the same where you hope, by punishing one man, to deter others from wrong actions. You believe that the fear of punishment will cause those who might otherwise do evil to do well.

We act on the same principle with non-human, and even with inanimate, things, if they do not behave in the way we think they ought to behave. The rose bushes in the garden produce only small and poor blooms, whereas we want large and rich ones. We supply a cause which will produce large blooms, namely fertilizer. Our automobile does not go properly. We supply a cause which will make it go better, namely oil in the works. The punishment for the man, the fertilizer for the plant, and the oil for the car, are all justified by the same principle and in the same way. The only difference is that different kinds of things require different kinds of causes to make them do what they should. Pain may be the appropriate remedy to apply, in certain cases, to human beings, and oil to the machine. It is, of course, of no use to inject motor oil into the boy or to beat the machine.

Thus we see that moral responsibility is not only consistent with determinism, but requires it. The assumption on which punishment is based is that human behavior is causally determined. If pain could not be a cause of truth-telling there would be no justification at all for punishing lies. If human actions and volitions were uncaused, it would be useless either to punish or reward, or indeed to do anything else to correct people's bad behavior. For nothing that you could do would in any way influence them. Thus moral responsibility would entirely disappear. If there were no determinism of human beings at all, their actions would be completely unpredictable and capricious, and therefore irresponsible. And this is in itself a strong argument against the common view of philosophers that free will means being undetermined by causes.

C. A. CAMPBELL
(1897–1974) Scottish Philosopher

Libertarianism*

I

. . . It is something of a truism that in philosophic enquiry the exact formulation of a problem often takes one a long way on the road to its solution. In the case of

*From C. A. Campbell, *On Selfhood and Godhood* (London: Allen & Unwin, 1957).

the Free Will problem I think there is a rather special need of careful formulation. For there are many sorts of human freedom; and it can easily happen that one wastes a great deal of labour in proving or disproving a freedom which has almost nothing to do with the freedom which is at issue in the traditional problem of Free Will. The abortiveness of so much of the argument for and against Free Will in contemporary philosophical literature seems to me due in the main to insufficient pains being taken over the preliminary definition of the problem. . . .

Fortunately we can at least make a beginning with a certain amount of confidence. It is not seriously disputable that the kind of freedom in question is the freedom which is commonly recognized to be in some sense a precondition of moral responsibility. Clearly, it is on account of this integral connection with moral responsibility that such exceptional importance has always been felt to attach to the Free Will problem. But in what precise sense is free will a precondition of moral responsibility, and thus a postulate of the moral life in general? This is an exceedingly troublesome question; but until we have satisfied ourselves about the answer to it, we are not in a position to state, let alone decide, the question whether "Free Will" in its traditional, ethical, significance is a reality. . . .

The first point to note is that the freedom at issue (as indeed the very name "Free *Will* Problem" indicates) pertains primarily not to overt acts but to inner acts. The nature of things has decreed that, save in the case of one's self it is only overt acts which one can directly observe. But a very little reflection serves to show that in our moral judgments upon others their overt acts are regarded as significant only in so far as they are the expression of inner acts. We do not consider the acts of a robot to be morally responsible acts; nor do we consider the acts of a man to be so save in so far as they are distinguishable from those of a robot by reflecting an inner life of choice. Similarly, from the other side, if we are satisfied (as we may on occasion be, at least in the case of ourselves) that a person has definitely elected to follow a course which he believes to be wrong, but has been prevented by external circumstances from translating his inner choice into an overt act, we still regard him as morally blameworthy. Moral freedom, then pertains to *inner* acts.

The next point seems at first sight equally obvious and uncontroversial; but, as we shall see, it has awkward implications if we are in real earnest with it (as almost nobody is). It is the simple point that the act must be one of which the person judged can be regarded as the *sole* author. It seems plain enough that if there are any *other* determinants of the act, external to the self, to that extent the act is not an act which the *self* determines, and to that extent not an act for which the self can be held morally responsible. The self is only part-author of the act, and his moral responsibility can logically extend only to those elements within the act (assuming for the moment that these can be isolated) of which he is the *sole* author. . . .

Thirdly, we come to a point over which much recent controversy has raged. We may approach it by raising the following question. Granted an act of which the agent is sole author, does this "sole authorship" suffice to make the act a morally free act? We may be inclined to think that it does, until we contemplate the possibility that an act of which the agent is sole author might conceivably occur as a necessary expression of the agent's nature; the way in which, e.g. some philosophers have supposed the Divine act of creation to occur. This consideration excites a legitimate doubt; for it is far from easy to see how a person can be regarded as a proper subject for moral praise or blame in respect of an act which he *cannot help* performing—even if it be his own "nature" which necessitates it. Must we not recognize it as a condition of the morally free act that the agent "could have acted otherwise" than he in fact did? It is true, indeed, that we sometimes praise or blame a man for an act about which we are prepared to say, in the light of our knowledge of his established character, that he "could no other." But I think that a little reflection shows that in such cases we are not praising or blaming the man strictly for what he does *now* (or at any rate we ought not to be), but rather for those past acts of his which have generated the firm habit of mind from which his *present* act follows "necessarily." In other words, our praise and blame, so far as justified, are really retrospective, being directed not to the agent *qua* performing *this* act, but to the agent *qua* performing those past acts which have built up his present character, and in respect to which we presume that he *could* have acted otherwise, that there really *were* open possibilities before him. These cases, therefore, seem to me to constitute no valid exception to what I must take to be the rule, viz. that a man can be morally praised or blamed for an act only if he could have acted otherwise.

Now philosophers today are fairly well agreed that it is a postulate of the morally responsible act that the agent "could have acted otherwise" in *some* sense of that phrase. But sharp differences of opinion have arisen over the way in which the phrase ought to be interpreted. There is a strong disposition to water down its apparent meaning by insisting that it is not (as a postulate of moral responsibility) to be understood as a straightforward categorical proposition, but rather as a disguised hypothetical proposition. All that we really require to be assured of, in order to justify our holding X morally responsible for an act, is, we are told, that X could have acted otherwise *if* he had *chosen* otherwise or perhaps that X could have acted otherwise *if* he had had a different character, or *if* he had been placed in different circumstances.

I think it is easy to understand, and even, in a measure, to sympathise with, the motives which induce philosophers to offer these counterinterpretations. It is not just the fact that "X could have acted otherwise," as a bald categorical statement, is incompatible with the universal sway of causal law—though this is, to some philosophers, a serious stone of stumbling. The more wide-spread objection is that at least it looks as though it were incompatible with that causal continuity of an agent's character with his conduct which is implied when we believe (surely with justice) that we can often tell the sort of thing a man will do from our knowledge of the sort of man he is.

We shall have to make our accounts with that particular difficulty later. At this stage I wish merely to show that neither of the hypothetical propositions suggested—and I think the same could be shown for *any* hypothetical alternative—is an acceptable substitute for the categorical proposition "X could have acted otherwise" as the presupposition of moral responsibility.

Let us look first at the earlier suggestion—"X could have acted otherwise *if* he had chosen otherwise." Now clearly there are a great many acts with regard to which we are entirely satisfied that the agent is thus situated. We are often perfectly sure that—for this is all it amounts to—if X had chosen otherwise, the circumstances presented no external obstacle to the translation of that choice into action. For example, we often have no doubt at all that X, who in point of fact told a lie, could have told the truth *if* he had so chosen. But does our confidence on this score allay all legitimate doubts about whether X is really blameworthy? Does it entail that X is free in the sense required for moral responsibility? Surely not. The obvious question immediately arises: "But *could* X have *chosen* otherwise than he did?" It is doubt about the true answer to *that* question which leads most people to doubt the reality of moral responsibility. Yet on this crucial question the hypothetical proposition which is offered as a sufficient statement of the condition justifying the ascription of moral responsibility gives us no information whatsoever.

Indeed this hypothetical substitute for the categorical "X could have acted otherwise" seems to me to lack all plausibility unless one contrives to forget why it is, after all, that we ever come to feel fundamental doubts about man's moral responsibility. Such doubts are born, surely, when one becomes aware of certain reputable world-views in religion or philosophy, or of certain reputable scientific beliefs, which in their several ways imply that man's actions are necessitated, and thus could not be otherwise than they in fact are. But clearly a doubt so based is not even touched by the recognition that a man could very often act otherwise *if* he so chose. That proposition is entirely compatible with the necessitarian theories which generate our doubt: indeed it is this very compatibility that has recommended it to some philosophers, who are reluctant to give up either moral responsibility or Determinism. The proposition which we *must* be able to affirm if moral praise or blame of X is to be justified is the categorical proposition that X could have acted otherwise because—not if—he could have chosen otherwise; or, since it is essentially the inner side of the act that matters, the proposition simply that X could have chosen otherwise.

For the second of the alternative formulae suggested we cannot spare more than a few moments. But its inability to meet the demands it is required to meet is almost transparent. "X could have acted otherwise," as a statement of a precondition of X's moral responsibility, really means (we are told) "X could have acted otherwise *if* he were differently constituted, or *if* he had been placed in different circumstances." It seems a sufficient reply to this to point out that the person whose moral responsibility is at issue is X; a specific individual, in a specific set of circumstances. It is totally irrelevant to X's moral responsibility that we should be able to say that some person differently constituted from X, or X in a different set of circumstances, could have done something different from what X did. . . .

II

That brings me to the second, and more constructive, part of this lecture. From now on I shall be considering whether it is reasonable to believe that man does in fact possess a free will of the kind specified in the first part of the lecture. If so, just how and where within the complex fabric of the volitional life are we to locate it?—for although free will must presumably belong (if anywhere) to the volitional side of human experience, it is pretty clear from the way in which we have been forced to define it that it does not pertain simply to volition as such; not even to all volitions that are commonly dignified with the name of "choices." It has been, I think, one of the more serious impediments to profitable discussion of the Free Will problem that Libertarians and Determinists alike have so often failed to appreciate the comparatively narrow area within which the free will that is necessary to "save" morality is required to operate. It goes without saying that this failure has been gravely prejudicial to the case for Libertarianism. I attach a good deal of importance, therefore, to the problem of locating free will correctly within the volitional orbit. Its solution forestalls and annuls, I believe, some of the more tiresome clichés of Determinist criticism.

We saw earlier that Common Sense's practice of "making allowances" in its moral judgments for the influence of heredity and environment indicates Common Sense's conviction, both that a just moral judgment must discount determinants of choice over which the agent has no control, and also (since it still accepts moral judgments as legitimate) that *something* of moral relevance survives which can be regarded as genuinely self-originated. We are now to try to discover what this "something" is. And I think we may still usefully take Common Sense as our guide. Suppose one asks the ordinary intelligent citizen *why* he deems it proper to make allowances for X, whose heredity and/or environment are unfortunate. He will tend to reply, I think, in some such terms as these: that X has more and stronger temptations to deviate from what is right than Y or Z, who are normally circumstanced, so that he must put forth a *stronger moral effort* if he is to achieve the same level of external conduct. The intended implication seems to be that X is just as morally praiseworthy as Y or Z *if* he exerts an equivalent moral effort, even though he may not thereby achieve an equal success in conforming his will to the "concrete" demands of duty. And this implies, again, Common Sense's belief that *in moral effort* we have something for which a man is responsible *without qualification*, something that is *not* affected by heredity and environment but depends *solely* upon the self itself.

Now in my opinion Common Sense has here, in principle, hit upon the one and only defensible answer. Here, and here alone, so far as I can see, in the act of deciding whether to put forth or withhold the moral effort required to resist temptation and rise to duty, is to be found an act which is free in the sense required for moral responsibility; an act of which the self is sole author, and of which it is true to say that "it could be" (or, after the event, "could have been") "otherwise." Such is the thesis which we shall now try to establish.

The species of argument appropriate to the establishment of a thesis of this sort should fall, I think, into two phases. First, there should be a consideration of the evidence of the moral agent's own inner experience. What *is* the act of moral decision, and what does it imply, from the standpoint of the actual participant? Since there is no way of knowing the act of moral decision—or for that matter any other form of activity—except by actual participation in it, the evidence of the subject, or agent, is on an issue of this kind of palmary importance. It can hardly, however, be taken as in itself conclusive. For even if that evidence should be overwhelmingly to the effect that moral decision does have the characteristics required by moral freedom, the question is bound to be raised—and in view of considerations from other quarters pointing in a contrary direction is *rightly* raised—Can we *trust* the evidence of inner experience? That brings us to what will be the second phase of the argument. We shall have to go on to show, if we are to make good our case, that the extraneous considerations so often supposed to be fatal to the belief in moral freedom are in fact innocuous to it. . . .

These arguments can, I think, be reduced in principle to no more than two: first, the argument from "predictability"; second, the argument from the alleged meaninglessness of an act supposed to be the self's act and yet not an expression of the self's character. Contemporary criticism of free will seems to me to consist almost exclusively of variations on these two themes. I shall deal with each in turn.

Let us remind ourselves briefly of the setting within which, on our view, free will functions. There is X, the course which we believe we ought to follow, and Y, the course towards which we feel our desire is strongest. The freedom which we ascribe to the agent is the freedom to put forth or refrain from putting forth the moral effort required to resist the pressure of desire and do what he thinks he ought to do.

But then there is surely an immense range of practical situations—covering by far the greater part of life—in which there is no question of a conflict within the self between what he most desires to do and what he thinks he ought to do. Indeed such conflict is a comparatively rare phenomenon for the majority of men. Yet over that whole vast range there is nothing whatever in our version of Libertarianism to prevent our agreeing that character determines conduct. In the absence, real or supposed, of any "moral" issue, what a man chooses will be simply that course which, after such reflection as seems called for, he deems most likely to bring him what he most strongly desires; and that is the same as to say the course to which his present character inclines him.

Over by far the greater area of human choices, then, our theory offers no more barrier to successful prediction on the basis of character than any other theory. For where there is no clash of strongest desire with duty, the free will we are defending has no business. There is just nothing for it to do.

But what about the situations—rare enough though they may be—in which there *is* this clash and in which free will does therefore operate? Does our theory entail that there at any rate, as the critic seems to suppose, "anything may happen"?

Not by any manner of means. In the first place, and by the very nature of the case, the range of the agent's possible choices is bounded by what he thinks he ought to do on the one hand, and what he most strongly desires on the other. The freedom claimed for him is a freedom of decision to make or withhold the effort required to do what he thinks he ought to do. There is no question of a freedom to act in some "wild" fashion, out of all relation to his characteristic beliefs and desires. This so-called "freedom of caprice," so often charged against the Libertarian, is, to put it bluntly, a sheer figment of the critic's imagination, with no *habitat* in serious Libertarian theory. Even in situations where free will does come into play it is perfectly possible, on a view like ours, given the appropriate knowledge of a man's character, to predict within certain limits how he will respond.

I claim, therefore, that the view of free will I have been putting forward is consistent with predictability of conduct on the basis of character over a very wide field indeed. And I make the further claim that that field will cover all the situations in life concerning which there is any empirical evidence that successful prediction is possible.

Let us pass on to consider the second main line of criticism. This is, I think, much the more illuminating of the two, if only because it compels the Libertarian to make explicit certain concepts which are indispensable to him, but which, being desperately hard to state clearly, are apt not to be stated at all. The critic's fundamental point might be stated somewhat as follows:

"Free will as you describe it is completely unintelligible. On your own showing no *reason* can be given, because there just *is* no reason, why a man decides to exert rather than to withhold moral effort, or *vice versa*. But such an act—or more properly, such an 'occurrence'—it is nonsense to speak of as an act of a *self*. If there is nothing in the self's character to which it is, even in principle, in any way traceable, the self has nothing to do with it. Your so-called 'freedom,' therefore, so far from supporting the self's moral responsibility, destroys it as surely as the crudest Determinism could do."

If we are to discuss this criticism usefully, it is important, I think, to begin by getting clear about two different senses of the word "intelligible."

If, in the first place, we mean by an "intelligible" act one whose occurrence is in principle capable of being inferred, since it follows necessarily from something (though we may not know in fact from what), then it is certainly true that the Libertarian's free will is unintelligible. But that is only saying, is it not, that the Libertarian's "free" act is not an act which follows necessarily from something! This can hardly rank as a *criticism* of Libertarianism. It is just a description of it. That there can be nothing unintelligible in *this* sense is precisely what the Determinist has got to *prove*.

Yet it is surprising how often the critic of Libertarianism involves himself in this circular mode of argument. Repeatedly it is urged against the Libertarian, with a great air of triumph, that on this view he can't say *why* I now decide to rise to duty or now decide to follow my strongest desire in defiance of duty. Of course he can't. If he could he wouldn't *be* a Libertarian. To "account for" a "free" act is a contradiction in terms. A free will is *ex hypothesi* the sort of thing of which the request for an *explanation* is absurd. The assumption that an explanation must be in principle possible for the act of moral decision deserves to rank as a classic example of the ancient fallacy of "begging the question."

But the critic usually has in mind another sense of the word "unintelligible." He is apt to take it for granted that an act which is unintelligible in the *above* sense (as the morally free act of the Libertarian undoubtedly is) is unintelligible in the *further* sense that we can attach no meaning to it. And this is an altogether more serious matter. If it could really be shown that the Libertarian's "free will" were unintelligible in this sense of being meaningless, that, for myself at any rate, would be the end of the affair. Libertarianism would have been conclusively refuted.

But it seems to me manifest that this can *not* be shown. The critic has allowed himself, I submit, to become the victim of a widely accepted but fundamentally vicious assumption. He has assumed that whatever is meaningful must exhibit its meaningfulness to those who view it from the standpoint of external observation. Now if one chooses thus to limit one's self to the rôle of external observer, it is, I think, perfectly true that one can attach no meaning to an act which is the act of something we call a "self" and yet follows from nothing in that self's character. But then *why should we* so limit ourselves, when what is under consideration is a subjective activity? For the apprehension of subjective acts there is *another* standpoint available, that of *inner experience*, of the practical consciousness in its actual functioning. If our free will should turn out to be something to which we can attach a meaning from *this* standpoint, no more is required. And no more ought to be expected. For I must repeat that only from the inner standpoint of living experience *could* anything of the nature of "activity" be directly grasped. Observation from without is in the nature of the case impotent to apprehend the active *qua* active. We can from without observe sequences of states. If into these we read activity (as we sometimes do), this can only be on the basis of what we discern in ourselves from the inner standpoint. It follows that if anyone insists upon taking his criterion of the meaningful simply from the standpoint of external observation, he is really deciding in advance of the evidence that the notion of activity, and *a fortiori* the notion of a free will, is "meaningless." He looks for the free act through a medium which is in the nature of the case incapable of revealing it, and then, because inevitably he doesn't find it, he declares that it doesn't exist!

But if, as we surely ought in this context, we adopt the inner standpoint, then (I am suggesting) things appear in a totally different light. From the inner standpoint, it seems to me plain, there is no difficulty whatever in attaching meaning to an act which is the self's act and which nevertheless does not follow from the self's character. So much I claim has been established by the phenomenological analysis, in this and the previous lecture, of the act of moral decision in face of moral temptation. It is thrown into particularly clear relief where the moral decision is to make the moral effort required to rise to duty. For the very function of moral effort, as it appears to the agent engaged in the act, is to enable the self to act against the line of least resistance, against the line to which his character as so far formed most strongly inclines him. But if the self is thus conscious here of *combating* his formed character, he surely cannot possibly suppose that the act, although his own act, *issues from* his formed character? I submit, therefore, that the self knows very well indeed—from the inner standpoint—what is meant by an act which is the *self's* act and which nevertheless does not follow from the self's *character.*

What this implies—and it seems to me to be an implication of cardinal importance for any theory of the self that aims at being more than superficial—is that the nature of the self is for itself something more than just its character as so far formed. The "nature" of the self and what we commonly call the "character" of the self are by no means the same thing, and it is utterly vital that they should not be confused. The "nature" of the self comprehends, but is not without remainder reducible to, its "character"; it must, if we are to be true to the testimony of our experience of it, be taken as including *also* the authentic creative power of fashioning and re-fashioning "character."

PETER VAN INWAGEN

Contemporary Philosopher

On Two Arguments for Compatibilism*

The two most popular arguments for the compatibility of free will and determinism are probably the following.

The *Ethics* Argument[1]

Analysis shows that statements of ability are disguised conditionals. More exactly, the correct analysis of "X could have done A" is "If X had decided (chosen willed. . .) to do A, X would have done A." Therefore, having acted freely—having been able to act otherwise than one in fact did—is compatible with determinism (with the causal determination of one's acts).

The *Mind* Argument

If one's acts were undetermined, they would be "bolts from the blue"; they would no more be *free* acts than they would if they had been caused by the manipulations of one's nervous system by a freakish demon. Therefore, free action is not merely *compatible* with determinism; it *entails* determinism.

I do not believe that it has been noticed that these two arguments are incompatible. That is: if either argument is sound (if its conclusion follows from its premises and if those premises are true), then the other is unsound.

To show this, we must first show that if the premise of the *Ethics* Argument is true, then free will is compatible not only with determinism but with *indeterminism* as well. To show this we need only tell a story having these three features: (1) in the story, an agent acts, and his act is causally undetermined; (2) in the story, his act is free, and (3) if statements of ability are disguised conditionals, then that story is internally consistent.

A story having these features is easy to construct. Suppose that Miss X has been deliberating about whether to tell the truth or to lie. Suppose that she has decided to tell the truth (and that, acting on this decision, she *has* told the truth). Suppose that this event—her having come to a decision to tell the truth—was not determined by earlier events or states: if God created a perfect duplicate of her as she was a moment before she made her decision to tell the truth, and if God placed that duplicate in circumstances identical with her circumstances at that moment, the duplicate might very well decide to lie. Suppose further that if X *had* chosen to lie, she would have lied. It is evident that (i) this story is consistent, and (ii) if "X could have lied" is equivalent to "if X had decided to lie, X would have lied," then the story entails the following three propositions:

---

*Peter van Inwagen, "On Two Arguments for Compatibilism," reprinted from *Analysis* 45 (1985): 161–63.
[1] Compare Inwagen's depiction of these two arguments to Stace's treatment. —ED.

- X told the truth
- X could have lied
- X's telling the truth was causally undetermined.

(I take the first two of these propositions jointly to entail "X told the truth freely.") It would seem that we have told a story with the required features, and have therefore demonstrated that if statements of ability are disguised conditionals, then free will is compatible with indeterminism. (It would seem that we have told a story with the required features, and have therefore demonstrated that if statements of ability are disguised conditionals, then free will is compatible with indeterminism. (It may be objected that there are available more sophisticated analyses of ability-statements as conditionals than the one that figures in the above argument. This is true, but I do not think that the argument would fail if it were reconstructed so as to involve any of these more sophisticated conditional analyses of ability. Of course, one could always offer *this* analysis: "X could have done A" means "If X had decided to do A, X would have done A, and either X's decision to do A or the non-occurrence of a decision by X to do A—whichever of the two in fact occurred—was causally determined." But no one *has* ever offered any such analysis, and I can see no motivation for doing so, other than a desire to devise a version of the *Ethics* argument that is compatible with the *Mind* argument. But what could move anyone to devise a version of the *Ethics* argument that had *that* particular feature? A desire to have available as many arguments for compatibilism as possible?)

The promised conclusion is now easy to demonstrate. If the *Ethics* Argument is sound, then "X could have done A" means "If X had decided to do A, X would have done A." If "X could have done A" means "If X had decided to do A, X would have done A," then (as we have seen) free will is compatible with indeterminism. If the *Mind Argument is sound, then free will entails determinism. If free will entails determinism, then free will is not compatible with indeterminism. Therefore, if either argument is sound, the other is unsound.*

Mind and Body

From *The Extasie*

Where, like a pillow on a bed,
A Pregnant banke swell'd up, to rest
The violets reclining head,
Sat we two, one anothers best.
Our hands were firmely cimented
With a fast balme, which thence did spring,
Our eye-beames twisted, and did thred
Our eyes, upon one double string;
So to 'entergraft our hands, as yet
Was all the meanes to make us one,
And pictures in our eyes to get
Was all our propagation.
As 'twixt two equall Armies, Fate
Suspends uncertaine victorie,
Our soules, (which to advance their state,
Were gone out,) hung 'twixt her, and mee.
And whil'st our soules negotiate there,
Wee like sepulchrall statues lay;
All day, the same our postures were,
And wee said nothing, all the day.

John Donne

ARISTOTLE

(384–322 B.C.) Greek Philosopher

From *On the Soul**

Book II

1. Let the foregoing suffice as our account of the views concerning the soul which have been handed on by our predecessors; let us now dismiss them and make as it were a completely fresh start, endeavouring to give a precise answer to the question, What is soul? i.e. to formulate the most general possible definition of it.

   We are in the habit of recognizing, as one determinate kind of what is, substance, and that in several senses, (*a*) in the sense of matter or that which in itself is not "a this," and (*b*) in the sense of form or essence, which is that precisely in virtue of which a thing is called "a this," and thirdly (*c*) in the sense of that which is compounded of both (*a*) and (*b*). Now matter is potentiality, form actuality; of the latter there are two grades related to one another as e.g. knowledge to the exercise of knowledge.

   Among substances are by general consent reckoned bodies and especially natural bodies; for they are the principles of all other bodies. Of natural bodies some have life in them, others not; by life we mean self-nutrition and growth (with its correlative decay). It follows that every natural body which has life in it is a substance in the sense of a composite.

   But since it is also a *body* of such a kind, viz. having life, the *body* cannot be soul; the body is the subject or matter, not what is attributed to it. Hence the soul must be a substance in the sense of the form of a natural body having life potentially within it. But substance is actuality, and thus soul is the actuality of a body as above characterized. Now the word actuality has two senses corresponding respectively to the possession of knowledge and the actual exercise of knowledge. It is obvious that the soul is actuality in the first sense, viz. that of knowledge as possessed, for both sleeping and waking presuppose the existence of soul, and of these waking corresponds to actual knowing, sleeping to knowledge possessed but not employed, and, in the history of the individual, knowledge comes before its employment or exercise.

   That is why the soul is the first grade of actuality of a natural body having life potentially in it. The body so described is a body which is organized. The parts of plants in spite of their extreme simplicity are "organs";

---

*From Aristotle, *On the Soul*, trans. by J. A. Smith, in *Oxford Translation of the Works of Aristotle*, ed. by J. A. Smith and W. D. Ross (Oxford: Oxford University Press, 1908–1952).

e.g. the leaf serves to shelter the pericarp, the pericarp to shelter the fruit, while the roots of plants are analogous to the mouth of animals, both serving for the absorption of food. If, then, we have to give a general formula applicable to all kinds of soul, we must describe it as the first grade of actuality of a natural organized body. That is why we can wholly dismiss as unnecessary the question whether the soul and the body are one: it is as meaningless as to ask whether the wax and the shape given to it by the stamp are one, or generally the matter of a thing and that of which it is the matter. Unity has many senses (as many as "is" has), but the most proper and fundamental sense of both is the relation of an actuality to that of which it is the actuality.

We have now given an answer to the question, What is soul?—an answer which applies to it in its full extent. It is substance in the sense which corresponds to the definitive formula of a thing"s essence. That means that it is "the essential whatness" of a body of the character just assigned. Suppose that what is literally an "organ," like an axe, were a *natural* body, its "essential whatness," would have been its essence, and so its soul; if this disappeared from it, it would have ceased to be an axe, except in name. As it is, it is just an axe; it wants the character which is required to make its whatness or formulable essence a soul; for that, it would have had to be a *natural* body of a particular kind, viz. one having *in itself* the power of setting itself in movement and arresting itself. Next, apply this doctrine in the case of the "parts" of the living body. Suppose that the eye were an animal—sight would have been its soul, for sight is the substance or essence of the eye which corresponds to the formula, the eye being merely the matter of seeing; when seeing is removed the eye is no longer an eye, except in name—it is no more a real eye than the eye of a statue or of a painted figure. We must now extend our consideration from the "parts" to the whole living body; for what the departmental sense is to the bodily part which is its organ, that the whole faculty of sense is to the whole sensitive body as such.

We must not understand by that which is "potentially capable of living" what has lost the soul it had, but only what still retains it; but seeds and fruits are bodies which possess the qualification. Consequently, while waking is actuality in a sense corresponding to the cutting and the seeing, the soul is actuality in the sense corresponding to the power of sight and the power in the tool; the body corresponds to what exists in potentiality; as the pupil *plus* the power of sight constitutes the eye, so the soul *plus* the body constitutes the animal.

From this it indubitably follows that the soul is inseparable from its body, or at any rate that certain parts of it are (if it has parts)—for the actuality of some of them is nothing but the actualities of their bodily parts. Yet some may be separable because they are not the actualities of any body at all. Further, we have no light on the problem whether the soul may not be the actuality of its body in the sense in which the sailor is the actuality of the ship. This must suffice as our sketch or outline determination of the nature of soul.

2. Since what is clear or logically more evident emerges from what in itself is confused but more observable by us, we must reconsider our results from this point of view. For it is not enough for a definitive formula to express as most now do the mere fact; it must include and exhibit the ground also. At present definitions are given in a form analogous to the conclusion of a syllogism; e.g. What is squaring? The construction of an equilateral rectangle equal to a given oblong rectangle. Such a definition is in form equivalent to a conclusion. One that tells us that squaring is the discovery of a line which is a mean proportional between the two unequal sides of the given rectangle discloses the ground of what is defined.

    We resume our inquiry from a fresh starting-point by calling attention to the fact that what has soul in it differs from what has not in that the former displays life. Now this word has more than one sense, and provided any one alone of these is found in a thing we say that thing is living. Living, that is, may mean thinking or perception or local movement and rest, or movement in the sense of nutrition, decay and growth. Hence we think of plants also as living, for they are observed to possess in themselves an originative power through which they increase or decrease in all spatial directions; they grow up *and* down, and everything that grows increases its bulk alike in both directions or indeed in all, and continues to live so long as it can absorb nutriment.

    This power of self-nutrition can be isolated from the other powers mentioned, but not they from it—in mortal beings at least. The fact is obvious in plants; for it is the only psychic power they possess.

    This is the originative power the possession of which leads us to speak of things as *living* at all, but it is the possession of sensation that leads us for the first time to speak of living things as animals; for even those beings which possess no power of local movement but do possess the power of sensation we call animals and not merely living things.

    The primary form of sense is touch, which belongs to all animals. Just as the power of self-nutrition can be isolated from touch and sensation generally, so touch can be isolated from all other forms of sense. (By the power of self-nutrition we mean that departmental power of the soul which is common to plants and animals: all animals whatsoever are observed to have the sense of touch.) What the explanation of these two facts is, we must discuss later. At present we must confine ourselves to saying that soul is the source of these phenomena and is characterized by them, viz. by the powers of self-nutrition, sensation, thinking, and motivity.

    Is each of these a soul or a part of a soul? And if a part, a part in what sense? A part merely distinguishable by definition or a part distinct in local situation as well? In the case of certain of these powers, the answers to these questions are easy, in the case of others we are puzzled what to say. Just as in the case of plants which when divided are observed to continue to live though removed to a distance from one another (thus showing that in *their* case the soul of each individual plant before division was actually one, potentially many), so we notice a similar result in other varieties of soul, i.e. in insects which have been cut in two; each of the segments possesses both sensation and local movement; and if sensation, necessarily also imagination and appetition; for, where there is sensation, there is also pleasure and pain, and, where these, necessarily also desire.

We have no evidence as yet about mind or the power to think; it seems to be a widely different kind of soul, differing as what is eternal from what is perishable; it alone is capable of existence in isolation from all other psychic powers. All the other parts of soul, it is evident from what we have said, are, in spite of certain statements to the contrary, incapable of separate existence though, of course, distinguishable by definition. If opining is distinct from perceiving, to be capable of opining and to be capable of perceiving must be distinct, and so with all the other forms of living above enumerated. Further, some animals possess all these parts of soul, some certain of them only, others one only (this is what enables us to classify animals); the cause must be considered later. A similar arrangement is found also within the field of the senses; some classes of animals have all the senses, some only certain of them, others only one, the most indispensable, touch.

Since the expression "that whereby we live and perceive" has two meanings, just like the expression "that whereby we know"—that may mean either (*a*) knowledge or (*b*) the soul, for we can speak of knowing *by* or *with* either, and similarly that whereby we are in health may be either (*a*) health or (*b*) the body or some part of the body; and since of the two terms thus contrasted knowledge or health is the name of a form, essence, or ratio, or if we so express it an actuality of a recipient matter—knowledge of what is capable of knowing, health of what is capable of being made healthy (for the operation of that which is capable of originating change terminates and has its seat in what is changed or altered); further, since it is the soul by or with which primarily we live, perceive, and think:—it follows that the soul must be a ratio or formulable essence, not a matter or subject. For, as we said, the word substance has three meanings—form, matter, and the complex of both—and of these three what is called matter is potentiality, what is called form actuality. Since then the complex here is the living thing, the body cannot be the actuality of the soul; it is the soul which is the actuality of a certain kind of body. Hence the rightness of the view that the soul cannot be without a body, while it cannot *be* a body; it is not a body but something relative to a body. That is why it is *in* a body, and a body of a definite kind. It was a mistake, therefore, to do as former thinkers did, merely to fit it into a body without adding a definite specification of the kind or character of that body. Reflection confirms the observed fact; the actuality of any given thing can only be realized in what is already potentially that thing, i.e. in a matter of its own appropriate to it. From all this it follows that soul is an actuality or formulable essence of something that possesses a potentiality of being besouled.

3. Of the psychic powers above enumerated some kinds of living things, as we have said, possess all, some less than all, others one only. Those we have

mentioned are the nutritive, the appetitive, the sensory, the locomotive, and the power of thinking. Plants have none but the first, the nutritive, while another order of living things has this *plus* the sensory. If any order of living things has the sensory, it must also have the appetitive; for appetite is the genus of which desire, passion, and wish are the species; now all animals have one sense at least, viz. touch, and whatever has a sense has the capacity for pleasure and pain and therefore has pleasant and painful objects present to it, and wherever these are present, there is desire, for desire is just appetition of what is pleasant. Further, all animals have the sense for food (for touch is the sense for food); the food of all living things consists of what is dry, moist, hot, cold, and these are the qualities apprehended by touch; all other sensible qualities are apprehended by touch only indirectly. Sounds, colours, and odours contribute nothing to nutriment; flavours fall within the field of tangible qualities. Hunger and thirst are forms of desire, hunger a desire for what is dry and hot, thirst a desire for what is cold and moist; flavour is a sort of seasoning added to both. We must later clear up these points, but at present it may be enough to say that all animals that possess the sense of touch have also appetition. The case of imagination is obscure; we must examine it later. Certain kinds of animals possess in addition the power of locomotion, and still another order of animate beings, i.e. man and possibly another order like man or superior to him, the power of thinking, i.e. mind. It is now evident that a single definition can be given of soul only in the same sense as one can be given of figure. For, as in that case there is no figure distinguishable and apart from triangle, &c., so here there is no soul apart from the forms of soul just enumerated. It is true that a highly general definition can be given for figure which will fit all figures without expressing the peculiar nature of any figure. So here in the case of soul and its specific forms. Hence it is absurd in this and similar cases to demand an absolutely general definition, which will fail to express the peculiar nature of anything that *is*, or again, omitting this, to look for separate definitions corresponding to each *infima species*. The cases of figure and soul are exactly parallel; for the particulars subsumed under the common name in both cases—figures and living beings—constitute a series, each successive term of which potentially contains its predecessor, e.g. the square the triangle, the sensory power the self-nutritive. Hence we must ask in the case of each order of living things, What is its soul, i.e. What is the soul of plant, animal, man? Why the terms are related in this serial way must form the subject of later examination. But the facts are that the power of perception is never found apart from the power of self-nutrition, while—in plants—the latter is found isolated from the former. Again, no sense is found apart from that of touch, while touch *is* found by itself; many animals have neither sight, hearing, nor smell. Again, among living things that possess sense some have the power of locomotion, some not. Lastly, certain living beings—a small minority—possess calculation and thought, for (among mortal beings) those which possess calculation have all the other powers above mentioned, while the converse does not hold—indeed some live by imagination alone, while others have not even imagination. The mind that knows with immediate intuition presents a different problem.

It is evident that the way to give the most adequate definition of soul is to seek in the case of *each* of its forms for the most appropriate definition.

4. It is necessary for the student of these forms of soul first to find a definition of each, expressive of what it is, and then to investigate its derivative properties, &c. But if we are to express what each is, viz. what the thinking power is, or the perceptive, or the nutritive, we must go farther back and first give an account of thinking or perceiving, for in the order of investigation the question of what an agent does precedes the question, what enables it to do what it does. If this is correct, we must on the same ground go yet another step farther back and have some clear view of the objects of each; thus we must *start* with these objects, e.g. with food, with what is perceptible, or with what is intelligible.

It follows that first of all we must treat of nutrition and reproduction, for the nutritive soul is found along with all the others and is the most primitive and widely distributed power of soul, being indeed that one in virtue of which all are said to have life. The acts in which it manifests itself are reproduction and the use of food—reproduction, I say, because for any living thing that has reached its normal development and which is unmutilated, and whose mode of generation is not spontaneous, the most natural act is the production of another like itself, an animal producing an animal, a plant a plant, in order that, as far as its nature allows, it may partake in the eternal and divine. That is the goal towards which all things strive, that for the sake of which they do whatsoever their nature renders possible. The phrase "for the sake of which" is ambiguous; it may mean either (*a*) the end to achieve which, or (*b*) the being in whose interest, the act is done. Since then no living thing is able to partake in what is eternal and divine by uninterrupted continuance (for nothing perishable can for ever remain one and the same), it tries to achieve that end in the only way possible to it, and success is possible in varying degrees; so it remains not indeed as the selfsame individual but continues its existence in something *like* itself—not numerically but specifically one.

The soul is the cause or source of the living body. The terms cause and source have many senses. But the soul is the cause of its body alike in all three senses which we explicitly recognize. It is (*a*) the source or origin of movement, it is (*b*) the end, it is (*c*) the essence of the whole living body.[1]

That it is the last, is clear; for in everything the essence is identical with the ground of its being, and here, in the case of living things, their being is to live, and of their being and their living the soul in them is the cause or source. Further, the actuality of whatever is potential is identical with its formulable essence.

It is manifest that the soul is also the final cause of its body. For Nature, like mind, always does whatever it does for the sake of something, which

[1] These refer to three of the four Aristolian causes; efficient, final, and formal. —ED.

something is its end. To that something corresponds in the case of animals the soul and in this it follows the order of nature; all natural bodies are organs of the soul. This is true of those that enter into the constitution of plants as well as of those which enter into that of animals. This shows that that for the sake of which they are is soul. We must here recall the two senses of 'that for the sake of which', viz. (*a*) the end to achieve which, and (*b*) the being in whose interest, anything is or is done.

We must maintain, further, that the soul is also the cause of the living body as the original source of local movement. The power of locomotion is not found, however, in all living things. But change of quality and change of quantity are also due to the soul. Sensation is held to be a qualitative alteration, and nothing except what has soul in it is capable of sensation. The same holds of the quantitative changes which constitute growth and decay; nothing grows or decays naturally except what feeds itself, and nothing feeds itself except what has a share of soul in it.

TITUS LUCRETIUS CARUS
(c. 99–55 B.C.) Roman Philosopher

From *On the Nature of Things**

The Structure of Soul (III, 417–430)

Now come that you might know
That the minds and light souls
Of all living creatures
Have their birth and later death.
I will fashion a poem
Worthy of your attention:
The sweet labor of my long investigations.

One name I shall employ
To designate them both.
For when I choose to speak of soul
And show it to be mortal
Understand, I speak of mind as well
Since both are one united substance.

---

*Editor's translation. Text used: Lucretius, *De rerum natura*, ed. by C. Bailey (Oxford: Clarendon Press, 1900).

First of all, because I have already
Shown the soul to be be
A fabric of much intricacy
Formed of minute bodies—
Atoms finer than
Water, mist, or smoke.
In its nimble penetration
It far exceeds both smoke and mist
Though lighter cause had prompted it. . . .

The Soul and Mind are Material (III, 136–176)

Mind and soul I do declare
Are closely joined and form a single nature.
But the ruler supreme
In all the body is the mind.
It lies beneath the breast.[1]
Here, fear and terror flaunt themselves.
Here also dwells beneath the breast
The balm of soothing joys.
And therefore here must also be
The mind or understanding.

The balance of the soul, though
Scattered throughout the body,
Is moved by the motion of the mind—[2]
Which by itself alone can think
And please itself without affecting
Either body or soul in any way.[3]
When the head or eye is suffering,
The pain is not uniformly
Spread throughout the body.
The mind can pine alone
Or raise itself with joy
While the soul residing
In limbs and frame
Is stirred by no sensation.

But when the shock is more severe
We note the whole soul's unity.

[1] Aristotle held that the mind was located in the chest. —ED.

[2] Compare to the doctrine of Aristotle's causes of motion. Here the mind is depicted as the first mover of the body. —ED.

[3] Lucretius thus supports mental events without physical instantiations. This will go against the behaviorists, cf. Ryle's (p. 348) and Fodor's discussions. (p. 357) —ED.

In the limbs sweat and pallor spread
Through all the body: the tongue falters,
The voice breaks, the eyes blur
The ears ring, the joints collapse—
In short, a man may drop
When the mind is full of terror.
Hence, anyone can see
The soul is closely joined to the mind,
And when stirred by the mind,
It responds by moving the body.

This very same argument shows
The nature of mind and soul
To be material.
For when the limbs are moved,
The body roused from sleep
And countenance changes as the
Whole person is turned and guided,
Then we must conclude the mind
And soul to be material
Since none of this could happen
If there were no contact *between,*
And without body, contact fails.

Likewise, it is together that
The mind suffers and the body feels.
If a spear should tear
Into bones laid bare
And slice the gut but life be spared
Yet there ensues a dizzy fall
And on the ground the jumbled mind
Can't decide but part inclines to rise.
Thus the mind is shown to be material
Since by virtue of a spear
A newly suffering mind appears.

RENÉ DESCARTES

(1596–1650) French Philosopher

From *The Passions of the Soul*[1]*

Part First.

Of the Passions in General, and Incidentally of the Whole Nature of Man.

Article I. That what in respect of a subject is passion, is in some other regard always action. There is nothing in which the defective nature of the sciences which we have received from the ancients appears more clearly than in what they have written on the passions; for, although this is a matter which has at all times been the object of much investigation, and though it would not appear to be one of the most difficult, inasmuch as since every one has experience of the passions within himself, there is no necessity to borrow one's observations from elsewhere in order to discover their nature; yet that which the ancients have taught regarding them is both so slight, and for the most part so far from credible, that I am unable to entertain any hope of approximating to the truth excepting by shunning the paths which they have followed. This is why I shall be here obliged to write just as though I were treating of a matter which no one had ever touched on before me; and, to begin with, I consider that all that which occurs or that happens anew, is by the philosophers, generally speaking, termed a passion, in as far as the subject to which it occurs is concerned, and an action in respect of him who causes it to occur. Thus although the agent and the recipient [patient] are frequently very different, the action and the passion are always one and the same thing, although having different names, because of the two diverse subjects to which it may be related.

Article II. That in order to understand the passions of the soul its functions must be distinguished from those of body. Next I note also that we do not observe the existence of any subject which more immediately acts upon our soul than the body to which it is joined, and that we must consequently consider that what in the soul is a passion is in the body commonly speaking an action; so that there is no better means of arriving at a knowledge of our passions than to examine the difference which exists between soul and body in order to know to which of the two we must attribute each one of the functions which are within us.

---

*From René Descartes, *The Passions of the Soul*, trans. by Elizabeth Haldane and G. R. T. Ross (Cambridge and London: Cambridge University Press, 1911; original work published 1649).
[1] The expression "Passion" in this Treatise is used in its etymological significance.

Article III. What rule we must follow to bring about this result. As to this we shall not find much difficulty if we realise that all that we experience as being in us, and that to observation may exist in wholly inanimate bodies, must be attributed to our body alone; and, on the other hand, that all that which is in us and which we cannot in any way conceive as possibly pertaining to a body, must be attributed to our soul.

Article IV. That the heat and movement of the members proceed from the body, the thoughts from the soul. Thus because we have no conception of the body as thinking in any way, we have reason to believe that every kind of thought which exists in us belongs to the soul; and because we do not doubt there being inanimate bodies which can move in as many as or in more diverse modes than can ours, and which have as much heat[2] or more (experience demonstrates this to us in flame, which of itself has much more heat and movement than any of our members), we must believe that all the heat and all the movements which are in us pertain only to body, inasmuch as they do not depend on thought at all.

Article V. That it is an error to believe that the soul supplies the movement and heat to body. By this means we shall avoid a very considerable error into which many have fallen; so much so that I am of opinion that this is the primary cause which has prevented our being able hitherto satisfactorily to explain the passions and the other properties of the soul. It arises from the fact that from observing that all dead bodies are devoid of heat and consequently of movement, it has been thought that it was the absence of soul which caused these movements and this heat to cease; and thus, without any reason, it was thought that our natural heat and all the movements of our body depend on the soul: while in fact we ought on the contrary to believe that the soul quits us on death only because this heat ceases, and the organs which serve to move the body disintegrate.

Article VI. The difference that exists between a living body and a dead body. In order, then, that we may avoid this error, let us consider that death never comes to pass by reason of the soul, but only because some one of the principal parts of the body decays; and we may judge that the body of a living man differs from that of a dead man just as does a watch or other automaton (i.e. a machine that moves of itself), when it is wound up and contains in itself the corporeal principle of those movements for which it is designed along with all that is requisite for its action, from the same watch or other machine when it is broken and when the principle of its movement ceases to act. . . .

Article X. How the animal spirits are produced in the brain. But what is here most worthy of remark is that all the most animated and subtle portions of the blood which the heat has rarefied in the heart, enter ceaselessly in large quantities into the

---

[2] In the ancient world heat was often associated with soul. This theory was tied to the notion that the mind was located near the heart (thought to be the hottest place in the body because that was where blood was manufactured). Descartes here distances himself from these traditional views. —ED.

cavities of the brain. And the reason which causes them to go there rather than elsewhere, is that all the blood which issues from the heart by the great artery [3] takes its course in a straight line towards that place, and not being able to enter it in its entirety, because there are only very narrow passages there,[4] those of its parts which are the most agitated and the most subtle alone pass through, while the rest spreads abroad in all the other portions of the body. But these very subtle parts of the blood form the animal spirits; and for this end they have no need to experience any other change in the brain, unless it be that they are separated from the other less subtle portions of the blood; for what I here name spirits are nothing but material bodies and their one peculiarity is that they are bodies of extreme minuteness and that they move very quickly like the particles of the flame which issues from a torch. Thus it is that they never remain at rest in any spot, and just as some of them enter into the cavities of the brain, others issue forth by the pores which are in its substance, which pores conduct them into the nerves,[5] and from there into the muscles, by means of which they move the body in all the different ways in which it can be moved. . . .

Article XV. . . . We see in the case of those who have drunk much wine—that the vapours of this wine entering quickly into the blood, rise from the heart to the brain, where they become converted into animal spirits, which, being stronger and more abundant than those ordinarily there, are capable of moving the body in many strange fashions. . . .

Article XXX. That the soul is united to all the portions of the body conjointly. But in order to understand all these things more perfectly, we must know that the soul is really joined to the whole body, and that we cannot, properly speaking, say that it exists in any one of its parts to the exclusion of the others, because it is one and in some manner indivisible, owing to the disposition of its organs, which are so related to one another that when any one of them is removed, that renders the whole body defective; and because it is of a nature which has no relation to extension, nor dimensions, nor other properties of the matter of which the body is composed, but only to the whole conglomerate of its organs, as appears from the fact that we could not in any way conceive of the half or the third of a soul, nor of the space it occupies, and because it does not become smaller owing to the cutting off of some portion of the body, but separates itself from it entirely when the union of its assembled organs is dissolved.

Article XXXI. That there is a small gland in the brain in which the soul exercises its functions more particularly than in the other parts. It is likewise necessary to know that although the soul is joined to the whole body, there is yet in that a certain part in which it exercises its functions more particularly than in all the others; and it is

---

[3] Aorta —ED.
[4] Carotid rete and the circle of Willis —ED.
[5] The nerves were thought to be hollow tubes. This belief goes back to Galen. —ED.

usually believed that this part is the brain, or possibly the heart: the brain, because it is with it that the organs of sense are connected, and the heart because it is apparently in it that we experience the passions. But, in examining the matter with care, it seems as though I had clearly ascertained that the part of the body in which the soul exercises its functions immediately is in nowise the heart, nor the whole of the brain, but merely the most inward of all its parts, to wit, a certain very small gland which is situated in the middle of its substance and so suspended above the duct whereby the animal spirits in its anterior cavities have communication with those in the posterior, that the slightest movements which take place in it may alter very greatly the course of these spirits; and reciprocally that the smallest changes which occur in the course of the spirits may do much to change the movements of this gland.

Article XXXII. How we know that this gland is the main seat of the soul. The reason which persuades me that the soul cannot have any other seat in all the body than this gland wherein to exercise its functions immediately, is that I reflect that the other parts of our brain are all of them double, just as we have two eyes, two hands, two ears, and finally all the organs of our outside senses are double; and inasmuch as we have but one solitary and simple thought of one particular thing at one and the same moment, it must necessarily be the case that there must somewhere be a place where the two images which come to us by the two eyes, where the two other impressions which proceed from a single object by means of the double organs of the other senses, can unite before arriving at the soul, in order that they may not represent to it two objects instead of one. And it is easy to apprehend how these images or other impressions might unite in this gland by the intermission of the spirits which fill the cavities of the brain: but there is no other place in the body where they can be thus united unless they are so in this gland.

Article XXXIII. That the seat of the passions is not in the heart. As to the opinion of those who think that the soul receives its passions in the heart, it is not of much consideration, for it is only founded on the fact that the passions cause us to feel some change taking place there; and it is easy to see that this change is not felt in the heart excepting through the medium of a small nerve which descends from the brain towards it, just as pain is felt as in the foot by means of the nerves of the foot, and the stars are perceived as in the heavens by means of their light and of the optic nerves; so that it is not more necessary that our soul should exercise its functions immediately in the heart, in order to feel its passions there, than it is necessary for the soul to be in the heavens in order to see the stars there.

Article XXXIV. How the soul and the body act on one another. Let us then conceive here that the soul has its principal seat in the little gland which exists in the middle of the brain, from whence it radiates forth through all the remainder of the body by means of the animal spirits, nerves, and even the blood, which, participating in the impressions of the spirits, can carry them by the arteries into all the members. And recollecting what has been said above about the machine of our body, i.e. that the little filaments of our nerves are so distributed in all its parts, that on the occasion of the diverse movements which are there excited by sensible objects, they open in diverse ways the pores of the brain, which causes the animal spirits contained in these cavities to enter in diverse ways into the muscles, by which means they can move the members in all the different ways in which they are capable of being moved; and also that all the other causes which are capable of moving the spirits in diverse ways suffice to conduct them into diverse muscles; let us here add that the small gland which is the main seat of the soul is so suspended between the cavities which contain the spirits that it can be moved by them in as many different ways as there are sensible diversities in the object, but that it may also be moved in diverse ways by the soul, whose nature is such that it receives in itself as many diverse impressions, that is to say, that it possesses as many diverse perceptions as there are diverse movements in this gland. Reciprocally, likewise, the machine of the body is so formed that from the simple fact that this gland is diversely moved by the soul, or by such other cause, whatever it is, it thrusts the spirits which surround it towards the pores of the brain, which conduct them by the nerves into the muscles, by which means it causes them to move the limbs.

Article XXXV. Example of the mode in which the impressions of the objects unite in the gland which is in the middle of the brain. Thus, for example, if we see some animal approach us, the light reflected from its body depicts two images of it, one in each of our eyes, and these two images form two others, by means of the optic nerves, in the interior surface of the brain which faces its cavities; then from there, by means of the animal spirits with which its cavities are filled, these images so radiate towards the little gland which is surrounded by these spirits, that the movement which forms each point of one of the images tends towards the same point of the gland towards which tends the movement which forms the point of the other image, which represents the same part of this animal. By this means the two images which are in the brain form but one upon the gland, which, acting immediately upon the soul, causes it to see the form of this animal.

Article XXXVI. Example of the way in which the passions are excited in the soul. And, besides that, if this figure is very strange and frightful—that is, if it has a close relationship with the things which have been formerly hurtful to the body, that excites the passion of apprehension in the soul and then that of courage, or else that of fear and consternation according to the particular temperament of the body or the strength of the soul, and according as we have to begin with been secured by defence or by flight against the hurtful things to which the present impression is related. For in certain persons that disposes the brain in such a way that the spirits reflected from the image thus formed on the gland, proceed thence to take their places partly in the nerves which serve to turn the back and dispose the legs for flight, and partly in those which so increase or diminish the orifices of the heart, or at least which so agitate the other parts from whence the blood is sent to it, that this blood being there rarefied in a different manner from usual, sends to the brain the spirits which are adapted for the maintenance and strengthening of the passion of fear, i.e. which are adapted to the holding open, or at least reopening, of the pores of the brain which conduct them into the same nerves. For from the fact alone that these spirits enter into these pores, they excite a particular movement in this gland which is instituted by nature in order to cause the soul to be sensible of this passion; and because these pores are principally in relation with the little nerves which serve to contract or enlarge the orifices of the heart, that causes the soul to be sensible of it for the most part as in the heart.

GILBERT RYLE
(1900–1976) English Philosopher

Descartes' Myth*

(1) The Official Doctrine

There is a doctrine about the nature and place of minds which is so prevalent among theorists and even among laymen that it deserves to be described as the official theory. Most philosophers, psychologists and religious teachers subscribe, with minor reservations, to its main articles and, although they admit certain theoretical difficulties in it, they tend to assume that these can be overcome without serious modifications being made to the architecture of the theory. It will be argued here that the central principles of the doctrine are unsound and conflict with the whole body of what we know about minds when we are not speculating about them.

The official doctrine, which hails chiefly from Descartes, is something like this. With the doubtful exceptions of idiots and infants in arms every human being has both a body and a mind. Some would prefer to say that every human being is both a body and a mind. His body and his mind are ordinarily harnessed together, but after the death of the body his mind may continue to exist and function.

Human bodies are in space and are subject to the mechanical laws which govern all other bodies in space. Bodily processes and states can be inspected by external observers. So a man's bodily life is as much a public affair as are the lives of animals and reptiles and even as the careers of trees, crystals and planets.

But minds are not in space, nor are their operations subject to mechanical laws. The workings of one mind are not witnessable by other observers; its career is private. Only I can take direct cognisance of the states and processes of my own mind. A person therefore lives through two collateral histories, one consisting of

---

*From Gilbert Ryle, *The Concept of Mind* (London: Hutchinson & Co., 1949), pp. 11–24.

what happens in and to his body, the other consisting of what happens in and to his mind. The first is public, the second private. The events in the first history are events in the physical world, those in the second are events in the mental world.

It has been disputed whether a person does or can directly monitor all or only some of the episodes of his own private history; but, according to the official doctrine, of at least some of these episodes he has direct and unchallengeable cognisance. In consciousness, self-consciousness and introspection he is directly and authentically apprised of the present states and operations of his mind. He may have great or small uncertainties about concurrent and adjacent episodes in the physical world, but he can have none about at least part of what is momentarily occupying his mind.

It is customary to express this bifurcation of his two lives and of his two worlds by saying that the things and events which belong to the physical world, including his own body, are external, while the workings of his own mind are internal. This antithesis of outer and inner is of course meant to be construed as a metaphor, since minds, not being in space, could not be described as being spatially inside anything else, or as having things going on spatially inside themselves. But relapses from this good intention are common and theorists are found speculating how stimuli, the physical sources of which are yards or miles outside a person's skin, can generate mental responses inside his skull, or how decisions framed inside his cranium can set going movements of his extremities.

Even when "inner" and "outer" are construed as metaphors, the problem how a person's mind and body influence one another is notoriously charged with theoretical difficulties. What the mind wills, the legs, arms and the tongue execute; what affects the ear and the eye has something to do with what the mind perceives; grimaces and smiles betray the mind's moods and bodily castigations lead, it is hoped, to moral improvement. But the actual transactions between the episodes of the private history and those of the public history remain mysterious, since by definition they can belong to neither series. They could not be reported among the happenings described in a person's autobiography of his inner life, but nor could they be reported among those described in some one else's biography of that person's overt career. They can be inspected neither by introspection nor by laboratory experiment. They are theoretical shuttlecocks which are forever being bandied from the physiologist back to the psychologist and from the psychologist back to the physiologist.

Underlying this partly metaphorical representation of the bifurcation of a person's two lives there is a seemingly more profound and philosophical assumption. It is assumed that there are two different kinds of existence or status. What exists or happens may have the status of physical existence, or it may have the status of mental existence. Somewhat as the faces of coins are either heads or tails, or somewhat as living creatures are either male or female, so, it is supposed, some existing is physical existing, other existing is mental existing. It is a necessary feature of what has physical existence that it is in space and time, it is a necessary feature of what has mental existence that it is in time but not in space. What has physical existence is composed of matter, or else is a function of matter; what has mental existence consists of consciousness, or else is a function of consciousness.

There is thus a polar opposition between mind and matter, an opposition which is often brought out as follows. Material objects are situated in a common field, known as "space," and what happens to one body in one part of space is mechanically connected with what happens to other bodies in other parts of space. But mental happenings occur in insulated fields, known as "minds," and there is, apart maybe from telepathy, no direct causal connection between what happens in one mind and what happens in another. Only through the medium of the public physical world can the mind of one person make a difference to the mind of another. The mind is its own place and in his inner life each of us lives the life of a ghostly Robinson Crusoe. People can see, hear and jolt one another's bodies, but they are irremediably blind and deaf to the workings of one another's minds and inoperative upon them.

What sort of knowledge can be secured of the workings of a mind? On the one side, according to the official theory, a person has direct knowledge of the best imaginable kind of the workings of his own mind. Mental states and processes are (or are normally) conscious states and processes, and the consciousness which irradiates them can engender no illusions and leaves the door open for no doubts. A person's present thinkings, feelings and willings, his perceivings, rememberings and imaginings are intrinsically "phosphorescent"; their existence and their nature are inevitably betrayed to their owner. The inner life is a stream of consciousness of such a sort that it would be absurd to suggest that the mind whose life is that stream might be unaware of what is passing down it.

True, the evidence adduced recently by Freud seems to show that there exist channels tributary to this stream, which run hidden from their owner. People are actuated by impulses the existence of which they vigorously disavow; some of their thoughts differ from the thoughts which they acknowledge; and some of the actions which they think they will to perform they do not really will. They are thoroughly gulled by some of their own hypocrisies and they successfully ignore facts about their mental lives which on the official theory ought to be patent to them. Holders of the official theory tend, however, to maintain that anyhow in normal circumstances a person must be directly and authentically seized of the present state and workings of his own mind.

Besides being currently supplied with these alleged immediate data of consciousness, a person is also generally supposed to be able to exercise from time to time a special kind of perception, namely inner perception, or introspection. He can take a (non-optical) "look" at what is passing in his mind. Not only can he view and scrutinize a flower through his sense of sight and listen to and discriminate the notes of a bell through his sense of hearing; he can also reflectively or introspectively watch, without any bodily organ of sense, the current episodes of his inner life. This self-observation is also commonly supposed to be immune from illusion, confusion or doubt. A mind's reports of its own affairs have a certainty superior to the best that is possessed by its reports of matters in the physical world. Sense-perceptions can, but consciousness and introspection cannot, be mistaken or confused.

On the other side, one person has no direct access of any sort to the events of the inner life of another. He cannot do better than make problematic inferences from the observed behaviour of the other person's body to the states of mind which, by analogy from his own conduct, he supposes to be signalised by that behaviour. Direct access to the workings of a mind is the privilege of that mind itself; in default of such privileged access, the workings of one mind are inevitably occult to everyone else. For the supposed arguments from bodily movements similar to their own to mental workings similar to their own would lack any possibility of observational corroboration. Not unnaturally, therefore, an adherent of the official theory finds it difficult to resist this consequence of his premises, that he has no good reason to believe that there do exist minds other than his own. Even if he prefers to believe that to other human bodies there are harnessed minds not unlike his own, he cannot claim to be able to discover their individual characteristics, or the particular things that they undergo and do. Absolute solitude is on this showing the ineluctable destiny of the soul. Only our bodies can meet.

As a necessary corollary of this general scheme there is implicitly prescribed a special way of construing our ordinary concepts of mental powers and operations. The verbs, nouns and adjectives, with which in ordinary life we describe the wits, characters and higher-grade performances of the people with whom we have do, are required to be construed as signifying special episodes in their secret histories, or else as signifying tendencies for such episodes to occur. When someone is described as knowing, believing or guessing something, as hoping, dreading, intending or shirking something, as designing this or being amused at that, these verbs are supposed to denote the occurrence of specific modifications in his (to us) occult stream of consciousness. Only his own privileged access to this stream in direct awareness and introspection could provide authentic testimony that these mental-conduct verbs were correctly or incorrectly applied. The onlooker, be he teacher, critic, biographer or friend, can never assure himself that his comments have any vestige of truth. Yet it was just because we do in fact all know how to make such comments, make them with general correctness and correct them when they turn out to be confused or mistaken, that philosophers found it necessary to construct their theories of the nature and place of minds. Finding mental-conduct concepts being regularly and effectively used, they properly sought to fix their logical geography. But the logical geography officially recommended would entail that there could be no regular or effective use of these mental-conduct concepts in our descriptions of, and prescriptions for, other people's minds.

(2) The Absurdity of the Official Doctrine

Such in outline is the official theory. I shall often speak of it, with deliberate abusiveness, as "the dogma of the Ghost in the Machine." I hope to prove that it is entirely false, and false not in detail but in principle. It is not merely an assemblage of particular mistakes. It is one big mistake and a mistake of a special kind. It is, namely, a category-mistake. It represents the facts of mental life as if they belonged to one logical type or category (or range of types or categories), when they actually belong to another. The dogma is therefore a philosopher's myth. In attempting to explode the myth I shall probably be taken to be denying well-known facts about the mental life of human beings, and my plea that I aim at doing nothing more than rectify the logic of mental-conduct concepts will probably be disallowed as mere subterfuge.

I must first indicate what is meant by the phrase "Category-mistake." This I do in a series of illustrations.

A foreigner visiting Oxford or Cambridge for the first time is shown a number of colleges, libraries, playing fields, museums, scientific departments and administrative offices. He then asks "But where is the University? I have seen where the members of the Colleges live, where the Registrar works, where the scientists experiment and the rest. But I have not yet seen the University in which reside and work the members of your University." It has then to be explained to him that the University is not another collateral institution, some ulterior counterpart to the colleges, laboratories and offices which he has seen. The University is just the way in which all that he has already seen is organized. When they are seen and when their co-ordination is understood, the University has been seen. His mistake lay in his innocent assumption that it was correct to speak of Christ Church, the Bodleian Library, The Ashmolean Museum *and* the University, to speak, that is, as if "the University" stood for an extra member of the class of which these other units are members. He was mistakenly allocating the University to the same category as that to which the other institutions belong.

The same mistake would be made by a child witnessing the march-past of a division, who, having had pointed out to him such and such battalions, batteries, squadrons, etc., asked when the division was going to appear. He would be supposing that a division was counterpart to the units already seen, partly similar to them and partly unlike them. He would be shown his mistake by being told that in watching the battalions, batteries and squadrons marching past he had been watching the division marking past. The march-past was not a parade of battalions, batteries, squadrons *and* a division; it was a parade of the battalions, batteries and squadrons *of* a division.

One more illustration. A foreigner watching his first game of cricket learns what are the functions of the bowlers, the batsmen, the fielders, the umpires and the scorers. He then says "But there is no one left on the field to contribute the famous element of team-spirit. I see who does the bowling, the batting and the wicket-keeping; but I do not see whose role it is to exercise *esprit de corps*." Once more, it would have to be explained that he was looking for the wrong type of thing. Team-spirit is not another cricketing-operation supplementary to all of the other special tasks. It is, roughly, the keenness with which each of the special tasks is performed, and performing a task keenly is not performing two tasks. Certainly exhibiting team-spirit is not the same thing as bowling or catching, but nor is it a third thing such that we can say that the bowler first bowls *and* then exhibits team-spirit or that a fielder is at a given moment *either* catching *or* displaying *esprit de corps*.

These illustrations of category-mistakes have a common feature which must be noticed. The mistakes were made by people who did not know how to wield the concepts *University, division* and *team-spirit*. Their puzzles arose from inability to use certain items in the English vocabulary.

The theoretically interesting category-mistakes are those made by people who are perfectly competent to apply concepts, at least in the situations with which they are familiar, but are still liable in their abstract thinking to allocate those concepts to logical types to which they do not belong. An instance of a mistake of this sort would be the following story. A student of politics has learned the main differences between the British, the French and the American Constitutions, and has learned also the differences and connections between the Cabinet, Parliament, the various Ministries, the Judicature and the Church of England. But he still becomes embarrassed when asked questions about the connections between the Church of England, the Home Office and the British Constitution. For while the Church and the Home Office are institutions, the British Constitution is not another institution in the same sense of that noun. So inter-institutional relations which can be asserted or denied to hold between the Church and the Home Office cannot be asserted or denied to hold between either of them and the British Constitution. "The British Constitution" is not a term of the same logical type as "the Home Office" and "the Church of England." In a partially similar way, John Doe may be a relative, a friend, an enemy or a stranger to Richard Roe; but he cannot be any of these things to the Average Taxpayer. He knows how to talk sense in certain sorts of discussions about the Average Taxpayer, but he is baffled to say why he could not come across him in the street as he can come across Richard Roe.

It is pertinent to our main subject to notice that, so long as the student of politics continues to think of the British Constitution as a counterpart to the other institutions, he will tend to describe it as a mysteriously occult institution; and so long as John Doe continues to think of the Average Taxpayer as a fellow-citizen, he will tend to think of him as an elusive insubstantial man, a ghost who is everywhere yet nowhere.

My destructive purpose is to show that a family of radical category-mistakes is the source of the double-life theory. The representation of a person as a ghost mysteriously ensconced in a machine derives from this argument. Because, as is true, a person's thinking, feeling and purposive doing cannot be described solely in the idioms of physics, chemistry and physiology, therefore they must be described in counterpart idioms. As the human body is a complex organised unit, so the human mind must be another complex organised unit, though one made of a different sort of stuff and with a different sort of structure. Or, again, as the human body, like any other parcel of matter, is a field of causes and effects, so the mind must be another field of causes and effects, though not (Heaven be praised) mechanical causes and effects.

(3) The Origin of the Category-Mistake

One of the chief intellectual origins of what I have yet to prove to be the Cartesian category-mistake seems to be this. When Galileo showed that his methods of scientific discovery were competent to provide a mechanical theory which should cover every occupant of space, Descartes found in himself two conflicting motives. As a man of scientific genius he could not but endorse the claims of mechanics, yet as a religious and moral man he could not accept, as Hobbes accepted, the discouraging rider to those claims, namely that human nature differs only in degree of complexity from clockwork. The mental could not be just a variety of the mechanical.

He and subsequent philosophers naturally but erroneously availed themselves of the following escape-route. Since mental-conduct words are not to be construed as signifying the occurrence of mechanical processes, they must be construed as signifying the occurrence of non-mechanical processes; since mechanical laws explain movements in space as the effects of other movements in space, other laws must explain some of the non-spatial workings of minds as the effects of other non-spatial workings of minds. The difference between the human behaviours which we describe as intelligent and those which we describe as unintelligent must be a difference in their causation; so, while some movements of human tongues and limbs are the effects of mechanical causes, others must be the effects of non-mechanical causes, i.e. some issue from movements of particles of matter, others from workings of the mind.

The differences between the physical and the mental were thus represented as differences inside the common framework of the categories of "thing," "stuff," "attribute," "stage," "process," "change," "cause," and "effect." Minds are things, but different sorts of things from bodies; mental processes are causes and effects but different sorts of causes and effects from bodily movements. And so on. Somewhat as the foreigner expected the University to be an extra edifice, rather like a college but also considerably different, so the repudiators of mechanism represented minds as extra centers of causal processes, rather like machines but also considerably different from them. Their theory was a para-mechanical hypothesis.

That this assumption was at the heart of the doctrine is shown by the fact that there was from the beginning felt to be a major theoretical difficulty in explaining how minds can influence and be influenced by bodies. How can a mental process, such as willing, cause spatial movements like the movements of the tongue? How can a physical change in the optic nerve have among its effects a mind's perception of a flash of light? This notorious crux by itself shows the logical mould into which Descartes pressed his theory of the mind. It was the self-same mould into which he and Galileo set their mechanics. Still unwittingly adhering to the grammar of mechanics, he tried to avert disaster by describing minds in what was merely an obverse vocabulary. The workings of minds had to be described by the mere negatives of the specific descriptions given to bodies; they are not in space, they are not motions, they are not modifications of matter, they are not accessible to public observation. Minds are not bits of clockwork, they are just bits of not-clockwork.

As thus represented, minds are not merely ghosts harnessed to machines, they are themselves just spectral machines. Though the human body is an engine, it is not quite an ordinary engine, since some of its workings are governed by another engine inside it—this interior governor-engine being one of a very special sort. It is invisible, inaudible and it has no size or weight. It cannot be taken to bits and the laws it obeys are not those known to ordinary engineers. Nothing is known of how it governs the bodily engine.

A second major crux points the same moral. Since, according to the doctrine, minds belong to the same category as bodies and since bodies are rigidly governed by mechanical laws, it seemed to many theorists to follow that minds must be similarly governed by rigid non-mechanical laws. The physical world is a deterministic system, so the mental world must be a deterministic system. Bodies cannot help the modifications that they undergo, so minds cannot help pursuing the careers fixed for them. *Responsibility, choice, merit* and *demerit* are therefore inapplicable concepts—unless the compromise solution is adopted of saying that the laws governing mental processes, unlike those governing physical processes, have the congenial attribute of being only rather rigid. The problem of the Freedom of the Will was the problem how to reconcile the hypothesis that minds are to be described in terms drawn from the categories of mechanics with the knowledge that higher-grade human conduct is not of a piece with the behavior of machines.

It is an historical curiosity that it was not noticed that the entire argument was broken-backed. Theorists correctly assumed that any sane man could already recognise the differences between, say, rational and non-rational utterances or between purposive and automatic behaviour. Else there would have been nothing requiring to be salved from mechanism. Yet the explanation given presupposed that one person could in principle never recognise the difference between the rational and the irrational utterances issuing from other human bodies, since he could never get access to the postulated immaterial causes of some of their utterances. Save for the doubtful exception of himself, he could never tell the difference between a man and a Robot. It would have to be conceded, for example, that, for all that we can tell, the inner lives of persons who are classed as idiots or lunatics are as rational as those of anyone else. Perhaps only their overt behaviour is disappointing; that is to say, perhaps "idiots" are not really idiotic, or "lunatics" lunatic. Perhaps, too, some of those who are classed as sane are really idiots. According to the theory, external observers could never know how the overt behaviour of others is correlated with their mental powers and processes and so they could never know or even plausibly conjuncture whether their applications of mental-conduct concepts to these other people were correct or incorrect. It would then be hazardous or impossible for a man to claim sanity or logical consistency even for himself, since he would be debarred from comparing his own performances with those of others. In short, our characterisations of persons and their performances as intelligent, prudent and virtuous or as stupid, hypocritical and cowardly could never have been made, so the problem of providing a special causal hypothesis to serve as the basis of such diagnoses would never have arisen. The question, "How do persons differ from machines?" arose just because everyone already knew how to apply mental-conduct concepts before the new causal hypothesis was introduced. This causal hypothesis could not therefore be the source of the criteria used in those applications. Nor, of course, has the causal hypothesis in any degree improved our handling of those criteria. We still distinguish good from bad arithmetic, politic from impolitic conduct and fertile from infertile imaginations in the ways in which Descartes himself distinguished them before and after he speculated how the applicability of these criteria was compatible with the principle of mechanical causation.

He had mistaken the logic of his problem. Instead of asking by what criteria intelligent behaviour is actually distinguished from non-intelligent behaviour, he asked "Given that the principle of mechanical causation does not tell us the difference, what other causal principle will tell it us?" He realised that the problem was not one of mechanics and assumed that it must therefore be one of some counterpart to mechanics. Not unnaturally psychology is often cast for just this role.

When two terms belong to the same category, it is proper to construct conjunctive propositions embodying them. Thus a purchaser may say that he bought a left-hand glove and a right-hand glove, but not that he bought a left-hand glove, a right-hand glove and a pair of gloves. "She came home in a flood of tears and a sedan-chair" is a well-known joke based on the absurdity of conjoining terms of different types. It would have been equally ridiculous to construct the disjunction "She came home either in a flood of tears or else in a sedan-chair." Now the dogma of the Ghost in the Machine does just this. It maintains that there exist both bodies and minds; that there occur physical processes and mental processes; that there are mechanical causes of corporeal movements and mental causes of corporeal movements. I shall argue that these and other analogous conjunctions are absurd; but, it must be noticed, the argument will not show that either of the illegitimately conjoined propositions is absurd in itself. I am not, for example, denying that there occur mental processes. Doing long division is a mental process and so is making a joke. But I am saying that the phrase "there occur mental processes" does not mean the same sort of thing as "there occur physical processes," and, therefore, that it makes no sense to conjoin or disjoin the two.

If my argument is successful, there will follow some interesting consequences. First, the hallowed contrast between Mind and Matter will be dissipated, but dissipated not by either of the equally hallowed absorptions of Mind by Matter or of Matter by Mind, but in quite a different way. For the seeming contrast of the two will be shown to be as illegitimate as would be the contrast of "she came home in a flood of tears" and "she came home in a sedan-chair." The belief that there is a polar opposition between Mind and Matter is the belief that they are terms of the same logical type.

It will also follow that both Idealism and Materialism are answers to an improper question. The "reduction" of the material world to mental states and processes, as well as the "reduction" of mental states and processes to physical states and processes, presuppose the legitimacy of the disjunction "Either there exist minds or there exist bodies (but not both)." It would be like saying, "Either she bought a left-hand and a right-hand glove or she bought a pair of gloves (but not both)."

It is perfectly proper to say, in one logical tone of voice, that there exist minds and to say, in another logical tone of voice, that there exist bodies. But these expressions do not indicate two different species of existence, for "existence" is not a generic word like "coloured" or "sexed." They indicate two different senses of "exist," somewhat as "rising" has different senses in "the tide is rising," "hopes are rising," and "the average age of death is rising." A man would be thought to be making a poor joke who said that three things are now rising, namely the tide, hopes and the average age of death. It would be just as good or bad a joke to say that there exist prime numbers and Wednesdays and public opinions and navies; or that there exist both minds and bodies. . . .

(4) Historical Note

It would not be true to say that the official theory derives solely from Descartes's theories, or even from a more widespread anxiety about the implications of seventeenth century mechanics. Scholastic and Reformation theology had schooled the intellects of the scientists as well as of the laymen, philosophers and clerics of that age. Stoic-Augustinian theories of the will were embedded in the Calvinist doctrines of sin and grace: Platonic and Aristotelian theories of the intellect shaped the orthodox doctrines of the immortality of the soul. Descartes was reformulating already prevalent theological doctrines of the soul in the new syntax of Galileo. The theologian's privacy of conscience became the philosopher's privacy of consciousness, and what had been the bogy of Predestination reappeared as the bogy of Determinism.

It would also not be true to say that the two-worlds myth did no theoretical good. Myths often do a lot of theoretical good, while they are still new. One benefit bestowed by the para-mechanical myth was that it partly superannuated the then prevalent para-political myth. Minds and their Faculties had previously been described by analogies with political superiors and political subordinates. The idioms used were those of ruling, obeying, collaborating and rebelling. They survived and still survive in many ethical and some epistemological discussions. As, in physics, the new myth of occult Forces was a scientific improvement on the old myth of Final Causes, so in anthropological and psychological theory, the new myth of hidden operations, impulses and agencies was an improvement on the old myth of dictations, deferrences and disobediences.

JERRY A. FODOR
Contemporary Philosopher of Psychology

The Mind-Body Problem*

Modern philosophy of science has been devoted largely to the formal and systematic description of the successful practices of working scientists. The philosopher does not try to dictate how scientific inquiry and argument ought to be conducted. Instead he tries to enumerate the principles and practices that have contributed to good science. The philosopher has devoted the most attention to analyzing the methodological peculiarities of the physical sciences. The analysis has helped to clarify the nature of confirmation, the logical structure of scientific theories, the formal properties of statements that express laws and the question of whether theoretical entities actually exist.

It is only rather recently that philosophers have become seriously interested in the methodological tenets of psychology. Psychological explanations of behavior refer liberally to the mind and to states, operations and processes of the mind.

*From *Scientific-American* 244 (1981), pp. 114–23.

The philosophical difficulty comes in stating in unambiguous language what such references imply.

Traditional philosophies of mind can be divided into two broad categories: dualist theories and materialist theories. In the dualist approach the mind is a nonphysical substance. In materialist theories the mental is not distinct from the physical; indeed, all mental states, properties, processes and operations are in principle identical with physical states, properties, processes and operations. Some materialists, known as behaviorists, maintain that all talk of mental causes can be eliminated from the language of psychology in favor of talk of environmental stimuli and behavioral responses. Other materialists, the identity theorists, contend that there are mental causes and that they are identical with neurophysiological events in the brain.

In the past 15 years a philosophy of mind called functionalism that is neither dualist nor materialist has emerged from philosophical reflection on developments in artificial intelligence, computational theory, linguistics, cybernetics and psychology. All these fields, which are collectively known as the cognitive sciences, have in common a certain level of abstraction and a concern with systems that process information. Functionalism, which seeks to provide a philosophical account of this level of abstraction, recognizes the possibility that systems as diverse as human beings, calculating machines and disembodied spirits could all have mental states. In the functionalist view the psychology of a system depends not on the stuff it is made of (living cells, metal or spiritual energy) but on how the stuff is put together. Functionalism is a difficult concept, and one way of coming to grips with it is to review the deficiencies of the dualist and materialist philosophies of mind it aims to displace.

The chief drawback of dualism is its failure to account adequately for mental causation. If the mind is nonphysical, it has no position in physical space. How, then, can a mental cause give rise to a behavioral effect that has a position in space? To put it another way, how can the nonphysical give rise to the physical without violating the laws of the conservation of mass, of energy and of momentum?

The dualist might respond that the problem of how an immaterial substance can cause physical events is not much obscurer than the problem of how one physical event can cause another. Yet there is an important difference: there are many clear cases of physical causation but not one clear case of non-physical causation. Physical interaction is something philosophers, like all other people, have to live with. Nonphysical interaction, however, may be no more than an artifact of the immaterialist construal of the mental. Most philosophers now agree that no argument has successfully demonstrated why mind-body causation should not be regarded as a species of physical causation.

Dualism is also incompatible with the practices of working psychologists. The psychologist frequently applies the experimental methods of the physical sciences to the study of the mind. If mental processes were different in kind from physical processes, there would be no reason to expect these methods to work in the realm of the mental. In order to justify their experimental methods many psychologists urgently sought an alternative to dualism.

In the 1920's John B. Watson of Johns Hopkins University made the radical suggestion that behavior does not have mental causes. He regarded the behavior of an organism as its observable responses to stimuli, which he took to be the causes of its behavior. Over the next 30 years psychologists such as B. F. Skinner of Harvard University developed Watson's ideas into an elaborate world view in which the role of psychology was to catalogue the laws that determine causal relations between stimuli and responses. In this "radical behaviorist" view the problem of explaining the nature of the mind-body interaction vanishes; there is no such interaction.

Radical behaviorism has always worn an air of paradox. For better or worse, the idea of mental causation is deeply ingrained in our everyday language and in our ways of understanding our fellow men and ourselves. For example, people commonly attribute behavior to beliefs, to knowledge and to expectations. Brown puts gas in his tank because he believes the car will not run without it. Jones writes not "acheive" but "achieve" because he knows the rule about putting *i* before *e*. Even when a behavioral response is closely tied to an environmental stimulus, mental processes often intervene. Smith carries an umbrella because the sky is cloudy, but the weather is only part of the story. There are apparently also mental links in the causal chain: observation and expectation. The clouds affect Smith's behavior only because he observes them and because they induce in him an expectation of rain.

The radical behaviorist is unmoved by appeals to such cases. He is prepared to dismiss references to mental causes, however plausible they may seem, as the residue of outworn creeds. The radical behaviorist predicts that as psychologists come to understand more about the relations between stimuli and responses they will find it increasingly possible to explain behavior without postulating mental causes.

The strongest argument against behaviorism is that psychology has not turned out this way; the opposite has happened. As psychology has matured, the framework of mental states and processes that is apparently needed to account for experimental observations has grown all the more elaborate. Particularly in the case of human behavior psychological theories satisfying the methodological tenets of radical behaviorism have proved largely sterile, as would be expected if the postulated mental processes are real and causally effective.

Nevertheless, many philosophers were initially drawn to radical behaviorism because, paradoxes and all, it seemed better than dualism. Since a psychology committed to immaterial substances was unacceptable, philosophers turned to radical behaviorism because it seemed to be the only alternative materialist philosophy of mind. The choice, as they saw it, was between radical behaviorism and ghosts.

By the early 1960's philosophers began to have doubts that dualism and radical behaviorism exhausted the possible approaches to the philosophy of mind. Since the two theories seemed unattractive, the right strategy might be to develop a materialist philosophy of mind that nonetheless allowed for mental causes. Two such philosophies emerged, one called logical behaviorism and the other called the central-state identity theory.

Logical behaviorism is a semantic theory about what mental terms mean. The basic idea is that attributing a mental state (say thirst) to an organism is the same as saying that the organism is disposed to behave in a particular way (for example to drink if there is water available). On this view every mental ascription is equivalent in meaning to an if-then statement (called a behavioral hypothetical) that expresses a behavioral disposition. For example, "Smith is thirsty" might be taken to be equivalent to the dispositional statement "If there were water available, then Smith would drink some." By definition a behavioral hypothetical includes no mental terms. The if-clause of the hypothetical speaks only of stimuli and the then-clause speaks only of behavioral responses. Since stimuli and responses are physical events, logical behaviorism is a species of materialism.

The strength of logical behaviorism is that by translating mental language into the language of stimuli and responses it provides an interpretation of psychological explanations in which behavioral effects are attributed to mental causes. Mental causation is simply the manifestation of a behavioral disposition. More precisely, mental causation is what happens when an organism has a behavioral disposition and the if-clause of the behavioral hypothetical expressing the disposition happens to be true. For example, the causal statement "Smith drank some water because he was thirsty" might be taken to mean "If there were water available, then Smith would drink some, and there was water available."

I have somewhat oversimplified logical behaviorism by assuming that each mental ascription can be translated by a unique behavioral hypothetical. Actually the logical behaviorist often maintains that it takes an open-ended set (perhaps an infinite set) of behavioral hypotheticals to spell out the behavioral disposition expressed by a mental term. The mental ascription "Smith is thirsty" might also be satisfied by the hypothetical "If there were orange juice available, then Smith would drink some" and by a host of other hypotheticals. In any event the logical behaviorist does not usually maintain he can actually enumerate all the hypotheticals that correspond to a behavioral disposition expressing a given mental term. He only insists that in principle the meaning of any mental term can be conveyed by behavioral hypotheticals.

The way the logical behaviorist has interpreted a mental term such as thirsty is modeled after the way many philosophers have interpreted a physical disposition such as fragility. The physical disposition "The glass is fragile" is often taken to mean something like "If the glass were struck, then it would break." By the same token the logical behaviorist's analysis of mental causation is similar to the received analysis of one kind of physical causation. The causal statement "The glass broke because it was fragile" is taken to mean something like "If the glass were struck, then it would break, and the glass was struck."

By equating mental terms with behavioral dispositions the logical behaviorist has put mental terms on a par with the nonbehavioral dispositions of the physical sciences. That is a promising move, because the analysis of nonbehavioral dispositions is on relatively solid philosophical ground. An explanation attributing the breaking of a glass to its fragility is surely something even the staunchest materialist can accept. By arguing that mental terms are synonymous with dispositional terms, the logical behaviorist has provided something the radical behaviorist could not: a materialist account of mental causation.

Nevertheless, the analogy between mental causation as construed by the logical behaviorist and physical causation goes only so far. The logical behaviorist treats the manifestation of a disposition as the sole form of mental causation, whereas the physical sciences recognize additional kinds of causation. There is the kind of causation where one physical event causes another, as when the breaking of a glass is attributed to its having been struck. In fact, explanations that involve event-event causation are presumably more basic than dispositional explanations, because the manifestation of a disposition (the breaking of a fragile glass) always involves event-event causation and not vice versa. In the realm of the mental many examples of event-event causation involve one mental state's causing another, and for this kind of causation logical behaviorism provides no analysis. As a result the logical behaviorist is committed to the tacit and implausible assumption that psychology requires a less robust notion of causation than the physical sciences require.

Event-event causation actually seems to be quite common in the realm of the mental. Mental causes typically give rise to behavioral effects by virtue of their interaction with other mental causes. For example, having a headache causes a disposition to take aspirin only if one also has the desire to get rid of the headache, the belief that aspirin exists, the belief that taking aspirin reduces headaches and so on. Since mental states interact in generating behavior, it will be necessary to find a construal of psychological explanations that posits mental processes: causal sequences of mental events. It is this construal that logical behaviorism fails to provide.

Such considerations bring out a fundamental way in which logical behaviorism is quite similar to radical behaviorism. It is true that the logical behaviorist, unlike the radical behaviorist, acknowledges the existence of mental states. Yet since the underlying tenet of logical behaviorism is that references to mental states can be translated out of psychological explanations by employing behavioral hypotheticals, all talk of mental states and processes is in a sense heuristic. The only facts to which the behaviorist is actually committed are facts about relations between stimuli and responses. In this respect logical behaviorism is just radical behaviorism in a semantic form. Although the former theory offers a construal of mental causation, the construal is Pickwickian. What does not really exist cannot cause anything, and the logical behaviorist, like the radical behaviorist, believes deep down that mental causes do not exist.

An alternative materialist theory of the mind to logical behaviorism is the central-state identity theory. According to this theory, mental events, states and processes are identical with neurophysiological events in the brain, and the property of being in a certain mental state (such as having a headache or believing it will rain) is identical with the property of being in a certain neurophysiological state. On this basis it is easy to make sense of the idea that a behavioral effect might sometimes have a chain of mental causes; that will be the case whenever a behavioral effect is contingent on the appropriate sequence of neurophysiological events.

The central-state identity theory acknowledges that it is possible for mental causes to interact causally without ever giving rise to any behavioral effect, as when a person thinks for a while about what he ought to do and then decides to do nothing. If mental processes are neurophysiological, they must have the causal properties of neurophysiological processes. Since neurophysiological processes are presumably physical processes, the central-state identity theory ensures that the concept of mental causation is as rich as the concept of physical causation.

The central-state identity theory provides a satisfactory account of what the mental terms in psychological explanations refer to, and so it is favored by psychologists who are dissatisfied with behaviorism. The behaviorist maintains that mental terms refer to nothing or that they refer to the parameters of stimulus-response relations. Either way the existence of mental entities is only illusory. The identity theorist, on the other hand, argues that mental terms refer to neurophysiological states. Thus he can take seriously the project of explaining behavior by appealing to its mental causes.

The chief advantage of the identity theory is that it takes the explanatory constructs of psychology at face value, which is surely something a philosophy of mind ought to do if it can. The identity theory shows how the mentalist explanations of psychology could be not mere heuristics but literal accounts of the causal history of behavior. Moreover, since the identity theory is not a semantic thesis, it is immune to many arguments that cast in doubt logical behaviorism. A drawback of logical behaviorism is that the observation "John has a headache" does not seem to mean the same thing as a statement of the form "John is disposed to behave in such and such a way." The identity theorist, however, can live with the fact that "John has a headache" and "John is in such and such a brain state" are not synonymous. The assertion of the identity theorist is not that these sentences mean the same thing but only that they are rendered true (or false) by the same neurophysiological phenomena.

The identity theory can be held either as a doctrine about mental particulars (John's current pain or Bill's fear of animals) or as a doctrine about mental universals, or properties (having a pain or being afraid of animals). The two doctrines, called respectively token physicalism and type physicalism, differ in strength and plausibility. Token physicalism maintains only that all the mental particulars that happen to exist are neurophysiological, whereas type physicalism makes the more sweeping assertion that all the mental particulars there could possibly be are neurophysiological. Token physicalism does not rule out the logical possibility of machines and disembodied spirits having mental properties. Type physicalism dismisses this possibility because neither machines nor disembodied spirits have neurons.

Type physicalism is not a plausible doctrine about mental properties even if token physicalism is right about mental particulars. The problem with type physicalism is that the psychological constitution of a system seems to depend not on its hardware, or physical composition, but on its software, or program. Why should the philosopher dismiss the possibility that silicon-based Martians have pains, assuming that the silicon is properly organized? And why should the philosopher rule out the possibility of machines having beliefs, assuming that the machines are correctly programmed? If it is logically possible that Martians and machines could have mental properties, then mental properties and neurophysiological processes cannot be identical, however much they may prove to be coextensive.

What it all comes down to is that there seems to be a level of abstraction at which the generalizations of psychology are most naturally pitched. This level of abstraction cuts across differences in the physical composition of the systems to which psychological generalizations apply. In the cognitive sciences, at least, the natural domain for psychological theorizing seems to be all systems that process information. The problem with type physicalism is that there are possible information-processing systems with the same psychological constitution as human beings but not the same physical organization. In principle all kinds of physically different things could have human software.

This situation calls for a relational account of mental properties that abstracts them from the physical structure of their bearers. In spite of the objections to logical behaviorism that I presented above, logical behaviorism was at least on the right track in offering a relational interpretation of mental properties: to have a headache is to be disposed to exhibit a certain pattern of relations between the stimuli one encounters and the responses one exhibits. If that is what having a headache is, however, there is no reason in principle why only heads that are physically similar to ours can ache. Indeed, according to logical behaviorism, it is a necessary truth that any system that has our stimulus-response contingencies also has our headaches.

All of this emerged 10 or 15 years ago as a nasty dilemma for the materialist program in the philosophy of mind. On the one hand the identity theorist (and not the logical behaviorist) had got right the causal character of the interactions of mind and body. On the other the logical behaviorist (and not the identity theorist) had got right the relational character of mental properties. Functionalism has apparently been able to resolve the dilemma. By stressing the distinction computer science draws between hardware and software the functionalist can make sense of both the causal and the relational character of the mental.

The intuition underlying functionalism is that what determines the psychological type to which a mental particular belongs is the causal role of the particular in the mental life of the organism. Functional individuation is differentiation with respect to causal role. A headache, for example, is identified with the type of mental state that among other things causes a disposition for taking aspirin in people who believe aspirin relieves a headache, causes a desire to rid oneself of the pain one is feeling, often causes someone who speaks English to say such things as "I have a headache" and is brought on by overwork, eyestrain and tension. This list is presumably not complete. More will be known about the nature of a headache as psychological and physiological research discovers more about its causal role.

Functionalism construes the concept of causal role in such a way that a mental state can be defined by its causal relations to other mental states. In this respect functionalism is completely different from logical behaviorism. Another major difference is that functionalism is not a reductionist thesis. It does not foresee, even in principle, the elimination of mentalistic concepts from the explanatory apparatus of psychological theories.

The difference between functionalism and logical behaviorism is brought out by the fact that functionalism is fully compatible with token physicalism. The functionalist would not be disturbed if brain events turn out to be the only things with the functional properties that define mental states. Indeed, most functionalists fully expect it will turn out that way.

Since functionalism recognizes that mental particulars may be physical, it is compatible with the idea that mental causation is a species of physical causation. In other words, functionalism tolerates the materialist solution to the mind-body problem provided by the central-state identity theory. It is possible for the functionalist to assert both that mental properties are typically defined in terms of their relations and that interactions of mind and body are typically causal in however robust a notion of causality is required by psychological explanations. The logical behaviorist can endorse only the first assertion and the type physicalist only the second. As a result functionalism seems to capture the best features of the materialist alternatives to dualism. It is no wonder that functionalism has become increasingly popular.

Machines provide good examples of two concepts that are central to functionalism: the concept that mental states are interdefined and the concept that they can be realized by many systems. Imagine the difference between a behavioristic Coke machine and a mentalistic one. Both machines dispense a Coke for 10 cents. (The price has not been affected by inflation.) The states of the machines are defined by reference to their causal roles, but only the behavioristic machine would satisfy the behaviorist. Its single state ($S0$) is completely specified in terms of stimuli and responses. $S0$ is the state a machine is in if, and only if, given a dime as the input, it dispenses a Coke as the output.

The mentalistic machine has interdefined states ($S1$ and $S2$), which are characteristic of functionalism. $S1$ is the state a machine is in if, and only if, (1) given a nickel, it dispenses nothing and proceeds to $S2$, and (2) given a dime, it dispenses a Coke and stays in $S1$. $S2$ is the state a machine is in if, and only if, (1) given a nickel, it dispenses a Coke and proceeds to $S1$, and (2) given a dime, it dispenses a Coke and a nickel and proceeds to $S1$. What $S1$ and $S2$ jointly amount to is the machine's dispensing a Coke if it is given a dime, dispensing a Coke and a nickel if it is given a dime and a nickel and waiting to be given a second nickel if it has been given a first one.

Since $S1$ and $S2$ are each defined by hypothetical statements, they can be viewed as dispositions. Nevertheless, they are not behavioral dispositions because the consequences an input has for a machine in $S1$ or $S2$ are not specified solely in terms of the output of the machine. Rather, the consequences also involve the machine's internal states.

Nothing about the way I have described the behavioristic and mentalistic Coke machines puts constraints on what they could be made of. Any system whose states bore the proper relations to inputs, outputs and other states could be one of these machines. No doubt it is reasonable to expect such a system to be constructed out of such things as wheels, levers and diodes (token physicalism for Coke machines). Similarly, it is reasonable to expect that our minds may prove to be neurophysiological (token physicalism for human beings).

Nevertheless, the software description of a Coke machine does not logically require wheels, levers and diodes for its concrete realization. By the same token, the software description of the mind does not logically require neurons. As far as functionalism is concerned a Coke machine with states $S1$ and $S2$ could be made of ectoplasm, if there is such stuff and if its states have the right causal properties. Functionalism allows for the possibility of disembodied Coke machines in exactly the same way and to the same extent that it allows for the possibility of disembodied minds.

To say that *S1* and *S2* are interdefined and realizable by different kinds of hardware is not, of course, to say that a Coke machine has a mind. Although interdefinition and functional specification are typical features of mental states, they are clearly not sufficient for mentality. What more is required is a question to which I shall return below.

Some philosophers are suspicious of functionalism because it seems too easy. Since functionalism licenses the individuation of states by reference to their causal role, it appears to allow a trivial explanation of any observed event *E*, that is, it appears to postulate an *E*-causer. For example, what makes the valves in a machine open? Why, the operation of a valve opener. And what is a valve opener? Why, anything that has the functionally defined property of causing valves to open.

In psychology this kind of question-begging often takes the form of theories that in effect postulate homunculi with the selfsame intellectual capacities the theorist set out to explain. Such is the case when visual perception is explained by simply postulating psychological mechanisms that process visual information. The behaviorist has often charged the mentalist, sometimes justifiably, of mongering this kind of question-begging pseudo explanation. The charge will have to be met if functionally defined mental states are to have a serious role in psychological theories.

The burden of the accusation is not untruth but triviality. There can be no doubt that it is a valve opener that opens valves, and it is likely that visual perception is mediated by the processing of visual information. The charge is that such putative functional explanations are mere platitudes. The functionalist can meet this objection by allowing functionally defined theoretical constructs only where mechanisms exist that can carry out the function and only where he has some notion of what such mechanisms might be like. One way of imposing this requirement is to identify the mental processes that, psychology postulates with the operations of the restricted class of possible computers called Turing machines.

A Turing machine can be informally characterized as a mechanism with a finite number of program states. The inputs and outputs of the machine are written on a tape that is divided into squares each of which includes a symbol from a finite alphabet. The machine scans the tape one square at a time. It can erase the symbol on a scanned square and print a new one in its place. The machine can execute only the elementary mechanical operations of scanning, erasing, printing, moving the tape and changing state.

The program states of the Turing machine are defined solely in terms of the input symbols on the tape, the output symbols on the tape, the elementary operations and the other states of the program. Each program state is therefore functionally defined by the part it plays in the overall operation of the machine. Since the functional role of a state depends on the relation of the state to other states as well as to inputs and outputs, the relational character of the mental is captured by the Turing-machine version of functionalism. Since the definition of a program state never refers to the physical structure of the system running the program, the Turing-machine version of functionalism also captures the idea that the character of a mental state is independent of its physical realization. A human being, a roomful of people, a computer and a disembodied spirit would all be a Turing machine if they operated according to a Turing-machine program.

The proposal is to restrict the functional definition of psychological states to those that can be expressed in terms of the program states of Turing machines. If this restriction can be enforced, it provides a guarantee that psychological theories will be compatible with the demands of mechanisms. Since Turing machines are very simple devices, they are in principle quite easy to build. Consequently by formulating a psychological explanation as a Turing-machine program the psychologist ensures that the explanation is mechanistic, even though the hardware realizing the mechanism is left open.

There are many kinds of computational mechanisms other than Turing machines, and so the formulation of a functionalist psychological theory in Turing machine-notation provides only a sufficient condition for the theory's being mechanically realizable. What makes the condition interesting, however, is that the simple Turing machine can perform many complex tasks. Although the elementary operations of the Turing machine are restricted, iterations of the operations enable the machine to carry out any well-defined computation on discrete symbols.

An important tendency in the cognitive sciences is to treat the mind chiefly as a device that manipulates symbols. If a mental process can be functionally defined as an operation on symbols, there is a Turing machine capable of carrying out the computation and a variety of mechanisms for realizing the Turing machine. Where the manipulation of symbols is important the Turing machine provides a connection between functional explanation and mechanistic explanation.

The reduction of a psychological theory to a program for a Turing machine is a way of exorcising the homunculi. The reduction ensures that no operations have been postulated except those that could be performed by a familiar mechanism. Of course, the working psychologist usually cannot specify the reduction for each functionally individuated process in every theory he is prepared to take seriously. In practice the argument usually goes in the opposite direction; if the postulation of a mental operation is essential to some cherished psychological explanation, the theory tends to assume that there must be program for a Turing machine that will carry out that operation.

The "black boxes" that are common in flow charts drawn by psychologists often serve to indicate postulated mental processes for which Turing reductions are wanting. Even so, the possibility in principle of such reduction serves as a methodological constraint on psychological theorizing by determining what functional definitions are to be allowed and what it would be like to know that everything has been explained that could possibly need explanation.

Such is the origin, the provenance and the promise of contemporary functionalism. How much has it actually paid off? This question is not easy to answer because much of what is now happening in the philosophy of mind and the cognitive sciences is directed at exploring the scope and limits of the functionalist explanations of behavior. I shall, however, give a brief overview.

An obvious objection to functionalism as a theory of the mind is that the functionalist definition is not limited to mental states and processes. Catalysts, Coke machines, valve openers, pencil sharpeners, mousetraps and ministers of finance are all in one way or another concepts that are functionally defined, but none is a mental concept such as pain, belief and desire. What, then, characterizes the mental? And can it be captured in a functionalist framework?

The traditional view in the philosophy of mind has it that mental states are distinguished by their having what are called either qualitative content or intentional content. I shall discuss qualitative content first.

It is not easy to say what qualitative content is; indeed, according to some theories, it is not even possible to say what it is because it can be known not by description but only by direct experience. I shall nonetheless attempt to describe it. Try to imagine looking at a blank wall through a red filter. Now change the filter to a green one and leave everything else exactly the way it was. Something about the character of your experience changes when the filter does, and it is this kind of thing that philosophers call qualitative content. I am not entirely comfortable about introducing qualitative content in this way, but it is a subject with which many philosophers are not comfortable.

The reason qualitative content is a problem for functionalism is straight-forward. Functionalism is committed to defining mental states in terms of their causes and effects. It seems, however, as if two mental states could have all the same causal relations and yet could differ in their qualitative content. Let me illustrate this with the classic puzzle of the inverted spectrum.

It seems possible to imagine two observers who are alike in all relevant psychological respects except that experiences having the qualitative content of red for one observer would have the qualitative content of green for the other. Nothing about their behavior need reveal the difference because both of them see ripe tomatoes and flaming sunsets as being similar in color and both of them call that color "red." Moreover, the causal connection between their (qualitatively distinct) experiences and their other mental states could also be identical. Perhaps they both think of Little Red Riding Hood when they see ripe tomatoes, feel depressed when they see the color green and so on. It seems as if anything that could be packed into the notion of the causal role of their experiences could be shared by them, and yet the qualitative content of the experiences could be as different as you like. If this is possible, then the functionalist account does not work for mental states that have qualitative content. If one person is having a green experience while another person is having a red one, then surely they must be in different mental states.

The example of the inverted spectrum is more than a verbal puzzle. Having qualitative content is supposed to be a chief factor in what makes a mental state conscious. Many psychologists who are inclined to accept the functionalist framework are nonetheless worried about the failure of functionalism to reveal much about the nature of consciousness. Functionalists have made a few ingenious attempts to talk themselves and their colleagues out of this worry, but they have not, in my view, done so with much success. (For example, perhaps one is wrong in thinking one can imagine what an inverted spectrum would be like.) As matters stand, the problem of qualitative content poses a serious threat to the assertion that functionalism can provide a general theory of the mental.

Functionalism has fared much better with the intentional content of mental states. Indeed, it is here that the major achievements of recent cognitive science are found. To say that a mental state has intentional content is to say that it has certain semantic properties. For example, for Enrico to believe Galileo was Italian apparently involves a three-way relation between Enrico, a belief and a proposition that is the content of the belief (namely the proposition that Galileo was Italian). In particular it is an essential property of Enrico's belief that it is about Galileo (and not about, say, Newton) and that it is true if, and only if, Galileo was indeed Italian. Philosophers are divided on how these considerations fit together, but it is widely agreed that beliefs involve semantic properties such as expressing a proposition, being true or false and being about one thing rather than another.

It is important to understand the semantic properties of beliefs because theories in the cognitive sciences are largely about the beliefs organisms have. Theories of learning and perception, for example, are chiefly accounts of how the host of beliefs an organism has are determined by the character of its experiences and its genetic endowment. The functionalist account of mental states does not by itself provide the required insights. Mousetraps are functionally defined, yet mousetraps do not express propositions and they are not true or false.

There is at least one kind of thing other than a mental state that has intentional content: a symbol. Like thoughts, symbols seem to be about things. If someone says "Galileo was Italian," his utterance, like Enrico's belief, expresses a proposition about Galileo that is true or false depending on Galileo's homeland. This parallel between the symbol and the mental underlies the traditional quest for a unified treatment of language and mind. Cognitive science is now trying to provide such a treatment.

The basic concept is simple but striking. Assume that there are such things as mental symbols (mental representations) and that mental symbols have semantic properties. On this view having a belief involves being related to a mental symbol, and the belief inherits its semantic properties from the mental symbol that figures in the relation. Mental processes (thinking, perceiving, learning and so on) involve causal interactions among relational states such as having a belief. The semantic properties of the words and sentences we utter are in turn inherited from the semantic properties of the mental states that language expresses.

Associating the semantic properties of mental states with those of mental symbols is fully compatible with the computer metaphor, because it is natural to think of the computer as a mechanism that manipulates symbols. A computation is a causal chain of computer states and the links in the chain are operations on semantically interpreted formulas in a machine code. To think of a system (such as the nervous system) as a computer is to raise questions about the nature of the code in which it computes and the semantic properties of the symbols in the code. In fact, the analogy between minds and computers actually implies the postulation of mental symbols. There is no computation without representation.

The representational account of the mind, however, predates considerably the invention of the computing machine. It is a throwback to classical epistemology, which is a tradition that includes philosophers as diverse as John Locke, David Hume, George Berkeley, René Descartes, Immanuel Kant, John Stuart Mill and William James.

Hume, for one, developed a representational theory of the mind that included five points. First, there exist "Ideas," which are a species of mental symbol. Second, having a belief involves entertaining an Idea. Third, mental processes are causal associations of Ideas. Fourth, Ideas are like pictures. And fifth, Ideas have their semantic properties by virtue of what they resemble: the Idea of John is about John because it looks like him.

Contemporary cognitive psychologists do not accept the details of Hume's theory, although they endorse much of its spirit. Theories of computation provide a far richer account of mental processes than the mere association of Ideas. And only a few psychologists still think that imagery is the chief vehicle of mental representation. Nevertheless, the most significant break with Hume's theory lies in the abandoning of resemblance as an explanation of the semantic properties of mental representations.

Many philosophers, starting with Berkeley, have argued that there is something seriously wrong with the suggestion that the semantic relation between a thought and what the thought is about could be one of resemblance. Consider the thought that John is tall. Clearly the thought is true only of the state of affairs consisting of John's being tall. A theory of the semantic properties of a thought should therefore explain how this particular thought is related to this particular state of affairs. According to the resemblance theory, entertaining the thought involves having a mental image that shows John to be tall. To put it another way, the relation between the thought that John is tall and his being tall is like the relation between a tall man and his portrait.

The difficulty with the resemblance theory is that any portrait showing John to be tall must also show him to be many other things: clothed or naked, lying, standing or sitting, having a head or not having one, and so on. A portrait of a tall man who is sitting down resembles a man's being seated as much as it resembles a man's being tall. On the resemblance theory it is not clear what distinguishes thoughts about John's height from thoughts about his posture.

The resemblance theory turns out to encounter paradoxes at every turn. The possibility of construing beliefs as involving relations to semantically interpreted mental representations clearly depends on having an acceptable account of where the semantic properties of the mental representations come from. If resemblance will not provide this account, what will?

The current idea is that the semantic properties of a mental representation are determined by aspects of its functional role. In other words, a sufficient condition for having semantic properties can be specified in causal terms. This is the connection between functionalism and the representational theory of the mind. Modern cognitive psychology rests largely on the hope that these two doctrines can be made to support each other.

No philosopher is now prepared to say exactly how the functional role of a mental representation determines its semantic properties. Nevertheless, the functionalist recognizes three types of causal relation among psychological states involving mental representations, and they might serve to fix the semantic properties of mental representations. The three types are causal relations among mental states and stimuli, mental states and responses and some mental states and other ones.

Consider the belief that John is tall. Presumably the following facts, which correspond respectively to the three types of causal relation, are relevant to determining the semantic properties of the mental representation involved in the belief. First, the belief is a normal effect of certain stimulations, such as seeing John in circumstances that reveal his height. Second, the belief is the normal cause of certain behavioral effects, such as uttering "John is tall." Third, the belief is a normal cause of certain other beliefs and a normal effect of certain other beliefs. For example, anyone who believes John is tall is very likely also to believe someone is tall. Having the first belief is normally causally sufficient for having the second belief. And anyone who believes everyone in the room is tall and also believes John is in the room will very likely believe John is tall. The third belief is a normal effect of the first two. In short, the functionalist maintains that the proposition expressed by a given mental representation depends on the causal properties of the mental states in which that mental representation figures.

The concept that the semantic properties of mental representations are determined by aspects of their functional role is at the center of current work in the cognitive sciences. Nevertheless, the concept may not be true. Many philosophers who are unsympathetic to the cognitive turn in modern psychology doubt its truth, and many psychologists would probably reject it in the bald and unelaborated way that I have sketched it. Yet even in its skeletal form, there is this much to be said in its favor: It legitimizes the notion of mental representation, which has become increasingly important to theorizing in every branch of the cognitive sciences. Recent advances in formulating and testing hypotheses about the character of mental representations in fields ranging from phonetics to computer vision suggest that the concept of mental representation is fundamental to empirical theories of the mind.

The behaviorist has rejected the appeal to mental representation because it runs counter to his view of the explanatory mechanisms that can figure in psychological theories. Nevertheless, the science of mental representation is now flourishing. The history of science reveals that when a successful theory comes into conflict with a methodological scruple, it is generally the scruple that gives way. Accordingly the functionalist has relaxed the behaviorist constraints on psychological explanations. There is probably no better way to decide what is methodologically permissible in science than by investigating what successful science requires.

MAURICE MERLEAU-PONTY
(1908–1961) French Philosopher

The Synthesis of One's Own Body*

The analysis of bodily space has led us to results which may be generalized. We notice for the first time, with regard to our own body, what is true of all perceived things: that the perception of space and the perception of the thing, the spatiality of the thing and its being as a thing are not two distinct problems. The Cartesian and Kantian tradition already teaches us this; it makes the object's spatial limits its essence; it shows in existence *partes extra partes,* and in spatial distribution, the only possible significance of existence in itself. But it elucidates the perception of the object through the perception of space, whereas the experience of our own body teaches us to realize space as rooted in existence. Intellectualism clearly sees that the "motive of the thing" and "the motive of space" are interwoven, but reduces the former to the latter. Experience discloses beneath objective space, in which the body eventually finds its place, a primitive spatiality of which experience is merely the outer covering and which merges with the body's very being. To be a body, is to be tied to a certain world, as we have seen; our body is not primarily *in* space; it is of it. Anosognosics who describe their arm as "like a snake," long and cold, do not, strictly speaking, fail to recognize its objective outline and, even when the patient looks unsuccessfully for his arm or fastens it in order not to lose it, he *knows* well enough where his arm is, since that is where he looks for it and fastens it. If, however, patients experience their arm's space as something alien, if generally speaking I can feel my body's space as vast or minute despite the evidence of my senses, this is because there exists an affective presence and enlargement for which objective spatiality is not a sufficient condition, as anosognosia shows, and indeed not even a necessary condition, as is shown by the phantom arm. Bodily spatiality is the deployment of one's bodily being, the way in which the body comes into being as a body. In trying to analyse it, we were therefore simply anticipating what we have to say about bodily synthesis in general.

We find in the unity of the body the same implicatory structure as we have already described in discussing space. The various parts of my body, its visual, tactile and motor aspects are not simply coordinated. If I am sitting at my table and I want to reach the telephone, the movement of my hand towards it, the straightening of the upper part of the body, the tautening of the leg muscles are superimposed on each other. I desire a certain result and the relevant tasks are

*From Maurice Merleau-Ponty, *The Phenomenology of Perception,* trans. by Colin Smith (London: Routledge & Kegan Paul; New York: Humanities Press, 1967)

spontaneously distributed amongst the appropriate segments, the possible combinations being presented in advance as equivalent: I can continue leaning back in my chair provided that I stretch my arm further, or lean forward, or even partly stand up. All these movements are available to us in virtue of their common meaning. That is why, in their first attempts at grasping, children look, not at their hand, but at the object: the various parts of the body are known to us through their functional value only, and their co-ordination is not learnt. Similarly, when I am sitting at my table, I can instantly visualize the parts of my body which are hidden from me. As I contract my foot in my shoe, I can see it. This power belongs to me even with respect to parts of the body which I have never seen. Thus certain patients have the hallucination of their own face *seen from inside*. It has been possible to show that we do not recognize our own hand in a photograph, and that many subjects are even uncertain about identifying their own handwriting among others, and yet that everyone recognizes his own silhouette or his own walk when it is filmed. Thus we do not recognize the appearance of what we have often seen, and on the other hand we immediately recognize the visual representation of what is invisible to us in our own body. In heautoscopy the double which the subject sees in front of him is not always recognized by certain visible details, yet he feels convinced that it is himself, and consequently declares that he sees his double. Each of us sees himself as it were through an inner eye which from a few yards away is looking at us from the head to the knees. Thus the connecting link between the parts of our body and that between our visual and tactile experience are not forged gradually and cumulatively. I do not translate the "data of touch into the language of seeing" or *vice versa*—I do not bring together one by one the parts of my body; this translation and this unification are performed once and for all within me: they are my body itself. Are we then to say that we perceive our body in virtue of its law of construction, as we know in advance all the possible facets of a cube in virtue of its geometrical structure? But—to say nothing at this stage about external objects—our own body acquaints us with a species of unity which is not a matter of subsumption under a law. In so far as it stands before me and presents its systematic variations to the observer, the external object lends itself to a cursory mental examination of its elements and it may, at least by way of preliminary approximation, be defined in terms of the law of their variation. But I am not in front of my body, I am in it, or rather I am it. Neither its variations nor their constant can, therefore, be expressly posited. We do not merely behold as spectators the relations between the parts of our body, and the correlations between the visual and tactile body: we are ourselves the unifier of these arms and legs, the person who both sees and touches them. The body is, to use Leibnitz's term, the "effective law" of its changes. If we can still speak of interpretation in relation to the perception of one's own body, we shall have to say that it interprets itself. Here the "visual data" make their appearance only through the sense of touch, tactile data through sight, each localized movement against a background of some inclusive position, each bodily event, whatever the "analyser" which reveals it, against a background of significance in which its remotest repercussions are at least foreshadowed and the possibility of an intersensory parity immediately furnished. What unites "tactile sensations" in the hand and links them to visual perceptions of the same hand, and to perceptions of other bodily areas, is a certain style informing my manual gestures and implying in turn a certain style of finger movements, and contributing, in the last resort, to a certain bodily bearing. The body is to be compared, not to a physical object, but rather to a work of art. In a picture or a piece of music the idea is incommunicable by means other than the display of colours and sounds. Any analysis of Cézanne's work, if I have not seen his pictures, leaves me with a choice between several possible Cézannes, and it is the sight of the pictures which provides me with the only existing Cézanne, and therein the analyses find their full meaning. The same is true of a poem or a novel, although they are made up of words. It is well known that a poem, though it has a superficial meaning translatable into prose, leads, in the reader's mind, a further existence which makes it a poem. Just as the spoken word is significant not only through the medium of individual words, but also through that of accent, intonation, gesture and facial expression, and as these additional meanings no longer reveal the speaker's thoughts but the source of his thoughts and his fundamental manner of being, so poetry, which is perhaps accidentally narrative and in that way informative, is essentially a variety of existence. It is distinguishable from the cry, because the cry makes use of the body as nature gave it to us: poor in expressive means; whereas the poem uses language, and even a particular language, in such a way that the existential modulation, instead of being dissipated at the very instant of its expression, finds in poetic art a means of making itself eternal. But although it is independent of the gesture which is inseparable from living expression, the poem is not independent of every material aid, and it would be irrecoverably lost if its text were not preserved down to the last detail. Its meaning is not arbitrary and does not dwell in the firmament of ideas: it is locked in the words printed on some perishable page. In that sense, like every work of art, the poem exists as a thing and does not eternally survive as does a truth. As for the novel, although its plot can be summarized and the "thought" of the writer lends itself to abstract expression, this conceptual significance is extracted from a wider one, as the description of a person is extracted from the actual appearance of his face. The novelist's task is not to expound ideas or even analyse characters, but to depict an inter-human event, ripening and bursting it upon us with no ideological commentary, to such an extent that any change in the order of the narrative or in choice of viewpoint would alter the *literary* meaning of the event. A novel, poem, picture or musical work are individuals, that is, beings in which the expression is indistinguishable from the thing expressed, their meaning, accessible only through direct contact, being radiated with no change of their temporal and spatial situation. It is in this sense that our body is comparable to a work of art. It is a focal point of living meanings, not the function of a certain number of mutually variable terms. A certain experience of touch felt in the upper arm signifies a certain feeling in the forearm and shoulder along with a certain appearance of the same arm, not because the various tactile perceptions among themselves, or the tactile and visual ones, are all involved in one intelligible arm, as the different facets of a cube are related to the idea of a cube, but because the arm seen and the arm touched, like the different segments of the arm, together *perform* one and the same action.

Just as we saw earlier that motor habit threw light on the particular nature of bodily space, so here habit in general enables us to understand the general synthesis of one's own body. And, just as the analysis of bodily spatiality foreshadowed that of the unity of one's own body, so we may extend to all habits what we have said about motor ones. In fact every habit is both motor and perceptual, because it lies, as we have said, between explicit perception and actual movement, in the basic function which sets boundaries to our field of vision and our field of action. Learning to find one's way among things with a stick, which we gave a little earlier as an example of motor habit, is equally an example of perceptual habit. Once the stick has become a familiar instrument, the world of feelable things recedes and now begins, not at the outer skin of the hand, but at the end of the stick. One is tempted to say that through the sensations produced by the pressure of the stick on the hand, the blind man builds up the stick along with its various positions, and that the latter then mediate a second order object, the external thing. It would appear in this case that perception is always a reading off from the same sense-data, but constantly accelerated, and operating with ever more attenuated signals. But habit does not *consist* in interpreting the pressures of the stick on the hand as indications of certain positions of the stick, and these as signs of an external object, since it *relieves us of the necessity* of doing so. The pressures on the hand and the stick are no longer given; the stick is no longer an object perceived by the blind man, but an instrument *with* which he perceives. It is a bodily auxiliary, an extension of the bodily synthesis. Correspondingly, the external object is not the flat projection or invariant of a set of perspectives, but something towards which the stick leads us, and the perspectives of which, according to perceptual evidence, are not signs, but aspects. Intellectualism cannot conceive any passage from the perspective to the thing itself, or from sign to significance otherwise than as an interpretation, an apperception, a cognitive intention. According to this view sense-data and perspectives are at each level contents grasped as (*aufgefasst als*) manifestations of one and the same intelligible core. But this analysis distorts both the sign and the meaning; it separates out, by a process of objectification of both, the sense-content, which is already "pregnant" with a meaning, and the invariant core, which is not a law but a thing: it conceals the organic relationship between subject and world, the active transcendence of consciousness, the momentum which carries it into a thing and into a world by means of its organs and instruments. The analysis of motor habit as an extension of existence leads on, then, to an analysis of perceptual habit as the coming into possession of a world. Conversely, every perceptual habit is still a motor habit and here equally the process of grasping a meaning is performed by the body. When a child grows accustomed to distinguishing blue from red, it is observed that the habit cultivated in relation to these two colours helps with the rest. Is it, then, the case that through the pair blue-red the child has perceived the meaning: "colour"? Is the crucial moment of habit-formation in that coming to awareness, that arrival at a "point of view of colour," that intellectual analysis which subsumes the data under one category? But for the child to be able to perceive blue and red under the category of colour, the category must be rooted in the data, otherwise no subsumption could recognize it in them. It is necessary that, on the "blue" and "red" panels presented to him, the particular kind of vibration and impression on the eye known as blue and red should be represented. In the gaze we have at our disposal a natural instrument analogous to the blind man's stick. The gaze gets more or less from things according to the way in which it questions them, ranges over or dwells on them. To learn to see colours is to acquire a certain style of seeing, a new use of one's own body; it is to enrich and recast the body image. Whether a system of motor or perceptual powers, our body is not an object for an "I think," it is a grouping of lived-through meanings which moves towards its equilibrium. Sometimes a new cluster of meanings is formed: our former movements are integrated into a fresh motor entity, the first visual data into a fresh sensory entity, our natural powers suddenly come together in a richer meaning, which hitherto has been merely foreshadowed in our perceptual or practical field, and which has made itself felt in our experience by no more than a certain lack, and which by its coming suddenly reshuffles the elements of our equilibrium and fulfils our blind expectation.

CONCLUSIONS

Here are conclusions for some of the important arguments in the Part Four Section entitled "Freedom and Determinism."

Locke
1. *The proof of freedom is the exercise of freedom.*
2. *Freedom means desires can be suspended.*

Hobbes
1. *The liberty of man consists in his finding no restraint in fulfilling inclinations.*
2. *Liberty and necessity are consistent.*

Skinner
1. *Descriptive freedom is rejected; prescriptive freedom is to be accepted.*
2. *Freedom is about certain contingencies of reinforcements.*

Wilson
1. *Altruism is the result of genetic expression.*
2. *We choose not to kill ourselves because of genetically transmitted behavior.*

Kant
1. *Man may consider himself both determined and free.*
2. *Reason cannot explain freedom.*

Stace
1. *The compatibility of determinism and freewill is shown by the following conditional: "If X wanted to do A, then X could have done A."*
2. *Moral responsibility demands both freewill and determinism.*

Campbell
1. *The proposition which we must be able to affirm, if moral praise or blame of X is to be justified, is the categorical proposition that X could have acted otherwise because—not if—he could have chosen otherwise.*

> 2. *The "nature" of self comprehends but is not reducible to its "character"; it must be taken as including also the authentic creative power of fashioning and re-fashioning character.*

van Inwagen

> 1. *If either the Mind Argument or the Ethics Argument is sound, then the other is unsound.*

Here are conclusions for some of the important arguments in the Part Four Section entitled *"Mind and Body."*

Aristotle

> 1. *The soul cannot be separated from the body.*
> 2. *Soul is the efficient, formal, and final cause of the body.*

Lucretius

> 1. *Mind and soul are corporeal.*

Descartes

> 1. *Thought is a property of the soul.*
> 2. *Body and soul interact via the tiny gland and animal spirits.*

Ryle

> 1. *There is no polar opposition between mind and matter.*

Fodor

> 1. *The problem of qualitative content poses a serious threat to the assertion that functionalism can provide a general theory of the mental.*
> 2. *Modern psychology seems empirically to confirm the truth of functionalism.*

Merleau-Ponty

> 1. *Experience discloses a merger of objective space and the subject's very being.*

Evaluating and Writing a Logical Argument

The Pro Essay

It's always easier to be *against* something than to be *for* something. Nevertheless, the student must acquire the skill to support a position. The basic strategy is this: Advance the discussion, not repeat it; therefore, open a conversation with a hypothetical critique and defend the author against this critique. Just as in the "con" evaluation, the outline and brainstorm list will give focus and direction to the writing process.

The essay will, again, be about one thousand words (three to four sides of notebook paper). The entire process can be summed up as follows:

Step 1: Create a logical outline of the argument to be examined.

Step 2: Brainstorm a thought-list.

Step 3: Choose the premise which stimulated the most thoughts in both directions—pro and con. This is your "crucial premise."

Step 4: Define a hypothetical detractor's point of view and add this to your thought-list. The detractor will be against the premise in question. The detractor's objection should be developed in around two hundred words (three-quarters of a page of notebook paper).

Step 5: Create a set of responses to your objector. These responses will defend the premise in question. Feel free to make slight modifications in the premise (so long as these stay true to the spirit of your author).

Step 6: Develop some give and take between you and the hypothetical detractor. The goal is to answer the searching objections raised.

Step 7: Set out your introduction and begin!

What you are doing in your "pro" essay is defending your author's argument at its most controversial point. (It was the one you had the most to say about, both pro and con, on your brainstorm list.) By defending the argument *at* its weakest point *from* its strongest attackers, you have done your author a service. Your defense extends the discussion *beyond* the presentation in the book and your narrow focus allows analytic precision.

The most common problems students have are:

1. *The objection is too easily defeated.* Many students, when they first attempt "pro" essays, create a shallow objection that is easily refuted. This is unwise. Don't choose a "straw man." You do not extend the discussion by bringing up trivial objections. Instead, try seeing the issue from "the other side."

2. *Students can't see the other side.* Some students cannot develop an objection because they only see plausibility for the position they hold. This is intellectually dangerous because it is a form of prejudice. Try to project yourself into the persona of the "other side." Do mental role playing. Become an actor of sorts and "transform" into the sort of person who might advocate an opposite viewpoint. Remember the "principle of fairness" (see the logical exercise at the end of Part Three). Make the objection as plausible as possible.

3. *The objection is underdeveloped.* Once you have a strong objection, you need to devote adequate space to illustrate the implications of the detractor's position. By not developing the objection, you shortchange your material for counter-refutation.

4. *There is no clear connection between the objection and the student's response.* Sometimes an essay will be written in which an objection is raised and then never answered. This is not good because it leaves your author unprotected. Instead, try to create parallel responses on your brainstorm list. This will give you a visual connection between the objections and your counter-refutations.

A sample opening paragraph for a "pro" essay might look like this:

The author of the argument believes [insert conclusion of the argument]. She (he) bases this conclusion on an argument that has as its basis a pivotal premise which states [insert crucial premise from your brainstorm list]. This premise is necessary to the author's conclusion and it is here that detractors are likely to concentrate. This essay will examine two possible objections to this thesis and then show why these objections are mistaken.

Freedom and Determinism, Mind and Body in Literature

*Making an End to Things**
H. G. Wells

1

Mr. Polly designed his suicide with considerable care and a quite remarkable altruism.

His passionate hatred for Miriam vanished directly the idea of getting away from her for ever became clear in his mind. He found himself full of solicitude then for her welfare. He did not want to buy his release at her expense. He had not the remotest intention of leaving her unprotected, with a painfully dead husband and a bankrupt shop on her hands. It seemed to him that he could contrive to secure for her the full benefit of both his life insurance and his fire insurance if he managed things in a tactful manner. He felt happier than he had done for years scheming out this undertaking, albeit it was, perhaps, a larger and somberer kind of happiness than had fallen to his lot before. It amazed him to think he had endured his monotony of misery and failure for so long.

But there were some queer doubts and questions in the dim, half-lit background of his mind that he had very resolutely to ignore.

"Sick of it," he had to repeat to himself aloud to keep his determination clear and firm. His life was a failure; there was nothing more to hope for but unhappiness. Why shouldn't he?

His project was to begin the fire with the stairs that led from the ground floor to the underground kitchen and scullery. This he would soak with paraffin, and assist with firewood and paper and a brisk fire in the coal cellar underneath. He would smash a hole or so in the stairs to ventilate the blaze, and have a good pile of boxes and paper, and a convenient chair or so, in the shop above. He would have the paraffin can upset, and the shop lamp, as if awaiting refilling, at convenient distances in the scullery ready to catch. Then he would smash the house lamp on the staircase—a fall with that in his hand was to be the ostensible cause of the blaze—and he would cut his throat at the top of the kitchen stairs, which would then become his funeral pyre. He would do all this on Sunday evening while Miriam was at church, and it would appear that he had fallen downstairs with the lamp and been burned to death. There was really no flaw whatever that he could see in the scheme. He was quite sure he knew how to cut his throat, deep at the side and not to saw at the windpipe, and he was reasonably sure it wouldn't hurt him very much. And then everything would be at an end.

There was no particular hurry to get the thing done, of course, and meanwhile he occupied his mind with possible variations of the scheme.

It needed a particularly dry and dusty east wind, a Sunday dinner of exceptional virulence, a conclusive letter from Konk, Maybrick, Ghool, and Gabbitas, his principal

---

*From H. G. Wells, *The History of Mr. Polly* (New York: Dodd, Mead & Co., 1909).

and most urgent creditors, and a conversation with Miriam, arising out of arrears of rent and leading on to mutual character sketching, before Mr. Polly could be brought to the necessary pitch of despair to carry out his plans. He went for an embittering walk, and came back to find Miriam in a bad temper over the tea things, with the brewings of three-quarters of an hour in the pot and hot buttered muffins gone leathery. He sat eating in silence with his resolution made.

"Coming to church?" said Miriam after she had cleared away.

"Rather. I got a lot to be grateful for," said Mr. Polly.

"You got what you deserve," said Miriam.

"Suppose I have," said Mr. Polly, and went and stared out of the back window at a despondent horse in the hotel yard.

He was still standing there when Miriam came downstairs dressed for church. Something in his immobility struck home to her. "You'd better come to church than mope," she said.

"I shan't mope," he answered.

She remained still. Her presence irritated him. He felt that in another moment he should say something absurd to her, make some last appeal for that understanding she had never been able to give. "Oh! *go* to church," he said.

In another moment the outer door slammed upon her. "Good riddance!" said Mr. Polly.

He turned about. "I've had my whack," he said.

He reflected. "I don't see she'll have any cause to holler," he said. "Beastly Home! Beastly Life!"

For a space he remained thoughtful. "Here goes!" he said at last.

2

For twenty minutes Mr. Polly busied himself about the house, making his preparations very neatly and methodically.

He opened the attic windows, in order to make sure of a good draught through the house, and drew down the blinds at the back and shut the kitchen door to conceal his arrangements from casual observation. At the end he would open the door on the yard and so make a clean, clear draught right through the house. He hacked at, and wedged off, the tread of a stair. He cleared out the coals from under the staircase, and built a neat fire of firewood and paper there; he splashed about paraffin and arranged the lamps and can even as he had designed, and made a fine, inflammable pile of things in the little parlour behind the shop. "Looks pretty arsonical," he said, as he surveyed it all. "Wouldn't do to have a caller now. Now for the stairs!"

"Plenty of time," he assured himself, and took the lamp which was to explain the whole affair, and went to the head of the staircase between the scullery and the parlour. He sat down in the twilight, with the unlit lamp beside him, and surveyed things. He must light the fire in the coal cellar under the stairs, open the back door, then come up them very quickly and light the paraffin puddles on each step, then sit down here again and cut his throat. He drew his razor from his pocket and felt the edge. It wouldn't hurt much, and in ten minutes he would be indistinguishable ashes in the blaze.

And this was the end of life for him!

The end! And it seemed to him now that life had never begun for him, never! It was as if his soul had been cramped and his eyes bandaged from the hour of his birth. Why had he lived such a life? Why had he submitted to things, blundered into things? Why had he never insisted on the things he thought beautiful and the things he desired, never sought them, fought for them, taken any risk for them, died rather than abandon them? They were the things that mattered. Safety did not matter. A living did not matter unless there were things to live for. . . .

He had been a fool, a coward and a fool; he had been fooled, too, for no one had ever warned him to take a firm hold upon life, no one had ever told him of the littleness of fear or pain or death. But what was the good of going through it now again. It was over and done with.

The clock in the back parlour pinged the half-hour.

"Time!" said Mr. Polly, and stood up.

For an instant he battled with an impulse to put it all back, hastily, guiltily, and abandon this desperate plan of suicide for ever.

But Miriam would smell the paraffin!

"No way out this time, O'Man," said Mr. Polly, and went slowly downstairs, matchbox in hand.

He paused for five seconds, perhaps to listen to noises in the yard of the Royal Fishbourne Hotel before he struck his match. It trembled a little in his hand. The paper blackened, and an edge of blue flame ran outward and spread. The fire burned up readily, and in an instant the wood was crackling cheerfully.

Some one might hear. He must hurry.

He lit a pool of paraffin on the scullery floor, and instantly a nest of wavering blue flame became agog for prey. He went up the stairs three steps at a time, with one eager blue flicker in pursuit of him. He seized the lamp at the top. "Now!" he said, and flung it smashing. The chimney broke, but the glass receiver stood the shock and rolled to the bottom, a potential bomb. Old Rumbold would hear that and wonder what it was. . . . He'd know soon enough!

Then Mr. Polly stood hesitating, razor in hand, and then sat down. He was trembling violently, but quite unafraid.

He drew the blade lightly under one ear. "Lord!" but it stung like a nettle!

Then he perceived a little blue thread of flame running up his leg. It arrested his attention, and for a moment he sat, razor in hand, staring at it. It must be paraffin! On his trousers that had caught fire on the stairs. Of course his legs were wet with paraffin! He smacked the flicker with his hand to put it out, and felt his leg burn as he did so. But his trousers still charred and glowed. It seemed to him necessary that he must put this out before he cut his throat. He put down the razor beside him to smack with both hands very eagerly. And as he did so a thin, tall, red flame came up through the hole in the stairs he had made and stood still, quite still, as it seemed, and looked at him. It was a strange-looking flame, a flattish, salmon colour, redly streaked. It was so queer and quiet-mannered that the sight of it held Mr. Polly agape.

"Whuff!" went the can of paraffin below, and boiled over with stinking white fire. At the outbreak, the salmon-coloured flames shivered and ducked and then doubled and vanished, and instantly all the staircase was noisily ablaze.

Mr. Polly sprang up and backwards, as though the uprushing tongues of fire were a pack of eager wolves.

"Good Lord!" he cried, like a man who wakes up from a dream.

He swore sharply, and slapped again at a recrudescent flame upon his leg.

"What the Deuce shall I do? I'm soaked with the confounded stuff!"

He had nerved himself for throat-cutting, but this was fire!

He wanted to delay things; to put the fire out for a moment while he did his business. The idea of arresting all this hurry with water occurred to him.

There was no water in the little parlour and none in the shop. He hesitated for a moment whether he should not run upstairs to the bedroom and get a ewer of water to throw on the flames. At this rate Rumbold's would be ablaze in five minutes. Things were going all too fast for Mr. Polly. He ran towards the staircase door, and its hot breath pulled him up sharply. Then he dashed out through the shop. The catch of the front door was sometimes obstinate; it was now, and instantly he became frantic. He rattled and stormed and felt the parlour already ablaze behind him. In another moment he was in the High Street with the door wide open.

The staircase behind him was crackling now like horsewhips and pistol-shots.

He had a vague sense that he wasn't doing as he had proposed, but the chief thing was his sense of that uncontrolled fire within. What was he going to do? There was the fire-brigade station next door but one.

The Fishbourne High Street had never seemed so empty.

Far off, at the corner by the God's Providence Inn, a group of three stiff hobbledehoys in their black, neat clothes conversed intermittently with Taplow, the policeman.

"Hi!" bawled Mr. Polly to them. "Fire! Fire!" and, struck by a horrible thought, he thought of Rumbold's deaf mother-in-law upstairs, began to bang and kick and rattle with the utmost fury at Rumbold's shop door.

"Hi!" he repeated, "Fire!"

That was the beginning of the great Fishbourne fire, which burned its way sideways into Mr. Rusper's piles of crates and straw, and backwards to the petrol and stabling of the Royal Fishbourne Hotel, and spread from that basis until it seemed half Fishbourne would be ablaze. The east wind, which had been gathering in strength all that day, fanned the flames; everything was dry and ready, and the little shed beyond Rumbold's, in which the local fire brigade kept its manual, was alight before the Fishbourne fire-hose could be saved from disaster. In a marvellously short time a great column of black smoke, shot with red streamers, rose out of the middle of the High Street, and all Fishbourne was alive with excitement.

Then the public-houses began to vomit forth the less desirable elements of Fishbourne society; boys and men were moved to run and shout, and more windows went up as the stir increased. Tashingford, the chemist, appeared at his door, in shirt sleeves and an apron, with his photographic plate-holders in his hand. And then, like a vision of purpose, came Mr. Gambell, the greengrocer, running out of Gayford's alley and buttoning on his jacket as he ran. His great brass fireman's helmet was on his head, hiding it all but the sharp nose, the firm mouth, the intrepid chin. He ran straight to the fire station and tried the door, and turned about and met the eye of Boomer still at his upper window. "The key!" cried Mr. Gambell, "the key!"

Mr. Boomer made some inaudible explanation about his trousers and half a minute.

"Seen old Rumbold?" cried Mr. Polly, approaching Mr. Gambell.

"Gone over Downford for a walk," said Mr. Gambell. "He told me! But look 'ere! We 'aven't got the key!"

"Lord!" said Mr. Polly, and regarded the china shop with open eyes. He knew the old woman must be there alone. He went back to the shop front, and stood surveying it in infinite perplexity. The other activities in the street did not interest him. A deaf old lady somewhere upstairs there! Precious moments passing! Suddenly he was struck by an idea, and vanished from public vision into the open door of the Royal Fishbourne Tap.

And now the street was getting crowded, and people were laying their hands to this and that.

Suddenly, in the midst of it all a woman in the crowd screamed, "Look up on the roof there! Two people on the roof!"

Her eyes had not deceived her. Two figures, which had emerged from the upper staircase window of Mr. Rumbold's and had got, after a perilous paddle in his cistern, on to the fire station, were now slowly but resolutely clambering up the outhouse roof towards the back of the main premises of Messrs. Mantell and Throbsons'. They clambered slowly, and one urged and helped the other, slipping and pausing ever and again amidst a constant trickle of fragments of broken tile.

One was Mr. Polly, with his hair wildly disordered, his face covered with black smudges and streaked with perspiration, and his trouser legs scorched and blackened; the other was an elderly lady, quietly but becomingly dressed in black with small white frills at her neck and wrists, and a Sunday cap of écru lace enlivened with a black velvet bow. Her hair was brushed back from her wrinkled brow and plastered down tightly, meeting in a small knob behind; her wrinkled mouth bore that expression of supreme resolution common with the toothless aged. She was shaky, not with fear, but with the vibrations natural to her years, and she spoke with a slow, quavering firmness.

"I don't mind scrambling," she said with piping inflexibility, "but I can't jump, and I won't jump."

"Scramble, old lady, then, scramble!" said Mr. Polly, pulling her arm. "It's one up and two down on these blessed tiles."

"It's not what I'm used to," she said.

"Stick to it," said Mr. Polly. "Live and learn," and got to the ridge and grasped at her arm to pull her after him.

"I can't jump, mind ye," she repeated, pressing her lips together. "And old ladies like me mustn't be hurried."

"Well, let's get as high as possible, anyhow," said Mr. Polly, urging her gently upwards. "Shinning up a waterspout in your line? Near as you'll get to Heaven."

"I *can't* jump," she said. "I can do anything but jump."

"Hold on," said Mr. Polly, "while I give you a boost. That's—wonderful."

"So long as it isn't jumping. . . ."

The old lady grasped the parapet above, and there was a moment of intense struggle.

"Urup!" said Mr. Polly. "Hold on! Gollys! where's she gone to? . . ."

Then an ill-mended, wavering, yet very reassuring spring-side boot appeared for an instant.

"Thought perhaps there wasn't any roof there!" he explained, scrambling up over the parapet beside her.

"I've never been out on a roof before," said the old lady. "I'm all disconnected. It's very bumpy. Especially that last bit. Can't we sit here for a bit and rest? I'm not the girl I used to be."

"You sit here ten minutes," shouted Mr. Polly, "and you'll pop like a roast chestnut. Don't understand me? *Roast Chestnut!* ROAST CHESTNUT! POP! There ought to be a limit to deafness. Come on round to the front and see if we can find an attic window. Look at this smoke!"

"Nasty!" said the old lady, her eyes following his gesture, puckering her face into an expression of great distaste.

"Come on!"

"Can't hear a word you say."

He pulled her arms. "Come on!"

She paused for a moment to relieve herself of a series of entirely unexpected chuckles. "Such goings on!" she said. "I never did! Where's he going now?" and came along behind the parapet to the front of the drapery establishment.

Below, the street was now fully alive to their presence, and encouraged the appearance of their heads by shouts and cheers. A sort of free fight was going on round the fire-escape, order represented by Mr. Boomer and the very young policeman, and disorder by some partially intoxicated volunteers with views of their own about the manipulation of the apparatus. Two or three lengths of Mr. Rusper's garden hose appeared to have twined themselves round the ladder. Mr. Polly watched the struggle with a certain impatience, and glanced ever and again over his shoulder at the increasing volume of smoke and steam that was pouring up from the burning fire station. He decided to break an attic window, and with some difficulty, got her into the attic, but the staircase, he found, was full of suffocating smoke, and he dared not venture below the next floor. He took her into a long dormitory, shut the door on those pungent and pervasive fumes, and opened the window, to discover the fire-escape was now against the house, and all Fishbourne boiling with excitement as an immensely helmeted and active and resolute little figure ascended. In another moment the rescuer stared over the window-sill, heroic but just a trifle self-conscious and grotesque.

"Lawks-a-mussy!" said the old lady. "Wonders and Wonders Why! it's Mr. Gambell! 'Iding 'is 'ead in that thing! I *never* did!"

"Can we get her out?" said Mr. Gambell. "There's not much time."

"He might git stuck in it."

"*You'll* get stuck in it," said Mr. Polly; "come along!"

"Not for jumpin' I don't," said the old lady, understanding his gestures rather than his words. "Not a bit of it. I bain't no good at jumping, and I *wun't.*"

They urged her gently but firmly towards the window.

"You lemme do it my own way," said the old lady at the sill. . . .

Mr. Gambell hovered protectingly below. Mr. Polly steered her aged limbs from above. An anxious crowd below babbled advice and did its best to upset the fire-escape. Within, streamers of black smoke were pouring up through the cracks in the floor. For some seconds the world waited while the old lady gave herself up to reckless mirth again. "Sich times!" she said. "Poor Rumbold!"

Slowly they descended; and Mr. Polly remained at the post of danger, steadying the long ladder, until the old lady was in safety below and sheltered by Mr. Rumbold (who was in tears) and the young policeman from the urgent congratulations of the crowd. The crowd was full of an impotent passion to participate. Those nearest wanted to shake her hand, those remoter cheered.

"The fust fire I was ever in, and likely to be my last. It's a scurryin', 'urryin' business, but I'm real glad I haven't missed it," said the old lady, as she was borne rather than led towards the refuge of the Temperance Hotel.

Also she was heard to remark: "'E was saying something about 'ot chestnuts. *I* haven't 'ad no 'ot chestnuts."

Then the crowd became aware of Mr. Polly awkwardly negotiating the top rungs of the fire-escape. "'Ere 'e comes!" proclaimed a voice; and Mr. Polly descended into the world again out of the conflagration he had lit to be his funeral-pyre, moist, excited, and tremendously alive, amidst a tempest of applause. As he got lower and lower, the crowd howled like a pack of dogs at him. Impatient men, unable to wait for him, seized and shook his descending boots, and so brought him to earth with a run. He was rescued with difficulty from an enthusiast who wished to slake at his own expense and to his own accompaniment a thirst altogether heroic. He was hauled into the Temperance Hotel and flung like a sack, breathless and helpless, into the tear-wet embrace of Miriam.

Questions For Discussion

1. Mr. Polly is very unhappy. He feels he has blundered into his life instead of choosing it. For the first time in his existence, he will make a decision and master events instead of letting them master him: he will commit suicide. Through an act of the will his mind will conquer his body. What happens?

2. How do the events which occur relate to Mr. Polly's assessment of life? of freedom? of the relation between body and soul?

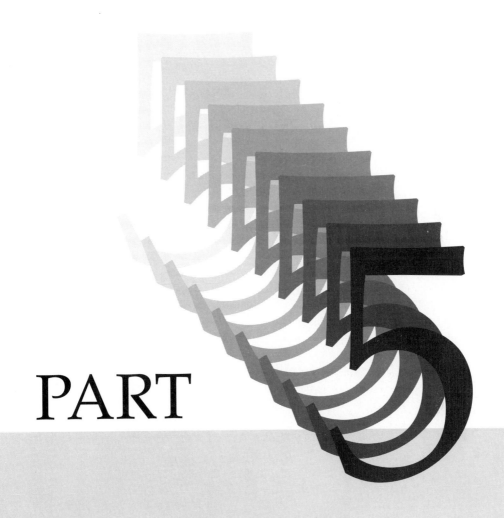

PART 5

Belief in God

Alvin Plantinga

University of Notre Dame

Belief in God

Some two-thirds of the world's population of approximately five billion people profess belief in God—the God of Abraham, Isaac, and Jacob, God as he is conceived of by Jews, Moslems, Christians, and others. So thought of, God is an immaterial person who is all-knowing, all-powerful, perfectly good, and the creator and sustainer of the world. First, God is a *person* (though not of course a *human* person): that is, he has aims and goals, he acts so as to achieve these aims and goals, and he has awareness and knowledge. Second, God is *immaterial:* he is not a material object and has no body, but is instead a spirit, a person without a body. Third, as Jews, Moslems, and Christians think of him, God is *omniscient*, that is, all-knowing: he not only has *some* knowledge, but he knows everything, or everything that can be known. (Perhaps there are certain things about the future that can't be known—for instance, what you will freely decide to have for breakfast tomorrow morning; but God knows whatever can be known.) Fourth, God is thought of as *omnipotent*—that is to say, all-powerful. The idea is not that God can do just *anything*, no matter how ridiculous. He can't draw round squares, for example, or create married bachelors. He can't change the past. He can't cause it to be the case that there never was any such person as Abraham, or that the Second World War never took place; it's too late for that. Nor can God lie or sin. The idea, rather, is that God has the maximum possible degree of power; he has a degree of

power such that it is not possible that there be something with more power than that. Further, God is wholly *good* and benevolently disposed to mankind. Still further, God is the creator and sustainer of the universe. He has created the world out of nothing: that is not to say that *nothing* is a sort of thin, gossamer material out of which he created the world, but rather that he created it and didn't create it *out* of anything at all. He also *sustains* the world from moment to moment, keeps it in existence.

This characterization of God is what we might call *standard theism;* but of course not all theists are standard theists. Some theists depart from one or another of the elements of standard theism: some, for example, think that God is very powerful, but not omnipotent; others—"deists" as they are called—think he created the world and set it going but does not now sustain it or act in or on it; still others (Mormons, for example) think God has a body or that the world is his body. Some believers in God depart even further from standard theism. Still others refer to themselves as theists but depart so far from standard theism that it isn't clear that they are theists at all. Thus Matthew Arnold said he thought God was "the power not ourselves that makes for goodness" (to which F. H. Bradley retorted that *he* thought *soap* was the power not ourselves that makes for cleanliness); and the contemporary theologian Gordon Kaufman suggests that (in this nuclear age) we should think of God as "the evolutionary-historical process that has brought us into being."[1]

Now there are many interesting philosophical questions and problems about God: how is he related to the world, and what in detail is it to be omnipotent, or omniscient, or the sustainer of the world, or a person without a body? But in contemporary philosophy (contemporary western philosophy anyway), perhaps the most widely discussed philosophical problem about belief in God is really about *belief* in God. This question is something like this: is it rational, or reasonable, or sensible, or intellectually acceptable, or in accord with one's intellectual obligations to believe in God? (This question has been very much with us for at least the last couple of hundred years, ever since the Enlightenment.) Many apparently think not; they think contemporary science, or modern historical methods, or perhaps just what those who are enlightened and in the know now think—they think these things make it unreasonable to believe in God, or at any rate unreasonable for those who are sufficiently aware of contemporary science and culture. This question—the reasonableness or rationality of belief in God—is the topic of this part of this book.

I

Arguments for and Against Belief in God
The most widely accepted method of approaching this question is to consider the arguments for and against belief in God. What more natural than to look at the evidence? If the arguments *for* the existence of God (theistic arguments, as they are called) are stronger than the arguments *against* his existence, then it is rational or reasonable to believe in God; on the other hand, if the arguments against theism outweigh the arguments for it, then the rational procedure is to reject belief in God in favor of atheism or agnosticism. Thus Bertrand Russell (see pg. 419) devotes a good share of his effort to elegant if superficial refutations of

some arguments for the existence of God; and J. L. Mackie (see pg. 430) argues that the existence of evil is an impressive argument against the existence of God. On the other side, many thinkers have offered arguments for the existence of God; among contemporary theistic arguments, perhaps the most powerful and highly developed is that offered by Richard Swinburne in his book *The Existence of God.*[2] As I say, this procedure seems initially sensible; and in the first part of this essay I shall briefly consider some of these arguments. In the second part, however, I shall argue that this is not the only way or even the best way to approach this question about the rationality of belief in God.

Arguments for the Existence of God
There are many arguments for the existence of God; they have been discussed for a long time by many acute philosophers and theologians; here it won't be possible to do more than barely indicate some of the most important arguments and some of the most important lines of discussion. Theistic arguments go back at least to the time of Aristotle (and perhaps considerably further back than that). Such arguments were extensively studied and discussed in the Middle Ages; one thinks particularly of Anselm's Ontological Argument and of Thomas Aquinas's celebrated five ways (five theistic proofs) at the beginning of his massive and monumental *Summa Theologiae.* In the Middle Ages, the principal reason for constructing theistic proofs was not to convince people that there really is such a person as God (then, as now, most people already believed that) but to show that we human beings can *know* that there is such a person, can have *scientific* or *demonstrative* knowledge of

---

[1] Gordon Kaufman, *Theology for a Nuclear Age* (Manchester: Manchester University Press, 1985), pp. 43.

[2] Richard Swinburne, *The Existence of God* (Oxford: Oxford University Press, 1979).

the existence of God.[3] Early modern philosophy and the Enlightenment saw a great flurry of theistic proofs; Descartes, Locke, Leibniz, Malebranche, Berkeley, Paley, and many others all offered proofs or arguments for the existence of God (prompting the remark that nobody doubted the existence of God until the philosophers tried to prove it). Here the aim wasn't so much to show that we can have demonstrative knowledge of the existence of God as to show that it is reasonable or rational to accept theistic belief. This attempt to provide good theistic arguments continues to the present day.

Traditional Theistic Arguments Immanuel Kant, one of the greatest commentators on the theistic arguments, divided them into three large categories: **Ontological Arguments, Cosmological Arguments,** and **Teleological Arguments.** In some ways the most interesting of these is the utterly fascinating **Ontological Argument,** first offered in the eleventh century by Anselm of Canterbury (1033–1109). Anselm states his argument as follows:

> And so Lord, do thou, who dost give understanding to faith, give me, so far as thou knowest it to be profitable, to understand that thou art as we believe and that thou art that which we believe. And indeed, we believe that thou art a being than which nothing greater can be conceived. Or is there no such nature, since the fool has said in his heart, there is no God? But at any rate this very fool, when he hears of this being of which I speak—a being than which nothing greater can be conceived—understands what he hears, and what he understands is in his understanding; although he does not understand it to exist.
>
> For it is one thing for any object to be in the understanding and another to understand that the object exists. When a painter first conceives of what he will afterwards perform he has it

in his understanding, but he does not yet understand it to be, because he has not yet performed it. But after he has made the painting, he both has it in his understanding, and he understands that it exists, because he has made it.

> Hence even the fool is convinced that something exists in the understanding, at least, than which nothing greater can be conceived. For suppose it exists in the understanding alone; then it can be conceived to exist in reality; which is greater.
>
> Therefore, if that, than which nothing greater can be conceived, exists in the understanding alone, the very being, than which nothing greater can be conceived, is one, than which a greater can be conceived. But obviously this is impossible. Hence, there is no doubt that there exists a being, than which nothing greater can be conceived, and it exists both in the understanding and in reality.[4]

Anselm's argument has been the subject of enormous controversy ever since he had the temerity to spring it on an unsuspecting world. It has fascinated nearly every great philosopher from Anselm's day to the present. Many utterly reject it; Kant claimed to have finally and definitively refuted it; Schopenhauer thought it was a charming joke; many philosophers since have thought it was a joke alright, but more like a *dumb* joke. And indeed the argument does have about it a suggestion of trumpery and deceit. Nonetheless there have been and are many who think some version of this argument a perfectly valid argument for the existence of

[3] See Nicholas Wolterstorff, "The Migration of the Theistic Proofs," in *Rationality, Religious Belief and Moral Commitment*, ed. by Robert Audi and William Wainwright (Ithaca, NY: Cornell University Press, 1986).

[4] S. Anselm, "Proslogion," Chapter 2 in S. Anselmi, *Opera Omnia*, ed. F. S. Schmitt, 6 vols. (Edinburgh University Press, 1946–1961).

God; it does not lack for contemporary defenders.[5]

Turn now to **Cosmological Arguments.** These arguments typically proceed from some very general fact about the world—that there is *motion,* for example, or *causation;* they then move to the conclusion that there must be a first unmoved mover or first uncaused cause—a being that is not itself caused to exist by anything else, but causes everything else to exist. An interesting variant is presented by the argument from *contingency.* This argument begins from the fact that there are many contingent beings—beings that (like you and me) *do* exist, but could have *failed* to exist; it moves to the conclusion that there is a *necessary* being, a being such that it is not possible that it fail to exist. (It would remain to be shown that such a being would be God.) Perhaps the strongest version of the Cosmological Arguments would combine the argument from contingency with first cause and first mover arguments.[6]

The third kind of argument, says Kant, is the **Teleological Argument** or argument from design—more exactly, the teleological arguments, since there are several different arguments of this type. A fine formulation of such an argument is given by David Hume (who, however, does not himself accept it):

Look round the world: contemplate the whole and every part of it: you will find it to be nothing but one great machine, subdivided into an infinite number of lesser machines, which again admit of subdivisions, to a degree beyond what human faculties can trace and explain. All these various machines, and even their most minute parts, are adjusted to each other with an accuracy, which ravishes into admiration all men, who have ever contemplated them. The curious adapting of means to ends, throughout all nature, resembles exactly, though it much exceeds the productions of human contrivance; of

human design, thought, wisdom and intelligence. Since therefore the effects resemble one another, we are led to infer, by all the rules of analogy, that the causes also resemble; and that the author of nature is somewhat similar to the mind of man; though possessed of much larger faculties, proportioned to the grandeur of the work which he has executed.[7]

Many facets of the universe strongly suggest that it has been created or designed: the delicate articulated beauty of a tiny flower, the night sky viewed from the side of a mountain, the fact that the cosmological constants (including in particular the rate of expansion of the universe) must be extremely accurately adjusted if there is to be intelligent life in the universe, and so on.

Now these classical arguments as classically presented typically take the form of *conclusive* or *coercive* arguments, or rather would-be conclusive or coercive arguments. They take the form of attempted *demonstrations;* the idea is that any rational person who is intellectually honest will believe the premises and will see that the premises do indeed entail the intended conclusions. Taken as coercive demonstrations, it is fair to say, I think, that they fail. None of these arguments seems to be a real demonstration. None seems to be the sort of argument which (like, say, the Pythagorean Theorem or Kurt Gödel's demonstration of the

[5] See, for example, Charles Hartshorne's *Man's Vision of God* (New York: Harper and Row, Inc., 1941); and Norman Malcolm's "Anselm's Ontological Arguments" (*Philosophical Review,* 1960). There is a development and defense of a version of this argument in my *God Freedom and Evil* (Grand Rapids: Eerdman's Publishing Co., 1978) and *The Nature of Necessity* (Oxford: Oxford University Press, 1974) Chap. 10.

[6] As in David Braine's *The Reality of Time and the Existence of God* (Oxford: Oxford University Press, 1988).

[7] *Dialogues Concerning Natural Religion,* ed. with an introduction by Norman Kemp Smith (Indianapolis: Bobbs-Merrill, 1947), pp. 143.

incompleteness of arithmetic) really leaves no room for doubt or disagreement. Taken as *demonstrations,* the theistic arguments fail. But why should they be taken like that? After all, scarcely any arguments for any serious philosophical conclusion qualify as real demonstrations—are really such that anyone who understands them is obliged to accept them on pain of irrationality or intellectual dishonesty. Take your favorite argument for any serious philosophical conclusion; there will be plenty of people who don't accept that argument, and are not thereby shown to be either unusually dense or intellectually dishonest. So why should it be different with theistic arguments? Even if there aren't any knockdown drag-out *demonstrations* for the existence of God, there might still be plenty of good arguments. A good argument would be one that started from premises many people rationally accept (or are inclined to accept) and proceeds via steps many people reasonably endorse to the conclusion that there is such a person as God. Perhaps there aren't any demonstrations; it doesn't follow that there aren't any good arguments. As a matter of fact, I think we can see that there are a host of good theistic arguments. The traditional argument from design is certainly one such an argument; many find it simply incredible that the world as we find it, with all its apparent traces of design, should have arisen by chance or natural necessity. As Kant says, this argument

> always deserves to be mentioned with respect. It is the oldest, the clearest, and the most accordant with the common reason of mankind. It enlivens the study of nature, just as it itself derives its existence and gains ever new vigor from that source. . . . Reason, constantly upheld by this ever-increasing evidence which, though empirical, is yet so powerful, cannot be so depressed through doubts suggested by subtle and abstruse

> speculation, that it is not at once aroused from the indecision of all melancholy reflection, as from a dream, by one glance at the wonders of nature and the majesty of the universe—ascending from height to height up to the all-highest.[8]

Some people claim that the Theory of Evolution, neo-Darwinian Evolution, undercuts this argument by showing how it could be that all of contemporary life could have arisen without any intelligent design at all: the suggestion is that these forms of life could have arisen by way of random or chance genetic mutation together with natural selection. Said Darwin himself: "the old argument from design, as given by Paley, which formerly seemed to me so conclusive, fails now that the law of natural selection has been discovered."[9]

But here we must make a distinction. There is apparently good evidence that contemporary forms of life have arisen by way of development over millions of years from simpler antecedents. So suppose we concede that there has indeed been the sort of biological development we learned about in high school.[10] A further and very different question is whether the mechanisms neo-Darwinians posit (random genetic mutation and natural selection) provide a good *explanation* for this development. This is a totally different question. Take, for example, the human eye. Do we really have an

[8] Imanuel Kant, *Critique of Pure Reason*, trans. by Norman Kemp Smith (New York: St. Martin's Press, 1929), pp. 520. (Kant speaks thus approvingly of this argument but did not himself accept it.)

[9] *The Autobiography of Charles Darwin*, ed. Nora Barlow (London: Collins, 1958) pp. 50–51.

[10] Even here, however, a certain wariness is probably appropriate; according to Stephen Gould, who should certainly know, the fossil record shows nearly no transitional forms: "The extreme rarity of transitional forms in the fossil record persists as the trade secret of paleontology. The evolutionary trees that adorn our textbooks have data only at the tips and nodes of their branches; the rest is inference, however reasonable, not the evidence of fossils."

evolutionary explanation of its development? Given how little is known about the rate of genetic mutations in the relevant populations at the relevant times, the length of time necessary for a mutation to become dominant in the relevant populations, the proportion of those mutations that would be adaptive, and the proportion of them that would both be adaptive and a step on the way to the development of the eye, all we can really say with any show of plausibility is that we don't know that it is impossible. (And perhaps we don't know that it is impossible only because we don't know much at all here.) But of course that is a long way from having a good explanation; what we have is not an explanation at all, but only a explanation-candidate.

So suppose we take these theistic proofs in a different spirit (in the spirit appropriate to philosophical arguments generally): not as knockdown drag-out arguments which no sane person can honestly reject, but instead as arguments whose premises and inferential moves will be found attractive by many who reflect on the matter. Then I think we must conclude that the ontological argument, even in the forms in which it commits no fallacies, doesn't have a great deal of force (despite the fact that, as I think, it is a perfectly valid argument). Perhaps it has *some* force; but probably not many who reflect on the argument and understand it will find the premise—that it is possible that there be a greatest possible being—plausible unless they already accept the conclusion. The cosmological argument, however, is much stronger, and the teleological arguments, stronger yet.

Non-traditional Arguments So far the traditional arguments. In addition to these, however, there are also a large number of other theistic arguments, some of which resist easy statement and don't fall easily under the traditional rubrics. First, there is a wide variety of *metaphysical* arguments of various types. I shall

mention just one: the Argument from Intentionality. Consider *propositions:* the things that are true or false, that are capable of being believed, and that stand in logical relations to one another; examples would be **All men are mortal,** $7 + 5 = 12$, **Roger Bannister is the first human being to run a four-minute mile,** and **The population of Australia is about that of metropolitan New York.** (Propositions are not sentences, or linguistic items, but what sentences express; the same proposition may be expressed by different sentences, and the same sentence on different occasions may express different propositions.) Propositions also have another property: *aboutness* or *intentionality.* Propositions *represent* reality or some part of it *as being thus and so.* (Thus the second proposition above represents Roger Bannister as being the first human being to run a four-minute mile, and the first represents 7 and 5 as being such that their sum is 12.) It is because of this representational property that propositions are either true or false; a proposition is true if the part of reality it represents as being a certain way, is in fact the way the proposition represents it.

Now many have thought it incredible that propositions should exist apart from the activity of minds. How could they just *be* there if never thought of, or entertained by a mind? This idea is connected with the intentionality of propositions. *Representing things as being thus and so,* being *about* something or other—these seem to be properties or activities of *minds* or perhaps *thoughts.* So it seems plausible to think that propositions are ontologically dependent upon mental or intellectual activity—dependent in such a way that either they just *are* thoughts, or else at any rate couldn't exist if they were not thought of. But if they have to be thought of by *human* thinkers, then there is a real problem: there are many propositions no human being has ever thought of, because there are many too complicated for any human being to grasp.

Further, there are far too many propositions for them to be human thoughts.
Clearly, there are at least as many propositions as there are real numbers: for, for
every real number **r,** there is the proposition **r is a real number.** On the other hand,
if propositions were *divine* thoughts,
there would be no problem here. So perhaps the best way to think of propositions is as divine thoughts. Then in our
thinking we would literally be thinking
God's thoughts after him. This argument
will appeal to those who think (a) that
intentionality is a characteristic of propositions, (b) that there are very many
propositions, or propositions no human
being can grasp, and (c) that intentionality or aboutness is dependent upon mind
in such a way that there couldn't be a
proposition **p** about something where **p**
had never been thought of.

This argument is just one of a sizeable
class of arguments: there are similar
arguments involving sets, properties,
and natural numbers, as well as a fairly
similar argument from the nature of
counterfactuals. But these metaphysical
arguments are just the beginning; there
is also a wide variety of *epistemological*
arguments, arguments that take their
premises or starting points in some fact
about human knowledge. Consider, for
example, The Argument from the Confluence of Proper Function and Reliability, which goes as follows. Most of us
assume that when our intellectual or cognitive faculties are functioning properly
(in the right sort of environment, the sort
of environment for which they seem to
be designed), they are for the most part
reliable; for the most part the beliefs they
produce are true. According to theism,
God has created us in his image; he has
created us in such a way as to resemble
him in being able to know the truth over
a wide range of topics and subjects. This
provides an easy, natural explanation of
the fact (as we see it) that when our cognitive faculties are not subject to dys-
function, the beliefs they produce are for
the most part true.

And this explanation has no real com-
petitors (at least among beliefs that are
live options for us.) It is sometimes suggested that nontheistic evolutionism is
such a competitor; but this is a mistake.
First, there is the problem I noted above:
we don't have an evolutionary explanation of human cognitive capacities, and
we don't even know that it is possible that
there be one. But second, nontheistic
evolution would at best explain our faculties' being reliable with respect to
beliefs that have survival value. (That
would exclude [among others] beliefs
involving reasonably recondite mathematical truths, relativity theory, and
quantum mechanics, and, more
poignantly, scientific beliefs of the sort
involved in thinking evolution is a plausible explanation of the flora and fauna we
see around us.) "At best," I say; but it
wouldn't really explain even that. True
beliefs *as such* don't have survival value;
they have to be linked with the right
kind of dispositions to behavior. What
evolution really requires is that our *behavior* have survival value, not necessarily
that our beliefs be true; it is sufficient for
the demand of evolution that we be pro-
gramed to act in adaptive ways. But there
are many ways in which our behavior
could be adaptive, even if our beliefs
were for the most part false. (For example, our whole belief structure might be a
sort of by-product or epiphenomenon,
having no real connection with truth,
and no real connection with our action.)
So there is no explanation in evolution
for the confluence of proper function and
reliability. As Patricia Churchland (not
noted as a defender of theism) puts it,
from an evolutionary point of view, "The
principal chore of nervous systems is to
get the body parts where they should be
in order that the organism may survive. . . . Truth, whatever that is, definitely takes the hindmost."[11]

[11] Patricia Churchland, "Epistemology in the Age of
Neuroscience," *Journal of Philosophy* 84 (October,
1987), pp. 548.

The argument from the confluence of reliability and proper function is one epistemological theistic argument; but there are many more. For example, there are arguments from the nature of warrant or positive epistemic status, from induction, from the rejection of global skepticism, from reference, from modal intuition, and from intuition generally. But there are also a variety of *moral* arguments, arguments from the phenomena of morality. Among the best are Robert Adams' favored version[12] which, stated in simple fashion, goes as follows. A person might find herself utterly convinced (as I do) that (1) morality is objective, not dependent upon what human beings know or think, that (2) the rightness or wrongness of an action (for example, the wrongness of the action of killing someone just for the thrill of it) cannot be explained in terms of any "natural" facts about human beings or other things— that is, it can't ultimately be explained in terms of physical, chemical, or biological facts, and that (3) there couldn't *be* such objective non-natural moral facts unless there were such a person as God who, in one way or another, brings them into being, or legislates them. This is the obverse side of the thought that in a naturalistic universe, objective moral facts somehow wouldn't make sense, wouldn't fit in.[13]

In addition to moral, epistemological, and metaphysical arguments, there are several others that don't fit well into those categories. For example, there are arguments from love, from beauty and the appreciation of beauty, from play, enjoyment, humor, and adventure. (At bottom, these arguments claim that love in its many manifestations, or a Mozart piano concerto, or a great adventure have a kind of value that can't be explained in naturalistic terms.) There are also arguments from colors and flavors, and from the meaning of life.

The most important thing to see here, I think, is this. Once we recognize that a good theistic argument doesn't have to

be a proof that will coerce any reasonable intellect (once we apply the same standards to theistic arguments that we apply to other arguments), we see that there are a large number of good theistic arguments—in fact it is extremely difficult to think of any other important philosophical thesis for which there are so many importantly different arguments. Indeed, the fact that there *are* so many different arguments (the fact that theism is of explanatory value in so many and so many different areas of thought) is itself still another argument in its favor.

Anti-Theistic Arguments

Of course there are also many arguments *against* theism. Some of these don't amount to much: for example, the first Russian cosmonaut, upon returning to earth, claimed that he had confirmed official Marxist atheism: he had very carefully looked around for God but had not seen him. But of course there are also many much more serious antitheistic arguments. For example, there is the Wittgensteinian argument that there is no God, since God, if he existed, would be a person without a body, and it is impossible that there be a person without a body. It has also been argued that even if there could be a spirit (a person without a body), such a person could have no causal effects in the hard, heavy, mass of physical world; but then such a person could not be God. Still further, there is the claim that there couldn't be an *omniscient* being, one who knows whatever could be known, because for each of us there are truths about ourselves that can be known alright, but can't be known by any other person (for example, what I

[12] C. Delaney, "Moral Argument for Theistic Belief," in *Rationality, Religious Belief and Moral Commitment*, ed. by Robert Audi and Richard Wainright (Ithaca, NY: Cornell University Press, 1986).
[13] See George Mavrodes, "Religion and the Queerness of Morality," in *Rationality, Religious Belief and Moral Commitment*, ed. by Robert Audi and William Wainright (Ithaca, NY: Cornell University Press, 1986).

know when I know that *I* am in pain). Similar arguments are used to try to show that it is not possible that there be an omnipotent being: the whole idea of omnipotence, it is sometimes said, is incoherent.[14] I can't comment on these arguments here, but none of them seems at all conclusive.

A more widely accepted argument for atheism or agnosticism is the oft-repeated claim that modern science casts a great deal of doubt upon the idea that there is such a person as God. It isn't easy to see how this argument is supposed to go; does physics, or astronomy, or chemistry, for example, suggest that there is no such person as God? It certainly isn't easy to see how. Possibly biology would be a better candidate. Indeed, William Provine argues that biology shows that there is no such person as God, because it shows that evolutionary development goes by way of *chance* or *random* genetic mutation and natural selection; but if there were such an all-knowing person as God, such mutations could not be really random. (God would know of them in advance and plan for their use in the development of life.) But here it is at best exceedingly hard to see how biology could possibly show that these mutations are random in *that* sense—that is, random in such a way that it follows that there is no divine person orchestrating the biological developments in question. What is more plausible, perhaps, is the claim, not that that biology provides an argument *against* theistic belief, but that it undercuts one of the reasons for accepting theistic belief, by showing a natural way in which it could be the case that all contemporary forms of life developed from simpler forms of life and ultimately from non-living matter. As I argued above, however, it is extremely dubious that we have anything like an explanation here at all; what evolutionary scenarios really show is that we don't know it couldn't have happened that way. (Of course we also don't know that it *could* have happened that

way, and we certainly don't know that it *did* happen that way.)

Still another kind of objection to theistic belief isn't exactly an *argument* so much as a sort of sociological comment: it is claimed that (among educated people, anyway) fewer and fewer are serious believers in God; mankind come of age, it is sometimes said, can't really believe in God as traditionally thought of. Of course there seem to be a large number of highly educated contemporaries who *do* believe in God; a large number of people with Ph.D.'s in physics and in engineering, for example, claim to believe in God, and in the United States, some 10 percent of those who teach philosophy in colleges and universities are members of the Society of Christian Philosophers. So if the objector's claim is that educated contemporaries don't in fact believe in God, the claim must be modified; obviously great numbers of educated contemporaries do. Perhaps this objection is less an objection than a sort of bludgeon or threat: if you believe in God, you will be out of step with the majority of your educated contemporaries. (Of course the fact that you and I are out of step doesn't show that it is you who is marching poorly.) On the other hand, perhaps the objector thinks that those educated contemporaries who do believe are to be discounted somehow—perhaps they haven't properly appreciated the good reasons there are for giving up belief in God. But then he is really falling back on the other arguments.

There are two atheological arguments that are particularly impressive. First, there is the radical *ambiguity* of the world. The world is ambiguous in that it seems to fit well both with belief in God and with atheism. The committed theist can plausibly interpret his experience in terms of theism (although certain kinds of evil can give him pause); the committed atheist can do the same for atheism (although he may be distressed

---

[14] See pp. 430 ffp.

by the place to which art, music, literature, intellectual endeavor, love, and morality are consigned on a coherently naturalistic way of thinking about the world). But (so the argument goes) isn't this ambiguity itself an argument for atheism? If there really *were* a God of the sort Christians, Muslims, and Jews worship, wouldn't his existence be much more *evident*? Why does God remain *hidden*, if indeed there is such a person? Why doesn't he show himself?

But what would it be for God *not* to be hidden? Perhaps it would be for us to be so constituted that we would find belief in God natural and inevitable. And the fact is, of course, that belief in God *does* seem natural and inevitable for many. Whether God is hidden or not depends on whom you talk to. But the objector can persist: even if God is evident to some of us, why isn't he evident to us *all*? Compare belief in God with, say, belief in the past, or other minds, or an external world. Scarcely anyone (apart from an occasional and very eccentric solipsist) is doubtful about the existence of other persons. If God is really there, wouldn't we expect his presence to be as evident to us as that of other persons? After all, if he *is* there, that is perhaps the most important truth of all.

Theists have made several suggestions as to why God might seem to be hidden from many. It is suggested, for example, that what God wants from us is spontaneous and uncoerced belief in him; but if he were as evident to us as other persons, that would not be possible. Or it is suggested that what God wants is a personal relationship with us, the sort of relationship that good friends enjoy; but this would be difficult or impossible if he were really evident to us in all his greatness and majesty; as Aristotle says, friendship is possible only among equals (or perceived equals). I doubt that these reasons and others like them are really convincing. Perhaps the theist must acknowledge that she doesn't really know why God

remains hidden from so many so much of the time.

Of course the fact that we don't know why God does what he does is not of great significance; and this brings us to what is by far the most important atheological argument: the celebrated argument from evil. This argument goes all the way back to Epicurus.[15] The objector begins by reminding us of the sheer *extent* of suffering and evil in the world; and indeed there is an enormous amount of it. There is also the cruelly ironic character of some evil; a man who drives a cement mixer truck comes home for lunch, lingers a bit too long in the warmth and love of his family, hurriedly jumps into his truck, backs out—and kills his three-year-old daughter who had been playing behind the wheels. Why didn't God prevent something so savagely ironic? A woman in a Nazi concentration camp is compelled to choose which of her two children shall go to the gas chamber and which shall be saved; here we have evil naked and unalloyed; and if God is what theists claim he is— omnipotent and wholly good—then why does he permit such abominations in his world? As David Hume (echoing Epicurus) put it,

> Is he willing to prevent evil, but not able? Then he is impotent. Is he able, but not willing? Then he is malevolent. Is he both able and willing? Whence then is evil?

and

> Why is there any misery at all in the world? Not by chance, surely. From some cause, then. Is it from the intention of the deity? But he is perfectly benevolent. Is it contrary to his intention? But he is almighty. Nothing can shake the solidity of this reasoning, so short, so clear, so decisive. . . .[16]

[15] Diogenes Laertius, *Lives of Eminent Philosophers*, trans. by R. D. Hicks (Cambridge: Harvard, 1979), 8K. X, 80–82.

[16] *Dialogues Concerning Natural Religion*, ed. by Nelson Pike (New York: Bobbs-Merrill Co. Inc., 1970), pp. 88, 91.

So the objector begins with this question: if God is omnipotent and wholly good, then why is there all this evil? The theist must concede, I think, that she doesn't know—that is, she doesn't know in any detail. On a quite general level, she may know or think she knows that God permits evil because he can achieve a world he sees as better by permitting evil than by preventing it; and what God sees as better is, of course, better. But we cannot see why *our* world, with all its ills, would be better than others we think we can imagine, nor what, in any detail, is God's reason for permitting a given specific evil. Not only can we not see this, we can't, I think, envision any very good possibilities. And here I must remark that most of the attempts to explain why God permits evil—*theodicies,* as we might call them—seem to me tepid and shallow.

Of course the fact that the theist can't answer Epicurus' question—the fact that for many or most specific evils, she has no real idea what God's reason for permitting that specific evil might be—that fact does not in itself prove much of anything. Our grasp of the fundamental way of things is at best limited; there is no reason to think that if God *did* have a reason for permitting the evil in question, we would be the first to know. Something further must be added, if the objector is to make worthwhile point. Granted: we don't know why God permits evil; but where, so far, is the problem?

Here the objector is quick to oblige. And (at least until recently) his most popular response has been to offer some version of the *deductive anti-theistic argument from evil*—as in J. L. Mackie's article (see pg. 430). Mackie claims that the existence of evil—and of course the theist will himself agree that there is evil—entails that there is no God, or at any rate no God as conceived by standard theism. Mackie puts the claim as follows:

I think, however, that a more telling criticism [of theism] can be made by way of the traditional problem of evil.

Here it can be shown, not merely that religious beliefs lack rational support, but that they are positively irrational, that the several parts of the essential theological doctrine are inconsistent with one another.[17]

He goes on to argue that the existence of God is incompatible with the existence of evil; he concludes that since the theist is committed to both God and evil, theistic belief is irrational. It ought to be discouraged; and those who accept it, presumably, ought to give it up.

At present, I think, it is fairly widely conceded (contrary to Mackie's claim) that there is nothing like straightforward contradiction or inconsistency or necessary falsehood in the joint affirmation of God and evil. It is logically possible that God should have a reason for permitting all the evil there is; but if so, then the existence of God is not incompatible with the existence of the evil the world displays. This suggestion is developed, for example, in the Free Will Defense, according to which God must put up with at least some evil if he is to create genuinely free creatures. The Free Will Defense goes all the way back to Augustine in the fifth century and is widely accepted at present.[18]

Accordingly, atheologians have turned from deductive to *probabilistic* arguments from evil. The typical atheological claim at present is not that the existence of God is logically *incompatible* with that of evil. The claim is instead that

[17] "Evil and Omnipotence", below, pp. 736. In Mackie's posthumous *The Miracle of Theism* (Oxford: Oxford University Press, 1982), Mackie wavers between his earlier claim that the existence of God is straightforwardly inconsistent with that of evil, and the claim that the existence of evil is powerful but not conclusive evidence against the existence of God. (See pp. 150–175, and see my "Is Theism Really a Miracle?" in *Faith and Philosophy*, 3, April 1986), pp. 298–313.

[18] And (as I see it) rightly so; see my *The Nature of Necessity* (Oxford: Clarendon Press, 1974), Chap. IX, and *God Freedom and Evil* (New York: Harper and Row, 1974; and Grand Rapids: W. B. Eerdman's, 1980), pp. 7–64.

(1) there is an omnipotent, omniscient and perfectly good God

is *improbable* or *unlikely* with respect to

(2) There are 10^{13} turps of evil (where the *turp* is the basic unit of evil).

According to William Rowe, for example, it is probable that

(3) "There exist instances of intense suffering which an omnipotent, omniscient being could have prevented without thereby losing some greater good or permitting some evil equally bad or worse";[19]

this is probable, he says, because

It seems quite unlikely that *all* the instances of intense suffering occurring daily in our world are intimately related to the occurrence of greater goods or the prevention of evils at least as bad; and even more unlikely, should they somehow all be so related, that an omnipotent omniscient being could not have achieved at least some of these goods (or prevented some of those evils) without permitting the instances of intense suffering that are supposedly related to them.[20]

The atheologian, therefore, claims that (1) is improbable with respect to (2). But he doesn't make this point for the sheer academic charm of it all; something further is supposed to follow. The fact, if it is a fact, that (1) is thus improbable is supposed to show that there is something wrong or misguided about belief in God, that it is irrational, or intellectually irresponsible, or noetically second class, or not such as to measure up to the appropriate standards for proper belief.

But *is* (1) improbable on (2) (or some other reasonably plausible proposition about evil)? Why should we think so? Rowe's claim is that there is much *apparently pointless* evil; there is much which is such that we have no idea what reason

God (if there is such a person) could have for permitting it. He considers a hypothetical state of affairs in which a fawn is burned in a forest fire and refers to the fawn's "apparently pointless" suffering; this suffering he says, "was preventable, and so far as we can see, pointless."[21] He seems to be arguing that (1) is improbable with respect to (2) because

(3) Many cases of evil are apparently pointless,

that is, many cases of evil are apparently not such that an omniscient and omnipotent God would be obliged to put up with them in order to achieve a world as good as ours.

But how shall we understand Rowe here? In particular, how shall we understand this "apparently pointless"? Here there are two possibilities. First, he may be holding that

(4) In fact there *are* many cases of evil such that *it is apparent that* an omnipotent and omniscient God, if he existed, would not have a reason for permitting them.

But this is much too strong. There aren't cases of evil such that it is just *obvious* or *apparent* that God could have no reason for permitting them. The most we can sensibly say is that there are many cases of evil such that we can't think of any good reason why he would permit them; but of course that doesn't mean that it is apparent to us that he doesn't *have* a reason. As Stephen Wykstra quite properly points out,[22] we could sensibly claim this latter only if we had reason to think that if such a God *did* have a reason for

[19] William Rowe, "The Problem of Evil and Some Varieties of Atheism," *American Philosophical Quarterly* 16 (1979), pp. 336. (My [3] is Rowe's [1]).

[20] Ibid., pp. 337–38.

[21] Ibid., pp. 337.

[22] Stephen Wykstra, "The Humean Obstacle to Evidential Arguments from Suffering: on Avoiding the Evils of Appearance," *International Journal for the Philosophy of Religion* 16 (1984), pp. 85.

permitting such evils, we would be likely to have some insight into what it is. But why think *that*? There is no reason to think that if there is such a person as God, and if he had a reason for permitting a particular evil state of affairs, *we* would have a pretty good idea of what that reason might be. On the theistic conception our cognitive powers, as opposed to God's, are a bit slim for that. God might have reasons we cannot so much as understand; he might have reasons involving other creatures—angels, devils, the principalities and powers of whom St. Paul speaks—creatures of whose nature and activities we have no knowledge.

Shall we take (3) as pointing out, then, that there are many evils such that we have no idea what God's reason, if any, is for permitting them? That seems right; but why suppose it shows that (1) is improbable with respect to (2)? We could sensibly claim *that* only if we had good reason to think that we would be privy to God's reasons for permitting evil, if he had some; but of course we don't have good reason to think that. We know very little of God's alternatives; perhaps, for example, we and our suffering figure into transactions involving beings we know nothing at all about.

This is the lesson of the book of Job, one of the great classic discussions of evil. Job suffers; he has done no particular wrong, so he thinks God is treating him unjustly in permitting this evil. He wants to go to court with God; he can't see any reason why God should allow him to be afflicted as he is; he concludes, unthinkingly, that God doesn't *have* a good reason. As a matter of fact, according to the story, God *does* have a good reason, but the reason involves a transaction among beings of some of whom Job has no awareness at all. The point here is that the reason for Job's sufferings is something entirely beyond his ken, so that the fact that he can't see what sort of reason God might have for permitting his suffering doesn't at all tend to show that God

has no reason. And when God replies to Job, he doesn't tell him the reason for his suffering (perhaps Job couldn't so much as grasp or comprehend God's reason); instead, God tells him how little he knows (compared to God):

> Then the Lord answered Job out of the tempest: Who is this whose ignorant words darken counsel? Brace yourself and stand up like a man; I will ask questions and you shall answer. Where were you when I laid the earth's foundations? Tell me, if you know and understand! Who settled its dimensions? Surely you should know! Who stretched his measuring-line over it? On what do its supporting pillars rest? Who set its corner-stone in place, when the morning stars sang together and all the sons of God shouted for joy? . . . Have you descended to the springs of the sea or walked in the unfathomable deep? Have the gates of death been revealed to you? Have you ever seen the doorkeepers of the place of darkness? Have you comprehended the vast expanse of the world? Come, tell me all this, if you know! Which is the way to the home of light and where does darkness dwell? And can you then take each to its appointed bound and escort it on its homeward path? Doubtless you know all this; for you were born already, so long is the span of your life![23]

Job complains that God has no good reason for permitting the evil that befalls him. He believes that God doesn't have a good reason because he, Job, can't imagine what that reason might be. In reply, God does not tell him what the reason is; instead, he attacks Job's unthinking assumption that if he can't imagine what reason God might have, then probably God doesn't have a reason at all. And God attacks this assumption by pointing

[23]Job 38, verses 1–7, 16–31.

out that Job's knowledge is really very limited along these lines. No doubt he can't think what God's reason might be; but nothing of interest follows from this. In particular it doesn't follow that probably God doesn't *have* a reason. "All right, Job, if you're so smart, if you know so much, tell me about it! Tell me how the universe was created; tell me about the sons of God who shouted with joy upon its creation! [No doubt you were there!]" And Job sees the point:". . . I have spoken of great things which I have not understood, things too wonderful for me to know."[24]

Say that an evil is *inscrutable* if it is such that we can't think of any reason God (if there is such a person) could have for permitting it. Clearly, the crucial problem for this probabilistic argument from evil is just the fact that nothing much follows from the fact that some evils are inscrutable; if theism is true, we would expect that there would be inscrutable evil. Indeed, it is only *hubris* which would tempt us to think that we could so much as grasp God's plans here, even if he proposed to divulge them to us. But then the fact that there is inscrutable evil does not make it improbable that God exists.[25] The argument from evil, therefore, may have some degree of strength, but its weaknesses are evident.

II

Is Argument Required for Belief in God?
As I said at the beginning, perhaps the most widely discussed philosophical question having to do with belief in God is the question whether such belief is rational, or reasonable, or intellectually up to snuff, or such that a person who was reasonable and well informed could accept it. And the typical way of approaching this question has been to examine the arguments for and against the existence of God. But is it really clear that discussing those arguments is the only or best way to approach this question of the rational justification of theistic

belief? The assumption seems to be that if the arguments for theism are stronger than those for atheism, then belief in God is rational; but if the arguments for atheism are stronger, then atheism, or at any rate agnosticism, is the more reasonable attitude. But why suppose that the rational status of theistic beliefs—its reasonability or intellectual acceptability—depends upon whether there are good theistic arguments available? Consider an analogy. We all believe that there has been a past and that we know something about it. As Bertrand Russell pointed out, however, it is possible (possible in the broadly logical sense) that the world is only five minutes old, having been created just five minutes ago complete with all its apparent traces of the past, all the apparent memories, dusty books, faded pictures, crumbling mountains, massive oak trees, and the like. So what about the belief that there has been a substantial

---

[24] Job 42, verse 3.

[25] We can put this more formally in terms of the calculus of probability. The conditional probability of inscrutable evil on the existence of God (P(IE/G)) is about the same as the antecedent probability of inscrutable evil (P(IE))P; Now consider Bayes' Theorem:

$$P(G/IE) = \frac{P(G) \times P(IE/G)}{P(IE)}$$

What this says is that the conditional probability of the existence of God on the existence of inscrutable evil (P(G/IE)) is equal to the antecedent probability of the existence of God (P(G)) multiplied by the conditional probability of inscrutable evil on the existence of God (P(IE/G)), this product being divided by the antecedent probability of inscrutable evil (P(IE)). What we have seen is that (P(IE/G)) is about the same as P(IE); on the supposition that theism is true, the existence of inscrutable evil is about as likely as it is apart from the consideration of the existence of God. But then,

$$\frac{P(IE/G)}{P(IE)}$$

will be nearly equal to 1, in which case P(G/IE) will be nearly equal to (P(G)). That is, the conditional probability of the existence of God on the existence of inscrutable evil is nearly equal to the antecedent probability of the existence of God, so that the existence of inscrutable evil does not significantly disconfirm (that is, lower the antecedent probability of) the existence of God.

past, that the world has been here for more than five minutes? Surely that belief is rational, justified, and reasonable. But is there a good non-circular, non-question begging *argument* for it? (Of course if we are content with *circular* arguments, the theist can produce plenty of such arguments for theism.) It is certainly hard to see what they might be; no one, so far as I know, has ever come up with much of a candidate. So our belief in the past is rational or justified even though we don't have a good non-circular argument for it; so a belief can be justified in the absence of such reason; so why suppose we need arguments or evidence (evidence in the sense of other supporting beliefs) for the existence of God? Why can't belief in God be properly basic?

We can approach this same question from a slightly different direction. Many philosophers (and others as well) object that theistic belief is irrational or intellectually sub par because, as they say, there is *insufficient evidence* for it. Bertrand Russell was once asked what he would say if, after dying, he were brought into the presence of God and asked why he hadn't been a believer. Russell's reply: "I'd say 'Not enough evidence God! Not enough evidence!'"[26] We needn't speculate as to how such a reply would be received; what is clear is that Russell held theistic belief to be unreasonable because there is insufficient evidence for it. W. K. Clifford, that "delicious *enfant terrible*" as William James called him, insisted that it is wrong, immoral, wicked, and monstrous to accept a belief for which you don't have sufficient evidence. As he puts it in his characteristically restrained fashion, "Whoso would deserve well of his fellows in this matter will guard the purity of his belief with a very fanaticism of jealous care, lest at any time it should rest on an unworthy object, and catch a stain which can never be wiped away"; and he concludes by saying "To sum up: it is wrong always, everywhere, and for anyone to believe

anything upon insufficient evidence."[27] So it is wrong to accept belief in God without sufficient evidence; numberless hordes of philosophers have joined Clifford in this opinion, and in the further opinion that indeed there is not sufficient evidence for belief in God.[28]

So the evidentialist objection has two premises:

(a) It is irrational to believe in God unless there is sufficient evidence (good arguments) for theistic belief

and

(b) there is no evidence, or at least no sufficient evidence, for theistic belief.

Now I have already argued that (b) is at best dubious. There are many good theistic arguments, and putting them all together results in an impressive case indeed. But our present concern is the *other* premise of the objector's argument: the claim that in the absence of evidence, belief in God is irrational or unjustifiable or intellectually unacceptable. Why should we believe a thing like that? Why do those who offer the evidentialist objection believe it? We don't think the same thing about belief in other minds, the past, material objects. So why here? One answer, I think, is that those who think thus, think of theism as a *scientific*

---

[26] Bertrand Russell, quoted in W. Salmon's "Religion and Science: a New Look at Hume's Dialogues," *Philosophical Studies* 33 (1978), pp. 176.

[27] W. K. Clifford, "The Ethics of Belief," in *Lectures and Essays* (London: Macmillan, 1879), pp. 345 ff.

[28] For example, Brand Blanshard, *Reason and Belief* (London: Allen and Unwin, 1974), pg. 400 ff.; Antony Flew, *The Presumption of Atheism* (London: Pemberton, 1976), pp. 87 ff.; Bertrand Russell, "Why I am not a Christian," in *Why I am not a Christian* (New York: Simon and Schuster, 1957), pg. 3 ff.; J. L. Mackie, *The Miracle of Theism* (Oxford: The Clarendon Press, 1982); Michael Scriven, *Primary Philosophy* (New York: McGraw-Hill, 1966) pp. 87 ff.; and many others. This objection is even more popular in the oral tradition than in published work; and it ordinarily has the character of an unspoken assumption more than that of an explicit objection.

hypothesis, or a quasi-scientific hypothesis, or relevantly *like* a scientific hypothesis—something like Special Relativity, for example, or Quantum Mechanics, or the Theory of Evolution. According to J. L. Mackie, for example, "Against the rival theistic hypothesis we should have to score the (significant) improbability that if there were a god he (or it) would create a world with causal laws, and one with our specific causal laws and constants, but also the great improbability of there being a process of the unmediated fulfillment of will."[29] And speaking of religious experience, he makes the following characteristic remark: "Here, as elsewhere, the supernaturalist hypothesis fails because there is an adequate and much more economical naturalistic alternative."[30] Clearly these remarks are relevant only if we think of belief in God as or as like a sort of scientific hypothesis, a theory designed to explain some body of evidence, and acceptable to the degree that it explains that evidence. On this way of looking at the matter, there is a relevant body of evidence shared by believer and unbeliever alike; theism is a hypothesis designed to explain that body of evidence; and theism is rationally defensible only to the extent that it is a good explanation thereof.

But why should we think of theism like this? Clearly there are perfectly sensible alternatives. Consider our beliefs about the past: one could take a Mackie-like view here as well. One could hold that our beliefs about the past are best thought of as like a scientific hypothesis, designed to explain such present phenomena as (among other things) apparent memories; and if there were a more "economical" explanation of these phenomena that did not postulate past facts, then our usual beliefs in the past "could not be rationally defended." But here this seems clearly mistaken (not to say silly); the availability of such an "explanation" wouldn't in any way tell against our ordinary belief that there has really been a past. Why couldn't the same hold for theism?

In responding to Hume, Thomas Reid brilliantly discusses a similar network of questions. Here the topic under discussion is not God, but material objects or an external world. Suppose it is proposed that my belief in material objects is "rationally defensible" only if it is more probable than not with respect to a body of knowledge that includes no physical object propositions but only, say, self-evident truths together with experiential propositions specifying how I am appeared to. Add (as the history of modern philosophy strongly suggests) that it is impossible to show that physical object statements *are* more probable than not with respect to such a body of evidence; or add, more strongly, that in fact physical object propositions are *not* more probable than not with respect to such propositions. What would follow from that? One of Reid's most important and enduring contributions was to point out that nothing of much interest would follow from that. In particular it would not follow that belief in physical objects ought to be discouraged as somehow improper, or irrational, or intellectually out of order.

But why, then, should we think it follows in the case of theism? Suppose theistic belief is not more probable than not with respect to the body of beliefs shared by theists and non-theists: why should we conclude that it is not rationally defensible? Perhaps it is perfectly rational to take belief in God in the way we ordinarily take belief in other minds, material objects, the past, and the like. Why isn't it perfectly sensible to *start with* belief in God? Why does belief in God have to be probable with respect to some *other* body of evidence in order to be rationally defensible?

This brings us to the papers by Alston and Wolterstorff. As they see this matter, it isn't necessary, in order for belief in God to be rationally justified or justified rationally, that it be accepted on the basis

[29] Mackie, *The Miracle of Theism,* pp. 252–53.
[30] Ibid., pp. 198.

of arguments. Wolterstorff argues that a believer in God can be perfectly rational even if he doesn't believe on the basis of arguments, even if in fact there aren't any good theistic arguments. Of course it doesn't follow that the believer in God who doesn't have *that* sort of grounds for his belief—that is, the sort provided by arguments or evidence from other beliefs—has no grounds at all; and Alston's article explains how these grounds might be, broadly speaking, *experiential*. His idea is that at least some believers in God might have the same sort of grounds (broadly speaking) for theistic belief as we have for perceptual beliefs, or memory beliefs, or beliefs about other persons. Here Alston stands in a long tradition, a tradition going back nearly to the beginnings of Christian thought. Essential to this tradition is the thought that our knowledge and awareness of God does not typically come by way of inference from other beliefs we have, but much more directly. John Calvin, for example, held that God has created us with a *"Sensus Divinitatis,"* an *awareness* of God, a disposition (activated in a variety of circumstances) to form beliefs about God:

> 'There is within the human mind, and indeed by natural instinct, an awareness of divinity.' This we take to be beyond controversy. To prevent anyone from taking refuge in the pretense of ignorance, God himself has implanted in all men a certain understanding of his divine majesty. Ever renewing its memory, he repeatedly sheds fresh drops. Since, therefore, men one and all perceive that there is a God and that he is their Maker, . . . From this we conclude that it is not a doctrine that must first be learned in school, but one of which each of us is master from his mother's womb and which nature itself permits no one to forget.[31]

Calvin's claim is that God has created us in such a way that we have a strong tendency or disposition to form beliefs

about him. This disposition is actualized or triggered in a wide variety of situations including, for example, perception of the world around us:

> Lest anyone, then, be excluded from access to happiness, he not only sowed in men's minds that seed of religion of which we have spoken, but revealed himself and daily discloses himself in the whole workmanship of the universe.[32]

Like Kant, Calvin is especially impressed, in this regard, by the starry heavens above:

> Even the common folk and the most untutored, who have been taught only by the aid of the eyes, cannot be unaware of the excellence of divine art, for it reveals itself in this innumerable and yet distinct and well-ordered variety of the heavenly host.[33]

So Calvin's basic idea here is that human beings have a sort of natural disposition or propensity to form beliefs about God in a wide variety of circumstances. When a human being is functioning properly from a cognitive point of view, she will form beliefs about God—**God has created all this; God is my Maker; I owe God allegiance and obedience**—in a wide variety of situations. These beliefs will not typically be reached by virtue of argument from other beliefs; they will not typically be evidentially based upon other beliefs she has; they will be accepted as basic. In this they will be like memory beliefs, perceptual beliefs, *a priori* beliefs, and many others.

So the question about the rationality of theistic belief can't anywhere nearly be settled just by paying attention to the arguments for and against belief in God. At least as important is the question whether belief in God is properly basic—

[31] John Calvin, *Institutes of the Christian Religion*, trans. by Ford Lewis Battles (Philadelphia: Westminster Press, 1960), Bk. I, Chap. 3, pp. 43–44.
[32] Ibid., pp. 51.
[33] Ibid., pp. 50.

whether, that is, proper and rational belief in God can resemble (say) memory beliefs in not ordinarily being accepted by way of reliance upon arguments or evidential support from other beliefs. The most promising way to investigate that question, I think, is to consider what rationality, or warrant, or positive epistemic status *is;* once we are clear about that, then we can ask whether basic belief in God can have it. I myself believe such investigation reveals that belief in God taken in the basic way is perfectly proper, and rational, and acceptable; indeed, I think we can *know* that God exists without believing on the basis of arguments. But that is a topic for another time.

Belief in God

The Tyger

Tyger Tyger, burning bright,
In the forests of the night;
What immortal hand or eye,
Could frame thy fearful symmetry?

In what distant deeps or skies
Burnt the fire of thine eyes!
On what wings dare he aspire?
What the hand, dare seize the fire?

And what shoulder, & what art,
Could twist the sinews of thy heart?
And when thy heart began to beat,
What dread hand? & what dread feet?

What the hammer? what the chain,
In what furnace was thy brain?
What the anvil? what dread grasp,
Dare its deadly terrors clasp?

When the stars threw down their spears
And water'd heaven with their tears:
Did he smile his work to see?
Did he who made the Lamb make thee?

Tyger, Tyger burning bright,
In the forests of the night:
What immortal hand or eye,
Dare frame thy fearful symmetry?

William Blake

THOMAS AQUINAS
(1225–1274) Italian Philosopher and Theologian

Whether God Exists?*

We proceed thus to the Third Article:

Objection 1. It seems that God does not exist; because if one of two contraries be infinite, the other would be altogether destroyed. But the name *God* means that He is infinite goodness. If, therefore, God existed, there would be no evil discoverable; but there is evil in the world. Therefore God does not exist.

Obj. 2. Further, it is superfluous to suppose that what can be accounted for by a few principles has been produced by many. But it seems that everything we see in the world can be accounted for by other principles, supposing God did not exist. For all natural things can be reduced to one principle, which is nature; and all voluntary things can be reduced to one principle, which is human reason, or will. Therefore there is no need to suppose God's existence.

On the contrary, It is said in the person of God: *I am Who am* (Exod. iii. 14).

I answer that, The existence of God can be proved in five ways.

The first and more manifest way is the argument from motion. It is certain, and evident to our senses, that in the world some things are in motion. Now whatever is moved is moved by another, for nothing can be moved except it is in potentiality to that towards which it is moved; whereas a thing moves inasmuch as it is in act. For motion is nothing else than the reduction of something from potentiality to actuality. But nothing can be reduced from potentiality to actuality, except by something in a state of actuality. Thus that which is actually hot, as fire, makes wood, which is potentially hot, to be actually hot, and thereby moves and changes it. Now it is not possible that the same thing should be at once in actuality and potentiality in the same respect, but only in different respects. For what is actually hot cannot simultaneously be potentially hot; but it is simultaneously potentially cold. It is therefore impossible that in the same respect and in the same way a thing should be both mover and moved, *i.e.*, that it should move itself. Therefore, whatever is moved must be moved by another. If that by which it is moved be itself moved, then this also must needs be moved by another, and that by another again. But this cannot go on to infinity, because then there would be no first mover, and, consequently, no other mover, seeing that subsequent movers move only inasmuch as they are moved by the first mover; as the staff moves only because it is moved by the hand. Therefore it is necessary to arrive at a first mover, moved by no other; and this everyone understands to be God.

*From Thomas Aquinas, *Summa Theologica* I, q. 2, article 3, in *Basic Writings of Saint Thomas Aquinas*, Vol. 1, ed. by Anton C. Pegis, (New York: Random House, 1945), pp. 21–23.

The second way is from the nature of efficient cause.[1] In the world of sensible things we find there is an order of efficient causes. There is no case known (neither is it, indeed, possible) in which a thing is found to be the efficient cause of itself; for so it would be prior to itself, which is impossible. Now in efficient causes it is not possible to go on to infinity, because in all efficient causes following in order, the first is the cause of the intermediate cause, and the intermediate is the cause of the ultimate cause, whether the intermediate cause be several, or one only. Now to take away the cause is to take away the effect. Therefore, if there be no first cause among efficient causes, there will be no ultimate, nor any intermediate, cause. But if in efficient causes it is possible to go on to infinity, there will be no first efficient cause, neither will there be an ultimate effect, nor any intermediate efficient causes; all of which is plainly false. Therefore it is necessary to admit a first efficient cause, to which everyone gives the name of God.

The third way is taken from possibility and necessity, and runs thus. We find in nature things that are possible to be and not to be, since they are found to be generated, and to be corrupted, and consequently, it is possible for them to be and not to be. But it is impossible for these always to exist, for that which can not-be at some time is not. Therefore, if everything can not-be, then at one time there was nothing in existence. Now if this were true, even now there would be nothing in existence, because that which does not exist begins to exist only through something already existing. Therefore, if at one time nothing was in existence, it would have been impossible for anything to have begun to exist; and thus even now nothing would be in existence—which is absurd. Therefore, not all beings are merely possible, but there must exist something the existence of which is necessary. But every necessary thing either has its necessity caused by another, or not. Now it is impossible to go on to infinity in necessary things which have their necessity caused by another, as has been already proved in regard to efficient causes. Therefore we cannot but admit the existence of some being having of itself its own necessity, and not receiving it from another, but rather causing in others their necessity. This all men speak of as God.

The fourth way is taken from the gradation to be found in things. Among beings there are some more and some less good, true, noble, and the like. But *more* and *less* are predicted of different things according as they resemble in their different ways something which is the maximum, as a thing is said to be hotter according as it more nearly resembles that which is hottest; so that there is something which is truest, something best, something noblest, and, consequently, something which is most being, for those things that are greatest in truth are greatest in being, as it is written in *Metaph*. ii. Now the maximum in any genus is the cause of all in that genus, as fire, which is the maximum of heat, is the cause of all hot things, as is said in the same book. Therefore there must also be something which is to all beings the cause of their being, goodness, and every other perfection; and this we call God.

The fifth way is taken from the governance of the world. We see that things which lack knowledge, such as natural bodies, act for an end, and this is evident from their acting always, or nearly always, in the same way, so as to obtain the

---

[1] The efficient cause is one of Aristotle's four causes. —ED.

best result. Hence it is plain that they achieve their end, not fortuitously, but designedly. Now whatever lacks knowledge cannot move towards an end, unless it be directed by some being endowed with knowledge and intelligence; as the arrow is directed by the archer. Therefore some intelligent being exists by whom all natural things are directed to their end; and this being we call God.

Reply Obj. 1. As Augustine says: *Since God is the highest good, He would not allow any evil to exist in His works, unless His omnipotence and goodness were such as to bring good even out of evil.* This is part of the infinite goodness of God, that He should allow evil to exist, and out of it produce good.

Reply Obj. 2. Since nature works for a determinate end under the direction of a higher agent, whatever is done by nature must be traced back to God as to its first cause. So likewise whatever is done voluntarily must be traced back to some higher cause other than human reason and will, since these can change and fail; for all things that are changeable and capable of defect must be traced back to an immovable and self-necessary first principle, as has been shown.

RENÉ DESCARTES
(1596–1650) French Philosopher

Meditations III and V*

Meditation III

The Cosmological Proof

To speak the truth, I see nothing in all that I have just said which by the light of nature is not manifest to anyone who desires to think attentively on the subject; but when I slightly relax my attention, my mind, finding its vision somewhat obscured and so to speak blinded by the images of sensible objects, I do not easily recollect the reason why the idea that I possess of a being more perfect than I, must necessarily have been placed in me by a being which is really more perfect; and this is why I wish here to go on to inquire whether I, who have this idea, can exist if no such being exists.

And I ask, from whom do I then derive my existence? Perhaps from myself or from my parents, or from some other source less perfect than God; for we can imagine nothing more perfect than God, or even as perfect as He is.

*From *Meditations on First Philosophy,* trans. by Elizabeth S. Haldane and G.R.T. Ross, in *The Philosophical Writings of Descartes,* Vol. 1 (Cambridge: Cambridge University Press, 1911, reprinted 1931).

But [were I independent of every other and] were I myself the author of my being, I should doubt nothing and I should desire nothing, and finally no perfection would be lacking to me; for I should have bestowed on myself every perfection of which I possessed any idea and should thus be God. And it must not be imagined that those things that are lacking to me are perhaps more difficult of attainment than those which I already possess; for, on the contrary, it is quite evident that it was a matter of much greater difficulty to bring to pass that I, that is to say, a thing or a substance that thinks, should emerge out of nothing, than it would be to attain to the knowledge of many things of which I am ignorant, and which are only the accidents of this thinking substance. But it is clear that if I had of myself possessed this greater perfection of which I have just spoken [that is to say, if I had been the author of my own existence], I should not at least have denied myself the things which are the more easy to acquire [to wit, many branches of knowledge of which my nature is destitute], nor should I have deprived myself of any of the things contained in the idea which I form of God, because there are none of them which seem to me specially difficult to acquire: and if there were any that were more difficult to acquire, they would certainly appear to me to be such (supposing I myself were the origin of the other things which I possess) since I should discover in them that my powers were limited.

But though I assume that perhaps I have always existed just as I am at present, neither can I escape the force of this reasoning, and imagine that the conclusion to be drawn from this is, that I need not seek for any author of my existence. For all the course of my life may be divided into an infinite number of parts, none of which is in any way dependent on the other; and thus from the fact that I was in existence a short time ago it does not follow that I must be in existence now, unless some cause at this instant, so to speak, produces me anew, that is to say, conserves me. It is as a matter of fact perfectly clear and evident to those who consider with attention the nature of time, that, in order to be conserved in each moment in which it endures, a substance has need of the same power and action as would be necessary to produce and create it anew supposing it did not yet exist, so that the light of nature shows us clearly that the distinction between creation and conservation is solely a distinction of the reason.

All that I thus require here is that I should interrogate myself, if I wish to know whether I possess a power which is capable of bringing it to pass that I who now am shall still be in the future; for since I am nothing but a thinking thing, or at least since thus far it is only this portion of myself which is precisely in question at present, if such a power did reside in me, I should certainly be conscious of it. But I am conscious of nothing of the kind, and by this I know clearly that I depend on some being different from myself.

Possibly, however, this being on which I depend is not that which I call God, and I am created either by my parents or by some other cause less perfect than God. This cannot be, because, as I have just said, it is perfectly evident that there must be at least so much reality in the cause as in the effect; and thus since I am a thinking thing, and possess an idea of God within me, whatever in the end be the cause assigned to my existence, it must be allowed that it is likewise a thinking thing and that is possesses in itself the idea of all the perfection which I attribute to God. We may again inquire whether this cause derives its origin from itself or from some other thing. For if from itself, it follows by the reasons before brought forward, that this cause must itself be God; for since it possesses the virtue of self-existence, it must also without doubt have the power of actually possessing all the perfections of which it has the idea, that is, all those which I conceive as existing in God. But if it derives its existence from some other cause than itself, we shall again ask, for the same reason, whether this second cause exists by itself or through another, until from one step to another, we finally arrive at an ultimate cause, which will be God.

And it is perfectly manifest that in this there can be no regression into infinity, since what is in question is not so much the cause which formerly created me, as that which conserves me at the present time.

Nor can we suppose that several causes may have concurred in my production, and that from one I have received the idea of one of the perfections which I attribute to God, and from another the idea of some other, so that all these perfections indeed exist somewhere in the universe, but not as complete in one unity which is God. On the contrary, the unity, the simplicity or the inseparability of all things which are in God is one of the principal perfections which I conceive to be in Him. And certainly the idea of this unity of all Devine perfections cannot have been placed in me by any cause from which I have not likewise received the ideas of all the other perfections; for this cause could not make me able to comprehend them as joined together in an inseparable unity without having at the same time caused me in some measure to know what they are [and in some way to recognise each one of them].

Finally, so far as my parents [from whom it appears I have sprung] are concerned, although all that I have ever been able to believe of them were true, that does not make it follow that it is they who conserve me, nor are they even the authors of my being in any sense, in so far as I am a thinking being; since what they did was merely to implant certain dispositions in that matter in which the self—i.e. the mind, which alone I at present identify with myself—is by me deemed to exist. And thus there can be no difficulty in their regard, but we must of necessity conclude from the fact alone that I exist, or that the idea of a Being supremely perfect—that is of God—is in me, that the proof of God's existence is grounded on the highest evidence.

Meditation V

The Ontological Proof
But now, if just because I can draw the idea of something from my thought, it follows that all which I know clearly and distinctly as pertaining to this object does really belong to it, may I not derive from this an argument demonstrating the existence of God? It is certain that I no less find the idea of God, that is to say, the idea of a supremely perfect Being, in me, than that of any figure or number whatever it is; and I do not know any less clearly and distinctly that an [actual and] eternal existence pertains to this nature than I know that all that which I am able to demonstrate of some figure or number truly pertains to the nature of this

figure or number, and therefore, although all that I concluded in the preceding Meditations were found to be false, the existence of God would pass with me as at least as certain as I have ever held the truths of mathematics (which concern only numbers and figures) to be.

This indeed is not at first manifest, since it would seem to present some appearance of being a sophism. For being accustomed in all other things to make a distinction between existence and essence, I easily persuade myself that the existence can be separated from the essence of God, and that we can thus conceive God as not actually existing. But, nevertheless, when I think of it with more attention, I clearly see that existence can no more be separated from the essence of God than can its having its three angles equal to two right angles be separated from the essence of a [rectilinear] triangle, or the idea of a mountain from the idea of a valley; and so there is not any less repugnance to our conceiving a God (that is, a Being supremely perfect) to whom existence is lacking (that is to say, to whom a certain perfection is lacking), than to conceive of a mountain which has no valley.

But although I cannot really conceive of a God without existence any more than a mountain without a valley, still from the fact that I conceive of a mountain with a valley, it does not follow that there is such a mountain in the world; similarly although I conceive of God as possessing existence, it would seem that it does not follow that there is a God which exists; for my thought does not impose any necessity upon things, and just as I may imagine a winged horse, although no horse with wings exists, so I could perhaps attribute existence to God, although no God existed.

But a sophism is concealed in this objection; for from the fact that I cannot conceive a mountain without a valley, it does not follow that there is any mountain or any valley in existence, but only that the mountain and the valley, whether they exist or do not exist, cannot in any way be separated one from the other. While from the fact that I cannot conceive God without existence, it follows that existence is inseparable from Him, and hence that He really exists; not that my thought can bring this to pass, or impose any necessity on things, but, on the contrary, because the necessity which lies in the thing itself, i.e. the necessity of the existence of God determines me to think in this way. For it is not within my power to think of God without existence (that is of a supremely perfect Being devoid of a supreme perfection) though it is in my power to imagine a horse either with wings or without wings.

And we must not here object that it is in truth necessary for me to assert that God exists after having presupposed that He possesses every sort of perfection, since existence is one of these, but that as a matter of fact my original supposition was not necessary, just as it is not necessary to consider that all quadrilateral figures can be inscribed in the circle; for supposing I thought this, I should be constrained to admit that the rhombus might be inscribed in the circle since it is a quadrilateral figure, which, however, is manifestly false. [We must not, I say, make any such allegations because] although it is not necessary that I should at any time entertain the notion of God, nevertheless whenever it happens that I think of a first and a sovereign Being, and, so to speak, derive the idea of Him from the storehouse of my mind, it is necessary that I should attribute to Him every sort of perfection, although I do not get so far as to enumerate them all, or to apply my mind to each one in particular. And this necessity suffices to make me conclude (after having recognised that existence is a perfection) that this first and sovereign Being really exists; just as though it is not necessary for me ever to imagine any triangle, yet, whenever I wish to consider a rectilinear figure composed only of three angles, it is absolutely essential that I should attribute to it all those properties which serve to bring about the conclusion that its three angles are not greater than two right angles, even although I may not then be considering this point in particular. But when I consider which figures are capable of being inscribed in the circle, it is in no wise necessary that I should think that all quadrilateral figures are of this number; on the contrary, I cannot even pretend that this is the case, so long as I do not desire to accept anything which I cannot conceive clearly and distinctly. And in consequence there is a great difference between the false suppositions such as this, and the true ideas born within me, the first and principal of which is that of God. For really I discern in many ways that this idea is not something factitious, and depending solely on my thought, but that it is the image of a true and immutable nature; first of all, because I cannot conceive anything but God himself to whose essence existence [necessarily] pertains; in the second place because it is not possible for me to conceive two or more Gods in this same position; and, granted that there is one such God who now exists, I see clearly that it is necessary that He should have existed from all eternity, and that He must exist eternally; and finally, because I know an infinitude of other properties in God, none of which I can either diminish or change.

For the rest, whatever proof or argument I avail myself of, we must always return to the point that it is only those things which we conceive clearly and distinctly that have the power of persuading me entirely. And although amongst the matters which I conceive of in this way, some indeed are manifestly obvious to all, while others only manifest themselves to those who consider them closely and examine them attentively; still, after they have once been discovered, the latter are not esteemed as any less certain than the former. For example, in the case of every right-angled triangle, although it does not so manifestly appear that the square of the base is equal to the squares of the two other sides as that this base is opposite to the greatest angle; still, when this has once been apprehended, we are just as certain of its truth as of the truth of the other. And as regards God, if my mind were not pre-occupied with prejudices, and if my thought did not find itself on all hands diverted by the continual pressure of sensible things, there would be nothing which I could know more immediately and more easily than Him. For is there anything more manifest than that there is a God, that is to say, a Supreme Being, to whose essence alone existence pertains?

IMMANUEL KANT

(1724–1804) German Philosopher

The Impossibility of an Ontological Proof of the Existence of God*

It is evident, from what has been said, that the concept of an absolutely necessary being is a concept of pure reason, that is, a mere idea the objective reality of which is very far from being proved by the fact that reason requires it. For the idea instructs us only in regard to a certain unattainable completeness, and so serves rather to limit the understanding than to extend it to new objects. But we are here faced by what is indeed strange and perplexing, namely, that while the inference from a given existence in general to some absolutely necessary being seems to be both imperative and legitimate, all those conditions under which alone the understanding can form a concept of such a necessity are so many obstacles in the way of our doing so.

In all ages men have spoken of an *absolutely necessary* being, and in so doing have endeavoured, not so much to understand whether and how a thing of this kind allows even of being thought, but rather to prove its existence. There is, of course, no difficulty in giving a verbal definition of the concept, namely, that it is something the non-existence of which is impossible. But this yields no insight into the conditions which make it necessary to regard the non-existence of a thing as absolutely unthinkable. It is precisely these conditions that we desire to know, in order that we may determine whether or not, in resorting to this concept, we are thinking anything at all. The expedient of removing all those conditions which the understanding indispensably requires in order to regard something as necessary, simply through the introduction of the word *unconditioned*, is very far from sufficing to show whether I am still thinking anything in the concept of the unconditionally necessary, or perhaps rather nothing at all.

Nay more, this concept, at first ventured upon blindly, and now become so completely familiar, has been supposed to have its meaning exhibited in a number of examples; and on this account all further enquiry into its intelligibility has seemed to be quite needless. Thus the fact that every geometrical proposition, as, for instance, that a triangle has three angles, is absolutely necessary, has been taken as justifying us in speaking of an object which lies entirely outside the sphere of our understanding as if we understood perfectly what it is that we intend to convey by the concept of that object.

All the alleged examples are, without exception, taken from *judgments*, not from *things* and their existence. But the unconditioned necessity of judgments is

*From Immanuel Kant, *Critique of Pure Reason*, trans. by Norman Kemp Smith (New York: St. Martin's Press, 1929).

not the same as an absolute necessity of things. The absolute necessity of the judgment is only a conditioned necessity of the thing, or of the predicate in the judgment. The above proposition does not declare that three angles are absolutely necessary, but that, under the condition that there is a triangle (that is, that a triangle is given), three angles will necessarily be found in it. So great, indeed, is the deluding influence exercised by this logical necessity that, by the simple device of forming an *a priori* concept of a thing in such a manner as to include existence within the scope of its meaning, we have supposed ourselves to have justified the conclusion that because existence necessarily belongs to the object of this concept—always under the condition that we posit the thing as given (as existing)—we are also of necessity, in accordance with the law of identity, required to posit the existence of its object, and that this being is therefore itself absolutely necessary—and this, to repeat, for the reason that the existence of this being has already been thought in a concept which is assumed arbitrarily and on condition that we posit its object.

If, in an identical proposition, I reject the predicate while retaining the subject, contradiction results; and I therefore say that the former belongs necessarily to the latter. But if we reject subject and predicate alike, there is no contradiction; for nothing is then left that can be contradicted. To posit a triangle, and yet to reject its three angles, is self-contradictory; but there is no contradiction in rejecting the triangle together with its three angles. The same holds true of the concept of an absolutely necessary being. If its existence is rejected, we reject the thing itself with all its predicates; and no question of contradiction can then arise. There is nothing outside it that would then be contradicted, since the necessity of the thing is not supposed to be derived from anything external; nor is there anything internal that would be contradicted, since in rejecting the thing itself we have at the same time rejected all its internal properties. "God is omnipotent" is a necessary judgment. The omnipotence cannot be rejected if we posit a Deity, that is, an infinite being; for the two concepts are identical. But if we say, "There is no God," neither the omnipotence nor any other of its predicates is given; they are one and all rejected together with the subject, and there is therefore not the least contradiction in such a judgment.

We have thus seen that if the predicate of a judgment is rejected together with the subject, no internal contradiction can result, and that this holds no matter what the predicate may be. The only way of evading this conclusion is to argue that there are subjects which cannot be removed, and must always remain. That, however, would only be another way of saying that there are absolutely necessary subjects; and that is the very assumption which I have called in question, and the possibility of which the above argument professes to establish. For I cannot form the least concept of a thing which, should it be rejected with all its predicates, leaves behind a contradiction; and in the absence of contradiction I have, through pure *a priori* concepts alone, no criterion of impossibility.

Notwithstanding all these general considerations, in which every one must concur, we may be challenged with a case which is brought forward as proof that in actual fact the contrary holds, namely, that there is one concept, and indeed only one, in reference to which the not-being or rejection of its object is in itself contradictory, namely, the concept of the *ens realissimum*. It is declared that it possesses all reality, and that we are justified in assuming that such a being is possible (the fact that a concept does not contradict itself by no means proves the possibility of its object: but the contrary assertion I am for the moment willing to allow).[1] Now [the argument proceeds] "all reality" includes existence; existence is therefore contained in the concept of a thing that is possible. If then, this thing is rejected, the internal possibility of the thing is rejected—which is self-contradictory.

My answer is as follows. There is already a contradiction in introducing the concept of existence—no matter under what title it may be disguised—into the concept of a thing which we profess to be thinking solely in reference to its possibility. If that be allowed as legitimate, a seeming victory has been won; but in actual fact nothing at all is said: the assertion is a mere tautology. We must ask: Is the proposition that *this or that thing* (which, whatever it may be, is allowed as possible) *exists*, an analytic or a synthetic proposition? If it is analytic, the assertion of the existence of the thing adds nothing to the thought of the thing; but in that case either the thought, which is in us, is the thing itself, or we have presupposed an existence as belonging to the realm of the possible, and have then, on that pretext, inferred its existence from its internal possibility—which is nothing but a miserable tautology. The word "reality," which in the concept of the thing sounds other than the word "existence" in the concept of the predicate, is of no avail in meeting this objection. For if all positing (no matter what it may be that is posited) is entitled reality, the thing with all its predicates is already posited in the concept of the subject, and is assumed as actual; and in the predicate this is merely repeated. But if, on the other hand, we admit, as every reasonable person must, that all existential propositions are synthetic, how can we profess to maintain that the predicate of existence cannot be rejected without contradiction? This is a feature which is found only in analytic propositions, and is indeed precisely what constitutes their analytic character.

I should have hoped to put an end to these idle and fruitless disputations in a direct manner, by an accurate determination of the concept of existence, had I not found that the illusion which is caused by the confusion of a logical with a real predicate (that is, with a predicate which determines a thing) is almost beyond correction. Anything we please can be made to serve as a logical predicate; the subject can even be predicated of itself; for logic abstracts from all content. But a *determining* predicate is a predicate which is added to the concept of the subject and enlarges it. Consequently, it must not be already contained in the concept.

"Being" is obviously not a real predicate; that is, it is not a concept of something which could be added to the concept of a thing. It is merely the positing of a thing, or of certain determinations, as existing in themselves. Logically, it is merely the copula of a judgment. The proposition, "God is omnipotent," contains two concepts, each of which has its object—God and omnipotence. The small

---

[1] A concept is always probable if it is not self-contradictory. This is the logical criterion of possibility, and by it the object of the concept is distinguishable from the *nihil negativum*. But it may none the less be an empty concept, unless the objective reality of the synthesis through which the concept is generated has been specifically proved; and such proof, as we have shown above, rests on principles of possible experience, and not on the principle of analysis (the law of contradiction). This is a warning against arguing directly from the logical possibility of concepts to the real possibility of things.

word "is" adds no new predicate, but only serves to posit the predicate *in its relation* to the subject. If, now, we take the subject (God) with all its predicates (among which is omnipotence), and say "God is," or "There is a God," we attach no new predicate to the concept of God, but only posit the subject in itself with all its predicates, and indeed posit it as being an *object* that stands in relation to my *concept*. The content of both must be one and the same; nothing can have been added to the concept, which expresses merely what is possible, by my thinking its object (through the expression "it is") as given absolutely. Otherwise stated, the real contains no more than the merely possible. A hundred real thalers do not contain the least coin more than a hundred possible thalers. For as the latter signify the concept, and the former the object and the positing of the object, should the former contain more than the latter, my concept would not, in that case, express the whole object, and would not therefore be an adequate concept of it. My financial position is, however, affected very differently by a hundred real thalers than it is by the mere concept of them (that is, of their possibility). For the object, as it actually exists, is not analytically contained in my concept, but is added to my concept (which is a determination of my state) synthetically; and yet the conceived hundred thalers are not themselves in the least increased through thus acquiring existence outside my concept.

By whatever and by however many predicates we may think a thing—even if we completely determine it—we do not make the least addition to the thing when we further declare that this thing *is*. Otherwise, it would not be exactly the same thing that exists, but something more than we had thought in the concept; and we could not, therefore, say that the exact object of my concept exists. If we think in a thing every feature of reality except one, the missing reality is not added by my saying that this defective thing exists. On the contrary, it exists with the same defect with which I have thought it, since otherwise what exists would be something different from what I thought. When, therefore, I think a being as the supreme reality, without any defect, the question still remains whether it exists or not. For though, in my concept, nothing may be lacking of the possible real content of a thing in general, something is still lacking in its relation to my whole state of thought, namely, [in so far as I am unable to assert] that knowledge of this object is also possible *a posteriori*. And here we find the source of our present difficulty. Were we dealing with an object of the senses, we could not confound the existence of the thing with the mere concept of it. For through the concept the object is thought only as conforming to the *universal conditions* of possible empirical knowledge in general, whereas through its existence it is thought as belonging to the context of experience as a whole. In being thus connected with the *content* of experience as a whole, the concept of the object is not, however, in the least enlarged; all that has happened is that our thought has thereby obtained an additional possible perception. It is not, therefore, surprising that, if we attempt to think existence through the pure category alone, we cannot specify a single mark distinguishing it from mere possibility.

Whatever, therefore, and however much, our concept of an object may contain, we must go outside it, if we are to ascribe existence to the object. In the case of objects of the senses, this takes place through their connection with some one of our perceptions, in accordance with empirical laws. But in dealing with objects of pure thought, we have no means whatsoever of knowing their existence, since it would have to be known in a completely *a priori* manner. Our consciousness of all existence (whether immediately through perception, or mediately through inferences which connect something with perception) belongs exclusively to the unity of experience; any [alleged] existence outside this field, while not indeed such as we can declare to be absolutely impossible, is of the nature of an assumption which we can never be in a position to justify.

The concept of a supreme being is in many respects a very useful idea; but just because it is a mere idea, it is altogether incapable, by itself alone, of enlarging our knowledge in regard to what exists. It is not even competent to enlighten us as to the *possibility* of any existence beyond that which is known in and through experience. The analytic criterion of possibility, as consisting in the principle that bare positives (realities) give rise to no contradiction, cannot be denied to it. But since the realities are not given to us in their specific characters; since even if they were, we should still not be in a position to pass judgment; since the criterion of the possibility of synthetic knowledge is never to be looked for save in experience, to which the object of an idea cannot belong, the connection of all real properties in a thing is a synthesis, the possibility of which we are unable to determine *a priori*. And thus the celebrated Leibniz is far from having succeeded in what he plumed himself on achieving—the comprehension *a priori* of the possibility of this sublime ideal being.

The attempt to establish the existence of a supreme being by means of the famous ontological argument of Descartes is therefore merely so much labour and effort lost; we can no more extend our stock of [theoretical] insight by mere ideas, than a merchant can better his position by adding a few noughts to his cash account.

BERTRAND RUSSELL
(1872–1970) English Philosopher

Why I Am Not a Christian

As your Chairman has told you, the subject about which I am going to speak to you tonight is "Why I Am Not a Christian." Perhaps it would be as well, first of all, to try to make out what one means by the word "Christian." It is used in these days in a very loose sense by a great many people. Some people mean no more by it than a person who attempts to live a good life. In that sense I suppose there would be Christians in all sects and creeds; but I do not think that that is

Bertrand Russell, "Why I Am Not a Christian," *The Rationalist Annual* (London: Watts & Company, 1927).

the proper sense of the word, if only because it would imply that all the people who are not Christians—all the Buddhists, Confucians, Mohammedans, and so on—are not trying to live a good life. I do not mean by a Christian any person who tries to live decently according to his lights. I think that you must have a certain amount of definite belief before you have a right to call yourself a Christian. The word does not have quite such a full-blooded meaning now as it had in the times of St. Augustine and St. Thomas Aquinas. In those days, if a man said that he was a Christian it was known what he meant. You accepted a whole collection of creeds which were set out with great precision, and every single syllable of those creeds you believed with the whole strength of your convictions.

What Is a Christian?

Nowadays it is not quite that. We have to be a little more vague in our meaning of Christianity. I think, however, that there are two different items which are quite essential to anybody calling himself a Christian. The first is one of a dogmatic nature—namely, that you must believe in God and in immortality. If you do not believe in those two things, I do not think that you can properly call yourself a Christian. Then, further than that, as the name implies, you must have some kind of belief about Christ. The Mohammedans, for instance, also believe in God and in immortality, and yet they would not call themselves Christians. I think you must have at the very lowest the belief that Christ was, if not divine, at least the best and the wisest of men. If you are not going to believe that much about Christ, I do not think that you have any right to call yourself a Christian. Of course there is another sense which you find in *Whitaker's Almanack* and in geography books, where the population of the world is said to be divided into Christians, Mohammedans, Buddhists, fetish worshippers, and so on; and in that sense we are all Christians. The geography books count us all in, but that is a purely geographical sense, which I suppose we can ignore. Therefore I take it that when I tell you why I am not a Christian I have to tell you two different things: first, why I do not believe in God and in immortality; and, secondly, why I do not think that Christ was the best and the wisest of men, although I grant him a very high degree of moral goodness.

But for the successful efforts of unbelievers in the past, I could not take so elastic a definition of Christianity as that. As I said before, in olden days it had a much more full-blooded sense. For instance, it included the belief in hell. Belief in eternal hell fire was an essential item of Christian belief until pretty recent times. In this country, as you know, it ceased to be an essential item because of a decision of the Privy Council, and from that decision the Archbishop of Canterbury and the Archbishop of York dissented; but in this country our religion is settled by Act of Parliament, and therefore the Privy Council was able to override their Graces, and hell was no longer necessary to a Christian. Consequently I shall not insist that a Christian must believe in hell.

The Existence of God

To come to this question of the existence of God, it is a large and serious question, and if I were to attempt to deal with it in any adequate manner I should have to keep you here until Kingdom Come, so that you will have to excuse me if I deal with it in a somewhat summary fashion. You know, of course, that the Catholic Church has laid it down as a dogma that the existence of God can be proved by the unaided reason. That is a somewhat curious dogma, but it is one of their dogmas. They had to introduce it because at one time the Freethinkers adopted the habit of saying that there were such and such arguments which mere reason might urge against the existence of God, but of course they knew as a matter of faith that God did exist. The arguments and the reasons were set out at great length, and the Catholic Church felt that they must stop it. Therefore they laid it down that the existence of God can be proved by the unaided reason, and they had to set up what they considered were arguments to prove it. There are, of course, a number of them, but I shall take only a few.

The First Cause Argument
Perhaps the simplest and easiest to understand is the argument of the First Cause. It is maintained that everything we see in this world has a cause, and as you go back in the chain of causes further and further you must come to a First Cause, and to that First Cause you give the name God. That argument, I suppose, does not carry very much weight nowadays, because, in the first place, cause is not quite what it used to be. The philosophers and the men of science have got going on cause, and it has not anything like the vitality that it used to have; but, apart from that, you can see that the argument that there must be a First Cause is one that cannot have any validity. I may say that when I was a young man, and was debating these questions very seriously in my mind, I for a long time accepted the argument of the First Cause, until one day, at the age of eighteen, I read John Stuart Mill's *Autobiography,* and I there found this sentence: "My father taught me that the question, Who made me? cannot be answered, since it immediately suggests the further question, Who made God?" That very simple sentence showed me, as I still think, the fallacy in the argument of the First Cause. If everything must have a cause, then God must have a cause. If there can be anything without a cause, it may just as well be the world as God, so that there cannot be any validity in that argument. It is exactly of the same nature as the Indian's view, that the world rested upon an elephant and the elephant rested upon a tortoise; and when they said, "How about the tortoise?" the Indian said, "Suppose we change the subject." The argument is really no better than that. There is no reason why the world could not have come into being without a cause; nor, on the other hand, is there any reason why it should not have always existed. There is no reason to suppose that the world had a beginning at all. The idea that things must have a beginning is really due to the poverty of our imagination. Therefore, perhaps, I need not waste any more time upon the argument about the First Cause.

The Natural Law Argument
Then there is a very common argument from natural law. That was a favorite argument all through the eighteenth century, especially under the influence of Sir Isaac Newton and his cosmogony. People observed the planets going round the sun according to the law of gravitation, and they thought that God had given a behest to these planets to move in that particular fashion, and that was why

they did so. That was, of course, a convenient and simple explanation that saved them the trouble of looking any further for explanations of the law of gravitation. Nowadays we explain the law of gravitation in a somewhat complicated fashion that Einstein has introduced. I do not propose to give you a lecture on the law of gravitation, as interpreted by Einstein, because that again would take some time; at any rate, you no longer have the sort of natural law that you had in the Newtonian system, where, for some reason that nobody could understand, nature behaved in a uniform fashion. We now find that a great many things that we thought were natural laws are really human conventions. You know that even in the remotest depths of stellar space there are still three feet to a yard. That is, no doubt, a very remarkable fact, but you would hardly call it a law of nature. And a great many things that have been regarded as laws of nature are of that kind. On the other hand, where you can get down to any knowledge of what atoms actually do, you find that they are much less subject to law than people thought, and that the laws at which you arrive are statistical averages of just the sort that would emerge from chance. There is, as we all know, a law that if you throw dice you will get double sixes only about once in thirty-six times, and we do not regard that as evidence that the fall of the dice is regulated by design; on the contrary, if the double sixes came every time we should think that there was design. The laws of nature are of that sort as regards a great many of them. They are statistical averages such as would emerge from the laws of chance; and that makes this whole business of natural law much less impressive than it formerly was. Quite apart from that, which represents the momentary state of science that may change tomorrow, the whole idea that natural laws imply a lawgiver is due to a confusion between natural and human laws. Human laws are behests commanding you to behave in a certain way, in which way you may choose to behave, or you may choose not to behave; but natural laws are a description of how things do in fact behave, and, being a mere description of what they in fact do, you cannot argue that there must be somebody who told them to do that, because even supposing that there were you are then faced with the question, Why did God issue just those natural laws and no others? If you say that he did it simply from his own good pleasure, and without any reason, you then find that there is something which is not subject to law, and so your train of natural law is interrupted. If you say, as more orthodox theologians do, that in all the laws which God issued he had a reason for giving those laws rather than others—the reason, of course, being to create the best universe, although you would never think it to look at it—if there was a reason for the laws which God gave, then God himself was subject to law, and therefore you do not get any advantage by introducing God as an intermediary. You have really a law outside and anterior to the divine edicts, and God does not serve your purpose, because he is not the ultimate lawgiver. In short, this whole argument about natural law no longer has anything like the strength that it used to have. I am travelling on in time in my review of the arguments. The arguments that are used for the existence of God change their character as time goes on. They were at first hard intellectual arguments embodying certain quite definite fallacies. As we come to modern times they become less respectable intellectually and more and more affected by a kind of moralizing vagueness.

The Argument from Design

The next step in this process brings us to the argument from design. You all know the argument from design: everything in the world is made just so that we can manage to live in the world, and if the world was ever so little different we could not manage to live in it. That is the argument from design. It sometimes takes rather a curious form; for instance, it is argued that rabbits have white tails in order to be easy to shoot. I do not know how rabbits would view that application. It is an easy argument to parody. You all know Voltaire's remark, that obviously the nose was designed to be such as to fit spectacles. That sort of parody has turned out to be not nearly so wide of the mark as it might have seemed in the eighteenth century, because since the time of Darwin we understand much better why living creatures are adapted to their environment. It is not that their environment was made to be suitable to them, but that they grew to be suitable to it, and that is the basis of adaptation. There is no evidence of design about it.

When you come to look into this argument from design, it is a most astonishing thing that people can believe that this world, with all the things that are in it, with all its defects, should be the best that omnipotence and omniscience has been able to produce in millions of years. I really cannot believe it. Do you think that, if you were granted omnipotence and omniscience and millions of years in which to perfect your world, you could produce nothing better than the Ku Klux Klan, the Fascisti, and Mr. Winston Churchill? Really I am not much impressed with the people who say: "Look at me: I am such a splendid product that there must have been design in the universe." I am not very much impressed by the splendor of those people. Therefore I think that this argument of design is really a very poor argument indeed. Moreover, if you accept the ordinary laws of science, you have to suppose that human life and life in general on this planet will die out in due course: it is merely a flash in the pan; it is a stage in the decay of the solar system; at a certain stage of decay you get the sort of conditions of temperature and so forth which are suitable to protoplasm, and there is life for a short time in the life of the whole solar system. You see in the moon the sort of thing to which the earth is tending—something dead, cold, and lifeless.

I am told that that sort of view is depressing, and people will sometimes tell you that if they believed that they would not be able to go on living. Do not believe it; it is all nonsense. Nobody really worries much about what is going to happen millions of years hence. Even if they think they are worrying much about that, they are really deceiving themselves. They are worried about something much more mundane, or it may merely be a bad digestion; but nobody is really seriously rendered unhappy by the thought of something that is going to happen to this world millions and millions of years hence. Therefore, although it is of course a gloomy view to suppose that life will die out—at least I suppose we may say so, although sometimes when I contemplate the things that people do with their lives I think it is almost a consolation—it is not such as to render life miserable. It merely makes you turn your attention to other things.

The Moral Arguments for Deity

Now we reach one stage further in what I shall call the intellectual descent that the Theists have made in their argumentations, and we come to what are called the moral arguments for the existence of God. You all know, of course, that there used to be in the old days three intellectual arguments for the existence of God, all of which were disposed of by Immanuel Kant in the *Critique of Pure Reason;* but no sooner had he disposed of those arguments than he invented a new one, a moral argument, and that quite convinced him. He was like many people: in intellectual matters he was skeptical, but in moral matters he believed implicitly in the maxims that he had imbibed at his mother's knee. That illustrates what the psychoanalysts so much emphasize—the immensely stronger hold upon us that our very early associations have than those of later times.

Kant, as I say, invented a new moral argument for the existence of God, and that in varying forms was extremely popular during the nineteenth century. It has all sorts of forms. One form is to say that there would be no right or wrong unless God existed. I am not for the moment concerned with whether there is a difference between right and wrong, or whether there is not: that is another question. The point I am concerned with is that, if you are quite sure there is a difference between right and wrong, you are then in this situation: Is that difference due to God's fiat or is it not? If it is due to God's fiat, then for God himself there is no difference between right and wrong, and it is no longer a significant statement to say that God is good. If you are going to say, as theologians do, that God is good, you must then say that right and wrong have some meaning which is independent of God's fiat, because God's fiats are good and not bad independently of the mere fact that he made them. If you are going to say that, you will then have to say that it is not only through God that right and wrong come into being, but that they are in their essence logically anterior to God. You could, of course, if you liked, say that there was a superior deity who gave orders to the God who made this world, or you could take up the line that some of the gnostics took up— a line which I often thought was a very plausible one—that as a matter of fact this world that we know was made by the devil at a moment when God was not looking. There is a good deal to be said for that, and I am not concerned to refute it.

The Argument for the Remedying of Injustice

Then there is another very curious form of moral argument, which is this: they say that the existence of God is required in order to bring justice into the world. In the part of this universe that we know there is great injustice, and often the good suffer, and often the wicked prosper, and one hardly knows which of those is the more annoying; but if you are going to have justice in the universe as a whole you have to suppose a future life to redress the balance of life here on earth, and so they say that there must be a God, and there must be a heaven and hell in order that in the long run there may be justice. That is a very curious argument. If you looked at the matter from a scientific point of view, you would say: "After all, I know only this world. I do not know about the rest of the universe, but so far as one can argue at all on probabilities one would say that probably this world is a fair sample, and if there is injustice here the odds are that there is injustice elsewhere also." Supposing you got a crate of oranges that you opened, and you found all the top layer of oranges bad, you would not argue: "The underneath ones must be good, so as to redress the balance." You would say: "Probably the whole lot is a bad consignment"; and that is really what a scientific person would argue about the universe. He would say: "Here we find in this world a great deal of injustice, and so far as that goes that is a reason for supposing that justice does not rule in the world; and therefore so far as it goes it affords a moral argument against a deity and not in favor of one." Of course I know that the sort of intellectual arguments that I have been talking to you about are not what really moves people. What really moves people to believe in God is not any intellectual argument at all. Most people believe in God because they have been taught from early infancy to do it, and that is the main reason.

Then I think that the next most powerful reason is the wish for safety, a sort of feeling that there is a big brother who will look after you. That plays a very profound part in influencing people's desire for a belief in God.

The Character of Christ

I now want to say a few words upon a topic which I often think is not quite sufficiently dealt with by Rationalists, and that is the question whether Christ was the best and the wisest of men. It is generally taken for granted that we should all agree that that was so. I do not myself. I think that there are a good many points upon which I agree with Christ a great deal more than the professing Christians do. I do not know that I could go with him all the way, but I could go with him much further than most professing Christians can. You will remember that he said: "Resist not evil, but whosoever shall smite thee on thy right cheek, turn to him the other also." That is not a new precept or a new principle. It was used by Lao-Tse and Buddha some 500 or 600 years before Christ, but it is not a principle which as a matter of fact Christians accept. I have no doubt that the present Prime Minister, for instance, is a most sincere Christian, but I should not advise any of you to go and smite him on one cheek. I think that you might find that he thought this text was intended in a figurative sense.

Then there is another point which I consider is excellent. You will remember that Christ said: "Judge not lest ye be judged." That principle I do not think you would find was popular in the law courts of Christian countries. I have known in my time quite a number of judges who were very earnest Christians, and they none of them felt that they were acting contrary to Christian principles in what they did. Then Christ says: "Give to him that asketh of thee, and from him that would borrow of thee turn not thou away." That is a very good principle. Your Chairman has reminded you that we are not here to talk politics, but I cannot help observing that the last General Election was fought on the question of how desirable it was to turn away from him that would borrow of thee, so that one must assume that the Liberals and Conservatives of this country are composed of people who do not agree with the teaching of Christ, because they certainly did very emphatically turn away on that occasion.

Then there is one other maxim of Christ which I think has a great deal in it, but I do not find that it is very popular among some of our Christian friends. He says: "If thou wilt be perfect, go and sell that which thou hast, and give to the poor."

That is a very excellent maxim, but, as I say, it is not much practiced. All these, I think, are good maxims, although they are a little difficult to live up to. I do not profess to live up to them myself; but then, after all, I am not by way of doing so, and it is not quite the same thing as for a Christian.

Defects In Christ's Teaching

Having granted the excellence of these maxims, I come to certain points in which I do not believe that one can grant either the superlative wisdom or the superlative goodness of Christ as depicted in the Gospels; and here I may say that one is not concerned with the historical question. Historically it is quite doubtful whether Christ ever existed at all, and if he did we do not know anything about him, so that I am not concerned with the historical question, which is a very difficult one. I am concerned with Christ as he appears in the Gospels, taking the Gospel narrative as it stands, and there one does find some things that do not seem to be very wise. For one thing, he certainly thought that his second coming would occur in clouds of glory before the death of all the people who were living at that time. There are a great many texts that prove that. He says, for instance: "Ye shall not have gone over the cities of Israel till the Son of Man be come." Then he says: "There are some standing here which shall not taste death till the Son of Man come into his kingdom"; and there are a lot of places where it is quite clear that he believed that his second coming would happen during the lifetime of many then living. That was the belief of his earlier followers, and it was the basis of a good deal of his moral teaching. When he said, "Take no thought for the morrow," and things of that sort, it was very largely because he thought that the second coming was going to be very soon, and that all ordinary mundane affairs did not count. I have, as a matter of fact, known some Christians who did believe that the second coming was imminent. I knew a parson who frightened his congregation terribly by telling them that the second coming was very imminent indeed, but they were much consoled when they found that he was planting trees in his garden. The early Christians did really believe it, and they did abstain from such things as planting trees in their gardens, because they did accept from Christ the belief that the second coming was imminent. In that respect clearly he was not so wise as some other people have been, and he was certainly not superlatively wise.

The Moral Problem

Then you came to moral questions. There is one very serious defect to my mind in Christ's moral character, and that is that he believed in hell. I do not myself feel that any person who is really profoundly humane can believe in everlasting punishment. Christ certainly as depicted in the Gospels did believe in everlasting punishment, and one does find repeatedly a vindictive fury against those people who would not listen to his preaching—an attitude which is not uncommon with preachers, but which does somewhat detract from superlative excellence. You do not, for instance, find that attitude in Socrates. You find him quite bland and urbane towards the people who would not listen to him; and it is, to my mind, far more worthy of a sage to take that line than to take the line of indignation. You probably all remember the sort of things that Socrates was saying when he was dying, and the sort of things that he generally did say to people who did not agree with him.

You will find that in the Gospels Christ said: "Ye serpents, ye generation of vipers, how can ye escape the damnation of hell." That was said to people who did not like his preaching. It is not really to my mind quite the best tone, and there are a great many of these things about hell. There is, of course, the familiar text about the sin against the Holy Ghost: "Whosoever speaketh against the Holy Ghost it shall not be forgiven him neither in this world nor in the world to come." That text has caused an unspeakable amount of misery in the world, for all sorts of people have imagined that they have committed the sin against the Holy Ghost, and thought that it would not be forgiven them either in this world or in the world to come. I really do not think that a person with a proper degree of kindliness in his nature would have put fears and terrors of that sort into the world.

Then Christ says: "The Son of Man shall send forth his angels, and they shall gather out of his kingdom all things that offend, and them which do iniquity, and shall cast them into a furnace of fire; there shall be wailing and gnashing of teeth"; and he goes on about the wailing and gnashing of teeth. It comes in one verse after another, and it is quite manifest to the reader that there is a certain pleasure in contemplating wailing and gnashing of teeth, or else it would not occur so often. Then you all, of course, remember about the sheep and the goats; how at the second coming he is going to divide the sheep from the goats, and he is going to say to the goats: "Depart from me, ye cursed, into everlasting fire." He continues: "And these shall go away into everlasting fire." Then he says again: "If thy hand offend thee, cut it off; it is better for thee to enter into life maimed, than having two hands to go into hell, into the fire that never shall be quenched; where their worm dieth not and the fire is not quenched." He repeats that again and again also. I must say that I think all this doctrine, that hell fire is a punishment for sin, is a doctrine of cruelty. It is a doctrine that put cruelty into the world and gave the world generations of cruel torture; and the Christ of the Gospels, if you could take him as his chroniclers represent him, would certainly have to be considered partly responsible for that.

There are other things of less importance. There is the instance of the Gadarene swine, where it certainly was not very kind to the pigs to put the devils into them and make them rush down the hill to the sea. You must remember that he was omnipotent, and he could have made the devils simply go away; but he chooses to send them into the pigs. Then there is the curious story of the fig-tree, which always rather puzzled me. You remember what happened about the fig-tree. "He was hungry; and seeing a fig-tree afar off having leaves; he came if haply he might find anything thereon; and when he came to it he found nothing but leaves, for the time of figs was not yet. And Jesus answered and said unto it: 'No man eat fruit of thee hereafter for ever' . . . and Peter . . . saith unto him: 'Master, behold the fig-tree which thou cursedst is withered away.'" That is a very curious story, because it was not the right time of year for figs, and you really could not blame the tree. I cannot myself feel that either in the matter of wisdom or in the matter of virtue Christ stands quite as high as some other people known to history. I think I should put Buddha and Socrates above him in those respects. As I said before, I do not think that the real reason why people accept religion is anything to do with argumentation. They accept religion on emotional grounds. One is often told that it is a very wrong thing to attack religion, because religion makes men virtuous. So I am told; I have not noticed it. You know, of course, the parody of that argument in Samuel Butler's book, *Erewhon Revisited*. You will remember that in *Erewhon* there is a certain Higgs who arrives in a remote country, and after spending some time there he escapes from that country in a balloon. Twenty years later he comes back to that country and finds a new religion, in which he is worshipped under the name of the "Sun Child"; and it is said that he ascended into heaven. He finds that the Feast of the Ascension is about to be celebrated, and he hears Professors Hanky and Panky say to each other that they never set eyes on the man Higgs, and they hope they never will; but they are the high priests of the religion of the Sun Child. He is very indignant, and he comes up to them, and he says: "I am going to expose all this humbug and tell the people of Erewhon that it was only I, the man Higgs, and I went up in a balloon." He was told: "You must not do that, because all the morals of this country are bound round his myth, and if they once know that you did not ascend into heaven they will all become wicked"; and so he is persuaded of that, and he goes away quite quietly.

That is the idea—that we should all be wicked if we did not hold to the Christian religion. It seems to me that the people who have held to it have been for the most part extremely wicked. You find this curious fact, that the more intense has been the religion of any period and the more profound has been the dogmatic belief, the greater has been the cruelty and the worse has been the state of affairs. In the so-called ages of faith, when men really did believe the Christian religion in all its completeness, there was the Inquisition, with its tortures; there were millions of unfortunate women burnt as witches; and there was every kind of cruelty practiced upon all sorts of people in the name of religion.

You find as you look round the world that every single bit of progress in humane feeling, every improvement in the criminal law, every step towards the diminution of war, every step towards better treatment of the colored races, or every mitigation of slavery, every moral progress that there has been in the world, has been consistently opposed by the organized Churches of the world. I say quite deliberately that the Christian religion, as organized in its Churches, has been and still is the principal enemy of moral progress in the world.

How the Churches Have Retarded Progress

You may think that I am going too far when I say that that is still so. I do not think that I am. Take one fact. You will bear with me if I mention it. It is not a pleasant fact, but the Churches compel one to mention facts that are not pleasant. Supposing that in this world that we live in today an inexperienced girl is married to a syphilitic man, in that case the Catholic Church says: "This is an indissoluble sacrament. You must stay together for life," and no steps of any sort must be taken by that women to prevent herself from giving birth to syphilitic children. That is what the Catholic Church says. I say that that is fiendish cruelty, and nobody whose natural sympathies have not been warped by dogma, or whose moral nature was not absolutely dead to all sense of suffering, could maintain that it is right and proper that that state of things should continue.

That is only an example. There are a great many ways in which at the present moment the Church, by its insistence upon what it chooses to call morality, inflicts upon all sorts of people undeserved and unnecessary suffering. And of course, as we know, it is in its major part an opponent still of progress and of improvement in all the ways that diminish suffering in the world, because it has chosen to label as morality a certain narrow set of rules of conduct which have nothing to do with human happiness; and when you say that this or that ought to be done because it would make for human happiness, they think that has nothing to do with the matter at all. "What has human happiness to do with morals? The object of morals is not to make people happy. It is to fit them for heaven." It certainly seems to unfit them for this world.

Fear for the Foundation of Religion

Religion is based, I think, primarily and mainly upon fear. It is partly the terror of the unknown, and partly, as I have said, the wish to feel that you have a kind of elder brother who will stand by you in all your troubles and disputes. Fear is the basis of the whole thing—fear of the mysterious, fear of defeat, fear of death. Fear is the parent of cruelty, and therefore it is no wonder if cruelty and religion have gone hand-in-hand. It is because fear is at the basis of those two things. In this world we can now begin a little to understand things, and a little to master them by the help of science, which has forced its way step by step against the Christian religion, against the Churches, and against the opposition of all the old precepts. Science can help us to get over this craven fear in which mankind has lived for so many generations. Science can teach us, and I think our own hearts can teach us, no longer to look round for imaginary supports, no longer to invent allies in the sky, but rather to look to our own efforts here below to make this world a fit place to live in, instead of the sort of place that the Churches in all these centuries have made it.

What We Must Do

We want to stand upon our own feet and look fair and square at the world—its good facts, its bad facts, its beauties, and its ugliness; see the world as it is, and be not afraid of it. Conquer the world by intelligence, and not merely by being slavishly subdued by the terror that comes from it. The whole conception of God is a conception derived from the ancient Oriental despotisms. It is a conception quite unworthy of free men. When you hear people in church debasing themselves and saying that they are miserable sinners, and all the rest of it, it seems contemptible and not worthy of self-respecting human beings. We ought to stand up and look the world frankly in the face. We ought to make the best we can of the world, and if it is not so good as we wish, after all it will still be better than what these others have made of it in all these ages. A good world needs knowledge, kindliness, and courage; it does not need a regretful hankering after the past, or a fettering of the free intelligence by the words uttered long ago by ignorant men. It needs a fearless outlook and a free intelligence. It needs hope for the future, not looking back all the time towards a past that is dead, which we trust will be far surpassed by the future that our intelligence can create.

J. L. MACKIE
(1917–1981) Australian Philosopher

Evil and Omnipotence*

The traditional arguments for the existence of God have been fairly thoroughly criticised by philosophers. But the theologian can, if he wishes, accept this criticism. He can admit that no rational proof of God's existence is possible. And he can still retain all that is essential to his position, by holding that God's existence is known in some other, non-rational way. I think, however, that a more telling criticism can be made by way of the traditional problem of evil. Here it can be shown, not that religious beliefs lack rational support, but that they are positively irrational, that the several parts of the essential theological doctrine are inconsistent with one another, so that the theologian can maintain his position as a whole only by a much more extreme rejection of reason than in the former case. He must now be prepared to believe, not merely what cannot be proved, but what can be *disproved* from other beliefs that he also holds.

The problem of evil, in the sense in which I shall be using the phrase, is a problem only for someone who believes that there is a God who is both omnipotent and wholly good. And it is a logical problem, the problem of clarifying and reconciling a number of beliefs: it is not a scientific problem that might be solved by further observations, or a practical problem that might be solved by a decision or an action. These points are obvious; I mention them only because they are sometimes ignored by theologians, who sometimes parry a statement of the problem with such remarks as "Well, can you solve the problem yourself?" or "This is a mystery which may be revealed to us later" or "Evil is something to be faced and overcome, not to be merely discussed."

In its simplest form the problem is this: God is omnipotent; God is wholly good; and yet evil exists. There seems to be some contradiction between these three propositions, so that if any two of them were true the third would be false. But at the same time all three are essential parts of most theological positions: the theologian, it seems, at once *must* adhere and *cannot consistently* adhere to all

*From *Mind* 64 (April 1955), pp. 200–212.

three. (The problem does not arise only for theists, but I shall discuss it in the form in which it presents itself for ordinary theism.)

However, the contradiction does not arise immediately; to show it we need some additional premises, or perhaps some quasi-logical rules connecting the terms "good," "evil," and "omnipotent." These additional principles are that good is opposed to evil, in such a way that a good thing always eliminates evil as far as it can, and that there are no limits to what an omnipotent thing can do. From these it follows that a good omnipotent thing eliminates evil completely, and then the propositions that a good omnipotent thing exists, and that evil exists, are incompatible.

A. Adequate Solutions

Now once the problem is fully stated it is clear that it can be solved, in the sense that the problem will not arise if one gives up at least one of the propositions that constitute it. If you are prepared to say that God is not wholly good, or not quite omnipotent, or that evil does not exist, or that good is not opposed to the kind of evil that exists, or that there are limits to what an omnipotent thing can do, then the problem of evil will not arise for you.

There are, then, quite a number of adequate solutions of the problem of evil, and some of these have been adopted, or almost adopted, by various thinkers. For example, a few have been prepared to deny God's omnipotence, and rather more have been prepared to keep the term "omnipotence" but severely to restrict its meaning, recording quite a number of things that an omnipotent being cannot do. Some have said that evil is an illusion, perhaps because they held that the whole world of temporal, changing things is an illusion, and that what we call evil belongs only to this world, or perhaps because they held that although temporal things *are* much as we see them, those that we call evil are not really evil. Some have said that what we call evil is merely the privation of good, that evil in a positive sense, evil that would really be opposed to good, does not exist. Many have agreed with Pope that disorder is harmony not understood, and that partial evil is universal good. Whether any of these views is *true* is, of course, another question. But each of them gives an adequate solution of the problem of evil in the sense that if you accept it this problem does not arise for you, though you may, of course, have *other* problems to face.

But often enough these adequate solutions are only *almost* adopted. The thinkers who restrict God's power, but keep the term "omnipotence," may reasonably be suspected of thinking, in other contexts, that his power is really unlimited. Those who say that evil is an illusion may also be thinking, inconsistently, that this illusion is itself an evil. Those who say that "evil" is merely privation of good may also be thinking, inconsistently, that privation of good is an evil. (The fallacy here is akin to some forms of the "naturalistic fallacy" in ethics, where some think, for example, that "good" is just what contributes to evolutionary progress, and that evolutionary progress is itself good.) If Pope meant what he said in the first line of his couplet, that "disorder" is only harmony not understood, the "partial evil" of the second line must, for consistency, mean "that which, taken in isolation, falsely appears to be evil," but it would more naturally mean "that which, in isolation, really is evil." The second line, in fact, hesitates between two views, that "partial evil" isn't really evil, since only the universal quality is real, and that "partial evil" is really an evil, but only a little one.

In addition, therefore, to adequate solutions, we must recognise unsatisfactory inconsistent solutions, in which there is only a half-hearted or temporary rejection of one of the propositions which together constitute the problem. In these, one of the constituent propositions is explicitly rejected, but it is covertly re-asserted or assumed elsewhere in the system.

B. Fallacious Solutions

Besides these half-hearted solutions, which explicitly reject but implicitly assert one of the constituent propositions, there are definitely fallacious solutions which explicitly maintain all the constituent propositions, but implicitly reject at least one of them in the course of the argument that explains away the problem of evil.

There are, in fact, many so-called solutions which purport to remove the con-tradiction without abandoning any of its constituent propositions. These must be fallacious, as we can see from the very statement of the problem, but it is not so easy to see in each case precisely where the fallacy lies. I suggest that in all cases the fallacy has the general form suggested above: in order to solve the problem one (or perhaps more) of its constituent propositions is given up, but in such a way that it appears to have been retained, and can therefore be asserted without qualification in other contexts. Sometimes there is a further complication: the supposed solution moves to and fro between, say, two of the constituent proposi-tions, at one point asserting the first of these but covertly abandoning the second, at another point asserting the second but covertly abandoning the first. These fallacious solutions often turn upon some equivocation with the words "good" and "evil," or upon some vagueness about the way in which good and evil are opposed to one another, or about how much is meant by "omnipotence." I pro-pose to examine some of these so-called solutions, and to exhibit their fallacies in detail. Incidentally, I shall also be considering whether an adequate solution could be reached by a minor modification of one or more of the constituent propo-sitions, which would, however, still satisfy all the essential requirements of ordi-nary theism.

1. "Good cannot exist without evil" or "Evil is necessary as a counterpart to good."

It is sometimes suggested that evil is necessary as a counterpart to good, that if there were no evil there could be no good either, and that this solves the problem of evil. It is true that it points to an answer to the question "Why should there be evil?" But it does so only by qualifying some of the propositions that constitute the problem.

First, it sets a limit to what God can do, saying that God *cannot* create good without simultaneously creating evil, and this means either that God is not omnipotent or that there are *some* limits to what an omnipotent thing can do. It may be replied that these limits are always presupposed, that omnipotence has never meant the power to do what is logically impossible, and on the present view the existence of good without evil would be a logical impossibility. This interpretation of omnipotence may, indeed, be accepted as a modification of our original account which does not reject anything that is essential to theism, and I shall in general assume it in the subsequent discussion. It is, perhaps, the most common theistic view, but I think that some theists at least have maintained that God can do what is logically impossible. Many theists, at any rate, have held that logic itself is created or laid down by God, that logic is the way in which God arbitrarily chooses to think. (This is, of course, parallel to the ethical view that morally right actions are those which God arbitrarily chooses to command, and the two views encounter similar difficulties.) And *this* account of logic is clearly inconsistent with the view that God is bound by logical necessities—unless it is possible for an omnipotent being to bind himself, an issue which we shall consider later, when we come to the Paradox of Omnipotence. This solution of the problem of evil cannot, therefore, be consistently adopted along with the view that logic is itself created by God.

But, secondly, this solution denies that evil is opposed to good in our original sense. If good and evil are counterparts, a good thing will not "eliminate evil as far as it can." Indeed, this view suggests that good and evil are not strictly qualities of things at all. Perhaps the suggestion is that good and evil are related in much the same way as great and small. Certainly, when the term "great" is used relatively as a condensation of "greater than so-and-so," and "small" is used correspondingly, greatness and smallness are counterparts and cannot exist without each other. But in this sense greatness is not a quality, not an intrinsic feature of anything; and it would be absurd to think of a movement in favour of greatness and against smallness in this sense. Such a movement would be self-defeating, since relative greatness can be promoted only by a simultaneous promotion of relative smallness. I feel sure that no theists would be content to regard God's goodness as analogous to this—as if what he supports were not the *good* but the *better*, and as if he had the paradoxical aim that all things should be better than other things.

This point is obscured by the fact that "great" and "small" seem to have an absolute as well as a relative sense. I cannot discuss here whether there is absolute magnitude or not, but if there is, there could be an absolute sense for "great," it could mean of at least a certain size, and it would make sense to speak of all things getting bigger, of a universe that was expanding all over, and therefore it would make sense to speak of promoting greatness. But in *this* sense great and small are not logically necessary counterparts: either quality could exist without the other. There would be no logical impossibility in everything's being small or in everything's being great.

Neither in the absolute nor in the relative sense, then, of "great" and "small" do these terms provide an analogy of the sort that would be needed to support this solution of the problem of evil. In neither case are greatness and smallness *both* necessary counterparts *and* mutually opposed forces or possible objects for support and attack.

It may be replied that good and evil are necessary counterparts in the same way as any quality and its logical opposite: redness can occur, it is suggested, only if non-redness also occurs. But unless evil is merely the privation of good, they are not logical opposites, and some further argument would be needed to show that they are counterparts in the same way as genuine logical opposites. Let us assume that this could be given. There is still doubt of the correctness of the metaphysical principle that a quality must have a real opposite: I suggest that it is not really impossible that everything should be, say, red, that the truth is merely that if everything were red we should not notice redness, and so we should have no word "red"; we observe and give names to qualities only if they have real opposites. If so, the principle that a term must have an opposite would belong only to our language or to our thought, and would not be an ontological principle, and, correspondingly, the rule that good cannot exist without evil would not state a logical necessity of a sort that God would just have to put up with. God might have made everything good, though we should not have noticed it if he had.

But, finally, even if we concede that this *is* an ontological principle, it will provide a solution for the problem of evil only if one is prepared to say, "Evil exists, but only just enough evil to serve as the counterpart of good." I doubt whether any theist will accept this. After all, the *ontological* requirement that non-redness should occur would be satisfied even if all the universe, except for a minute speck, were red, and, if there were a corresponding requirement for evil as a counterpart to good, a minute dose of evil would presumably do. But theists are not usually willing to say, in all contexts, that all the evil that occurs is a minute and necessary dose.

2. "Evil is necessary as a means to good."
It is sometimes suggested that evil is necessary for good not as a counterpart but as a means. In its simple form this has little plausibility as a solution of the problem of evil, since it obviously implies a severe restriction of God's power. It would be a *causal* law that you cannot have a certain end without a certain means, so that if God has to introduce evil as a means to good, he must be subject to at least some causal laws. This certainly conflicts with what a theist normally means by omnipotence. This view of God as limited by causal laws also conflicts with the view that causal laws are themselves made by God, which is more widely held than the corresponding view about the laws of logic. This conflict would, indeed, be resolved if it were possible for an omnipotent being to bind himself, and this possibility has still to be considered. Unless a favourable answer can be given to this question, the suggestion that evil is necessary as a means to good solves the problem of evil only by denying one of its constituent propositions, either that God is omnipotent or that "omnipotent" means what it says.

3. "The universe is better with some evil in it than it could be if there were no evil."
Much more important is a solution which at first seems to be a mere variant of the previous one, that evil may contribute to the goodness of a whole in which it is found, so that the universe as a whole is better as it is, with some evil in it, than it would be if there were no evil. This solution may be developed in either of two ways. It may be supported by an aesthetic analogy, by the fact that contrasts heighten beauty, that in a musical work, for example, there may occur discords which somehow add to the beauty of the work as a whole. Alternatively, it may be worked out in connexion with the notion of progress, that the best possible

organisation of the universe will not be static, but progressive, that the gradual overcoming of evil by good is really a finer thing than would be the eternal unchallenged supremacy of good.

In either case, this solution usually starts from the assumption that the evil whose existence gives rise to the problem of evil is primarily what is called physical evil, that is to say, pain. In Hume's rather half-hearted presentation of the problem of evil, the evils that he stresses are pain and disease, and those who reply to him argue that the existence of pain and disease makes possible the existence of sympathy, benevolence, heroism, and the gradually successful struggle of doctors and reformers to overcome these evils. In fact, theists often seize the opportunity to accuse those who stress the problem of evil of taking a low, materialistic view of good and evil, equating these with pleasure and pain, and of ignoring the more spiritual goods which can arise in the struggle against evils.

But let us see exactly what is being done here. Let us call pain and misery "first order evil" or "evil (1)." What contrasts with this, namely, pleasure and happiness, will be called "first order good" or "good (1)." Distinct from this is "second order good" or "good (2)" which somehow emerges in a complex situation in which evil (1) is a necessary component—logically, not merely causally, necessary. (Exactly *how* it emerges does not matter: in the crudest version of this solution good (2) is simply the heightening of happiness by the contrast with misery, in other versions it includes sympathy with suffering, heroism in facing danger, and the gradual decrease of first order evil and increase of first order good.) It is also being assumed that second order good is more important than first order good or evil, in particular that it more than outweighs the first order evil it involves.

Now this is a particularly subtle attempt to solve the problem of evil. It defends God's goodness and omnipotence on the ground that (on a sufficiently long view) this is the best of all logically possible worlds, because it includes the important second order goods, and yet it admits that real evils, namely first order evils, exist. But does it still hold that good and evil are opposed? Not, clearly, in the sense that we set out originally: good does not tend to eliminate evil in general. Instead, we have a modified, a more complex pattern. First order good (*e.g.* happiness) *contrasts with* first order evil (*e.g.* misery): these two are opposed in a fairly mechanical way; some second order goods (*e.g.* benevolence) try to maximise first order good and minimise first order evil; but God's goodness is not this, it is rather the will to maximise *second* order good. We might, therefore, call God's goodness an example of a third order goodness, or good (3). While this account is different from our original one, it might well be held to be an improvement on it, to give a more accurate description of the way in which good is opposed to evil, and to be consistent with the essential theist position.

There might, however, be several objections to this solution.

First, some might argue that such qualities as benevolence—and a *fortiori* the third order goodness which promotes benevolence—have a merely derivative value, that they are not higher sorts of good, but merely means to good (1), that is, to happiness, so that it would be absurd for God to keep misery in existence in order to make possible the virtues of benevolence, heroism, etc. The theist who adopts the present solution must, of course, deny this, but he can do so with some plausibility, so I should not press this objection.

Secondly, it follows from this solution that God is not in our sense benevolent or sympathetic: he is not concerned to minimise evil (1), but only to promote good (2); and this might be a disturbing conclusion for some theists.

But, thirdly, the fatal objection is this. Our analysis shows clearly the possibility of the existence of a *second* order evil, an evil (2) contrasting with good (2) as evil (1) contrasts with good (1). This would include malevolence, cruelty, callousness, cowardice, and states in which good (1) is decreasing and evil (1) increasing. And just as good (2) is held to be the important kind of good, the kind that God is concerned to promote, so evil (2) will, by analogy, be the important kind of evil, the kind which God, if he were wholly good and omnipotent, would eliminate. And yet evil (2) plainly exists, and indeed most theists (in other contexts) stress its existence more than that of evil (1). We should, therefore, state the problem of evil in terms of second order evil, and against this form of the problem the present solution is useless.

An attempt might be made to use this solution again, at a higher level, to explain the occurrence of evil (2): indeed the next main solution that we shall examine does just this, with the help of some new notions. Without any fresh notions, such a solution would have little plausibility: for example, we could hardly say that the really important good was a good (3), such as the increase of benevolence in proportion to cruelty, which logically required for its occurrence the occurrence of some second order evil. But even if evil (2) could be explained in this way, it is fairly clear that there would be third order evils contrasting with this third order good: and we should be well on the way to an infinite regress, where the solution of a problem of evil, stated in terms of evil (n), indicated the existence of an evil ($n + 1$), and a further problem to be solved.

4. "Evil is due to human free will."

Perhaps the most important proposed solution of the problem of evil is that evil is not to be ascribed to God at all, but to the independent actions of human beings, supposed to have been endowed by God with freedom of the will. This solution may be combined with the preceding one: first order evil (*e.g.* pain) may be justified as a logically necessary component in second order good (*e.g.* sympathy) while second order evil (*e.g.* cruelty) is not *justified*, but is so ascribed to human beings that God cannot be held responsible for it. This combination evades my third criticism of the preceding solution.

The freewill solution also involves the preceding solution at a higher level. To explain why a wholly good God gave men freewill although it would lead to some important evils, it must be argued that it is better on the whole that men should act freely, and sometimes err, than that they should be innocent automata, acting rightly in a wholly determined way. Freedom, that is to say, is now treated as a third order good, and as being more valuable than second order goods (such as sympathy and heroism) would be if they were deterministically produced, and it is being assumed that second order evils, such as cruelty, are logically necessary accompaniments of freedom, just as pain is a logically necessary pre-condition of sympathy.

I think that this solution is unsatisfactory primarily because of the incoherence of the notion of freedom of the will: but I cannot discuss this topic adequately here, although some of my criticisms will touch upon it.

First I should query the assumption that second order evils are logically necessary accompaniments of freedom. I should ask this: if God has made men such that in their free choices they sometimes prefer what is good and sometimes what is evil, why could he not have made men such that they always freely choose the good? If there is no logical impossibility in a man's freely choosing the good on one, or on several, occasions, there cannot be a logical impossibility in his freely choosing the good on every occasion. God was not, then, faced with a choice between making innocent automata and making beings who, in acting freely, would sometimes go wrong: there was open to him the obviously better possibility of making beings who would act freely but always go right. Clearly, his failure to avail himself of this possibility is inconsistent with his being both omnipotent and wholly good.

If it is replied that this objection is absurd, that the making of some wrong choices is logically necessary for freedom, it would seem that "freedom" must here mean complete randomness or indeterminacy, including randomness with regard to the alternatives good and evil, in other words that men's choices and consequent actions can be "free" only if they are not determined by their characters. Only on this assumption can God escape the responsibility for men's actions; for if he made them as they are, but did not determine their wrong choices, this can only be because the wrong choices are not determined by men as they are. But then if freedom is randomness, how can it be a characteristic of *will*? And, still more, how can it be the most important good? What value or merit would there be in free choices if these were random actions which were not determined by the nature of the agent?

I conclude that to make this solution plausible two different senses of "freedom" must be confused, one sense which will justify the view that freedom is a third order good, more valuable than other goods would be without it, and another sense, sheer randomness, to prevent us from ascribing to God a decision to make men such that they sometimes go wrong when he might have made them such that they would always freely go right.

This criticism is sufficient to dispose of this solution. But besides this there is a fundamental difficulty in the notion of an omnipotent God creating men with free will, for if men's wills are really free this must mean that even God cannot control them, that is, that God is no longer omnipotent. It may be objected that God's gift of freedom to men does not mean that he *cannot* control their wills, but that he always *refrains* from controlling their wills. But why, we may ask, should God refrain from controlling evil wills? Why should he not leave men free to will rightly, but intervene when he sees them beginning to will wrongly? If God could do this, but does not, and if he is wholly good, the only explanation could be that even a wrong free act of will is not really evil, that its freedom is a value which outweighs its wrongness, so that there would be a loss of value if God took away the wrongness and the freedom together. But this is utterly opposed to what theists say about sin in other contexts. The present solution of the problem of evil, then, can be maintained only in the form that God has made men so free that he *cannot* control their wills.

This leads us to what I call the Paradox of Omnipotence: can an omnipotent being make things which he cannot subsequently control? Or, what is practically equivalent to this, can an omnipotent being make rules which then bind himself? (These are practically equivalent because any such rules could be regarded as setting certain things beyond his control, and *vice versa.*) The second of these formulations is relevant to the suggestions that we have already met, that an omnipotent God creates the rules of logic or causal laws, and is then bound by them.

It is clear that this is a paradox: the questions cannot be answered satisfactorily either in the affirmative or in the negative. If we answer "Yes," it follows that if God actually makes things which he cannot control, or makes rules which bind himself, he is not omnipotent once he has made them: there are *then* things which he cannot do. But if we answer "No," we are immediately asserting that there are things which he cannot do, that is to say that he is already not omnipotent.

It cannot be replied that the question which sets this paradox is not a proper question. It would make perfectly good sense to say that a human mechanic has made a machine which he cannot control: if there is any difficulty about the question it lies in the notion of omnipotence itself.

This, incidentally, shows that although we have approached this paradox from the free will theory, it is equally a problem for a theological determinist. No one thinks that machines have free will, yet they may well be beyond the control of their makers. The determinist might reply that anyone who makes anything determines its ways of acting, and so determines its subsequent behaviour: even the human mechanic does this by his *choice* of materials and structure for his machine, though he does not know all about either of these: the mechanic thus determines, though he may not foresee, his machine's actions. And since God is omniscient, and since his creation of things is total, he both determines and foresees the ways in which his creatures will act. We may grant this, but it is beside the point. The question is not whether God *originally* determined the future actions of his creatures, but whether he can *subsequently* control their actions, or whether he was able in his original creation to put things beyond his subsequent control. Even on determinist principles the answers "Yes" and "No" are equally irreconcilable with God's omnipotence.

Before suggesting a solution of this paradox, I would point out that there is a parallel Paradox of Sovereignty. Can a legal sovereign make a law restricting its own future legislative power? For example, could the British parliament make a law forbidding any future parliament to socialise banking, and also forbidding the future repeal of this law itself? Or could the British parliament, which was legally sovereign in Australia in, say, 1899, pass a valid law, or series of laws, which made it no longer sovereign in 1933? Again, neither the affirmative nor the negative answer is really satisfactory. If we were to answer "Yes," we should be admitting the validity of a law which, if it were actually made, would mean that parliament was no longer sovereign. If we were to answer "No," we should be admitting that there is a law, not logically absurd, which parliament cannot validly make, that is, that parliament a not now a legal sovereign. This paradox can be solved in the following way. We should distinguish between first order laws, that is laws governing the actions of individuals and bodies other than the legislature, and second order laws, that is laws about laws, laws governing the actions of the legislature itself. Correspondingly, we should distinguish two orders of sovereignty, first order sovereignty (sovereignty (1)) which is unlimited authority to make first order laws, and second order sovereignty (sovereignty (2)) which is unlimited authority to make second order laws. If we say that parliament is sovereign we might mean that any parliament at any time has sovereignty (1), or we might mean that parliament has both sovereignty (1) and sovereignty (2) at present, but we cannot without contradiction mean both that the present parliament has sovereignty (2) and that every parliament at every time has sovereignty (1), for if the present parliament has sovereignty (2) it may use it to take away the sovereignty (1) of later parliaments. What the paradox shows is that we cannot ascribe to any continuing institution legal sovereignty in an inclusive sense.

The analogy between omnipotence and sovereignty shows that the paradox of omnipotence can be solved in a similar way. We must distinguish between first order omnipotence (omnipotence (1)), that is unlimited power to act, and second order omnipotence (omnipotence (2)), that is unlimited power to determine what powers to act things shall have. Then we could consistently say that God all the time has omnipotence (1), but if so no beings at any time have powers to act independently of God. Or we could say that God at one time had omnipotence (2), and used it to assign independent powers to act to certain things, so that God thereafter did not have omnipotence (1). But what the paradox shows is that we cannot consistently ascribe to any continuing being omnipotence in an inclusive sense.

An alternative solution of this paradox would be simply to deny that God is a continuing being, that any times can be assigned to his actions at all. But on this assumption (which also has difficulties of its own) no meaning can be given to the assertion that God made men with wills so free that he could not control them. The paradox of omnipotence can be avoided by putting God outside time, but the free will solution of the problem of evil cannot be saved in this way, and equally it remains impossible to hold that an omnipotent God *binds himself* by causal or logical laws.

Conclusion

Of the proposed solutions of the problem of evil which we have examined, none has stood up to criticism. There may be other solutions which require examination, but this study strongly suggests that there is no valid solution of the problem which does not modify at least one of the constituent propositions in a way which would seriously affect the essential core of the theistic position.

Quite apart from the problem of evil, the paradox of omnipotence has shown that God's omnipotence must in any case be restricted in one way or another, that unqualified omnipotence cannot be ascribed to any being that continues through time. And if God and his actions are not in time, can omnipotence, or power of any sort, be meaningfully ascribed to him?

NICHOLAS WOLTERSTORFF
Contemporary Philosopher

Can Belief in God Be Rational if it Has No Foundations?*

I

Locke assumes—rightly in my judgment—that we have an obligation to govern our assent with the goal in mind of getting more amply in touch with reality. Likewise he assumes—also rightly, I think—that this goal has the two sides of seeking to increase our stock of true beliefs and of seeking to avoid or eliminate false beliefs. Let us scrutinize these assumptions a bit, beginning with a consideration of that latter assumption. To do so it will be helpful to consider Roderick Chisholm's formulation of our intellectual duties. "Each person," he says, "is subject to two quite different requirements in connection with any proposition he considers: (1) he should try his best to bring it about that if that proposition is true then he believes it; and (2) he should try his best to bring it about that if that proposition is false then he not believe it."

Now suppose one took the second of these two requirements seriously but not the first. That is, suppose one had it as one's sole goal to snare as few falsehoods in one's net of belief as possible. What strategy would then be appropriate? Quite obviously the strategy of undertaking to believe as few as possible of the propositions that cross one's mind. There is nothing better than this that one could do (though even this might well not achieve the result of eliminating all falsehoods, for many of the things we believe, we do so ineluctably). If one wants above all to avoid catching trash fish, one goes fishing as little as possible. But though a serious pursuit of this strategy would be likely to diminish significantly the number of falsehoods believed, that merit would be purchased at the cost of missing out on a great deal of truth. And surely that is an important deficiency in this strategy of incredulity. The extent to which one had gotten in touch with reality would be severely limited.

Suppose, on the other hand, that one took the first of these two requirements seriously but paid no attention to the second. Suppose one had it as one's sole goal to snare as many truths as possible in one's net of belief. What strategy would then be appropriate? Quite obviously the strategy of undertaking to believe as many as possible of the propositions that come to mind—with this proviso: if one cannot believe both a proposition which comes to mind and its contradictory, then one strives to believe that member of the pair, if either, for which one

---

*From "Can Belief in God Be Rational if it Has No Foundations?" in A. Plantinga and N. Wolterstorff, eds., *Faith and Rationality* (South Bend, Indiana: University of Notre Dame Press, 1984), pp. 135–186.

has better evidence. There seems no better strategy than this strategy of gullibility for achieving the goal. If catching as many edible fish as possible is one's only goal, one nets fish indiscriminately—unless one has to make a choice here and there. But though the serious pursuit of this strategy would increase the number of truths one believes, it is also likely to increase substantially one's stock of false beliefs. And that, surely, is a deficiency. False beliefs mark a failure fully to get in touch with reality.

So both goals are necessary: the goal of increasing one's stock of true beliefs and the goal of avoiding or eliminating false beliefs. Accordingly, more subtle strategies will have to be adopted than either that comprehensive strategy of incredulity or that comprehensive strategy of gullibility.

Of course, once we allow that the pursuit of both these goals is necessary for getting in touch with reality, we must also acknowledge the possibility that in specific cases the two goals will yield conflicting results. Upon doing one's best to ascertain whether a proposition is true or false, one may discover that the evidence pro and con is equally balanced. In such a case one has to weigh up which is the worse outcome—that of missing out on truth or that of falling into error.

Yet another matter, pertaining to our obligation to get more amply in touch with reality, must be raised at this point. With respect to which propositions does one have an obligation to bring it about that one believes them if they are true and disbelieves them if they are false? The answer Chisholm gives is *any proposition one considers.* But that seems hardly correct on a couple of counts. Suppose, upon looking at a bean bag, that the thought crosses my mind that it contains exactly 2019 beans. Suppose I then consider that proposition. Is it really the case, in ordinary circumstances, that I then have an obligation to bring it about that I believe this if and only if it is true? Is not the acquisition of true, and the avoidance of false, belief on this matter so unimportant to my life that I have no such obligation—not even *prima facie?* Of course propositions are not in general inherently trivial or important. There may be tasks which *you* have that make it important for *you* to seek to bring it about that you believe there are 2019 beans in the bag just in case there are. But I have no such tasks.

Neither is it the case that our obligation to attain truth pertains just to the propositions we *consider.* Some of the propositions we have never considered are nonetheless propositions that we ought to believe. It may be that we *ought* to have considered them—and having considered, to believe. Or alternatively, it may be that though we have no obligation to *consider* them, nonetheless we do have an obligation to *believe* them. After all, there are ways of coming to believe propositions which do not require *considering* those propositions. Many of the things we believe, and ought to believe, have never been *considered* by us. Considering is involved in only some modes of belief acquisition. . . .

It was the eighteenth-century Scottish philosopher Thomas Reid's great genius to perceive that if we want to understand knowledge and rationality, we cannot talk only about the abstract relations holding among propositions, along the way making unreflective assumptions about the "mechanisms" which form our beliefs. We must look head-on at the psychological "mechanisms" involved in belief formation. Articulate epistemology requires articulate psychology.

At the very foundation of Reid's approach is his claim that at any point in our lives we each have a variety of dispositions, inclinations, propensities, to believe things—*belief dispositions* we may call them. What accounts for our beliefs, in the vast majority of cases anyway, is the triggering of one and another such disposition. For example, we are all so constituted that upon having memory experiences in certain situations, we are disposed to have certain beliefs about the past. We are all disposed, upon having certain sensations in certain situations, to have certain beliefs about the external physical world. Upon having certain other sensations in certain situations, we are all disposed to have certain beliefs about our persons. Likewise we are all so constituted as to be disposed in certain circumstances to believe what we apprehend people as telling us—the *credulity* disposition, as Reid rather fetchingly called it.

To the belief dispositions of which Reid took note we may add those rather ignoble belief dispositions of which Marx and Freud made so much: our disposition to believe what gives us a sense of security, our disposition to believe what serves to perpetuate our positions of economic privilege, our disposition to adopt clusters of beliefs which function as ideologies and rationalizations to conceal from our conscious awareness the ignobility of those other dispositions, and so on.

The belief dispositions which I have cited thus far are all dispositions which produce their effects *immediately.* We do not normally infer, from other beliefs of ours which we take as good evidence for it, that a person is before us. Rather, upon having certain sensations in certain situations we just immediately believe this. Likewise our memory experiences produce immediately in us certain convictions about the past. Remembering does not consist in going through a process of inferring a belief about the past from other beliefs.

There is, though, another disposition in us of which these remarks are not true. In addition to the features of our constitution thus far mentioned, we are all so constituted that upon judging some proposition which we already believe as being good evidence for another proposition not yet believed, we are disposed to believe that other proposition as well. To this disposition Reid assigned the name of reason. Let me call it the *reasoning disposition.* What the tradition called *mediate* beliefs can now be singled out as those produced by the reasoning disposition, and what it called *immediate* beliefs, those produced by some one of our other belief dispositions. . . .

To a great extent it is in our power to *govern* the workings of our belief dispositions—not now to alter them, but to govern their workings. And often it is because it is in our power to govern their workings that we are culpable for our believings and our failings to believe. For one thing, it is often in our power to determine whether a triggering event for some disposition will occur. For example, it was in my power to go over and look at the tire; if I had, the sensations received would have triggered in me the belief that the tire was flat. There are also more subtle and interesting examples than ones like this, however. Often it is in our power to bring it about that we will *notice* something when in situations where that is noticeable. For example, one can set oneself, or fail to set oneself, to notice speed-limit signs when entering villages; and setting oneself to do so makes it highly likely that one will. It is for this reason that police officers are often right in holding us accountable for not knowing what the speed limit in a given village is. So too one can try, or fail to try, to *remember* something; and making an effort to remember often makes it much more likely that one will. For this reason one can often rightly be held accountable for not remembering something—for not having correct beliefs on a certain matter. (Strictly speaking, this last case is a case, not of having it in one's power to determine whether a certain belief disposition will be triggered, but of having it in one's power to determine whether a certain belief is *sustained*. Believing is not an event but an enduring state. A full discussion of the matter would systematically distinguish between factors *initiating* such a state and factors *sustaining* such a state.)

Not only is it often in our power to determine whether a certain triggering event for some belief disposition will occur; likewise it is sometimes in our power, even when an event does occur that characteristically would trigger the disposition, to determine whether or not the disposition will become operative. We can *resolve* or *determine* that a disposition will not become operative, and sometimes at least such a resolution is effective. For example, one can resolve to resist the workings of one's credulity disposition and come to no belief as to what transpired in marital disputes until one has heard out both parties; in the absence of the resolution one would have believed the tale of the first party. Or again: one can resolve to resist the workings of one's memory disposition and no longer to believe that what one seems to remember as having happened when one was in situations of great stress did in fact happen. So, too, one can resolve to resist the workings of one's reasoning disposition and hold no belief about the size of one's checking-account balance until one has gone over the figures at least twice. Obviously, repeatedly resolving to resist the operation of some belief disposition in certain sorts of situations may eventually result in that disposition's being extinguished for those sorts of cases.

The resolve to resist the activation of a belief disposition, even in the presence of an event which, were it not for this resolve, would trigger the disposition, may sometimes take the form of leaving one, not in a state of suspension of belief, but in a state of continuing to believe as one did. Suppose, for example, that a certain belief of Vern's is deeply embedded in the whole structure of his personality, his life-style, his career, and so on. It gives him great comfort. Or he has spent twenty years of work in physics on the premise that this is true. In short, he has deep motivations for hanging on to this belief. Suppose that then someone comes along and presents him with evidence that this belief is false. It would seem that in some such cases it is in Vern's power to accept the evidence and change his mind, but equally in his power to resist changing his mind. That is to say, it is true not merely that in some such cases his mind *is changed* but also that in some such cases it is in his power *to change* his mind, or at least to *let* his mind *be changed*. It is in his power to acknowledge the force of the evidence, give up his resistance to the conclusion, and change his mind; but equally it is in his power to cling stubbornly to what he has always believed and treat the evidence as not conclusive.

And now what about the case so dear to the heart of the classical epistemologist: the case of a person considering some proposition and then deciding to believe it, or to disbelieve it? Perhaps the *considering* is here unimportant. Does it ever happen that we *decide* to believe something? Must a full picture of our belief-forming processes, and of our capacity to govern them, have this sort of case in mind as well?

Perhaps so. Of course it may be that some cases of resolving to resist the working of some belief disposition are also cases of deciding to believe or not to believe so-and-so. Perhaps that is true of the last case considered, the case of Vern. But be that as it may, let us consider a case in which a resolution to resist is not in the picture. Suppose that one is a member of a jury and has agonized long hours over which of two conflicting witnesses to believe on a certain matter. May it be that eventually one *decides to believe* what one of them said and to disbelieve what the other said? One could have made the opposite decision, but as a matter of fact this is what one decides to believe. In some cases of conflicting testimony one just finds oneself persuaded that one witness is speaking truth and the other not. May it be that in other cases one decides? If so, that decision is probably accompanied by a decision to the effect that the *evidence* for the veracity of the one witness is slightly stronger than the evidence for the veracity of the other. This would then be a second point at which a decision to believe occurs in such a case.

So the full picture that emerges is something like this: we each have a variety of belief dispositions, some of which we share with all normal, mature human beings, some of which we do not; some of which we have as part of our native endowment, some of which are the result of one and another form of conditioning, and probably some of which are the result of having resolved to resist the workings of some native or conditioned disposition. In addition, we each have a variety of capacities for governing the workings of these dispositions. To some extent it is in our power to determine whether a certain (sort of) triggering event for a disposition will occur. And to some extent it is in our power to determine whether the disposition will be activated even if an event does occur which characteristically would activate it. Perhaps we also have the capacity in certain (relatively rare) circumstances to *decide* whether to believe something.

It must be clearly noted that rationality, thus conceived, is in good measure person specific and situation specific. When I was young, there were things which it was rational for me to believe which now, when I am older, it is no longer rational for me to believe. And for a person reared in a traditional tribal society who never comes into contact with another society or culture, there will be things rational to believe which for me, a member of the modern Western intelligentsia, would not be rational to believe. Rationality of belief can only be determined in context—historical and social contexts, and, even more narrowly, personal context. It has long been the habit of philosophers to ask in abstract, nonspecific fashion whether it is rational to believe that God exists, whether it is rational to believe that there is an external world, whether it is rational to believe that there are other persons, and so on. Mountains of confusion have resulted. The proper question is always and only whether it is rational for this or that particular person in this or that situation, or for a person of this or that particular type in this or that type of situation, to believe so-and-so. Rationality is always *situated* rationality. (Some thinkers in the modern world seem to have concluded from the fact that a nonsituated theory of rationality is untenable that the concept of rationality itself must be discarded. They have become historicists. We have seen, and will see, no reason whatsoever to draw this conclusion.)

II

And now it is easy to see why the theist cannot simply dismiss out of hand the charge that his theistic convictions are nonrational. Nonrationality in one's beliefs is the sure sign that some of one's obligations have been violated. Accordingly, a person cannot meet the charge that one of his beliefs is nonrational by announcing that he has chosen not to live by the canons of rationality, anymore than he can meet the charge that he has acted immorally by announcing that he has chosen not to live by moral obligations. He can meet it only by *contesting* the charge.

There is yet a deeper reason why the theist, at least if he is a Christian, Jew, or Muslim, cannot just dismiss out of hand the demands of rationality. Such a person will always perceive our human obligations as related, in one way or another, to the will of God. God wills that we do what we ought to do. When a theist believes nonrationally, he acts in violation of the will of the very God in whom he believes—unless it be the case that there are extenuating circumstances.

However, it is also easy to see now that the charge lodged against the theist, that he holds his theistic convictions nonrationally, is not a *decisive* charge, in the sense that it does not *follow* from the nonrationality of the belief that he ought to give up believing that. We can see, in short, that one of the two principal components in the evidentialist challenge to theistic conviction is untenable.

The most obvious, and perhaps least important, point to make here is that what grounds the nonrationality of some beliefs is not *what* is believed but *how* it is believed: it is believed with the wrong degree of firmness. Hence, from being told that someone holds some one of his beliefs nonrationally one cannot infer that he ought not to believe that.

But second, the nonrationality of a belief—as, following Locke, we have conceived it—results from the fact that one has not done as well as one ought to have done in governing one's belief-forming "mechanisms" toward the goal of getting more amply in touch with reality. But as we have already seen, one can presumably conduct such governance with other goals in mind; and perhaps with respect to such alternative governance there are also obligations. If so, it may well be that though a given belief represents inadequate governance with respect to the goal of getting more amply in touch with reality and is, accordingly, a nonrational belief, it represents *adequate* governance with respect to some other goal. Further, it may well be that governance with respect to that other goal has priority over governance with respect to getting more amply in touch with reality. We in the West for several centuries now have assumed that nothing could take priority in belief governance over our obligation to expand our hold on truth and to avoid or eliminate falsehood in our beliefs. It is difficult to perceive, though, what defense could be given for this. And if the assumption is in fact false, then here is a second way in which it may come about that a person is permitted to believe something that is not rational for him to believe. Maybe in some cases it is even true that he *ought* to believe it in spite of its nonrationality.

Lastly, there is more to life than governing aright the *what* and the *how* of one's assent—and so too there is more to life's obligations than the obligation to govern aright one's belief-forming "mechanisms." Sometimes these other obligations of life take precedence over those governance obligations, again with the result that one is permitted to believe something that is not rational to believe. Perhaps I did not calculate my bank account figures carefully enough for me to believe rationally that the balance is $53.09. But perhaps I had to choose between spending more time calculating and taking my son to see the Phillies play in the World Series. In this conflict of obligations I may have made the right decision, to calculate quickly and go off to the game. Our obligation to govern our assent aright often takes time to carry out, and sometimes the time taken is wrongly taken from the time needed to carry out some other obligation. For this reason, too, from the fact that someone holds a belief nonrationally it does not in general follow that he ought not to hold it.

When we speak of a person as *justified* in holding some belief, often, perhaps always, what we mean is that the person is *permitted* to hold that belief. So another way of putting the point above is that a person may be justified in holding a belief even though he does not hold it rationally. What is true, of course, is that if a person holds a belief rationally, then *other things being equal,* he is justified in holding it—or to put the same point in other words, then he is *prima facie* justified in holding it. But other things may not be equal, with the result that though he holds it rationally, he is nonetheless not justified in holding it. It will sometimes be convenient in what follows to say of the person who believes some proposition rationally that he is *rationally* justified in holding it—from which it does not follow that he is justified *tout court* in holding it.

Now that we have introduced the word "justified" into our discussion, a few cautions should be sounded. For one thing, *being justified* in one's belief that so-and-so is different from *justifying* one's belief that so-and-so. To be justified in believing that so-and-so is to be in a certain *state.* To justify one's belief that so-and-so is to perform a certain *action.* Most of the beliefs we are justified in holding are such that we never justify them—never even attempt to do so. Probably most are such that we could not do so—depending, of course, on the standards adopted for success in performing the action of justifying.

Second, we speak sometimes of one proposition justifying another, but that too is a different matter. One proposition justifies another when it is good evidence for the other. But justification, on the concept I am using, is not a relation between propositions. It is a relation between a *person* and some one of his *believings.*

Last, an unjustified belief of a person is, not one that he ought to give up, but one that he ought not to have had. Thinkably, now that he has it, he *cannot* give it up. Similarly, the immoral act is not the act that the person ought to undo, nor, always, the act that the person ought to cease doing. It is the act that the person ought not to have done.

WILLIAM P. ALSTON
Contemporary Philosopher

Christian Experience and Christian Belief*

Let PP stand for "perceptual practice" (our familiar way of objectifying sense experience). Let CP stand for the practice of objectifying certain ranges of experience in Christian terms.

With this, let us tackle the question of whether one can be justified in PP and in CP. In order to get a handle on this question, we will have to determine what intellectual obligations we have vis-à-vis epistemic practices. Since our basic cognitive aims are to come into possession of as much truth as possible and to avoid false beliefs, it would seem that one's basic intellectual obligation vis-à-vis practices of belief formation would be to do what one can (or at least as much as could reasonably be expected of one) to see to it that these practices are as reliable as possible. But this still leaves us with an option between a stronger and a weaker view of this obligation, corresponding to the famous Clifford-James confrontation over the ethics of belief. To oversimplify, Clifford held that we are obligated to refrain from believing that p unless we have adequate reasons for that belief, whereas James held that we are permitted to believe that p unless we have adequate reasons for supposing it false. Transposing this to the epistemology of practices, the harsher Cliffordian view is that one is obliged to refrain from engaging in a practice unless one has adequate reasons for supposing it to be reliable. Hence one is justified in engaging in a practice *if and only if* one has such reasons. In the absence of sufficient reasons for considering the practice reliable, one is not justified in it. Practices are guilty until proved innocent. While on the more latitudinarian Jamesian view one is justified in engaging in a practice provided one does not have sufficient reasons for regarding it as unreliable. Practices are innocent until proved guilty.[1] Let us take J_{ns} as an abbreviation for "justified in the normative sense on the stronger (Cliffordian) requirement," and J_{nw} as an abbreviation for "justified in the normative sense on the weaker (Jamesian) requirement."[2]

---

*From "Christian Experience and Christian Belief," in A. Plantinga and N. Wolterstroff, eds., *Faith and Rationality* (South Bend, Indiana: University of Notre Dame Press, 1984), pp. 116–134.

[1] *Glossary of Abbreviations:* PP = Perceptual practice (our familiar way of objectifying sense experience. CP = Practice of objectifying certain ranges of experience in Christian terms. J_{ns} = Justified in the normative sense on the stronger (Cliffordian) requirement. J_{nw} = Justified in the normative sense on the weaker (Jamesian) requirement.

For the Clifford-James debate see pp. 195–203. —ED.

[2] In giving these formulations I have been making the simplifying assumption that we have complete (direct or indirect) control over what epistemic practices we engage in. If that is the case, then when on the stronger version I have an obligation to do what I can to avoid engaging in practice P because I lack adequate reason for

Jamesian Justifications in PP

Now let us consider whether we are justified, in one or another sense, in engaging in PP. And let us begin with J_{nw}. Except for those who, like Parmenides and Bradley, have argued that there are ineradicable inconsistencies in the conceptual scheme involved in PP, philosophers have not supposed that we can show that sense perception is an unreliable guide to our immediate surroundings. Sceptics about sense perception have generally confined themselves to arguing that we cannot show that sense perception is reliable: that is, they have argued that PP is not J_{ns}. I shall assume without further argument that our perceptual practice is J_{nw}. . . .

It would seem that PP is what we might call a "basic practice," one that constitutes our basic access to its subject matter. We can learn about our physical environment only by perceiving it, by receiving reports of the perceptions of others, and by carrying out inferences from what we learn in these first two ways. We cannot know anything a priori about these matters, nor do we have any other sort of experiential access to the physical world. If this is correct, then the attempt to determine the reliability of perceptual practice faces problems very different from those faced by an attempt to determine the reliability of some restricted method or procedure that is imbedded in some wider practice, the rest of which is taken for granted. Suppose I ask whether the process that led up to my present visual perception of a typewriter is of a sort that is generally reliable. Here I am only putting this particular process in question; I am taking for granted the reliability of PP generally, and I am assuming what we suppose ourselves to have learned about the physical world from that practice and from reasoning based on its products. In this case it is certainly possible to obtain evidence to settle the question. Again, if I ask, in the same spirit, about the reliability of the practice of using mercury thermometers for certain kinds of temperature readings, there would again be a very favorable prospect of settling the matter. In all such cases the rest of the total practice in which these procedures are imbedded (or enough of the rest) is assumed to be reliable; hence we can use those other subpractices, and what has been learned from them, to investigate the point in question. But where a total basic practice is under investigation, we have no such resources. Since this practice, and what is based on it, constitutes our sole access to the subject matter, we cannot carry out a direct investigation of its reliability by comparing its deliverances with how the object matter is, since we have no other way of determining the latter. How, then, can we proceed?

Since this issue has been in the forefront of the European philosophical consciousness for several hundred years, a number of ideas have been broached that could be construed as attempts to provide such a justification, though the

---

regarding it as reliable, that will be an obligation to avoid P; and so it will be true that I am justified in engaging in P *iff* (if and only if) I have adequate reason to regard it as reliable. We can generalize the formulations so as to avoid reliance on this assumption by simply putting lack of control as another alternative. Thus the stronger version would become: *S* is justified in engaging in P *iff* either (a) *S* has adequate reason for regarding P as reliable or (b) *S* is unable to prevent himself from engaging in P.

question has rarely been put in just these terms. In the interests of getting to my own positive suggestions I shall just issue a few *obiter dicta* concerning a few samples.

1. There are straightforward attempts at justification, typified by Descartes' appeal to the goodness of God, that make use of premises that have not been obtained from PP itself and hence do not suffer from circularity. However, they are all dubitable, at best, either with respect to the premises or with respect to the support those premises give the conclusion.

2. A recent survey of my colleagues revealed a considerable degree of support for "transcendental" arguments of the Kantian or the Strawsonian type, in which it is claimed that the objectification of sense experience by use of the physical-object scheme is necessary for us to have any experience of anything, or for us to have any conception of ourselves, or. . . . I think that all these arguments exhibit various sorts of difficulties in detail. But even if one of them should succeed, it would still, at best, have shown that our customary perceptual practice is even more deeply embedded in other aspects of our cognitive practices than we had supposed. Or, alternatively, it would show that we are unable to envisage, in any thoroughgoing way, any alternative to this familiar practice. But both of these results would fall short of showing that this practice is a reliable way of finding out how something actually is.

3. Finally, there are various more popular "pragmatic" arguments. "This practice 'works'; it serves as a basis for accurate prediction; it permits general agreement;" and so on. The basic trouble with all this is that it is blatantly circular. We have to use PP to determine that the predictions we make on the basis of perceptual beliefs often turn out to be correct, and to determine that there is a large measure of agreement in perceptual beliefs. We do not discover this by using a crystal ball or being told by an angel.

This survey would indicate that prospects are not good for providing adequate noncircular reasons for regarding PP as reliable. If no such reasons can be provided, we cannot be J_{ns} in that practice. It does not follow, of course, that the practice is not reliable, and hence it does not follow that the practice is not justifiable; but it does follow that we cannot have adequate reasons for supposing it to be justifiable. This leaves us with J_{nw}. Since, so far as I know, no one has unearthed any sufficient reason for regarding PP as unreliable, I shall take it that we do lack such reasons, and hence that the practice is J_{nw}.

If we take it that being J_{nw} in engaging in PP is enough to make it reasonable for us to do so, and if we generalize this to all epistemic practices, we will arrive at a general perspective on epistemology that has been enunciated by various thinkers in the last two hundred years but, to my mind, never more persuasively than by the eighteenth-century Scottish philosopher Thomas Reid. According to Reid we have several ultimate sources of belief. These include at least "self-consciousness" (in the sense of awareness of one's own current conscious states), sense perception, memory, rational intuition (that is, "seeing" with the mind's eye that certain things are self-evidently so, for example, two quantities equal to the same quantity are equal to each other), and reasoning, which itself is of various sorts. All normal human beings are endowed by God or nature, or both, with a strong tendency to trust these sources, that is, to form firm beliefs on their basis. Moreover, we do this, for the most part, unhesitatingly and uncritically, though we may question one of these sources on a particular occasion if there is special reason to do so. But are we rationally justified in according such trust? What reason do we have for regarding these sources as reliable? When we consider this question generally, as we did above for sense perception, we see that we are unable to give an adequate noncircular justification for any of the sources. Our only reason for supposing that memory is generally reliable is that its past track record is a good one, and we have no way of ascertaining that without relying on our memory. Again, it is obviously impossible to *argue* for the reliability of reasoning without relying on reasoning to do so. And so on.

Thus, if we are to have any chance of acquiring knowledge, we must simply go along with our natural reactions of trust with respect to at least some basic sources of belief, provided we lack sufficient reason for regarding them as unreliable. In the above terms we must be content with being J_{nw}. And if some, why not all? Of course we could, if we chose, accept some sources without any positive basis, such as intuition and reasoning, and then require that other candidates be certified by the former, that is, require J_{ns} for these latter. This is, in effect, what Descartes[3] and many other philosophers have done, when, for example, they held sense perception suspect until its reliability could be shown to follow from self-evident premises. But, as Reid points out, this is to be guilty of arbitrary partiality. Why accept intuition and reasoning without any basis, while refusing to do the same for sense perception? Moreover, these attempts have never met with success. In any event nature has not left us any real choice with respect to the sources listed above. In the absence of special reasons for doubt, we do accept the deliverances of sense and memory willy-nilly, whatever our reflective philosophical views. These matters are too important to be left to the vagaries of philosophical reasoning. . . .

Jamesian Justification in CP

I believe that many people are inclined to take CP to be discredited by certain ways in which it differs from PP, by the lack of certain salient features of PP. These include the following:

1. Within PP there are standard ways of checking the accuracy of any particular perceptual belief. If, by looking at a cup, I form the belief that there is coffee in it, I can check this belief for accuracy by smelling or tasting the contents; I can get other observers to look at it, smell it, or taste it; I can run chemical tests on it and get other people to do so.

2. By engaging in PP we can discover regularities in the behavior of objects putatively observed, and on this basis we can, to a certain extent, effectively predict the course of events.

3. Capacity for PP, and practice of it, is found universally among normal adult human beings.

[3] See Descartes pp. 185; cf. pp. 410. —ED.

4. All normal adult human beings, whatever their culture, use basically the same conceptual scheme in objectifying their sense experience. . . .[4]

One could quibble over whether the contrast is as sharp as is alleged. Questions could be raised about both sides of the putative divide. On the PP side is it really true that all cultures have objectified sense experience in the same way? Many anthropologists have thought not. And what about the idea that all *normal* adult human beings engage in the same perceptual practice? Are we not loading the dice by taking participation in what we regard as standard perceptual practice as our basic criterion for normality? On the CP side is it really the case that this practice reveals no regularities to us, or only that they are very different from regularities in the physical world? What about the point that God is faithful to His promises? Or that the pure in heart will see God? However, I believe that when all legitimate quibbles have been duly registered there will still be very significant differences between the two practices in these respects. So rather than contest the factual allegations, I will concentrate on the *de jure* issue as to what bearing these differences have on epistemic status.

If the lack of these features is to prevent CP from being J_{nw}, then that lack will have to constitute an adequate reason for regarding CP as unreliable.[5] And why should we suppose that? I am prepared to agree that 1–4 are desiderata for an epistemic practice. If we were shaping the world to our heart's desire, I dare say that we would arrange for our practices to exhibit these features.[6] Where we have 3, each of us can feel reassured about the practice by noting that everyone else does it. Where we have 2 and 1, we cannot only acquire the handle on prediction and explanation that we get from a knowledge of regularities, but we are able to distinguish effectively between correct and incorrect reports. Where 4 is present, we are saved the agonizing necessity of choosing between radically divergent conceptual schemes and correspondingly radically different beliefs about the subject matter. Things go more smoothly, more satisfyingly, from a cognitive point of view where these features are exhibited. Since PP possesses these virtues and CP does not, the former is, to that extent and in that way, superior from a cognitive view where these features are exhibited. Since PP possesses these virtues and CP does not, the former is, to that extent and in that way, superior from a cognitive point of view.[7] But granting all this, why should we suppose that the lack of these

---

[4] In attributing these features to PP we are enriching our conception of that practice by including the storage of perceptual beliefs in memory and various kinds of reasonings from those beliefs, as well as their initial formation. We may enlarge our conception of CP in a similar way and even include PP in CP as well. Then in considering whether CP possesses these features we will be thinking of the distinctive portion of CP by virtue of which it "goes beyond" PP.

[5] To be sure, even if it does constitute an adequate reason it will not follow that no one can be J_{nw} in engaging in CP. For there may well be persons who do not know that CP lacks these features. Such a person will not have an adequate reason (at least not this adequate reason) for taking CP to be unreliable. Normative justification of practices, like normative justification of beliefs, is situation relative. What I am justified in believing or doing may not be the same as what you are justified in believing or doing. In thinking that these lacks would inhibit J_{nw} if they were an adequate reason for unreliability, we are thinking of persons who are fully cognizant of the relevant facts.

[6] At least those practices that deal with objects that act or change through time. Otherwise 2 would be inapplicable.

[7] In fact, if we could have things our own way we would, no doubt, bring it about that PP exhibits these features to a higher degree than it does. Our perception, and reasoning thereon, could conceivably reveal regularities

features indicates unreliability? Why suppose that any practice that lacks *these* cognitive virtues will be, or will be likely to be, unreliable, that is, fail to yield generally correct truths about its subject matter? Why suppose that the lack of those virtues carries with it the lack of this further virtue? . . .

The reality CP claims to put us in touch with is conceived to be vastly different from the physical environment. Why should not the sorts of procedures required to put us in effective cognitive touch with this reality be equally different? Why suppose that the distinctive features of PP set an appropriate standard for the cognitive approach to God? I shall sketch out a possible state of affairs in which CP is quite trustworthy while lacking 1–4, and then suggest that we have no reason to suppose that this state of affairs does not obtain.

Suppose, then, that (A) God is too different from created beings, too "wholly other," for us to be able to grasp any regularities in His behavior. Suppose further that (B) for the same reason we can only attain the faintest, sketchiest, and most insecure grasp of what God is like. Finally, suppose that (C) God has decreed that a human being will be aware of His presence in any clear and unmistakable fashion only when certain special and difficult conditions are satisfied. If all this is the case, then it is the reverse of surprising that CP should lack 1–4, even if it does involve a genuine experience of God. It would lack 1–2 because of (A). It is quite understandable that it should lack 4 because of (B). If our cognitive powers are not fitted to frame an adequate conception of God, it is not at all surprising that there should be wide variation in attempts to do so. This is what typically happens in science when investigators are grappling with a phenomenon no one really understands. A variety of models, analogues, metaphors, hypotheses, hunches are propounded, and it is impossible to secure universal agreement. 3 is missing because of (C). If very difficult conditions are set, it is not surprising that few are chosen. Now it is compatible with (A)–(C) that (D) religious experience should, in general, constitute a genuine awareness of the divine; that (E) although any particular articulation of such an experience might be mistaken to a greater or lesser extent, indeed even though all such articulations might miss the mark to some extent, still such judgments will, for the most part, contain some measure of truth; and that (F) God's designs contain provision for correction and refinement, for increasing the accuracy of the beliefs derived from religious experience. If something like (A)–(F) is the case, then CP is trustworthy even though it lacks features 1–4. This is a conceivable way in which CP would constitute a road to the truth, while differing from PP in respects 1–4. If (A)–(F) represents the way it is with God and our situation vis-á-vis God, then the absence of 1–4 does not betoken unreliability of CP, nor would their presence betoken reliability of CP. Quite the contrary. If this is the way things are, then if an epistemic practice were to lead us to suppose that we had discovered regular patterns in the divine behavior or that divine activity is equally discernible by all, that would be a reason for regarding the practice as *unreliable*. Therefore, unless we have adequate reason for

---

to us much more readily and extensively than it does; and if it did then, by the same considerations we would be even better off. And would we not have been better off if there had not been such divergencies as have existed between ways of objectifying sense experience in different cultures?

supposing that (A)–(F) does not obtain, we are not warranted in taking the lack of 1–4 to be an adequate reason for a judgment of untrustworthiness.

Moreover, it is not just that (A)–(C) constitute a bare possibility. In the practice of CP we seem to learn that this is the way things are. As for (A) and (B) it is the common teaching of all the higher religions that God is of a radically different order of being from finite substances and, therefore, that we cannot expect to attain the grasp of His nature and His doings that we have of worldly objects. As for (C) it is a basic theme in Christianity, and in other religions as well, that one finds God within one's experience, to any considerable degree, only as one progresses in the spiritual life. God is not available for *voyeurs*. Awareness of God, and understanding of His nature and His will for us, is not a purely cognitive achievement; it requires the involvement of the whole person; it takes a practical commitment and a practice of the life of the spirit, as well as the exercise of cognitive faculties. "Blessed are the pure in heart, for they shall see God." "If we love one another, God dwells in us." God is always present; we do not have to travel to distant climes or distant planets to see Him and enjoy His presence. But He reveals Himself clearly, unmistakably, and in detail, only to those who have responded to His call, have made a stable commitment to Him, have put Him at the center of their lives, and have opened themselves to His influence.

To be sure, if in the last paragraph I were arguing for the reliability of CP by alleging that (A)–(C) obtain, then that argument would be vitiated with circularity, since we have no reason for supposing that (A)–(C) obtain, apart from assuming the reliability of CP or some analogous religious epistemic practice. But that was not the point. In calling attention to the fact that CP yields (A)–(C) I was merely reinforcing the negative point that we lack adequate reason for supposing that these conditions do not obtain. So far from that being the case, insofar as any epistemic practice claims to tell us anything about the matter, what it tells us is that they do obtain. Thus the basic point is still the negative one. We do not have adequate reason for supposing that (A)–(F) do not obtain, and, therefore, we are not justified in taking the absence of 1–4 to provide an adequate reason for the unreliability of CP.[8]

CP Through Christian Experience

Suppose the points I have made so far are granted. More specifically, suppose it to be granted that a fully reflective, knowledgeable person in our society can be J_{nw} in engaging in CP and that she cannot be justified in any other sense in engaging in PP and other commonly accepted, basic epistemic practices. Let us suppose it granted, furthermore, that CP yields a picture of its subject matter that is such as to tend to protect it from imputations of unreliability and so, in this way, is self-supporting. Nevertheless, one might still feel the need for some further recommendation of CP. Granted that we cannot reasonably expect to be able to develop a cogent noncircular argument for the reliability of CP, one still might

---

[8] There is also the following subsidiary point. Since CP yields the conclusion that (A)–(C) hold, if we were to take it that they do not hold, in the absence of overriding reason for supposing them not to hold, we would be begging the question against CP. We would be presupposing that it is unreliable in the course of arriving at a judgment on the matter.

wonder if there is some way in which CP "proves itself," as PP does with its pay-offs of prediction and control of the course of events. Those are the fruits of PP with which it rewards its devotees. Are there analogous fruits of the practice of CP, fruits which provide its devotees with a token of its authenticity that may serve to encourage them to persevere?

Perceptual practice proves itself, insofar as it does, by providing us with a "map" of the physical and social environment that enables us to find our way around in it, to anticipate the course of events, and to adjust our behavior to what we encounter so as to satisfy our needs and achieve our ends. This is the basic function of sense perception in our lives, and it carries out that function with rea-sonable success, as it itself testifies. To discover the appropriate fruits of the Chris-tian enterprise, we have to ask what its basic purpose or function is. It is clear that it is not primarily a theoretical or speculative function, any more than in the for-mer case, but it is not the same kind of practical function either. It is rather the transformation of the individual into what God intended him to be. This is what, from within the Christian life, its basic goal is revealed to be. It would seem, then, that Christian practice proves itself insofar as it enables the individual to transform himself, or to be transformed, in ways that when they occur will be seen by the individual as supremely fulfilling, as the actualization of his real nature, as what God had planned for him.

At this point it may help us to bring in another epistemological practice hith-erto unmentioned, namely, interpersonal perception, our awareness of other per-sons as persons. There is controversy over whether to regard this as an autonomous practice or simply as a department of perceptual practice, but I shall adopt the former view. That is, I shall suppose that we have a practice of objectify-ing certain ranges of our experience in terms of the presence, condition, charac-teristics, and activities of other persons, and that this practice can no more be justified from the outside than any of the others we have been considering. It is, in a way, intermediate between PP and CP. In particular, and this is the point I want to stress at the moment, its internal self-justification is not so purely in terms of predictive efficacy as is PP. To be sure, by perceiving what we do of other persons we are thereby enabled to anticipate their behavior to some extent, and this is of pragmatic value. But persons are notoriously less predictable than things, and the value of this practice for our lives is not restricted to that payoff. To compensate for this relative unpredictability there is the possibility of entering into communication, fellowship, competition, and so on with other persons. And, most basically, that is what this practice enables us to do. We might, analogously, rephrase the above statement about the function of CP by saying that it enables us to enter into communication with God and thereby to become what God has intended us to become.

Please note that I am not suggesting that we can justify particular Christian beliefs by pointing out that one will become a better person if he accepts them or anything of the sort. I am rather suggesting that the feature just imputed to CP is a favorable one, one that enables it to satisfy our basic needs.

But *does* Christian practice prove itself in this way? It follows from points that I have been repeating too often that this cannot be decided except from inside, though outsiders can find out something about this from hearing what insiders say, seeing what they do, and reading what they write. That is the stance I will be taking. And at this point I must make explicit something that has been suppressed, or at least unmentioned, up to this point. It is really inappropriate to compare the situation of the ordinary Christian believer, even the serious, devout, and committed Christian believer, vis-á-vis CP with the situation of the normal adult human being vis-á-vis PP. For we are all masters of the latter practice. We emerged from our apprenticeship in early childhood, long before we reached the stage of philosophical reflection on these matters. But in Christian practice we are, almost all of us, at the stage of early infancy, just beginning to learn to distinguish the other reality from ourselves, just beginning to learn to recognize the major outlines of the landscape, and, one should add, just beginning to learn to respond to them appropriately. Hence we must look outside our own experience to the tiny minority that qualify as masters of the spiritual life, both for some intimation of what mastery of this practice is like and for an answer to the question of whether this enterprise proves itself by its fruits. We cannot hope to arrive at a definitive answer to that question from the outside. Of course there is a remedy for that—to get inside. But that is an arduous and time-consuming task, not one to be attempted in the course of an essay. Meanwhile we must glean such hints as we can from the lives, works, and thoughts of the likes of Mother Teresa of Calcutta as to what it is to be more than babes in the experience of God, and as to what it is to respond to this experience in the ways it indicates.

But I fear that the course of the argument has led me into a region that calls for the expertise of a preacher or a spiritual director rather than that of a philosopher, and so I must take my leave.

CONCLUSIONS

Here are conclusions for some of the important arguments in Part Five.

Aquinas
>   1. *God exists.*

Descartes
>   1. *God exists (cosmological argument).*
>   2. *God exists (ontological argument).*

Kant
>   1. *The ontological proof fails.*

Russell
>   1. *Arguments for God's existence fail.*
>   2. *Jesus was neither the best nor the wisest of men.*

Mackie
>   1. *At least one of the following propositions must be false: (a) God is all powerful; (b) God is all good; (c) Evil exists.*
>   2. *God's omnipotence must be limited.*

Wolterstorff
>   1. *Rationality is always situated rationality.*

2. *It does not follow from the charge that theism is non-rational that one should give it up.*

Alston

1. *In the absence of special reasons to doubt the reliability of PP, we should accept it as J_{nw}.*
2. *There is no adequate reason to doubt the reliability of CP, and CP should be accepted as J_{nw}.*
3. *Positive proof of CP is only available to those insiders who have mastered it.*

Evaluating and Writing a Logical Argument
The Term Paper

There are many varieties of term papers. The one that this logic exercise examines deals with the same kind of critical analysis as the 1,000-word essay. The main difference is length. The term paper should be about 2,500 words (eight typed pages). Some instructors assign longer papers. The following comments should be readily adaptable to term papers of varying lengths.

Just as in the shorter essay, the student should adopt a "pro" or "con" position to an argument or group of arguments within the text. It is important not to cast your net too widely. Logical analysis presupposes a tight, focused approach that is centered around a textual argument(s). The additional length allows you to examine additional premises in an effort to achieve a more comprehensive treatment.

Some important differences between the term paper and the 1,000-word essay are:

1. *The term paper allows for a more elaborate treatment.* The term paper's greater length requires you to define and justify the approach you are taking. This may mean that you set your logical outline in the text itself. From this you can discuss the rationale for choosing the crucial premise. What general implications does the argument as a whole have? Why should we be interested in it? Why are your observations a contribution to this subject area?

2. *The term paper enables the student to follow the consequences of several premises.* Whether you adopt a pro or con position (or anything in between), you need to coordinate your exposition so that it is balanced. If you find you have a disproportionate amount on one point, perhaps the focus is not what you thought it was. Go back and see if you should revise the introduction/justification to fit the actual exposition.

3. *The term paper enables students to integrate insights.* If you find that you are moving in many different directions, your paper will not be unified. Unity of exposition is important. Remember, the focus of your comments is always the argument from the text. This argument dictates your logical outline, brainstorm list, and term paper.

   Stray from the text only as you follow logical consequences of various interpretations. In the end, you have to return to the argument itself and show how your ruminations have advanced a judgment on the logical correctness of the argument under examination. Thus, though you may leave some threads hanging in the body of your paper, be sure to return to them and tie them together in your conclusion.

   Unity in a longer work is vital. Do not ignore it.

4. *The term paper allows students to keep promises.* In the introduction you promised the reader you'd prove or disprove the truth of certain premises. The general significance of the premises to the argument and the larger context of the argument itself were also set out. Now it is time to return to that sequence and tell what happened. How do the parts of the essay interrelate? How do these pertain to the argument(s)

to be examined? Finally, why should your exposition command our attention? This final point speaks to the significance of your paper.

5. *The term paper allows for the use of secondary sources.* You may or may not be required or encouraged to use secondary sources. These are books and articles written by people who have thought about the argument you are studying. They can be useful because they may stimulate you to think about an issue in a new way. However, they can be dangerous, too. Some students may move to secondary sources too soon and therefore become too dependent upon the thinking of these scholars. When this happens the student may begin to distrust his or her own opinions and the paper may becomes a mere pastiche of other people's thoughts.[1]

   To avoid such overreliance on secondary sources, do not consult them until *after* you have finished your brainstorm lists. These are the touchstones of *your own* thinking on the argument. They are records of how *you* responded. Use the intellectual directions that these brainstorm lists provide to help you search through various periodical indexes and/or books your professor may recommend.

   Try to see where your preliminary examination fits in with these published philosophers. In this way you may see distinctions you'd never thought about or areas of development that you failed to follow in your brainstorm list.

   Acknowledge and document this input and then return to your brainstorm list and revise it accordingly. The result of using secondary sources should be to broaden and deepen your own understanding of the arguments at hand.

6. *The term paper encourages the student to see the larger picture.* Last is the larger picture that should emerge from your preparation. Analysis breaks up the argument and then reconstructs it. The process of reconstruction should initiate speculation on larger questions as well. Examples of some large questions may be found in the titles of the subparts in this textbook: "Morality and Self-Interest"; "Moral Relativism and Absolutism"; "Rights"; "The Problem of Skepticism"; "Appearance and Reality"; "The Sources of Knowledge"; "Freedom and Determinism"; "Mind and Body"; and "Belief in God." How does your analysis aid you in your understanding of these larger issues?

   So often, people who try to address the larger issues straightaway become hopelessly vague and superficial. By basing your observations upon the foundation of an argument within a text, you have a more reliable structure to support your observations.

   This larger picture is your ultimate goal.

The logic exercise sections have been designed to help students approach the arguments presented in this text. This includes understanding, reconstructing, and responding to these arguments. These skills are transferable to any situation in which argument is involved. Logical analysis is thus a valuable skill to develop—not only for use in philosophy class, but also for your life as a rational creature living in a sometimes irrational world.

---

[1] Such treatments are at best a survey of the literature and at worst can result in plagiarism.

ISAAC BASHEVIS SINGER
(1904–1991) Polish Novelist and Short-Story Writer

*Gimpel the Fool**

I

I am Gimpel the Fool. I don't think myself a fool. On the contrary. But that's what folks call me. They gave me the name while I was still in school. I had seven names in all: imbecile, donkey, flax-head, dope, glump, ninny, and fool. The last name stuck. What did my foolishness consist of? I was easy to take in. They said, "Gimpel, you know the rabbi's wife has been brought to childbed?" So I skipped school. Well, it turned out to be a lie. How was I supposed to know? She hadn't had a big belly. But I never looked at her belly. Was that really so foolish? The gang laughed and hee-hawed, stomped and danced and chanted a good-night prayer. And instead of the raisins they give when a woman's lying in, they stuffed my hand full of goat turds. I was no weakling. If I slapped someone he'd see all the way to Cracow. But I'm really not a slugger by nature. I think to myself: Let it pass. So they take advantage of me.

I was coming home from school and heard a dog barking. I'm not afraid of dogs, but of course I never want to start up with them. One of them may be mad, and if he bites there's not a Tartar in the world who can help you. So I made tracks. Then I looked around and saw the whole market place wild with laughter. It was no dog at all but Wolf-Leib the Thief. How was I supposed to know it was he? It sounded like a howling bitch.

When the pranksters and leg-pullers found that I was easy to fool, every one of them tried his luck with me. "Gimpel, the Czar is coming to Frampol; Gimpel, the moon fell down in Turbeen; Gimpel, little Hodel Furpiece found a treasure behind the bathhouse." And I like a golem believed everyone. In the first place, everything is possible, as it is written in the Wisdom of the Fathers, I've forgotten just how. Second, I had to believe when the whole town came down on me! If I ever dared to say, "Ah, you're kidding!" there was trouble. People got angry. "What do you mean! You want to call everyone a liar?" What was I to do? I believed them, and I hope at least that did them some good.

I was an orphan. My grandfather who brought me up was already bent toward the grave. So they turned me over to a baker, and what a time they gave me there! Every woman or girl who came to bake a batch of noodles had to fool me at least once. "Gimpel, there's a fair in heaven; Gimpel, the rabbi gave birth to a calf in the seventh month; Gimpel, a cow flew over the roof and laid brass eggs." A student from the yeshiva came once to buy a roll, and he said, "You, Gimpel, while you stand here scraping with your baker's shovel the Messiah has come. The dead have arisen." "What do you mean?" I said. "I heard no one blowing the ram's horn!" He said, "Are you deaf?" And

---

*Published in Yiddish in *The Jewish Daily Forward*; published in English in *The Partisan Review*, trans. by Saul Bellow; reprinted (New York: Farrar, Straus & Giroux, 1953).

all began to cry, "We heard it, we heard!" Then in came Rietze the Candle-dipper and called out in her hoarse voice, "Gimpel, your father and mother have stood up from the grave. They're looking for you."

To tell the truth, I knew very well that nothing of the sort had happened, but all the same, as folks were talking, I threw on my wool vest and went out. Maybe something had happened. What did I stand to lose by looking? Well, what a cat music went up! And then I took a vow to believe nothing more. But that was no go either. They confused me so that I didn't know the big end from the small.

I went to the rabbi to get some advice. He said, "It is written, better to be a fool all your days than for one hour to be evil. You are not a fool. They are the fools. For he who causes his neighbor to feel shame loses Paradise himself." Nevertheless the rabbi's daughter took me in. As I left the rabbinical court she said, "Have you kissed the wall yet?" I said, "No; what for?" She answered, "It's the law; you've got to do it after every visit." Well, there didn't seem to be any harm in it. And she burst out laughing. It was a fine trick. She put one over on me, all right.

I wanted to go off to another town, but then everyone got busy matchmaking, and they were after me so they nearly tore my coat tails off. They talked at me and talked until I got water on the ear. She was no chaste maiden, but they told me she was virgin pure. She had a limp, and they said it was deliberate, from coyness. She had a bastard, and they told me the child was her little brother. I cried, "You're wasting your time. I'll never marry that whore." But they said indignantly, "What a way to talk! Aren't you ashamed of yourself? We can take you to the rabbi and have you fined for giving her a bad name." I saw then that I wouldn't escape them so easily and I thought: They're set on making me their butt. But when you're married the husband's the master, and if that's all right with her it's agreeable to me too. Besides, you can't pass through life unscathed, nor expect to.

I went to her clay house, which was built on the sand, and the whole gang, hollering and chorusing, came after me. They acted like bear-baiters. When we came to the well they stopped all the same. They were afraid to start anything with Elka. Her mouth would open as if it were on a hinge, and she had a fierce tongue. I entered the house. Lines were strung from wall to wall and clothes were drying. Barefoot she stood by the tub, doing the wash. She was dressed in a worn hand-me-down gown of plush. She had her hair put up in braids and pinned across her head. It took my breath away, almost, the reek of it all.

Evidently she knew who I was. She took a look at me and said, "Look who's here! He's come, the drip. Grab a seat."

I told her all; I denied nothing. "Tell me the truth," I said, "are you really a virgin, and is that mischievous Yechiel actually your little brother? Don't be deceitful with me, for I'm an orphan."

"I'm an orphan myself," she answered, "and whoever tries to twist you up, may the end of his nose take a twist. But don't let them think they can take advantage of me. I want a dowry of fifty guilders, and let them take up a collection besides. Otherwise they can kiss my you-know-what." She was very plainspoken. I said, "It's the bride and not the groom who gives a dowry." Then she said, "Don't bargain with me. Either a flat 'yes' or a flat 'no'—Go back where you came from."

I thought: No bread will ever be baked from *this* dough. But ours is not a poor town. They consented to everything and proceeded with the wedding. It so happened that there was a dysentery epidemic at the time. The ceremony was held at the cemetery gates, near the little corpse-washing hut. The fellows got drunk. While the marriage contract was being drawn up I heard the most pious high rabbi ask, "Is the bride a widow or a divorced woman?" And the sexton's wife answered for her, "Both a widow and divorced." It was a black moment for me. But what was I to do, run away from under the marriage canopy?

There was singing and dancing. An old granny danced opposite me, hugging a braided white *chalah.* The master of revels made a "God 'a mercy" in memory of the bride's parents. The schoolboys threw burrs, as on Tishe b'Av fast day. There were a lot of gifts after the sermon: a noodle board, a kneading trough, a bucket, brooms, ladles, household articles galore. Then I took a look and saw two strapping young men carrying a crib. "What do we need this for?" I asked. So they said, "Don't rack your brains about it. It's all right, it'll come in handy." I realized I was going to be rooked. Take it another way though, what did I stand to lose? I reflected: I'll see what comes of it. A whole town can't go altogether crazy.

II

At night I came where my wife lay, but she wouldn't let me in. "Say, look here, is this what they married us for?" I said. And she said, "My monthly has come." "But yesterday they took you to the ritual bath, and that's afterward, isn't it supposed to be?" "Today isn't yesterday," said she, "and yesterday's not today. You can beat it if you don't like it." In short, I waited.

Not four months later she was in childbed. The townsfolk hid their laughter with their knuckles. But what could I do? She suffered intolerable pains and clawed at the walls. "Gimpel," she cried, "I'm going. Forgive me!" The house filled with women. They were boiling pans of water. The screams rose to the welkin.

The thing to do was to go to the House of Prayer to repeat Psalms, and that was what I did.

The townsfolk liked that, all right. I stood in a corner saying Psalms and prayers, and they shook their heads at me. "Pray, pray!" they told me. "Prayer never made any woman pregnant." One of the congregation put a straw to my mouth and said, "Hay for the cows." There was something to that too, by God!

She gave birth to a boy. Friday at the synagogue the sexton stood up before the Ark, pounded on the reading table, and announced, "The wealthy Reb Gimpel invites the congregation to a feast in honor of the birth of a son." The whole House of Prayer rang with laughter. My face was flaming. But there was nothing I could do. After all, I *was* the one responsible for the circumcision honors and rituals.

Half the town came running. You couldn't wedge another soul in. Women brought peppered chick-peas, and there was a keg of beer from the tavern. I ate and drank as much as anyone, and they all congratulated me. Then there was a circumcision, and I named the boy after my father, may he rest in peace. When all were gone and I was left with my wife alone, she thrust her head through the bed-curtain and called me to her.

"Gimpel," said she, "why are you silent? Has your ship gone and sunk?"

"What shall I say?" I answered. "A fine thing you've done to me! If my mother had known of it she'd have died a second time."

She said, "Are you crazy, or what?"

"How can you make such a fool," I said, "of one who should be the lord and master?"

"What's the matter with you?" she said. "What have you taken it into your head to imagine?"

I saw that I must speak bluntly and openly. "Do you think this is the way to use an orphan?" I said. "You have borne a bastard."

She answered, "Drive this foolishness out of your head. The child is yours."

"How can he be mine?" I argued. "He was born seventeen weeks after the wedding."

She told me then that he was premature. I said, "Isn't he a little too premature?" She said, she had had a grandmother who carried just as short a time and she resembled this grandmother of hers as one drop of water does another. She swore to it with such oaths that you would have believed a peasant at the fair if he had used them. To tell the plain truth, I didn't believe her; but when I talked it over next day with the schoolmaster he told me that the very same thing had happened to Adam and Eve. Two they went up to bed, and four they descended.

"There isn't a woman in the world who is not the granddaughter of Eve," he said.

That was how it was; they argued me dumb. But then, who really knows how such things are?

I began to forget my sorrow. I loved the child madly, and he loved me too. As soon as he saw me he'd wave his little hands and want me to pick him up, and when he was colicky I was the only one who could pacify him. I bought him a little bone teething ring and a little gilded cap. He was forever catching the evil eye from someone, and then I had to run to get one of those abracadabras for him that would get him out of it. I worked like an ox. You know how expenses go up when there's an infant in the house. I don't want to lie about it; I didn't dislike Elka either, for that matter. She swore at me and cursed, and I couldn't get enough of her. What strength she had! One of her looks could rob you of the power of speech. And her orations! Pitch and sulphur, that's what they were full of, and yet somehow also full of charm. I adored her every word. She gave me bloody wounds though.

In the evening I brought her a white loaf as well as a dark one, and also poppyseed rolls I baked myself. I thieved because of her and swiped everything I could lay hands on: macaroons, raisins, almonds, cakes. I hope I may be forgiven for stealing from the Saturday pots the women left to warm in the baker's oven. I would take out scraps of meat, a chunk of pudding, a chicken leg or head, a piece of tripe, whatever I could nip quickly. She ate and became fat and handsome.

I had to sleep away from home all during the week, at the bakery. On Friday nights when I got home she always made an excuse of some sort. Either she had heartburn, or a stitch in the side, or hiccups, or headaches. You know what women's excuses are. I had a bitter time of it. It was rough. To add to it, this little brother of hers, the bastard, was growing bigger. He'd put lumps on me, and when I wanted to hit back she'd open her mouth and curse so powerfully I saw a green haze floating before my eyes. Ten times a day she threatened to divorce me. Another man in my place would have taken French leave and disappeared. But I'm the type that bears it and says nothing. What's one to do? Shoulders are from God, and burdens too.

One night there was a calamity in the bakery; the oven burst, and we almost had a fire. There was nothing to do but go home, so I went home. Let me, I thought, also taste the joy of sleeping in bed in mid-week. I didn't want to wake the sleeping mite and tiptoed into the house. Coming in, it seemed to me that I heard not the snoring of one but, as it were, a double snore, one a thin enough snore and the other like the snoring of a slaughtered ox. Oh, I didn't like that! I didn't like it at all. I went up to the bed, and things suddenly turned black. Next to Elka lay a man's form. Another in my place would have made an uproar, and enough noise to rouse the whole town, but the thought occurred to me that I might wake the child. A little thing like that—why frighten a little swallow, I thought. All right then, I went back to the bakery and stretched out on a sack of flour and till morning I never shut an eye. I shivered as if I had had malaria. "Enough of being a donkey," I said to myself. "Gimpel isn't going to be a sucker all his life. There's a limit even to the foolishness of a fool like Gimpel."

In the morning I went to the rabbi to get advice, and it made a great commotion in the town. They sent the beadle for Elka right away. She came, carrying the child. And what do you think she did? She denied it, denied everything, bone and stone! "He's out of his head," she said. "I know nothing of dreams or divinations." They yelled at her, warned her, hammered on the table, but she stuck to her guns: it was a false accusation, she said.

The butchers and the horse-traders took her part. One of the lads from the slaughterhouse came by and said to me, "We've got our eye on you, you're a marked man." Meanwhile the child started to bear down and soiled itself. In the rabbinical court there was an Ark of the Covenant, and they couldn't allow that, so they sent Elka away.

I said to the rabbi, "What shall I do?"

"You must divorce her at once," said he.

"And what if she refuses?" I asked.

He said, "You must serve the divorce. That's all you'll have to do."

I said, "Well, all right, Rabbi. Let me think about it."

"There's nothing to think about," said he. "You mustn't remain under the same roof with her."

"And if I want to see the child?" I asked.

"Let her go, the harlot," said he, "and her brood of bastards with her."

The verdict he gave was that I mustn't even cross her threshold—never again, as long as I should live.

During the day it didn't bother me so much. I thought: It was bound to happen, the abscess had to burst. But at night when I stretched out upon the sacks I felt it all very bitterly. A longing took me, for her and for the child. I wanted to be angry, but that's my misfortune exactly, I don't have it in me to be really angry. In the first place—this was how my thoughts went—there's bound to be a slip sometimes. You can't live without errors. Probably that lad who was with her led her on and gave her presents and what not, and women are often long on hair and short on sense, and so he got around her. And then since she denies it so, maybe I was only seeing things? Hallucinations do happen. You see a figure or a mannikin or something, but when you come up closer it's nothing, there's not a thing there. And if that's so, I'm doing her an injustice. And when I got so far in my thoughts I started to weep. I sobbed so that I wet the flour where I lay. In the morning I went to the rabbi and told him that I had made a mistake.

The rabbi wrote on with his quill, and he said that if that were so he would have to reconsider the whole case. Until he had finished I wasn't to go near my wife, but I might send her bread and money by messenger.

III

Nine months passed before all the rabbis could come to an agreement. Letters went back and forth. I hadn't realized that there could be so much erudition about a matter like this.

Meanwhile Elka gave birth to still another child, a girl this time. On the Sabbath I went to the synagogue and invoked a blessing on her. They called me up to the Torah, and I named the child for my mother-in-law—may she rest in peace. The louts and loudmouths of the town who came into the bakery gave me a going over. All Frampol refreshed its spirits because of my trouble and grief. However, I resolved that I would always believe what I was told. What's the good of *not* believing? Today it's your wife and you don't believe; tomorrow it's God Himself you won't take stock in.

By an apprentice who was her neighbor I sent her daily a corn or a wheat loaf, or a piece of pastry, rolls or bagels, or, when I got the chance, a slab of pudding, a slice of honeycake, or wedding strudel—whatever came my way. The apprentice was a goodhearted lad, and more than once he added something on his own. He had formerly annoyed me a lot, plucking my nose and digging me in the ribs, but when he started to be a visitor to my house he became kind and friendly. "Hey, you, Gimpel," he said to me, "you have a very decent little wife and two fine kids. You don't deserve them."

"But the things people say about her," I said.

"Well, they have long tongues," he said, "and nothing to do with them but babble. Ignore it as you ignore the cold of last winter."

One day the rabbi sent for me and said, "Are you certain, Gimpel, that you were wrong about your wife?"

I said, "I'm certain."

"Why, but look here! You yourself saw it."

"It must have been a shadow," I said.

"The shadow of what?"

"Just of one of the beams, I think."

"You can go home then. You owe thanks to the Yanover rabbi. He found an obscure reference in Maimonides that favored you."

I seized the rabbi's hand and kissed it.

I wanted to run home immediately. It's no small thing to be separated for so long a time from wife and child. Then I reflected: I'd better go back to work now, and go home in the evening. I said nothing to anyone, although as far as my heart was concerned it was like one of the Holy Days. The women teased and twitted me as they did every day, but my thought was: Go on, with your loose talk. The truth is out, like the oil upon the water. Maimonides says it's right, and therefore it is right!

At night, when I had covered the dough to let it rise, I took my share of bread and a little sack of flour and started homeward. The moon was full and the stars were glistening, something to terrify the soul. I hurried onward, and before me darted a long shadow. It was winter, and a fresh snow had fallen. I had a mind to sing, but it was growing late and I didn't want to wake the householders. Then I felt like whistling, but I remembered that you don't whistle at night because it brings the demons out. So I was silent and walked as fast as I could.

Dogs in the Christian yards barked at me when I passed, but I thought: Bark your teeth out! What are you but mere dogs? Whereas I am a man, the husband of a fine wife, the father of promising children.

As I approached the house my heart started to pound as though it were the heart of a criminal. I felt no fear, but my heart went thump! thump! Well, no drawing back. I quietly lifted the latch and went in. Elka was asleep. I looked at the infant's cradle. The shutter was closed, but the moon forced its way through the cracks. I saw the newborn child's face and loved it as soon as I saw it—immediately—each tiny bone.

Then I came nearer to the bed. And what did I see but the apprentice lying there beside Elka. The moon went out all at once. It was utterly black, and I trembled. My teeth chattered. The bread fell from my hands, and my wife waked and said, "Who is that, ah?"

I muttered, "It's me."

"Gimpel?" she asked. "How come you're here? I thought it was forbidden."

"The rabbi said," I answered and shook as with a fever.

"Listen to me, Gimpel," she said, "go out to the shed and see if the goat's all right. It seems she's been sick." I have forgotten to say that we had a goat. When I heard she was unwell I went into the yard. The nannygoat was a good little creature. I had a nearly human feeling for her.

With hesitant steps I went up to the shed and opened the door. The goat stood there on her four feet. I felt her everywhere, drew her by the horns, examined her udders, and found nothing wrong. She had probably eaten too much bark. "Good night, little goat," I said. "Keep well." And the little beast answered with a "Maa" as though to thank me for the good will.

I went back. The apprentice had vanished.

"Where," I asked, "is the lad?"

"What lad?" my wife answered.

"What do you mean?" I said. "The apprentice. You were sleeping with him."

"The things I have dreamed this night and the night before," she said, "may they come true and lay you low, body and soul! An evil spirit has taken root in you and dazzles your sight." She screamed out, "You hateful creature! You moon calf! You spook! You uncouth man! Get out, or I'll scream all Frampol out of bed!"

Before I could move, her brother sprang out from behind the oven and struck me a blow on the back of the head. I thought he had broken my neck. I felt that something about me was deeply wrong, and I said, "Don't make a scandal. All that's needed now is that people should accuse me of raising spooks and *dybbuks.*" For that was what she had meant. "No one will touch bread of my baking."

In short, I somehow calmed her.

"Well," she said, "that's enough. Lie down, and be shattered by wheels."

Next morning I called the apprentice aside. "Listen here, brother!" I said. And so on and so forth. "What do you say?" He stared at me as though I had dropped from the roof or something.

"I swear," he said, "you'd better go to an herb doctor or some healer. I'm afraid you have a screw loose, but I'll hush it up for you." And that's how the thing stood.

To make a long story short, I lived twenty years with my wife. She bore me six children, four daughters and two sons. All kinds of things happened, but I neither saw nor heard. I believed, and that's all. The rabbi recently said to me, "Belief in itself is beneficial. It is written that a good man lives by his faith."

Suddenly my wife took sick. It began with a trifle, a little growth upon the breast. But she evidently was not destined to live long; she had no years. I spent a fortune on her. I have forgotten to say that by this time I had a bakery of my own and in Frampol was considered to be something of a rich man. Daily the healer came, and every witch doctor in the neighborhood was brought. They decided to use leeches, and after that to try cupping. They even called a doctor from Lublin, but it was too late. Before she died she called me to her bed and said, "Forgive me, Gimpel."

I said, "What is there to forgive? You have been a good and faithful wife."

"Woe, Gimpel!" she said. "It was ugly how I deceived you all these years. I want to go clean to my Maker, and so I have to tell you that the children are not yours."

If I had been clouted on the head with a piece of wood it couldn't have bewildered me more.

"Whose are they?" I asked.

"I don't know," she said. "There were a lot . . . but they're not yours." And as she spoke she tossed her head to the side, her eyes turned glassy, and it was all up with Elka. On her whitened lips there remained a smile.

I imagined that, dead as she was, she was saying, "I deceived Gimpel. That was the meaning of my brief life."

IV

One night, when the period of mourning was done, as I lay dreaming on the flour sacks, there came the Spirit of Evil himself and said to me, "Gimpel, why do you sleep?"

I said, "What should I be doing? Eating *kreplach?*"

"The whole world deceives you," he said, "and you ought to deceive the world in your turn."

"How can I deceive all the world?" I asked him.

He answered, "You might accumulate a bucket of urine every day and at night pour it into the dough. Let the sages of Frampol eat filth."

"What about the judgment in the world to come?" I said.

"There is no world to come," he said. "They've sold you a bill of goods and talked you into believing you carried a cat in your belly. What nonsense!"

"Well then," I said, "and is there a God?"

He answered, "There is no God either."

"What," I said, "*is* there, then?"

"A thick mire."

He stood before my eyes with a goatish beard and horn, long-toothed, and with a tail. Hearing such words, I wanted to snatch him by the tail, but I tumbled from the flour sacks and nearly broke a rib. Then it happened that I had to answer the call of nature, and, passing, I saw the risen dough, which seemed to say to me, "Do it!" In brief, I let myself be persuaded.

At dawn the apprentice came. We kneaded the bread, scattered caraway seeds on it, and set it to bake. Then the apprentice went away, and I was left sitting in the little trench by the oven, on a pile of rags. Well, Gimpel, I thought, you've revenged yourself on them for all the shame they've put on you. Outside the frost glittered, but it was warm beside the oven. The flames heated my face. I bent my head and fell into a doze.

I saw in a dream, at once, Elka in her shroud. She called to me, "What have you done, Gimpel?"

I said to her, "It's all your fault," and started to cry.

"You fool!" she said. "You fool! Because I was false is everything false too? I never deceived anyone but myself. I'm paying for it all, Gimpel. They spare you nothing here."

I looked at her face. It was black; I was startled and waked, and remained sitting dumb. I sensed that everything hung in the balance. A false step now and I'd lose Eternal Life. But God gave me His help. I seized the long shovel and took out the loaves, carried them into the yard, and started to dig a hole in the frozen earth.

My apprentice came back as I was doing it. "What are you doing boss?" he said, and grew pale as a corpse.

"I know what I'm doing," I said, and I buried it all before his very eyes.

Then I went home, took my hoard from its hiding place, and divided it among the children. "I saw your mother tonight," I said. "She's turning black, poor thing."

They were so astounded they couldn't speak a word.

"Be well," I said, "and forget that such a one as Gimpel ever existed." I put on my short coat, a pair of boots, took the bag that held my prayer shawl in one hand, my stock in the other, and kissed the *mezzuzah*. When people saw me in the street they were greatly surprised.

"Where are you going?" they said.

I answered, "Into the world." And so I departed from Frampol.

I wandered over the land, and good people did not neglect me. After many years I became old and white; I heard a great deal, many lies and falsehoods, but the longer I lived the more I understood that there were really no lies. Whatever doesn't really happen is dreamed at night. It happens to one if it doesn't happen to another, tomorrow if not today, or a century hence if not next year. What difference can it make? Often I heard tales of which I said, "Now this is a thing that cannot happen." But before a year had elapsed I heard that it actually had come to pass somewhere.

Going from place to place, eating at strange tables, it often happens that I spin yarns—improbable things that could never have happened—about devils, magicians, windmills, and the like. The children run after me, calling, "Grandfather, tell us a story." Sometimes they ask for particular stories, and I try to please them. A fat young boy once said to me, "Grandfather, it's the same story you told us before." The little rogue, he was right.

So it is with dreams too. It is many years since I left Frampol, but as soon as I shut my eyes I am there again. And whom do you think I see? Elka. She is standing by the washtub, as at our first encounter, but her face is shining and her eyes are as radiant as the eyes of a saint, and she speaks outlandish words to me, strange things. When I wake I have forgotten it all. But while the dreams lasts I am comforted. She answers all my queries, and what comes out is that all is right. I weep and implore, "Let me be with you." And she consoles me and tells me to be patient. The time is nearer than it is far. Sometimes she strokes and kisses me and weeps upon my face. When I awaken I feel her lips and taste the salt of her tears.

No doubt the world is entirely an imaginary world, but it is only once removed from the true world. At the door of the hovel where I lie, there stands the plank on which the dead are taken away. The gravedigger Jew has his spade ready. The grave waits and the worms are hungry; the shrouds are prepared—I carry them in my beggar's sack. Another *shnorrer* is waiting to inherit my bed of straw. When the time comes I will go joyfully. Whatever may be there, it will be real, without complication, without ridicule, without deception. God be praised: there even Gimpel cannot be deceived.

Questions for Discussion

1. Is it foolish to believe?

2. Who is the real loser in the final scheme of things—the one who may become a fool because he believes in something that turns out to be false or someone whom no one tricks?

3. What is illusion? Is it true that there are no lies?

Further Readings

Part One: Self-Interest and Moral Relativism
Traditional Treatments

Aquinas, St. Thomas. *Summa Theologica.* Book I, Part I. Questions 40–43. Translated by the Dominican Fathers. New York: Benzinger Brothers, 1925.

Augustine, St. of Hippo. *The City of God.* Books 12–14, xxi. Translated by M. Dods. New York: Modern Library, 1950.

Benedict, Ruth. *Patterns of Culture.* Chaps. 1–3. Boston: Houghton Mifflin, 1934.

Bradley, F. H. "Why Should I be Moral?" *Ethical Studies.* Essay II. 53–74. London: Oxford University Press, 1927.

Broad, C.D. "Certain Features in Moore's Ethical Doctrines." In *The Philosophy of G.E. Moore.* Edited by Paul A. Schilpp, 43–57. Evanston, Illinois: Northwestern University Press, 1942.

Butler, Joseph. *Five Sermons.* Edited by Stuart M. Brown, Jr. Indianapolis: Bobbs-Merrill, 1950.

Cudworth, R. *Treatise Concerning Eternal and Immutable Morality.* London: J. & J. Knapton, 1731.

Hegel, G.W.F. *The Philosophy of Right.* Translated by T.M. Knox. Oxford: Clarendon Press, 1953.

Nietzsche, F. "The Genealogy of Morals." In *The Philosophy of Nietzsche.* Translated by Walter Kaufman. New York: Modern Library, 1950.

Prichard, H.A. *Moral Obligation.* Oxford: Clarendon Press, 1949.

Sharp, F.C. *Ethics.* Chaps. 22–23. New York: The Century Company, 1928.

Stace, W.T. *The Concept of Morals.* New York: Macmillan, 1937.

Toulmin, Stephen. *An Examination of the Place of Reason in Ethics.* Part III. London: Cambridge University Press, 1950.

Contemporary Treatments

Allen, R.E. "The Speech of Glaucon in Plato's *Republic.*" *Journal of the History of Philosophy* 25 (January 1987): 3–11.

Edelman, John. *An Audience for Moral Philosophy?* New York: St. Martin's, 1991.

Epstein, Richard. "The Varieties of Self-Interest." *Social and Political Philosophy* 8.1 (Autumn 1990): 102–120.

Firth, Raymond. *Elements of Social Organization.* Chap. 6. London: Watts, 1951.

Gewirth, Alan. *Reason and Morality.* Chicago: University of Chicago Press, 1978.

———. "Moral Rationality." In *Freedom and Morality.* Edited by John Bricke, 113–150. Lawrence: University of Kansas Press, 1976.

Ladd, J., ed. *Ethical Relativism.* Belmont: Wadsworth, 1973.

MacIntyre, Alasdair. "Egoism and Altruism." In *The Encyclopedia of Philosophy.* Edited by Paul Edwards, vol. 2, 462–466. New York: Macmillan, 1967.

Mackie, J. *Ethics: Inventing Right and Wrong.* Baltimore: Penguin, 1977.

Mansbridge, Jane. "Self-Interest in Political Life." *Political Theory* 18.1 (February 1990): 132–153.

Milo, Ronald, ed. *Egoism and Altruism.* Belmont: Wadsworth, 1973.

Nielsen, Kai. "Is 'Why Should I be Moral?' An Absurdity?" *Australasian Journal of Philosophy.* (1958).

Olson, Robert. *The Morality of Self-Interest.* New York: Harcourt Brace Jovanovich, 1965.

Prichard, H.A. "Does Moral Philosophy Rest upon a Mistake?" *Mind* 21 (1912): 487–499.

Putnam, Hilary. "Why Is a Philosopher?" In *The Institution of Philosophy: A Discipline in Crisis?* Edited by Auner Cohen, 67–85. Lasalle: Open Court, 1989.

Radnitzky, Gerard. "Against Relativism." *Conceptus* 23.60 (1989): 99–110.

Rescher, Nicholas. *Moral Absolutes: An Essay on the Nature and Rationale of Morality.* Lanham: Rowman and Allenheld, 1989.

Rorty, Amélie O. "Relativism, Persons and Practices." In *Relativism.* Edited by Michael Krausz, 418–440. Notre Dame: University of Notre Dame Press, 1989.

Seller, Anne. "Realism Versus Relativism." In *Feminist Perspectives in Philosophy.* Edited by Morwenna Griffiths, 169–186. Bloomington: University of Indiana Press, 1988.

Singer, M.G. *Generalization in Ethics.* New York: Knopf, 1961.

Slote, Michael. "An Empirical Basis for Psychological Egoism." *Journal of Philosophy* 61.18 (October 1964): 530–537.

Werhane, Patricia. "The Role of Self-Interest in Adam Smith's *Wealth of Nations.*" *Journal of Philosophy* 86.11 (November 1989): 669–680.

Wong, David. "Relativism." *A Companion to Ethics.* Edited by Peter Singer, 442–450. Cambridge: Cambridge University Press, 1991.

Part Two: Rights

Traditional Treatments

Austin, John. *The Province of Jurisprudence Determined.* Edited by Robert Campbell, 5th ed. 2 vols. London: John Murray, 1885.

Benn, S. I. and Peters, R. S. *Social Principle and the Democratic State.* London: Allen & Unwin, 1959.

Dias, R. W. M. *A Bibliography of Jurisprudence.* London: Butterworths, 1964.

Frankena, William. "Natural and Inalienable Rights." *Philosophical Review* 64 (1955): 212–232.

Hart, H. L. A. "Are There Any Natural Rights?" *The Philosophical Review* 64 (April 1955): 175–91.

Vlastos, Gregory. "Justice and Equality." In *Social Justice.* Edited by R. B. Brandt. Englewood Cliffs: Prentice-Hall, 1962.

Hohfeld, Wesley. *Fundamental Legal Conceptions.* New Haven: Yale University Press, 1919.

Maritain, Jacques. *Les Droits de l'Homme et la Loi Naturelle.* New York: Éditions de la Maison Français, 1942.

Passerin d'Entreves, A. *Natural Law.* London: Hutchinson's University Library, 1951.

Pound, Roscoe. *Jurisprudence.* Vol. 4. St. Paul: West Publishing Co., 1959.

Ritchie, David. *Natural Rights.* London: Macmillan, 1894.

Ross, W. D. *The Right and the Good.* Oxford: Oxford University Press, 1930.

Contemporary Treatments

Almond, Brenda. "Rights." In *A Companion to Ethics.* Edited by Peter Singer, 259–269. Cambridge: Cambridge University Press, 1991.

Cranston, Maurice. *What Are Human Rights?* London: Bodley Head, 1973.

Donnelly, Jack. *The Concept of Human Rights.* New York: St. Martin's Press, 1985.

Gilbert, Alan. "Rights and Resources." *Journal of Value Inquiry* 23.3 (Summer 1989): 227–247.

Hajdin, Mane. "A Defence of Rights-Duties Correlativism." In *Contemporary Yugoslav Philosophy.* Edited by Aleksandar Parkovic, 97–119. Dordrecht: Kluwer, 1988.

Lyons, David, ed. *Rights.* Belmont: Wadsworth, 1979.

Melden, A. I., ed. *Human Rights.* Belmont: Wadsworth, 1970.

————. *Rights and Persons.* Berkeley: University of California Press, 1977.

Milne, A. J. M. *Human Rights and Human Diversity.* Albany: State University of New York Press, 1986.

Nickel, James W. *Making Sense of Human Rights.* Berkeley: University of California Press, 1987.

Pennock, J. R. and Chapman, J. W., eds. *Nomos XXIII: Human Rights.* New York: New York University Press, 1981.

Raphael, D. D., ed. *Political Theory and the Rights of Man.* London: Macmillan, 1967.

Shue, Henry. *Basic Rights.* Princeton: Princeton University Press, 1980.

Social Philosophy and Policy 1.2 (Spring 1984). Issue entitled "Human Rights."

Sumner, L. W. *The Moral Foundation of Rights.* Oxford: Oxford University Press, 1987.

UNESCO. *Human Rights: Comments and Interpretations: A Symposium.* 1949. Reprint. New York: Columbia University Press, 1973.

Vincent, R. J. *Human Rights and International Relations.* Cambridge: Cambridge University Press, 1986.

Waldron, Jeremy, ed. *Theories of Rights.* Oxford: Oxford University Press, 1984.

Warren, Mary Anne. "The Moral Significance of Birth." *Hypatia* 4.3 (Fall 1989): 46–65.

Part Three: Epistemology: Skepticism, Appearance, and Reality

Traditional Treatments

Aquinas, St. Thomas. *Summa Theologica.* Translated by the Dominican Fathers. Ia, 2,2; Ia 84, 7; Ia, 86,1. New York: Benzinger Brothers, 1925.

Aristotle, "Metaphysics." I.1; I. 8–9; XIII., "De Anima." II.5; III. 3–8., "Posterior Analytics." II.19. In *The Basic Works of Aristotle.* Edited by Richard McKeon. New York: Random House, 1941.

Augustine, St. of Hippo. *Contra academicos.* Translated by Mary Garvey. Milwaukee: Marquette University Press, 1978.

————. *On the Free Choice of the Will.* Translated by Anna S. Benjamin and L. H. Hackstaff. New York: Macmillan, 1964.

Ayer, A. J. *The Problem of Knowledge.* New York: St. Martin's, 1956.

Berkeley, George. *Berkeley: Philosophical Writings.* Edited by T. E. Jessop. Austin: University of Texas Press, 1953.

Black, Max. *Problems of Analysis.* Ithaca: Cornell University Press, 1954.

Bosanquet, B. *Knowledge and Reality.* London: K. Paul & Trench & Co., 1885.

Bradley, F. H. *Appearance and Reality.* 2nd ed. London: Macmillan, 1897.

Cassierer, E. *Liebinz System in Seinen Wissenschaftlichen Grundlagen.* Marburg: N.G. Elwert, 1902.

Coffey, Peter. *Epistemology or the Theory of Knowledge.* New York: Longmans, Green & Co., 1917.

Cornford, F. M. *Plato's Theory of Knowledge.* Indianapolis: Bobbs-Merrill, 1957.

Cunningham, G. W. *Thought and Reality in Hegel's System.* New York: Longmans, Green & Co., 1910.

Curley, E. M. "Locke, Boyle and the Distinction between Primary and Secondary Qualities." *Philosophical Review* 81 (1972): 438–464.

Déscartes, René. *The Philosophical Works of Déscartes.* Translated by E. S. Haldane and G. R. T. Ross. 2 vols. Cambridge: Cambridge University Press, 1911–1912.

Fichte, I. H. *The Science of Knowledge.* Translated by A. E. Kroeger. Philadelphia: J. B. Lippincott, 1868.

Frankfurth, Henry. *Demons, Dreamers, and Madmen.* Indianapolis: Bobbs-Merrill, 1970.

Empiricus, Sextus. *Sextus Empiricus.* Translated by R. G. Bury. 4 vols. Cambridge: Loeb/Harvard University Press, 1933–1953.

Flew, Anthony. *Hume's Philosophy of Belief.* New York: Humanities Press, 1966.

Hegel, G. W. F. *Phenomology of Mind.* Translated by William Wallace. Oxford: Clarendon Press, 1971.

Hicks, R. D. *Stoic and Epicurean.* New York: Russell & Russell, 1962.

Hume, David. *Treatise of Human Nature.* Edited by L. A. Selby-Bigge. Oxford: Oxford University Press, 1888.

————. *Essay Concerning Human Understanding.* Edited by L. A. Selby-Bigge. Oxford: Oxford University Press, 1902.

James, William. *The Will to Believe.* 1897. Reprint. New York: Longmans, Green & Son, 1931.

Kant, Immanuel. *Critique of Pure Reason.* Translated by Norman Kemp Smith. New York: St. Martin's, 1933.

Laërtius, Diogenes. *Lives of Eminent Philosophers.* Translated by R. D. Hicks. 2 vols. Cambridge: Loeb/Harvard University Press, 1959.

Leibniz, Gottfried. *New Essays Concerning Human Understanding.* Edited by Robert Latta. Oxford: Clarendon Press, 1948.

Lewis, C. I. *An Analysis of Knowledge and Valuation.* Lasalle: Open Court, 1947.

Lloyd, G. E. R. *Magic, Reason & Experience: Studies in the Origin & Development of Greek Science.* Cambridge University Press, 1979.

Locke, John. *Essay Concerning Human Understanding.* Edited by Seth Pattison. Oxford: Clarendon Press, 1924.

Lucretius. *De rerum natura.* Edited by Cyril Bailey. Oxford: Clarendon Press, 1900.

Mehta, Ved Parkash. *The Fly and the Fly-Bottle.* Boston: Little, Brown & Company, 1962.

Mill, John Stuart. *A System of Logic.* 1863. Reprint. Toronto: University of Toronto Press, 1966.

Nagel, Ernest. "The Ground of Induction." Part II, Chap. 7. In *Logic Without Metaphysics.* New York: Free Press, 1961.

Ockam, William. *Philosophical Writings.* Translated by Philotheus Boehner, OFM. Indianapolis: Bobbs-Merrill, 1957.

Peirce, Charles Sanders. *Collected Papers of Charles Sanders Peirce.* Edited by C. Hartshorne and P. Weiss. 8 vols. Cambridge: Harvard University Press, 1931–1935.

Plato. "Meno, Sophist, Theaetetus." In *The Collected Dialogues of Plato.* Edited by Edith Hamilton and Huntington Cairns. Princeton: Bollingen/Princeton University Press, 1963.

Reichenbach, Hans. *The Rise of Scientific Philosophy.* Berkeley: University of California Press, 1958.

Reid, Thomas. "Essays on the Intellectual Powers of Man." In *The Works of Thomas Reid.* Edited by Sir William Hamilton. London: Longman, Brown, Green and Longmans, 1884.

Robin, Léon. *Pyrrhon et le scepticisme grec.* Paris: Vrin, 1944.

Russell, Bertrand. *Human Knowledge.* Parts III and VI. New York: Simon and Schuster, 1962.

––––––. *Problems of Philosophy.* Chapts. 1–4. London: Oxford University Press, 1912.

Scotus, John Duns. *Philosophical Writings.* Translated by Allan Wolter, OFM. Indianapolis: Bobbs-Merrill, 1962.

Spinoza, Baruch. *Tractatus de intellectus emendatione.* 1899. Reprint. Translated by W. Hale White. Freeport: Books for Libraries Press, 1969.

Reid, Thomas. *Inquiry and Essays.* Edited by R. Beanblossom and K. Lehrer. Indianapolis: Hackett, 1983.

Warnock, G. J. *Berkeley.* Baltimore: Penguin, 1969.

Contemporary Treatments

Audi, Robert. *Belief, Justification & Knowledge: An Introduction to Epistemology.* Belmont: Wadsworth, 1988.

Bonjour, Lawrence. *The Structure of Empirical Knowledge.* Cambridge: Harvard University Press, 1985.

Chisholm, Roderick. *Theory of Knowledge.* 3rd ed. Englewood Cliffs: Prentice-Hall, 1989.

Foley, Richard. *The Theory of Empirical Rationality.* Cambridge: Harvard University Press, 1987.

Garnett, A. C. *The Perceptual Process.* London: Allen and Unwin, 1965.

Goldman, Alvin. *Epistemology and Cognition.* Cambridge: Harvard University Press, 1985.

Hamlyn, D. W. *The Theory of Knowledge.* Garden City: Doubleday, 1978.

Harman, Gilbert. "Justification, Truth, Goals and Pragmatism: Comments on Stich's 'Fragmentation of Reason.'" *Philosophy and Phenomenological Research* 51.1 (March 1991): 195–199.

Lehrer, Keith. *Theory of Knowledge.* Boulder: Westview Press, 1990.

Logino, Helen. "Feminism and Philosophy of Science." *Journal of Social Philosophy* 21.2–3 (Fall and Winter 1990): 150–159.

Mandelbaum, M. *Philosophy, Science and Sense Perception.* Baltimore: Johns Hopkins University Press, 1964.

Moser, Paul. *Empirical Justifications.* Dordrecht: D. Reidel Publishers, 1986.

Pitcher, George. *A Theory of Perception.* Princeton: Princeton University Press, 1971.

Pollock, John. *Contemporary Theories of Knowledge.* Totowa: Rowman and Littlefield, 1986.

Putnam, Hilary. *Reason, Truth and History.* Cambridge: Cambridge University Press, 1981.

Quine, W. V. O. *From a Logical Point of View.* 2nd ed. New York: Harper and Row, 1961.

Summerfield, Donna. "Modest A Priori Knowledge." *Philosophy and Phenomenological Research* 51.1 (March 1991): 195–199.

Part Four: Freedom and Determinism, Mind and Body
Traditional Treatments

Augustine, St. of Hippo. *On the Free Choice of the Will.* Translated by Anna S. Benjamin and L. H. Hackstaff. New York: Macmillan, 1964.

Adams, M. M. and Kretzmann, N. *William Ockham: Predestination, God's Foreknowledge and Future Contingents.* 1969. Reprint. Indianapolis: Hackett, 1982.

Anscombe, G. E. M. *Intention.* Oxford: Clarendon Press, 1959.

Berkeley, George. *Treatise Concerning Principles of Human Knowledge.* In *The Works of George Berkeley Bishop of Cloyne.* 9 vols. London: Nelson, 1948–57.

Bradley, Francis Herbert. *Appearance and Reality.* 2nd ed. London: Macmillan, 1897.

Broad, C. D. *The Mind and Its Place in Nature.* New York: Harcourt, Brace & Co., 1925.

Campbell, C. A. "Is Free-Will a Pseudo-Problem?" *Mind* 60 (1951): 441–465.

Cranston, Maurice. *Freedom: A New Analysis.* London: Longmans, 1953.

Ducasse, C. J. *Nature, Mind and Death.* LaSalle: Open Court, 1951.

Edwards, Jonathan. *Freedom of the Will.* Edited by Paul Ramsey. New Haven: Yale University Press, 1957.

Goldman, Alvin. *A Theory of Human Action.* Englewood Cliffs: Prentice-Hall, 1970.

Hampshire, Stuart. *Thought and Action.* London: Chatto and Windus, 1982.

Hempel, Carl. "The Logical Analysis of Psychology." Revue de Synthese 10 (1935). Reprinted in *Readings in Philosophical Analysis.* H. Feigl and W. Sellars. New York: Appleton-Century-Crofts, 1949. pp. 373–384.

Hook, Sydney. "Necessity, Indeterminism and Sentimentalism." In *Determinism and Freedom in the Age of Modern Science.* Edited by Sydney Hook, 187–192. New York: Collier, 1961.

Hospers, John. *An Introduction to Philosophical Analysis.* Chap. 5. London: Routledge & Paul, 1956.

_____. "Free Will and Psychoanalysis." In *A Modern Introduction to Philosophy.* Edited by Paul Edwards and Arthur Pap. Glencoe: Free Press, 1957.

Hume, David. *Treatise of Human Nature.* Edited by L. A. Selby-Bigge, II, 3, 1–3. Oxford: Oxford University Press, 1888.

Köhler, Wolfgang. *Gestalt Psychology.* New York: Liverwright, 1947.

MacIntyre, A. C. "Determinism." *Mind* 66 (1957): 28–41.

Maher, Michael. *Psychology.* 9th ed. New York: Longman, Green & Co., 1933.

Nowell-Smith, P. H. *Ethics.* Chaps. 19–21. London: Penguin, 1954.

Pratt, J. B. *Matter and Spirit.* 1922. Reprint. Westport: Greenwood Press, 1970.

Ryle, Gilbert. *The Concept of Mind.* London: Hutchinson's University Library, 1949.

Shaffer, Jerome A. "Could Mental States Be Brain Processes?" *Journal of Philosophy* 58 (1961): 813–822.

Smart, J. J. C. "Sensations and Brain Processes." *The Philosophical Review* 68 (1959): 141–156.

Stevenson, C. L. *Ethics and Language.* Chap. 14. New Haven: Yale University Press, 1944.

Schlick, Moritz. *Problems of Ethics.* Chap 7. New York: Dover, 1962.

Watson, J. B. *Behaviorism.* New York: W. W. Norton, 1925.

Contemporary Treatments

Annas, Julia. "Epicurus' Philosophy of Mind." In *Psychology* (Companions to Ancient Thought: 2). Edited by Stephen Everson, 84–101. New York: Cambridge University Press, 1991.

Beloff, John. *The Existence of the Mind.* New York: Citadel, 1964.

Churchland, Paul. *Matter and Consciousness.* Cambridge: MIT Press, 1984.

Clark, Mary T. "Willing Freely According to Thomas Aquinas." In *A Straight Path: Studies in Medieval Philosophy and Culture.* Edited by Ruth Link-Salinger, 49–56. Washington: Catholic University Press, 1988.

Davidson, Donald. *Essays on Actions and Events.* Oxford: Clarendon Press, 1980.

Dennett, Daniel C. *Elbow Room.* Cambridge: MIT Press, 1984.

Donagan, Alan. *The Theory of Morality.* Chicago: University of Chicago Press, 1977.

Dreyfus, Hubert L. and Stuart E. *Mind over Machine.* New York: Macmillan, 1986.

Fischer, John Martin. *Moral Responsibility.* Ithaca: Cornell University Press, 1982.

Flax, Jane. *Thinking Fragments: Psychoanalysis, Feminism and Postmodernism in the Contemporary West.* Berkeley: University of California Press, 1989.

Fodor, Jerry. "Making Mind Matter More." *Philosophical Topics* 17.1 (Spring 1989): 59–79.

Markham, Ian. "Hume Revisited: A Problem with the Free Will Defense." *Modern Theology* 7.3 (April 1991): 181–190.

Rorty, Amélie. *Mind in Action: Essays in the Philosophy of Mind.* Boston: Beacon Press, 1991.

Searle, John. "Consciousness, Unconsciousness and Intentionality." *Philosophical Topics* 17.1 (Spring 1989): 193–209.

Smilansky, S. "Free Will and Being a Victim." *International Journal of Moral and Social Studies* 6.1 (1991): 19–32.

Slote, Michael. "Ethics without Free Will." *Social Theory and Practice* 16.3 (Fall 1990): 369–383.

Taylor, Richard. *Metaphysics.* 3rd ed. Chap. 5. Englewood Cliffs: Prentice-Hall, 1983.

Trusted, Jennifer. *Freewill and Responsibility.* Oxford: Oxford University Press, 1984.

Part Five: Belief in God

Traditional Treatments

Carnes, R. D. "Descartes and the Ontological Argument." *Philosophy and Phenomenological Research* 24 (1964): 502–511.

Crahay, F. "L' Argumnt ontologique chez Déscartes et Liebniz et la critique Kantienne." *Revue philosophique de Louvain* 47 (1949): 458–468.

Collingwood, R. G. *An Essay on Philosophical Method.* 123–36. Oxford: Clarendon Press, 1933.

Engel, S. M. "Kant's 'Refutation' of the Ontological Argument." *Philosophy and Phenomenological Research* 24 (1963): 20–35.

Findlay, J. N. "Can God's Existence be Disproved?" *Mind* 57 (1948): 176–183.

Flimons, S. "Kant and the Proofs for the Existence of God." *American Catholic Quarterly* 48 (1923): 14–48.

Hartshorne, Charles. *Man's Vision of God and the Logic of Theism.* Chicago: University of Chicago Press, 1941.

Hume, David. *Dialogues on Natural Religion.* Edited by Norman Kemp Smith. Indianapolis: Bobbs-Merrill, 1947.

Koyré, A. *Essai sur l'idée de Dieu et les preuves de son existence chez Déscartes.* 174–193. Paris: Vrin, 1922.

―――. *L'idée de Dieu dans la Philosophie de St. Anselme.* Paris: Vrin, 1984.

Malcolm, Norman. "Anselm's Ontological Argument." *Philosophical Review* 69 (1960): 41–62.

Miller, Robert. "The Ontological Argument in St. Anselm and Descartes." *The Modern Schoolman* 33 (1955–56): 31–38.

Du Noüv, Lecomte. *Human Destiny.* New York: Longmans, 1947.

Russell, Bertrand. "The Existential Import of Propositions." *Mind* 14 (1905): 398–401.

Contemporary Treatments

Abraham, William. *An Introduction to the Philosophy of Religion.* Englewood Cliffs: Prentice-Hall, 1985.

Audi, Robert and Wainwright, William, eds. *Rationality, Religious Belief and Moral Commitment.* Notre Dame: University of Notre Dame Press, 1986.

Braine, Davis. *The Reality of Time and the Existence of God*. London: Oxford University Press, 1988.

Brinton, Alan. "Agnosticism and Atheism." *Sophia* 28.3 (October 1989): 2–6.

Brody, Baruch. *Readings in the Philosophy of Religion*. Englewood Cliffs: Prentice-Hall, 1974.

Chrzan, Keith. "Plantinga and Probabilistic Atheism." *International Journal for the Philosophy of Religion* 30.1 (1991): 21–27.

Clark, Kelly James. *Return to Reason: Critique of Enlightenment Evidentialism and a Defense of Reason and Belief in God*. Grand Rapids: Eerdmans Publishing Company, 1990.

Clark, Stephen. "Limited Explanation." *Philosophy* 27 (1990 supplement): 195–210.

Diamond, Michael. "A Modern Theistic Argument." *Modern Theology* 6.3 (April 1990): 287–293.

Hick, John. *Philosophy of Religion*. 3rd ed. Englewood Cliffs: Prentice-Hall, 1983.

Lauder, Robert. "The Accuracy of Atheism and the Truth of Theism." *Sophia* 28.3 (October 1989): 40–48.

Mackie, J. L. *The Miracle of Theism*. Oxford: Clarendon Press, 1982.

Nielsen, Kai. *Philosophy and Atheism*. Buffalo: Prometheus, 1985.

———. *God, Scepticism and Modernity*. Ottawa: University of Ottawa Press, 1989.

Plantinga, Alvin. *God, Freedom and Evil*. Grand Rapids: Eerdmans Publishing Company, 1978.

———. *The Nature of Necessity*. Oxford: Oxford University Press, 1974.

Shaw, Marvin. "The Moral Stance of Theism without the Transcent God: Wieman and Heidegger." *Process Studies* 18.3 (Fall 1989): 173–180.

Smith, George. *Atheism: The Case Against God*. Buffalo: Prometheus, 1979.

Swinburne, Richard. *The Existence of God*. Oxford: Clarendon Press, 1979.

———. "The Limits of Explanation." *Philosophy* 27 (1990 supplement): 177–193.

Yandell, Keith E. *Christianity and Philosophy*. Grand Rapids: Eerdmans Publishing Company, 1984.

Copyrights and Acknowledgments